S0-AXY-357

includes some of what we would call "green" in its word for blue, and others in its word for yellow. Experiments have demonstrated that people from cultures with large and precise color vocabularies are better able to remember and pick out colors they have been previously shown. Having words for colors helps us remember them.

Everyone knows the axiom that Eskimos have hundreds of words for snow. Although this has been overstated—actually, Eskimo languages don't have all that many root words for different kinds of snow, but form specialized words by building on root words—it is still true that people in northern climates speak of (and thus also see and consider) their ice- and snowbound environments with a keen precision. There are important survival distinctions to be made between a snow that can easily be cut into blocks for building shelter and one that will soon turn to rain. Alaska's Aleuts have a word that translates as "the snow that melts the snow," to designate the wet snowfall of spring—that which hastens the melt of the old snow beneath it. (Since I learned this concept, I've come to think of spring snow with a new appreciation, a more accepting attitude toward winter's end.) In sharp contrast, the Aztec language has a single word—with different endings—for snow, ice, and cold.

Here at home, the Dena'ina have an entire lexicon with which to describe kinds of streams and trails. It makes a difference if a stream is a river, a tributary, the outlet of a lake, a straight stretch of water, a place of fast or slow current, covered with slush ice or overflow ice. Likewise, a trail is not just a trail; it's a packed-snow trail or a trail with snow drifted over, an animal trail, a snowshoe or sled trail, a trapline trail, or a trail used for getting wood.

The same wealth of Dena'ina language applies to salmon and other fish—not only the names of the fish but specialized words to distinguish between dried fish, half-dried fish, a bundle of dried fish, fish dried in one day's wind, fish dried with eggs inside, fish dried ungutted, fish dried flat, smoked fish, half-smoked fish, the backbone of the fish, the fish belly, the fat, the fatty part just in front of the king's dorsal fin, the roe, dried roe, fermented roe, frozen roe, salted roe, and roe soup. To know these words is to share in the universe of salmon.

Along my trail in Dena'ina country, I try to imagine how differently—or more clearly—I might see my world if I had the Dena'ina language precision with which to know my surroundings and my place in them. I look at a fern and think "fern." But if instead I thought of *uh t'una*, I would know that I was seeing and thinking about the leafy part of the plant, in contrast to *uh*, its underground parts used for food. And if I thought of another part of the plant, *elnen tselts'egha* (literally "ground's coiled rectum"), I would find humor in the fiddlehead fern.

Unfortunately, few of these words are spoken anymore, one person to another in the course of daily living. Of the original five dialects of Dena'ina Athabaskan, one is long gone, the second's fluency died with Peter Kalifornsky, and two of the other three are spoken only by elders. Only one, in an isolated village, is still spoken by young adults. What remains of the various dialects has been assembled in dictionary form by linguist James Kari of the University of Alaska's Native Language Center. If not for Kari, Dena'ina words would be scattering silently and irretrievably into the winds.

Once there were between 10,000 and 15,000 languages in the world. Today there are barely 6,000, and half of those are no longer being learned by children and will probably become extinct within the next century. "They are beyond endangerment," says University of Alaska linguist Michael Krauss. "They are the living dead."

Of North American's 300-some Native languages, about 210 are still spoken. (About 50 of those are in California, the world's most linguistically diverse region after New Guinea and the Caucasus.) Very few of the 210 are, however, still spoken by children. Even Navajo, by far the largest language group with 200,000 speakers, appears to be in trouble. A generation ago, 90 percent of Navajo children entering school spoke their language; today, the reverse is true—90 percent of Navajo children entering school speak English, but not Navajo. In Alaska, only two of the 20 Native languages are still spoken by children and one language—Eyak—has one remaining elderly speaker. Krauss believes that despite bilingual programs in schools, all Native American languages are today threatened.

The cause, of course, is the unfinished conquest of Native peoples and the eradication of their cultures. Even after the wars and removals ended and were replaced with assimilation policies, most white Americans believed that Natives would be best off abandoning their "inferior" cultures and adopting the English-only, mainstream American one. Until the 1960s, Natives were forbidden to speak their own languages in schools, and children were punished for doing so. Parents were told that they were holding their children back by speaking their languages at home, and so they too were silenced.

Even the best bilingual programs can't compensate for traditional family-to-child language learning. Language loss is further exacerbated by the influence of television and "global culture." At this late date, perhaps the best that can be done is to teach Native languages as second or even third languages, so that coming generations can learn enough of their ancestral tongues to maintain respect for them and for their heritage, and to continue some ceremonial and artistic uses.

Preservation, Tlingit oral historians Richard and Nora Marks Dauenhauer remind us, is what we do to berries in jam jars and salmon in cans. Preserved foods are different from thriving berry patches and surging runs of salmon, and dictionaries are not the same as speech. Books and recordings can preserve languages, but only people and communities can keep them alive.

Most people are now aware of and concerned about the mass extinction of animals and plants. We understand the need for diversity, and the imperative to protect what we can. As with species, once a language is lost it is gone forever. Every extinguished language diminishes the world by robbing us of the ability to know that world with the millennia of accumulated wisdom of groups such as California's Pomo, or the New Guinea Dani, or the Gwich'in of Alaska.

Back at my fishcamp, the sky opens, and a hard, dumping rain pounds onto the metal roof, the alders, the squally inlet. When the rain stops I walk behind the cabin to pick fireweed shoots for a salad. The air is fragrant with plant oils and wet earth, and all the leaves and grasses are magnified by the droplets caught in their creases and dangling from their tips. A warm white light suffuses the breaking clouds; its shafts pierce the mosaic of green and gray inlet waters. There's a Dena'ina word for this—this fresh-scrubbed, brightened, new-world look. *Htashtch'ul.* The world everywhere after a rain looks fresh and lovely, but to have a word to put to it—a word that came from this land, that is as native as the blue-backed salmon and alder thickets, that tells me what the first people saw and what significance they gave by naming it—makes me feel even more a part of this place.

Words have power. Languages connected to place help us to respect local knowledge, to ask and answer the tough questions about how the human and nonhuman can live together in a tolerant and dignified way. They can help us extend our sense of community; what we hold ourselves responsible for, what we must do to live right and well.

The Dena'ina greeting is *Yaghali du?* "Is it good?" Not, "How are you?" but, "Is it good?" There is, in the question, the assumption that something larger is at stake than the feelings of the two speakers, something less anthropocentric, less egocentric. If it is good, then we shall all—me, you, our community, the larger world—prosper together, not the one individual at the expense of others.

Yaghali du? Yaghali du? The answer we want is *Aa'yaghali.* Yes, it is good. It is all good.

═══

FOR DISCUSSION AND REVIEW

1. Why do native Alaskans use waterways instead of the sun and the stars to define direction and location? How does this affect the structure of their languages?

2. What parallel may be drawn between the use of prefixes and suffixes in Dena'ina and verb tenses in English?

3. Why does Lord refer to the native language of her chosen home as coevolutionary? What relationships exist between a place and the human language spoken there?

4. Why did Thoreau value the Abenaki names of things for which he already knew the English scientific names?

5. What is the central idea in Whorf's theory of "linguistic relativity"? What lasting effect, according to Lord, did his theory have on our understanding of the nature of languages?

6. How does the Hopi concept of time, as Whorf describes it, differ from ours? What role does language play in a person's development and understanding of concepts?

7. Give several reasons why the number of living languages in the world is shrinking so rapidly.

8. According to Lord, why does the loss of a language "diminish the world"?

9. What specific powers does Lord ascribe to words?

4

Shakespeare in the Bush

Laura Bohannan

Are people alike everywhere? Are all peoples subject to the same feelings, driven by the same motivations? Do great stories of human endeavor carry identical messages to every audience, regardless of its background? Laura Bohannan, an anthropologist from the University of Illinois at Chicago, believed in the universality of human experience when she attempted to retell the story of Hamlet to members of a tribe in West Africa. She found that it was very difficult indeed to translate a classic tale from one language and culture to another. An audience that has no concept of ghosts, is accustomed to chiefs who have many wives, and ascribes madness to witchcraft must necessarily reinterpret Hamlet in ways so fundamental that the thrust of the original story is lost. In both word and concept, Shakespeare's vision of human tragedy becomes unrecognizable when its "true meaning" is interpreted by the wise elders of a distant, illiterate tribe whose existence he could not have imagined.

Just before I left Oxford for the Tiv in West Africa, conversation turned to the season at Stratford. "You Americans," said a friend, "often have difficulty with Shakespeare. He was, after all, a very English poet, and one can easily misinterpret the universal by misunderstanding the particular."

I protested that human nature is pretty much the same the whole world over; at least the general plot and motivation of the greater tragedies would always be clear—everywhere—although some details of custom might have to be explained and difficulties of translation might produce other slight changes. To end an argument we could not conclude, my friend gave me a copy of *Hamlet* to study in the African bush: it would, he hoped, lift my mind above its primitive surroundings, and possibly I might, by prolonged meditation, achieve the grace of correct interpretation.

It was my second field trip to that African tribe, and I thought myself ready to live in one of its remote sections—an area difficult to cross even on foot. I eventually settled on the hillock of a very knowledgeable old man, the head of a homestead of some hundred and forty people, all of whom were either his close relatives or their wives and children. Like the other elders of the vicinity, the old man spent most of his time performing ceremonies seldom seen these days in the more accessible parts of the tribe. I was delighted. Soon there would be three months of enforced isolation and leisure, between the harvest that takes place just before the rising of the swamps and the clearing of new farms when the water goes down. Then, I thought, they would have even more time to perform ceremonies and explain them to me.

I was quite mistaken. Most of the ceremonies demanded the presence of elders from several homesteads. As the swamps rose, the old men found it too difficult to walk from one homestead to the next, and the ceremonies gradually ceased. As the swamps rose even higher, all activities but one came to an end. The women brewed beer from maize and millet. Men, women, and children sat on their hillocks and drank it.

People began to drink at dawn. By midmorning the whole homestead was singing, dancing, and drumming. When it rained, people had to sit inside their huts: there they drank and sang or they drank and told stories. In any case, by noon or before, I either had to join the party or retire to my own hut and my books. "One does not discuss serious matters when there is beer. Come, drink with us." Since I lacked their capacity for the thick native beer, I spent more and more time with *Hamlet*. Before the end of the second month, grace descended on me. I was quite sure that *Hamlet* had only one possible interpretation, and that one universally obvious.

Early every morning, in the hope of having some serious talk before the beer party, I used to call on the old man at his reception hut—a circle of posts supporting a thatched roof above a low mud wall to keep out wind and rain. One day I crawled through the low doorway and found most of the men of the homestead sitting huddled in their ragged cloths on stools, low plank beds, and reclining chairs, warming themselves against the chill of the rain around a smoky fire. In the center were three pots of beer. The party had started.

The old man greeted me cordially. "Sit down and drink." I accepted a large calabash full of beer, poured some into a small drinking gourd, and tossed it down. Then I poured some more into the same gourd for the man second in seniority to my host before I handed my calabash over to a young man for further distribution. Important people shouldn't ladle beer themselves.

"It is better like this," the old man said, looking at me approvingly and plucking at the thatch that had caught in my hair. "You should sit and drink with us more often. Your servants tell me that when you are not with us, you sit inside your hut looking at a paper."

The old man was acquainted with four kinds of "papers": tax receipts, bride price receipts, court fee receipts, and letters. The messenger who brought him letters from the chief used them mainly as a badge of office, for he always knew what was in them and told the old man. Personal letters for the few who had relatives in the government or mission stations were kept until someone went to a large market where there was a letter writer and reader. Since my arrival, letters were brought to me to be read. A few men also brought me bride price receipts, privately, with requests to change the figures to a higher sum. I found moral arguments were of no avail, since in-laws are fair game, and the technical hazards of forgery difficult to explain to an illiterate people. I did not wish them to think me silly enough to look at any such papers for days on end, and I hastily explained that my "paper" was one of the "things of long ago" of my country.

"Ah," said the old man. "Tell us."

I protested that I was not a storyteller. Story telling is a skilled art among them; their standards are high, and the audiences critical—and vocal in their criticism. I protested in vain. This morning they wanted to hear a story while they drank. They threatened to tell me no more stories until I told them one of mine. Finally, the old man promised that no one would criticize my style "for we know you are struggling with our language." "But," put in one of the elders, "you must explain what we do not understand, as we do when we tell you our stories." Realizing that here was my chance to prove *Hamlet* universally intelligible, I agreed.

The old man handed me some more beer to help me on with my storytelling. Men filled their long wooden pipes and knocked coals from the fire to place in the pipe bowls; then, puffing contentedly, they sat back to listen. I began in the proper style, "Not yesterday, not yesterday, but long ago, a thing occurred. One night three men were keeping watch outside the homestead of the great chief, when suddenly they saw the former chief approach them."

"Why was he no longer their chief?"

"He was dead," I explained. "That is why they were troubled and afraid when they saw him."

"Impossible," began one of the elders, handing his pipe on to his neighbor, who interrupted, "Of course it wasn't the dead chief. It was an omen sent by a witch. Go on."

Slightly shaken, I continued. "One of these three was a man who knew things"—the closest translation for scholar, but unfortunately it also meant witch. The second elder looked triumphantly at the first. "So he spoke to the dead chief saying, 'Tell us what we must do so you may rest in your grave,' but the dead chief did not answer. He vanished, and they could see him no more. Then the man who knew things—his name was Horatio—said this event was the affair of the dead chief's son, Hamlet."

There was a general shaking of heads round the circle. "Had the dead chief no living brothers? Or was this son the chief?"

"No," I replied. "That is, he had one living brother who became the chief when the elder brother died."

The old men muttered: such omens were matters for chiefs and elders, not for youngsters; no good could come of going behind a chief's back; clearly Horatio was not a man who knew things.

"Yes, he was," I insisted, shooing a chicken away from my beer. "In our country the son is next to the father. The dead chief's younger brother had become the great chief. He had also married his elder brother's widow only about a month after the funeral."

"He did well," the old man beamed and announced to the others, "I told you that if we knew more about Europeans, we would find they really were very like us. In our country also," he added to me, "the younger brother marries the elder brother's widow and becomes the father of his children. Now, if your uncle, who married your widowed mother, is your father's full brother, then he will be a real father to you. Did Hamlet's father and uncle have one mother?"

His question barely penetrated my mind; I was too upset and thrown too far off balance by having one of the most important elements of *Hamlet* knocked straight out of the picture. Rather uncertainly I said that I thought they had the same mother, but I wasn't sure—the story didn't say. The old man told me severely that these genealogical details made all the difference and that when I got home I must ask the elders about it. He shouted out the door to one of his younger wives to bring his goatskin bag.

Determined to save what I could of the mother motif, I took a deep breath and began again. "The son Hamlet was very sad because his mother had married again so quickly. There was no need for her to do so, and it is our custom for a widow not to go to her next husband until she has mourned for two years."

"Two years is too long," objected the wife, who had appeared with the old man's battered goatskin bag. "Who will hoe your farms for you while you have no husband?"

"Hamlet," I retorted without thinking, "was old enough to hoe his mother's farms himself. There was no need for her to remarry." No one looked convinced. I gave up. "His mother and the great chief told Hamlet not to be sad, for the great chief himself would be a father to Hamlet. Furthermore, Hamlet would be the next chief: therefore he must stay to learn the things of a chief. Hamlet agreed to remain, and all the rest went off to drink beer."

While I paused, perplexed at how to render Hamlet's disgusted soliloquy to an audience convinced that Claudius and Gertrude had behaved in the best possible manner, one of the younger men asked me who had married the other wives of the dead chief.

"He had no other wives," I told him.

"But a chief must have many wives! How else can he brew beer and prepare food for all his guests?"

I said firmly that in our country even chiefs had only one wife, that they had servants to do their work, and that they paid them from tax money.

It was better, they returned, for a chief to have many wives and sons who would help him hoe his farms and feed his people; then everyone loved the chief who gave much and took nothing—taxes were a bad thing.

I agreed with the last comment, but for the rest fell back on their favorite way of fobbing off my questions: "That is the way it is done, so that is how we do it."

I decided to skip the soliloquy. Even if Claudius was here thought quite right to marry his brother's widow, there remained the poison motif, and I knew they would disapprove of fratricide. More hopefully I resumed, "That night Hamlet kept watch with the three who had seen his dead father. The dead chief again appeared, and although the others were afraid, Hamlet followed his dead father off to one side. When they were alone, Hamlet's dead father spoke."

"Omens can't talk!" The old man was emphatic.

"Hamlet's dead father wasn't an omen. Seeing him might have been an omen, but he was not." My audience looked as confused as I sounded. "It *was* Hamlet's dead father. It was a thing we call a 'ghost.'" I had to use the English word, for unlike many of the neighboring tribes, these people didn't believe in the survival after death of any individuating part of the personality.

"What is a 'ghost'? An omen?"

"No, a 'ghost' is someone who is dead but who walks around and can talk, and people can hear him and see him but not touch him."

They objected. "One can touch zombis."

"No, no! It was not a dead body the witches had animated to sacrifice and eat. No one else made Hamlet's dead father walk. He did it himself."

"Dead men can't walk," protested my audience as one man.

I was quite willing to compromise. "A 'ghost' is the dead man's shadow."

But again they objected. "Dead men cast no shadows."

"They do in my country," I snapped.

The old man quelled the babble of disbelief that arose immediately and told me with that insincere, but courteous, agreement one extends to the fancies of the young, ignorant, and superstitious, "No doubt in your country the dead can also walk without being zombis." From the depths of his bag he produced a withered fragment of kola nut, bit off one end to show it wasn't poisoned, and handed me the rest as a peace offering.

"Anyhow," I resumed, "Hamlet's dead father said that his own brother, the one who became chief, had poisoned him. He wanted Hamlet to avenge him. Hamlet believed this in his heart, for he did not like his father's brother." I took another swallow of beer. "In the country of the great chief, living in the same homestead, for it was a very large one, was an important elder who was often with the chief to advise and help him. His name was Polonius. Hamlet was courting his daughter, but her father and her brother . . . [I cast hastily about for some tribal analogy] warned her not to let Hamlet visit her when she was alone on her farm, for he would be a great chief and so could not marry her."

"Why not?" asked the wife, who had settled down on the edge of the old man's chair. He frowned at her for asking stupid questions and growled, "They lived in the same homestead."

"This was not the reason," I informed them. "Polonius was a stranger who lived in the homestead because he helped the chief, not because he was a relative."

"Then why couldn't Hamlet marry her?"

"He could have," I explained, "but Polonius didn't think he would. After all, Hamlet was a man of great importance who ought to marry a chief's daughter, for in his country a man could have only one wife.

Polonius was afraid that if Hamlet made love to his daughter, then no one else would give a high price for her."

"That might be true," remarked one of the shrewder elders, "but a chief's son would give his mistress's father enough presents and patronage to more than make up the difference. Polonius sounds like a fool to me."

"Many people think he was," I agreed. "Meanwhile Polonius sent his son Laertes off to Paris to learn the things of the country, for it was the homestead of a very great chief indeed. Because he was afraid that Laertes might waste a lot of money on beer and women and gambling, or get into trouble by fighting, he sent one of his servants to Paris secretly, to spy out what Laertes was doing. One day Hamlet came upon Polonius's daughter Ophelia. He behaved so oddly he frightened her. Indeed"—I was fumbling for words to express the dubious quality of Hamlet's madness—"the chief and many others had also noticed that when Hamlet talked one could understand the words but not what they meant. Many people thought that he had become mad." My audience suddenly became much more attentive. "The great chief wanted to know what was wrong with Hamlet, so he sent for two of Hamlet's age mates [school friends would have taken long explanation] to talk to Hamlet and find out what troubled his heart. Hamlet, seeing that they had been bribed by the chief to betray him, told them nothing. Polonius, however, insisted that Hamlet was mad because he had been forbidden to see Ophelia, whom he loved."

"Why," inquired a bewildered voice, "should anyone bewitch Hamlet on that account?"

"Bewitch him?"

"Yes, only witchcraft can make anyone mad, unless, of course, one sees the beings that lurk in the forest."

I stopped being a storyteller, took out my notebook and demanded to be told more about these two causes of madness. Even while they spoke and I jotted notes, I tried to calculate the effect of this new factor on the plot. Hamlet had not been exposed to the beings that lurk in the forests. Only his relatives in the male line could bewitch him. Barring relatives not mentioned by Shakespeare, it had to be Claudius who was attempting to harm him. And, of course, it was.

For the moment I staved off questions by saying that the great chief also refused to believe that Hamlet was mad for the love of Ophelia and nothing else. "He was sure that something much more important was troubling Hamlet's heart."

"Now Hamlet's age mates," I continued, "had brought with them a famous storyteller. Hamlet decided to have this man tell the chief and all his homestead a story about a man who had poisoned his brother because he desired his brother's wife and wished to be chief himself. Hamlet was sure the great chief could not hear the story without making a sign if he was indeed guilty, and then he would discover whether his dead father had told him the truth."

The old man interrupted, with deep cunning, "Why should a father lie to his son?" he asked.

I hedged: "Hamlet wasn't sure that it really was his dead father." It was impossible to say anything, in that language, about devil-inspired visions.

"You mean," he said, "it actually was an omen, and he knew witches sometimes send false ones. Hamlet was a fool not to go to one skilled in reading omens and divining the truth in the first place. A man-who-sees-the-truth could have told him how his father died, if he really had been poisoned, and if there was witchcraft in it; then Hamlet could have called the elders to settle the matter."

The shrewd elder ventured to disagree. "Because his father's brother was a great chief, one-who-sees-the-truth might therefore have been afraid to tell it. I think it was for that reason that a friend of Hamlet's father—a witch and an elder—sent an omen so his friend's son would know. Was the omen true?"

"Yes," I said, abandoning ghosts and the devil; a witch-sent omen it would have to be. "It was true, for when the storyteller was telling his tale before all the homestead, the great chief rose in fear. Afraid that Hamlet knew his secret, he planned to have him killed."

The stage set of the next bit presented some difficulties of translation. I began cautiously. "The great chief told Hamlet's mother to find out from her son what he knew. But because a woman's children are always first in her heart, he had the important elder Polonius hide behind a cloth that hung against the wall of Hamlet's mother's sleeping hut. Hamlet started to scold his mother for what she had done."

There was a shocked murmur from everyone. A man should never scold his mother.

"She called out in fear, and Polonius moved behind the cloth. Shouting, 'A rat!' Hamlet took his machete and slashed through the cloth." I paused for dramatic effect. "He had killed Polonius!"

The old men looked at each other in supreme disgust. "That Polonius truly was a fool and a man who knew nothing! What child would not know enough to shout, 'It's me!'" With a pang, I remembered that these people are ardent hunters, always armed with bow, arrow, and machete; at the first rustle in the grass an arrow is aimed and ready, and the hunter shouts "Game!" If no human voice answers immediately, the arrow speeds on its way. Like a good hunter Hamlet had shouted, "A rat!"

I rushed in, to save Polonius's reputation. "Polonius did speak. Hamlet heard him. But he thought it was the chief and wished to kill him earlier that evening. . . ." I broke down, unable to describe to these pagans, who had no belief in individual after-life, the difference between dying at one's prayers and dying "unhousell'd, disappointed, unaneled."

This time I had shocked my audience seriously. "For a man to raise his hand against his father's brother and the one who has become his father—that is a terrible thing. The elders ought to let such a man be bewitched."

I nibbled at my kola nut in some perplexity, then pointed out that after all the man had killed Hamlet's father.

"No," pronounced the old man, speaking less to me than to the young men sitting behind the elders. "If your father's brother has killed your father, you must appeal to your father's age mates; *they* may avenge him. No man may use violence against his senior relative." Another thought struck him, "But if his father's brother had indeed been wicked enough to bewitch Hamlet and make him mad that would be a good story indeed, for it would be his fault that Hamlet, being mad, no longer had any sense and thus was ready to kill his father's brother."

There was a murmur of applause. *Hamlet* was again a good story to them, but it no longer seemed quite the same story to me. As I thought over the coming complications of plot and motive, I lost courage and decided to skim over dangerous ground quickly.

"The great chief," I went on, "was not sorry that Hamlet had killed Polonius. It gave him a reason to send Hamlet away, with his two treacherous mates, with letters to a chief of a far country, saying that Hamlet should be killed. But Hamlet changed the writing on their papers, so that the chief killed his age mates instead." I encountered a reproachful glare from one of the men whom I had told undetectable forgery was not merely immoral but beyond human skill. I looked the other way.

"Before Hamlet could return, Laertes came back for his father's funeral. The great chief told him Hamlet had killed Polonius. Laertes swore to kill Hamlet because of this, and because his sister Ophelia, hearing her father had been killed by the man she loved, went mad and drowned in the river."

"Have you already forgotten what we told you?" The old man was reproachful. "One cannot take vengeance on a madman; Hamlet killed Polonius in his madness. As for the girl, she not only went mad, she was drowned. Only witches can make people drown. Water itself can't hurt anything. It is merely something one drinks and bathes in."

I began to get cross. "If you don't like the story, I'll stop."

The old man made soothing noises and himself poured me some more beer. "You tell the story well, and we are listening. But it is clear that the elders of your country have never told you what the story really means. No, don't interrupt! We believe you when you say your marriage customs are different, or your clothes and weapons. But people are the same everywhere; therefore, there are always witches and it is we, the elders, who know how witches work. We told you it was the great chief who wished to kill Hamlet, and now your own words have proved us right. Who were Ophelia's male relatives?"

"There were only her father and her brother." *Hamlet* was clearly out of my hands.

"There must have been many more; this also you must ask of your elders when you get back to your country. From what you tell us, since Polonius was dead, it must have been Laertes who killed Ophelia, although I do not see the reason for it."

We had emptied one pot of beer, and the old men argued the point with slightly tipsy interest. Finally one of them demanded of me, "What did the servant of Polonius say on his return?"

With difficulty I recollected Reynaldo and his mission. "I don't think he did return before Polonius was killed."

"Listen," said the elder, "and I will tell you how it was and how your story will go, then you may tell me if I am right. Polonius knew his son would get into trouble, and so he did. He had many fines to pay for fighting, and debts from gambling. But he had only two ways of getting money quickly. One was to marry off his sister at once, but it is difficult to find a man who will marry a woman desired by the son of a chief. For if the chief's heir commits adultery with your wife, what can you do? Only a fool calls a case against a man who will someday be his judge. Therefore Laertes had to take the second way: he killed his sister by witchcraft, drowning her so he could secretly sell her body to the witches."

I raised an objection. "They found her body and buried it. Indeed Laertes jumped into the grave to see his sister once more—so, you see, the body was truly there. Hamlet, who had just come back, jumped in after him."

"What did I tell you?" The elder appealed to the others. "Laertes was up to no good with his sister's body. Hamlet prevented him, because the chief's heir, like a chief, does not wish any other man to grow rich and powerful. Laertes would be angry, because he would have killed his sister without benefit to himself. In our country he would try to kill Hamlet for that reason. Is this not what happened?"

"More or less," I admitted. "When the great chief found Hamlet was still alive, he encouraged Laertes to try to kill Hamlet and arranged a fight with machetes between them. In the fight both young men were wounded to death. Hamlet's mother drank the poisoned beer that the chief meant for Hamlet in case he won the fight. When he saw his mother die of poison, Hamlet, dying, managed to kill his father's brother with his machete."

"You see, I was right!" exclaimed the elder.

"That was a very good story," added the old man, "and you told it with very few mistakes. There was just one more error, at the very end. The poison Hamlet's mother drank was obviously meant for the survivor of the fight, whichever it was. If Laertes had won, the great chief would have poisoned him, for no one would know that he arranged Hamlet's death. Then, too, he need not fear Laertes' witchcraft; it takes a strong heart to kill one's only sister by witchcraft.

"Sometime," concluded the old man, gathering his ragged toga about him, "you must tell us some more stories of your country. We, who are elders, will instruct you in their true meaning, so that when you return to your own land your elders will see that you have not been sitting in the bush, but among those who know things and who have taught you wisdom."

FOR DISCUSSION AND REVIEW

1. In the opening paragraph, Bohannan quotes her English friend as saying, "one can easily misinterpret the universal by misunderstanding the particular." How does this comment relate to Bohannan's own interpretation of *Hamlet*? How does it relate to the response to *Hamlet* of her African audience?

2. For what reason does Bohannan agree to tell the story of Hamlet to the tribespeople?

3. The tone of the essay is humorous throughout. What is the author's central purpose, and how does humor serve it?

4. Bohannan intersperses her retelling of *Hamlet* with a narrative about the behavior of the tribal members listening to the story. Why does she include details about their sharing the beer and the kola nut? Why does she bring in the commentary of the old man's wife and that of the "shrewd" elder?

5. What are some familiar English words that Bohannan was unable to translate directly into the language of her audience? What are some of the misunderstandings that arose as a result?

6. What are some familiar English cultural concepts that Bohannan was unable to transmit effectively within the context of the story of *Hamlet*? What are some of the misunderstandings that arose as a result?

7. At one point, Bohannan abandons *Hamlet* for a few moments in order to take notes. Both she and the elders are authorities in their own culture; when it comes to storytelling, however, they behave very differently. Discuss these differences and the reasons for them.

8. Near the end of the essay, the old man remarks that "people are the same everywhere." How does this comment reflect Bohannan's theme? Why is it ironic? What do both the comment and the theme have to do with language?

Projects for "Language and Personal Identity"

1. Two of the essays in this section were written by women born into a foreign culture and thrust early in life into American schools and communities. There are many fine autobiographies written by immigrants to America whose native language was not English. Maxine Hong Kingston's *The Woman Warrior* is one of the best examples, because issues of language are at the core of her story; others are *A Romantic Education* by Patricia Hampl and *Meatless Days* by Sara Suleri. Read one of these autobiographies, or another of your choice, and write an analysis that explores the impact of a new language on the author's sense of personal and cultural identity.

2. Interview in depth a member of your immediate family or community who had to make a transition from one country and language to another. Write an oral history emphasizing the effects of this transition on the person.

3. Edite Cunha's family moved from Portugal to an immigrant community in Massachusetts; Maxine Hong Kingston was born in San Francisco's Chinatown. Many immigrant groups have set up their own communities in the "new world," maintaining a culture within a culture. Locate an immigrant community near you that maintains characteristics of its original culture. Interview one or more of the older people in the community to learn why, when, and from where they came, how they established their new neighborhood, and how they adapted to their new culture, including its language, educational system, and work environment. What changes have they observed in the community over time?

4. Most large communities in the United States have one or more organizations that teach English as a second language (ESL). Interview the director or one of the teachers in your local ESL organization. What sorts of students do they attract? What are their goals and techniques? What difficulties do they encounter?

5. We know that the English language includes many words that have been adopted and modified from other languages. Proper names are no exception. One telephone directory in northern New England, for example, lists the surnames Bosher, Bouche, Boucher, Boushey, Bushee, Bushey, Bushway, Busse, and Bussey—all variations of the original French surname Boucher. On the other hand, many given names have come to America already modified by their earlier travels from culture to culture and language to language. How many variations of the common names John and Mary can you find? What are their countries of origin? Choose two or three other familiar given names and find out how they are spelled and pronounced in other parts of the world. Choose two or three familiar surnames from your area of the country and see how many variations you can find.

6. There is currently considerable public interest in the issue of whether or not legislation should be passed to make English the official language of the United States. With several classmates, research both sides of the argument and present a debate. As an alternative, write a well-researched, persuasive essay defending your own opinion on the issue.

7. Having come under attack by some modern linguists, the Sapir-Whorf theory of "linguistic relativity" is now the subject of considerable controversy in the field. Read several articles that call this theory into question. Good examples are "The Great Eskimo Vocabulary Hoax" by Geoffrey Pullum in a book by the same title and "Mentalese" in *The Language Instinct* by Steven Pinker. Prepare a brief talk for the class, reviewing the basic tenets of "linguistic relativity" and clearly presenting the arguments against them.

8. Storytellers in an oral culture, like the Tiv elders in Laura Bohannan's essay, occupy a place of major importance within the community. Research and write a brief paper describing the powers and responsibilities generally ascribed to the native storyteller.

9. Before printed language was widely available, the bard, minstrel, and troubadour played a role in Western culture somewhat analogous to that of the storyteller in an oral culture. Research and write a brief paper about the role of minstrels in early Greece or in Europe during the Middle Ages.

10. Laura Bohannan may have been "quite sure that *Hamlet* had only one possible interpretation, and that one universally obvious," but she is not the only interpreter of the play to struggle with her audience over concepts such as ghosts, madness, and incest. English-speaking audiences experience the same problems with a 400-year-old story about a quasi-historical event obscured in the mists of medieval Europe, though perhaps not to the extent the Tiv did. There are several excellent versions of *Hamlet* available on film, notably those featuring the performances of Laurence Olivier, Mel Gibson, and Kenneth Branagh. View the Olivier version, followed by either or both of the others, and analyze their differences in interpreting the three concepts.

Selected Bibliography

Angelou, Maya. *I Know Why the Caged Bird Sings*. New York: Random House, 1970. [Language repression and language recovery in a classic African American woman's autobiography.]

Anzaldua, Gloria. *Borderlands/La Frontera: The New Mestiza*. San Francisco: Aunt Lute Books, 1987. [Recounts the Mexican-Anglo conflicts of this Chicana writer.]

Edwards, J. *Language, Society, and Identity*. Oxford: Blackwell, 1985. [Explores issues in language planning, i.e., choosing and promulgating an official language within a particular social setting.]

Freeman, David E., and Yvonne S. Freeman. *Between Worlds: Access to Second Language Acquisition*. Portsmouth, NH: Heinemann, 1994. [Issues in teaching and learning a second language.]

Hoffman, Eva. *Lost in Translation: A Life in a New Language*. New York: Penguin, 1989. [Describes her experiences as a Polish-speaking Jew in English-only Canadian schools.]

Jesperson, O. *Mankind, Nation, and Individual*. London: Allen & Unwin, 1946. [Includes a discussion of magic and taboo in language.]

Kando, Dorinne K. *Crafting Selves: Power, Gender, and Discourses of Identity in a Japanese Workplace*. Chicago: University of Chicago Press, 1990. [Insightful commentary by a woman caught between Japanese and American cultures.]

Lorde, Audre. *Zami: A New Spelling of My Name*. Freedom, CA: Crossing Press, 1982. [Narrates her early experiences in school; see especially chapter 3, "How I Became a Poet."]

Mandelbaum, D. G., ed. *Selected Writings in Language, Culture, and Personality*. Berkeley and Los Angeles: University of California Press, 1949. [An exploration of the work of Edward Sapir.]

McKay, Sandra Lee, and Nancy Hornberger, eds. *Sociolinguistics and Language Teaching*. Cambridge: Cambridge University Press, 1996. [Highly recommended general text in sociolinguistics.]

Ortiz, Simon. "The Language We Know," In *I Tell You Now: Autobiographical Essays by Native American Writers*. Eds. Brian Swann and Arnold Krupat. Lincoln: University of Nebraska Press, 1987. [Account of attempts to Americanize the author by teaching him English.]

Pinker, Steven. *The Language Instinct: How the Mind Creates Language*. New York: Morrow, 1994. [See especially chapter 3, "Mentalese."]

Rodriguez, Richard. *Hunger of Memory*. Boston: Godine, 1982. [Raises serious questions about the effectiveness of bilingual education.]

Romaine, Suzanne. *Language in Society: An Introduction to Sociolinguistics*. Oxford: Oxford University Press, 1994. [A good contemporary basic text.]

Rose, Mike. *Lives on the Boundary: The Struggles and Achievements of America's Underprepared*. New York: Free Press, 1989. [A highly readable account of the author's many years teaching disadvantaged students.]

Sapir, Edward. *Language: An Introduction to the Study of Speech*. 1921. Reprint, New York: Harcourt Brace & World, 1949. [Explores the relationship between speech and culture.]

Silko, Leslie Marmon. "Language and Literature from a Pueblo Indian Perspective." In *English Literature: Opening Up the Canon*, ed. Leslie A. Fiedler and Houston A. Baker, Jr. Baltimore: Johns Hopkins University Press, 1979. [Draws a sharp cultural contrast to American language and literature.]

Wardhaugh, Ronald. *An Introduction to Sociolinguistics*, 2nd ed. Oxford: Blackwell, 1986. [A recommended introductory text.]

Whorf, Benjamin Lee. *Language, Thought, and Reality*. Ed. John B. Carroll. Cambridge: MIT Press, 1956. [A classic work on the relationship between language and culture.]

LANGUAGE AND ITS STUDY

Language is not only the principal medium of human communication, but it also binds us to each other and to our respective cultures. To understand our humanity, we must understand how language makes us human. The study of language, then, is a practical, as well as challenging, pursuit. In beginning this study, we will consider some fundamental questions: What is language? What are its unique characteristics? Are there some commonly held misconceptions that impede our understanding of language? What are they? What effect does language have on a people and its culture? The selections in Part Two raise these basic questions and suggest some answers.

Most people take their language ability for granted; speaking and understanding what is spoken seem as natural as breathing and sleeping. But human language is extremely complex and has unique characteristics. In the first selection, Harvey A. Daniels discusses nine ideas about language that most contemporary linguists believe to be demonstrably true. These "facts" are important in their own right; in addition, they will enhance your understanding and enjoyment of selections in other parts of this book.

Following Daniels's definition of language, W. F. Bolton discusses the properties of human language and explains the intricate physiological adaptations that make speech and hearing possible. He also points out that all languages are systematic and that no language is "simple" or "primitive," and he alerts us to the harm of ethnocentric attitudes.

Human beings are not the only species able to communicate, however; many birds, animals, and insects are capable of sending and receiving messages. The article "True Language?" compares human language with some of the communication systems of other species. It concludes that there are several characteristics that make "true" language uniquely human.

In "Sign Language," Karen Emmorey demonstrates that vocalization, which might appear fundamental to human communication, is not a necessary component of language. She demonstrates exact parallels between the phonology, morphology, and syntax of spoken language and their soundless equivalents in American Sign Language (ASL). And in "Nonverbal Communication," George A. Miller explores the role of various types of body language—adornment, ritualized gesture, spatial relations, and eye contact—in human communication systems. These nonverbal signals vary from culture to culture, and they are frequently as necessary as words and sentence structures to our understanding of one another.

5

Nine Ideas about Language

Harvey A. Daniels

In the following chapter adapted from his book Famous Last Words: The American Language Crisis Reconsidered, *Professor Harvey A. Daniels presents nine fundamental ideas about language that are widely accepted by contemporary linguists. In doing so, he dispels a number of myths about language that are all too prevalent among Americans. The ideas introduced here provide a foundation for readings in later parts of this book, where they are discussed in more detail.*

Assuming we agree that the English language has in fact survived all of the predictions of doom which have been prevalent since at least the early eighteenth century, we also have reason to believe that current reports of the death of our language are similarly exaggerated. The managers of the present crisis of course disagree, and their efforts may even result in the reinstatement of the linguistic loyalty oath of the 1920s or of some updated equivalent ("I promise to use good American unsplit infinitives") in our schools. But it won't make much difference. The English language, if history is any guide at all, will remain useful and vibrant as long as it is spoken, whether we eagerly try to tend and nurture and prune its growth or if we just leave it alone.

Contemporary language critics recognize that language is changing, that people use a lot of jargon, that few people consistently speak the standard dialect, that much writing done in our society is ineffective, and so forth—but they have no other way of viewing these phenomena except with alarm. But most of the uses of and apparent changes in language which worry the critics *can* be explained and understood in unalarming ways. Such explanations have been provided by linguists during the past seventy-five years.

I have said that in order to understand the errors and misrepresentations of the language critics, we need to examine not only history but also "the facts." Of course, facts about language are a somewhat elusive commodity, and we may never be able to answer all of our questions about this wonderfully complex activity. But linguists have made a good start during this century toward describing some of the basic features, structures, and operations of human speech. This section presents a series of nine fundamental ideas about language that form, if not exactly a list of facts, at least a fair summary of the consensus of most linguistic scholars.

1. Children learn their native language swiftly, efficiently, and largely without instruction. Language is a species-specific trait of human beings. All children, unless they are severely retarded or completely deprived of exposure to speech, will acquire their oral language as naturally as they learn to walk. Many linguists even assert that the human brain is prewired for language, and some have also postulated that the underlying linguistic features which are common to all languages are present in the brain at birth. This latter theory comes from the discovery that all languages have certain procedures in common: ways of making statements, questions, and commands; ways of referring to past time; the ability to negate, and so on.[1] In spite of the underlying similarities of all languages, though, it is important to remember that children will acquire the language which they hear around them—whether that is Ukrainian, Swahili, Cantonese, or Appalachian American English.

In spite of the commonsense notions of parents, they do not "teach" their children to talk. Children *learn* to talk, using the language of their parents, siblings, friends, and others as sources and examples—and by using other speakers as testing devices for their own emerging ideas about language. When we acknowledge the complexity of adult speech, with its ability to generate an unlimited number of new, meaningful utterances, it is clear that this skill cannot be the end result of simple instruction. Parents do not explain to their children, for example, that adjectives generally precede the noun in English, nor do they lecture them on the rules governing formation of the past participle. While parents do correct some kinds of mistakes on a piecemeal basis, discovering the underlying rules which make up the language is the child's job.

From what we know, children appear to learn language partly by imitation but even more by hypothesis-testing. Consider a child who is just beginning to form past tenses. In the earliest efforts, the child is likely to produce such incorrect and unheard forms as *I goed to the store* or *I seed a dog*, along with other conventional uses of the past tense: *I walked to Grandma's*. This process reveals that the child has learned the basic, general rule about the formation of the past tense—you add *-ed* to the verb—but has not yet mastered the other rules, the exceptions and irregularities. The production of forms that the child has never heard suggests that imitation is not central in language learning and that the child's main strategy is hypothesizing—deducing from the language she hears an idea about the underlying rule, and then trying it out.

My own son, who is now two-and-a-half, has just been working on the -ed problem. Until recently, he used present tense verb forms for all situations: *Daddy go work?* (for: *Did Daddy go to work?*) and *We take a bath today?* (for: *Will we take a bath today?*). Once he discovered that wonderful past tag, he attached it with gusto to any verb he could think up and produced, predictably enough, *goed, eated, flied,* and many other

---

[1] Victoria Fromkin and Robert Rodman, *An Introduction to Language* (New York: Holt, Rinehart and Winston, 1978), 329–342.

overgeneralizations of his initial hypothetical rule for the formation of past tenses. He was so excited about his new discovery, in fact, that he would often give extra emphasis to the marker: *Dad, I swallow-ed the cookie*. Nicky will soon learn to deemphasize the sound of *-ed* (as well as to master all those irregular past forms) by listening to more language and by revising and expanding his own internal set of language rules.

Linguists and educators sometimes debate about what percentage of adult forms is learned by a given age. A common estimate is that 90 percent of adult structures are acquired by the time a child is seven. Obviously, it is quite difficult to attach proportions to such a complex process, but the central point is clear: schoolchildren of primary age have already learned the great majority of the rules governing their native language, and can produce virtually all the kinds of sentences that it permits. With the passing years, all children will add some additional capabilities, but the main growth from this point forward will not so much be in acquiring new rules as in using new combinations of them to express increasingly sophisticated ideas, and in learning how to use language effectively in a widening variety of social settings.

It is important to reiterate that we are talking here about the child's acquisition of her native language. It may be that the child has been born into a community of standard English or French or Urdu speakers, or into a community of nonstandard English, French, or Urdu speakers. But the language of the child's home and community *is* the native language, and it would be impossible for her to somehow grow up speaking a language to which she was never, or rarely, exposed.

2. Language operates by rules. As the *-ed* saga suggests, when a child begins learning his native language, what he is doing is acquiring a vast system of mostly subconscious rules which allow him to make meaningful and increasingly complex utterances. These rules concern sounds, words, the arrangement of strings of words, and aspects of the social act of speaking. Obviously, children who grow up speaking different languages will acquire generally different sets of rules. This fact reminds us that human language is, in an important sense, arbitrary.

Except for a few onomatopoetic words (*bang, hiss, grunt*), the assignment of meanings to certain combinations of sounds is arbitrary. We English speakers might just as well call a chair a *glotz* or a *blurg*, as long as we all agreed that these combinations of sounds meant *chair*. In fact, not just the words but the individual sounds used in English have been arbitrarily selected from a much larger inventory of sounds which the human vocal organs are capable of producing. The existence of African languages employing musical tones or clicks reminds us that the forty phonemes used in English represent an arbitrary selection from hundreds of available sounds. Grammar, too, is arbitrary. We have a rule in English which requires most adjectives to appear before the noun which they modify (*the blue chair*). In French, the syntax is reversed (*la chaise bleue*), and in some languages, like Latin, either order is allowed.

Given that any language requires a complex set of arbitrary choices regarding sounds, words, and syntax, it is clear that the foundation of a language lies not in any "natural" meaning or appropriateness of its features, but in its system of rules—the implicit agreement among speakers that they will use certain sounds consistently, that certain combinations of sounds will mean the same thing over and over, and that they will observe certain grammatical patterns in order to convey messages. It takes thousands of such rules to make up a language. Many linguists believe that when each of us learned these countless rules, as very young children, we accomplished the most complex cognitive task of our lives.

Our agreement about the rules of language, of course, is only a general one. Every speaker of a language is unique; no one sounds exactly like anyone else. The language differs from region to region, between social, occupational and ethnic groups, and even from one speech situation to the next. These variations are not mistakes or deviations from some basic tongue, but are simply the rule-governed alternatives which make up any language. Still, in America our assorted variations of English are mostly mutually intelligible, reflecting the fact that most of our language rules do overlap, whatever group we belong to, or whatever situation we are in.

3. All languages have three major components: a sound system, a vocabulary, and a system of grammar. This statement underscores what has already been suggested: that any human speaker makes meaning by manipulating sounds, words, and their order according to an internalized system of rules which other speakers of that language largely share.

The sound system of a language—its phonology—is the inventory of vocal noises, and combinations of noises, that it employs. Children learn the selected sounds of their own language in the same way they learn the other elements: by listening, hypothesizing, testing, and listening again. They do not, though it may seem logical, learn the sounds first (after all, English has only forty) and then go on to words and then to grammar. My son, for example, can say nearly anything he needs to say, in sentences of eight or ten or fourteen words, but he couldn't utter the sound of *th* to save his life.

The vocabulary, or lexicon, of a language is the individual's storehouse of words. Obviously, one of the young child's most conspicuous efforts is aimed at expanding his lexical inventory. Two- and three-year-olds are notorious for asking "What's that?" a good deal more often than even the most doting parents can tolerate. And not only do children constantly and spontaneously try to enlarge their vocabularies, but they are always working to build categories, to establish classes of words, to add connotative meanings, to hone and refine their sense of the semantic properties—the meanings—of the words they are learning. My awareness of these latter processes was heightened a few months ago as we were driving home from a trip in the country during which Nicky had delighted in learning the names of various features of the rural landscape. As we drove past the Chicago skyline, Nicky looked up at the tall buildings and announced "Look at those silos, Dad!" I asked him what he thought they kept in the Sears Tower, and he replied confidently, "Animal food." His parents' laughter presumably helped him to begin reevaluating his lexical hypothesis that any tall narrow structure was a silo.

Linguists, who look at language descriptively rather than prescriptively, use two different definitions of *grammar*. The first, which I am using, says that grammar is the system of rules we use to arrange words into meaningful English sentences. For example, my lexicon and my phonology may provide me with the appropriate strings of sounds to say the words: *eat four yesterday cat crocodile the*. It is my knowledge of grammar which allows me to arrange these elements into a sentence: *Yesterday the crocodile ate four cats*. Not only does my grammar arrange these elements in a meaningful order, it also provides me with the necessary markers of plurality, tense, and agreement. Explaining the series of rules by which I subconsciously constructed this sentence describes some of my "grammar" in this sense.

The second definition of *grammar* often used by linguists refers to the whole system of rules which makes up a language—not just the rules for the arrangement and appropriate marking of elements in a sentence, but all of the lexical, phonological, and syntactic patterns which a language uses. In this sense, *everything* I know about my language, all the conscious and unconscious operations I can perform when speaking or listening, constitutes my grammar. It is this second definition of grammar to which linguists sometimes refer when they speak of describing a language in terms of its grammar.

4. Everyone speaks a dialect. Among linguists the term *dialect* simply designates a variety of a particular language which has a certain set of lexical, phonological, and grammatical rules that distinguish it from other dialects. The most familiar definition of dialects in America is geographical: we recognize, for example, that some features of New England language—the dropping *r*'s (*pahk the cah in Hahvahd yahd*) and the use of *bubbler* for *drinking fountain*—distinguish the speech of this region. The native speaker of Bostonian English is not making mistakes, of course; he or she simply observes systematic rules which happen to differ from those observed in other regions.

Where do these different varieties of a language come from and how are they maintained? The underlying factors are isolation and language change. Imagine a group of people which lives, works, and talks together constantly. Among them, there is a good deal of natural pressure to keep the language relatively uniform. But if one part of the group moves away to a remote location, and has no further contact with the other, the language of the two groups will gradually diverge. This will happen not just because of the differing needs of the two different environments, but also because of the inexorable and sometimes arbitrary process of language change itself. In other words, there is no likelihood that the language of these two groups, though identical at the beginning, will now change in the same ways. Ultimately, if the isolation is lengthy and complete, the two hypothetical groups will probably develop separate, mutu-

ally unintelligible languages. If the isolation is only partial, if interchange occurs between the two groups, and if they have some need to
continue communicating (as with the American and British peoples) less
divergence will occur.

This same principle of isolation also applies, in a less dramatic way,
to contemporary American dialects. New England speakers are partially
isolated from southern speakers, and so some of the differences between
these two dialects are maintained. Other factors, such as travel and the
mass media, bring them into contact with each other and tend to prevent
drastic divergences. But the isolation that produces or maintains language differences may not be only geographical. In many American cities
we find people living within miles, or even blocks of each other, who
speak markedly different and quite enduring dialects. Black English and
mid-western English are examples of such pairs. Here, the isolation is
partially spatial, but more importantly it is social, economic, occupational, educational, and political. And as long as this effective separation
of speech communities persists, so will the differences in their dialects.

Many of the world's languages have a "standard" dialect. In some
countries, the term *standard* refers more to a *lingua franca* than to an
indigenous dialect. In Nigeria, for example, where there are more than
150 mostly mutually unintelligible languages and dialects, English was
selected as the official standard. In America, we enjoy this kind of
national standardization because the vast majority of us speak some
mutually intelligible dialect of English. But we also have ideas about a
standard English which is not just a *lingua franca* but a prestige or preferred dialect. Similarly, the British have Received Pronunciation, the
Germans have High German, and the French, backed by the authority of
the Académie Française, have "Le Vrai Français." These languages are
typically defined as the speech of the upper, or at least educated, classes
of the society, are the predominant dialect of written communication,
and are commonly taught to schoolchildren. In the past, these prestige
dialects have sometimes been markers which conveniently set the ruling classes apart from the rabble—as once was the case with Norman
French. But in most modern societies the standard dialect is a mutually
intelligible version of the country's common tongue which is accorded a
special status.

A standard dialect is not *inherently* superior to any other dialect of
the same language. It may, however, confer considerable social, political,
and economic power on its users, because of prevailing attitudes about
the dialect's worthiness.

Recently, American linguists have been working to describe some of
the nonstandard dialects of English, and we now seem to have a better
description of some of these dialects than of our shadowy standard. Black
English is a case in point. The most important finding of all this research
has been that Black English is just as "logical" and "ordered" as any
other English dialect, in spite of the fact that it is commonly viewed by
white speakers as being somehow inferior, deformed, or limited.

5. Speakers of all languages employ a range of styles and a set of sub-dialects or jargons. Just as soon as we accept the notion that we all speak a dialect, it is necessary to complicate things further. We may realize that we do belong to a speech community, although we may not like to call it a dialect, but we often forget that our speech patterns vary greatly during the course of our everyday routine. In the morning, at home, communication with our spouses may consist of grumbled fragments of a private code:

Uhhh.

Yeah.

More?

Um-hmm.

You gonna . . . ?

Yeah, if . . .

'Kay.

Yet half an hour later, we may be standing in a meeting and talking quite differently: "The cost-effectiveness curve of the Peoria facility has declined to the point at which management is compelled to consider terminating production." These two samples of speech suggest that we constantly range between formal and informal styles of speech—and this is an adjustment which speakers of all languages constantly make. Learning the sociolinguistic rules which tell us what sort of speech is appropriate in differing social situations is as much a part of language acquisition as learning how to produce the sound of /b/ or /t/. We talk differently to our acquaintances than to strangers, differently to our bosses than to our subordinates, differently to children than to adults. We speak in one way on the racquetball court and in another way in the courtroom; we perhaps talk differently to stewardesses than to stewards.

The ability to adjust our language forms to the social context is something which we acquire as children, along with sounds, words, and syntax. We learn, in other words, not just to say things, but also how and when and to whom. Children discover, for example, that while the purpose of most language is to communicate meaning (if it weren't they could never learn it in the first place), we sometimes use words as mere acknowledgments. (Hi. How are you doing? Fine. Bye.) Youngsters also learn that to get what you want, you have to address people as your social relation with them dictates (Miss Jones, may I please feed the hamster today?). And, of course, children learn that in some situations one doesn't use certain words at all—though such learning may sometimes seem cruelly delayed to parents whose offspring loudly announce in restaurants: "I hafta go toilet!"

Interestingly, these sociolinguistic rules are learned quite late in the game. While a child of seven or eight does command a remarkably sophisticated array of sentence types, for example, he has a great deal left to learn about the social regulations governing language use. This seems logical, given that children *do* learn language mostly by listening and experimenting. Only as a child grows old enough to encounter a widening range of social relationships and roles will he have the experience necessary to help him discover the sociolinguistic dimensions of them.

While there are many ways of describing the different styles, or registers, of language which all speakers learn, it is helpful to consider them in terms of levels of formality. One well-known example of such a scheme was developed by Martin Joos, who posited five basic styles, which he called *intimate, casual, consultative, formal*, and *frozen*.[2] While Joos's model is only one of many attempts to find a scale for the range of human speech styles, and is certainly not the final word on the subject, it does illuminate some of the ways in which day-to-day language varies. At the bottom of Joos's model is the *intimate* style, a kind of language which "fuses two separate personalities" and can only occur between individuals with a close personal relationship. A husband and wife, for example, may sometimes speak to each other in what sounds like a very fragmentary and clipped code that they alone understand. Such utterances are characterized by their "extraction"—the use of extracts of potentially complete sentences, made possible by an intricate, personal, shared system of private symbols. The *intimate* style, in sum, is personal, fragmentary, and implicit.

The *casual* style also depends on social groupings. When people share understandings and meanings which are not complete enough to be called intimate, they tend to employ the *casual* style. The earmarks of this pattern are ellipsis and slang. Ellipsis is the shorthand of shared meaning; slang often expresses these meanings in a way that defines the group and excludes others. The *casual* style is reserved for friends and insiders, or those whom we choose to make friends and insiders. The *consultative* style "produces cooperation without the integration, profiting from the lack of it."[3] In this style, the speaker provides more explicit background information because the listener may not understand without it. This is the style used by strangers or near-strangers in routine transactions: co-workers dealing with a problem, a buyer making a purchase from a clerk, and so forth. An important feature of this style is the participation of the listener, who uses frequent interjections such as *Yeah, Uh-huh* or *I see* to signal understanding.

This element of listener participation disappears in the *formal* style. Speech in this mode is defined by the listener's lack of participation, as well as by the speaker's opportunity to plan his utterances ahead of time and in detail. The *formal* style is most often found in speeches, lectures, sermons, television newscasts, and the like. The *frozen* style is reserved for print, and particularly for literature. This style can be densely packed and repacked with meanings by its "speaker," and it can be read and reread by its "listener." The immediacy of interaction between the participants is sacrificed in the interests of permanence, elegance, and precision.

---

[2] Martin Joos, *The Five Clocks* (New York: Harcourt, Brace and World, 1962).
[3] Ibid., 40.

Whether or not we accept Joos's scheme to classify the different gradations of formality, we can probably sense the truth of the basic proposition: we do make such adjustments in our speech constantly, mostly unconsciously, and in response to the social situation in which we are speaking. What we sometimes forget is that no one style can accurately be called better or worse than another, apart from the context in which it is used. Though we have much reverence for the formal and frozen styles, they can be utterly dysfunctional in certain circumstances. If I said to my wife: "Let us consider the possibility of driving our automobile into the central business district of Chicago in order to contemplate the possible purchase of denim trousers," she would certainly find my way of speaking strange, if not positively disturbing. All of us need to shift between the intimate, casual, and consultative styles in everyday life, not because one or another of these is a better way of talking, but because each is required in certain contexts. Many of us also need to master the formal style for the talking and writing demanded by our jobs. But as Joos has pointed out, few of us actually need to control the frozen style, which is reserved primarily for literature.[4]

Besides having a range of speech styles, each speaker also uses a number of jargons based upon his or her affiliation with certain groups. The most familiar of these jargons are occupational: doctors, lawyers, accountants, farmers, electricians, plumbers, truckers, and social workers each have a job-related jargon into which they can shift when the situation demands it. Sometimes these special languages are a source of amusement or consternation to outsiders, but usually the outsiders also speak jargons of their own, though they may not recognize them. Jargons may also be based on other kinds of affiliations. Teenagers, it is often remarked by bemused parents, have a language of their own. So they do, and so do other age groups. Some of the games and chants of youngsters reflect a kind of childhood dialect, and much older persons may have a jargon of their own as well, reflecting concerns with aging, illness, and finances. Sports fans obviously use and understand various abstruse athletic terms, while people interested in needlecrafts use words that are equally impenetrable to the uninitiated. For every human enterprise we can think of, there will probably be a jargon attached to it.

But simply noting that all speakers control a range of styles and a set of jargons does not tell the whole story. For every time we speak, we do so not just in a social context, but for certain purposes of our own. When talking with a dialectologist, for example, I may use linguistic jargon simply to facilitate our sharing of information, or instead to convince him that I know enough technical linguistics to be taken seriously—or both. In other words, my purposes—the functions of my language—affect the way I talk. The British linguist M. A. K. Halliday has studied children in an attempt to determine how people's varying purposes affect their speech.[5]

---

[4] Ibid., 39–67.

[5] M. A. K. Halliday, *Explorations in the Functions of Language* (London: Edward Arnold, 1973).

Halliday *had* to consider children, in fact, because the purposes of any given adult utterance are usually so complex and overlapping that it is extremely difficult to isolate the individual purposes. By examining the relatively simpler language of children, he was able to discover seven main uses, functions, or purposes for talking: *instrumental, regulatory, interactional, personal, heuristic, imaginative,* and *representational.*

The *instrumental* function, Halliday explains, is for getting things done; it is the *I want* function. Close to it is the *regulatory* function, which seeks to control the actions of others around the speaker. The *interactional* function is used to define groups and relationships, to get along with others. The *personal* function allows people to express what they are and how they feel; Halliday calls this the *here I come* function. The *heuristic* function is in operation when the speaker is using language to learn, by asking questions and testing hypotheses. In the *imaginative* function, a speaker may use language to create a world just as he or she wants it, or may simply use it as a toy, making amusing combinations of sounds and words. In the *representational* function, the speaker uses language to express propositions, give information, or communicate subject matter.

Absent from Halliday's list of functions, interestingly, is one of the most common and enduring purposes of human language: lying. Perhaps lying could be included in the representational or interactional functions, in the sense that a person may deceive in order to be a more congenial companion. Or perhaps each of Halliday's seven functions could be assigned a reverse, false version. In any case, common sense, human history, and our own experience all tell us that lying—or misleading or covering up or shading the truth—is one of the main ends to which language is put.

As we look back over these three forms of language variation—styles, jargons, and functions—we may well marvel at the astounding complexity of language. For not only do all speakers master the intricate sound, lexical, and grammatical patterns of their native tongue, but they also learn countless, systematic alternative ways of applying their linguistic knowledge to varying situations and needs. We are reminded, in short, that language is as beautifully varied and fascinating as the creatures who use it.

6. Language change is normal. This fact, while often acknowledged by critics of contemporary English, has rarely been fully understood or accepted by them. It is easy enough to welcome into the language such innocent neologisms as *astronaut, transistor,* or *jet lag.* These terms serve obvious needs, responding to certain changes in society which virtually require them. But language also changes in many ways that don't seem so logical or necessary. The dreaded dangling *hopefully,* which now attaches itself to the beginning of sentences with the meaning *I hope,* appears to be driving out the connotation *full of hope.* As Jean Stafford has angrily pointed out, the word *relevant* has broadened to denote almost any kind of "with-it-ness." But these kinds of lexical changes are not new, and simply demonstrate an age-old process at work in the present. The word *dog* (actually, *dogge*), for example, used to refer to one specific breed, but now serves as a general term for a quite varied family of animals. Perhaps similarly, *dialogue* has now broadened to include exchanges of views between (or among) any number of speakers. But word meanings can also narrow over time, as the word *deer* shrank from indicating any game animal to just one specific type.

The sounds of language also change, though usually in slower and less noticeable ways than vocabulary. Perhaps fifty years ago, the majority of American speakers produced distinctly different consonant sounds in the middle of *latter* and *ladder*. Today, most younger people and many adults pronounce the two words is if they were the same. Another sound change in progress is the weakening distinction between the vowel sounds in *dawn* and *Don*, or *hawk* and *hock*. Taking the longer view, of course, we realize that modern pronunciation is the product of centuries of gradual sound changes.

Shifts in grammar are more comparable to the slow process of sound change than the sometimes sudden one of lexical change. Today we find that the *shall/will* distinction, which is still maintained among some upper-class Britishers, has effectively disappeared from spoken American English. A similar fate seems to await the *who/whom* contrast, which is upheld by fewer and fewer speakers. Our pronouns, as a matter of fact, seem to be a quite volatile corner of our grammar. In spite of the efforts of teachers, textbooks, style manuals, and the SAT tests, most American speakers now find nothing wrong with *Everyone should bring their books to class* or even *John and me went to the Cubs game*. And even the hoary old double negative (which is an obligatory feature of degraded tongues like French) seems to be making steady, if slow progress. We may be only a generation or two from the day when we will again say, with Shakespeare, "I will not budge for no man's pleasure."

While we may recognize that language does inexorably change, we cannot always explain the causes or the sequences of each individual change. Sometimes changes move toward simplification, as with the shedding of vowel distinctions. Other changes tend to regularize the language, as when we de-Latinize words like *medium/media* (The newspapers are one media of communication), or when we abandon *dreamt* and *burnt* in favor of the regular forms *dreamed* and *burned*. And some coinages will always reflect the need to represent new inventions, ideas, or events: *quark, simulcast, pulsar, stagflation*. Yet there is plenty of language change which seems to happen spontaneously, sporadically, and without apparent purpose. Why should *irregardless* substitute for *regardless*, meaning the same thing? Why should handy distinctions like that between *imply* and *infer* be lost? But even if we can never explain the reasons for such mysterious changes—or perhaps *because* we can't—we must accept the fact that language does change. Today, we would certainly be thought odd to call cattle *kine*, to pronounce *saw* as *saux*, or to ask about "thy health," however ordinary such language might have been centuries ago. Of course, the more recent changes, and especially the changes in progress, make us most uncomfortable.

But then our sense of the pace of language change is often exaggerated. When we cringe (as do so many of the language critics) at the sudden reassignment of the word *gay* to a new referent, we tend to forget that we can still read Shakespeare. In other words, even if many conspicuous (and almost invariably lexical) changes are in progress, this doesn't necessarily mean that the language as a whole is undergoing a rapid or wholesale transformation.

However, once we start looking for language change, it seems to be everywhere, and we are sorely tempted to overestimate its importance. Sometimes we even discover changes which aren't changes at all. Various language critics have propounded the notion that we are being inundated by a host of very new and particularly insidious coinages. Here are some of the most notorious ones, along with the date of their earliest citation in the *Oxford English Dictionary* for the meaning presently viewed as modern and dangerous: *you know* (1350); *anxious* for *eager* (1742); *between you and I* (1640); *super* for *good* (1850); *decimate* for *diminish* by other than one-tenth (1663); *inoperative* for nonmechanical phenomena (1631); *near-perfect* for *nearly perfect* (1635); *host* as in *to host a gathering* (1485); *gifted*, as in *He gifted his associates* (1660); *aggravate* for *annoy* (1611).[6]

If we find ourselves being aggravated (or annoyed) by any of these crotchety old neologisms, we can always look to the Mobil Oil Corporation for a comforting discussion of the problem. In one of its self-serving public service magazine ads, Mobil intoned: "Change upsets people. Always has. Disrupts routine and habit patterns. Demands constant adaptation. But change is inevitable. And essential. Inability to change can be fatal."[7] And Mobil inadvertently gives us one last example of a language change currently in progress: the increasing use of sentence fragments in formal written English.

7. Languages are intimately related to the societies and individuals who use them. Every human language has been shaped by, and changes to meet, the needs of its speakers. In this limited sense, all human languages can be said to be both equal and perfect. Some Eskimo languages, for example, have many words for different types of snow: wet snow, powdery snow, blowing snow, and so forth. This extensive vocabulary obviously results from the importance of snow in the Eskimo environment and the need to be able to talk about it in detailed ways. In Chicago, where snow is just an occasional annoyance, we get along quite nicely with a few basic terms—snow, slush, and sleet—and a number of adjectival modifiers. Richard Mitchell has described a hypothetical primitive society where the main preoccupation is banging on tree-bark to

---

[6] With many thanks to Jim Quinn and his *American Tongue and Cheek* (New York: Pantheon, 1981).

[7] "Business Is Bound to Change," Mobil Oil advertisement, *Chicago Tribune*, January 5, 1977.

harvest edible insects, and this particular people has developed a large, specialized vocabulary for talking about the different kinds of rocks and trees involved in this process. In each of these cases, the language in question is well adapted to the needs of its speakers. Each language allows its speakers to easily talk about whatever it is important to discuss in that society.

This does not mean, however, that any given language will work "perfectly" or be "equal" to any other in a cross-cultural setting. If I take my Chicago dialect to the tundra, I may have trouble conversing with people who distinguish, in Eskimo, ten more kinds of snow than I do. Or if one of Mitchell's tree-bangers came to Chicago, his elaborate rock-and-bark vocabulary would be of little use. Still, neither of these languages is inherently inferior or superior; inside its normal sphere of use, each is just what it needs to be.

There is a related question concerning the differences between languages. Many linguists have tried to determine the extent to which our native language conditions our thought processes. For all the talk of similarities between languages, there are also some quite remarkable differences from one language to another. The famous studies of American Indian languages by Benjamin Lee Whorf and Edward Sapir have suggested, for example, that Hopi speakers do not conceptualize time in the same way as speakers of English.[8] To the Hopi, time is a continuing process, an unfolding that cannot be segmented into chunks to be used or "wasted." The words and constructions of the Hopi language reflect this perception. Similarly, some languages do not describe the same color spectrum which we speakers of English normally regard as a given physical phenomenon. Some of these name only two, others three, and so on. Are we, then, hopelessly caught in the grasp of the language which we happen to grow up speaking? Are all our ideas about the world controlled by our language, so that our reality is what we *say* rather than what objectively, verifiably exists?

The best judgment of linguists on this subject comes down to this: we are conditioned to some degree by the language we speak, and our language does teach us habitual ways of looking at the world. But on the other hand, human adaptability enables us to transcend the limitations of a language—to learn to see the world in new ways and voice new concepts—when we must. While it is probably true that some ideas are easier to communicate in one language than another, both languages and speakers can change to meet new needs. The grip which language has on us is firm, but it does not strangle; we make language more than language makes us.

It is also important to realize that a language is not just an asset of a culture or group, but of individual human beings. Our native language is the speech of our parents, siblings, friends, and community. It is the code

---

[8] See Edward Sapir, *Culture, Language, and Personality* (Berkeley: University of California Press, 1949).

we use to communicate in the most powerful and intimate experiences of our lives. It is a central part of our personality, an expression and a mirror of what we are and wish to be. Our language is as personal and as integral to each of us as our bodies and our brains, and in our own unique ways, we all treasure it. And all of us, when we are honest, have to admit that criticism of the way we talk is hard not to take personally. This reaction is nothing to be ashamed of: it is simply a reflection of the natural and profound importance of language to every individual human being.

To summarize: all human languages and the concept systems which they embody are efficient in their native speech communities. The languages of the world also vary in some important ways, so that people sometimes falsely assume that certain tongues are inherently superior to others. Yet it is marvelous that these differences exist. It is good that the Eskimo language facilitates talk about snow, that the Hopi language supports that culture's view of time, and I suppose, that Chicago speech has ample resources for discussing drizzle, wind, and inept baseball teams.

8. Value judgments about different languages or dialects are matters of taste. One of the things we seem to acquire right along with our native tongue is a set of attitudes about the value of other people's language. If we think for a moment about any of the world's major languages, we will find that we usually have some idea—usually a prejudice or stereotype—about it. French is the sweet music of love. German is harsh, martial, overbearing. The language of Spain is exotic, romantic. The Spanish of Latin Americans is alien, uneducated. Scandinavian tongues have a kind of silly rhythm, as the Muppet Show's Swedish chef demonstrates weekly. British English is refined and intelligent. New York dialect (especially on Toity-Toid Street) is crude and loud. Almost all southern American speakers (especially rural sheriffs) are either cruelly crafty or just plain dumb. Oriental languages have a funny, high-pitched, singsong sound. And Black English, well, it just goes to show. None of these notions about different languages and dialects says anything about the way these tongues function in their native speech communities. By definition—by the biological and social order of things—they function efficiently. Each is a fully formed, logical, rule-governed variant of human speech.

It is easy enough to assert that all languages are equal and efficient in their own sphere of use. But most of us do not really believe in this idea, and certainly do not act as if we did. We constantly make judgments about other people and other nations on the basis of the language they use. Especially when we consider the question of mutually intelligible American dialects, we are able to see that most ideas about language differences are purely matters of taste. It isn't that we cannot understand each other—Southerners, Northerners, Californians, New Yorkers, blacks, whites, Appalachian folk—with only the slightest effort we can communicate just fine. But because of our history of experiences with each other, or perhaps just out of perversity, we have developed prejudices toward other people's language which sometimes affect our behavior. Such prejudices, however irrational, generate much pressure for speakers of disfavored dialects to abandon their native speech for some approved pattern. But as the linguist Einar Haugen has warned:

> And yet, who are we to call for linguistic genocide in the name of efficiency? Let us recall that although a language is a tool and an instrument of communication, that is not all it is. A language is also a part of one's personality, a form of behavior that has its roots in our earliest experience. Whether it is a so-called rural or ghetto dialect, or a peasant language, or a "primitive" idiom, it fulfills exactly the same needs and performs the same services in the daily lives of its speakers as does the most advanced language of culture. Every language, dialect, patois, or lingo is a structurally complete framework into which can be poured any subtlety of emotion or thought that its users are capable of experiencing. Whatever it lacks at any given time or place in the way of vocabulary and syntax can be supplied in very short order by borrowing and imitation from other languages. *Any scorn for the language of others is scorn for those who use it, and as such is a form of social discrimination.* [Emphasis mine.][9]

It is not Haugen's purpose—nor is it mine—to deny that social acceptability and economic success in America may be linked in certain ways to the mastery of approved patterns of speech. Yet all of us must realize that the need for such mastery arises *only* out of the prejudices of the dominant speech community and not from any intrinsic shortcomings of nonstandard American dialects.

9. Writing is derivative of speech. Writing systems are always based upon systems of oral language which of necessity develop first. People have been talking for at least a half million years, but the earliest known writing system appeared fewer than 5,000 years ago. Of all the world's languages, only about 5 percent have developed indigenous writing systems. In other words, wherever there are human beings, we will always find language, but not necessarily writing. If language is indeed a biologically programmed trait of the species, writing does not seem to be part of the standard equipment.

Although the English writing system is essentially phonemic—an attempt to represent the sounds of language in graphic form—it is notoriously irregular and confusing. Some other languages, like Czech, Finnish, and Spanish, come close to having perfect sound-symbol correspondence: each letter in the writing system stands for one, and only one, sound. English, unfortunately, uses some 2,000 letters and combinations of letters to represent its forty or so separate sounds. This causes problems. For example, in the sentence: *Did he believe that Caesar could see the people seize the seas?* there are seven different spellings for the vowel sound /ē/. The sentence: *The silly amoeba stole the key to the machine* yields four more spellings of the same vowel sound. George

---

[9] Einar Haugen, "The Curse of Babel," in Einar Haugen and Morton Bloomfield, *Language as a Human Problem* (New York: W. W. Norton, 1974), 41.

Bernard Shaw once noted that a reasonable spelling of the word *fish* might be *ghoti*: *gh* as in *enough*, *o* as in *women*, and *ti* as in *nation*. In spite of all its irregularities, however, the English spelling system is nevertheless phonemic at heart, as our ability to easily read and pronounce nonsense words like *mimsy* or *proat* demonstrates.

Writing, like speech, may be put to a whole range of often overlapping uses. And shifts in the level of formality occur in writing just as they do in talk. An author, like a speaker, must adjust the style of her message to the audience and the occasion. A woman composing a scholarly article, for example, makes some systematically different linguistic choices than those she makes when leaving a note for her husband on the refrigerator. Both writers and speakers (even good ones) employ various jargons or specialized vocabularies that seem comfortable and convenient to the people they are addressing. Rules change with time in both writing and speech. Most obviously, changes in speech habits are reflected in writing: today we readily pen words which weren't even invented ten or a hundred years ago. And even some of the rules which are enforced in writing after they have been abandoned in speech do eventually break down. Today, for example, split infinitives and sentence fragments are increasingly accepted in writing. Our personal tastes and social prejudices, which often guide our reactions to other people's speech, can also dictate our response to other people's writing.

Our beliefs about writing are also bound up with our literary tradition. We have come to revere certain works of literature and exposition which have "stood the test of time," which speak across the centuries to successive generations of readers. These masterpieces, like most enduring published writing, tend to employ what Joos would call formal and frozen styles of language. They were written in such language, of course, because their authors had to accommodate the subject, audience, and purpose at hand—and the making of sonnets and declarations of independence generally calls for considerable linguistic formality. Given our affection for these classics, we quite naturally admire not only their content but their form. We find ourselves feeling that only in the nineteenth or sixteenth century could writers "really use the language" correctly and beautifully. Frequently, we teach this notion in our schools, encouraging students to see the language of written literature as the only true and correct style of English. We require students not only to mimic the formal literary style in their writing, but even to transplant certain of its features into their speech—in both cases without reference to the *students'* subject, audience, or purpose. All of this is not meant to demean literature or the cultivation of its appreciation among teenagers. It simply reminds us of how the mere existence of a system of writing and a literature can be a conservative influence on the language. The study, occasionally the official worship, of language forms that are both old and formal may retard linguistic changes currently in progress, as well as reinforce our mistaken belief that one style of language is always and truly the best.

The preceding nine ideas about language are not entirely new. Many of them have been proclaimed by loud, if lonely, voices in centuries long past. It has only been in the last seventy or eighty years, however, that these ideas have begun to form a coherent picture of how language works, thanks to the work of the descriptive and historical linguists. It is their research which has been, I hope, accurately if broadly summarized here.

A look at the history of past crises offered a general kind of reassurance about the present language panic. It suggested that such spasms of insecurity and intolerance are a regular, cyclical feature of the human chronicle, and result more from social and political tensions than from actual changes in the language. The review of research presented in this section broadens that perspective and deflates the urgency of the 1983-model literary crisis in some other ways. It shows us that our language cannot "die" as long as people speak it; that language change is a healthy and inevitable process; that all human languages are rule governed, ordered, and logical; that variations between different groups of speakers are normal and predictable; that all speakers employ a variety of speech forms and styles in response to changing social settings; and that most of our attitudes about language are based upon social rather than linguistic judgments.

And so, if we are to believe the evidence of historical and linguistic research, our current language crisis seems rather curious. This is a crisis which is not critical, which does not actually pose the dangers widely attributed to it. If anything, the crisis is merely a description of linguistic business as usual, drawn by the critics in rather bizarre and hysterical strokes. It seems fair to ask at this point: What's the problem?

FOR DISCUSSION AND REVIEW

1. In presenting his "nine ideas about language," Daniels attempts to dispel some commonly held but inaccurate beliefs about language. List as many of these myths as you can. How successful is Daniels in dispelling them?

2. As Daniels notes, children learn relatively late the "rules" about the kinds of speech that are appropriate in various circumstances. From your own experience, give some examples of children's use of language that, given the social context, was inappropriate.

3. You probably would describe a particular event—for example, a party, a camping trip, an evening with a friend—differently to different people. Jot down the way you would tell a good friend about some event. Then write down the way you would describe the same occurrence to your parents. When you compare the two accounts, what differences do you find? Are they the differences that Daniels leads you to expect?

4. Daniels believes that most people have "some idea—usually a prejudice or stereotype"—about different languages and dialects. Define
   the terms *prejudice* and *stereotype*. Then test Daniels's theory by
   asking five people what they think of (a) the languages and dialects
   or (b) the speakers of the languages and dialects that Daniels mentioned under point 8 on pp. 56–57. Study the responses and describe
   any prejudices or stereotypes that you find.

6

Language: An Introduction

W. F. Bolton

The ability to use language is the most distinctive human characteristic, and yet most people take this ability for granted, never considering its richness and complexity. In the following selection, Professor W. F. Bolton analyzes the intricate physiological mechanisms involved in speech production and in speech reception, or hearing. Especially interesting is his discussion of the differences between "speech breathing" and "quiet breathing." Professor Bolton also explains the "design features" that characterize human language; this explanation is important for understanding many of the later selections in this book. His concluding warning against ethnocentricity is particularly important today.

Language is so built into the way people live that it has become an axiom of being human. It is the attribute that most clearly distinguishes our species from all others; it is what makes possible much of what we do, and perhaps even what we think. Without language we could not specify our wishes, our needs, the practical instructions that make possible cooperative endeavor ("You hold it while I hit it"). Without language we would have to grunt and gesture and touch rather than tell. And through writing systems or word of mouth we are in touch with distant places we will never visit, people we will never meet, a past and a future of which we can have no direct experience. Without language we would live in isolation from our ancestors and our descendants, condemned to learn only from our own experiences and to take our knowledge to the grave.

Of course other species communicate too, sometimes in ways that seem almost human. A pet dog or cat can make its needs and wishes known quite effectively, not only to others of its own species but to its human owner. But is this language? Porpoises make extremely complex sequences of sounds that may suggest equally complex messages, but so far no way has been found to verify the suggestion. Chimpanzees have been taught several humanly understandable languages, notably AMES-LAN [American Sign Language] and a computer language, but there has been heated debate whether their uses of these languages are like ours or merely learned performances of rather greater subtlety than those of trained circus animals. If the accomplishments of dolphins and chimpanzees remain open questions, however, there is no question but that human uses of language, both everyday and in the building of human cultures, are of a scope and power unequaled on our planet.

It seems likely that language arose in humans about a hundred thousand years ago. How this happened is at least as unknowable as how the universe began, and for the same reason: there was nobody there capable of writing us a report of the great event. Language, like the universe, has its creation myths; indeed, in St. John's Gospel both come together in the grand formulation, "In the beginning was the Word, and the Word was with God, and the Word was God." Modern linguists, like modern cosmologists, have adopted an evolutionary hypothesis. Somehow, over the millennia, both the human brain and those parts of the human body now loosely classed as the organs of speech have evolved so that speech is now a part of human nature. Babies start to talk at a certain stage of their development, whether or not their parents consciously try to teach them; only prolonged isolation from the sounds of speech can keep them from learning.

Writing is another matter. When the topic of language comes up, our first thoughts are likely to be of written words. But the majority of the world's languages have never been reduced to writing (though they all could be), and illiteracy is a natural state: we learn to write only laboriously and with much instruction. This is hardly surprising, since compared with speech, writing is a very recent invention—within the past 5,000 years. Still more recently there have been invented complex languages of gesture for use by and with people unable to hear or speak; these too must be painstakingly learned. What do the spoken, written, and sign languages have in common that distinguishes them from other ways to communicate?

PROPERTIES OF LANGUAGE

Perhaps the most distinctive property of language is that its users can create sentences never before known, and yet perfectly understandable to their hearers and readers. We don't have to be able to say "I've heard that one before!" in order to be able to say, "I see what you mean." And so language can meet our expressive needs virtually without limit, no matter how little we have read or heard before, or what our new experiences call on us to express. Another way of describing this property is to say that language is *productive*. We take this productivity for granted in our uses of language, but in fact it is one of the things that make human communication unique.

Less obvious is the fact that language is *arbitrary*: the word for something seldom has any necessary connection with the thing itself. We say *one, two, three*—but the Chinese say *yi, er, san*. Neither language has the "right" word for the numerals, because there is no such thing. (It might seem that a dog's barking, or a blackbird's call, were equally arbitrary, as both might be translated into various languages as "Go away!" or "Allez-vous-en!"—but within the species the sound is universally understand-able. A chow and a German shepherd understand each other without translation—unlike speakers of Chinese and German.)

Even the sounds of a language are arbitrary. English can be spoken using only 36 significantly different sounds, and these are not all the same as the sounds needed to speak other languages. These 36 sounds are in turn arbitrarily represented by 26 letters, some standing for two or more sounds, others overlapping. (Consider *c, s,* and *k.*) And the patterns into which these sounds, and indeed words, may be arranged are also arbitrary. We all know too well what *tax* means, but, in English at least, there is no such word as *xat*. In English we usually put an adjective before its noun—*fat man;* in French it's the other way round, *homme gros.* This patterning is the key to the productivity of language. If we use intelligible words in proper patterns, we can be sure of being understood by others who speak our language. Indeed, we seem to understand non-sense, provided it is fitted into proper patterns—the silly nonsense of doubletalk, the impressive nonsense of much bureaucratese.

This ability to attach meaning to arbitrary clusters of sounds or words is like the use and understanding of symbolism in literature and art. The word *one* does not somehow represent the numeral, somehow embody its essence the way a three-sided plane figure represents the essence of triangularity. Rather, *one* merely stands for the prime numeral 1, giving a physical form to the concept, just as the word *rosebuds* gives a physical form to the concept "the pleasures of youth" in the poetic line, "Gather ye rosebuds while ye may." Thus the sound /wʌn/, spelled *one*, has a dual quality as a sound and as a concept. This can be seen from the fact that /wʌn/, spelled *won*, matches the identical sound to a wholly different concept. This feature of *duality* is both characteristic of and apparently unique in human communication, and so linguists use it as a test to distinguish language from other kinds of communication in which a sound can have only a single meaning. (Such sounds are called signs, to distinguish them from the symbols that are human words.)

Sounds can be made into meaningful combinations, such as language, only if they are first perceived as meaningfully distinct, or *discrete*. We can find an analogy in music. Musical pitch rises continuously without steps from the lowest frequency we can hear to the highest, sliding upward like the sound of a siren. But most of music is not continuous; it consists of notes that move upwards in discrete steps, as in a scale (from *scalae*, the Latin for "stairs"). This is why we can talk about notes being the same or different, as we could not easily do if all possible tones from low to high were distributed along a continuous line. Similarly, in speech we can slide through all the vowels from "ee" in the front of the mouth to "aw" in the throat—but then how could we tell *key* from *Kay* from *coo* from *caw*? Likewise we distinguish between *v* and *f*, so that *view* is different from *few*. But these distinctions are arbitrary. They are not even common to all languages. For example, in

German the letters *v* and *f* both represent the sound /f/, the letter *w* represents the sound /v/—and there is no sound /w/. What all languages do have in common, however, is the property of discreteness.

These four properties, or "design features," of language were first set down by Charles Hockett in 1958 as part of an attempt to see how human language differs from animal communication systems. There are of course other design features—their number has varied from seven to sixteen but these four (discreteness, arbitrariness, duality, and productivity) appear to be the most important. Among the others:

Human language uses the *channel of sound*, generated by the vocal organs and perceived by the ear, as its primary mode. As a consequence, speech is *nondirectional*: anyone within hearing can pick it up, and we can hear from sources which we cannot see. Our hearing, being stereophonic, can also tell from what direction the sound is coming. Also, our language acts *fade rapidly* (unless recorded on tape or in writing). We do not, as a rule, repeat these acts the way animals often do their signals.

In human language, *any speaker can be a listener and any listener can be a speaker*, at least normally. Some kinds of animal communication, such as courtship behavior, are one-way. And we get *feedback* of our own utterances through our ears and through bone conduction. Nonsound animal communication, like the dances of bees, can often only be invisible to the originator of the message.

Our language acts are *specialized*. That is to say, they have to do only with communication; they do not serve any other function. For example, speech is not necessary for breathing, nor is it the same as other sounds we make, such as a laugh or a cry of pain or fear. Of course, such sounds can communicate, but only by accident to those within earshot. Their main purpose is a reflexive one: they happen more or less involuntarily, like the jerk of a tapped knee.

Italian children grow up speaking Italian; Chinese children learn Chinese. *Human language is transmitted by the cultures we live in*, not by our parentage: if the Chinese infant is adopted by an Italian couple living in Italy, he or she will grow up speaking perfect Italian. But a kitten growing up among human beings speaks neither Italian nor Chinese; it says *meow*. Its communication is determined by its genetic makeup, not by its cultural context.

THE PHYSIOLOGY OF SPEECH

Speech is a kind of specialized exhalation, so it follows that we breathe while we speak. But the two sorts of breathing are not at all the same. "Quiet" breathing is more rapid and shallow than breathing during speech. Quiet breathing is also more even and restful than speech breathing, for during speech the air is taken in quickly and then expelled slowly against the resistance of the speech organs. Quiet breathing is mostly through the nose, speech breathing through the mouth. These differences, and others, would normally affect the accumulation of carbon dioxide (CO_2) in the blood, and the level of CO_2 is the main regulator of breathing—the rate or volume of breathing responds to the level of CO_2 so as to keep us from getting too uncomfortable. If we consciously use "speech" breathing but remain silent, we resist this response and our discomfort grows rapidly. That discomfort does not take place during actual speech, however; some other mechanism comes into play.

> Thus, it is quite clear that breathing undergoes peculiar changes during speech. What is astonishing is that man can tolerate these modifications for an apparently unlimited period of time without experiencing respiratory distress, as is well demonstrated by the interminable speech with which many a statesman embellishes his political existence. Cloture is dictated by motor fatigue and limited receptivity in the audience—never by respiratory demands.[1]

Our neural and biochemical makeup is in fact specially adapted so that we can sustain the speech act. Other animal species are equally adapted to their systems of communication, but none of them can be taught ours because ours is species-specific, a set of abilities that have evolved in humankind over a very long time. The evolution has included the most intricate adaptations of the body and its workings, particularly the neural system (including, above all, the brain); the motor system (especially the muscles that the neural system controls); and the sensory system (especially hearing, of course, but also touch).

The speech act involves an input of meaning and an output of sound on the part of the speaker, the reverse on the part of the listener. But a great deal takes place between the input and the output, and it takes place in the brain. That means that the organ for thinking, the brain, is by definition the seat of language. And the brain is also the control center for the intricate virtuoso muscular performance we call speech, commanding the vocal activities and—most important—ensuring their coordination and sequencing.

The brain is not just an undifferentiated mass in which the whole organ does all of its tasks. The different tasks that the brain does are localized, and in a more general way, the whole brain is lateralized. In most people, the right half (or hemisphere) controls the left half of the body and vice versa, and many brain functions are also lateralized. Language is one of them; it is localized in several areas of the left hemisphere. The language centers are not motor control centers for the production of speech. Instead, they are "boardrooms" in which decisions are made, decisions that motor control centers in both hemispheres of the brain implement by issuing the orders to the body. The orders are carried by electric impulses from the central nervous system (brain and spinal cord) into the peripheral nervous system (activating the muscles).

---

[1] Eric H. Lenneberg, *Biological Foundations of Language* (New York: John Wiley & Sons, Inc., 1967), 80.

Wernicke's area lies in the left hemisphere of the brain, just above the ear. It takes its name from the German Carl Wernicke (1848–1905), who in 1874 showed that damage to that part of the brain leads to a disrupted flow of meaning in speech. A decade earlier the Frenchman Paul Broca (1824–1880) had shown that damage to another area of the left hemisphere, several inches further downward, led instead to disrupted pronunciation and grammar. There are also differences in the areas when it comes to receptive ability: damage to Broca's area does not much affect comprehension, but damage to Wernicke's area disrupts it seriously.

These differences suggest that the two chief language areas of the brain have functions that are distinct but complementary. It seems that the utterance gets its basic structure in Wernicke's area, which sends it on to Broca's area through a bundle of nerve fibers called the *arcuate fasciculus*. In Broca's area the basic structure is translated into the orders of the speech act itself, which go on to the appropriate motor control area for implementation. In reverse order, a signal from the hearing or the visual system (speech or writing) is relayed to Wernicke's area for decoding from language to linguistic meaning. Broca's area, which seems to write the program for the speech act, is not so important to listening or reading as Wernicke's area is.

All of this, naturally, is inferential: the evidence as we know it points to these conclusions, but no one has ever actually seen these brain activities taking place. The conclusions are also incredible. It is difficult to imagine all that activity for a simple "Hi!" But those conclusions are the simplest ones that will account adequately for the evidence.

All sound, whether a cat's meow, a runner's "Hi!," or a sonar beep, is a disturbance of the air or other medium (water, for example) in which it is produced. When the sound is speech it can be studied in terms of its production (articulatory phonetics), its physical properties in the air (acoustic phonetics), or its reception by the ear and other organs of hearing (auditory phonetics). The first of these is the easiest to study without special instruments, and it is the only one of the three that directly involves the motor system.

The vocal organs are those that produce speech. They form an irregular tube from the lungs, the windpipe, the larynx (and the vocal cords it contains), and the throat, to the mouth (including the tongue and lips) and nose [Fig. 6.1]. All the organs except the larynx have other functions, so not all their activities are speech activities. The lungs are central to breathing, for example, to provide oxygen to the blood, and so many animals that cannot speak have lungs. In that sense speech is a secondary function of the lungs and of all the vocal organs; it has been said that they are "vocal organs" only in the sense that the knees are prayer organs. The action of forming the sound we write with the letter *p* is very similar to that of spitting, but *p* is a part of a language system while spitting is not.

Nonetheless, to regard the speech function of these organs as secondary is to overlook the profound language adaptation of the whole human anatomy. The language functions of the motor system are not simply "overlaid" on their other functions, for the language functions in many ways conflict with the others: the tongue is far more agile than is needed for eating, the ear more sensitive than is needed for nonspeech sounds, and the esophagus much too close to the pharynx for safety (hence the need for the Heimlich maneuver). In human beings, there is nothing really secondary about the speech activities of the vocal organs.

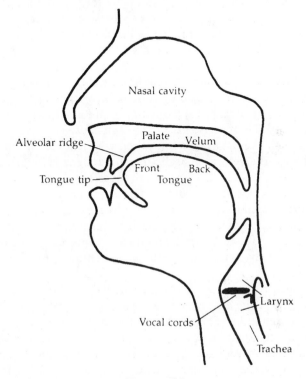

FIGURE 6.1

The lungs produce a steady stream of exhaled air which the other speech organs specialize into speech. For vowels and for many consonants, the air is set into rapid vibration by the vocal cords in the larynx or "Adam's apple." The more rapid the vibration, the higher the pitch of the speech. The air can also be set in motion by a partial constriction farther up the vocal tract in the mouth, or by a complete stoppage followed by an abrupt release. The vocal cords produce a buzzlike vibration, constriction produces a hissing sound, stoppage and release produce a small explosion. A buzz alone gives us one or another of the vowels, such as the *u* in *buzz*. A stop without buzz will be like the *p* in *stoppage*, with buzz like the *b* in *buzz*.

Whether buzzing or not, the column of air driven by the lungs next passes through the pharynx, a tube that extends from the larynx through the back of the mouth as far as the rear opening of the nasal cavity. The nasal cavity itself is a chamber about four inches long, opening in front at the nostrils and at the rear into the pharynx. The nasal cavity is divided in two by the septum. The nostrils cannot open and close, but the entrance into the pharynx is controlled by the soft palate or velum. The velum is open for n and m (and often for sounds adjacent to them), closed for other sounds. You can probably feel, or with a mirror even see, the velum open at the end of a word like *hang*.

Within the mouth, the air column is molded by the tongue and the lips. The lips can cause constriction or stoppage; they constrict the air when the upper teeth touch the lower lip to make an *f* or *v* sound, and they stop the air when they close to make a *p* or *b* sound. They also close for the *m* sound, which is emitted through the nose, not the mouth. The lips can further mold the air by rounding, as they do when making the vowel sound in *do* or the consonant sound in *we*, among others.

The tongue—which has a surprising shape for those familiar only with the tip and the upper surface of it—can cause constriction or stoppage of the airflow at any point from the back of the teeth to the roof of the mouth near the velum. Like the lips, the tongue is involved in making both vowel sounds and consonant sounds. It makes both with the tip in a word like *eat*. Or the rear of the tongue can arch up toward the roof of the mouth to make a "back" consonant or vowel. It makes both in a word like *goo*. The tongue can approach the roof of the mouth in other positions farther forward as well, and it can change the shape of the oral cavity in other ways without actually approaching or touching the roof of the mouth.

So the speech sounds are formed in the larynx, in the mouth, and in the nasal cavity. They are formed by the action of the larynx, the velum, the tongue, and the lips. The lips may touch the teeth, and the tongue may touch the teeth or the roof of the mouth. That sounds a trifle complicated, but it is only a small part of what goes on in the motor system. To begin with, all the vocal organs are controlled by muscles, from those that cause the lungs to inhale and exhale air to those that shape the lips in speech. These muscles are not single—a lung muscle, a lip muscle, and so forth—but arranged in intricate groups. In reality, the vocal organs are not only those that articulate but those that activate the articulators.

Other parts of the anatomy too are involved in articulations although we do not usually think of them as vocal organs. The pharynx changes shape as we talk, and so do the cheeks. Some of the vocal organs move in ways that coordinate with articulation but do not seem to be part of it: the larynx moves up and down, for example, in speaking as it does more obviously in swallowing.

Finally, all the vocal organs are in constant motion during speech. The vowels in *house* and in *white* are formed by a change of position in the mouth, not by a single position. And as the mouth moves from the first consonants in these words, through the complex vowel sound, to the final consonants, it is always in motion. What is more, these actions must be coordinated. To take a simple example, the buzz of the larynx must be "on" for the first sounds of *mat* but "off" for the *t*; meanwhile, the mouth closes and the velum opens for the *m*, but they reverse roles for the *a* and *t*. The whole performance adds up to a virtuoso display that far exceeds in complexity . . . the minute adjustments required for even the finest violinist's playing. To observe that "The cat is on the mat" is, from the standpoint of the motor skills required, so demanding that we would think it impossible if we paused to analyze it. We usually do not.

THE SENSORY SYSTEM

In a way, the main sensory system of language, hearing, is the reverse of speech. Speech turns meaning into sound, while hearing turns sound into meaning. Speech encodes meaning as language in the brain, and the brain sends neural messages to the motor system for action; the motor system produces speech. Hearing turns the speech sounds back into neural messages which go to the brain where they are decoded into language and interpreted for meaning.

Sound, as we have seen, is a disturbance of the air—a kind of applied energy. The ear is designed to pick up and process that energy, often in incredibly small amounts. The ear is good not only at amplifying small sounds but at damping loud ones, within limits: a very sudden, very loud noise, or even sound that is not sudden (if it is loud enough), can cause damage to the sensitive sound-gathering mechanisms of the ear, damage which if severe or prolonged can be permanent.

What we usually mean by *ear* is the appendage earrings hang from, but that is only the ear's most visible part. In fact it has three divisions: the outer ear, which extends into the eardrum; the middle ear; and the inner ear. The outer ear collects the sound, passes it through the ear canal, and focuses it on the eardrum. The eardrum is a tightly stretched membrane which is set into motion by the vibrations of sound energy; it is really a "drum" in reverse, for while the bass drum in a marching band converts the energy of motion (a blow from a drumstick) into sound waves, the eardrum converts sound waves into motion energy which is picked up in the middle ear. That motion is carried through the middle ear by three tiny bones; here weak sounds are amplified and very strong sounds are damped. The last of the three bones delivers the sound motion to a membrane called the oval window, which is smaller than the eardrum; the difference in size helps to concentrate the sound energy.

The oval window divides the middle ear from the inner ear. The inner ear is composed of several cavities in the bones of the skull; in one of these, the cochlea, the energy that arrived at the outer ear as sound, and is now motion, will be converted by a set of intricate organs into electrical impulses and fed into the central nervous system for delivery to the auditory center of the brain. The remaining steps in the process are then neural, not sensory.

The process here described, and our idea of hearing in general, relates to sound that reaches us from outside by conduction through the air, water, or other medium. But there is another way in which we can receive sound. A vibrating tuning fork held against the skull will be "heard" by conduction through the bone itself, even if the ear-hole is effectively plugged. Bone-conduction helps us monitor our own speech by providing continuous feedback; thus we can pick out our own words even when surrounded by loud conversation or noise. Bone-conduction has a different sound quality from air-conduction, which is why your voice sounds to you one way when you are speaking and another when you hear it played back from a tape. And bone-conduction can sometimes substitute for air-conduction—for example, when a hearing aid "plays" sound waves directly into the bones of the skull.

LANGUAGE AND CULTURE

Language is species-specific to humankind. By *humankind* we mean the genus *Homo*, species *sapiens*—no other species of this genus survives. Any smaller subdivisions, such as sex or race, may differ among themselves in other very visible ways, but the neural, motor, and sensory equipment necessary to language is common to all. Not that the equipment is identical, otherwise everyone would speak at about the same pitch. But racial, sexual, or individual differences in the shape and size of the nose and lips, or of the internal speech organs, do not override the structural similarity of the vocal organs among all human groups, and they definitely do not result in any functional differences. The members of any group, that is, have the vocal organs to articulate any human language with complete mastery. The same is true of other genetic factors: the intellectual ability to use language is the same in all the varieties of humankind and in all normal individuals.

That is not the same as saying that adult individuals can learn a foreign language as easily as they learned their own in childhood. The physiological habits of the speech organs are complex, and they are learned early. We observe that a native speaker of Chinese has difficulty with the sound of *r* in *very*, a native speaker of Japanese with the sound of *l* in *hello*. That is because their native languages have given them no opportunity to practice those sounds. On the contrary, the languages have reinforced other sounds that tend to crop up when the Chinese speaker attempts English *r* or the Japanese speaker English *l*. The problem, however, is one of habit and not heredity. An American of Chinese ancestry has no trouble with the sounds of English, including *r*, while a person of European ancestry raised to speak Chinese would.

Our virtuosity in our own language carries with it other commitments, some easily understandable and some less so. Speakers of English easily handle a system of pronouns that distinguishes among masculine (*he*), feminine (*she*), and neuter (*it*) forms. They may have trouble with a language like German, however, where the nouns, adjectives, and articles (equivalents of *the* and *a*) make a similar three-way distinction, often in apparent disregard of the sex of the noun—a *maiden* (*das Mädchen*) is neuter, [but changes to feminine] when she becomes a *wife* (*die Frau*)—or with a language like French which makes only a two-way distinction between masculine and feminine, so that *table* is feminine (*la table*) but *floor* is masculine (*le plancher*).

We should not rush to conclude, however, that the Germans and the French see sexual characteristics in inanimate objects or concepts, or do not see them in people. Rather, their languages have grammatical features that English lacks. True, words like *he, she,* and *it* do reflect the sex of their antecedent (except for a few oddities, like referring to a ship as "she"). But their equivalents in French and German refer not to sex but to *gender*, which is an entirely linguistic, and therefore arbitrary, matter. No French speaker regards a table as having any feminine properties other than grammatical ones.

In more remote languages the differences are still greater. When a Chinese speaker counts items, he or she puts a "measure word" between the number and the item: "one [measure word] book," and so forth. There is nothing quite like this in English, although when we arrange numbers in order we signify that we are ordering rather than counting by inserting expressions like *number, No.,* or #: "We're number 1," "Love Potion No. Nine," and the like. But our practice is invariable, while the Chinese measure word is not; it varies according to the thing being counted. The most common one is *ga,* "one *ga* book." But for flat objects it is *zhang,* "one *zhang* table"; and for other kinds of objects there are many other measure words. Sometimes it is far from obvious what the objects have in common that makes them take a common measure word: the measure word *ba* is used for both chairs and umbrellas!

This all sounds formidably difficult, but only to us—not to the Chinese. The Mandarin variety of Chinese is the native language of over half a billion people in the world today, and they all master their language at the same rate and by the same age as English speakers do. No language, no matter how strange and difficult it may seem to outsiders, is too hard for its native speakers to master. All languages are systematic, which makes their complexities intelligible to their native speakers but each system is arbitrary in its own way, which makes it something of a closed book to others.

Equally, no language is especially "simple," if by that word we mean lacking complexity in its phonological and grammatical systems. More likely, people who speak of simplicity in language have a restricted vocabulary in mind. But even this judgment needs to be well-informed if it is to be at all valid. Of course, some languages have larger vocabularies than others; English may comprise half a million words, depending on your manner of counting, while a small tribal group out of touch with the complexities of industrial and urban civilization would probably have a markedly smaller vocabulary. But that vocabulary might be more subtle than English in those areas of thought and experience vital to its users. For example, Eskimos have many different words for different kinds of snow. Moreover, the tribal vocabulary could rapidly expand to deal with new needs as they come along, by borrowing or creating new words. Borrowing, indeed, is one of the most important ways that the English vocabulary has grown to such size. (And, of course, no individual speaker of English has all its half-million words at his or her disposal.)

So the equation of language with culture, one we tend to make, has two possibilities of misleading us. First, we are likely to judge another culture as "simple" because we do not understand it or even know much about it; cultural anthropologists would quickly remedy that error for us. Second, we are likely to think that a "primitive" culture has a primitive language. Yet such remote languages, we now know, seem forbiddingly complex to outsiders who try to learn them.

These attitudes are forms of *ethnocentricity*—a point of view in which one culture is at the center of things and all others are more or less "off the target," either because they never got on target (they are too primitive) or they have wandered away from it (they are decadent). Language is very fertile ground for ethnocentricity. We are quick to judge even small differences from our own variety of English as "wrong," either laughably or disgustingly. When another people's language is different in more than just small ways, we are inclined to doubt the native intelligence of those who use it, its adequacy for serious purposes, or both.

A more enlightened and indeed more realistic view is the opposite of ethnocentricity. It often goes by the name of "cultural relativism," but learning the name is not the same thing as adopting the view. Only an objective eye on the facts, and a careful eye on our own attitudes, will raise us above ethnocentricity.

To compare linguistics with the study of other forms of human behavior is instructive, but a still grander comparison comes to mind: In many ways the study of language is like the study of life itself. Languages, like species, come into being, grow, change, are sometimes grafted to each other, and occasionally become extinct; they have their histories and, in the written record, their fossils. The origins of both life and language, and their processes, are mysteries that can be penetrated (if at all) by reasoning from incomplete and perhaps ultimately inadequate evidence. And linguists, the scientists of language, study language and its environment with a biologist's care and intensity in order to approach an understanding of the nature of language itself—the most characteristic attribute of all humanity.

FOR DISCUSSION AND REVIEW

1. Why is the fact that human language is *productive* one of its most distinctive properties? In answering this question, consider both

your ability to create sentences you have never seen or heard before and also your ability to understand such sentences.

2. Another important property of human language is that it is *arbitrary*. Discuss the several aspects of language characterized by this property.

3. Two other significant "design features" of human language are *duality* and *discreteness*. One way to be sure that you understand these concepts is to try to explain them in your own words to someone else. Write brief explanations of these two concepts, and ask a friend to evaluate the clarity of your explanations.

4. Review the seven additional "design features" discussed by Bolton. Do they seem to you to be of equal importance? Why or why not?

5. In what ways does human physiology support the conclusion that speech is not simply an "overlaid function"?

6. Summarize the differences between "quiet" breathing and "speech" breathing. *Without speaking*, use "speech" breathing for at least a minute. Write a brief description of your physical sensations.

7. Explain the functions in the hearing process of (a) the outer ear, (b) the middle ear, and (c) the inner ear.

8. For what reasons does Bolton insist that "all languages are systematic" and that "no language is especially 'simple'"? In what way is an understanding of these principles important to our understanding of different cultures and their peoples? What is *ethnocentricity*?

9. In the preface to this book, we quote the philosopher Ludwig Wittgenstein: "The limits of my language mean the limits of my world." Discuss the implications of this statement, considering the points Bolton makes and paying particular attention to the concepts of *ethnocentricity* and *cultural relativism*.

10. Bolton asserts that "we seem to understand nonsense, provided it is fitted into proper patterns." Consider the following "nonsense," the opening stanza of "Jabberwocky" by Lewis Carroll (Charles Lutwidge Dodgson [1832–1898]):

> 'Twas brillig, and the slithy toves
>> Did gyre and gimble in the wabe;
> All mimsy were the borogroves,
>> And the mome raths outgrabe.

What do you "know" about the meaning of this stanza? For example, can you identify any nouns? Any verbs? Do you know that something will or did happen? If so, what is that something? Try to describe *how* you "understand" these and other aspects of the stanza.

7

True Language?

The Ohio State University Language Files

People tend to think of language as a uniquely human achievement, one of the few characteristics by which we distinguish ourselves from other living creatures. However, when we explore the myriad ways in which other species communicate with their own kind, we find that the specific properties of language are not easily identified. Bees dance in order to instruct each other where to find food; dogs warn each other off with a show of teeth; birds sing to establish the borders of their territories. How, then, do we define language? Are there any clear criteria by which to differentiate human language from animal communication? This article, based on the work of linguist Charles Hockett, does not seek to define language. Instead, it examines the qualities shared by all communication systems, describes characteristics that belong to some but not others, and separates out those that are particular to human beings. We see that two characteristics distinguish true (human) language: first, although the potential for true language is innate, all its forms must be learned; second, true language is open communication, in that its elements can be combined in a number of ways to convey a variety of meanings.

Humans are not the only creatures that communicate. All varieties of birds make short calls and sing songs, cats meow to be fed or let outside, dogs bark to announce the arrival of strangers or growl and bare their teeth to indicate their intent to attack, and so on. The fact that other animals send and receive messages is in evidence all around us. One approach to determining the nature of language is to investigate the way other animals communicate and to explore the possibility that some species use a system that is fundamentally the same as human language. Most people assume that only humans use language—it is something that sets us apart from all other creatures. But is it possible that when we examine animal communication systems we will discover our assumption was wrong?

The task of comparing human language with various animal communication systems is not an easy one. First, we need a suitable working definition of "language" on which to base our comparisons. Unfortunately, no definition seems to adequately define language or be agreeable to everyone. One approach to getting around this problem, suggested by the linguist Charles Hockett, is that we identify some descriptive characteristics of language rather than attempt to define its fundamental nature. Then we can determine whether a particular animal communication system exhibits these characteristics as well. His list of characteristics, known as "design features," has been modified over the years, but a standard list is provided below. From what we now know about animal communication systems, we have found that none possesses *all* of these features, and thus we conclude that no nonhuman species uses language. Instead, they communicate with each other in systems called signal codes.

All communication systems have some features in common:

1. *A Mode of Communication.* This refers to the means by which the messages are transmitted. The mode of communication may be vocal-auditory, as in most human and most animal systems—the signals are transmitted by sound produced in the vocal tract and are received by the auditory system. The mode may be visual (e.g., apes' gestural signals), tactile (e.g., bees), or even chemical (e.g., moths).
2. *Semanticity.* The signals in any communication system have meaning.
3. *Pragmatic Function.* All systems of communication serve some useful purpose, from helping the species to stay alive to influencing others' behavior.

Some communication systems exhibit these features as well:

4. *Interchangeability.* This refers to the ability of individuals to both send and receive messages. Human language exhibits this feature because each individual human can both send messages (usually by speaking) and comprehend the messages of others (usually by listening). But not all animals can both send and receive messages. For example, the *Bombyx mori* (silkworm) moth uses a chemical communication system. When the female is ready to mate, she secretes a chemical that males can trace back to her. The males themselves cannot secrete this chemical; they can only be receivers.
5. *Cultural Transmission.* This is the need for some aspect of a communication system to be learned through communicative interaction with other users of the system. Human language exhibits this feature because humans must learn languages (even though the ability to learn those languages is innate). Thus a child of Russian parents will learn English if that is the language it is exposed to. In most organisms, the actual signal code itself is innate, or genetically programmed, so an individual can no more learn a code different from the one it is programmed for than it can grow an extra eye. However, in a few systems, including certain bird songs and chimpanzee signals, some of the signals seem to be genetically programmed or instinctive, while others are learned. Therefore these systems, too, exhibit cultural transmission. Humans, of course, must learn *all* the signals of their language.
6. *Arbitrariness.* This refers to the property of having signals for which the form of the signal is not logically related to its meaning. The word *cat*, for example, does not sound like a cat or represent a cat in any logical way. We know what the word *cat* refers to because we learned the word as English speakers. If we were Spanish, the word

would be *gato*, and if we were Russian it would be *koshka*. When the relationship between a signal and its meaning is arbitrary, then, there is nothing inherent in the form that designates its meaning. The meaning must be learned. Most animal systems use iconic signals that in some way directly represent their meaning, for instance, when a dog bares its teeth to indicate that it is ready to attack.

7. *Discreteness*. This is the property of having complex messages that are built up out of smaller parts. Consider a sentence from a human language. It is composed of discrete units, independent words, which are in turn composed of even smaller discrete units, individual sounds. The messages in the animal communication systems with which we are familiar do not have this property. Each message is an indivisible unit. Even when some animals imitate human sounds so well, say parrots for example, these animals are merely memorizing a whole sequence that they reproduce, but they cannot break down the sequence into its discrete units. A parrot trained to say *Polly want a cracker* and *Don't go in there!* will never recombine the words of the sentence to say *Polly* don't *want a cracker* or recombine the sounds involved to say *Scram, rat!*

True language has, in addition to the above, the following characteristics:

8. *Displacement*. This refers to the ability to communicate about things that are not present in space or time. In human language, we can talk about the color red when we are not actually seeing it, or we can talk about a friend who lives in another state when he is not with us. We can talk about a class we had last year, or the class we will take next year. No animal communication system appears to display this feature.

9. *Productivity*. This refers to the ability to produce and understand any number of messages that have never been expressed before and that may express novel ideas. Human language is an "open-ended" system. However, in all animal communication systems, the number of signals is fixed. Even if some of the signals are complex (i.e., the system exhibits feature 7, discreteness), there is no mechanism for systematically combining discrete units to create new signals. These systems are thus called closed communication systems.

In the comparison of human language with animal communication systems, a debate has arisen about whether the two systems are *qualitatively* or *quantitatively* different. If there is merely a quantitative difference, then we would find an animal system that possessed *all* of these features, but some would not be present to the degree that they are found in human language. If, however, the two systems differ qualitatively, we would find no animal communication system that possessed each and every design feature. While this seems straightforward enough, there is still some disagreement on the application of this point.

Consider the feature of displacement, for example. It seems as if the bees' signal code exhibits this to a limited degree, since they communicate about food that is not visible while they are transmitting their message. But note that we can "translate" the message of their behavior in a number of ways. We're in the habit of interpreting the bees' message as something like "there's a food source 40 feet from the hive at a 45° angle from the sun." In other words, our translation assumes they're relaying a message *about* a distant, invisible object. But the message can be represented differently—more simply, e.g., "perform this behavior now," that is, "fly 45° for 2 minutes." This is no different from most messages sent in animal systems. Think, for example, of a chimpanzee who adopts a grooming posture. This communicates the chimp's desire for another chimp to perform a particular behavior. The bees' messages are of this type—messages sent to alter the behavior of other individuals; their signals may not *represent* objects not present. Thus, some linguists claim the bees' system exhibits *limited* displacement, while others maintain it does not possess this feature in any degree.

At any rate, we say that a communication system must have *all* the design features to be considered qualitatively the same as human language, and no animal communication system has been identified to date that meets this criterion.

FOR DISCUSSION AND REVIEW

1. According to this article, how does one distinguish between a communication system and language?

2. How does Charles Hockett resolve the problem of defining the term *language*? In your opinion, is his solution valid? Why or why not?

3. What is the primary difference between language and signal codes? Are signal codes synonymous with communication systems? If not, how do they differ?

4. What are the three characteristics common to all communication systems?

5. What is the difference between an iconic symbol and an arbitrary symbol? Why is the arbitrary symbol characteristic of true language?

6. When a parrot is able to convey a meaningful message in acceptable English terms by saying, "Polly want a cracker," why is this not considered true language?

7. What is the difference between innate acquisition and cultural learning of a communication system? What aspect of communication is innate in human beings? What is learned?

8. According to this article, what are the two distinguishing characteristics of true language?

8

Sign Language

Karen Emmorey

Sound would appear to be one of the most obvious properties of language. People speak; people listen and hear. One major branch of linguistics analyzes sound patterns in language, another studies the physiological attributes that allow human beings to produce and receive those patterns. It was a long-held belief that the deaf were disadvantaged in their linguistic capabilities; sign language as a form of communication is still widely considered a poor second best, a mimed pidgin version of the language spoken by the hearing community. In the following essay, Karen Emmorey, Senior Staff Scientist at the Salk Institute of Biological Studies, decisively lays to rest any prevailing myths that stigmatize sign language as an inferior form of communication. Commenting on the purposes of her research, she notes, "The study of signed language provides a window into the nature of human language, into the relation between language and spatial cognition, and into the determinants of brain organization for language." Basing her conclusions on a study of American Sign Language (ASL), Emmorey finds that sign language shares—albeit in a different format—all the characteristics and complex structural patterns of spoken languages.

Sign languages are used primarily by deaf people throughout the world. They are languages that have evolved in a completely different medium, using the hands and face rather than the vocal tract and perceived by eye rather than by ear. They have arisen as autonomous languages not derived from spoken language and are passed down from one generation of deaf people to the next. Deaf children with deaf parents acquire sign language in the same way that hearing children learn spoken language. Sign languages are rich and complex linguistic systems which conform to the universal properties found in all human languages. As with spoken language, the left hemisphere of the brain is critically involved in processing sign language, indicating that the general brain basis for language is modality independent. American Sign Language (ASL) is the language used by deaf people in the United States and parts of Canada.

MYTHS ABOUT SIGN LANGUAGE

Myth 1: Sign language is universal. Sign language is *not* a universal language shared by deaf peoples of the world. There are many different sign languages that have evolved independently of each other. Just as spoken languages differ in grammatical structure, in the types of rules that they contain, and in historical relationships, signed languages also differ along these parameters. For example, despite the fact that American Sign Language (ASL) and British Sign Language are surrounded by the same spoken language, they are mutually unintelligible. Sign languages are generally named for the country or area in which they are used (e.g., Austrian Sign Language, German Sign Language, Hong Kong Sign Language). The exact number of sign languages in the world is not known.

Myth 2: Sign language is made up of pictorial gestures and is similar to mime. An important property of human language is that the form of words is generally arbitrary. For example, there is no relation between the English word "frog" or the French word "grenouille" and an actual frog. In contrast, many signs have a discernible relation to the concepts that they denote. For example, the sign for "tree" in American Sign Language is made with the forearm held upright with the fingers spread wide. One could say that the forearm represents the trunk and the fingers represent the branches of the tree. In Danish Sign Language the sign for "tree" differs from the ASL sign, but it also bears a perceptible relation to a tree: the two hands outline the shape of a tree starting with a round top and ending with the trunk. Although both of these signs are iconic and resemble mime, they have been conventionalized in different ways by the two sign languages.

Although some signs have iconic properties, most signs do not bear a clear resemblance to what they denote. For example, the ASL sign for "apple" is made with the knuckle of the index finger touching the cheek and bears no resemblance to an apple or to eating an apple. For most signs, the relationship between the form and the meaning is not transparent. In addition, the iconicity of signs is generally irrelevant to the way the language is organized and processed.

Furthermore, pantomime differs from a linguistic system of signs in important and systematic ways. The space in which signs are articulated is much more restricted than that available for pantomime. For example, pantomime can involve movement of the entire body as well as any part of the body. In contrast, signing is constrained to a space extending from just below the waist to the top of the head, and the entire body is never involved. In addition, sign languages have an intricate compositional structure in which smaller units (such as words) are combined to create higher level structures (such as sentences), and this compositional structure is found at all linguistic levels (phonology, morphology, syntax, and discourse). This complex and hierarchical compositional structure is not present in pantomime.

Myth 3: Sign language is a pidgin form of spoken language using the hands and has no grammar of its own. American Sign Language has been mistakenly thought to be "English on the hands." However, ASL has an independent grammar that is quite different from the grammar of English. For example, ASL allows much freer word order compared to English. English contains tense markers (e.g., *-ed* to express past tense), but ASL (like many languages) does not have tense markers that are part of the morphology of a word; rather tense is expressed lexically (e.g., by adverbs such as "yesterday"). There are no indigenous signed languages that are simply a transformation of a spoken language to the hands.

One might ask "If sign languages are not based on spoken languages, then where did they come from?" However, this question is as difficult to answer as the question "Where did language come from?" We know very little about the very first spoken or signed languages of the world, but research is beginning to uncover the historical relationships between sign languages, as has been done for spoken languages. For example, part of the origin of American Sign Language can be traced to the establishment of a large community of deaf people in France in 1761. These people attended the first public school for the deaf, and the sign language that arose within this community is still used today in France. In 1817, Laurent Clerc, a deaf teacher from this French school, established the first deaf public school in the United States and brought with him French Sign Language. The gestural systems of the American children attending this school mixed with French Sign Language to create a new form that was no longer recognizable as French Sign Language. ASL still contains a historical resemblance to French Sign Language, but both languages are mutually unintelligible.

Myth 4: Sign language cannot convey the same subtleties and complex meanings that spoken languages can. On the contrary, sign languages are equipped with the same expressive power that is inherent in spoken languages. Sign languages can express complicated and intricate concepts with the same degree of explicitness and eloquence as spoken languages. The linguistic structuring which permits such expressive power is described in the next section.

LINGUISTIC STRUCTURE OF AMERICAN SIGN LANGUAGE

American Sign Language is one of the most widely studied sign languages. A brief description of ASL structure is provided here—a complete description would require a large volume (the full characterization of any grammar is lengthy). The description is designed to illustrate that signed languages exhibit the same properties and follow the same universal principles as spoken languages and that signed languages provide unique insight into the nature of language itself.

Phonology

Phonology is the study of the sound patterns found in human languages; it is also the term used to refer to the system of knowledge that speakers have about the sound patterns of their particular language. But do sign languages have a phonology? Is it possible to have a phonological system that is not based on sound? In spoken languages, words are constructed out of sounds which in and of themselves have no meaning. The words "cat" and "pat" differ only in the initial sounds which have no inherent meanings of their own. Sounds may be combined in different ways to create different words: "bad" differs from "dab" only in how the sounds are sequenced. Similarly, signs are constructed out of components that are themselves meaningless and are combined to create words.

Signs are composed of four basic phonological parameters: handshape, location, movement, and palm orientation. American Sign Language contrasts about 36 different handshapes, but not all sign languages share the same handshape inventory. For example, the "t" handshape in ASL (the thumb is inserted between the index and middle fingers of a fist) is not used by Danish Sign Language; Swedish Sign Language contains a handshape formed with an open hand with all fingers extended except for the ring finger which is bent—this hand configuration is not used in ASL. Figure 8.1A illustrates three ASL signs that differ only in handshape. Signs also differ according to where they are made on the body or face. Figure 8.1B shows three signs that differ only in location. Movement is another contrasting phonological parameter that distinguishes minimally between signs as shown in Figure 8.1C. Several different path movement types occur in ASL, e.g., circling, arc, straight; and signs can contain "internal" movement such as wiggling of the fingers or changes in handshape. Finally, signs can differ solely in the orientation of the palm; for example, the sign WANT (signs are notated as English glosses in uppercase) is produced with a spread hand with the palm up, and FREEZE is produced with the same handshape and movement (bending of the fingers and movement toward the body), but the palm is facing downward. These meaningless phonological elements are combined and sequenced to create lexical signs.

ASL exhibits other phonological properties that were once thought to be only found in speech. For example, ASL contains phonological rules similar to those found in spoken languages. ASL contains deletion rules in which an element (such as a movement or a handshape) is deleted from a sign and assimilation rules in which one element is made more similar to a neighboring element. ASL signs also have a level of syllabic structure which is governed by rules similar to those that apply to syllables in spoken languages. The fact that signed languages exhibit phonological properties despite the completely different set of articulators (e.g., the hands vs. the tongue) attests to the universality and abstractness of sublexical structure in human languages.

Morphology

ASL contains the same basic form classes as spoken languages, nouns, verbs, adjectives, pronouns, and adverbs, but it has a very differ-

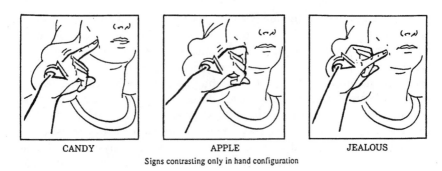

CANDY   APPLE   JEALOUS

Signs contrasting only in hand configuration

FIGURE 8.1A

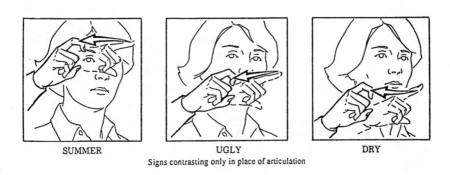

SUMMER   UGLY   DRY

Signs contrasting only in place of articulation

FIGURE 8.1B

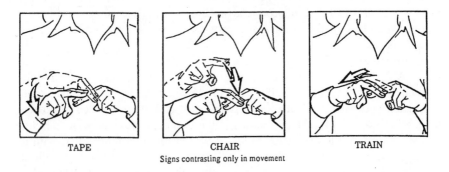

TAPE   CHAIR   TRAIN

Signs contrasting only in movement

FIGURE 8.1C

FIGURE 8.1   Illustration of Part of the Phonological System of American Sign Language. These signs contrast the different phonological parameters of ASL, which are themselves meaningless but can be combined to create lexically meaningful signs.

ent system of word formation. In English and in most spoken languages, morphologically complex words are most often formed by adding prefixes or suffixes to a word stem. In ASL, these forms are created by nesting a sign stem within dynamic movement contours and planes in space. Figure 8.2A illustrates the base form GIVE along with several inflected forms which can be embedded within one another and which convey slightly different meanings. ASL has many verbal inflections which convey temporal information about the action, e.g., whether the action was habitual, iterative, or continual. These inflections do not occur in English, but they are found in other languages of the world.

Another set of inflections applies to a subset of ASL verbs and indicates the subject and/or object of the verb (see Fig. 8.2B). In ASL, noun phrases are associated with points in a plane of signing space, and verbs can move between these spatial points to indicate the subject or object. For example, if MOTHER has been associated with a point on the signer's right and BOY with a point on the signer's left, then if the verb FORCE moves from right to left, it would mean "She forces him" (see Fig. 8.2B). If the verb were to move left to right, it would mean "He forces her." The first spatial endpoint of the verb agrees with the subject, and the final endpoint agrees with the object; thus, these verbs are called "agreeing" verbs. Other inflections can also be added to indicate plural objects or reciprocal ("each other").

Like English, ASL has rules that govern how compound nouns and verbs are formed. An example of an English compound is the word "blackboard" which does not mean a board that is black (blackboards can even be white) and which has a different stress pattern than the phrase "black board." ASL compounds also have different meanings and stress patterns compared to noun phrases. For example, the ASL compound BLACK-NAME which means "bad reputation" is formed by combining the sign BLACK with the sign NAME. In isolation the sign NAME contains two beats, but within the compound it contains only one beat. Compounding is a common morphological process in ASL, as it is in many languages.

Finally, ASL does not have many prepositions, and instead encodes spatial relations through morphological devices. ASL uses a system of classifiers which are pronominal forms that classify an object according to its semantic and/or visual-geometric properties. Many of the world's languages have classifier systems (especially Bantu languages) in which a different pronoun is used for humans, for animals, for inanimate objects, etc. ASL classifiers are embedded in verbs of motion and location which describe the movement and position of objects and/or people in space. For example, to express "the bicycle is beside the fence" a vehicle classifier is used for bicycle and is positioned in space next to a visual-geometric classifier for fence ("long-sectioned-rectangular object"). The ASL expression tends to be much more explicit compared to the English preposition "beside" because the ASL classifier verbs of location also indicate the orientation and precise location of the fence and bicycle with respect to each other (e.g., whether the bicycle is close to the fence, facing the fence, etc.). Again, although this system appears mimetic, it is not. ASL expressions of location and motion have an internal structure comprised of a limited set of movements, locations, and manners of movement which are constrained by linguistic rules.

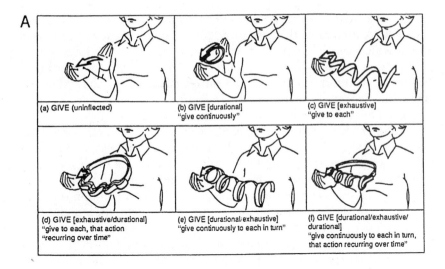

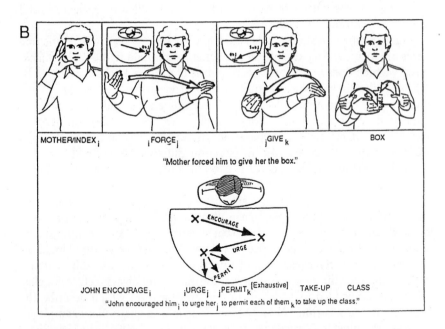

FIGURE 8.2 Morphology and Syntax in American Sign Language   (A) The uninflected sign GIVE is illustrated in (a), and GIVE with single inflections is shown in (b) and (c). The figure shows different embedded combinations of inflections which have distinct meanings (d, e, and f). Note that these inflections are produced simultaneously rather than as prefixes or suffixes. (B) Syntactic spatial mechanisms in ASL. The figure illustrates the association of nouns with loci in space (indicated by subscripts), and movements of verbs between these loci (indicated by arrows). The spatial endpoints of these verbs agree with the spatial loci established for the subject and object of the sentence.

Syntax

The basic canonical word order for ASL is subject–verb–object; however, ASL word order is much more flexible compared to English. ASL morphology can mark the relationship between words, and ASL does not need to rely on word order to convey grammatical relations such as subject or object. For example, the object of the verb can appear as the first word of the sentence, if it is morphologically marked as a topic, e.g., CAT (topic), DOG CHASE. "As for the cat, the dog chased it." Topics are distinguished by a specific facial expression (see below). Similar to Italian and unlike English, ASL allows "subjectless" sentences. For example, it is possible to sign the following: TODAY SUNDAY. MUST VISIT MY MOTHER. In English these two sentences would require subjects (subjects are bolded): "Today, **it**'s Sunday. **I** must visit my mother." The constraint on overt subjects is just one of the ways in which the syntax of ASL differs from English (but is similar to other languages).

Personal pronouns in ASL are expressed with either a flat handshape (fingers together) to indicate possessive case ("my," "your") or with a closed fist and extended index finger (pointing) to indicate nominative ("I," "you"). For referents that are physically present, the pronominal sign is directed at the physical referent; thus, first person reference is made by the signer pointing to his or her own chest, and second-person pronominal reference is made by pointing to the addressee's chest. Similarly, when referents are actually present, third-person pronouns are produced by pointing to the appropriate persons. Although these pronoun signs appear to be simple pointing gestures, they are not. The ASL system of pronouns has the same grammatical properties found in spoken languages. For example, the pronominal signs are compositional unlike pointing gestures, and the component parts convey different grammatical distinctions. Hand orientation indicates grammatical person (e.g., first vs. second person), handshape contrasts grammatical case (e.g., possessive vs. nominative), and movement (an arc vs. pointing) indicates grammatical number (plural vs. singular).

Many of the syntactic functions that are fulfilled in spoken languages by word order or case marking are expressed in ASL by spatial mechanisms. For example, when noun phrases are introduced into ASL discourse, they may be assigned an arbitrary locus in the plane of signing space. Once a referent has been associated with a locus, the signer may then refer to that referent by using a pronominal sign directed at the locus. In addition, verbs can move with respect to these loci to indicate subject and object relations. Generally, these loci remain fixed in space, but under certain discourse conditions, the loci can *shift* such that they are associated with different referents. In addition, spatial loci can be embedded within different subspaces of the reference plane, and there is evidence for more than one signing plane (e.g., nonspecific reference and counterfactuals may use diagonal and/or higher planes of space). Overall, the syntactic system of ASL is used to express the same linguistic *functions* found in the world's languages, but the *form* these functions take is explicitly spatial. The use of space for syntactic functions is a unique resource afforded by the visual modality of sign language.

Linguistic and Emotional Facial Expression

The face carries both linguistic and emotional information for ASL signers. Both hearing and deaf people use their face in the same way to convey emotional information—these expressions (e.g., happy, sad, angry) are universal. However, ASL signers also use facial expressions to convey linguistic contrasts. Linguistic and emotional facial expressions differ in their scope and timing and in the face muscles that are used. Grammatical facial expressions have a clear onset and offset, and they are coordinated with specific parts of the signed sentence. Emotional expressions have more global and inconsistent onset and offset patterns, and they are not timed to co-occur with specific signs or parts of a signed sentence. Examples of linguistic facial expression include marking for adverbials, topics, questions, conditionals, and relative clauses.

Grammatical facial expressions are critical to the syntax of ASL because they distinguish several different syntactic structures. For example, consider the following two ASL clauses: TODAY SNOW, TRIP CANCEL ("It's snowing today; the trip is canceled"). These are two co-ordinate main clauses. However, if the first clause is produced with a conditional facial expression (the eyebrows are raised, the head is tilted slightly to the side, and the shoulders move slightly forward), the syntactic structure is altered. The first clause becomes a conditional subordinate clause, and the meaning changes to "If it snows today, the trip will be canceled." The only difference between the two structures is the facial marking that co-occurs with the first clause. Facial behaviors also represent adverbs which appear in predicates and carry different specific meanings. For example, two ASL sentences may have exactly the same signs and differ only in the facial adverbials which co-occur with the signs. The facial expression "mm" (lips pressed together and protruded) indicates an action done effortlessly; whereas the facial expression "th" (tongue protrudes between the teeth) means "awkwardly" or "carelessly." These two facial expressions accompanying the same verb (e.g., DRIVE) convey quite different meanings ("drive effortlessly" or "drive carelessly").

Researchers are studying facial expressions in ASL for insight into the interface between biology and behavior. Emotional expressions are produced consistently and universally by children by 1 year of age. Emotional facial expressions also appear to be associated with specific neural substrates that are distinct from those involved in language. How does the linguistic system underlying the use of grammatical facial expressions interact with the biologically programmed use of emotional facial expressions? Current research suggests that different neural systems may subserve linguistic and emotional facial expressions—the left hemisphere appears to be involved in producing linguistic facial expressions, whereas the right hemisphere is important for producing emotional facial expressions. In addition, although deaf children produce emotional facial expressions very early (as do hearing children), they acquire linguistic facial expressions later and with a quite different pattern of development, which reflects their (unconscious) analysis of these facial signals as part of a linguistic system.

Fingerspelling and the Manual Alphabet

The manual alphabet used in ASL consists of 26 different handshapes which correspond to the 26 letters of the English alphabet. Other signed languages have different fingerspelling systems; for example, British fingerspelling uses a two-handed system. Fingerspelling is often used when there is no existing ASL sign (e.g., for place names) and is somewhat separate from the grammar of ASL—grammatical rules do not apply to *novel* fingerspelled words.

However, fingerspelled words can become "lexicalized" or enter the sign vocabulary if they are used repeatedly in one or several contexts. These fingerspelled signs are quite distinct from fingerspelled English words because they have undergone significant phonological reshaping and have become incorporated into the ASL grammar over time. For example, N-O was a fingerspelled word meaning "no" which has been incorporated into the ASL lexicon. The sign #NO (the # indicates a lexicalized fingerspelled sign) has a different movement than the fingerspelled word (N-O moves to the right slightly whereas #NO moves forward slightly), and #NO contains modified alphabet handshapes such that neither the N nor the O handshapes appear as they do in the original fingerspelled word. Further evidence that the sign #NO is part of the ASL lexicon is that it can undergo a morphological rule which creates a verb which can be inflected. The verb SAY-NO-TO is derived from #NO and can inflect for subject and object as an agreeing verb.

Dialects, Accents, and Language Use

Very often speakers in different geographic regions or from different social groups show systematic differences in language use, and these groups are said to speak different dialects of the same language. The same phenomenon occurs for signed languages. For example, ASL signers from the Northeast and Southern regions of the United States often use different signs for the same object (compare British and American dialectal differences in word use: gas/petrol, diaper/nappy, elevator/lift). Southern signers also produce the two-handed form of signs more often than non-Southerners (some signs have both one-handed and two-handed forms that do not differ in meaning). The deaf black community in the United States also has its own dialect of ASL. Certain signs (e.g., FLIRT, SCHOOL) have black forms which originate from the time when schools for the deaf were racially segregated. These signs are used most often when black deaf individuals interact with each other and form part of the culture of the black deaf community. Both regional and black signing dialects also differ phonologically, but these systematic differences in pronunciation have been less well studied. In some regional dialects, the thumb may be extended while producing certain signs without changing meaning (e.g., FUNNY, BUTTER); this difference in pronunciation may be perceived as an accent. Similarly, when signers of Chinese Sign Language learn ASL, they may have an accent derived from small phonetic differences between CSL and ASL. For example, the closed fist handshape is slightly different for ASL and CSL. In ASL, the hand is relaxed and only the very tip of the thumb protrudes above the fist, but in CSL the fist is more rigid, and the entire top joint of the thumb protrudes. When CSL signers produce ASL signs, they may maintain the handshape from CSL, and this phonological difference may be perceived as a foreign accent.

In addition to regional and social dialects, different "situational dialects" or language styles can be found for users of ASL. The signing style used for formal lectures differs from that used for informal conversations or narratives. Formal ASL is slower paced, uses a larger signing space, tends to use two-handed variants of signs, and shows less coarticulation. In contrast, for casual or informal signing, signs that are made near the face may be produced lower down, one-handed signs predominate, and signs are often articulated such that they "overlap." For example, the sign THINK is made with an "l" handshape touching the forehead, and the sign PLAY is made with an "Y" handshape (thumb and pinky extended, other fingers closed). When THINK occurs before PLAY in casual signing, the signer may "anticipate" the handshape for PLAY and produce THINK with a "Y" handshape and extended index finger. This kind of anticipation or coarticulation does not occur as frequently in formal signing. These phonological and lexical changes are not unlike those found for formal and informal speech.

Sign Poetry and Song

Poetry and song are forms of artistic expression that make use of linguistic patternings of sound, rhythm, and grammar. How are poems and songs expressed in a language without sound? ASL poetry exhibits some internal structuring that is parallel to that found in oral languages, but it also contains poetic structure that is intrinsic to its visual-spatial modality. Like spoken poetry and song, ASL can rhyme by manipulating the phonological structure of words. Signs can rhyme if they share the same handshape or the same movement, and a poem may contain signs that all share a single handshape or group of handshapes that are formationally similar.

Rhythmic structure within a sign poem can be created by manipulating the flow of movement between signs and by rhythmically balancing the two hands. The use of space is a poetic device that is intrinsic to the visual modality. Signs move through space and are clustered and separated within space to produce an additional dimension of structure within a poem. Sign poetry also takes advantage of the visual modality by using "cinematic" techniques such as zooms, close-ups, and visual panning.

The poetic and literary tradition for English is hundreds of years old. For ASL, this tradition is developing within our generation through organizations such as the National Theater of the Deaf. The nature of ASL literature is similar to the "oral" literature of storytelling and poetry that exists in communities which do not have a writing system. Songs and stories are passed down from generation to generation which reflect the culture of the society. Similarly, deaf culture is strongly reflected in the themes of ASL stories and poems. For example, poems and stories often express the value of sign language to the deaf community—a common language is a major determinant of any culture. Other themes include the origins of the deaf community, the relationship between hearing and deaf people, and shared cultural experiences such as growing up in a residential school for the deaf.

SIGN LANGUAGE ACQUISITION

A child acquiring a sign language appears to be faced with a quite different task than a child acquiring a spoken language. A completely different set of articulators is involved, and the language is perceived with a different sensory system. Do the properties of sign languages affect the course and timing of language acquisition? For example, do the iconic properties of sign languages aid in their acquisition? Do the spatial properties of sign language present special challenges for the acquisition process? Recent research has added these questions, and the results are briefly described here. This research is based on deaf children acquiring ASL as a native language from their deaf parents. The general finding is that deaf children acquire sign language in the same way as hearing children acquire a spoken language: both groups pass through the same linguistic milestones at the same time. These findings suggest that the capacities which underlie language acquisition are maturationally controlled and that the psychological, linguistic, and neural mechanisms involved in language acquisition are not speech specific.

Babbling and First Signs

Just as hearing babies babble prior to producing their first word, deaf babies babble with their hands prior to producing their first sign. Babbling occurs between about 7 and 10 months of age, and is characterized by a rhythmic syllable organization for both speech and sign. Just like vocal babbling in hearing infants, manual babbling is produced with a subset of manual phonetic units found in sign languages of the world and is produced without meaning or reference. The fact that babbling occurs in babies exposed to sign language suggests that babbling in general is not simply a result of the maturation of the motor system governing vocal articulation, but rather babbling may be the product of the maturation of a modality-neutral linguistic capacity.

Children acquiring both spoken and signed languages go through a stage in which isolated single words are produced. There is some evidence that first signs in ASL emerge earlier than first words in English. First signs have been reported as early as 6 months, whereas first words tend to appear between 11 and 13 months. The apparent early appearance of first signs is not tied to iconicity since the majority of first signs are not particularly iconic. For example, MILK which is a frequent first sign (and first word) is made with movements similar to milking a cow. While this sign may be iconic for adults, it is not iconic for children. The ostensible early appearance of first signs may be due to the early motor development of the hands compared to the vocal tract. However, some recent research has questioned the early appearance of first signs and has suggested that first words and signs may appear at about the same time.

Similar to spoken languages, early lexical signs tend to be uninflected, i.e., just the stem or base form of the word is produced. In addition, children often make phonological substitutions and alterations within their first signs. Thus, just as hearing children acquiring English might say "baba" for "bottle," deaf children simplify and alter adult signs; e.g., the "baby" sign for MOMMY is often produced with an "l" handshape (loose fist with index finger extended) rather than the correct spread hand (fingers not touching) and contact to the chin is with the index finger rather than the thumb. The phonological alterations in both sign and speech tend to reflect articulatory ease, with more difficult sounds and handshapes acquired later.

The semantic relations that are expressed in children's early word combinations are also the same for speech and sign. Children sign and talk about the existence and nonexistence of objects, actions on objects, possession of objects, and locations of objects. The expression of semantic relations occurs in the same order for both signed and spoken languages: existence relations appear first, followed by action and state relations, then locative relations. The last semantic expressions to emerge for both types of languages are datives, instruments, causatives, and manners of action.

Acquisition of Morphology and Syntax

All children make "mistakes" when learning language, and deaf children learning ASL make the same kinds of errors that hearing children make when acquiring English. For example, English-speaking children go through a stage in which they overgeneralize the past tense marker -*ed*, producing forms such as *comed, goed,* and *broked*. Similarly, children acquiring ASL overgeneralize verb morphology. For example, once children have learned to inflect verbs for subject and object, they may overextend this marking to verbs which do not permit this inflection. These "mistakes" provide a view into the child's developing grammar and indicate that children do not simply imitate adult utterances but instead have an internal system of rules that may or may not match the adult grammar.

Children learning English (and other spoken languages) make errors with personal pronouns, substituting "you" for "me" and vice versa. Pronoun reversals are not that surprising in child speech, given the shifts that occur between speakers and listeners using "I" and "you." Children often construe "you" as a name for themselves. For ASL, one might predict a different course of acquisition for these pronouns because of their iconic properties, i.e., "you" is indicated by pointing to the addressee and "me" is indicated by pointing to oneself. Both hearing and deaf children use pointing gestures prelinguistically. This raises the question of how deaf children move from prelinguistic gestural communication to linguistic–symbolic communication when the form (pointing) is virtually identical. Is the acquisition of pronouns early and error-free for children acquiring ASL—do they capitalize on the iconic nature of ASL pronouns? The surprising answer is no; despite the transparency of pointing gestures, deaf children do not use ASL pronouns earlier than children acquiring English, and they make pronoun reversals in early signing. Children acquiring ASL seem to go through three stages: (1) the use of gestural (nonlinguistic) pointing, (2) the use and misuse of pronouns as lexical signs (i.e., "you" as a name), and (3) the correct use of pronouns within a grammatical system.

Children acquiring ASL must master the syntactic use of space, which is quite intricate and complex (see Syntax above). At age 3, children do not use spatially indexed pronouns to refer to people or objects that are not physically present. By age 4, children begin to associate noun phrases with abstract loci in space, but they make errors. For example, children may fail to correctly maintain the unique association between a locus and a noun phrase, producing sentences in which it is not clear who is doing what to whom. Similarly, children acquiring English produce sentences with unidentified "he's" and "she's." By age 5, ASL learning children provide an abstract locus for noun phrases when one is required, and generally maintain this association appropriately. Verb agreement between these loci is also produced correctly. The complete spatial reference system (including shifting space) is not acquired until age 7 or 8—the same age at which English-speaking children master the reference system of English.

Understanding the nature of language acquisition for a signed language has provided important and profound insight into the nature of human language and the human capacity for language. The maturational mechanisms underlying language are not tied specifically to speech but appear to be linked to a more abstract linguistic capacity such that the acquisition of visual–manual and aural–oral languages are acquired according to the same maturational time table. Furthermore, linguistic symbolic systems are essentially and fundamentally arbitrary, and children acquiring ASL ignore its potential iconicity and construct linguistic rules according to grammatical principles which are not grounded in form-meaning similarities.

Acquisition of Sign Language Late in Childhood: Evidence for a Critical Period for Language Acquisition

The majority (90 percent) of deaf children are first exposed to sign language later in life—only deaf children who have deaf signing parents are exposed to sign language from birth. Children who have hearing parents who do not sign may have no effective language exposure in infancy and early childhood. These children typically acquire sign language when they enter a residential school for the deaf and become immersed in the language, using it to converse with other deaf children and adults. Some children may not enter a residential school until high school. Unfortunately, deaf children rarely acquire competence in English and often have no primary language until they acquire a sign language. This population of deaf signers provides a unique opportunity to investigate the "critical period" hypothesis for language acquisition. Essentially, this hypothesis posits that a child must be exposed to language within a particular critical or sensitive period in development in order to acquire language normally and completely. Exposure to language past this critical period will result in imperfect and abnormal language acquisition. Because most individuals are exposed to their native language from birth, this hypothesis has been difficult to test.

Recent research with deaf adults who were not exposed to sign language until late in childhood or adulthood supports the critical period hypothesis for language acquisition. There is a nearly linear relationship between the age at which a deaf person was first exposed to ASL and their performance on tests of ASL grammar and processing—the later the exposure to language, the worse their grammatical knowledge and performance. Crucially, these differences are not due to the number of years of signing experience—the native signers and the "late" signers in these studies were equated for the number of years of practice with ASL, and most had been signing for 20 or 30 years. The production and comprehension of ASL morphology are strongly affected by age of acquisition, with those exposed to the language early in life outperforming those exposed at later ages. Late learners of ASL are not entirely incompetent in their use of ASL morphology, but they lack the grammatical analysis and highly consistent use of linguistic structures that is displayed by native signers. Similar critical period effects have also been found with spoken languages for second-language learning. Researchers hypothesize that these effects are due to the maturational state of the child at the time of language exposure. A precise account of the mechanisms underlying the maturational change involved in the critical period for language acquisition remains a goal for future research.

BRAIN ORGANIZATION FOR SIGN LANGUAGE

Sign language exhibits properties for which each of the cerebral hemispheres of hearing people shows different predominant functioning. The left hemisphere has been shown to subserve linguistic functions, whereas the right hemisphere subserves visual–spatial functions. Given that ASL expresses linguistic functions by manipulating spatial relations, what is the brain organization for sign language? Is sign language controlled by the right hemisphere along with other visual–spatial functions or does the left hemisphere subserve sign language as it does spoken language? Or is sign language represented equally in both hemispheres of the brain? Recent research has shown that the brain honors the distinction between language and nonlanguage visual–spatial functions. Thus, despite the modality, signed languages are represented primarily in the left hemisphere of deaf signers, whereas the right hemisphere is specialized for nonlinguistic visual–spatial processing in these signers.

Damage to the left hemisphere of the brain in deaf signers leads to sign aphasias similar to those observed with spoken language. Aphasias are disruptions of language that follow certain types of brain injury. For example, adult signers with left-hemisphere damage may produce "agrammatic" signing which is characterized by a lack of morphological and syntactic markings and is often accompanied by halting effortful signing. For example, an agrammatic signer will produce single sign utterances which lack the grammatically required inflectional movements and use of space. Similarly, "agrammatic" aphasia in spoken language is characterized by effortful speech and a lack of grammatical markers, such as the past tense -*ed* or plural -*s* in English. Lesions to a different area of the left hemisphere produce a different kind of aphasia characterized by fluent signing or speaking, but with errors in the selection of grammatical markers and syntactic errors. A signer with this type of lesion may sign fluently but will not correctly utilize syntactic spatial loci and will produce incorrectly inflected signs. Differential damage within the left hemisphere produces differential linguistic impairments, and these impairments reflect linguistically relevant components for both sign and speech.

In contrast, right-hemisphere damage produces impairments of many visual–spatial abilities, but does *not* produce sign language aphasias. When given tests of sign language comprehension and production, signers with right hemisphere damage perform normally, but these same signers show marked impairment on nonlinguistic tests of visual–spatial functions. For example, when given a set of colored blocks and asked to assemble them to match a model, right-hemisphere damaged signers have great difficulty and are unable to capture the overall configuration of the block design. Similar impairments on this task are found with hearing, speaking subjects with right-hemisphere damage. In contrast, left-hemisphere damage does not impair performance on most visual–spatial tasks for either signers or speakers. The poor performance of right-hemisphere damaged signers on nonlinguistic visual–spatial tasks, such as perceiving spatial orientation or understanding spatial relations between objects, stands in marked contrast to their unimpaired visual–spatial linguistic abilities. The brain exhibits a principled distinction between linguistic and nonlinguistic visual–spatial functions.

The brain organization for sign language indicates that left-hemispheric specialization for language is not based on hearing and speech. The underlying basis for left-hemisphere specialization is the fundamental nature of linguistic functions rather than the sensory modality which conveys the language. Investigations of the neural underpinnings of signed and spoken languages are currently making use of *in vivo* techniques which can probe linguistic and visual–spatial processing in the intact brain. By contrasting signed and spoken languages, these studies can illuminate in greater detail the determinants of brain substrate for language and visual–spatial cognition.

BIBLIOGRAPHY

Klima, E. S., and U. Bellugi. *Signs of Language.* Cambridge: Harvard University Press, 1988.

Newport, E., and R. Meier. "The Acquisition of American Sign Language." In *The Crosslinguistic Study of Language Acquisition.* Ed. D. Slobin. Vol. 1. Hillsdale, NJ: Erlbaum, 1985.

Padden, C. "Grammatical Theory and Signed Languages." In *Linguistics: The Cambridge Survey.* Ed. F. Newmeyer. Vol. 2. New York: Cambridge University Press, 1988.

Poizner, H., E. S. Klima, and U. Bellugi. *What the Hands Reveal about the Brain.* Cambridge: MIT Press, 1987.

Reilly, J., M. McIntire, and U. Bellugi. "Faces: The Relationship between Language and Affect." In *From Gesture to Language in Hearing and Deaf Children.* Ed. V. Volterra and C. Erting. New York: Springer-Verlag, 1991.

FOR DISCUSSION AND REVIEW

1. Review the four prevalent myths about sign language. How might each have arisen? How is each refuted?

2. The phonological elements of spoken language are based upon patterns of sound. What characteristics of sign language are analogous to the phonology of spoken language? For help in considering the answers to questions 2, 3, and 4, refer to the figures accompanying the article. You might also refer to two essays in Part Three, "Phonetics" by Edward Callary and "The Minimal Units of Meaning: Morphemes" from The Ohio State University Language Files for more detailed definitions of phonology and morphology.

3. How are morphological form changes created in English and most spoken languages? How are they created in ASL?

4. In English, as in most spoken languages, syntax is based largely on word order. Explain how the use of spatial mechanisms makes syntax more flexible in ASL. You might also refer to Part Four, "Syntax: The Structure of Sentences," by Frank Heny for a more detailed definition of syntax.

5. How are facial expressions used in sign language? How do they differ from normal expressions of emotion?

6. How are regional dialects and foreign accents perceived in ASL?

7. Just as hearing babies babble using sound, deaf babies babble using gesture. What does this suggest about the nature of the maturational process represented by babbling?

8. Identify some of the important parallels between the acquisition of language by hearing children born to hearing parents and by deaf children born to deaf parents.

9. What are the disadvantages of deaf children born to hearing parents? What does their experience suggest about language acquisition?

10. What does research show about the differences and similarities of language functions in the brains of speakers and signers? What do these findings imply about the nature of language?

11. Because, at the most obvious levels, sign language differs drastically from oral language, the similarities between them offer striking insights into the most fundamental characteristics of human language. Review the characteristics shared by sign languages and oral languages.

9

Nonverbal Communication

George A. Miller

The famous linguist Edward Sapir once described nonverbal behavior as "an elaborate and secret code that is written nowhere, known by none, and understood by all." His statement is to a great extent still true. Nonverbal behavior has been studied extensively, but our understanding of it is far from complete. Unfortunately, most of the popular books and articles about nonverbal communication—usually referred to as "body language"—have drastically oversimplified the subject, suggesting that one can easily learn to "read" the nonverbal signals unconsciously "sent" by other people. In fact, however, the study of nonverbal communication is complex and subtle, far more than a kind of game that anyone can play. Returning to Sapir's phrase, "understood by all," the "all" refers to members of the same culture. Cross-culturally, people continue to misunderstand one another because they have different nonverbal systems—different acceptable postures, ways of moving, gestures, facial expressions, eye behavior, and use of space and distance. In the following selection, Professor George A. Miller uses a variety of examples to explain how necessary it is to understand the nonverbal systems as well as the languages of other cultures.

When the German philosopher Nietzsche said that "success is the greatest liar," he meant that a successful person seems especially worthy to us even when his success is due to nothing more than good luck. But Nietzsche's observation can be interpreted more broadly.

People communicate in many different ways. One of the most important ways, of course, is through language. Moreover, when language is written it can be completely isolated from the context in which it occurs; it can be treated as if it were an independent and self-contained process. We have been so successful in using and describing and analyzing this special kind of communication that we sometimes act as if language were the *only* kind of communication that can occur between people. When we act that way, of course, we have been deceived by success, the greatest liar of them all.

Like animals, people communicate by their actions as well as by the noises they make. It is a sort of biological anomaly of man—something like the giraffe's neck, or the pelican's beak—that our vocal noises have so far outgrown in importance and frequency all our other methods of signaling to one another. Language is obviously essential for human beings, but it is not the whole story of human communication. Not by a long shot.

Consider the following familiar fact. When leaders in one of the less well developed countries decide that they are ready to introduce some technology that is already highly advanced in another country, they do not simply buy all the books that have been written about that technology and have their students read them. The books may exist and they may be very good, but just reading about the technology is not enough. The students must be sent to study in a country where the technology is already flourishing, where they can see it firsthand. Once they have been exposed to it in person and experienced it as part of their own lives, they are ready to understand and put to use the information that is in the books. But the verbal message, without the personal experience to back it up, is of little value.

Now what is it that the students learn by participating in a technology that they cannot learn by just reading about it? It seems obvious that they are learning something important, and that whatever it is they are learning is something that we don't know how to put into our verbal descriptions. There is a kind of nonverbal communication that occurs when students are personally involved in the technology and when they interact with people who are using and developing it.

Pictures are one kind of nonverbal communication, of course, and moving pictures can communicate some of the information that is difficult to capture in words. Pictures also have many of the properties that make language so useful—they can be taken in one situation at one time and viewed in an entirely different situation at any later time. Now that we have television satellites, pictures can be transmitted instantaneously all over the world, just as our words can be transmitted by radio. Perhaps the students who are trying to learn how to create a new technology in their own country could supplement their reading by watching moving pictures of people at work in the developed industry. Certainly the pictures would be a help, but they would be very expensive. And we don't really know whether words and pictures together would capture everything the students would be able to learn by going to a more advanced country and participating directly in the technology.

Let me take another familiar example. There are many different cultures in the world, and in each of them the children must learn a great many things that are expected of everyone who participates effectively in that culture. When I say they are taken for granted, I mean that nobody needs to describe them or write them down or try self-consciously to teach them to children. Indeed, the children begin to learn them before their linguistic skills are far enough developed to understand a verbal description of what they are learning. This kind of learning has sometimes been called "imitation," but that is much too simple an explanation for the complex processes that go on when a child learns what is normal and expected in his own community. Most of the norms are communicated to the child nonverbally, and he internalizes them as if no other possibilities existed. They are as much a part of him as his own body; he would no more question them than he would question the fact that he has two hands and two feet, but only one head.

These cultural norms can be described verbally, of course. Anthropologists who are interested in describing the differences among the many cultures of the world have developed a special sensitivity to cultural norms and have described them at length in their scholarly books. But if a child had to read those books in order to learn what was expected of him, he would never become an effective member of his own community.

What is an example of the sort of thing that children learn nonverbally? One of the simplest examples to observe and analyze and discuss is the way people use clothing and bodily ornamentation to communicate. At any particular time in any particular culture there is an accepted and normal way to dress and to arrange the hair and to paint the face and to wear one's jewelry. By adopting those conventions for dressing himself, a person communicates to the world that he wants to be treated according to the standards of the culture for which they are appropriate. When a black person in America rejects the normal American dress and puts on African clothing, he is communicating to the world that he wants to be treated as an Afro-American. When a white man lets his hair and beard grow, wears very informal clothing, and puts beads around his neck, he is communicating to the world that he rejects many of the traditional values of Western culture. On the surface, dressing up in unusual costumes would seem to be one of the more innocent forms of dissent that a person could express, but in fact it is deeply resented by many people who still feel bound by the traditional conventions of their culture and who become fearful or angry when those norms are violated. The nonverbal message that such a costume communicates is "I reject your culture and your values," and those who resent this message can be violent in their response.

The use of clothing as an avenue of communication is relatively obvious, of course. A somewhat subtler kind of communication occurs in the way people use their eyes. We are remarkably accurate in judging the direction of another person's gaze; psychologists have done experiments that have measured just how accurate such judgments are. From an observation of where a person is looking we can infer what he is looking at, and from knowing what he is looking at we can guess what he is interested in, and from what he is interested in and the general situation we can usually make a fairly good guess about what he is going to do. Thus eye movements can be a rich and important channel of nonverbal communication.

Most personal interaction is initiated by a short period during which two people look directly at one another. Direct eye contact is a signal that each has the other's attention, and that some further form of interaction can follow. In Western cultures, to look directly into another person's eyes is equivalent to saying, "I am open to you—let the action begin." Everyone knows how much lovers can communicate by their eyes, but aggressive eye contact can also be extremely informative.

In large cities, where people are crowded in together with others they neither know nor care about, many people develop a deliberate strategy of avoiding eye contacts. They want to mind their own business, they don't have time to interact with everyone they pass, and they communicate this fact by refusing to look at other people's faces. It is one of the things that make newcomers to the city feel that it is a hostile and unfriendly place.

Eye contact also has an important role in regulating conversational interactions. In America, a typical pattern is for the listener to signal that he is paying attention by looking at the talker's mouth or eyes. Since direct eye contact is often too intimate, the talker may let his eyes wander elsewhere. As the moment arrives for the talker to become a listener, and for his partner to begin talking, there will often be a preliminary eye signal. The talker will often look toward the listener, and the listener will signal that he is ready to talk by glancing away.

Such eye signals will vary, of course, depending on what the people are talking about and what the personal relation is between them. But whatever the pattern of eye signals that two people are using, they use them unconsciously. If you try to become aware of your own eye movements while you are talking to someone, you will find it extremely frustrating. As soon as you try to think self-consciously about your own eye movements, you do not know where you should be looking. If you want to study how the eyes communicate, therefore, you should do it by observing other people, not yourself. But if you watch other people too intently, of course, you may disturb them or make them angry. So be careful!

Even the pupils of your eyes communicate. When a person becomes excited or interested in something, the pupils of his eyes increase in size. In order to test whether we are sensitive to these changes in pupil size, a psychologist showed people two pictures of the face of a pretty girl. The two pictures were completely identical except that in one picture the girl's pupils were constricted, whereas in the other picture her pupils were dilated. The people were asked to say which picture they liked better, and they voted in favor of the picture with the large pupils. Many of the judges did not even realize consciously what the difference was, but apparently they were sensitive to the difference and preferred the eyes that communicated excitement and interest.

Eye communication seems to be particularly important for Americans. It is part of the American culture that people should be kept at a distance, and that contact with another person's body should be avoided in all but the most intimate situations. Because of this social convention of dealing with others at a distance, Americans have to place much reliance on their distance receptors, their eyes and ears, for personal communication. In other cultures, however, people normally come close together and bodily contact between conversational partners is as normal as eye contact is in America. In the Eastern Mediterranean cultures, for example, both the touch and the smell of the other person are expected.

The anthropologist Edward T. Hall has studied the spatial relations that seem appropriate to various kinds of interactions. They vary with intimacy, they depend on the possibility of eye contact, and they are different in different cultures. In America, for example, two strangers will converse impersonally at a distance of about four feet. If one moves closer, the other will back away. In a waiting room, strangers will keep apart, but friends will sit together, and members of a family may actually touch one another.

Other cultures have different spatial norms. In Latin America, for example, impersonal discussion normally occurs at a distance of two or three feet, which is the distance that is appropriate for personal discussion in North America. Consequently, it is impossible for a North and a South American both to be comfortable when they talk to one another unless one can adopt the zones that are normal for the other. If the South American advances to a distance that is comfortable for him, it will be too close for the North American, and he will withdraw, and one can chase the other all around the room unless something intervenes to end the conversation. The North American seems aloof and unfriendly to the South American. The South American seems hostile or oversexed to the North American. Hall mentions that North Americans sometimes cope with this difference by barricading themselves behind desks or tables, and that South Americans have been known literally to climb over these barriers in order to attain a comfortable distance at which to talk.

Within one's own culture these spatial signals are perfectly understood. If two North Americans are talking at a distance of one foot or less, you know that what they are saying is highly confidential. At a distance of two to three feet it will be some personal subject matter. At four or five feet it is impersonal, and if they are conversing at a distance of seven or eight feet, we know that they expect others to be listening to what they are saying. When talking to a group, a distance of ten to twenty feet is normal, and at greater distances only greetings are exchanged. These conventions are unconscious but highly reliable. For example, if you are having a personal conversation with a North American at a distance of two feet, you can shift it to an impersonal conversation by the simple procedure of moving back to a distance of four or five feet. If he can't follow you, he will find it quite impossible to maintain a personal discussion at that distance.

These examples should be enough to convince you—if you needed convincing—that we communicate a great deal of information that is not expressed in the words we utter. And I have not even mentioned yet the interesting kind of communication that occurs by means of gestures. A gesture is an expressive motion or action, usually made with the hands and arms, but also with the head or even the whole body. Gestures can occur with or without speech. As a part of the speech act, they usually emphasize what the person is saying, but they may occur without any speech at all. Some gestures are spontaneous, some are highly ritualized and have very specific meanings. And they differ enormously from one culture to another.

Misunderstanding of nonverbal communication is one of the most distressing and unnecessary sources of international friction. For example, few Americans understand how much the Chinese hate to be touched, or slapped on the back, or even to shake hands. How easy it would be for an American to avoid giving offense simply by avoiding these particular gestures that, to him, signify intimacy and friendliness. Or, to take another example, when Khrushchev placed his hands together over his head and shook them, most Americans interpreted it as an arrogant gesture of triumph, the sort of gesture a victorious prize fighter would make, even though Khrushchev seems to have intended it as a friendly gesture of international brotherhood. Sticking out the tongue and quickly drawing it back can be a gesture of self-castigation in one culture, an admission of a social mistake, but someone from another culture might interpret it as a gesture of ridicule or contempt, and in the Eskimo culture it would not be a gesture at all, but the conventional way of directing a current of air when blowing out a candle. Just a little better communication on the nonverbal level might go a long way toward improving international relations.

Ritualized gestures—the bow, the shrug, the smile, the wink, the military salute, the pointed finger, the thumbed nose, sticking out the tongue, and so on—are not really nonverbal communication, because such gestures are just a substitute for the verbal meanings that are associated with them. There are, however, many spontaneous gestures and actions that are unconscious, but communicate a great deal. If you take a moving picture of someone who is deeply engrossed in a conversation, and later show it to him, he will be quite surprised to see many of the gestures he used and the subtle effects they produced. Sometimes what a person is saying unconsciously by his actions may directly contradict what he is saying consciously with his words. Anthropologists have tried to develop a way to write down a description of these nonverbal actions, something like the notation that choreographers use to record the movements of a ballet dancer, but it is difficult to know exactly what the significance of these actions really is, or what the important features are that should be recorded. We can record them photographically, of course, but we still are not agreed on how the photographic record should be analyzed.

Finally, there is a whole spectrum of communication that is vocal, but not really verbal. The most obvious examples are spontaneous gasps of surprise or cries of pain. I suspect this kind of vocal communication is very similar for both man and animal. But our use of vocal signals goes far beyond such grunts and groans. It is a commonplace observation that the way you say something is as important as what you say, and often more important for telling the listener what your real intentions are. Exactly the same words may convey directly opposite messages according to the way they are said. For example, I can say, "Oh, isn't that *wonderful*" so that I sound enthusiastic, or I can say, "Oh, isn't *that* wonderful" in a sarcastic tone so that you know I don't think it is wonderful at all. Because the actual words uttered are often misleading, lawyers and judges in the courtroom have learned that it is sometimes important to have an actual recording and not just a written transcript of what a person is supposed to have said.

Rapid and highly inflected speech usually communicates excitement, extremely distinct speech usually communicates anger, very loud speech usually communicates pomposity, and a slow monotone usually communicates boredom. The emotional clues that are provided by the way a person talks are extremely subtle, and accomplished actors must practice for many years to bring them under conscious control.

A person's pronunciation also tells a great deal about him. If he has a foreign accent, a sensitive listener can generally tell where he was born. If he speaks with a local dialect, we can often guess what his social origins were and how much education he has had. Often a person will have several different styles of speaking, and will use them to communicate which social role he happens to be playing at the moment. This is such a rich source of social and psychological information, in fact, that a whole new field has recently developed to study it, a field called "sociology of language." . . .

One of the most significant signals that is vocal but nonverbal is the ungrammatical pause. . . . In careful speech most of our pauses are grammatical. That is to say, our pauses occur at the boundaries of grammatical segments, and serve as a kind of audible punctuation. By calling them "grammatical pauses" we imply that they are a normal part of the verbal message. An ungrammatical pause, however, is not a part of the verbal message. For example, when I . . . uh . . . pause within a . . . uh . . . grammatical unit, you cannot regard the pause as part of my verbal message. These ungrammatical pauses are better regarded as the places where the speaker is thinking, is searching for words, and is planning how to continue his utterance. For a linguist, of course, the grammatical pause is most interesting, since it reveals something about the structure of the verbal message. For a psychologist, however, the ungrammatical pause is more interesting, because it reveals something about the thought processes of the speaker.

When a skilled person reads a prepared text, there are few ungrammatical pauses. But spontaneous speech is a highly fragmented and discontinuous activity. Indeed, ungrammatical pausing is a reliable signal of spontaneity in speech. The pauses tend to occur at choice points in the message, and particularly before words that are rare or unusual and words that are chosen with particular care. An actor who wanted to make his rehearsed speech sound spontaneous would deliberately introduce ungrammatical pauses at these critical points.

Verbal communication uses only one of the many kinds of signals that people can exchange; for a balanced view of the communication process we should always keep in mind the great variety of other signals that can reinforce or contradict the verbal message. These subtleties are especially important in psychotherapy, where a patient tries to communicate his emotional troubles to a doctor, but may find it difficult or impossible to express in words the real source of his distress. Under such circumstances, a good therapist learns to listen for more than words, and to rely on nonverbal signals to help him interpret the verbal signals. For this reason, many psychologists have been persistently interested in nonverbal communication, and have perhaps been less likely than linguists to fall into the mistaken belief that language is the only way we can communicate.

The price of opening up one's attention to this wider range of events, however, is a certain vagueness about the kind of communication that is occurring—about what it means and how to study it. We have no dictionaries or grammars to help us analyze nonverbal communication, and there is much work that will have to be done in many cultures before we can formulate and test any interesting scientific theories about nonverbal communication. Nevertheless, the obvious fact that so much communication does occur nonverbally should persuade us not to give up, and not to be misled by our success in analyzing verbal messages.

Recognizing the great variety of communication channels that are available is probably only the first step toward a broader conception of communication as a psychological process. Not only must we study what a person says and how he says it, but we must try to understand why he says it. If we concentrate primarily on the words that people say, we are likely to think that the only purpose of language is to exchange information. That is one of its purposes, of course, but certainly not the only one. People exchange many things. Not only do they exchange information, but they also exchange money, goods, services, love, and status. In any particular interaction, a person may give one of these social commodities in exchange for another. He may give information in exchange for money or give services in exchange for status or love. Perhaps we should first characterize communication acts in terms of what people are trying to give and gain in their social interactions. Then, within that broader frame of reference, we might see better that verbal messages are more appropriate for some exchanges and nonverbal messages for others, and that both have their natural and complementary roles to play in the vast tapestry we call human society.

FOR DISCUSSION AND REVIEW

1. According to Miller, why is reading about some advanced technology developed in another country not enough? Why must students actually *go* to the country? In answering this question, try to use specific, original examples.

2. Miller asserts that, along with their language, children also learn certain nonverbal "cultural norms" that "are communicated to the child nonverbally." Drawing from your own experience, describe three of the cultural norms that American children learn.

3. Keep track for a day of the way people you meet use their eyes to

make or avoid eye contact. Write a brief description of the behavior you have observed. Do your findings agree with Miller's statements about the way Americans use their eyes? If not, what are the differences?

4. Miller uses two examples of the use of clothing to communicate. Based on your own experience, give two additional examples.

5. Spatial norms vary from culture to culture. Describe any differences between American norms and those of other countries that you have noticed while traveling abroad. If you haven't had such experiences, ask two or three of your friends about theirs.

Projects for "Language and Its Study"

1. In "Language: An Introduction," W. F. Bolton points out that "perhaps the most distinctive property of language is that its users can create sentences never before known, and yet perfectly understandable to their hearers and readers." He calls this property *productivity*. To illustrate Bolton's point, show a photograph or a cartoon to the members of your class, and ask each of them to describe in one sentence what they see. Write down the sentences, and have the class compare them. What conclusions can be drawn?

2. Discussing the origin of human language, Bolton writes: "How this happened is at least as unknowable as how the universe began." However, a number of theories (e.g., the ding-dong and bow-wow theories) about the origin of language that used to be taken seriously have now been discredited. Read about four of these early theories in your library, and prepare an oral or written report describing the theories and evaluating their adequacy. Good starting places for this research are such standard textbooks as *The Origins and Development of the English Language* (Thomas Pyles and John Algeo) and *A History of the English Language* (Albert C. Baugh and Thomas Cable).

3. In describing the vocal organs that produce speech, Bolton notes that all of them except the larynx have other functions. Although disease sometimes necessitates the removal of an individual's larynx, speech is not always impossible for such a person. Both the artificial larynx and a technique involving swallowing air and talking while the air is "exhaled" have made speech possible for many people who have had this surgery. Prepare a report on one of these techniques. A great deal of published material will be available in your library; you may also find it useful to interview a speech pathologist or a specialist in this kind of rehabilitative medicine.

4. In some cases of deafness, as Bolton indicates, "bone-conduction can sometimes substitute for air-conduction." Prepare a brief report describing how hearing aids work; you may want to pay particular attention to bone-conduction.

5. Harvey A. Daniels presents "nine fundamental ideas about language." List the nine one-sentence ideas, and show them to five people who are not in your class. Summarize their reactions. Are some of the ideas more controversial or less accepted than others?

6. On p. 55 Daniels describes the Sapir-Whorf hypothesis that the structure and vocabulary of people's languages influence their cultural and social beliefs, as well as their view of the world. Prepare a written or oral report explaining and analyzing the Sapir-Whorf hypothesis. Be sure to include examples of the ways in which language allegedly conditions perceptions.

7. An interesting group project is to debate the validity of the Sapir-Whorf hypothesis. An excellent summary of the pro and con arguments can be found in Danny D. Steinberg's *Psycholinguistics: Language, Mind*

and World (London and New York: Longman, 1982), pp. 101–120. See also, Steven Pinker, "Mentalese," in *The Language Instinct: How the Mind Creates Language* (New York: Morrow, 1994) and Geoffrey K. Pullum, *The Great Eskimo Vocabulary Hoax and Other Irreverent Essays on the Study of Language* (Chicago: University of Chicago Press, 1991).

8. In his book *The Word-A-Day Vocabulary Builder*, lexicographer Bergen Evans states:

> Words are the tools for the job of saying what you want to say. And what you want to say are your thoughts and feelings, your desires and your dislikes, your hopes and your fears, your business and your pleasure— almost everything, indeed, that makes up you. Except for our vegetable- like growth and our animal-like impulses, almost all that we are is relat- ed to our use of words. Man has been defined as a tool-using animal, but his most important tool, the one that distinguishes him from all other animals, is his speech.

Do you agree with Evans's statement? Is it possible to think with- out language? Are there some creative activities for which people do not need speech? Write a brief essay in which you defend your position.

9. As Daniels notes, "Although the English writing system is essen- tially phonemic—an attempt to represent the sounds of language in graph- ic form—it is notoriously irregular and confusing." (Consider, for example, the various ways the vowel sound in the word *keep* can be spelled: k*ee*p, k*ey*, tr*ea*t, p*eo*ple, qu*ay*, am*oe*ba, th*ie*f, rec*ei*ve.) It is no wonder that there have been many attempts to reform the spelling of English to make it more closely reflect its actual pronunciation. From Benjamin Franklin to Noah Webster, from Theodore Roosevelt to George Bernard Shaw, many people have devised "improved" spelling systems for English. Prepare a report on (a) the proposals of one of the major would-be reformers, or (b) the history of the spelling-reform movement as a whole, summarizing both the arguments for and against spelling reform.

10. Daniels's book *Famous Last Words: The American Language Crisis Reconsidered*, from which "Nine Ideas about Language" is taken, disputes the idea that the English language is deteriorating and argues against what Daniels believes to be the trivializing attacks of such self- proclaimed experts as Edwin Newman, William Safire, John Simon, and the authors of usage handbooks. The subjects of just what is "correct usage" and of whether English is deteriorating are fascinating ones about which people have strong opinions.

Divide the class into three groups. Basing its arguments on facts, not opinions, each group should prepare a logical, well-documented position paper on one of the following: (a) the English language is deteriorating; (b) the English language is not deteriorating; and (c) there is an absolute stan- dard for "correct" English and its basis is clear and defensible.

11. Consult at least four introductory linguistics texts (not dictionar- ies), and copy the definitions of *language* that each gives. After carefully comparing the definitions, write a paper discussing which points recur and

explaining their significance. (If you decide to do this assignment as a class project, class members should collect as many different definitions of *language* as they can, being sure to identify the source of each. Copy and distribute the definitions; discuss, as a group or in small groups, the significance of the similarities and differences among the definitions.)

12. Many schools for the deaf use a form of language called "Signed English" instead of ASL. Study the differences between the two and the reasons given for preferring one or the other in a school setting. Prepare a short paper in which you defend the language you would prefer, exploring the arguments for and against both sides.

13. Individually or in small groups, prepare answers to the following questions for a class discussion: (a) What are your three most common gestures? What are your instructor's three most common gestures? What conclusions (about personality, setting, etc.) can you draw from these? (b) In a conversation, how do you know when someone is losing interest? Is not losing interest? (c) What aspects of a person's appearance cause you to feel (at least initially) friendly? Hostile? (d) In what ways do you act differently at home from the way you do at a friend's? Why?

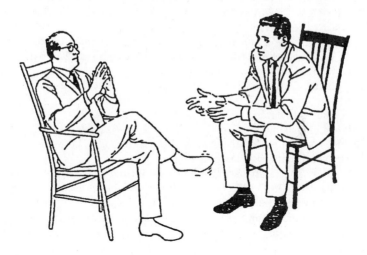

14. Study the above illustration of a typical buyer-seller relationship; the buyer is on the left and the seller on the right. Discuss the interaction between the buyer and the seller in terms of their gestures, their personal appearances, and their proxemic arrangement. What general statements can you make about the buyer? About the seller?

Selected Bibliography

Akmajian, Adrian, Richard A. Demers, and Robert M. Harnish. *Linguistics: An Introduction to Language and Communication*, 2nd ed. Cambridge: MIT Press, 1984. [An excellent introduction to the field of linguistics.]

Axtell, Roger E., and Mike Fornwald. *Gestures: The Do's and Taboos of Body Language around the World*. New York: Wiley, 1991. [Packed with anecdotes and hypothetical scenarios as well as historical facts and scientific theory.]

Baynton, Douglas C. *Forbidden Signs: American Culture and the Campaign against Sign Language*. Chicago: University of Chicago Press, 1996. [Documents the social and historical difficulties encountered by ASL users.]

Berko-Gleason, Jean. *The Development of Language*, 3rd ed. New York: Macmillan, 1993. [Revised extensively with many new features of the 2nd ed. An introductory text that studies language development as a lifelong process.]

Bloomfield, Leonard. *Language*. New York: Holt, Rinehart and Winston, 1933. [Still a classic work for students of linguistics.]

Bolinger, Dwight. *Aspects of Language*, 2nd ed. New York: Harcourt Brace Jovanovich, 1975. [An extensive and readable treatment of a wide variety of topics.]

———. *Language: The Loaded Weapon*. New York: Longman Group, 1980. [A short but insightful introduction to language, with an emphasis on the importance of meaning.]

Burling, Robbins. *Patterns of Language: Structure, Variation, Change*. San Diego: Academic Press, 1992. [Includes topics other introductory textbooks avoid with plenty of references from a variety of languages.]

Celee-Murcia, Marianne. *English as a Second or Foreign Language*. Boston: Heinle and Heinle, 1991. [A general text that discusses both the theory and practice of teaching and learning ESL.]

Cook, V. J. *Chomsky's Universal Grammar: An Introduction*, 2nd ed. New York: Basil Blackwell Inc., 1996. [Yet another invaluable collection of linguistic material from the field's master.]

Emmorey, Karen, and Judy S. Reilly, eds. *Language, Gesture, and Space*. Hillsdale, NJ: Erlbaum, 1995. [A useful recent collection including material on sign language.]

Farb, Peter. *Humankind*. Boston: Houghton Mifflin, 1978. [Very readable discussion of all aspects of human behavior, including language.]

———. *Word Play: What Happens When People Talk*. New York: Alfred A. Knopf, 1973; rpt. New York: Bantam, 1975. [Entertaining, knowledgeable discussion.]

Fromkin, Victoria, and Robert Rodman. *An Introduction to Language*, 5th ed. New York: Holt, Rinehart and Winston, 1993. [One of the most popular introductory books.]

Goffman, Erving. *Behavior in Public Places*. New York: The Free Press of Glencoe, 1963. [A psychiatrist's analysis of public behavior.]

———. *Gender Advertisements*. New York: Harper Colophon Books, 1979. [Goffman is a widely recognized social scientist; here he investigates advertisements and the way in which they do and do not reflect reality; highly recommended.]

———. *The Presentation of Self in Everyday Life.* New York: Doubleday, 1976. [An analysis of an individual's self-impressions when appearing before others.]

Hall, Edward T. *Beyond Culture.* Garden City, NY: Doubleday, 1976. [A study of how cultures use such factors as time and space to organize human behavior.]

———. "Proxemics." *Current Anthropology,* 9 (April–June 1968): 83–104. [A good introduction to proxemics with charts, comments by authorities, and bibliography.]

———. *The Hidden Dimension.* Garden City, NY: Doubleday, 1966. [A fascinating discussion of human and animal use of space.]

———. *The Silent Language.* Garden City, NY: Doubleday, 1973. [A pioneer work on space and language.]

Hattiangadi, J. N. *How Is Language Possible? Philosophical Reflections on the Evolution of Language and Knowledge.* La Salle, IL: Open Court Publishing, 1987. [An interesting philosophical look at everything from acquisition through development of language. A very accessible reference work.]

Hulit, Lloyd M., and M. R. Howard. *Born to Talk: An Introduction to Speech and Language Development.* New York: Macmillan, 1993. [An easily accessible detailed study of the "stages" of language development with inviting chapter titles and thorough exploration of the subject matter.]

Human Ancestors: Readings from "Scientific American." San Francisco: W. H. Freeman and Company, 1979. [A collection of eleven articles describing a number of aspects of the search for evidence regarding the origin and development of human beings.]

Kluckholm, Clyde. "The Gift of Tongues," In *Mirror for Man: The Relation of Anthropology to Modern Life.* New York: Whittlesey House, 1949. [An anthropologist's view of language, culture, and the Whorfian hypothesis.]

Knapp, Mark L., and Judith A. Hall. *Nonverbal Communication in Human Interaction,* 4th ed. San Diego: Harcourt Brace, 1996. [A very thorough survey of research, excellent notes and comprehensive bibliography.]

Langer, Suzanne K. *Philosophy in a New Key: A Study in the Symbolism of Reason, Rite, & Art,* 3rd ed. Cambridge: Harvard University Press, 1956. [A classic work on the human symbol-making process and its relationship to language.]

Lehmann, Winfred P. *Language: An Introduction.* New York: Random House, 1983. [A good, brief introduction to current areas of interest in linguistics.]

Lieberman, Philip. *On the Origins of Language.* New York: Macmillan, 1975. [A careful analysis of paleontological and archeological evidence.]

Michaels, Leonard, and Christopher Ricks, eds. *The State of the Language.* Berkeley: University of California Press, 1980. [A collection of sixty-three short, interesting essays on topics of widespread interest.]

Milner, Jean-Claude. *For the Love of Language.* New York: The Macmillan Press, 1990. [A translation of a 1978 publication with an extensive helpful introduction entitled "What Do Linguists Want?"]

Nilsen, Don L. F., and Alleen Pace Nilsen. *Language Play: An Introduction to Linguistics.* Rowley, MA: Newbury House Publishers, 1978. [Interesting; includes topics often omitted. See chapter 1, "What Is Language?"]

Pei, Mario. *The Story of Language.* Revised ed. Philadelphia: J. B. Lippincott, 1965. [A popular and readable introduction.]

Pinker, Steven. *The Language Instinct: How the Mind Creates Language.* New York: Morrow, 1994. [See especially chapter 3, "Mentalese," for arguments against linguistic determinism.]

Poyatos, Fernando. *Cross-Cultural Perspectives in Nonverbal Communication.* Lewiston, NY: C. J. Hogrefe, 1988. [Gestures, painting, photography, clothing, and architecture are included as forms of nonverbal communication in this interesting study.]

Quinn, Jim. *American Tongue and Cheek: A Populist Guide to Our Language.* New York: Penguin Books, 1982. [Delightful and informative; traces changing attitudes toward usage, takes on the current "usage experts," and demonstrates that the English language is alive and well.]

Sagan, Carl. *The Dragons of Eden: Speculations on the Evolution of Human Intelligence.* New York: Random House, 1977. [Controversial but fascinating.]

Salus, P. H., ed. *On Language: Plato to Von Humboldt.* New York: Holt, Rinehart & Winston, 1969. [Includes several essays on the nature and origin of language.]

Sapir, Edward. *Language: An Introduction to the Study of Speech.* 1921; Reprint, New York: Harcourt Brace & World, 1949. [A classic book that explores the relationship between speech and culture.]

Saussure, Ferdinand de. *Course in General Linguistics.* Trans. Wade Baskin; Ed. Charles Bally and Albert Sechehaye, 1915. Reprint, New York: Philosophical Library, 1959. [A classic; based on lecture notes collected by former students.]

Stam, J. *Inquiries in the Origin of Language: The Fate of a Question.* New York: Harper & Row, 1976. [Traces the history of theories about the origin of language.]

Steinberg, Danny D. *Psycholinguistics: Language, Mind and World.* London and New York: Longman, 1982. [Summarizes pro and con arguments about the Sapir-Whorf Hypothesis.]

Ullmann, Stephen. *Words and Their Use.* New York: Philosophical Library, 1951. [Contains an excellent chapter on the symbol-making process in language.]

Whorf, Benjamin Lee. *Language, Thought, and Reality.* Ed. John B. Carroll. Cambridge: MIT Press, 1956. [A classic work on the relationship between language and culture.]

Wilson, Edward O. *On Human Nature.* Cambridge: Harvard University Press, 1978. [Difficult but rewarding; attempt to join biological thought to the social sciences and the humanities.]

Wolkomir, Richard. "American Sigh-n Language: 'It's Not Mouth Stuff—It's Brain Stuff,'" *Smithsonian,* July 1992, 30–41. [A captivating study of how deaf people communicate in our spoken world.]

PHONETICS AND PHONOLOGY, AND MORPHOLOGY

The basic questions posed by any discipline vary over time. These variations are taken for granted in a field such as chemistry, but are less accepted in the study of language, or linguistics. And yet, in only seventy-five years, the fundamentals of traditional grammar, largely unquestioned for centuries, have been challenged, first by the proponents of structural grammar, and, more recently, by linguists advocating a generative approach to studying language. The basic goal of the latter group, who currently dominates serious linguistic work in the United States, is to explain what it means to know a language.

Most linguists agree that it is best to describe languages in terms of their basic systems, or divisions:

1. *phonetics and phonology:* the sounds of a language, and the rules describing how they are combined

2. *morphology:* the ways in which the words of a language are formed from smaller units, and the nature of these units

3. *syntax:* the finite set of rules that enable native speakers to combine words in order to form phrases and sentences

4. *semantics:* the analysis of the meaning of individual words and larger units such as phrases and sentences

5. *discourse:* the study of speech acts or how language is used in various contexts

It is possible to analyze each of these language components in terms of (1) the units that comprise it and (2) the rules or patterns of each system that human beings follow when they speak.

Part Three and Part Four deal with these basic language systems. Part Three discusses the first two systems: phonetics and phonology, and morphology. Phonetics and phonology are addressed first because it is often helpful, for example, to use phonetic transcriptions or to refer to phonemes and phonological processes when discussing subjects such as syntax, which is covered in Part Four.

The first selection, "Phonetics," by Professor Edward Callary, deals with the important science of speech sounds, both articulatory and acoustic, and also with the principles of phonetic transcription. Exercises in the text provide readers with an immediate opportunity to apply phonetic concepts and relate phonological patterns to English language words as they are spoken and written.

Morphology is then examined in "The Minimal Units of Meaning: Morphemes," from the Ohio State University *Language Files*. This focuses on the various kinds of English morphemes and the hierarchical way in which they combine to form words.

The following selection, "The Identification of Morphemes," by H. A. Gleason Jr., uses data primarily from Hebrew to describe the analytical process for identifying morphemes. Three exercises prepared by Professor Gleason that involve the morphological analysis of samples of Swahili, Ilocano, and Dinka follow his selection.

Words are built in systematic ways from morphemic units. In the next selection, "Word-Making," Professor W. Nelson Francis examines the processes of word formation in English and explains the processes that have been most influential at different times.

In the final article, Kelvin Don Nilsen and Alleen Pace Nilsen take the reader on a detailed, often humorous, journey through the newest sector of English word-making—"computer talk"—which has burgeoned in the last two decades as computers have become a part of our daily lives. While this rapid growth in language appears random and chaotic, it also clearly demonstrates the rules underlying all word formation. The concept of language as a rule-governed system recurs frequently in this anthology. Part 3 stresses this concept and part 4 covers it more extensively.

10

Phonetics

Edward Callary

Phonetics, which has been studied for many years, is one of the best known subfields of linguistics. Some knowledge of phonetics is an essential basis for further work in linguistics. In the following selection, written especially for this book, Professor Edward Callary of Northern Illinois University discusses some of the applications of current research in phonetics and clearly explains articulatory and acoustic phonetics. Then he explores two aspects of the "grammar of phonetics," aspects that are "known" by all native speakers of English: (1) some of the permissible sequences of sounds in English and how they can be described in terms of general rules, and (2) the regular changes in sounds made by speakers, changes that depend on the contexts in which the sounds occur. The exercises that appear throughout the article reinforce and clarify the author's points.

Phonetics is that part of linguistics concerned with the sounds and sound systems of language; it deals with how sounds are produced, their physical properties, and how the rules of language organize and change sounds from one context to another.

The study of phonetics provides information with practical applications in a variety of areas. Knowledge of how sounds are produced, perceived, and understood is necessary for clinicians who diagnose and remediate speech disorders; for language specialists who teach a nonnative language; for engineers who design more efficient telephones and create voice-based identification and security systems; and for linguists who analyze the properties common to all human languages.

As part of their work, phoneticians (people who study phonetics) analyze the characteristics of the sounds that make up the syllables, words, and sentences of spoken language. For a particular language, they ask the following: How many sounds are there (this is not as easy to answer as it sounds)? What is the best way to describe these sounds? How does the language organize sounds (how do the sounds change from one situation to another and how are they added to or deleted from words)? Ultimately, phoneticians want to know not only about individual languages but about language in general—those characteristics that are common to all languages and what they reveal about the structure and functioning of the human mind.

Since this is an introductory chapter, the examples and the problems are simplified and English examples are used almost exclusively; however, the principles are applicable to all languages, since human languages differ only in their details, although the details themselves are infinitely interesting.

It is extremely important to keep the following point in mind while reading this chapter: many of the ideas about language that we have assimilated are in conflict with the facts of how language actually works. In this chapter on phonetics, it is especially important to emphasize that language is *sound*, not *writing*. As educated people who have spent years learning to read and spell correctly, we may have the mistaken notion that writing is somehow "real" language and that speech is an often poor attempt to express the sounds that letters naturally possess. The idea that letters "have" sounds is not only mistaken but misleading as well, since it tends to blind us to the principles and rules of our spoken language. Rather than saying, for instance, that the letter *c* has the sound [s] or [k], it is truer to the facts of language to say that, in the English spelling system, the sounds [s] and [k] are sometimes represented by the letter *c*. (For the sake of clarity, square brackets enclose sounds, and italics indicate letters of the regular alphabet.) Remember, we learn to speak and understand a complex language well before we learn to read or write that language. Many languages, even those in use today, have never been recorded in writing and are just as legitimate (and just as phonetic) as those that have been written for centuries.

ENGLISH SPELLING AND THE PHONETIC ALPHABET

In order to communicate sounds in print, we need to be able to represent them in a way that all readers can understand. This is why alphabets were invented in the first place, to assign a permanence to the ephemeral air of speech. Unfortunately, the alphabet we already know and have spent such a long time learning, the familiar ABCs or Roman alphabet, is not adequate for this task.

The relationship between sounds and their spellings is not perfect in any living language, but in English it is particularly deceiving. If you have studied a language such as Spanish or Swahili, you know that your chances of correctly pronouncing a word on first sight are quite good and, conversely, your chances of correctly spelling a word on hearing it the first time are also good. But in English there are so many different ways to represent sounds and so many unsystematic spelling "rules" that reading mistakes and spelling mistakes are common.

While there are reasons for the many discrepancies between sound and spelling in English, two are particularly important. First, with the introduction of the printing press in England in the fifteenth century, spelling began to be standardized and standard spelling reflected the pronunciation of that time. However, pronunciation has changed dramatically in the past 500 years and spelling has not. Many of the "silent let-ters" in contemporary English represent pronunciations of the past; for instance, the *gh* of *light*, the *k* of *knee*, and the *h* of *whale* were pro-nounced in earlier times.

Second, today we often have either multiple spellings for the same sound or instances where the same letter represents first one sound and then another because of adoption. When we adopt a word from a foreign language, we often adopt its spelling as well. For example, the letter *i* rep-resents one sound in *ice* (a native English word) and a completely differ-ent sound in *police* (adopted from French).

There have been a number of attempts to modify English spelling in order to bring it into line with English pronunciation, such as writing *night* as *nite* and *though* as *tho* (the *Chicago Tribune* of the 1930s and 1940s was an especially active advocate of spelling reform); but these have come to naught and, with the advent of the spelling checker, there is even less motivation for spelling reform than before, despite the fact that attempts to represent the approximately forty sounds of English using the twenty-six letters of the regular alphabet are bound to create problems.

The inconsistencies of English spelling require an unambiguous alphabet with a consistent relationship between sound and spelling—where a given sound is always represented by the same symbol and where a given symbol always represents the same sound. Such an alpha-bet is called a *phonetic alphabet*. Many phonetic alphabets have been devised over the years (unfortunately the symbols they use are not con-sistent from one phonetic alphabet to another). The phonetic alphabet this text employs is based on the most famous phonetic alphabet cur-rently in use, the International Phonetic Alphabet (IPA), which was developed by a group of European phoneticians toward the end of the nineteenth century. One of the developers of the IPA was the English phonetician Henry Sweet, the model for Professor Henry Higgins in George Bernard Shaw's *Pygmalion* (and its musical offspring *My Fair Lady*). Higgins, who devises a universal alphabet in the play, could (according to Shaw) identify more than 130 vowels! The IPA is complex; it has been revised several times and now contains more than 100 sym-bols, plus diacritics and other specifying marks. This text uses far fewer symbols, since the aim is to represent the sounds of only a single lan-guage, English, and not to attempt to provide symbols for every sound in all languages, as the IPA does.

The symbols of our phonetic alphabet that represent English conso-nants follow, along with several words illustrating their sound values. Notice the different ways in which many of the sounds are spelled. Most of the symbols are already familiar to you, since they have the values you might expect from the way they are represented in the regular alphabet. Five symbols use modified Roman letters: ǰ, č, š, ž, and ŋ. Since these are single sounds in English, a single letter represents each one.

The consonant symbols shouldn't present problems, since most of

PHONETIC SYMBOL	AS IN:	PHONETIC SYMBOL	AS IN:
p	pit, happen	θ	thin, bath
b	bit, rubber	ð	this, bathe
t	bet, thyme	s	sincere, science
d	did, maddest	z	haze, lose
k	sheikh, catch	š	sure, shine
g	gone, ghost	ž	treasure, azure
f	stuff, phone	č	itch, concerto
v	of, savvy	ǰ	jam, gem
m	thumb, simmer		
n	none, foreign		
ŋ	bring, thanks		
l	pale, tall		
r	berry, rhythm		
y	yet, million		
w	with, suede		
h	help, who		

them are drawn from the regular alphabet and are closely related to the values we might expect. The vowels, however, present some difficulties because there are not enough vowel letters to cover all sound values. As you can see from the list below, contrary to what you learned in elementary school, there are more than a dozen vowels in English, not five. Look at the symbols and their sound values and try to pronounce the sounds (not the words) several times. Pay particular attention to the symbol [ə]; this symbol is called *schwa* and it represents one of the most frequent sounds in English. In the regular alphabet schwa is spelled using all the vowel letters: *a*bility, blasph*e*my, eas*i*ly, c*o*nnect, c*u*p and by using many combinations of vowel letters.

PHONETIC SYMBOL	AS IN:	PHONETIC SYMBOL	AS IN:
i	each, machine	e	able, they
ɪ	sieve, system	ɛ	said, guest
æ	at, plaid	o	load, foe
ə	about, son	ɔ	raw, fought
u	move, ooze	a	father, honor
ʊ	book, full	ay	sigh, buy
		aw	shout, cow
		oy	soy, lawyer

PHONETIC TRANSCRIPTION

One of the first things you must learn is how to represent words phonetically; that is, how to write words using the symbols of our phonetic alphabet. This is easy; all it requires is a little practice and a willingness to think phonetically rather than orthographically (in terms of standard spelling). Once you learn to transcribe words, you can explore more interesting areas, such as how a language organizes sounds and how sounds fit into general patterns as defined by the rules of that language.

In order to transcribe phonetically, you first need to determine how many sounds there are in a particular word. Then you need to determine the phonetic symbol from the previously provided lists that represents each of these sounds. Remember, there are exactly the same number of symbols as there are sounds. Use the word *shake* as an example. It has five letters, but only three sounds, so use three symbols to write it phonetically. From the consonant list you see that [š] represents the first sound, [e] represents the vowel, and [k] represents the final sound, so the word transcription is [šek]. (Remember that phonetic symbols are enclosed in square brackets.) As a second example, the word *knee*, although spelled with four letters, is transcribed [ni] because it is composed of two sounds.

EXERCISE 1

Transcribe each of the following words using the appropriate phonetic symbols from the consonant and vowel lists.

Group 1: Monosyllabic Words

shut	noise	scene	juice
eye	guess	owe	piece
wrong	ouch	phrase	school
gym	who	those	friend
tight	tongue	now	was
quick	rhyme	rough	those
shook	why	ache	one
axe	cheese	month	lounge
doubt	debt	of	off
says	moist	cheese	

Group 2: Bisyllabic Words

echo	unique	many	okay
hygiene	onion	penguin	champagne
biscuit	extinct	antique	although
chronic	healthy	physics	croquet
monkey	caffeine	issue	

The pronunciation of the words in these two groups varies little; generally, they are pronounced the same way throughout the country and in most situations. But many words have more than one pronunciation; one pronunciation is used in some parts of the country while another pronunciation is used in other parts. For example, large sections of the country pronounce *don* and *dawn* the same way, while other large sections do not. Most often, however, different pronunciations are the result of different contexts; we pronounce a word one way in one social setting and another way in a different social setting. For instance, the word *literature* is likely to be pronounced one way when we are talking informally with our friends and another way when we are giving a formal class presentation. The words *candidate* and *history*, as well, usually have formal and informal pronunciations. Can you describe them?

Unfortunately, Americans have long labored under the misguided assumption, especially where language is concerned, that there is one right way to do something, and all other ways are wrong. This is regrettable since, just as we wear different clothes for different occasions and use different words in different circumstances (you might say "shucks" or "darn it" when talking with your parents or other elders; this might differ from what you would say to your dormitory friends!), we use different pronunciations for different occasions. One is not right and the others wrong; each pronunciation is appropriate in its place, and to use variations of pronunciation interchangeably might label us as snooty, pretentious, or ignorant of the English language. It is impossible to overstress this point, since many people, no matter how well educated or well intentioned, honestly believe that informal pronunciation is sloppy, slovenly, ungrammatical, illiterate, lazy, and ignorant, or all of these. This is not true: most Americans pronounce the word *today* at least two ways, [təde] and [tude], and the phonetic alphabet also expresses both pronunciations. In addressing a formal gathering we might say "I am pleased to be here [tude]." But outside such a setting we are more likely to say "It's good to be here [təde]."

In the exercises below, it is important that you transcribe each of the words as you generally would pronounce them in informal American English. You may not use the informal pronunciations all the time or even most of the time; you may even regard some pronunciations as "wrong," but be aware of the fact that they are characteristic of American English. And be particularly wary of schwa. This exercise will seem artificial, since usually you do not pronounce in isolation; otherwise you might tend to substitute a different vowel for schwa. For instance, it is tempting to transcribe a word like *polite* as [polayt]. But it is important to recognize that, informally, it is usually pronounced [pəlayt]. Is it wrong to transcribe the word *salami* as [salami]? Or should it be [səlami]? The answer is yes—and no. It depends upon the pronunciation you want to represent. If you want to indicate the pronunciation used by your third grade teacher while giving a spelling test, [salami] is correct; if you want to represent the pronunciation of *salami* used by most Americans in general conversation, then [səlami] is correct. The differences will become clearer to you with practice.

EXERCISE 2

In this exercise, transcribe to represent informal American pronunciation.

Group 3

among	column	extra	achieve
Asia	supply	fatigue	command
succeed	Canada	mosquito	iguana
kangaroo	Miami	Achilles	apathy
bungalow	cathedral	odyssey	coincide
Hiawatha	macaroni	alfalfa	oxygen
business	brilliant	moustache	baloney

Group 4

zucchini	postpone	family	chestnut
buzzed	seconds	consumes	trucks
clothes	Wednesday	atom	atomic
relaxed	adjective	coughed	physicist

ARTICULATORY PHONETICS

In order to understand how language uses sounds, it is important to understand how sounds are produced by the human vocal apparatus; in other words, to know something about *articulatory phonetics*, so called because sounds are described by the actions (articulations) of the vocal tract as they are produced. Figure 10.1 is a diagram of the human vocal tract, with those areas that are especially important in speech production labeled. Refer to this diagram while reading this chapter as often as necessary and try to locate the relevant areas of your own vocal tract with your tongue or finger.

We produce speech sounds by modifying a stream of air as we push it by the lungs through the trachea and ultimately out of the oral or nasal cavities, or both. We modify the airstream by changing the size or shape, or both, of the cavities in which the airstream resonates. Just as we produce sounds of different pitches when we blow over the openings of different size bottles, we produce different sounds by changing the size and shape of the resonating cavities. With [i], for instance, we use a tiny resonating cavity, and the result is a high-pitched sound; the opposite is true for [a], where we open our mouth fully.

Stated this way the production of speech sounds seems trivial, obvious, and incredibly easy. But the facts of articulation prove otherwise. The production of even the simplest sound is the result of a marvelously complex activity that involves the coordination of dozens of muscles, all acting with the precision and timing of a ballet. The fact that this occurs unconsciously, thousands of times a day, is all the more remarkable.

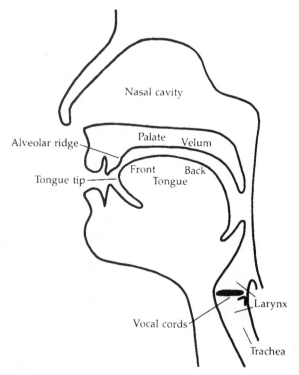

FIGURE 10.1.   **Anatomy Diagram.**

CONSONANTS

Consonants are sounds created by obstructing airflow, either completely as in the first sound of *dine,* or partially, as in the first sound of *fine.* Consonants are classified by three factors: (1) the location of the obstruction within the oral tract; (2) the nature of the obstruction; and (3) the state of the vocal cords. The sites in the vocal tract where we set up obstructions are called the *points of articulation,* and one way of describing consonants is by referring to these points. For English, there are six points of articulation:

1. *Bilabial* (bi, "two" + labia, "lips"). By completely blocking the airstream with both lips you produce [p], [b], or [m]. Therefore, [p], [b], and [m] are called *bilabial sounds.* Make each of these sounds, as well as those that follow, several times and pay particular attention to the action of your tongue and lips as you do.
2. *Labio-dental.* These sounds are made by bringing your lower lip into contact with your upper teeth. The sounds [f] and [v] are labio-dentals.

3. *Interdental.* As the term suggests, interdental sounds are made by placing your tongue tip between your teeth. There are two interdental sounds in English: [θ] and [ð]; both are usually spelled *th*.

4. *Alveolar.* The alveolar ridge is the bony crest that lies where your teeth join your palate. Most languages have a number of sounds articulated in the alveolar area; English has six: [t], [d], [n], [s], [z], and [l].

5. *Palatal.* The roof of the mouth is made up of two distinct parts: a hard, front part called the palate (from the Latin word for "plate," as in an artist's palette), and a soft, back part, called the velum. You can easily find the dividing line between the palate and the velum by sliding your tongue over your palate. In English there are six palatal sounds: [č], [ǰ], [š], [ž], [r], and [y].

6. *Velar.* As noted, the velum is the soft, fleshy area lying to the rear of the palate. Check its location in figure 10.1. In English, velar sounds are articulated by bringing the back of the tongue into contact with the velum; velar sounds are [k], [g], and [ŋ].

Point of articulation is only one parameter of consonant articulation, however; another is *manner of articulation.* Manner of articulation refers to the way in which the airstream is obstructed at any given point of articulation. In all languages there are several ways to obstruct the airstream; four of the major manners of articulation are:

1. *Stops* (an older term, but one you may still hear, is *plosive*, since these sounds are exploded). As the term suggests, stop refers to a complete blockage of the airstream. There are six stops in English: the bilabials, [p] and [b], in which the lips block the airstream; the alveolars, [t] and [d], where blockage is between the tongue tip and alveolar ridge; and the velars, [k] and [g], where the back of the tongue contacts the velum. (Make these sounds several times.)

2. *Fricatives* (related to the word *friction*). To produce fricatives, you narrow the vocal tract at one point and force air through the opening, setting up a turbulent airstream. In English, there are the labio-dental fricatives, [f] and [v]; the interdental fricatives, [θ] and [ð]; the alveolar fricatives [s] and [z]; and the palatal fricatives, [š] and [ž]. Other languages have different fricatives; if you have studied Spanish, you know that the *b* in *Cuba* is a bilabial fricative, made by bringing both lips close together and forcing air through the narrowing.

3. *Affricates* (not to be confused with fricatives). Affricates are combination sounds made by articulating a stop and a fricative in rapid succession, almost simultaneously. Affricates are found in the first sounds in *chin* and *gin*, and the final sounds in *itch* and *edge*. The affricate of *chin* is a combination of the stop [t] and the fricative [š], and the affricate of *gin* is a combination of the stop [d] and the fricative [ž]. You can think of affricates as single sounds since they function as single units in English; therefore, you represent them using single characters from the phonetic alphabet.

4. *Nasals.* The velum acts as a kind of drawbridge in articulation,

allowing or prohibiting airflow into the nasal cavity when necessary. If the velum is lowered, the pathway to the nasal cavity is open and air can resonate in both the oral and nasal cavities; if the velum is raised, it shuts off access to the nasal cavity. Sounds made with resonance in the nasal cavity are called *nasal sounds*; all other sounds are *oral sounds*. In English there are three nasals: [m], [n], and [ŋ].

The last item to consider in the production of sounds is the action of the vocal cords as a sound is articulated. This action is particularly important, since it is important in phonetic rules. Within the larynx, the cartilaginous structure known as the Adam's apple, lie two sheets of elastic tissue called the *vocal cords*, or *vocal folds* or *vocal bands*. For the purposes of describing speech sounds in this text, we will consider that the vocal cords assume one of two positions: relaxed and relatively far apart, or tensed and drawn close together, so that there is only a narrow opening (called the *glottis*) between them. The vocal cords are in the relaxed position when we make sounds such as [f] or [s], and in the tensed position when we articulate [v] or [z]. When we articulate [s] or [f], the vocal cords remain relatively still, but for [f] and [v] they vibrate rapidly; they open and close several thousand times each second. This vocal cord vibration is called *voice* and sounds produced with vocal cord vibration are called *voiced sounds*; all other sounds are *voiceless*.

You can easily check for the presence of voice by placing your fingers in your ears and articulating first one sound and then another. The buzzing you hear with some sounds but not others is voice. Try making a long *sssssss*, then a long *zzzzzzz*. Now make a long [θ] and a long [ð]. Which of these sounds is voiced, [s] or [z]? [θ] or [ð]? Is [m] voiced? How about [l]?

Each sound can be described as a combination of: (1) its point of articulation (bilabial, palatal, etc.), (2) its manner of articulation (fricative, nasal, etc.), and (3) whether or not it is voiced. For instance, [f] is a voiceless labio-dental fricative; [ǰ] is a voiced palatal affricate.

This information is summarized in figure 10.2, which shows each sound and indicates its point of articulation, its manner of articulation, and whether it is voiced or voiceless. The points of articulation appear as horizontal headings and the manners of articulation appear as vertical headings at the left. Not all consonants are included in figure 10.2, only those called *obstruents*, sounds that result from obstructing airflow:

	Bilabial	Labio-dental	Interdental	Alveolar	Palatal	Velar
Stop	p			t		k
	b			d		g
Fricative		f	θ	s	š	
		v	ð	z	ž	
Affricate					č	
					ǰ	
Nasal	m			n	ŋ	

FIGURE 10.2. **English Obstruents.**

stops, fricatives, affricates, and nasals. Notice that each cell in figure 10.2 is divided into two parts: a top part for the voiceless member of a pair and a bottom part for the voiced member. Since all nasals are voiced, the cells in this row are not divided.

Figure 10.2 shows clearly that sounds are not indivisible units but are made up of the smaller, fundamental components of point of articulation, manner of articulation, and voicing, which combine in unique ways to create different sounds. From this perspective, a phonetic symbol (or the sounds it represents) is merely a convenient way to represent a specific combination of a point of articulation, a manner of articulation, and voicing. Further discussion of this notion follows later, and there are many references to figure 10.2 in the following pages, since it provides information vital to understanding how English organizes its sounds into groups and changes those groups systematically from one context to another. For now, use figure 10.2 to grasp a general sense of how the sounds are arranged and how they relate to one another.

VARIATION IN SOUNDS

The opening paragraphs of this chapter mentioned that determining the number of sounds in a language is not as easy as it might seem; it is, in fact, often difficult and phoneticians argue frequently over what they consider to be a sound in a particular language. The reasons for the debate arise in part because it is difficult in many cases to determine if a sound is basic to the sound system of a language or if it should be considered a variant of another sound. There is a great deal of variability among sounds and, to illustrate the problems involved, consider the "sound" t. Notice that there are no brackets around t; we will see the reason for this shortly. Look at how we pronounce t in the set of words where t occurs initially—words like *top* and *tuck*—and contrast this pronunciation with that of t in the set of words in which t follows [s], such as *stop* and *stuck*. Put your fingers on your lips as you first say *top* and then *stop*, *tuck* and then *stuck*. Do this several times. You should notice that the t in one of these sets of words is accompanied by a puff of air (called aspiration), while the t of the other set is not. Which word has an aspirated t? *Top* or *stop*, *tuck* or *stuck*?

Now consider the t in the word *metal*. Is it more like the t of *top* or the t of *stop*? Is it different from both of these? Say the word to yourself several times and compare your pronunciation of *metal* with your pronunciation of *medal*. Are *metal* and *medal* pronounced identically or differently? In general conversation most Americans pronounce them exactly alike. Remember, if two words are pronounced the same they must be transcribed the same way. Would you say that the medial (middle) sound of both *metal* and *medal* is more like [t] or more like [d]?

As a final example, look at words like *pot* and *right*, where a final t occurs. In this case, English provides an option: you can pronounce *pot* with a puff of air accompanying the *t* as with *top*, or you can just block the airstream at the alveolar ridge and not release it at all. (You can see this nonrelease more clearly with a final *p*, as in *cup*, than with final *t*.)

These examples illustrate that *t* can appear in a number of different forms: sometimes it is accompanied by a puff of air and at other times it is not; sometimes it is pronounced more like [d] than [t], and sometimes it is not released at all. So, how many *t* sounds are there? One or four?

All sounds in all languages have variants such as those of *t*; usually these are called *positional variants*; that is, different forms of a sound occur at different positions in a word; in the case of the *t* variants, aspirated *t* occurs only at the beginning of a syllable, unaspirated *t* follows *s*, unreleased *t* can occur at the end of a word, etc. Notice that each of these phonetically different sounds is, in an important way, the "same" sound; each has an essential "*t*-ness" at its core; even the most different, the *t* of *metal*, appears as aspirated *t* in the related word *metallic*.

Phoneticians explain the relationships among these different sounds by saying that a language consists of a set of basic sounds, technically called *phonemes*, and a set of related variants, technically called *allophones*. The phoneme/allophone distinction is one of the most important concepts in linguistics; an analogy may help you understand it more fully. Among other devices, the English spelling system makes use of uppercase and lowercase letters, and italics—for example, Q, q, *Q*, and *q* (roman and italic). In an obvious way, these are all different, but in another sense they are all expressions of the same letter, since all have a basic "*q*-ness." We express both their differences and their similarities by the names we give them: capital *q*, lowercase *q*, capital italic *q*, lowercase italic *q*. For our purposes, it is important to remember that each can occur only in specific environments: we use capital italic *q* at the beginning of a sentence or a proper name that we want to emphasize, lowercase italic *q* for other emphasis, capital *q* at the beginning of a nonemphasized sentence or proper name, and lowercase *q* elsewhere. These usages lead us to conclude that there is a relatively abstract component that unites the four *q*s that we represent as Q, q, *Q*, or *q* (uppercase and lowercase roman and italic); the rules of English writing instruct us when to use each. Similarly, the phoneme /t/ includes the allophones aspirated *t*, unaspirated *t*, unreleased *t*, etc., and the rules of English pronunciation tell us when to pronounce each allophone.

Phoneticians call phonemes *contrastive units*, since they can distinguish one word from another: *top* is not *cop* is not *pop*, so /t/, /k/, and /p/ are separate phonemes. The particular variants of a phoneme, however, are not contrastive; substituting one for another does not result in a different word, but only a word that sounds unusual, as if it were spoken by an individual unfamiliar with the rules of the language. Try using the *t* of *top* (aspirated [t]) in the word *city*. It sounds odd, doesn't it? But you still recognize the word as *city*, not as *sissy* or *sicky*, so aspirated *t* and flap *t* (what phoneticians call the /t/ of *city*, *water*, *bitter*, and the like, since your tongue tip flaps once against your alveolar ridge) are variants of the phoneme /t/. Notice that the phoneme /t/ is placed between slant lines, while a particular allophone of [t] is enclosed in square brackets.

SOME ENGLISH ALLOPHONES

All languages have rules for the pronunciation of phonemes; they indicate which variant to use under which circumstances, when to use aspirated [t], when to use flap [t], etc. A study of several of the rules of English pronunciation follows, but first we need a clear definition of the term "rule." One of the problems in phonetics (and language study in general) is its terminology, and one of the more difficult terms is "rule." Linguists use the term "rule" differently from nonlinguists. Linguists regard rules as descriptions of the way language operates and not as evaluations of "good" or "bad" language use. The rules that linguists use concisely state the principles of a language. For instance, one rule in English is that the phoneme /t/, when it occurs between vowels, is usually pronounced as a voiced flap. This is a rule of American English only; the rules of British English are slightly different, and a speaker of British English might pronounce *city* with aspirated /t/. When you violate language rules, you don't necessarily make social errors, you just sound odd, or your words don't form sentences. Violating phonetic rules usually results in odd pronunciations, as if you learned English from a book but never heard it spoken. You can experience this by saying "Betty makes better butter" using all aspirated *t*'s. You were never taught the rules of English; you just picked them up as a child and you know them so well that you apply them repeatedly without a thought. Linguistics attempts to state rules formally in order to illustrate how a language works.

With phonemes, allophones, and rules in mind, let's look again at aspiration and write a descriptive rule that explains, first, which sounds are aspirated and, second, under what circumstances they are aspirated.

In English three phonemes have aspirated allophones: /p/, /t/, and /k/; they are aspirated whenever they occur at the beginning of a syllable—for example, *pin, tin, kin, upon, octane, occur.* We could simply state that /p/, /t/, and /k/ are aspirated at the beginning of a syllable; but we also want the rule to identify the set of which /p/, /t/, and /k/ are members and to specify why these particular phonemes, as opposed to others, should appear together and function as a group. To do this we need to consult figure 10.2 and examine the point of articulation, manner of articulation, and voicing for /p/, /t/, and /k/. We want to reduce these three sounds to a common factor. Notice that figure 10.2 indicates that /p/, /t/, and /k/ are stops and that they are voiceless; in fact, these three sounds are the only sounds that meet this description. We can use this information to conclude that English has a rule that all voiceless stops are aspirated at the beginning of a syllable.

Using figure 10.2, explain why it would be difficult to write a rule that refers to /p/, /m/, and /ĭ/ as a group.

≡

EXERCISE 3

1. Write a rule using the following information. In English, some vowels are held longer in some circumstances than in others. Say the words below out loud several times, paying particular attention to how long you sustain the vowel in each word as you speak. You should be able to put each of these words into one of two groups: a group with "shorter" vowels and a group with "longer" vowels. For instance, the [i] of *heed* is longer than the [i] of *heat*. (The actual length is not important; what is important is to recognize that some vowels are relatively longer than others.)

made	mate	edge	etch
dose	doze	pot	pod
prove	proof	pig	pick
seed	seat	ice	eyes

2. Make a list of those words with the longer vowels and another list of those words with the shorter vowels.

3. Now we need to determine the environment in which a vowel is lengthened. Look at the words with the longer vowels and consider the consonant at the end of each word. Using figure 10.2, determine the common component for all the consonants and write a rule that describes when a vowel is lengthened. Your rule should begin, "A vowel is lengthened when . . . ."

There are many more allophonic rules in English, but these examples give you an appreciation for the systematic variability of sounds and an understanding of how the rules of English transform a phoneme into a related group of sounds that we actually speak and hear.

VARIATION IN MORPHEMES

We can summarize this brief consideration of phonemes and their allophones as follows:

The sound system of language is made up of a relatively small number of abstract items (phonemes) that occur in a variety of forms (allophones), and the phonetic rules of a language describe where each allophone occurs. What is true for phonemes is also true for words, or, more precisely, for the parts of words called *morphemes*. Morpheme is another term with a precise meaning in linguistics. Your teacher can explain it further; for now we define a morpheme as the smallest part of a word that has a meaning. For instance, *lend* is a one-morpheme word; *lender* is a two-morpheme word consisting of *lend+er*; and *lenders* is a three-morpheme word, *lend+er+s*, where -*er* means "one who does" the verb and -*s* means plural. A particular morpheme may be expressed by one group of phonemes in one instance and by a different group of phonemes in another—yet we recognize it as the same morpheme in both instances. A morpheme often is spelled differently depending on the circumstances, but spelling is not a reliable guide to the identification of morphemes.

We are all familiar with morphemes and their different forms, called *alternates*. One common example is the morpheme we spell *the*, which appears as [ði] in the phrase *the apple*, *the end*, and *the outsider* but as [ðə] in *the city*, *the quarterback*, and *the visitor*. What determines the form?

The concept of alternates (and alternation) is important in linguistics, so we will consider a second example. There is a group of words in English that is built on the morpheme *pel*, which has the general meaning of "push" or "drive": *compel*, *repel*, *expel*, *propel*. This morpheme appears not only as *pel* but also as *pul* in words such as *compulsive*, *repulsion*, and *expulsion*. *Pel* and *pul* represent the same morpheme, and the rules of English tell us when to pronounce each (and, in this case, when to spell them differently). This situation is directly analogous to that of *Q* and *q*, in which the rules of English spelling indicate when to use the two representations of the same letter.

Now we can apply these concepts to another morpheme: the morpheme that means "5." (Notice the use of the numeral rather than the letters in order to allow the morpheme to remain rather abstract). In English we assume the spelling of the numeral 5 is *f i v e*. Actually, this is not entirely true. How about when we are using ordinals—*first, second, third, fourth, fifth* (*fifth*, not fiveth)? When we multiply 5 times 10 we get *fifty*, not fivety. Therefore, the morpheme 5 has two different forms: one spelled *five* and pronounced [fayv]; the other spelled *fif* and pronounced [fɪf]. We are concerned here only with the consonant change, so ignore the vowel difference between *five* and *fif*). Thus, the morpheme 5 has two variants that alternate with one another: [fayv] and [fɪf]. We will assume that *five* [fayv] is the basic form, and we want to know exactly what the change is and why it changes. To do this we notice that the only consonant difference between [fayv] and [fɪf] is that *fif* contains [f] where *five* contains [v]. The first thing we need to do is determine the phonetic difference between [f] and [v]. From figure 10.2, we see that the only difference between [f] and [v] is in voicing; [f] is voiceless and [v] is voiced. Notice that [f] occurs only when the morpheme 5 precedes the suffix [θ] or the suffix [ti]; in other words, when we add [θ] or [ti] to *five*, [fayv] changes to [fɪf] (we also change the spelling, which makes the phonetic change easier to see, but many phonetic changes do not include a change in spelling). Why do these words contain [f] rather than [v]? Why does the voiced sound [v] become the voiceless [f] in *fifty* and *fifth*? The reason for the change is *assimilation*, another important concept in linguistics. In phonetics, assimilation refers to the process in which a sound changes in such a way that it becomes more like another (usually neighboring) sound. In this case, the voiced [v] of *five* becomes voiceless in order to become more like the voiceless [θ] or [t] of the suffix; in the process [v] in effect becomes [f]. Whenever there is assimilation, there is one sound (or one group of sounds) that causes the assimilation and another sound that changes, or undergoes the assimilation. In this example, the [t] of *fifty* and the [θ] of *fifth* are the causes of the assimilation, and the final [v] of *five* is the sound that undergoes the assimilation.

Assimilation is a common and natural process that is found in all languages. The reasons for assimilation are simple. As speakers we try, whenever possible, to reduce the effort required for articulation, and we find that it is easier to pronounce some sequences of sounds than others. One way to make articulation easier is to produce one sound as much like a neighboring sound as possible. Consider the articulatory effort required to pronounce fivty (if the [v] were not assimilated). We would have to vibrate the vocal cords for the [v] and quickly stop the vibration for [t]. We can make the articulation easier by anticipating the voicelessness of [t] and extending voicelessness over both sounds. Since voice is the feature involved, this particular instance is an example of assimilation in voice.

The following is another example of assimilation in which the spelling helps to identify the sounds involved.

We have a number of ways of negating adjectives in English; one way is to use a prefix, but the form of the prefix can vary. We say *indecent*, yet we say *impartial*, because the rules of English do not allow us to say *imdecent or *inpartial. (Linguists use * to mark nongrammatical forms.) Two forms of this prefix are shown below:

Prefix Form	*Examples*
im-	imperfect, immature, implausible, improper
in-	indecent, intolerant, innumerable, indistinct

In order to understand why *imperfect* and *indecent* are spelled as they are (as opposed to *imdecent and *inperfect), look at the adjectives to which each form is attached and determine specifically what they have in common. Notice that all the adjectives to which *im-* are attached begin with either /m/ or /p/. Comparing /m/ and /p/ by using the articulatory characteristics of these sounds as shown in figure 10.2 indicates that /m/ and /p/ are both bilabial. To determine the characteristics of the adjectives to which *in-* attaches, it is necessary to ask why *im-*, and not *in-*, precedes the first group, while *in-*, and not *im-*, precedes the second group. Using figure 10.2, you will note that /m/, like /p/, is bilabial and /n/, like /t/ and /d/, is alveolar; in other words, the consonant of the prefix must have the same point of articulation as the first consonant of the adjective to which it is attached. This is an example of assimilation in point of articulation.

Many speakers, especially in more relaxed speech situations, use another form, /ɪŋ/ to negate adjectives like *complete, corruptible,* and *glorious.* Although spelled *in-*, this prefix is pronounced [ɪŋ] ([ɪŋkəmplit]).

Consider [ŋ] and the adjectives to which it is attached. How does this group fit into the pattern we saw with *im-* and *in-*? Explain.

Other forms of this prefix are as follows:

Prefix Form	Examples
ir-	irregular, irresponsible, irrelevant
il-	illegal, illegible, illogical

In what ways do *ir-* and *il-* fit the pattern and in what way are they slightly different? Are they actually more assimilated to their adjectives than *im-*, *in-*, or [ŋ]?

One way of looking at assimilation is to see it as a kind of phonetic agreement. You are already familiar with grammatical agreement—for example, English subjects and verbs must agree in number and Spanish articles and nouns must agree in gender. Just as there is grammatical agreement, there is phonetic agreement. Sounds must agree in voicing or point of articulation; several sounds must share the same point of articulation, or they must all be voiced (or voiceless). There are other phonetic agreements, but point of articulation and voicing agreement are probably the most common.

We are now ready to examine phonetic agreement and how we form the regular plural in English (there are a number of irregular plurals that do not follow particular patterns). In elementary school you probably learned that to form a plural noun you add "s" or "es." This is indeed how we write most plurals, but this rule obscures the way we actually form plurals when we speak. There is a single plural morpheme, and it takes several different forms.

EXERCISE 4

1. Listed below is a group of plural nouns, most of which you have seen before. Transcribe them, paying particular attention to how the plural is indicated for each word. What two variants are used to indicate the plural? (A discussion of an important third variant follows later.)

caves	tacks	cuffs	tags
smiths	buds	globes	loops
scouts			

2. Make a list of the singular nouns to which each of the two variants is attached and, using figure 10.2, determine the common components for the singulars in each group. Describe the agreement. Is the cause of the assimilation the singular or the plural morpheme? Is the assimilation in point of articulation or in voicing?

3. Transcribe each of the following words, again paying attention to the plural marker of each one:

     bees   lambs   cells   cars   tons   sighs

4. Noting the pattern of assimilation you gathered from the words in the first group, what can you say about the sounds /i/, /m/, /l/, /r/, /n/, and /ay/?

MORPHEMES IN CONTEXT

Earlier you transcribed words written in standard spelling using the symbols of our phonetic alphabet. As mentioned then, these were artificial exercises since it is unusual to encounter words in isolation. We don't say one (pause) word (pause) at (pause) a (pause) time (big pause). In normal speech words and sounds run together; one word affects another word, one sound affects another sound, and our everyday encounters with language sound closer to "jeet?" "na chet" and "haef tuh?" "godduh" than "did you eat?" "not yet" and "have to?" "got to." In real speech there are no spaces between words and no capital letters at the beginning of sentences or periods at the end. When we put one word next to another in context, a number of changes may occur in one word or the other, or both. In addition to the assimilation that changes sounds, sounds may be added to or deleted from words, or several sounds may be blended together. Usually these changes affect the sounds at the beginnings or ends of words. These changes are the result of the normal operation of phonetic rules. But be warned: our schooling and particularly our literacy can delude us into believing that a word is a word is a word (or that it should be). On the contrary, phonetically, a word in one context may be a different (phonetic) word in another context, and yet a different (phonetic) word in still another context. The point is that these differences are anything but arbitrary; they are the natural results of the regular rules of language. As mentioned earlier, there is often a considerable difference between the way we pronounce a word in isolation and the way we pronounce it in context. The word *a* in isolation is [e], but in context it is either [e] or [ə].

DISSIMILATION (SIMPLIFICATION)

We saw earlier that assimilation is a phonetic process that tends to make neighboring sounds more alike. Many phonetic rules are assimilating rules, which minimize the articulatory differences between sounds. However, it does not follow that sequences of sounds that are most alike are always easiest to pronounce. Sounds can be so much alike that they are nearly impossible to pronounce in sequence or even close to one another. Tongue twisters are wonderful examples. Try saying, at normal speed, "the sixth sick sheik's sixth sheep's sick," one of the worst (or best, depending upon your point of view) tongue twisters ever devised, as listed in the *Guinness Book of World Records*. When faced with a sequence of too-similar sounds, speakers regularly break up the sequence in one of two ways: by deleting one of the offending sounds or by inserting a sound (in English, usually schwa) into the sequence so that the troublesome sounds are separated. *Cupboard*, for instance is [kəbərd]; [kəpbɔrd] is non-English. Since there are two bilabial stops adjacent to one another, English speakers simplify the cluster by deleting [p].

English allows a maximum of three consonants at the beginning of a word (*stream, split*) and up to three consonants at the end (*desks*). (Many American dialects, however, allow only two consonants at the end of a word.) As a general rule, and depending on the specific sounds involved and other phonetic, grammatical, and social factors, English speakers tolerate at most two adjacent consonants in the middle of a word. When we form a compound or add a suffix that increases the number to three or more, we are phonetically overwhelmed and usually respond by dropping one of the three consonants. Thus, the word *sand* and the word *box* present no problems but *sandbox* is another matter; the usual pronunciation is [sænbaks], not [sændbaks]. This pronunciation is neither capricious nor idiosyncratic; a rule of English phonetics allows the deletion of this particular consonant only; to delete any of the others would not reflect English phonetics: *[sædbaks] or [*sændaks].

Once again, remember that pronunciations such as [sænbaks] are not "incorrect" and pronunciations such as [sændbaks] are not "correct." It is true that some speakers pronounce more formally than others, but it is misguided to believe that [sændbaks] is a "better" pronunciation than [sænbaks]. It is a social rather than a linguistic judgment to label one person a "better" pronouncer than another, and it ignores the facts of language. The rules of English provide the possibilities; they specify what can and cannot be done within the context of spoken English. Those who participate most fully in the richness of English know the rules and use the rules for their maximum effect.

EXERCISE 5

The examples below are either compounds or include suffixes that create three or more consonants medially. But in normal, rapid conversation, one of the consonants is usually deleted. Mark the deleted consonant in each word and state the English rule for deleting the consonant.

first grade	kindness	government	Christmas
second place	handbag	guest towel	waistcoat

Earlier, you did an exercise on English plurals; there was a discussion of two alternates and a third was mentioned. Words such as *judges, matches, classes,* and *sneezes* illustrate this third alternate. Refresh your memory of the general rule. Which of the two alternates is found in these words? Why does it not attach directly to the singular?

The English past tense marker has three regular variants or *allomorphs*: /t/, /d/, and /əd/ (or [ɪd]). They are illustrated by the words below:

/t/	/d/	/əd/
AS IN:	*AS IN:*	*AS IN:*
coughed	saved	sifted
touched	judged	waded
passed	buzzed	heated
flapped	rubbed	bounded
marked	sagged	divided
mashed	sealed	coated
asked	dimmed	handed
dressed	pleased	directed
faked	played	sorted
moped	labored	provided

In which environment do you find each of the three alternates? Why are they grouped this way? Are assimilation, simplification, or both involved?

This chapter provides you with only the barest outline of phonetics and a brief sample of the kinds of issues with which phoneticians concern themselves. As with all language study, phonetics attempts to understand the dimensions of human language, the kinds of rules that characterize languages, and what people know about their own language—the rules they carry around in their heads. Because these rules are complex, there is much to learn, and phoneticians will be busy for decades to come.

FOR DISCUSSION AND REVIEW

1. Identify and explain the importance of the three characteristics shared by all phonetic alphabets.

2. Define the terms *point of articulation, manner of articulation,* and *voicing (sound).* Give two original examples of ways in which an understanding of these concepts could be helpful to you.

3. Examine the charts of English consonant and vowel phonemes. Explain why it is significant that not every slot (or cell) is filled.

4. Explain the relationship between phonemes and allophones and their differing roles within a language.

5. Both *assimilation* and *dissimilation* are important phonetic processes. Define each term, and give two original examples of each.

6. How could you put phonetics to work in learning a second language?

7. What would be some advantages and disadvantages of changing English spelling to bring it more into line with pronunciation?

8. Do you think spell checkers will increase or decrease the likelihood of spelling reform? What are your reasons?

9. The following sentences were written by elementary school students:

   a. "I haf to go now."

   b. "Why won chew be my friend?"

   c. "I went to see my grampa."

   From what you know about phonetics, how can you explain their spelling errors?

11

The Minimal Units of Meaning: Morphemes

The Ohio State University Language Files

Phonemes by themselves have no meaning. However, as we have seen, one of the distinguishing features of human language is its duality of patterning, its multilayered quality. Thus, phonemes, in themselves meaningless, are combined to form units that do have meaning—morphemes. Not all languages use the same kinds of morphemes, but all languages do use various kinds of morphemes as building blocks to construct words, units larger than morphemes and harder to define. The first part of the following selection describes the kinds of morphemes that occur in English and identifies their various functions. The second part begins by examining the complex ways in which, in English, affixes combine with other units. It then explains the hierarchical internal structure of English words that results from these combinations.

A continuous stream of speech can be broken up by the listener (or linguist) into smaller, meaningful parts. A conversation, for example, can be divided into the sentences of the conversation, which can be divided up further into the words that make up each of the sentences. It is obvious to most people that a sentence has a meaning, and that each of the words in it has a meaning as well. Can we go further and divide words into smaller units which still have meanings? Many people think not; their immediate intuition is that words are the basic meaningful elements of a language. This is, however, not the case. Many words can be broken down into still smaller units. Think, for example, of words such as *unlucky, unhappy,* and *unsatisfied.* The *un-* in each of these words has the same meaning, loosely, that of "not," but *un* is not a word by itself. Thus, we have identified units—smaller than the word—that have meanings. These are called *morphemes.* Now consider the words *look, looks,* and *looked.* What about the *-s* in *looks* and the *-ed* in *looked*? These segments can be separated from the meaningful unit *look,* and although they do not really have an identifiable meaning themselves, each does have a particular function. The *-s* is required for agreement with certain subjects (*she looks,* but not **she look*), and the *-ed* signifies that the action of the verb *look* has already taken place. Segments such as these

134

are also considered morphemes. Thus, a morpheme is the smallest linguistic unit that has a meaning or grammatical function.

Some words, of course, are not composed of other morphemes. *Car*, *spider*, and *race*, for example, are words, but they are also morphemes since they cannot be broken down into smaller meaningful parts. Morphemes that are also words are called *free morphemes* since they can stand alone. *Bound morphemes*, on the other hand, never exist as words themselves, but are always attached to some other morpheme. Some examples of bound morphemes in English are *un-*, *-ed*, and *-s*.

When we identify the number and types of morphemes a given word consists of, we are looking at what is referred to as the *structure of* the word. Morphology is the study of how words are structured and how they are put together from smaller parts. Morphologists not only identify the different classes of morphemes but also study the patterns that occur in the combination of morphemes in a given language. For example, consider the words *rewrite, retake,* and *relive*. Notice that *re-* is a bound morpheme that attaches only to verbs, and, furthermore, attaches to the beginning of the verb, not the end. Every speaker of English knows you can't say *write-re* or *take-re* (where *re-* is connected to the end of the free morpheme), nor can you say *rechoice* or *repretty* (where *re-* is connected to a morpheme that is not a verb). In other words, part of a speaker's linguistic competence is knowing, in addition to the meaning of the morphemes of a language, the ways in which the morphemes are allowed to combine with other morphemes.

Morphemes can be classified as either bound or free, as we have seen. There are three additional ways of characterizing morphemes. The first is to label bound morphemes according to whether they attach to the beginning or end of a word. You are most likely familiar with these terms. A *prefix* attaches to the beginning and a *suffix* attaches to the end of a word. The general term for prefixes and suffixes is *affix*, so bound morphemes are also referred to as affixes. The second way of characterizing morphemes is to classify bound morphemes according to their function in the complex words of which they are a part. When some morphemes attach to words, they create, or *derive*, new words, either by changing the meaning of the word or by changing its part of speech. For example, *un-* in *unhappy* creates a new word with the opposite meaning of *happy*. Notice that both *unhappy* and *happy* are adjectives. The suffix *-ness* in *quickness*, however, changes the part of speech of *quick*, an adjective, into a noun, *quickness*. Morphemes that change the meaning or part of speech of a word they attach to are called *derivational* morphemes. Other morphemes do not alter words in this way, but only refine and give extra grammatical information about the word's already existing meaning. For example, *cat* and *cats* are both nouns that basically have the same meaning (i.e., they refer to the same sort of thing), but *cats*, with the plural morpheme *-s*, contains only the additional information that there are more than one of these things referred to. The morphemes that serve a purely grammatical function, never creating a new word but only a different *form* of the same word, are called *inflectional* morphemes.

TABLE 11.1   The Inflectional Suffixes of English

STEM	*SUFFIX*	*FUNCTION*	*EXAMPLE*
wait	-s	3rd per. sg. present	She waits there at noon.
wait	-ed	past tense	She waited there yesterday.
wait	-ing	progressive	She is waiting there now.
eat	-en	past participle	Jack has eaten the Oreos.
chair	-s	plural	The chairs are in the room.
chair	-'s	possessive	The chair's leg is broken.
fast	-er	comparative	Jill runs faster than Joe.
fast	-est	superlative	Tim runs fastest of all.

In every word we find that there is at least one free morpheme. In a morphologically complex word, i.e., one composed of a free morpheme and any number of bound affixes, the free morpheme is referred to as the *stem*, *root*, or *base*. However, if there is more than one affix in a word, we cannot say that all of the affixes attach to the stem. Consider the word *happenings*, for example. When -*ing* is added to *happen*, we note that a new word is derived; it is morphologically complex, but it is a word. The plural morpheme -*s* is added onto the word *happening*, not the suffix -*ing*.

In English the derivational morphemes are either prefixes or suffixes, but, by chance, the inflectional morphemes are all suffixes. Of course, this is not the same in other languages. There are only eight inflectional morphemes in English. They are listed above along with an example of the type of stem each can attach to.

The difference between inflectional and derivational morphemes is sometimes difficult to see at first. Some characteristics of each are listed below to help make the distinction clearer.

Derivational Morphemes

1. Derivational morphemes change the part of speech or the meaning of a word, e.g., -*ment* added to a verb forms a noun (*judg-ment*), and *re-activate* means "activate again."
2. Syntax does not require the presence of derivational morphemes. They typically indicate semantic relations *within* a word, but no syntactic relations outside the word (compare this with item 2 following), e.g., *un-kind* relates -*un* "not" to *kind*, but has no particular syntactic connections outside the word—note that the same word can be used in *he is unkind* and *they are unkind*.
3. Derivational morphemes are usually not very productive; they generally are selective about what they'll combine with. For example, the suffix -*hood* occurs with just a few nouns such as *brother*, *neighbor*, and *knight*, but not with most others, such as *friend*, *daughter*, or *candle*.

4. They typically occur before inflectional suffixes, e.g., *government-s.* *-ment,* a derivational suffix, precedes *-s,* an inflectional suffix.
5. They may be prefixes or suffixes (in English), e.g., *pre-arrange,* *arrange-ment.*

Inflectional Morphemes

1. They do not change meaning or part of speech, e.g., *big, bigg-er, bigg-est* are all adjectives.
2. They are required by syntax. They typically indicate syntactic or semantic relations *between* different words in a sentence, e.g., *Nim love-s bananas. -s* marks the third-person singular present form of the verb, relating it to the third singular subject *Nim.*
3. They are very productive. They typically occur with all members of some large class of morphemes, e.g., the plural morpheme /-s/ occurs with almost all nouns.
4. They occur at the margin of a word, after any derivational morphemes, e.g., *ration-al-iz-ation-s. -s* is inflectional, and appears at the very end of the word.
5. They are suffixes only (in English).

There is one final distinction between types of morphemes that is useful. Some morphemes have semantic content. That is, they either have some kind of independent, identifiable meaning or indicate a change in meaning when added to a word. Others serve only to provide information about grammatical function by relating certain words in a sentence to each other (see item 2 about inflectional morphemes, above). The former are called *content* morphemes, and the latter are called *function* morphemes. This might appear at first to be the same as the inflectional and derivational distinction. They do overlap, but not completely. All derivational morphemes are content morphemes, and all inflectional morphemes are function morphemes, as you might have surmised. However, some words can be merely function morphemes. Examples in English of such free morphemes that are also function morphemes are prepositions, articles, pronouns, and conjunctions.

In this file, we have been using conventional spelling to represent morphemes. But it is important to realize that morphemes are pairings of *sounds* with meanings, not spellings with meanings, and representing morphemes phonetically reveals some interesting facts. We find that just as different free morphemes can have the same phonetic representations, as in *ear* (for hearing) and *ear* (of corn), the same is true of bound morphemes. For example, the plural, possessive, and third-person singular suffixes can all sound identical in English (e.g., *cats* [kæts], *Frank's* [fræŋks], and *walks* [waks]). These three suffixes are completely different morphemes, they just happen to be homophonous, or sound alike, in English. Similarly, there are two morphemes in English which sound like [ɪn]. One means "not," as in *inoperable* or *intolerable,* and the other means "in," as in *intake* or *inside.*

One of the more interesting things revealed by transcribing morphemes phonetically is the interaction of phonological and morphological processes. For example, some morphemes have more than one phonetic representation depending on which sounds precede or follow them, but since each of the pronunciations serves the same function or has the same meaning, it is considered to be the same morpheme. In other words, the same morpheme can be pronounced differently depending upon the sounds which follow or precede it. Of course, these different pronunciations will be patterned. For example, the phonetic representation of the plural morpheme is either [s] as in *cats*, [z] as in *dogs*, or [əz] as in *churches*. Each of these three pronunciations is said to be an *allomorph* of the *same* morpheme because [s], [z], and [əz] all have the same function (making some word plural) and because they are similar phonetically. Note that this same phonological process that causes the plural morpheme /s/ to be pronounced as [s] after voiceless sounds, [z] after voiced sounds, and [əz] after sibilants also applies to the possessive morpheme /s/ and the third-person singular morpheme /s/. Consider the morpheme /ɪn/ that means "not" in the words *inoperable, incongruent,* and *impossible.* What are the allomorphs of this morpheme?

We now call your attention to a few pitfalls of identifying morphemes. First, don't confuse morphemes with syllables. A few examples will show that the number of morphemes and syllables in a word are independent of each other. Consider the word *coats.* It is a one-syllable word composed of two morphemes. *Coat* happens to be one morpheme and consist of a single syllable, but *-s* is not even a syllable, although it is a morpheme. Note that *syllable* is a three-syllable word composed only of one morpheme.

Second, note that a given morpheme has a particular sound or sound sequence associated with it, but not every instance of that sound sequence in the language represents that morpheme. For example, take the plural morpheme /s/. When you hear the word [karts] in isolation, you can't determine if the [s] is an instance of this plural morpheme (*the carts are back in the store*), or an instance of the possessive morpheme (*the cart's wheels turn funny*) or of the third-person singular morpheme (*he carts those books around every day*). That sound sequence may not even be a morpheme at all. The [s] in [sun], for example, is not a morpheme. Likewise, the [ɪn] of *inexcusable* is the morpheme that means "not," but the [ɪn] of *print* is not a morpheme.

Third, remember to analyze the phonetic representations of morphemes and not their spellings. A morpheme can have one or more allomorphs, and these allomorphs might be represented by the same or different spellings. The *-er* in *writer* is the same morpheme as the *-or* in *editor*, and the *-ar* in *liar*, since all three mean "one who," but they do not represent separate allomorphs since their pronunciations are identical, namely [ɾ]. On the other hand, the *-s* in *Mark's, John's,* and *Charles's* is the same morpheme, but represents three different allomorphs, since each is pronounced differently.

Finally, we include below a summary list of criteria that might help you to identify the different types of morphemes.

Given a morpheme,

1. Can it stand alone as a word?
   YES → it's a *free* morpheme (e.g., *bubble, orange*)
   NO → it's a *bound* morpheme (e.g., *-er* in *beater*, *-s* in *oranges*)

2. Does it have the principal meaning of the word it's in?

   YES → it's the *stem* (e.g., *happy* in *unhappiness*)
   NO → it's an *affix* (e.g., *-or* in *contributor*, *pre-* in *preview*)

3. Does it create a new word by changing the meaning and/or part of speech?

   YES → it's a *derivational* affix (e.g., *re-* in *rewind*, *-ist* in *artist*)
   NO → it's an *inflectional* affix (e.g., *-est* in *smartest*)

4. Does it have a meaning, or cause a change in meaning when added to a word?

   YES → it's a *content* morpheme (e.g., *-un* in *untrue*)
   NO → it's a *function* morpheme (e.g., *the, to, or, -s* in *books*)

THE HIERARCHICAL STRUCTURE OF WORDS

When we examine words composed of only two morphemes, we implicitly know two facts about the ways in which affixes join with their stems. First, the stems with which a given affix may combine normally belong to the same part of speech. For example, the suffix *-able* attaches freely to verbs, but not to adjectives or nouns; thus, we can add this suffix to the verbs *adjust, break, compare,* and *debate,* but not to the adjectives *asleep, lovely, happy,* and *strong,* nor to the nouns *anger, morning, student,* or *success.* Second, the words formed by the addition of a given affix to some word or morpheme also normally belong to the same part of speech. For example, the expressions resulting from the addition of *-able* to a verb are always adjectives; thus *adjustable, breakable, comparable,* and *debatable* are all adjectives.

These two facts have an important consequence for determining the way in which words with more than one affix must be formed. What it means is that words are formed in steps, with one affix attaching to a complete word, which can be a free morpheme or a morphologically complex word. Words with more than one affix are not formed in one single step with the affixes and stem just strung together. For example, consider the word *unusable,* which is composed of a prefix *un-,* a stem *use,* and a suffix *-able.* One possible way this morphologically complex word might be formed is all at once, as in: *un + use + able,* where the prefix and the suffix attach at the same time to the verb stem *use*. However, this cannot be the case, knowing what we know about how affixes attach only to certain parts of speech and create words of certain parts of speech. The prefix *un-*, meaning "not," attaches only to adjectives and creates new words that are also adjectives. (Compare with *unkind, unwise,* and *unhappy*.) The suffix *-able*, on the other hand, attaches to verbs and forms words that are adjectives. (Compare with *stoppable, doable,* and *washable*.) Therefore, *un-* cannot attach to *use*, since *use* is a verb and not an adjective. However, if *-able* attaches *first* to the stem *use*, then it creates an adjective, *usable*, and the prefix *-un* is allowed to combine with it. Thus the formation of the word *unusable* is a two-step process whereby *use* and *-able* attach first, then *un-* attaches to the word *usable*.

Recall that what we are analyzing is the internal *structure* of words. Words, since they are formed by steps, have a special type of structure characterized as *hierarchical*. This hierarchical structure can be schematically represented by means of a "tree" that indicates the steps involved in the formation of the word, i.e., which morphemes joined together first and so on. The tree for *unusable* is:

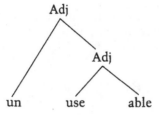

Now consider the word *reusable*. Both the prefix *re-* and the suffix *-able* attach to verbs, but we have already shown that one must attach first. Which is it? Notice that *reusable* cannot be regarded as the result of adding the prefix *re-* to the word *usable* since *re-* attaches only to verbs (compare with *redo, relive,* and *refuel*) and *usable* is an adjective. However, *-able* can attach to the verb *reuse* since *-able* attaches to verbs. Thus, our understanding of how the affixes *re-* and *-able* combine with other morphemes allows us to conclude that the verb *reuse*, but not the adjective *usable*, is a step in the formation of the adjective *reusable*.

Interestingly, some words are ambiguous in that they have more than one meaning. When we examine their internal structure, we find an explanation for this: their structure may be analyzed in more than one way. Consider, for example, the word *unlockable*. This could mean either "not able to be locked" or "able to be unlocked." If we made a list to determine the parts of speech the affix *un-* attaches to, we would discover that there are not one but two prefixes that sound like *un-*. The first combines with adjectives to form new adjectives, and means "not." (Compare with *unaware, unintelligent,* or *unwise*.) The second prefix *un-* combines with verbs to form new verbs, and means "do the reverse of." (Compare with *untie, undo,* or *undress*.)

Even though these prefixes sound alike, they are entirely different morphemes. Because of these two different sorts of *un-* in English, *unlockable* may be analyzed in two different ways. First, the suffix *-able* may join with the verb *lock* to form the adjective *lockable*. *Un-* may then join with this adjective to form the new adjective *unlockable*, with the meaning "not able to be locked." This way of forming *unlockable* is schematized in the following tree:

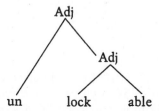

The second way of forming *unlockable* is as follows. The prefix *un-* joins with the verb *lock* to form the verb *unlock*. The suffix *-able* then joins with this verb to form the adjective *unlockable* with the meaning of "able to be unlocked." This manner of forming *unlockable* is represented by the following tree:

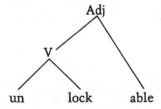

Some Suggestions

There are a few prefixes that do not attach exclusively to one part of speech. For example, consider the prefix *pre-*. *Pre-* attaches to verbs and does not change the part of speech, as the following examples show:

preexist

predecide

predetermine

predefine

premeditate

However, there are examples of words with the prefix *pre-* that do not follow the same pattern as those cited above:

preseason

predawn

prewar

pregame

In these words *pre-* attaches to a noun and forms an adjective (*the preseason game, the prewar propaganda, the pregame warmup.* However, the meaning of the prefix is the same as in *preexist, predecide,* etc. (although its function is different). In addition, there are sets such as:

prefrontal

predental

preinvasive

prehistoric

In these words, *pre-* is attaching to an adjective, forming adjectives, and has the same meaning as in *preexist, predecide,* etc. So this is a bit problematic. We don't want to throw out the idea that a given affix attaches only to one part of speech, since the overwhelming majority of affixes adhere to this pattern. Apparently, some morphemes become so productive that their combinatorial possibilities can be extended. Such must be the case with *pre-*. Note, however, that its combinations are nevertheless rule-governed. When *pre-* attaches to verbs, it forms only verbs. When it attaches to nouns, it forms only adjectives, and when it attaches to adjectives, it forms only adjectives. So, it is advisable to consider many examples when attempting to determine the rules by which a given affix combines.

EXERCISES

1. Draw tree diagrams for each of the following words:

   a. reconstruction
   b. unaffordable
   c. un-American
   d. manliness
   e. impersonal
   f. irreplaceability
   g. oversimplification
   h. unhappiness
   i. impotency

   j. international
   k. misunderstandable
   l. dehumidifier
   m. unrespectable
   n. nonrefundable
   o. mismanagement
   p. underspecification
   q. restatement
   r. inflammability

   s. unmistakable
   t. insincerity
   u. dysfunctional
   v. inconclusive
   w. premeditatedly
   x. overgeneralization
   y. reformer
   z. infertility
   aa. dishonesty

2. We said that polar opposite ("not") *un-* attaches only to adjectives, but two exceptions to this rule are *Uncola* and *Uncar.* Why are these

exceptions? Why would advertisers have made them up in the first place when the words fail to follow the rule?

≡

FOR DISCUSSION AND REVIEW

1. Explain the difference between derivational morphemes and inflectional morphemes. Illustrate each difference with an example not in the text.

2. What is the difference between content morphemes and function morphemes?

3. Describe the relationship between morphemes and syllables.

4. Explain what an *allomorph* is. Give an example of an English morpheme, in addition to the regular noun plural, that has more than one phonetic representation.

5. Allomorphs, unlike allophones, need not be phonetically similar. The productive plural morpheme in English has the forms /-s/, /-z/, /əz/; which one is used depends on the sound with which the noun to be made plural ends. These allomorphs are phonologically conditioned. Some nouns in English, however, do not form regular plurals. List as many "irregular" plurals as you can. Then try to divide them into groups (note: there are five types of morphologically conditioned plurals in English; four of them derive from Old English).

6. Explain the statement that "the internal structure of words is *hierarchical.*"

7. Explain the ambiguity of the words *bimonthly* and *biweekly*. Is it similar to or different from the ambiguity of *unlockable*? Explain.

12

The Identification of Morphemes

H. A. Gleason Jr.

As native speakers of English, we usually do not find it difficult to iden-
tify the morphemes in English words. We are, of course, relying in part
on our unconscious knowledge of the rules of English and in part on our
familiarity with much of the English vocabulary. Therefore, in order to
begin to understand the complexity of morphemic analysis, we need to
examine data from a language that we do not know well. In the follow-
ing excerpt from his book An Introduction to Descriptive Linguistics, *Professor H. A. Gleason uses some Hebrew verb forms to demonstrate*
the basic analytical technique for the identification of morphemes:
comparing groups of utterances which are (1) partially identical in both
expression and content and (2) partially different in both expression and
content. Note that both conditions must be met: we are looking for the
smallest change in content (i.e., structure) that results in a change in
meaning (i.e., expression). At the end of his analysis of Hebrew verb
forms, Professor Gleason introduces discontinuous morphemes, which
do not occur in all languages; the type of morpheme known as an
"infix"; "replacives," which do not occur in English; and the zero affix
(Ø), which also occurs in English.

The process of analysis [to identify morphemes] is best shown by detailed
discussion of an actual example. For this purpose we will use a series of
Hebrew verb forms. The data will be introduced a few words at a time.
This is an artificial feature of the presentation. The preceding step is merely implied: namely that we have selected from the corpus those pairs or
sets of items that can be profitably compared. The order of presentation is
not necessarily that which is most efficient for the analysis of the data, but
that which most effectively illustrates the methods used.

1. /zəkartíihuu/   "I remembered him"

2. /zəkartíihaa/   "I remembered her"

3. /zəkartíikaa/   "I remembered thee"

Comparison of items 1 and 2 reveals one contrast in expression,
/-uu/:/-aa/, and one in meaning, as shown by translation, and hence presumably in content "him": "her." This may (tentatively!) be considered
as a pair of morphemes. However, comparison of 1, 2, and 3 suggests that
the first identification was wrong. The contrast now seems to be /-huu/

"him":/-haa/ "her":/-kaa/ "thee." We can be reasonably sure that the morpheme meaning "him" includes the sounds /-uu/ or /-huu/, but until we can identify the remaining parts of the word we cannot be sure how much else is included.

4. /zəkarnúuhuu/ "we remembered him"

5. /zəkarnúuhaa/ "we remembered her"

6. /zəkarnúukaa/ "we remembered thee"

Comparison of 4, 5, and 6 with 1, 2, and 3 reveals a contrast in expression and meaning between /-tíi-/ "I" and /-núu-/ "we." However, as before, we cannot be sure how much is to be included until the remainders of the words are identified. It is conceivable that the morphemes might be /-rtíi-/ "I" and /-rnúu-/ "we." . . . .

7. /qətaltíihuu/ "I killed him"

8. /qətalnúuhuu/ "we killed him"

Comparison of 7 and 8 with the foregoing gives us a basis for identifying /zəkar-/ "remembered" and /qətal-/ "killed." By so doing we have tentatively assigned every portion of each word to a tentative morpheme. We have, however, no reason to be certain that each portion so isolated is only a single morpheme. We have only reasonable assurance that by dividing any of these words in a manner similar to /zəkar-tíi-huu/ we have divided between morphemes, so that each piece consists of one or more essentially complete morphemes; that is, each piece is probably either a morpheme or a morpheme sequence.

The problem is somewhat simpler if one sample is identical with another except for an additional item of meaning and of expression:

/koohéen/ "a priest"

/ləkoohéen/ "to a priest"

There can be little doubt as to the most likely place to divide, and we can be rather confident in identifying two tentative morphemes /lə-/ "to" and /koohéen/ "priest." Nevertheless, there are significant possibilities of error so that this sort of division must also be considered tentative. Consider the following English example:

/hím/ "a song used in church"

/hímnəl/ "a book containing /hímz/"

The obvious division is into two morphemes /hím/ and /-nəl/. Reference to the spelling (which is, of course, never conclusive evidence for anything in spoken language!), *hymn:hymnal* suggests that this is not very certain. Actually the two morphemes are /him ~ himn-/ and /-əl/, as may be shown by comparing additional data: *confession:confessional, hymnology:geology, hymnody:psalmody.*

9. /zəkaarúuhuu/ "they remembered him"

10. /zəkaaráthuu/ "she remembered him"

If we compare 9 and 10 with the foregoing we find /-huu/ "him," /-úu-/ "they," and /-át-/ "she." But where 1–6 have /zəkar-/, 9 and 10 have /zəkaar-/. There is an obvious similarity of form between /zəkar-/ and /zəkaar-/ and the meaning seems to be identical. We may guess that they are two different allomorphs of one morpheme, and proceed to check whether this hypothesis is adequate. . . . We must leave the question . . . but must anticipate the result. /zəkar-/ and /zəkaar-/ will be shown to be variants of one tentative morpheme.

But though we will proceed on the basis that the hypothesis can be sustained, we must recognize that there are certain other possibilities. (1) /zəkar-/ and /zəkaar-/ may be different morphemes. This seems unlikely because of the similarity of meaning, but we must always remember that English translation may be misleading. (2) A somewhat less remote possibility is that /zəkar-/ and /zəkaar-/ are each sequences of morphemes and contain two contrasting morphemes. We can do nothing with this possibility from the data at hand, because there is no evidence of a contrast in meaning, but this may well be the kind of difference that does not show up clearly in translation. (3) We may have divided wrongly. Perhaps "I" is not /-tíi-/ but /-a-tíi-/ and "they" is similarly /-aa-úu-/. This would mean that the morpheme for "remembered" would have to be /zək-r-/. Our only present reason for rejecting this possibility is the comparative rarity of discontinuous morphemes. We would ordinarily assume that morphemes are continuous sequences of phonemes unless there is cogent reason to believe the contrary.

11. /zəkartúunii/ "you remembered me"

We have as yet no item which forms a wholly satisfactory comparison with 11. We may, however, tentatively divide it into /zəkar-/ + /-túu-/ "you" + /-nii/ "me." We do this because we have come to expect words similar to this to be divisible into three pieces, stem + actor + person acted upon, in that order. A division on such a basis is legitimate if done with caution, though obviously such an identification is not as certain as it would be if based on contrasts for each morpheme separately.

12. /sə́martúuhaa/ "you guarded him"

13. /ləqaaxúunii/ "they took me"

Even without providing minimal pairs, 12 and 13 pretty well corroborate the conclusion which was drawn from 11 [above]. They thus confirm the two morphemes /-túu/ "you" and /-nii/ "me." Words 11, 12, and 13 would be rather unsatisfactory words from which to start an analysis. However, as the analysis proceeds, the requirements for satisfactory samples relax in some respects. This is because we are now able to make our comparisons within the framework of an emerging pattern. This pattern involves certain classes of elements, stems, actor affixes, and affixes stating the person acted upon. It involves certain regular types of arrangement of these elements. In short, the pattern we are uncovering is a portion of the structure of the language at a level a bit deeper than mere details of individual words.

14. /zəkaaróo/   "he remembered him"

This word cannot be analyzed by comparison with the foregoing only. We can easily identify the stem as /zəkaar-/, identical in form with that of 9 and 10. But the remainder /-óo/ neither seems to consist of the expected two parts (actor and person acted upon), nor to contain the morpheme /-huu/ "him" which meaning would lead us to expect. Since the pattern does not assist us here in the way it did with 11, we must seek some more direct type of evidence.

15. /zaakártii/   "I remembered"

16. /zaakárnuu/   "we remembered"

17. /zaakár/   "he remembered"

These three forms differ from all those examined before in that they do not express a person acted upon. If we compare these words with each other, and if we compare 15 and 16 with 1 and 4, we can easily identify the affixes expressing the actor. These are /-tii/ "I" and /-nuu/ "we," identical with those we found before except for a difference in the stress. In 17, however, there is no affix expressing actor. We will tentatively list Ø (zero) "he" with the other actor affixes. This is intended merely as a convenient notation for our conclusion that the actor "he" is expressed by the absence of any affix indicating some other actor. These three forms also show another variant of the stem: /zaakár/; we shall proceed on the hypothesis that like /zəkar-/ and /zəkaar-/, it is merely another conditioned variant. This proposal should be carefully checked by methods to be discussed later.

The analysis attained in the last paragraph suggests that item 14 can be considered as divisible as follows: /zəkaar-Ø-óo/. The zero is, of course, a fiction, but it does serve to indicate that the form does show a rather closer parallelism with the others than we could see at first. That is, it contains a stem and a suffix expressing the person acted upon, and these are in the same order that we have found before. Whereas the pattern we had found did not seem to fit this word, closer examination shows that it does fit in with only slight modification. The pattern is therefore valid.

One problem posed by item 14 is taken care of in this way, but the other remains. We have identified two forms meaning "him," /-huu/ and /-óo/. These are not so obviously similar in form as /zəkar-/ and /zəkaar-/, so the hypothesis that they are allomorphs of one morpheme is not so attractive. Nevertheless, the similarity in meaning, and certain peculiarities in distribution which would be evident in a larger body of data, should induce us to check such a hypothesis. It will be sustained; /-huu ~ -óo/ is one morpheme.

In the course of the discussion we have found four stems: /zəkar-/
"remembered," /qəṭal-/ "killed," /šəmar-/ "guarded," and /ləqaax-/
"took." Comparison of these forms reveals that they all have the same
vowels and differ only in consonants. /ləqaax-/ is not an exception, since
it compares directly with /zəkaar-/. More data would yield a much longer
list of such forms. This similarity in vowels could be a coincidence, but
that possibility is slight. Another hypothesis is that these forms consist
of two morphemes each. This is very attractive, but there is no means of
checking it without a contrast. The following will provide such:

18. /šoméer/   "watchman"

19. /zookéer/   "one who remembers"

20. /qooṭéel/   "killer"

By comparing these with some of the earlier samples we may identify the following morphemes: /z-k-r/ "remember," /q-ṭ-l/ "kill," /š-m-r/
"guard," /l-q-x/ "take," /-oo-ée-/ "one who," and /-ə-a- ~ -ə-aa- ~ -aa-á-/
"-ed." The first four of these are roots; the last two are some sort of affixes.

Note that we were wrong in considering /zəkar-/, /zəkaar-/, and
/zaakár/ as allomorphs of a single morpheme. No damage was done,
however, since these three forms, each composed of two morphemes, are
distributed in exactly the same way as are allomorphs. What we assumed
to condition the selection of one of these three (/zəkar-/, etc.) can just as
well be considered as conditioning the selection of one of the allomorphs
of the affix contained in these stems. Treating larger items as morphemes is, of course, wrong, but not seriously so at preliminary stages,
provided the larger units consist of associated morphemes. Ultimate
simplification is, however, attained by full analysis in any case like that
just discussed.

That the [preceding] analysis . . . should yield morphemes such as
/z-k-r/ and /-oo-ée-/ seems at first sight somewhat disconcerting. We
expect morphemes to be sequences of phonemes. These, however, are
discontinuous and interdigitated. Of course there is no reason why such
morphemes cannot occur, as in fact our sample has indicated they do.
They are much less common than compact sequences of phonemes, but
they occur in a wide variety of languages and are quite common in some.
Any combination of phonemes which regularly occur together and
which as a group are associated with some point in the content structure
is a morpheme. We need give no regard to any peculiarity of their
arrangement relative to each other and to other phonemes. Rarely do
morphemes consist of separate portions widely separated by intervening
material. A linguist must always be prepared for such a phenomenon,
however, rare as it may be.

Hebrew and related languages are unusual in the large number of discontinuous morphemes they contain. In fact the majority of the roots are
similar to {zkr}, consisting of three consonants. Various allomorphs
occur: /z-k-r/ in /zaakár/ "he remembered," /-zk-r/ in /yizkóor/ "he was

remembering," and /z-kr-/ in /zikríi/ "my remembrance." The three consonants never occur contiguously in any utterance; such roots are discontinuous in all their occurrences.

In other languages, discontinuous allomorphs of otherwise quite usual morphemes occur. These commonly arise as a byproduct of a special type of affix not mentioned before, an *infix*. An infix is a morpheme which is inserted into the stem with which it is associated. In comparison with suffixes and prefixes, infixes are comparatively rare but of sufficiently frequent occurrence to warrant notice. An example is the common Greek stem formative /-m-/ in /lambanɔ·/ "I take" from the root /lab-/. Another is Quileute (Oregon) /-¢-/ "plural" in /ho¢kᵂat'/ "white men" from /hokᵂat'/ "white person." Such infixes produce discontinuous allomorphs /la-b-/ and /ho-kᵂat'/ of the root morphemes with which they occur.

An affix should not be considered as an infix unless there is cogent reason to do so. Of course, any affix which actually interrupts another morpheme is an infix. In Tagalog *ginulay* "greenish blue" is formed from the root *gulay* "green vegetables." The *-in-* is clearly an infix. But it is not justifiable to consider English *-as-* in *reassign* as in infix. This word is made by two prefixes. First *as-* and *sign* form the stem *assign*. Then *re-* is added. The alternative would be to consider *re-* and *sign* as forming a stem *resign* to which an infix *-as-* is added. The latter would be immediately rejected by any native speaker of English, since he would sense that *reassign* has a much closer connection with *assign* than with *resign*. It is always better, unless there is good reason to the contrary, to consider words as being constructed of successive layers of affixes outward from the root.

Most English verbs have a form that is made by the addition of the suffix *-ed*/-d ~ -t ~ -ɨd/. This is usually known as the past. The verbs which lack this formation do, however, have some form which is used in all the same syntactic environments where we might expect such a form, and in comparable social and linguistic contexts. For example, in most of the places where *discover* /dɪskə́ver/ can be used, *find* /fáynd/ can also. Similarly, where *discovered* /dɪskə́vərd/ can be used, *found* /fáwnd/ generally can also. *Found* must therefore be considered as the past of *find* in the same sense that *discovered* is the past of *discover*.

Most of the past tenses which lack the *-ed* suffix are clearly differentiated from the base form by a difference of syllable nucleus. We may express the facts by the following equations:

discovered = *discover* + suffix *-ed*

found   = *find*   + difference of syllable nucleus

When it is so stated, it becomes evident that the difference of syllable nucleus functions in some ways like the suffix. We may consider such a difference in phonemes (they are not restricted to nuclei; consider *send:sent*) as a special type of morphemic element called a *replacive*.

We will use the following notation for a replacive: /aw ← (ay)/. This should be read as "/aw/ replaces /ay/." The equation above can be stated in the following form:

found   = *find*   + *ou* ← (*i*)

/fáwnd/ = /fáynd/ + /aw ← (ay)/

If this is done, then we must consider /aw ← (ay)/ as another allomorph of the morpheme whose most familiar form is *-ed* and which we can conveniently symbolize {-D$_1$}. This morpheme has a number of replacive allomorphs. . . . All of them are morphologically conditioned. {-Z$_1$}, the English noun plural affix, also has replacives among its allomorphs.

It is, of course, possible to describe a language like English without recourse to replacives. Thus, *geese* /gíys/ can be described as containing a root /g-s/ and an infix allomorph of the plural morpheme {-Z$_1$} of the form /-iy-/. Then the singular would have to be described as containing an infix /-uw-/, an allomorph of a singular morpheme *{X}. Except for the cases under consideration, there are no infixes, nor discontinuous morphemes in the language. To consider plurals like *geese* as formed by an infix turns out to involve many more complications than the alternative of describing replacives. As is often the case, the simpler explanation accords more closely with the native speaker's feeling about his language.

With replacives it is not easy to divide a word into its constituent morphemes. Obviously /giys/ is two morphemes, but the four phonemes cannot be neatly apportioned between them. A morpheme does not necessarily *consist* of phonemes, but all morphemes are statable in terms of phonemes. A replacive must be described in terms of two sets of phonemes: those that appear when it is present (/iy/ in *geese*) and those that appear when the replacive is absent (/uw/ in *goose*). A morpheme can consist of any recurring feature or features of the expression which can be described in terms of phonemes, without restriction of any sort.

A further, and in some respects more extreme, type of morphemic element can be seen in the past of some other English verbs. Words like *cut* and *hit* parallel such forms as *walked* in meaning and usage. There is, however, no phoneme difference of any kind between the past and the nonpast form. Nevertheless, it is in the interest of simplicity to consider all English past verb forms as consisting of a stem plus an affix. Moreover, the description must in some ways note the lack of any overt marker of the past. An expedient by which both can be done is to consider *cut* "past" as containing a root /kət/ plus a zero affix. (Zero is customarily symbolized Ø to avoid confusion with the letter O.) Ø is therefore another of the numerous allomorphs of {-D$_1$}.

The plural affix {-Z$_1$} also has a zero allomorph in *sheep*. The reason that it is necessary to describe these forms in this way rests ultimately in English content structure. Native speakers feel that the dichotomy between singular and plural is a basic characteristic of nouns. Every individual occurrence of any noun must be either singular or plural. *Sheep* is ambiguous, but not indifferent to the distinction. That is, in any given utterance the word is thought of by speaker and hearer as either singular or plural. Sometimes they may disagree, plural being intended and singular being perceived, or vice versa. It requires conscious effort for a person accustomed only to English patterns to conceive of noun referents without consideration of number. To attempt to do so impresses many people as being "too abstract." Yet they feel under no such compulsion to distinguish the exact number if it is more than two.

In other words, there is a covert difference between *sheep* "singular" and *sheep* "plural," and this is linguistically significant as may be seen from the fact that it controls the forms of certain other words in *This sheep is. . . .: These sheep are. . . .* The recognition of a Ø allomorph of {-Z₁} is merely a convenient device for entering all this into our description. . . .

FOR DISCUSSION AND REVIEW

The following three exercises by H. A. Gleason Jr., provide practice in morphemic analysis and will help you to assess your understanding of the concepts introduced in "The Identification of Morphemes." Believing that students of linguistics need to work with problems drawn from a variety of languages, Professor Gleason prepared a *Workbook in Descriptive Linguistics* to accompany his textbook *An Introduction to Descriptive Linguistics*. The following exercises have been taken from that workbook. In the preface to the workbook, Professor Gleason notes that although there is some inevitable distortion in presenting short samples of languages, "All the problems represent real languages" and "the complexities are all genuine."

Swahili (East Africa)

1.	atanipenda	he will like me
2.	atakupenda	he will like you
3.	atampenda	he will like him
4.	atatupenda	he will like us
5.	atawapenda	he will like them
6.	nitakupenda	I will like you
7.	nitampenda	I will like him
8.	nitawapenda	I will like them
9.	utanipenda	you will like me
10.	utampenda	you will like him
11.	tutampenda	we will like him
12.	watampenda	they will like him
13.	atakusumbua	he will annoy you

14. unamsumbua   you are annoying him
15. atanipiga   he will beat me
16. atakupiga   he will beat you
17. atampiga   he will beat him
18. ananipiga   he is beating me
19. anakupiga   he is beating you
20. anampiga   he is beating him
21. amenipiga   he has beaten me
22. amekupiga   he has beaten you
23. amempiga   he has beaten him
24. alinipiga   he beat me
25. alikupiga   he beat you
26. alimpiga   he beat him
27. wametulipa   they have paid us
28. tulikulipa   we paid you

Note: The forms glossed "he" could as well be glossed "she." The forms glossed "you" are all singular. The plural "you" is omitted from this problem because of a minor complication.

Give the morphemes associated with each of the following meanings:

subjects:	_____	I	objects:	_____	me
	_____	you		_____	you
	_____	he		_____	him
	_____	we		_____	us
	_____	they		_____	them
tenses:	_____	future	stems:	_____	like
	_____	present		_____	beat
	_____	perfect		_____	annoy
	_____	past		_____	pay

What is the order of the morphemes in a word?

Supply the probable forms for the following meanings:

_____ I have beaten them   _____ you have beaten us
_____ they are beating me   _____ we beat them
_____ they have annoyed me   _____ I am paying him

Supply the probable meanings for the following forms:

atanilipa   _____   walikupenda   _____
utawapiga   _____   nimemsumbua   _____

Ilocano (Philippine Islands)

1. píŋgan	dish	piŋpíŋgan	dishes
2. tálon	field	taltálon	fields
3. dálan	road	daldálan	roads
4. bíag	life	bibíag	lives
5. nuáŋ	carabao	nunuáŋ	caribao
6. úlo	head	ulúlo	heads

What type of affix is used to form the plural?

Describe its form and relationship to the stem. Be sure to make clear exactly how much is involved.

Given /múla/ "plant," what would be the most likely form meaning "plants"?

Given /tawtáwa/ "windows," what would be the most likely form meaning "window"?

Dinka (Sudan)

1. pal	knife	paal	knives	_____
2. bit	spear	biit	spears	_____
3. ɣot	hut	ɣoot	huts	_____
4. čiin	hand	čin	hands	_____
5. agɔɔk	monkey	agɔk	monkeys	_____
6. kat	frame	kɛt	frames	_____
7. mač	fire	měč	fires	_____
8. bɛñ	chief	bañ	chiefs	_____
9. dom	field	dum	fields	_____
10. dɔk	boy	dak	boys	_____
11. gɔl	clan	gal	clans	_____
12. tuɔŋ	egg	tɔŋ	eggs	_____
13. muɔr	bull	mior	bulls	_____
14. buɔl	rabbit	bial	rabbits	_____
15. met	child	miit	children	_____
16. jɔŋ	dog	jɔk	dogs	_____
17. yič	ear	yit	ears	_____

What type of affix is shown in [these] data? List the forms of the affixes in the spaces provided opposite the stems with which they are found. Do not attempt to find conditioning factors; the distribution of allomorphs is morphologically conditioned. This is very frequently true of this type of affix.

13

Word-Making:
Some Sources of New Words

W. Nelson Francis

English has the largest vocabulary of any language in the world—over 600,000 words—in part, at least, because English has borrowed words from every language with which it has had any contact. (The rate of borrowing, interestingly, appears to be slowing; and English has become an exporter of words, much to the dismay of the French, among others.) But even without borrowing, English, like all other living languages, has a variety of ways of forming new words. Sometimes, of course, we use an old word with a new meaning, as when cool ("chilly") became cool ("outstanding"). But many times we actually create new words; and when we do, we create them by very regular and predictable processes. In the following excerpt from his book The English Language: An Introduction, *Professor W. Nelson Francis discusses the major ways, in addition to borrowing from other languages and semantic change, that new words are created and become a part of the vocabulary of English.*

Though borrowing has been the most prolific source of addition to the vocabulary of English, we acquire or create new words in several other ways. Those which will be discussed here, in descending order of importance, are *derivation, compounding, functional shift, back formation* and *clipping, proper names, imitation, blending,* and *coinage.*

DERIVATION

The derivational process consists of using an existing word—or in some cases a bound morpheme* or morphemic structure—as a stem to which affixes are attached. Thus our imaginary word *pandle* might become the stem for such derivatives as *pandler, pandlette, depandle,*

---

*Editors' note: Francis earlier tells us: "The smallest meaningful units of language—those which cannot be subdivided into smaller meaningful units—are called *morphemes.* In combinations like *rooster, greenness, lucky, widen,* and *strongly,* all of which are made up of two morphemes, one morpheme carries the principal part of the meaning of the whole. This is called the *base* (or sometimes the *root*). The bases in the examples are *roost, green, luck, wide,* and *strong.* These . . . bases are capable of standing by themselves and of entering rather freely into grammatical combinations.

and *repandlize*. Affixes like these are called *productive*; all native speakers know their meanings and feel free to add them to various kinds of stems in accordance with analogy or the rules of English derivation. By this process any new word, whatever its source, may almost immediately become the nucleus of a cluster of derivatives. Thus *plane*, formed by clipping from *airplane*, had produced *emplane* and *deplane*, presumably by analogy with *entrain* and *detrain*, themselves formed by analogy with *embark* and *debark*, which were borrowed from French. When *telegraph* was formed by compounding of two Greek elements, it soon gave rise to *telegrapher*, *telegraphy*, *telegraphic*, and *telegraphist*, all of which were self-explaining derivatives.

So obvious is the process of forming derivatives with productive affixes that all of us probably do it much more frequently than we realize. The words we thus "create" in most cases have been frequently used before and are listed in the dictionary, but we may not know that. This process allows us to expand our vocabulary without specifically memorizing new words. But this reliance on analogical derivation may sometimes trap us into creating new words that are unnecessary because other derivatives already exist and have become standard. The student who wrote about Hamlet's *unableness to overcome his mental undecidedness* undoubtedly was familiar with *inability* and *indecision*, but under the pressure of an examination he forgot them and created his own derivatives instead.

COMPOUNDING

In a sense, compounding is a special form of derivation in which, instead of adding affixes (bound forms) to a stem, two or more words (or in some cases bound bases) are put together to make a new lexical unit. Compounding has been a source of new words in English since earliest times, and is particularly common in present-day English. Perusal of any daily paper will turn up countless examples of compounds that are new within the last few years or months: *launching pad, blast off, jet-port, freeway, ski-tow, freeloader, featherbedding, sit-in*. Out writing system does not indicate whether items like *weather satellite* are compounds or constructions. Many of them begin as constructions but then assume the characteristic stress patterns of compounds: some people still pronounce *ice cream* with the stress pattern of a construction (as in *iced tea*), but most treat it as a compound (as in *iceboat*). Some of the older compounds have gone through sound (and spelling) changes that have completely obscured their compound origin. Typical of these is *lord*, which began in

---

For this reason they are called *free bases*. Other bases cannot stand alone or enter freely into grammatical combinations but must always appear in close affiliation with other morphemes. These are called *bound bases*. We can recognize a common base *turb* in such words as *disturb*, *perturb*, and *turbulent*; it never stands alone as the *green* of *greenness* does, so it is a bound base."

early Old English as *hlāf-weard*, a compound of the ancestors of our *loaf* and *ward*, and passed through the stages of OE *hlāford* and ME *loverd* to its present monosyllabic form. Other examples are *woman*, originally a compound of the ancestors of *wife* and *man*, and *hussy*, from *house* and *wife*, hence etymologically a doublet of *housewife*.

The semantic relationships between the parts of compounds are very varied. If compounds are thought of as the product of a transformation process, this variety can be revealed by reconstructing the phrase from which the compound might have been created. This may range from a simple modification, in which the transformation involves only a change in stress pattern (*hot dog, blackboard, bluebird*), to complete predication, where the transformation involves complicated reordering and deletion (as in *salesman* from *man who makes sales* or *movie camera* from *camera that takes movies*). Compounds may themselves enter into compounds to produce elaborate structures like *aircraft carrier* and *real estate salesman*. These must be considered compounds, since they have the characteristic stress pattern with the strongest stress on the first element (*aírcràft càrrier, réal estàte sàlesman*), in contrast to the stress pattern of modification constructions (as in *aírcràft desígner* or *rèal estàte invéstment*).

One special group of compounds, most of them of quite recent origin, includes those words—mostly technical and scientific terms—which are made up of morphemes borrowed from Greek. Many of the elements so used were free forms—words—in Greek, but must be considered bound bases in English. The practice of compounding them began in Greek: *philosophia* is compounded from *philos* "fond of" and *sophia* "wisdom." Words of this sort were borrowed into Latin in ancient times, and ultimately reached English by way of French. Renaissance scholars, who knew Greek and recognized the combining elements, began to make new combinations which did not exist in the original Greek. With the growth of scientific knowledge from the seventeenth century on, new technical and scientific terms were commonly invented this way.

Words created can be roughly divided into two groups. The first includes those which have wide circulation in the general vocabulary—like *telephone*, *photograph*, and *thermometer*. These are constructed out of a relatively small number of morphemes, whose meanings are well known:

tele	"far, distant"	*meter*	"measure"
phone	"sound"	*dyna*	"power"
photo	"light"	*hydro*	"water, moisture"
graph	"write, mark"	*bio*	"life"
thermo	"heat"	*morph*	"shape, form"

Inventors and manufacturers of new products often create names for their inventions from elements of this sort. Sometimes the Greek elements are combined with Latin ones, as in *automobile* (Greek *autos* "self," Latin *mobilis* "movable") and *television*, or even with native English elements, as in *dynaflow*. Recent creations in this group are *astronaut* and *cosmonaut,* from Greek *aster* "star," *kosmos* "universe," and *nautes* "sailor." Actually *cosmonaut* was first used in Russian, whence it was borrowed, but since both of its bases were already in use in English (as in *cosmology* and *aeronaut*), it might just as well have originated in English.

The second group of Greek-based compounds comprises the large number of technical and scientific terms whose use is almost wholly restricted to specialists. As in the case of *cosmonaut,* most of these words are readily interchangeable among the languages in which scientific publication is extensive. Since it is often difficult if not impossible to determine the language in which they were first used, the Merriam-Webster editors have recently made use of the term *International Scientific Vocabulary* (abbreviated ISV) to describe them. A few examples of wide enough circulation to be included in an abridged dictionary are the following:

hypsography: "recording (*graphy*) of elevation (*hypso*)"

telethermoscope: "instrument that perceives (*scope*) heat (*thermo*) at a distance (*tele*)"

electroencephalograph: "instrument that records (*graph*) electric current (*electro*) within (*en*) the head (*cephalo*)"

schizogenesis: "reproduction (*genesis*) by division (*schizo*)"

In all cases, since at least two of the combining elements are bases, these words must be considered compounds. They may also give rise to derivatives formed by the addition of affixes in regular patterns, such as *electroencephalography* and *schizogenetic.* It is in this way, rather than by direct borrowing, that Greek has made its great contribution to the English vocabulary.

FUNCTIONAL SHIFT

Since the late Middle English period, when most of the inflections surviving from Old English finally disappeared, it has been easy to shift a word from one part of speech to another without altering its form, at least in the unmarked base form. A verb like *walk* can be turned into a noun simply by using it in a syntactic position reserved for nouns, as in *he took a walk,* where the determiner *a* marks *walk* as a noun, direct object of *took.* This process, called *functional shift,* is an important concomitant of the historical change of English from a synthetic to an analytic language, and has greatly enlarged the vocabulary in a very economical way. Since the words so created belong to a different part of speech and hence have a different grammatical distribution from that of the original, they must be considered new words, homonymous in the base form with the words from which they were derived, rather than merely extensions of meaning. From another point of view, they may be thought of as derivatives with zero affixes. In some cases they may take a different stress pattern in their new use: the noun *implement*, with weak stress and the weak central vowel /ə/ in the last syllable, when shifted to a verb took secondary stress on the last syllable, whose vowel was changed to /ɛ/. Since there is overt change in pronunciation, this is true derivation rather than functional shift. But the two processes are obviously closely related.

Older instances of functional shift commonly produced nouns from verbs: in addition to *walk*, already cited, we might mention *run, steal, laugh, touch, buy, break*, and many others. In present-day English the shift from noun to verb is much in favor. In the past, short words like *brush* and *perch* were sometimes shifted from noun to verb, but today, longer nouns like *implement, position, process, contact* are often used as verbs. Even compound nouns get shifted to verbs; the secretary who said "I didn't back-file the letter, I waste-basketed it" was speaking twentieth-century English, however inelegant.

BACK FORMATION AND CLIPPING

Back formation and clipping are two modes of word creation which can be classed together as different types of *reduction*. In each case, a shorter word is made from a longer one, so that the effect is the opposite of derivation and compounding. Back formation makes use of analogy to produce a sort of reverse derivation. The existence of *creation, create*, and *donation* readily suggests that if there is not a verb *donate* there should be. This seems so natural to us that it is hard to believe that less than a century ago *donate* was considered an American barbarism by many puristically inclined British speakers of Engligh.[1] Other words that have come into English by back formation are *edit* (from *editor*), *burgle* (from *burglar*), *enthuse* (from *enthusiasm*), *televise* (from *television*, by analogy with pairs like *supervise:supervision*), *automate* (from *automation*), *laze* (from *lazy*), and many more. Once pairs of words like these have become established, only the historical record proving prior use of the longer forms serves to distinguish them from normal derivational pairs.

Clippings, on the other hand, are shortenings without regard to derivational analogy. They are frequent in informal language, especially spoken, as in the campus and classroom use of *exam, lab, math*, and *dorm*. They are possible because often a single syllable, usually the one bearing the main stress, is sufficient to identify a word, especially in a rather closely restricted context, so that the remaining syllables are redundant and can be dropped. Most of them preserve a colloquial flavor and are limited to the special vocabularies of occupational groups. Others, however—often over the objections of purists—attain wide circulation and may

---

[1] See H. L. Mencken, *The American Language*, 4th ed. (New York: Alfred A. Knopf, 1936): 121, 165.

ultimately replace the longer forms on most or all levels of usage. Some that have done so are *van* (from *caravan*), *bus* (from *omnibus*), *cello* (from *violoncello*), *mob* (from Latin *mobile vulgus* "unstable crowd"), *piano* (from *pianoforte*), and *fan* (in the sense "ardent devotee," from *fanatic*). Others which are in acceptable, though perhaps characteristically informal, use alongside the longer unclipped words are *phone* (for *telephone*), *taxi* and *cab* (from *taxicab*) and *plane* (for *airplane* or older *aeroplane*). A rather special form of clipping is that which reduces long compounds or idiomatic fixed phrases to one of their elements—often the modifying element rather than the head—as in *express train*, *car* from *motor car*, and *outboard* from *outboard motor* (*boat*). This process often accounts for what otherwise seems strange transfers of meaning.

An extreme form of clipping is that which reduces words to their abbreviations and longer phrases to their initials. Abbreviation is, of course, a standard device of the writing system to save space by reducing the length of common or often repeated words. Usually it is confined to writing, and to rather informal writing at that. But some common abbreviations have been adopted in speech and ways have been found to pronounce them. The common abbreviations for the two halves of the day— A.M. and P.M.—which stand for the Latin phrases *ante meridiem* ("before noon") and *post meridiem* ("after noon") are frequently used in speech, where they are pronounced/é: + èm/ and /pí:èm/. These must indeed be considered words, though their spelling is that of abbreviations. The same is true of B.C. and A.D. in dates, O.K. (which has become an international word), U.S., G.I., L.P., TNT, TV, and DDT. In all these cases the pronunciation is simply the syllabic names of the letters, usually with the strongest stress on the last: /yù: + és/, /dì: + dì: + tí:/, and so on.

If the initial letters of a phrase, used as an abbreviation, happen to make a combination that is pronounceable, what results is an *acronym*— a word whose spelling represents the initial letters of a phrase. Though very popular in recent times, acronyms are by no means an innovation of the twentieth century. The early Christians made a famous one when they took the initials of the Greek phrase {Ιησοὺς Χριστὸϯ θεοῦ ὑὸς σωτήρ} ("Jesus Christ, son of God, Savior") to make the Greek word ϯχθύς ("fish") and adopted the fish as a symbol of Christ. Acronyms have become more frequent in English since World War II. Everyone talks about NATO, UNESCO, and NASA, often without being able to supply the longer title whose initials created the acronym. In fact, acronyms have become so popular that some longer titles have been created by a kind of back formation from the desired initials. It was certainly more than a happy accident that led the Navy in World War II to call its feminine branch "Women Assigned to Volunteer Emergency Service," or WAVES. More recently an organization devoted to finding foster parents for orphan children from foreign lands has called itself "World Adoption International Fund" so its initials would spell WAIF.

PROPER NAMES

The giving of individual names to persons, geographic features, deities, and sometimes to animals is a universal human practice, apparently as old as language itself. A proper name, since it is closely restricted to a single specific referent, does not have the general and varied distribution and reference that characterize ordinary nouns. But there is frequent interchange across the line separating proper names from other words. Many proper names, such as *Taylor, Smith, Clark,* and *Wright,* are derived from common nouns describing occupations; others like *Brown, Strong,* and *Wild* derive from adjectives that may once have described the person so named. Placenames also frequently show their derivation from common nouns, as in *Northfield, Portsmouth,* and *Fairmount.*

There has also been interchange in the other direction, by which the proper name of a person or place becomes generalized in meaning, usually to refer to a product or activity connected with the referent of the proper name. One famous example is the name *Caesar,* originally a nickname coined from the Latin verb *caedo* "to cut" to describe Julius Caesar, who was cut from his mother's womb by the operation still called *Caesarian section.* The name was assumed by Julius's nephew Octavius, the first Roman emperor, and then by the subsequent emperors, so that it became virtually a synonym for *imperator* "emperor." In its later history it was borrowed into Germanic, ultimately becoming German *Kaiser* (there was also a Middle English word *kayser,* now obsolete), and into Slavonic, whence came *tsar.* Another interesting set of words derived from names are the adjectives *mercurial, saturnine,* and *jovial,* referring to temperaments supposed to be characteristic of people under the dominance of the planets Mercury, Saturn, and Jupiter. The corresponding *venereal* (from *Venus*) has been restricted in meaning almost entirely to medical use, but *venery* is still a rather high-flown word for love-making. Those supposed to derive instability from the changeable moon used to be called *lunatic* (from Latin *luna,* the moon). The punishment visited upon Tantalus, forever doomed to be within sight of food and water that receded when he reached for it, has given us the verb *tantalize,* formed by adding the productive suffix *-ize* (itself ultimately derived from Greek) to his name. Also ultimately Greek in origin are *hector* ("a bully, to bully") from the Trojan hero in the *Iliad* and *mentor* ("teacher"—now often used in the sports pages for "athletic coach") from the adviser of Telemachus in the *Odyssey.*

During the history of English since the beginning of the Middle English period, various words have been derived from proper names. Some earlier ones are *dunce* (from the scholastic philosopher Duns Scotus—used in ridicule of scholastic philosophy in the later sixteenth century), *pander* (from the character Pandarus in Chaucer's *Troilus and Criseyde,* c. 1385), *mawmet* (from Mahomet; at first it meant "idol," later "puppet, doll"). The Bible, widely read from Reformation times on and frequently discussed for its symbolic, as well as its literal or historical meaning, has contributed many words of this sort, such as *jeremiad* ("a denunciatory tirade"), *babel, lazar* (from Lazarus; common for *leper* in Middle English), *maudlin* (from Mary Magdalen and her noted tears), and *simony* ("taking or giving money for church offices," from Simon Magus). On the border between proper and common nouns are names of Biblical and other personages taken in figurative meanings, though usually capitalized in writing, indicating that the transfer to common nouns is not complete: *the old Adam, raising Cain, a doubting Thomas, a Daniel come to judgment.*

Some proper names that have assumed general meanings have undergone pronunciation changes that obscure their origins. The adjective *tawdry* ("cheap and flashy") comes from a clipping of *Saint Audrey,* and presumably was first used to describe a kind of cheap lace sold at St. Audrey's Fair. *Bedlam,* which to us means "uproar, total confusion," was a proper name as late as the eighteenth century, when it was used as a short name for *St. Mary of Bethlehem,* a London insane asylum. The word *mawkin,* used dialectally in England for "scarecrow," comes from *Malkyn,* a girl's name, ultimately a nickname from *Mary.* The parallel nickname *Moll* gave rise to an American slang word for a criminal's girl. The history of *doll* is similar but more complicated; it passed from a clipped form of *Dorothy* to describe a miniature (usually female) figure, then to describe a small and pretty girl.

The names of historical characters—often those of unsavory reputation—have given us some rather common words. One of the most interesting of these is *guy,* from *Guy Fawkes,* used in England to describe the effigies of that notable traitor which are customarily carried in procession and burned on November 5, the anniversary of the discovery of his "Gunpowder Plot." The term came to mean "a figure of fun, a butt of scorn," and as a verb "to poke fun at, tease." In America it has become a universal colloquial term for any male not held in high respect. In phrases like *a nice guy* (when not used ironically), it has lost all of its original pejorative flavor.

Names of products derived from the names of their places of origin are rather plentiful in English. Textiles like *calico* (from *Calicut,* or *Calcutta*), *denim* (*serge de Nîmes*), *cashmere* (*Kashmir*), and *worsted* (from the name of a town in Norfolk, England) are well known. So are products like *china* (clipped from *chinaware* from *China ware*), *gin* (clipped from *Geneva*), *cognac,* and *cayenne.* Specialized and technical vocabularies are especially fond of words adapted from proper names. Skiing has its *telemark* and *christiania* (usually clipped to *christy*); librarians speak of *Dewey decimal classification* and *Cutter numbers;* horticulturists of *fuchsia, dahlia,* and *wisteria;* physicists of *roentgen rays, curies,* and *angstrom units;* electricians of *ohms, watts,* and *amperes;* doctors of *rickettsia* and *Bright's disease.*

IMITATION

A relatively small number of words in English apparently owe their origin to attempts to imitate natural sounds. *Bow-wow, meow, baa, moo,* and other words for animal cries are supposed to remind us of the noises made by dogs, cats, sheep, and cows. They are not accurate imitations, since they are pronounced with sounds characteristic of the sound-system of English, which these animals, not being native speakers of English, do not use. Other languages have other, often quite different imitative words. Both *cock-a-doodle-doo* and *kikiriki* are supposedly imitative of a rooster's crow; unless we assume that English and Greek roosters make quite different sounds, we must attribute the difference between these words to the differing sound-systems of the two languages.

Related to imitation is the phenomenon sometimes called *sound symbolism:* the habit of associating a certain type or class of meanings with a certain sound or cluster of sounds. There seems to be in English an association between the initial consonant cluster *sn-* and the nose (*snarl, sneer, sneeze, sniff, snivel, snore, snort, snout,* and *snuffle*). When slang words referred to or involving the nose are coined they may begin with this cluster, as in *snook* and *snoop.* English speakers associate the sound-combination spelled *-ash* (/æš/) with a sudden loud sound or rapid, turbulent, or destructive motion, as in *crash, dash, flash, smash,* and *splash;* and a final *-er* on verbs suggests rapidly repeated, often rhythmic motion, as in *flicker, flutter, hover, quiver, shimmer, waver.* This last example is perhaps a morpheme in its own right, though to call it one would give us a large number of bound bases that occur nowhere else. But it is well on the way to the morphemic status which certainly must be accorded to the *-le* or *-dle* of *handle, treadle,* and *spindle.*

Imitation was once considered so important as to be made the basis for a theory of the origin of language—the so-called "bow-wow theory." This theory is commonly discounted nowadays.

BLENDING

Blending is a combination of clipping and compounding, which makes new words by putting together fragments of existing words in new combinations. It differs from derivation in that the elements thus combined are not morphemes at the time the blends are made, though they may become so afterward as a result of the blending process, especially if several blends are made with the same element and the phenomenon of *false etymology* is present.

The poem "Jabberwocky" in Lewis Carroll's *Through the Looking Glass* contains many ingenious blends, though only a few of them (called *portmanteau* words by Humpty Dumpty in the book) have passed into the general vocabulary. Thus *slithy* (from *lithe* and *slimy*) and *mimsy* (from *miserable* and *flimsy*) are not used outside the poem, but *chortle* (*chuckle* and *snort*) and *galumphing* (*galloping* and *triumphing*) are not uncommon words, though they are usually restricted to colloquial or facetious use.

The history of *-burger* illustrates the way in which blending can give rise to a new morpheme. The name *Hamburger steak* (varying with *Hamburg steak*) was given to a kind of ground beef in America in the 1880s. It was soon shortened by phrase-clipping to *hamburger*, losing its proper-name quality in the process. The *-er* here is simply the normal German suffix for making an adjective from a proper noun (as in *Brandenburger Tor* "Brandenburg Gate"). But to those who did not know German, the word looked (and sounded) like a compound of *ham* and *burger*. So the *-burger* part was clipped and combined with various words or parts of words to make *cheeseburger, deerburger, buffaloburger*, and many more. These have the form of compounds made up of one free base and a bound base *-burger*. Meanwhile by further clipping, *hamburger*, already short for *hamburger steak sandwich*, was cut down to *burger*, which now became a free form—a word. Thus what began as the last two syllables of a German proper adjective has become first a bound morpheme and then a full word in English.

Other morphemes which owe their origin to blending are *-rama*, *-orium*, *-teria*, and *-omat*. The first of these began with words of Greek origin like *panorama* and *cyclorama*.[2] The combining elements in Greek were *pan* "all," *kyklos* "circle, wheel," and *horama* "view," a noun derived from the verb *horan* "see." But the *-rama* part of these words was blended with *cine* (from *cinema*) to make *cinerama*, describing a type of wide-screen motion picture. Subsequently *-rama* was blended with various other elements to make new words like *colorama* and *vistarama*, as well as many trade and commercial names. It certainly must now be considered a separate morpheme, conveying a vague notion of grandeur and sweep (or so its users hope) to the words in which it is used. Similarly *-orium*, split off from *emporium* (a rather fancy Latin loan-word for "shop"), *-teria*, split off from the Spanish loan-word *cafeteria*, and *-omat*, split off from the trade name *Automat*, itself a clipping from *automatic*, have become separate morphemes, as in *lubritorium, valeteria*, and *laundromat*. The process of blending has thus produced not only new words but new morphemes capable of entering with some freedom into new compounds and derivatives. Many of the words thus coined never get any farther than their first application by an enterprising advertiser or proprietor, and those that do usually have a brief life. But a few seem to fill a real need and remain as part of the general vocabulary of English.

---

[2] See John Lotz, "The Suffix '-rama,'" *American Speech* 39 (1954): 156–158.

COINAGE

Very few words are simply made up out of unrelated, meaningless elements. The other resources for making new words and the abundant vocabularies of other languages available for borrowing supply so many easy ways of producing new words that outright coinage seldom suggests itself. The outright coinage—unlike the compound, clipping, derivative, and blend—is also hard to remember because it has no familiar elements to aid the memory. So wholly new coinages are both harder to make and less likely to be remembered and used. It is no wonder that they are relatively rare. Some words, however, are indubitable coinages, and others for which etymologists have found no source may be tentatively assumed to be. Words like *quiz, pun, slang,* and *fun* have no cognates in other Germanic languages, cannot be traced to other languages as loanwords, and, since they are monosyllabic, are not compounds or derivatives, though they might be blends to which we have lost the key. One can imagine that *slang*—an eighteenth-century creation—combined elements from *slovenly* and *language,* but this is pure guesswork. These, together with more recent words, most of them facetious or slangy, like *hooch* and *pooch, snob* and *gob* ("sailor"), most probably originated as free coinages, sometimes involving sound symbolism.

More elaborate coinages, having more than one syllable, are likely to combine original elements with various other processes of word formation, especially derivation. Thus the stems of *segashuate, sockdologer,* and *spifflicated* seem to be coinages, but the suffixes are recognizable morphemes. In fact, it would be exceedingly unlikely for a native speaker to coin a word of more than one syllable without making use of one or more of the word-forming devices we have been discussing.

As even this brief chapter must have made obvious, the vocabulary of English is large, complex, highly diversified in origin, and constantly changing. No dictionary, however large, can contain it all. Or, if such a dictionary should be prepared, it would be out of date by the time it was printed, since new meanings, new borrowings, and new creations are being added every day. Nor can any single individual know it all. Speakers of English share a large vocabulary in common, it is true, but every individual speaker has his own unique inventory of the less commonly used words and meanings, reflecting his unique experience with language.

Many people—perhaps most people—go through life with a vocabulary adequate only to their daily needs, picking up new words when some new facet of life makes it necessary, but never indulging in curiosity and speculation about words. Others are wordlovers—collectors and connoisseurs. They like to measure one word against another, trace their etymologies and shifts of meaning, use them in new and exciting or amusing combinations. They play word-games like *Scrabble* and *Anagrams,* they do crossword puzzles, they make puns and rhymes and nonsense jingles. Some make poems, which are the highest form of word-game. But even those who aspire no further than to the writing of good clear expository prose must become at least amateur connoisseurs of words. Only this way—not by formal exercises or courses in vocabulary-building—will they learn to make the best possible use of the vast and remarkable lexicon of English.

FOR DISCUSSION AND REVIEW

1. Why is an understanding of morphology important in the study of word formation?

2. What role does analogy play in the process of forming words by derivation?

3. Compounding is of particular importance in areas involving extensive technological development. One study found that 19 percent of the words in a series of NASA reports were in nominal compounds, compared to only 3 percent in articles published in the *American Scholar*. Why might this situation exist?

4. Keep a list of nominal compounds that you encounter in your reading during the course of a week. Where are you most likely to find them? What is the longest one you found? (The author of the study referred to in question 3 found a nominal compound that contained 13 words!)

5. Consider the order of importance of the various methods of word formation listed by Francis in the first paragraph of this selection. Discuss the possible causes of this particular ordering or of some of its components. Why, for example, are derivation and compounding so important? Why are imitation and blending relatively unimportant?

6. Identify the process of word formation in the following words: *gas, contrail, happenstance, spa, diesel, flu, laser, smog, meow, syphilis.*

14

Literary Metaphors and Other Linguistic Innovations in Computer Language

Kelvin Don Nilsen and Alleen Pace Nilsen

Computers have burst onto the American cultural scene with the impact of an explosion, accompanied by a whole range of new technological tools and concepts for which no language previously existed. Probably even the least computer-literate among us have a passing familiarity by now with such terms as "hacker," "user-friendly," "bug," and "cyberspace." Kelvin Don Nilsen, who teaches computer science at Iowa State University, and Alleen Pace Nilsen, who teaches English at Arizona State University, combine their areas of expertise in this article to explore the sources and meanings of some specialized words and expressions known as "computer talk" or "jargon." The Nilsens discovered that many of the terms current among computer users are borrowed from literature, especially from the most familiar works of science fiction and from popular TV shows and films such as Star Trek *and* Star Wars. *In this article, the Nilsens suggest several activities to help readers familiarize themselves with the often clever and amusing language of "computer talk" and the ways in which it impacts, and is impacted by, traditional English usage.*

An important linguistic principle is that when speakers meet new concepts that they don't have words for, they are not likely to create new sets of sounds to arbitrarily attach to the new ideas; instead they will adapt old words to new concepts. Over the last three decades, we've seen this principle illustrated by people working with computers.

These people form a distinctive subculture which has developed its own language. We don't mean the language of "codes" that computer programmers use to communicate with their machines but instead the very human kind of language that people use to talk with each other about computers: While this language is based on English sound patterns and grammar and is built from English words (often with adapted spelling, capitalization, and spacing), the end result is nevertheless quite different from mainstream English. As an exploration of how a subculture goes about developing its own language, we have gathered examples of names, concepts, and allusions that have been adapted from literature and given new meanings in relation to computers.

166

Just as speakers who study a foreign language sometimes gain insights about their own language, an examination of aspects of language change brought about by computers will also provide insights. First, both teachers and students will increase their understanding of "computer language," and second, they will come to a greater understanding of how languages change in relation to changing needs.

WHO CREATES "COMPUTER TALK"?

The creators of "computer talk" come from two different camps. On one end are the *hackers* (see Notes), those individuals who spend inordinate amounts of time at computer terminals as they devise software, create challenges for themselves and their machines, and communicate with each other via electronic or *e-mail*. In the other camp are those the hackers call the *suits* or the *marketroids*. These are the company managers and the salespeople who create product names and manage the advertising campaigns. In between is a much larger group of people who use computers as a tool for their daily work but whose primary interest is not in the computer itself as much as in how it can help them accomplish their other goals. Hackers call the most computer-knowledgeable of these people *techies*, while they refer to those who barely get by as *lusers*—a pun on user and loser. Although some interesting product names have been created for both hardware and software, we are looking here at the more creative language bubbling up from computer hackers, some of which makes its way into technie language or even into mainstream English.

While hackers are connected electronically so that they exchange written messages almost instantaneously—either between individuals or with all members of a like-minded group—they are basically strangers to each other in that their messages lack the benefits of eye contact or voice intonation. This means that when a hacker relies on a literary reference, the communication will fail unless the receivers of the message are already familiar with the piece being cited and unless the image being invoked is clearly memorable.

LITERARY ORIGINS AND REFERENCES

For English teachers, an important point of interest is which literature satisfies these requirements for this cultural subset. Although hackers say that women are welcome and respected members of the community (in faceless and sometimes nameless communication, who's to know?), the literature that has become part of their vocabulary is what used to be labeled as "boys' books." We found no reference to Shakespeare or to romances, but lots of references to science fiction and fantasy. *Heavy wizardry* is a term used to talk about the integration and maintenance of components within large, complicated, poorly documented software systems, while *deep magic*, a term borrowed from C. S. Lewis's Narnia books, refers to the implementation of software that is based on difficult-to-understand mathematical principles.

Lovecraft, Orwell, Tolkien

The Internet is respectfully, or fearfully, spoken of as the *Shub-Internet*, a reference to H. P. Lovecraft's horror fiction and his evil *Shub-Niggurath*, the Black Goat with a Thousand Young. The definition in *The Jargon File* (see Notes) clarifies this harsh personification as:

> Beast of a Thousand Processes, Eater of Characters, Avatar of Line Noise, and Imp of Call Waiting: the hideous multi-tendriled entity formed of all the manifold connections of the net . . . its purpose is malign and evil, and is the cause of all network slowdown.

A slightly less malevolent reference is to *code police* as a comparison to the *thought police* in George Orwell's *1984*. Code police take upon themselves the responsibility of enforcing idealized styles and standards for programming language codes. The term is generally used pejoratively, and the feeling among the hacker community is that those who are most likely to assume this role are outsiders (management, ivy-tower academics) who rarely participate in the practice of software development. A closely related term is *net police*, which describes members of the network community who assume the role of enforcing protocol and etiquette standards. In public e-mail and electronic bulletin board forums, the net police shame anyone who violates the established rules.

Archaic operating systems that print only uppercase letters are called *Great Runes*, a usage probably influenced by the writings of J. R. R. Tolkien, who has contributed more words to hacker language than has any other author. Hackers talk of the pre-1980s as their *elder days*, while they use *Hobbit* to describe the high-order bit of a byte (see Notes). An infamous 1988 bugging of the Internet was called *The Great Worm*, named after Scatha and Glaurung, Tolkien's powerful and highly feared Middle Earth dragons. Printers, and especially the people who use printers to provide unnecessary paper copies, are called *Tree-killers* based on what Treebeard the Ent called the Orcs. *Elvish*, the name of the fictional language that Tolkien created in *The Lord of the Rings*, was first used to refer to a particularly elegant style of printing, but is now used more generally for any odd or unreadable typeface produced through graphics.

Science Fiction

Terms coming from various sources in the genre of science fiction include *hyperspace*, which describes an errant memory access (valid memory regions include *code* or *text space*, *static space*, *stack space*, and *heap space*; anything else is considered *hyperspace*); *cyberpunk*, which refers to an imagined world in which anthropomorphized computers participate in human interactions as if they were human; and *cyberspace*, which characterizes future human-computer systems in which humans communicate with the computer as if by mental telepathy. In cyberspace, computers display images directly within the user's mind, similar to prophetic visions as described in biblical writings. Similarly, the science fiction term *martian* is used to describe a network packet received from an unidentifiable network node.

Droid, from *android*, a science fiction term since the 1920s, was popularized in the *Star Trek* television series. Computer hackers frequently use droid or the suffix *-oid* in a derogatory way to imply that a person is acting mindlessly, as though programmed. Thus, *marketroids* and *sales droids* promise customers things which can't be delivered, while a *trendoid* is concerned only with being up-to-date with the latest fads.

The term *Vulcan nerve pinch* also comes from the original *Star Trek* television series. It describes the keyboard action of simultaneously pressing on three keys as when rebooting with the control, alternate, and delete keys.

When there is a need for a random number that people will recognize as such, 42 is often used because in *The Hitchhiker's Guide to the Galaxy* (1980, New York: Harmony) that's what Douglas Adams had his computer give as "The Answer to the Ultimate Question of Life, the Universe, and Everything."

Another interesting term is *Twonkie*, a software addition that is essentially useless but nevertheless appealing in some way, perhaps for marketing purposes. Its meaning is made clear by its resemblance to *Twinkie*, which has become almost a generic term for junk food. However, its source is thought to be the title of Lewis Padgett's 1942 short story "The Twonky," which has been frequently anthologized since its original publication in *Astounding Science Fiction*.

Grok, from Robert Heinlein's *Stranger in a Strange Land* (New York: Putnam, 1961), is used to mean that a computer program understands or is "one with" a particular idea or capability. Often, older versions of commercial software products can't grok data files produced by newer releases of the same product. In a more playful usage from Heinlein's *The Moon Is a Harsh Mistress* (New York: Putnam, 1966), the acronym *TANSTAAFL* has become a quick and socially acceptable way to tell someone "There Ain't No Such Thing As A Free Lunch." Another Heinlein usage is *Waldo*, taken from the title of his 1942 story in which he invented mechanical devices working under the control of a human hand or foot. Computer hackers prefer the term Waldo, but NASA, which hopes to use such devices to manipulate robot arms in space, has chosen the more technological-sounding name *telepresence* (see Notes).

Star Wars

Two of the cleverest science fiction references are based on the *Star*

Wars movies. *UTSL* is a shorthand way to send someone the message that they should do some research before they send out a network call for help. It is an acronym for "Use The Source, Luke!," a play on the line, "Use the Force, Luke!" (see Notes). An *Obi-Wan error*, a pun on the name of Obi-Wan Kenobi, refers to any computation that is off-by-one, as when a programmer started counting a particular quantity at 1 instead of 0. By analogy, an Obi-Wan code would give the name *HAL* (from the movie *2001*, each letter is one away from the corresponding letter in the original acronym) for IBM. In another *Star Wars* allusion, someone who uses computer skills for devious purposes is called a *dark-side hacker* (as opposed to a *Samurai*), meaning the person is like Darth Vader in having been seduced by the "dark side of the Force."

Children's Literature

There are relatively few references to traditional children's literature. However, in the 1960s people spoke of *IBM and the Seven Dwarves*, with the dwarves being Burroughs, Control Data, General Electric, Honeywell, NCR, RCA, and Univac. Lewis Carroll's *Snark* is an appropriate name for any unexplained foul-up that programmers have to go hunting for. In a classic computer hacker story about a conflict between Motorola and Xerox, two hackers at Motorola wrote a pair of "bandit" background processes they affectionately named *Robin Hood* and *Friar Tuck*. These two processes took over the Xerox developer's main computer system. The point of this activity was to get the attention of the Xerox team in order to deliver an important message that had been repeatedly ignored during the several months prior to the attack. The *Trojan Horse* legend provides the name for a program that is designed to get around security measures by sneaking into a system while disguised, perhaps as a game or a useful utility. When the program is invoked, it does unexpected and unwanted harm to a computer system, in addition to providing the advertised functionality.

Moby Dick

One of the most common references to a piece of traditional literature is *moby*, meaning something immense or huge. Although this comes from Herman Melville's *Moby Dick*, its use was popularized in precomputer days by model train fans and such usages as *Moby Pickle*. Hackers use it in such sentences as "The disk crash resulted in moby data lose," and "Writing a new back-end for the compiler would be a moby undertaking!" Several years ago when the University of California Library System named its library access program *Melvyl* after *Melvyl Dewey*, developer of the Dewey Decimal System, some users assumed a connection to Herman Melville because it was such a moby of a database.

OTHER REFERENCES FROM LITERATURE, FILM, AND TV

There's always a lag between the popularization of a term and its being adapted to a new use. However, today's instant communication shortens the lag as shown by two fairly recent references. *Feature Shock* is a play on the title of Alvin Toffler's *Future Shock* (New York: Random House, 1970). It describes a user's reaction to a program heavy on features, but light on explanations. The other recent usage is *Sagan* from the name of Carl Sagan, star of the TV series *Cosmos*, who is often heard repeating the phrase "billions and billions." His name is used as shorthand for any large number as in "There's a sagan different ways to tweak EMACS."

One thing this discussion shows is the importance of television and movies in contributing to the store of literary images from which hackers take their references. A *Godzillagram*, based on the hero of Japanese monster movies, is a network packet of maximum size or one broadcast to every conceivable receiver. *Dr. Mbogo*, the witch doctor from the old *Addams Family* television show, has his name memorialized in *Dr. Fred Mbogo* (hackers often use *Fred* as a random name because it's so easy to type) as a humorous identifier for someone with "bogus" skills.

Computer hackers are relatively young (ranging from teenagers to their mid-forties) and they grew up watching *Sesame Street*, hence the name *Cookie Monster* for a hacker who manages to deny computer access to other users of a system, thereby obtaining exclusive access for selfish purposes. *Double Bucky* is a play on the *Sesame Street* "Rubber Duckie" song. It originated as a joke when human-computer interface designers were trying to figure out how to get more characters from the same keyboard. One suggestion was that foot pedals be added to serve as extra shift keys which would allow typists to make more changes without moving their fingers from their home keys.

Real programmers (a reference to the book *Real Men Don't Eat Quiche*) refer to aspiring teenaged programmers as *Munchkins* in memory of the little people in *The Wizard of Oz*. Depending on their behavior, such hackers might also be called *Wabbits*, from cartoon character Elmer Fudd's famous "You wascawwy wabbit!" The specific meaning of the latter term is a trouble-making hacker who programs something so that it will keep repeating itself. In contrast, a protocol that accidentally includes a bug resulting in multiple messages being sent or multiple instances of a particular abstract object being created is described as being in *Sorcerer's Apprentice mode*, a reference to the Walt Disney movie *Fantasia*.

USING COMPUTER TALK IN THE CLASSROOM

One of the advantages of looking at these literary references from the perspective of a computer person is that we see the literature with fresh eyes. Something similar can happen in the classroom when we look at other metaphors and kinds of language change brought about by computers. While English teachers know more about processes of language development than do students, many students know more computer language than do their teachers. Because of this, bringing computer language into the English classroom sets up a good teacher/student partnership with information and insights coming from both sides of the table.

The following class activities can be done as a discussion with a whole class or assigned to small groups who will do their research and then present it to their classmates. Oral presentations can be supplemented with display posters, handouts, or mini-dictionaries. A bibliography of resources is attached, but the main resource should be students' own experiences and what they can find out from interviewing other students and adults who work with computers.

This is a unit designed to provide computer whiz kids their day of glory in the English classroom. And because computers are such a new part of American culture, students can have the experience of doing original field work.

Collect Semantically Related Metaphors

Using a broad definition of metaphor to mean any computer term that is based on a similarity between what is being named and what the base word refers to in standard English, search for terms taken from specific semantic areas. Help students compare the standard English meaning to the specialized computer meaning. Just as we collected computer metaphors related to literature above, different groups of students can collect metaphors related to transportation (*driver, bus, channel, map, information highway, hard-drive crash, cruising the Internet*), food and kitchen (*menu, byte, nybble, cooked, raw, fork, filter, fold, stack*), human activities (*handshaking, bootstrapping* or *booting, memory, massage, motherboard, daughtercard, "smart"* and *"dumb" terminals, "second"* and *"third" generations*), architecture (*back door, port, window, screen, pane, desk top, trap door,* and *pipe* or *pipeline*), and precomputer kinds of writing and printing (*envelope, mail, file, address, clipboard, format, scroll,* and *bulletin board*). This latter set is a good illustration of how new inventions are described with the language of their predecessors—as when cars were called horseless carriages and vans were named after the kinds of caravans that depended on camels and oxen instead of machines.

Collect Alternate Spellings

Computer users purposely "misspell" some of their words to identify them as computer words and to keep them from being confused with similar words. For example, *byte* is spelled with a *y* because it was important to distinguish it from *bit*. The *y* spelling caught on as "computer talk" and is also seen in *nybble*. *Luser*, as a pun on *loser* and *user*, influenced the spelling of *turist* as someone who out of curiosity temporarily joins various groups; *c.f.* TV channel surfing. Have students list standard spelling alongside "computer" spelling and see if they can figure out whether the change was simply to communicate a specialized use of the word or was commercially motivated as when a company creates a trademark that it wants to protect legally.

Look at Capitalization Patterns

In the dinosaur days of computers, some machines printed only capital letters. Ever since, computer users have had a unique attitude toward upper- and lowercase letters. Bicapitalization describes the practice of inserting caps inside words as with these trademarks: *WordPerfect, NeXt, GEnie, TeX, VisiCalc, dBASE, FrameMaker,* and *CompuServe* (often spelled playfully by hackers as *Compu$erve* because this public network access provider costs so much in comparison with university and employer facilities). Students could clip product names from old catalogs and make a poster to use as part of a discussion of whether the deviant capitalization helps the names to be memorable. (Another reason for the practice is so companies can register them as original trademarks.)

Collect Acronyms

Computer hackers even have acronyms for acronyms. *TLA* stands for Three Letter Acronym while *YABA* stands for Yet Another Bloody Acronym. When new names are chosen, creators check to make sure they are "*YABA* compatible," meaning the initials can be pronounced easily and won't make a suggestive or unpleasant word. But no matter how carefully acronyms are chosen, hackers will still try to create new meanings as when they say that the true meaning of *LISP* (LISt Processing language) is "Lots of Irritating Superfluous Parentheses." In discussing acronyms, students can talk about their space-saving features as compared to their potential for confusion. What's the difference between the ones that run together in people's minds and the ones like *GIGO* (Garbage In, Garbage Out) that are becoming part of mainstream English?

Trace the Influence of Computer
Language on Mainstream Language

The name of the television news program *Hard Copy*, which suggests both "hard line" and "hard core," was undoubtedly influenced by the computer term *hard copy* for something printed on paper (i.e., "documented") compared to soft copy for something in the machine. As a comparison to e-mail and Internet, people refer to the U.S. Postal Service as *USnail, snail mail,* or *papernet*. The widespread use of computers has also increased the general use of such words as *glitch, bug* and *debug, user-friendly, protocol, input, zap,* and *programming* or *deprogramming* people or things other than computers. Students can collect headlines and news clippings for a display of such new usages. They can then compare their specialized computer meanings with their original and now their new meanings in mainstream English.

Compare Brand Names

Steve Jobs was "into" health foods, and when it came time to choose a name for the new computer he had designed for ordinary people rather than professional computer whizzes, he settled on *Apple* to stand out from other companies' high-tech names. Apple included such positive connotations as "an apple for the teacher" and "an apple a day keeps the doctor away." It also provided for a "family tree" with such later names as *Macintosh* and *Newton. Lotus* software has an equally inspired name based on the comparison of a lotus blossom opening out and the creation of a spreadsheet. And what could be more persuasive in getting customers to buy a product than the name *WordPerfect*? Another tricky bit of persuasion is that when users want to get into their *Windows* program, they have to type *WIN*.

Once students have gathered a list of product names, both for hard- and software, they can pull out specialized lists; for example, names based on metaphors, names that include unorthodox spelling or capitalization, names made from morphemes (small units of words that carry meaning), and "families" of names that are designed to show relationships between one product and another. They might divide their list into names designed to appeal to the general public as contrasted with those for computer specialists. What differences will they find? In which group will they find code numbers and letters? In which group will they find such poetic techniques as rhyme, alliteration, and allusion?

Examples of Pejorative Language Play
Used to Relieve Frustrations

Its common for people who feel frustrated or out of control to make jokes that release some of the nervousness or hostility they are feeling. For example, the computer building at Stanford is named the Margaret Jacks Hall, but students refer to it as the *Marginal Hacks Hall*. Computer hackers also refer to the *IBM 360* as the *IBM Three-Sickly*, to a Macintosh as a *Macintoy* or *Macintrash*, and to programs coming from the University of California at Berkeley as *Berzerkeley*. And frustrated users of newly released technology often lament that they are living on the *bleeding edge* (a play on *leading edge*). Chances are that students in your school have their own share of pejorative jokes related to computing—some of which will be appropriate for sharing in the English class.

NOTES

Hackers: In common usage, hacker has several different connotations. Some readers will be more familiar with the following definition of hacker: "A malicious meddler who tries to discover sensitive information by poking around." E. Raymond's *The New Hacker's Dictionary*, Second Edition (Cambridge, MA: MIT Press, 1993), written and maintained by the community of friendly hackers (as defined in the main body of this text), suggests that the malicious meddler is more properly titled a *cracker*.

Bits and Bytes: Within a computer, all numbers are represented by strings of bits (a bit is a binary digit, each bit representing either a 0 or 1). A byte is a string of exactly eight bits. The least-significant bit represents the 1s, the next bit represents 2s, and the third represents 4s. The most-significant (high-order) bit within a byte represents 128s. Compare this with our base-ten numbering system in which the least-significant digit represents 1s, the next digit represents 10s, and so on.

Telepresence: Allows a human user on earth, for example, to manipulate a mechanical arm belonging to a robot walking on the surface of the moon. Visual and sensual feedback are provided to human operators in order to portray the illusion that they are actually present on the moon.

Source and Object Codes: Modern computer software is written in high-level programming languages designed to simplify programming effort. Compilers are programs that translate the high-level programming languages to the machine language required for execution of the program in a particular environment. The high-level program written by the user is called the source code, whereas the program's machine-language translation is called the object code. Most commercial applications are supplied only in object-code form, as the object code hides many of the developer's trade secrets. However, members of the hacker subculture regularly share source codes with one another. When user-level documentation is missing or unintelligible, hackers are encouraged to refer directly to the source code to better understand the program's features and capabilities.

The Jargon File: We could not have written this article without the help of innumerable hackers who over the past 15 years have contributed definitions and examples to *The Jargon File*, most recently edited by Eric Raymond (eric@snark.thyrsus.com). *The Jargon File* can be downloaded by anonymous ftp from prep.ai.mit.edu as pub/gnu/jarg300.txt.gz. The contents of this file were recently published as *The New Hacker's*

Dictionary, Second Edition. Many of the examples presented in this paper were prompted by this resource.

SUGGESTED REFERENCE MATERIAL
FOR CLASSROOM TEACHERS

Microsoft Press Computer Dictionary, Second Edition. Redmond, WA: Microsoft Press, 1994.

Raymond, E., ed. *The New Hacker's Dictionary,* Second Edition. Cambridge, MA: MIT Press, 1993.

Spencer, D., ed. *Webster's New World Dictionary of Computer Terms,* Fourth Edition Englewood Cliffs, NJ: Prentice-Hall, Inc., 1992.

Tidrow, R. and J. Boyce. *Windows for Non-Nerds.* Carmel, IN: New Riders Publishing, 1993. [The concluding chapter is a dictionary of computer terms.]

18-Section Insert on Computer Technology, *The Wall Street Journal,* 27 June 1994. [Reprints available for $2.00 from Technology/Dow Jones and Company, Inc., 200 Burnett Road, Chicopee, MA 01020.]

≡

FOR DISCUSSION AND REVIEW

1. What important linguistic principle is demonstrated by the new terms and expressions that have developed among computer users?

2. How is communication among computer users different from normal conversation? How does this difference affect the language they devise?

3. Which literary genres are most represented in computer talk? What reasons can you give to explain these choices?

4. What is the most obvious type of word-making featured in this article? What are some other types you can identify? Give examples. (See the previous essay in this section, "Word-Making: Some Sources of New Words" by W. Nelson Francis.)

Projects for "Phonetics and Phonology, and Morphology"

Note: Since a large number of exercises are included for the readings in part 3 and because short exercises are particularly useful for these topics, we have suggested fewer long projects than usual.

1. An excellent project, if you speak another language, is to compare the significant units of sound of the two languages. For example, German does not have the sound with which the English word *judge* begins and ends. As a variation of this project, you could make a similar comparison for two different dialects of English. In either case, try to make your data as complete as possible.

2. Examine the following: "These *foser glipses* have *volbicly merfed* and *wheeple* their *preebs.*"[1] Although you do not know the meaning of any of the italicized words (How big is a "wheeple"? How does one "merf"? Are "glipses" good to eat?), you do know a great deal about them. What can you say about the form, function, and meaning of the words? On what basis?

3. Using either *The Barnhart Dictionary of New English Since 1963* or *The Second Barnhart Dictionary of New English*, choose a random sample of at least 100 words and identify their source (e.g., borrowing, derivation, compounding). Prepare a report of your findings. Does your order of importance for processes of word formation coincide with that suggested by Francis? If not, try to suggest some reasons why it doesn't.

4. Read John Algeo's "Where Do All the New Words Come From?" in the Winter 1980 issue of *American Speech*. Prepare a report summarizing his findings. You may wish to compare them with what Francis says in his article in this section.

5. Many linguists and grammarians complain that our orthographic system contains too many ambiguities and too many uncertainties with regard to our pronunciations. One famous example is the spelling of "fish" by George Bernard Shaw as "g-h-o-t-i." He uses the "gh" from the word "enou*gh*," the "o" from the word "w*o*men," and the "ti" from the word "na*ti*on." Divide the class into groups of four or five and create your own lists of the names of the people in your class. How many of the names are decipherable by others? What does this tell you or reaffirm about our spelling system? What problems might this cause?

6. Select an article from your favorite magazine or journal and bring a copy to class. Form groups, select a paragraph or two, and simplify the spelling of the words in the article. Feel free to eliminate unnec-

---

[1] This example comes from Kenneth G. Wilson, "English Grammars and the Grammar of English," which appears in the front matter of *Funk & Wagnalls Standard College Dictionary*: Text Edition (New York: Harcourt, Brace & World, 1963).

essary letters and to simplify as many consonant clusters as you wish. In order to further simplify the spelling, you may choose to substitute letters for those in the printed words and eliminate others altogether. After your "cleaning" is done, reinsert the paragraph in your article and exchange with another group. Are your classmates able to read the passage? Which sounds in our language appear to have the greatest variety of spellings? Which letter appears to represent the greatest variety of sounds? What would you propose as a revised English alphabet? What have you learned about our spelling system? As a result of this exercise, do you foresee any difficulties for foreign-language speakers trying to learn English?

7. Nilsen and Nilsen describe "computer talk" as the jargon of a subculture. Most of us are familiar with some activity, hobby, or career that has a language of its own. Some examples would be fishing, automobile maintenance or enhancement, sewing, cooking, sailing—the list is endless. Explore the vocabulary that is special to an interest of your own. Have any of the words or expressions made an impact on English usage in general? If you are a cook, for example, think of "putting something on the back burner." Share with your classmates some of the words and expressions from your field of interest.

8. Marmo Soemarmo, Professor of Linguistics at Ohio University in Athens, Ohio, has developed a collection of linguistic card games that he calls "language games." Professor Soemarmo created his language games, basing them on familiar card games, to help the nonlinguistics major become familiar with the basic building blocks of language: phonetics and phonology, and morphology. He provides more information on his language games on the web:

http://ouvaxa.cats.ohiou.edu/~soemarmo/games/menu.htm

Professor Soemarmo invites people to log on and play these games and to suggest variations as well as games of their own. You might try this as one of your classroom activities.

Selected Bibliography

Adams, V. *An Introduction to Modern English Word Formation*. London: Longman, 1973. [A very thorough analysis.]

Anderson, Stephen R. *The Organization of Phonology*. New York: Academic Press, 1974. [Technical and comprehensive.]

Aronoff, Mark. *Word Formation in Generative Grammar*. Cambridge: MIT Press, 1976. [Excellent, but not for beginners.]

Chomsky, Noam, and Morris Halle. *The Sound Pattern of English*. New York: Harper & Row, 1968. [The first major application of transformational-generative theory to phonology.]

Denes, Peter, and E. N. Pinson. *The Speech Chain*. Garden City, NY: Harper & Row, 1968. [A clear introduction to speech perception, speech production, and acoustic phonetics.]

Dyson, Alice Tanner. "Phonetic Inventories of 2- and 3-Year-Old Children." *Journal of Speech and Hearing Disorders* (February 1988): 89–93. [A further detailed study into phonological acquisition of young children.]

Halle, Morris. "Knowledge Unlearned and Untaught: What Speakers Know about the Sounds of Their Language." In *Linguistic Theory and Psychological Reality*, ed. Morris Halle, Joan Bresnan, and George A. Miller. Cambridge: MIT Press, 1978. [Very interesting; nontechnical.]

Halle, Morris, and G. N. Clements. *Problem Book in Phonology: A Workbook for Introductory Courses in Linguistics and in Modern Phonology*. Cambridge: MIT Press, 1983. [Contains an excellent introduction [pp. 2–25] and six sections with exercises based on a wide variety of languages.]

Hyman, Larry M. *Phonology: Theory and Analysis*. New York: Holt, Rinehart and Winston, 1975. [Important but difficult.]

Kenstowicz, M., and C. Kisseberth. *Generative Phonology: Description and Theory*. New York: Academic Press, 1979. [Technical but important.]

Ladefoged, Peter. *A Course in Phonetics*, 2nd ed. New York: Harcourt Brace Jovanovich, 1982. [An excellent introduction. The author writes, "This is a *course* in phonetics, not a book about phonetics."]

Matthews, P. H. *Morphology: An Introduction to the Theory of Word-Structure*. Cambridge, England: Cambridge University Press, 1974. [A comprehensive introductory textbook.]

Preisser, Debra A., B. W. Hodson, and E. P. Paden. "Developmental Phonology: 18–29 Months." *Journal of Speech and Hearing Disorders* (May 1988): 125–130. [A detailed hands-on examination of the phonological processes of children.]

Schane, S. A. *Generative Phonology*. Englewood Cliffs, NJ: Prentice-Hall, 1973. [An introduction, but technical.]

Sommerstein, A. *Modern Phonology*. Baltimore: University Park Press, 1977. [Another very good introduction.]

Sproat, Richard. *Morphology and Computation*. Cambridge: MIT Press, 1992. [A useful overview of issues in morphology, computational morphology, and linguistics.]

SYNTAX AND SEMANTICS

The introduction to Part Three discussed the fact that most linguists agree that languages are best described in terms of their basic systems or divisions. In Part Four we focus on syntax and semantics. Syntax involves the study of the largely unconscious finite set of rules that enable speakers to create and understand sentences. It also explores the relationships among the components of sentences. Although most people take it for granted, the ability of native speakers to comprehend sentences that they have never heard and to utter sentences that they have never heard or spoken is remarkable. This is possible because all levels of language are rule-governed and because human beings are genetically predisposed to learn the kinds of rules that are inherent in language. A discussion of syntax provides an excellent opportunity to reemphasize the concept of language as a rule-governed system.

Syntax is central to a description of a native speaker's knowledge of his or her language. What do native speakers know that enables them to create novel utterances and to understand sentences they have never heard? The first two selections in Part Four address this question directly. First, Roderick A. Jacobs and Peter S. Rosenbaum, in "What Do Native Speakers Know about Their Language?" point out four seemingly trivial but in fact complex and crucial skills possessed by all native speakers. Next, Frank Heny, in "Syntax: The Structure of Sentences," examines some important syntactic structures and rules, using mainly English examples, to show the kinds of structures that are found in language and how some of these might relate directly to the way in which language is learned.

In the introduction to Part Three, we defined *semantics* as "the analysis of the meaning of individual words and of such larger units as phrases and sentences." However, this definition is too simple. As George L. Dillon writes, "Most writers on semantics would agree that it is the study of meaning. This is probably the only statement about the subject that all would subscribe to, and disagreement begins with what is properly meant by *meaning*." Part of this disagreement arises because linguists and logicians tend to use the word *semantics* in different ways.

Also, although semantics is currently the focus of a great deal of interest to linguists (and a field characterized by controversy), this interest developed only within the last twenty years as linguists realized that a complete description of what native speakers know about their language must include semantics.

The third and fourth selections in Part Four deal with semantics. When native speakers attempt to pin down the exact meanings of common words and utterances, they encounter ambiguity, contradiction, and redundancy. In "Bad Birds and Better Birds: Prototype Theories," Jean Aitchison presents the principles and uses of prototype theory as a means of explaining our ability to communicate despite the imprecision of language. Drawing on such word categories as birds, vegetables, furniture, and lies, she shows how prototype theory works, "how people are able to cope with word meaning when it is so fuzzy and fluid."

In the final essay, "The Tower of Babel," contemporary linguist Steven Pinker asks a question as old as the Bible: if human beings are born to communicate with language, why are there so many languages, most so different that the speakers of one can't understand the speakers of another? It would seem that the rules of semantics must be redefined within the context of each language and its cultural setting. Beneath the surface differences among languages, however, Pinker identifies the many precise rules of what he calls "Universal Grammar." He demonstrates that the ways in which languages differ are trivial compared to the profound structural similarities they all share. The particular language each of us speaks is determined by the times and culture in which we live; at its most fundamental level, the meaning of language lives within all human beings as the innate capability to speak, hear, and understand.

15

What Do Native Speakers Know about Their Language?

Roderick A. Jacobs and Peter S. Rosenbaum

In the following excerpt from their book Readings in English Transformational Grammar, *Professors Jacobs and Rosenbaum identify four kinds of knowledge that all native speakers of a language possess about that language. These kinds of knowledge involve the ability to distinguish a grammatical utterance from an ungrammatical one, to understand utterances even though a portion or portions thereof may have been deleted, to recognize both lexical and syntactic ambiguity, and to recognize both lexical and syntactic synonymy. We take these abilities for granted; in fact, we usually do not even recognize that they exist. But attempting to explain them, to account for these abilities, raises fundamental questions. What is language? How is it learned? What is it that is learned? As the authors point out, "When we attempt to explain these skills, we are really seeking to explain an important part of what makes us human."*

The mysteries about language that will be discussed here [may] seem trivial and obvious at first sight. For example: Every normal human being is capable of distinguishing the sentences of his language from all other objects in the universe. Yet, how can this fact be explained? A sentence is a *string* of words, but not every string of words is a sentence. The following strings are English sentences:

1. the trains are most crowded during the holidays
2. aren't you thinking of a perambulator?
3. wash that car before breakfast!

Suppose the word order of these strings was reversed:

4. *holidays the during crowded most are trains the
5. *perambulator a of thinking you aren't
6. *breakfast before car that wash

Every speaker of English knows, without a moment's hesitation, that these strings are not English sentences, even though they contain English words. (An asterisk is always placed before a string which is syntactically or semantically deviant.) What is it that you know when you distinguish between strings of words which are sentences of your language and strings which are not sentences of your language? And where did you get this knowledge?

One possible answer to the latter question is that you memorized the possible sentences of your language while learning it in your infancy, much as you memorized the faces or names of classmates and friends. But this is not the way a human being learns his language. It is impossible to memorize *all* sentences possible in your language, and you frequently utter or hear sentences that do not duplicate any of your past experience. (In fact, the sentence you are reading now has probably not occurred previously in your experience.) Nonetheless, you have been able to distinguish between the grammatical strings and those strings made ungrammatical by reversal of word order. Obviously, you have not learned your language by memorizing its sentences. This, then, is one important human ability that needs to be investigated: How is a normal human being capable of deciding whether a string of words is a sentence in his language, and how is he able to do this for any of a potentially infinite number of strings he has never seen nor heard before?

But this is far from all that needs to be explained. For example, a speaker of a language can almost always tell whether a string is peculiar because of its meaning (i.e., its semantic interpretation) or because of its form (its "syntax"). In his first book on transformational grammar, Noam Chomsky pointed out that the following string is grammatical[1]:

*colorless green ideas sleep furiously.

However, it is nonsensical. It could be described as well-formed grammatically but ill-formed semantically.

Finally, the meaning of a string may be quite clear, but the string may be ungrammatical:

*John and I jumps over wall and we shoots he

*you don't can putting your feet on the table in here

*is reading your father this book.

Thus we are often able to understand foreigners and others who do not correctly use the rules of English.

Furthermore, what is left unsaid may also be very important in a normal sentence of English. You would not be able to explain the full meaning of the following ungrammatical string:

*so was Norbert Wiener

but you would understand and be able to explain this string if it appeared as part of a grammatical string:

Yehudi Menuhin was a child prodigy and so was Norbert Wiener.

You understand the last four words to mean that Norbert Wiener was

---

[1] Noam Chomsky, *Syntactic Structures* (Gravenhage: Mouton, 1957), 15.

a child prodigy, although this is not stated in so many words. A speaker of a particular human language can often understand the full meaning of a sentence in his language without explicit statements in the words of the sentence. . . . Compare the following sentences:

1. Dr. Johnson asked someone to behave himself.
2. Dr. Johnson promised someone to behave himself.

When you read the first of these superficially similar sentences, you understood the person who was to behave to be "someone." But when you read the second sentence, you understood the person who was to behave to be "Dr. Johnson." In these two sentences, the items which you understood to refer to the person who was to behave were in different positions, although the sentences were identical on the surface except for one word. What is it that you know about English that enables you to understand the sentences correctly? How is it that you understand

finding the revolver in that drawer worried us

as meaning that *we* are the ones who found the revolver in that drawer? Your knowledge of your language includes the ability to reconstruct the full meaning of a sentence from a string of words which may not contain all the words necessary for an accurate interpretation if you were, say, a Thai learning English.

Frequently, a native speaker of English will understand a sentence as having more than one meaning, as being *ambiguous*. Sometimes just one word is ambiguous, as the word "bank" in

the police station was right by the bank.

Here "bank" could be either the bank where money may be deposited or the bank of a river. Sometimes, however, the ambiguity has to do with the grammatical structure of the sentence:

the lamb is too hot to eat.

This sentence means either that the lamb is so hot that it cannot eat anything or that the lamb is so hot that no one can eat it. Can you see the ambiguity in the following sentence?

visiting relatives can be a nuisance.

Sentences may be multiply ambiguous. Six possible interpretations of the following sentence are given below:
The seniors were told to stop demonstrating on campus.

1. The seniors were demonstrating on campus and were asked to desist.
2. The seniors were demonstrating and were asked, on campus, to desist.
3. The seniors were demonstrating and were asked to desist on campus (although they could demonstrate elsewhere).

4. People were demonstrating on campus, and seniors were asked to stop them.
5. People were demonstrating and seniors were asked, on campus, to stop them.
6. People were demonstrating and seniors were asked to stop them from doing this on the campus (although they could do it elsewhere).

This ability that you have to extract more than one meaning from some sentences of your language is matched by one other skill. You can usually tell when two or more sentences have the same meaning—when they are *synonymous*. Sometimes this synonymy arises from the existence of more than one word for a meaning, as in the joke translation of "Twinkle, twinkle, little star," which begins:

Scintillate, scintillate, diminutive asteroid,
How I speculate as to your identity.

Frequently the synonymy is a result of the way the sentences are structured, as demonstrated by the following sentences:

1. six out of seven salesmen agree that walruses have buck teeth.
2. that walruses have buck teeth is agreed by six out of seven salesmen.
3. it is agreed by six out of seven salesmen that walruses have buck teeth.

You have never seen nor heard these sentences before; yet you need little or no conscious thought to decide that all three of them have a common meaning—a meaning distinct from that of

six out of seven walruses believe that salesmen have buck teeth.

The simplest type of synonymy is word synonymy. As you saw in the alternative version of "Twinkle, twinkle, little star," different words may have the same meaning, though sometimes some alternatives may carry slightly differing connotations. Word synonymy is obviously responsible for the synonymy of the following pair of sentences:

oculists are expected to be well trained.
eye doctors are expected to be well trained.

Anyone who speaks English as his native language understands these sentences to be synonymous because he has memorized the meanings of "oculist" and "eye doctor." Since these meanings are the same, he knows that the otherwise identical sentences must have the same meaning.

It is not as simple, however, to explain the native speaker's ability to detect synonymy in such sentences as:

1. the chicken crossed the expressway.
   the expressway was crossed by the chicken.

2. it is believed that the framers of the Constitution met in Philadelphia.

   the framers of the Constitution are believed to have met in Philadelphia.

3. economists claim that a recession is not inevitable, and economists are not noted for optimism.

   economists, who are not noted for optimism, claim that a recession is not inevitable.

SUMMARY

When you use skills such as the four discussed in this article:

1. the ability to distinguish between the grammatical and ungrammatical strings of a potentially infinite set of utterances,
2. the ability to interpret certain grammatical strings even though elements of the interpretation may not be physically present in the string,
3. the ability to perceive ambiguity in a grammatical string,
4. the ability to perceive when two or more strings are synonymous,

you are making use of a kind of knowledge that can best be described as knowledge of the grammar of your language. This provides you with the grammatical information you need to understand and produce (or generate) the sentences of English. Although these four skills seem too obvious to bother with, they have never been satisfactorily explained. . . .

Language is a specifically human characteristic. Descartes noted in Part V of his *Discourse on Method*:

> It is a very remarkable fact that there are none so depraved and stupid, without even excepting idiots, that they cannot arrange different words together forming of them a statement by which they make known their thoughts; while, on the other hand, there is no other animal, however perfect and fortunately circumstanced it may be, which can do the same.[2]

The particular skills that human beings use when they speak and understand their own language are quite remarkable, especially when you realize that a language is basically an infinite set of sentences.

In a very real sense, then, the study of what a grammar must be like if it is to account for the sentences of our language is more than the study of the structure of English sentences and the processes which operate on these structures. The various linguistic skills reflect aspects of the intellectual abilities we possess by virtue of being human. When we attempt to explain these skills, we are really seeking to explain an important part of what makes us human.

---

[2] Quoted in Noam Chomsky, *Cartesian Linguistics* (New York: Harper & Row, 1966), 4.

===

FOR DISCUSSION AND REVIEW

1. Discuss the difference in the relationship between the italicized words in *a*, those in *b*, and those in *c* with respect to the phrase "to paint in Paris."

   a. *Whistler* persuaded *his mother* to paint in Paris.
   b. *Whistler* promised *his mother* to paint in Paris.
   c. *Whistler* left *his mother* to paint in Paris.

   Explain the ambiguity of c.

2. Explain the ambiguity of the following sentences:

   a. Eating apples can be enjoyable.
   b. She told me to leave at five o'clock.
   c. Could this be the invisible man's hair tonic?
   d. The old matron fed her dog biscuits.
   e. Every citizen may vote.

3. Describe the difference in the relationship of "Eberhart" to "please" in *a* and *b*:

   a. Eberhart is eager to please.
   b. Eberhart is easy to please.

4. Certain material has been deleted from the following sentences. Indicate the deleted material.

   a. She adopted forty-two cats simply because she wanted to.
   b. John likes Mary, Bill, and Sally.
   c. Oaks are taller than maples.
   d. Discovering the truth pleases scientists.
   e. Ladies wearing high heels are not welcome on tennis courts.

5. The following pairs of sentences are synonymous, but in a different way. Can you describe and explain the differences?

   a. My attorney specializes in copyright law.
      My lawyer specializes in copyright law.
   b. A proposal was made that bothered me.
      A proposal that bothered me was made.

16

Syntax: The Structure of Sentences

Frank Heny

A sentence is not just a string of words; it is a string of words in a certain order, a string that has structure. Thus, cat dog the the chased *is not a sentence; it is just a list of English words. But* the dog chased the cat *is a sentence (as is* the cat chased the dog*). A sentence, then, is more than the sum of its parts (i.e., its words); it is words ordered in a particular way, in this case according to the rules of English syntax. But how did we learn these rules, rules of which, to a large extent, we are unaware?*

In the following article, Professor Frank Heny suggests an answer to this question, and then examines some of the basic syntactic rules of English that we all use every day. No single article can possibly treat English syntax in depth. But by drawing examples from two kinds of English questions and from several other familiar constructions, Professor Heny is able to illustrate some fundamental principles of syntax and to demonstrate that children come to language learning with an inborn mechanism that "severely limit[s] what the language learner needs to take into account," one of the crucial concepts in contemporary linguistic theory.

LEARNING LANGUAGE
IS LEARNING STRUCTURE

It is easy to think of your language as a vast collection of words—like *easy* and *think* and *language* and *vast*. But as soon as you try to take this idea seriously, you realize that it can't be the whole truth. String together the words of the previous sentence in another order:

1. you to that as take idea this try realize truth the be soon it but can't whole seriously you as

The obvious difference between (1) and *But as soon as you try to take this idea seriously, you realize that it can't be the whole truth* is the order of the words; and it is almost equally obvious that what happens when you change the order is that you change how the words themselves interact with each other. Certain words now form coherent groups, like *the whole truth* or *as soon as you try to take this idea seriously*. Saying or writing the words in a particular order structures them into groups: they stop being just isolated words and turn into real language.

English is not just a huge dictionary. Learning it is not simply committing a vast list of words to memory. This may be more obvious if you think about a foreign language. To be able to speak German or French you must do much more than just learn the sounds and meanings of a whole lot of words! Of course you have to know vocabulary, but you could learn dozens of German words from a dictionary every day for the rest of your life and still never approach being able to speak the language.

Despite this fact, that language is so much more than just a huge store of isolated words, what you remember of learning your own native language is likely to be limited to memories of just that—the learning of new words. Think back as far as you can, and see if you can recall starting to learn English. You may well remember occasions in which you learned what a new word meant—perhaps even as far back as when you were two years old. (Indeed, it is probably still an everyday occurrence to learn the meaning of a new word.) But you will not remember a thing about learning how to form the structures those words are set in, the structures that make your language what it is. No native speaker of English remembers learning how to make different kinds of sentences (questions, commands, passive sentences and so on)—or even how to form phrases like *the whole truth*. To a typical native speaker of English, the sentence structure, the way phrases are built up and joined together, seems often so natural that it is hard to conceive of putting words together in any other way—almost as if the structure of the language itself had never had to be learned.

It will take only a moment to verify this. There are kinds of sentences that we use every day yet have never thought about consciously. In the previous paragraph, the expression "passive sentences" appears. Here is a group of English sentences. Try to pick out all the passive ones and jot down the numbers. (Don't worry if you can't do this; just read on after you have tried.)

2. a. I watched the prisoner from the tower.
   b. The tower was where I watched the prisoner from.
   c. The prisoner was being watched from the tower.
   d. I was watching the prisoner.
   e. Who was watching the prisoner?
   f. Who was being watched from the tower?

Unless you happen to have studied traditional grammar, or some linguistics, it is not likely that you were comfortable with this task. The sentences are perfectly simple. You use sentences similar in form to all of them every day. Examples (c) and (f) in fact are passive—but you certainly didn't need to know that in order to use them or others like them.

The purpose of showing you the examples above was not to test your knowledge of traditional grammar. In fact, we assumed that the expression "passive sentence" might be a little unfamiliar, and wanted to show that even if you had no idea which of the examples were passives you would find the sentences perfectly ordinary: you would have absolutely no difficulty using and understanding such structures. If you happened to be familiar with the term "passive" you would not normally be at all conscious of the construction itself, even when you used it, and you would not be in any way helped in your use of passive sentences by being able to identify them. Furthermore, whether or not you picked out (c) and (f), many readers would have failed to do so—yet would not have been less able than you to use and understand passives. Conscious knowledge about the passive construction seems unrelated to the native speaker's ability to deal with passive sentences.

Do not confuse learning the basic structure of your language (which had taken place before you were five years old) with the attempts of teachers, for example, to get you to say "It is I" instead of "It's me" or to distinguish nouns from adjectives. That kind of learning *about* language was a collection of facts or opinions about your language and how it is used. Compared to your original achievement in learning the language itself, this added knowledge was really quite insignificant. Your high school and college English teachers may have taught you a good deal about how to use the language effectively. In particular, they may well have contributed significantly to your ability to write effectively. Written language is an added, in part artificial, skill built upon the oral language that you developed for yourself. Writing you had to learn consciously, just as you have had to learn math or music. In contrast, you had somehow mastered, quite unconsciously, and without any formal teaching, before you first went to grade school, a system so complex that linguists have still not figured out how it works—your native language itself. How did you do it?

At the present time no one really knows for sure. However, some very interesting ideas are now being explored, which seem to come rather close to the truth. It is likely that you developed the structures of your native language so easily because there was actually very little you had to *learn*. Even learning the words was not a matter of learning thousands of quite arbitrary items piece by piece. You learned the words as parts of structures and the structures you did not really have to learn at all. For they were already there before you learned the language—much as the eye is there, with all the appropriate structure, waiting within the womb for the light and the sights it will see.

The underlying patterns of language, any language, were waiting within you in some sense, and all you had to do was select from those internally stored structures the ones into which you could fit the sounds and words of the language you heard around you. By the time you were a year or so old, surrounded by English, the sounds of that language had already begun to form themselves into patterns in your mind—not as a result of your own individual attempts to "discover" the structure of English (surely too much for any toddler) but rather through a process in which those sounds began to clothe some of the preexisting structures, the ones matching English. From this perspective, your learning English was no miracle or mysterious feat of super intelligence! Indeed it would have been a miracle if you, as an ordinary, normal human being had not, under normal circumstances, and surrounded by English, become a fluent English speaker.

To repeat: it was not so much that you *learned* your language as that it simply *developed*, fleshing out certain of a number of possible language structures which were in effect already waiting to develop. The language around you merely determined the particular choices among those structures that had to be made. Had you grown up exposed instead to French or Navajo or Japanese, you would have been forced by the patterns made by the sounds and words to select a different set of options. To see what this idea amounts to we need to understand a little more about what kinds of systems languages are. Ideally, this would mean looking at a number of languages. Because that would take too long, this account will be based almost entirely on English. However, it will be aimed at demonstrating not what *English* is like, but what *language* is like.

STRUCTURE IS MORE THAN JUST WORD ORDER

Let us first be quite clear that sentences are not just strings of words in a particular order, but really do have a complex internal structure. In pointing out the rather obvious fact that a sentence is not just a string of words put together in any old order, we noted that when the words are in a particular order they acquire a certain structure—and in doing so fit together to make up a sentence. This structure is more than just order, for a single string of words strung together in just one order can have two quite different meanings. These two distinct meanings correspond to two sentences. An example follows; make sure that you see that (3) is really two quite distinct sentences, with two distinct meanings, before you go further. The bracketing in (a) and (b) should help you to distinguish these meanings clearly.

3. I watched the prisoner from the tower.
    a. I watched [the prisoner from the tower].
    b. I watched [the prisoner] [from the tower].

The first way of interpreting this string treats [*the prisoner from the tower*] as a unit: it is the [prisoner from the tower] who is seen by the speaker. This same group of words, [*the prisoner from the tower*], functions as a single unit, a *constituent*, in other, similar sentences. In such sentences, the words *the prisoner from the tower* act together to characterize someone as a prisoner from some tower:

4. a. [The prisoner from the tower] was what I saw.
    b. [The prisoner from the tower] was being watched carefully.
    c. [The prisoner from the tower], I watched carefully.

In each of these examples, the phrase [*the prisoner from the tower*] could be replaced by other constituents such as [*the prisoner from Siberia*], [*a visitor from Mars*], or [*three men in dark glasses*]. Each of these, too, would be acting as a single unit in such sentences. Under this first interpretation, the sentence has nothing at all to say about where the watcher was, but does imply something about the prisoner.

The other interpretation of (3), on the other hand, represented by (3b), does have something to say about where the watcher was, and has nothing to say about the prisoner. The words *from the tower* are not applied to *the prisoner* at all. The two phrases act quite independently, as separate units. This is suggested by the bracketing in (3b). This time, *from the tower* is much more closely associated with the verb *watched*, or with the pronoun *I* than with *the prisoner*. The sentence is not about a prisoner from a tower at all, but reports that the speaker *watched from the tower*. Given this fact, it is not surprising that (3b) is very similar in meaning to another sentence in which the phrase *from the tower* occurs right at the beginning, next to *I*:

5. [From the tower], I watched [the prisoner].

Constructed out of the same English words as (3), this string can be understood only as having a structure in which *the prisoner* and *from the tower* are separate, unrelated constituents. This is also the case in the following rather closely related sentence:

6. [The prisoner], I watched [from the tower].

This last example may seem a little stilted, but there are occasions when most of us use such forms. It is possible that you could more readily use something like: *It was the prisoner that I watched from the tower* or *As for the prisoner, I watched him from the tower* or perhaps even a passive: *The prisoner was watched from the tower by me—and my friend*. (That extra bit added on—*and my friend*—does not change the structure of the sentence and has been added just to help make the sentence sound more natural.) In all these cases, the phrase [*the prisoner*] is separated from [*from the tower*], and the two are quite independent of each other in meaning. Contrast the unambiguous interpretation of (5) and (6), where *from the tower* is not linked to *the prisoner* in any way, with the equally unambiguous interpretation of all the sentences of (4)— where the whole phrase [*the prisoner from the tower*] was always interpreted as a single constituent, i.e., where each sentence is about a prisoner from some tower.

In the examples of (4) the word order somehow forces us to interpret the words *the prisoner* and *from the tower* together as a single constituent whereas in (5) and (6) the word order splits the two parts of this string and they must be interpreted as two distinct, unrelated constituents. In contrast, the order of words in (3) permits either interpretation depending on how we take the words to be structured: as a single constituent or as two. The word order does not force us to choose, as it does in (4) or (5). In a particular instance, when we hear, or utter, a string of words like (3), we determine (generally quite unconsciously) which structure to assign to it and hence which sentence we will regard it as representing, (3a) or (3b). Thus there are two structures associated with that one order of words: word order sometimes forces words to be structured in a particular way, but it doesn't always do so. Structure and word order are not the same thing.

WAYS OF MARKING OUT PHRASES

All languages are built up from phrases; the phrases are small groups of words interacting with each other in various ways to produce sentences. In English, the order of the words limits the ways in which words can interact to form phrases, though as we saw in the case of (3), word order does not determine the phrase structure completely.

In many languages word order plays little role; in Warlpiri, for example, a language spoken in Australia, the words from a single phrase may be scattered around in a sentence. Thus in Warlpiri it is almost (but not quite!) as if one could say *The from watched I prisoner tower the* and mean (3a). Here is an actual Warlpiri sentence:

7.	Wawirri	yalumpu	kapi-rna	panti-rni
	kangaroo	*that*	*spear*	*NONPAST*

I will spear that kangaroo.

This sentence means roughly *I will spear that kangaroo*. There is no obvious word meaning *I*, but the meaning is implied. We are not interested in this aspect of (7), but in the order of the words that *do* appear in the sentence. First, let us focus on the words meaning *that kangaroo*. In (7), those two words are next to each other, as in English, but in the order *kangaroo that*. Thus far, Warlpiri might seem to require a different word order from English. Such an impression is consistent with the fact that the verb meaning *to spear* comes near the end of the sentence, whereas in English it would come before the phrase *the kangaroo*. So in English we would have *spear that kangaroo*, while in (7) we have the equivalent Warlpiri words in the order *kangaroo that spear*—with about the same meaning. There are many languages that differ from English in that the order of the words in the various phrases is not the same as the English order.

But Warlpiri is more radically different. The words of (7) (like those of other Warlpiri sentences) can be moved around in all sorts of ways without changing the essential meaning. Thus, the following means the same as (7):

8.	Wawirri	kapi-rna	panti-rni	yalumpu
	kangaroo	*spear*	*NONPAST*	*that*

I will spear that kangaroo.

This example contains just the same words as (7), but in a totally different order. Most striking is the fact that the word meaning *that* comes right at the end of the sentence, while the word meaning *kangaroo* is at the beginning—yet the two words are interpreted in such a way that together they form a phrase meaning the same as the English *that kangaroo*. Of course, a language like Warlpiri obviously must have some way of indicating which of the words of a sentence go together; Warlpiri speakers don't know by magic that in this example *wawirri* and *yalumpu* belong together! We cannot describe here how this is achieved because to do so would mean discussing numerous unfamiliar Warlpiri sentences.

Which words go in which phrases is by no means always signaled by word order. In Warlpiri, for example, as suggested by our examples, the order of the words is practically irrelevant. Other languages vary; the word order in French, like that of English, is quite rigidly fixed and serves to group the words into phrases and the phrases into sentences. Latin was quite free, and other devices signaled which words were grouped into phrases or where the phrases belonged in a sentence. Finnish, Russian, and German fall somewhere in between, with some freedom in word order, and a number of devices (patterns of agreement and case marking, for example) that show what belongs with what and where everything fits into a sentence. Still, Warlpiri sentences, and the sentences of all the other languages that we know about, are constructed out of phrases, and for the most part phrases are much the same as English ones, however they are marked.

A child hearing English or Warlpiri, or any other language, will therefore not need to "figure out" that the babble of noise around it consists of phrases. As far as we can tell today (though our knowledge about such matters is still rather fragmentary), the human infant automatically assumes that any noise it interprets as language consists of words grouped, by one of a small number of devices, into meaningful phrases and hence into sentences. Thus, the child has only to discover whether word order or one of those other methods (such as agreement patterns like those you may have met in Latin or German) signals how words group together into phrases.

There is much that we do not know for sure yet about how a child develops a knowledge of syntax. For example, we do not know just what it is that signals that word order is what matters in English, but that some other option must be relevant when Warlpiri is the language to be learned. One possibility is that certain options are, as it were, "favored" or "unmarked," which is to say that unless a child encounters specific indicators to the contrary, it automatically selects the "unmarked" option whenever there is a choice.

Assume for the sake of argument that word order is the "unmarked" way of grouping words into phrases. A child (no matter what language it will eventually acquire) assumes, until that assumption won't work on the language it hears, that it is hearing words grouped together in some fixed order. The child will expect to find words recurring in fixed, ordered patterns, with adjectives occurring consistently either before or after the nouns they go with and so on.

This expectation is met in the case of English. When the word *that* occurs as part of a phrase built up around the word *kangaroo*, as in *that kangaroo*, they have to appear together. In fact, *that* must appear before *kangaroo*. We can't even say *I want kangaroo that* and still be talking English. (An asterisk before a string of words indicates that *that* string is not a proper sentence in the language; we place it before *I want kangaroo that* to indicate that that string is not an English sentence.) So a child growing up hearing English merely needs to discover *which* order works for English. A child growing up hearing Warlpiri, on the other hand, will need to do more "figuring out" to discover how the phrases in that language are grouped together. (In regard to other aspects of language structure, it will be Warlpiri and not English that follows "unmarked" patterns.)

EXERCISE 1

1. Imagine you are a child. You hear some of the following words grouped together to form English phrases like *several monkeys* or *some gold*:

   > books several yellow those that monkeys gold some inadequate little

   Try to form as many phrases as possible using various selections from these words (not all of them can occur together) and then try to give a general account of how the phrases are formed.
   To do this you will need to:

   a. Decide what orders are possible.
   b. Decide which words can occur at the same point in structure (for example, where *gold* can occur, *yellow* can generally occur as well). You will thus be grouping the words into small classes that act alike.
   c. Make up names for the word classes. If you have studied traditional grammar, it may be natural to call *little* and *gold* "adjectives," but what you call the classes matters little. You just need some way to refer to them. List the words that fall into each class.
   d. Add several words to each of the word classes you have identified. Make sure that your examples act like the original members of the class.
   e. Make up general rules for forming phrases that are built up out of the word classes you have named. Which words come before which other words? Are some word classes free to appear in alternative positions?

2. While continuing to deal only with phrases that seem to you to be

very similar to those you have been dealing with, like *several monkeys*, add more and more *classes of words*, and decide what order they occur in. Is the order ever free? That is, can English words ever occur in alternative orders while still (as far as you can tell) occurring within these phrases? (Hint: think of strings of adjectives, like *old*, *sick*, or *tired*.) Can you find words that do not ever occur within phrases of the sort you are dealing with? For example, does the word *unfortunately* ever occur as part of one of these phrases? Try to explain precisely what you mean if you claim that it (or some other word) cannot occur within these phrases.

3. If you know another language that seems to have fixed word order, try to find instances where this is (a) the same as in English for some given pair of word classes (e.g., adjectives and nouns), and (b) where it is different.

SOME SIMPLE PHRASES: NP AND PP

So far we have seen that a string of words, like *the prisoner from the tower*, may act as a single phrase or may be two independent phrases, *the prisoner* and *from the tower*, each a constituent adding its own meaning to the sentence—as in (3b). We have seen that English words, when occurring together in a sentence, are interpreted not just as *strings* of words, but as *structures*, i.e., phrases built up out of those words. The order of the words may determine completely how they group into phrases, as in (4), (5), and (6), or it may not, as in (3). It is the phrases rather than the words as such that form constituents of sentences: (3a) and (3b) contain the same words but different phrases—as suggested by the bracketing in those examples—and their distinct meanings. Phrases like [*the prisoner*], [*from the tower*], and [*the prisoner from the tower*] interact as units with the verb *watch* in a sentence like (3) to yield a meaningful sentence. Individual words like *from* or *the* or *prisoner* do not. Thus *the* was not watched, nor was *prisoner*, nor was the watching *from*. Rather it was [the prisoner] or [the prisoner from the tower] who was watched, and if we know anything about where the watching took place from, then we know that it was [from the tower].

We have seen that at the level of the sentence, it is not words but phrases that are significant, and have also seen how certain English phrases require that the words making them up occur in a fixed order. We have begun to build up a picture of how certain kinds of (so far undefined) phrases consist of various classes of words in certain specific orders. Only when those words occur together in a permitted order can they be grouped together to form a phrase. Now it is time to consider the structure of these phrases themselves, generalizing as precisely as possible about how they are constructed. In other words, we need to determine what may occur in such phrases. They can be very complex—or very short and simple. We could replace *the prisoner* in (5) with phrases of increasing complexity, without altering the essential structure of the sentence as a whole:

9. a. From the tower, I watched [*the prisoner with bare feet*].
    b. From the tower, I watched [*the prisoner in the yard with bare feet*].
    c. From the tower, I watched [*the prisoner in the yard with bare feet who was trying to run away*].

But we could also replace these complex phrases with just a single word:

9. d. From the tower, I watched [*John*].

A phrase does not have to be long, and in (9d) it consists of just that one word, *John*. In each example of (9), the phrase in square brackets refers to the person who is said to be being watched; thus the phrase in question, however long or short it may be, plays the same role in the meaning of the sentence as a whole. In (9c), for example, the prisoner is identified by a long and complex description: *The prisoner in the yard with bare feet who was trying to run away*. The length and complexity of this phrase in no way modifies the role of the phrase in the sentence, which is precisely the same as that of *John* in (9d); it identifies the object being watched.

The phrases of (9), despite their very different levels of complexity, are built up in essentially just one way. Each, no matter how complex (or simple), is constructed around a noun: *prisoner* in the first three, and *John* in the last. There are other nouns in these phrases, such as *yard* and *tower*. But these are just helping the main noun to build up the description, to identify precisely which thing or group of things the phrase refers to. We may call the phrase a noun phrase (NP). It is a phrase built up around a noun, the head noun of that phrase, which most directly identifies the kind of thing to which the phrase refers.

The word *John* is a noun that can act alone as a noun phrase. Most nouns can't. So we can't say **I was watching prisoner*; we have to say *I was watching* the *prisoner*. The noun *prisoner*, when it is in the singular, requires a determiner like *the* or *a*, though this is not always essential when the noun is plural, as in a sentence like *I was watching [prisoners] in the yard*. When *John* is used as the name of someone it does not generally even permit a determiner, and if we said *From the tower I was watching the john* we would probably want to spell the word *john* with a small letter—and mean something quite different from (9d)! Nouns differ in all sorts of ways regarding what they require or permit with them in their phrases; they are alike in that they allow an NP to be built around them, serving as its head.

Not every string of words containing a noun can act as an NP. In English (and this should now come as no surprise), the order of the words is significant. Whereas *the prisoner* is a perfectly fine NP, *prisoner the* is not. Nor is *from the tower the prisoner*. Hence a string like *from the tower the prisoner was watched carefully* can only be interpreted as a statement about how a prisoner, not further identified, was *watched from the tower.* Although right next to *the prisoner* and some distance away from the verb *watched,* the string *from the tower* goes unambiguously with *watched* and never with the NP *the prisoner.* There are many restrictions on what can form a noun phrase. Some are general restrictions; others, as we saw in the previous paragraph, depend on the special properties of the head noun.

Some strings simply cannot be rearranged in any way to form a single noun phrase. For example, there is no way at all to rearrange the words in the string **the suddenly prisoner* and end up with a single, well-formed NP. Similarly with strings like **the run prisoner,* or **that the prisoner three.* Noun phrases, like all the parts of a sentence, have a very precise syntax: they are constructed according to exact formulas. Learning the language may consist in part of learning these, though it seems likely that many regular patterns in NPs do not have to be learned, since they derive from principles that determine the very process of language learning in children. (One of the troublesome aspects of learning a language later in life is that we seem to have to learn far more of those word order rules than a young child does—something may be "blocking" our ability to make use of whatever linguistic principles are available to a young child.) How much of the syntax of noun phrases a child has to learn we do not yet know. If, as we have suggested may be the case, the "unmarked" way of grouping words into phrases is to have them occur in some fixed order, then all that an English-speaking child has to determine is the specific order in which the noun, adjectives, and so on have to be placed in the NP.

NPs do not constitute the only phrase-level building blocks of language. There are other phrases, for example, those like *from the tower.* Although not themselves noun phrases, these nevertheless contain noun phrases (*the tower* in this instance). In addition, they contain prepositions like *from.* Prepositions themselves vary greatly in behavior, just as nouns do. But just as the phrases built up around nouns have a great deal in common with each other, both from the point of view of what can occur inside them and from the point of view of where they can act in a sentence, so prepositional phrases (PPs), built up around prepositions, have a good deal in common. We will not deal in any detail with the syntax of prepositional phrases. We turn instead to the unit within which PPs and NPs have to occur—as do all other phrases and apparently isolated words that can occur in English, like *swiftly, perhaps,* or *as big as Peter.* This larger unit, which seems to be central in (virtually?) all languages, is the sentence.

BASIC ENGLISH SENTENCE PATTERNS

Phrases like NPs and PPs are very important constituents: they contribute a great deal to the structure of language. However, they do so only in interaction with verbs. Verbs, and the phrases built up around them, are what really determine the essentials of sentence structure. And ultimately a language consists of sentences rather than either isolated words or even just independent phrases. Sentences consist of phrases grouped together in certain specific ways, and these phrases consist of words grouped together in specific ways. It is sentence structure that we have to learn, over and above vocabulary, when we learn a foreign language. The syntax of our native language, English for most readers of this selection, is never consciously learned, and is often quite difficult for people to think about consciously. We are now attempting to do just that—to understand how sentences are constructed in language, using English as an example.

Generally it seems that a language will have one or two "normal" or "unmarked" sentence patterns, which are embodied in many of the commonest, most ordinary sentences. The verbs of the language are at the center of this structure, each verb occurring in some variant of the basic pattern. Here are some very simple examples of the English unmarked pattern:

10. a. [The cat] <u>slept</u>.
    b. [My friend] <u>likes</u> this puzzle.
    c. [The wanderer] <u>tramped</u> down the road.
    d. [The cat] <u>put</u> the mouse on the mat.

Each sentence in (10) contains a verb, which is underlined, and a phrase preceding it, the subject of the sentence, which is an NP (i.e., a noun phrase). The subjects are enclosed in square brackets.

Although every sentence in (10), and indeed every simple, "normal" English sentence, contains a verb preceded by a subject, there is a good deal of variation in what can *follow* the verb. Because of differences in the properties of the verbs, each sentence in (10) is forced to differ a little in structure from all the others—and these differences always concern what may, must, or must not occur to the right of that verb. So, for example, (10a) cannot incorporate the phrase *this puzzle* after the verb.

11. *The cat slept this puzzle.

The asterisk is again used to indicate that the string *The cat slept this puzzle* is not a well-formed English sentence. The verb *sleep* differs from *like*; it does not permit the phrase *this puzzle* to appear to its right. In fact, it will not permit any other noun phrase to appear there.

Conversely, the verb *like* cannot appear *without* an NP after it, as suggested by the ungrammaticality of the following:

12. *My friend likes.

What can, must, or must not appear to the right of the verb depends directly on that verb. After *sleep*, no phrase like *this puzzle*, no NP, may appear at all, whereas after *like*, an NP must appear.

Those two verbs, *sleep* and *like*, represent the simplest cases. The first will not permit an NP to its right, while the second requires one. There is a name for verbs like *sleep*; they are called intransitive. Verbs like *like* are called transitive. A transitive verb is one that requires an NP directly to its right; an intransitive verb will not permit a plain NP in that position. An NP directly to the right of a verb is called a direct object. Thus, while transitive verbs require a direct object, intransitive verbs do not permit one.

These two classes of verbs are the most basic, but there are many variations in the way English verbs require or permit the presence or absence of NPs and PPs to their right. For example, *put* requires both an NP and a PP. This is shown by the ungrammaticality of both (13a) and (13b). (Compare these two with the grammatical [10d].)

13. a. *The cat *put* the mouse.
    b. *The cat *put* on the mat.

Likewise, the verb *tramp* seems very strange when used without a PP.

14. *The wanderer tramped.

Tramp at least arguably requires a PP to its right. [This does not mean that we call *tramp* intransitive, for that term is confined to verbs requiring a direct object, i.e., requiring an NP and not a PP to the right.]

In general, then, a verb is often closely associated with certain phrases that may or must appear to its right; these phrases, which include noun phrases and PPs, are called its complements.

Verbs that never permit any kind of complement at all are rare, and so are verbs which, like *put*, require more than one phrase to occur in their complement structure. Many verbs seem to *prefer* rather than absolutely *require* certain complements. For example, both of the following are perfectly acceptable:

15. a. Bob Dylan sings.
    b. Bob Dylan sings his own compositions.

The first of these examples suggests that *sings* is intransitive; the second that it is transitive—i.e., requires a direct object. Thus, the meaning of the verb *sing* appears to be such that the verb can permit but does not absolutely require an NP in its complement.

When we say that some phrase is a complement of a verb we are not concerned merely with whether it is absolutely required or excluded by that verb, but with whether the phrase in question goes with the verb in such a way that the meaning of the phrase is actually part of the meaning of the verb. When material to the right of the verb is not part of its complement at all, it is not required and, more significantly, does not interact directly with the meaning of the verb so as to form a part of that meaning. Take a sentence like the following:

16. Jane watched your father on the Paris metro.

What are the complements of *watch*? There are at least two quite distinct constituents after the verb. Each can "move around" independently, much as *the prisoner* and *from the tower* could in (3):

17. a. [On the Paris metro], Jane watched your father.
    b. [Your father] Jane watched on the Paris metro.

Of the two phrases *on the Paris metro* and *your father*, one seems to be part of the complement of *watched*, the other does not. Before we say which is which it would be a good thing to think about the meaning of sentence (16). Which of the two phrases interacts most closely with the verb, building up the meaning of *watched*? That will be the one that is its complement.

The answer is the NP *your father* rather than the PP *on the Paris metro*. The latter adds more detail about where the act of seeing occurred, but it is the *seeing of your father* which is the act of seeing. The PP *on the Paris metro*, a *locative adjunct*, adds information about where the seeing took place, its "location"; the NP *your father* fleshes out the meaning of the verb *watched*: the seeing is a seeing of your father.

This account might be confusing if not further supplemented. For there are all manner of adverbs, among them *quickly* and *carefully*, as well as PPs that can act like adverbs, which seem to be much more closely related to verbs than a locative phrase like *on the Paris metro*:

18. a. Jane watched *carefully*.
    b. Jim sang *in a crazy way*.
    c. Jack ate *noisily*.

These expressions are clearly neither direct objects nor locatives. In fact, they can occur with both:

19. a. Jane watched [NP your father] *carefully* [PP on the Paris metro].
    b. Jim sang [NP the ditty] *in a crazy way* [PP in the bar].
    c. Jack ate [NP the sausage] *noisily* [PP behind my back].

They add to the meaning of the sentence something about the manner in which the watching, singing, or eating was performed (and are often in fact called manner adverbials).

Why are such adverbials not part of the complement of the verb? To put the question another way, how does *eating a sausage* differ (structurally) from *eating noisily*? Consider the sausage. It is part of *eating*—in fact, it is consumed in the process. Nothing happens to "noisily." There is no "noisily" to take part in the eating process; only Jack and the sausages are involved in that. At least in the clear cases, it should be possible to see that the complements of a verb refer to things that participate in the verbal activity. They are the phrases (if any) that build up the core meaning of the verb, and along with that verb form part of a higher-level phrase, the verb phrase. So, in example (16), *your father* is part of the verb phrase, along with *watched*, while *on the Paris metro* is not because *on the Paris metro* does not refer to anything that participates in the activity of watching, while *your father* does. *On the Paris metro* simply indicates where that activity takes place; it is a locative adjunct.

If we now put square brackets around the verb plus its complements in (10)—the verb phrase (VP)—then we see immediately that all four sentences have the same basic structure, an NP followed by a VP:

10. a. [NP The cat]   [VP *slept*].
    b. [NP My friend]   [VP *likes* this puzzle].
    c. [NP The wanderer   [VP *tramped* down the road].
    d. [NP The cat]   [VP *put* the mouse on the mat].

We can summarize what has been shown so far in this section in the following way: English sentences "normally" consist of an NP before the verb, i.e., a subject, followed by the verb itself and then the complements of that verb, if it has any. Whether a verb requires or permits complements, and if it does, then precisely how many—i.e., precisely how many NPs and/or PPs must or may follow it—is a property of the verb itself.

The complement structure of a verb depends largely on how complex the meaning of that verb is—how many distinct participants are involved in the relevant activity. Comparing the sentences of (10) with each other, it is easy to see how far the structure of each is directly dependent on the verb it contains and hence on the complements that must or may follow that verb. Sleeping is an activity that can involve only a single person; hence the verb *sleep* permits no complements in addition to the subject. You can't like without liking something, so there are two participants in the liking relationship. So *like* not only requires a subject (as do all verbs), but must also have an NP as its complement—a direct object. Tramping is an act that requires a place to tramp in (or down, or whatever)—not just fortuitously but as part of what it means to tramp. So *tramp* more or less requires a PP as its complement. Notice that although *down the road* in (10c) is a kind of locative, somewhat like *on the Paris metro* in (16), it is not an adjunct but a complement. It does not *add* to our information about where some activity took place, for part of the core meaning of tramping is that it involves a relationship between a person and a place—it is in fact an activity in which the subject *changes its place*. Finally, the verb *put* requires both an NP and a PP in its complement, reflecting the fact that putting involves a change of place in something which unlike tramping is brought about by some other entity. The subject of sentence (10d) refers to the "putter." The direct object refers to the thing that is put—i.e., the thing that changes place. And the PP *on the mat* characterizes the location to which the thing is moved. Again, this is a locative phrase. In a sentence like *Jane hit Bill on the mat* it would be a locative adjunct. But in (10d) it is a complement.

≡

EXERCISE 2

In the text we said that (14), *The wanderer tramped*, was not a possible

English sentence, that *tramped* is a verb that requires a PP complement. That may well be true, but what about:

> The wanderer tramped on and on.
> Sam tramped wearily away.

What is *on and on*? What is *away*? Think of some other sentences based on verbs that seem to act somewhat like *tramp*, and think of other expressions that could occur instead of *on and on* or *away* in these examples. See if you can provide some kind of coherent account of what is happening. You are not likely to find a clear solution; the problem involves some borderline cases. You may find it interesting, nevertheless, to explore it.

BASIC ENGLISH SENTENCES: A PHRASE STRUCTURE GRAMMAR

If there is a "normal" pattern that English sentences follow, and especially if it is true that the main lines of this pattern develop more or less automatically as a child constructs his or her own version of English, then it must surely be true that each of us who speaks English in some sense *knows* these basic sentence structures. This is one aspect of knowing the language that, in addition to a knowledge of the meanings of the words, is necessary in order to speak a language. Although, as with so much of language, we do not consciously know what the patterns are, it is clear (for example, when we try to learn another language) just how important that knowledge is.

It is still not clear how the patterns of language are stored in the mind. We know too little about how they develop, nor do we yet know exactly how the language user produces sentences that follow the stored patterns or recognizes that utterances conform to those patterns. Indeed it is still not certain what the crucial features of those patterns are. Structures like those in (10) can be represented in many ways, not all of them equivalent. The way of representing them that emphasizes those features that are truly significant is still subject to debate. That the patterns exist and are significant is perfectly clear, though, and linguists are now trying to find ways of representing these and other language patterns so their representations throw light on language development and use—and on other related aspects of human nature. To do this, they build models of sentence structures—much as a physicist builds models of atoms and molecules.

One of the most fruitful ways of modeling the basic structures of English has been by means of a *phrase structure grammar*. This is a way of directly representing the structure of every basic sentence of the language as a *tree*. Each tree corresponds to a particular sentence, being a model of (the structure of) that sentence. Some examples will help clarify this. The following trees might be assigned to the sentences of (10):

20. a.

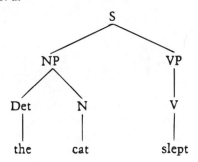

b.

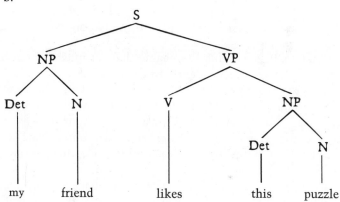

c.

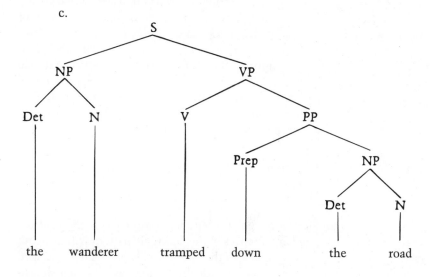

d.

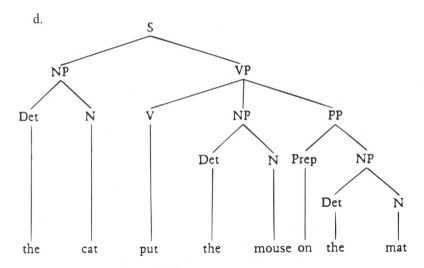

In principle, it is possible to imagine that we might store each sentence of our language independently in the mind, as a tree, like (20a–d), representing the structure of that sentence. However, a little reflection should be enough to make it clear that English cannot be represented in that way. Our knowledge of English cannot be thought of as simply a treelike structure stored with each sentence. We cannot store sentences individually in our brains. Apart from anything else, there are simply too many sentences. (In fact, there is an infinite number of possible sentences in the language, as in any human language.) Each of us deals effortlessly with hundreds of sentences every day that we have never heard before—every one not just a string of words but a structured string. Consequently, in learning English we must have acquired some way of assigning structure to *any* appropriate string of words.

This aspect of our language is represented in a phrase structure grammar by a set of rules that captures the main aspects of English sentence structure in the form of trees like those above, associated appropriately and automatically with every sentence of the language. For every (possible) sentence of English, the rules will construct a tree. The following set of rules would construct the trees of (20)—and others like them:

21. a. S → NP VP
   b. VP → V (NP) (PP)
   c. PP → Prep NP
   d. NP → (Det) N

These rules provide a "recipe" for building a number of related structural skeletons that English sentences of the "normal" pattern will flesh out once appropriate words are linked to the end symbols N, V, Prep, and Det. To yield a way of representing, automatically, a large class of English sentences, those like the sentences in (10), we need only add to the rules of (21) lists of nouns, verbs, prepositions, and determiners that can be linked to the lowest nodes of the trees built by these rules. Before we show precisely how the rules work, you should work through the following exercises.

EXERCISE 3

1. Make up lists of English words that would fall under the symbols N, V, Prep, and Det, and then draw several trees like those in (20), replacing the words in those trees with others from your lists.

2. Describe any problems that arose in completing the previous exercise.

3. If you know another language, try to make lists corresponding to those that you constructed for English, and then try to draw trees for comparable sentences to the ones given for English. Do you meet any problems in carrying out this assignment? If so, describe them.

Each rule in (21) may be thought of as building part of a tree. Let us start with the part built by the rule (21a): S → NP VP. In this tree (for each part of a tree is also itself a tree), the S to the left of the arrow in the rule in question is drawn above the NP and VP that appear to the right of the arrow, and it is linked directly to each of them. The symbols to the right of the arrow (i.e., NP and VP) appear in precisely the same order (from left to right) as they do in the rule itself. So, rule (21a) builds a little piece of structure that looks like this:

22.

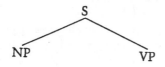

If you find it easier to think in terms of how *you* should interpret the rule, think of it as an instruction to write down the symbol to the left of the arrow and then to write, under it, and in the order in which they appear in the rule, all the symbols to the right of the arrow. And finally, link each of those lower symbols to the one above it. If you follow these instructions precisely, this should enable you to draw (22) as the structure (the *only* structure) resulting from the application of (21a) according to the interpretation we have just given to that rule. First you write down the "S." Then under it you write "NP VP." And finally, you link "NP" to "S," and "VP" to "S." The result is (22).

Now notice that this little tree forms a part of every one of the larger sentence trees given in (20). Make sure you follow this before going further. Either make a tracing of (22) and lay it over each of the trees given in (20), or simply look carefully at those four earlier trees and satisfy yourself that you *could* lay a tracing of (22) over each of them. (It would cover the *S* node at the top of each tree, and the NP and VP which are joined to it.)

This is not just a trivial fact, though at first you may not see why it is important. The real significance of having a rule like (21a) in our grammar of English—a rule that draws the sub-tree (22) as a part of every sentence—is that it directly represents an aspect of English structure that has been mentioned several times: the fact that all the "normal" sentence patterns of English contain a subject NP followed by a VP. This rule, (21a), contains NP + VP on the right-hand side, and is the only rule for S in the grammar, so it forces every tree to contain, below the S and connected to it, NP followed by VP. In this way, rule (21a) ensures that the language model of which it forms a central part will include only trees built with the structure NP + VP: every sentence will be associated with the structure NP + VP.

Although of itself quite a small point, it is a typical application of a basic methodology that is central to all current work in theoretical linguistics, and worth following closely for that reason. Let us look at it again from a slightly different angle: in order to discover just how language develops, we need to understand what kinds of structures may be included in a human language. In order to do that, we formulate hypotheses about the structure of language, representing these hypotheses by means of some clear formalism such as a phrase structure grammar. Put this way, the grammar (i.e., the set of rules) in (21) is a step towards understanding how we learn language and must be thought of as an attempt to build a model of the kinds of structure that we, as children, eventually assign to English sentences.

A linguist using the grammar of (21) in an account of English is thereby committed to the claim that a child ends up with a representation of the language that is essentially like that set of rules. The linguist is also committed to the representations for each of the sentences of (10) that are given in the trees drawn by those rules, namely (20a–d). It will be good to try and keep these underlying principles in mind as we proceed. The formal details are important, for it is only by understanding them that you can really grasp the significance of theoretical work on language, but it is all too easy to get bogged down in those formal details and to lose sight of the goals that give them their significance.

We can now fill in additional details, looking briefly at how the rules of (21b–d) provide "recipes" for drawing every aspect of the trees (20). First, we must extend the sub-tree (22). Look at the diagram once again. One branch ends in the symbol "VP." This is the symbol on the left of rule (21b). So when we apply the general instructions for tree-building to this particular rule, "VP" will be the symbol we write down first, just as "S" was with respect to rule (21a). Then we will need to write down, under "VP," the symbols to the right of the arrow in the rule. And so on. In practice, since "VP" is already written down, in (22), we take that as our starting point. We don't write it again. Any time the left-hand symbol of a rule we are applying is already part of an existing tree we proceed in this way: we simply write down the symbols that are on the right of the arrow, placing them under the existing left-hand symbol. So, in this case, we may write down "V NP PP" (all of which appear on the right of the VP rule). We write them immediately under the existing VP in the tree in question, namely (22), in the order they appear in the rule, and we obtain (23):

23.

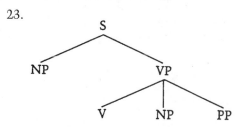

While it is perfectly true that application of rule (21b) to the VP in tree (22) does—and should—produce the above tree (which is a sub-tree of the tree given earlier in [20c]), we have ignored a small but quite significant property of rule (21b), which results in (23) being *not the only tree* drawn by that rule. In (21b) there are two symbols inside parentheses. These parentheses never appear in the trees at all; a tree never contains symbols inside parentheses. The parentheses are in fact not a part of the symbols themselves at all. They simply indicate, in the phrase structure rules, elements that *may*—but *need not*—appear in trees constructed by using those rules.

When we applied (21a), we had no choice but to write down both "NP" and "VP." There was no choice because there were no parentheses around either symbol; and the rule was written without parentheses around these symbols in order to represent English as a language in which every sentence has a subject NP followed by a VP. Rule (21b), on the other hand, allows us a number of choices when we apply it. This reflects the fact that the structure of VP differs from sentence to sentence—that is, not every VP has the same contents. In fact, as we emphasized early on, the structure of the VP of each sentence is dependent on what verb actually appears in it. Our general rules for constructing sentences must therefore permit the appropriate variation. The parentheses in rule (21b) are there, then, because a VP may contain an NP or a PP, both, or neither. Both the NP and the PP are optional, and this is marked by enclosing both symbols in parentheses. When we apply the rule, we have to make a choice; we do not need to write down "V NP PP" under the VP, but may leave out either NP or PP or both. So, under the VP, we may write down just "V NP," omitting the "PP." Or we may write down "V PP," or "V NP PP." Or just "V." We cannot leave out the "V" since that is not inside parentheses. But since everything else is, we may omit any or all of the other symbols.

The operation of the rule may be much easier to follow if we work through each of these possibilities one by one. First, here is the rule itself again:

VP → V (NP) (PP)

Omit both elements in parentheses and we obtain the shortest version of the rule—and, as suggested below, the simplest trees:

24. a. VP → V

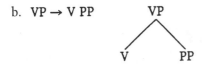

Omit only the NP and we have:

b. VP → V PP

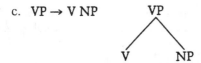

Omit the PP and we have:

c. VP → V NP

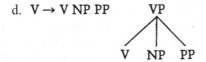

If both NP and PP are selected in applying the rule, so that the longest possible version applies and the right-hand side includes the symbols "V NP PP," then the result is a tree like the one already shown in (23). Using the same format as (24a–c), we obtain:

d. V → V NP PP

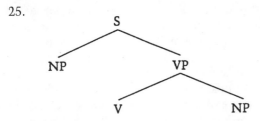

If, when we applied rule (21b) to the VP in tree (22), we had chosen just "V NP," instead of "V NP PP," then the result of applying that rule would not have been (23) but would instead have been:

25.

We could extend this figure so as to turn it into the tree shown in (20b). The structure we have in (25) is a "sub-tree" of (20b). That is to say, you could lay it over (20b) like a tracing, and (perhaps with a little stretching here and there) each symbol and line would match up precisely with a part of that larger, complete tree. To turn (25) into (20b) requires just two applications of rule (21d) to add the proper structure under NP—and then, of course, the right words have to be added at the ends of the branches. In a similar manner, all the sentences of (20) can be obtained from the rules of (21). It would be worth taking the time to try to derive each of these trees by applying those rules in proper order.

EXERCISE 4

1. Construct each of the trees of (20), using the rules in (21) in the manner described in the text.

2. Use the lists of words that you made for the exercise on page 207 to construct other trees for good English sentences having similar patterns to those of (20).

3. Describe briefly any difficulties you have encountered. If you are dissatisfied with the rules or with the way they work, state the problem briefly.

Notice that an un-English string of English words (like *on the mat the cat the mouse put*) will not be assigned a structure by any possible combination of the rules. We need to be clear about that. Why is it true? Here is one way of looking at it: Rule (21a), which starts each derivation off by getting the "S" for "sentence" in position, forces every sentence to consist of an NP followed by a VP. And the rule for VP insists that the verb appear at the beginning of the verb phrase—*followed* by NP or PP or both or neither. There is no rule that will get the verb to appear *preceded by* a string consisting of *on the mat the cat the mouse* since this string consists of PP (*on the mat*) + NP (*the cat*) + NP (*the mouse*). None of the sub-rules of (21) will place PP + NP + NP in that order, let alone place them before the verb. If English included sentences with such a pattern, we would need to add some rules to (21) to generate appropriate trees. For example, we might assign to this string a tree somewhat like the following:

26.

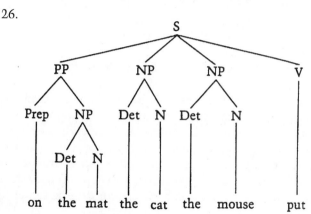

A rule that would generate (26) might, for example, be:

27. S → PP NP NP V

Since English does not permit these structures, of course, we don't add this rule to (21) and hence our grammar, correctly, never generates strings like *on the mat the cat the mouse put*. To that extent, it properly represents the English native speaker's internalized language, generating the sentences of (20) while excluding strings like that shown in (26).

BASIC SENTENCE PATTERNS IN THE MIND

We may regard the rules of (21) as a reasonable first approximation to the way the basic sentence structures of English eventually develop in the mind of a child. However, it is going much too far to conclude from this that rules like these do indeed represent how the English speaker stores those patterns. We cannot, without evidence from many sources, conclude that learning, or developing, a language is in part a matter of constructing a grammar like (21) to define trees for all the sentences of the language. To claim this, that a child acquiring English develops a phrase structure grammar like (21) as a mental representation of the basic patterns of the language, goes far beyond what can be concluded on the basis of the fact that those rules are a "reasonable first approximation" to the representation of English that the child must eventually develop. We have dealt thus far with only a very tiny part of English and there are many other ways of approximating the effect of rules like those in (21).

For a number of years, it seemed likely to most linguists that in learning a language a child does indeed build up a phrase structure grammar providing recipes for constructing all the sentences of the language. The grammar of English, according to this hypothesis about language, would include some rules very much like (21). Recently, it has become clear that a child probably never learns language in terms of rules like these. Rather than trying to discover a set of rules like (21), analyzing for this purpose the language she hears around her (which seemed for a time to be the most likely way for the child to learn language), it now seems probable that a young language learner engages in a much simpler task. To see what this might be, we must consider the task from the point of view of a young child.

Children learn languages other than English. In fact, every child could just as well learn any language, and languages differ from each other in their basic sentence patterns—but not in infinitely many ways. The basic patterns of all languages have much in common. So when a child learns English he needs to determine that the verb goes between the subject and the direct object. Learners of Japanese or Persian need to determine that the verb goes last in the sentence. Young Irish speakers (there are now very few!) find the verb at the very beginning of the sentence. Whether the verb goes at the end or beginning of the sentence or, as in English, after the subject, is probably something that has to be learned. Since the verb is such an important part of every sentence, it needs to be identified.

The position of the verb undoubtedly helps the child to find it. In a language like Warlpiri, of course, where word order is not important, other signals must identify the verb, but generally verbs cannot appear at just any point in a sentence; there are just a very few positions where a verb can be expected to appear. It is likely that when a child begins trying to analyze the language around her, the limitations on word order, etc., which are included in every child's "instinctive" knowledge of what can constitute a language, greatly simplify the task of discovering the verbs of the language to which the child is exposed, and hence of determining those many aspects of structure that depend crucially on the verb.

There seems to be a link, for example, between the position in which the verb appears in a language (first in the sentence, last, or after the subject) and the structure of PPs. A language with the verb in final position, which is to say one whose structure could be represented (in this respect) by a phrase structure rule something like (27), would not have prepositional phrases like those in English, with the preposition before the NP, but would place the preposition *after* the NP. (It would then be called a *postposition* by grammarians, but this difference in name does not reflect any real difference in the function of prepositions and postpositions.) A child exposed to a language in which the verb came last would quickly discover where the verb had to appear. The sentences of the language he heard would follow a rule with "V" on the far right, which we could represent by replacing rules (21a,b) with one like (27) (though probably with an NP in initial position), or perhaps replacing rule (21b) with a rule for VP like this:

VP → NP PP V

A child would not actually have to learn such a rule. Given the fact that language consists of sentences built around verbs having subjects, once the position of the verb was fixed there would be no need to learn, in addition, a specific rule like (27). Nor, given what has just been suggested about the linkage between the position of the verb and the position of prepositions/postpositions, there would be no need to learn a specific rule for PP. There would be only one rule available for PP (*post*positional phrase) in a language with the verb in final position: PP → NP Post. The Post would come last in its phrase, just as the verb comes last. And hence the rule would not need to be learned, let alone stored in the mind.

Now, whether this is indeed a case where the structure of human language is constrained by predetermined limitations built into the human mind is not yet certain. But it does seem very likely that specific rules directly corresponding to phrase structure rules do not often need to be learned by children developing language. In any case, the underlying point seems valid: the patterns of all human languages may well be derived by the application of a few deep, unlearned, "instinctive" principles that make it quite unnecessary to suppose that our native language is learned by constructing explicit grammars like the rules of (21).

Despite this fact, we will continue to present analyses of English in terms of phrase structure rules, just as if such rules really were how speakers of the language represented the patterns of their language. This is partly a matter of convenience: phrase structure rules provide the most transparent way known to us of characterizing the basic structures of a language as a whole. They are, as already pointed out, the best available approximation to those basic structures, even if in fact there is no explicit grammar of this sort that the language learner constructs.

SOME DEVIANT PATTERNS:
AUXILIARIES IN ENGLISH QUESTIONS

Not all sentences of English follow patterns that are covered by the rules of (21). In the simplest cases, we would need only to extend those rules. For example, our account of English makes no provision for NPs containing adjectives, such as *little* in *the little cat*. Nor does it allow us to introduce a PP inside an NP, such as (NP *the prisoner* [PP *from the tower*]), one of the very first constructions we noticed, in (3). In both of these instances, it would be quite a simple matter to add extra optional elements at the appropriate points in the rule for NP, (21d). We might, for example, modify the present version, NP → (Det) N, to read NP → (Det) (Adj) N (PP), extending this rule even further to take care of complex NPs like *the man with a huge mouse in one of the three tiniest cages in the world*—and so on!

Among other words that must be introduced into the sentence in this way are the *auxiliaries*. These are the little verblike words that may appear between the subject NP and the VP in any ordinary English statement. When we introduced the idea that there are basic, unmarked patterns in English, we could perfectly well have added one or more auxiliaries to the sentences of (10), for auxiliary verbs are part of the basic sentence structure of the language. We could have used examples like the following (compare them with the corresponding sentences of [10]):

28. a. [The cat] *has* [slept].
    b. [My friend] *could* [likes this puzzle].
    c. [The wanderer] *is* [tramping down the road].
    d. [The cat] *will* [put the mouse on the mat].

In each case, one auxiliary verb appears between the subject and the VP. This is perfectly normal. In fact up to three, and in passive sentences up to four, auxiliaries can appear in this position. They always appear in a fixed sequence. The examples above could have been more complex: *The cat* may have been *sleeping*, or *The wanderer* could be *tramping down the road*, and so on.

In an exhaustive account of the basic structure of English we would need to allow for these auxiliaries. Just as we suggested expanding the rule for NP (i.e., [21d]) to include adjectives (when it would read NP → (Det) (Adj) N (PP)), so we might add an extra symbol, say "AUX," between the NP and the VP of rule (21a) to accommodate auxiliaries: S → NP AUX VP.

Adding such a node would allow us to draw trees like the following:

29.

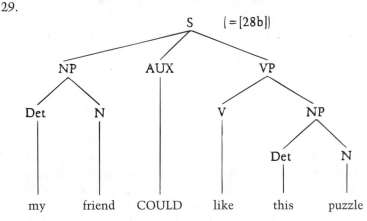

We cannot go into more detail about how to modify the basic structures of English so as to accommodate the auxiliaries in such sentences as these. For we are primarily concerned in this section with the fact that there are many English sentences whose structure differs from that of the "normal" patterns we have seen so far, and does so in ways that suggest that a grammar consisting only of rules like those of (21) does not adequately represent the full structure of a language like English—that human languages exhibit other kinds of structure in addition. The primary reason, therefore, for dealing with the auxiliaries is that in certain kinds of sentences they lead us on to structures that deviate in an interesting way from the "normal" patterns. Corresponding to each of (28a–d) there is a sentence which we may think of as its question counterpart. This question differs from the corresponding nonquestion only in that *the first auxiliary in the nonquestion appears before the subject NP in the question.*

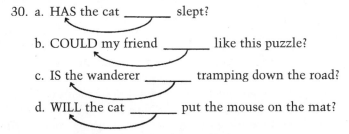

Questions like these are often called "yes-no questions." Each is related to its nonquestion counterpart in a very regular fashion: the first auxiliary verb is not in its "normal" position, but appears to the left of the subject NP. This is suggested by the gaps and arrows in (30). (In fact, there is just a single auxiliary in each of these particular examples, just as there was in their statement counterparts; but it is clear from examination of pairs like *the wanderer* could be *tramping down the road*/could *the wanderer* _____ be *tramping down the road*? that when there is more than one auxiliary in a sentence, as there often is, then only the *first* auxiliary "moves" to the left of the subject.)

The arrows and gaps in (30), which suggest that the first auxiliary "moves" to a position to the left of the subject NP, imply that the order SUBJECT + AUXILIARY is in some sense normal, primary, or as it is often called, "unmarked," and that when the first of the auxiliaries appears before the subject in questions, this is a "deviation" from the normal order—a "marked" order. There are good reasons for thinking that something along these lines is indeed the case.

We take the order of the auxiliaries in statements as basic, and the order found in questions as in some sense derived from that basic order, because if we do so, then the order of the auxiliaries, and the way they are ordered with respect to the subject NP in a statement and in its corresponding question can be systematically related to each other. Both are taken care of in the basic trees—the ones that questions have before the first auxiliary has moved, which are identical to the trees for the corresponding statements. If we do not take the statement order as basic, then it is hard to relate statements and their corresponding questions in any systematic way. (We do not have the space to show this here, but it is not too difficult to show.) Of course, it could be the case that the order of the auxiliaries in English questions is totally unrelated to their order in statements. But that is rather unlikely; there are simply too many ways in which they can be systematically related—provided we derive the questions from the statements by a *movement rule*, along the lines suggested by the gaps and arrows in (30).

Given an account involving movement of the first auxiliary, a sentence like (28a), *The cat has slept*, would be defined directly by phrase structure rules like those of (21). But its question counterpart, (30a), *Has the cat* _____ *slept*, would be defined in two steps: first, the phrase structure rules would yield a "normal" sentence, with *has* in the position it occupies in (28a), and then this word would be moved to its eventual position at the front of the sentence.

What stage have we reached in our account of syntactic structure? We began by developing a phrase structure grammar to represent the speaker's knowledge of the general patterns found in certain simple English sentences. We have just seen in outline how phrase structure rules would need to be supplemented by the addition of a movement rule in order to define the structure of English questions. However, we had already seen that there were good reasons for thinking that language learning is not a process by which a phrase structure grammar is constructed. In developing language, a child simply determines such things as the order of the verb and subject, of the verb and direct object, and so on. Speakers of English, Persian, Japanese, Irish and all other languages do not need to construct and store away phrase structure grammars to represent the basic sentence structures; those structures follow automatically once the correct choice is made between a limited number of alternative word orders such as the position of the verb. Now, what about movement rules? Does the English-speaking child learn a movement rule like "In order to form a question, move the first auxiliary in the corresponding statement to the left of the subject NP," and store this rule away in her mind?

The "movement" of the first auxiliary to the beginning of the sentence, which is so characteristic of English questions of all kinds (and occurs in a few other very minor constructions such as, "Boy, *can he* drink beer!"), is actually very rare in the languages of the world. There is probably no other language in which questions are marked by this auxiliary inversion rule—though the Germanic languages generally have the verb in initial position in yes-no questions, making them look superficially very much like (30a–d). It may be that at least certain aspects of this strange little construction do indeed have to be learned specifically by English speakers and stored away. However, there are other kinds of movement that seems so very widespread in the languages of the world that it is likely that they, like the phrase structure grammar which we eliminated as something that has to be learned, develop more or less automatically from general principles governing the structure of human language. In the next section, we look at one such widespread "movement" phenomenon as it appears in English.

WH-MOVEMENT

In addition to questions calling for "yes" or "no" as an answer, there are questions that ask for more detailed information; they are often called information questions. The following simple examples are quite typical:

31. a. Which cake *can* you make?
    b. What *has* Joe put on the table?
    c. Whose mouse *is* the boy looking for?

Like the examples of yes-no questions given earlier, each of these sentences exhibits subject-auxiliary inversion: each contains an auxiliary before the subject. This is perhaps easiest to see if we compare them to similar sentences that are statements rather than questions. Here are some examples that correspond directly to those of (31):

32. a. You *can* make this cake.
    b. Joe *has* put the book on the table.
    c. The boy *is* looking for his mouse.

In (31a) we find the sequence *can you* ("Which cake *can you* make?"); in the corresponding statement (32a), we find *you can* ("You can make this cake."| Similarly we find *has Joe* in the question (31b), but *Joe has* in the statement (32b). In the third pair, we find *is the boy* in the question, but *the boy is* in the statement.

These information questions not only exhibit the rather rare, perhaps uniquely English, phenomenon of auxiliary fronting already discussed, but they also begin with a phrase containing a question word—which corresponds to nothing at the beginning of their nonquestion counterparts. It is "movement" of this sort that is so common: the movement of some phrase to the very front of the sentence. In English questions what moves is a phrase containing a special question word. In the following representation of (31) this "*Wh*-phrase" (as it is called, for reasons that should be obvious) has been set in italic—and for clarity placed in square brackets.

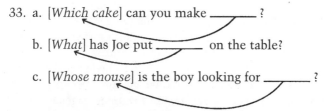

33. a. [*Which cake*] can you make _____ ?

 b. [*What*] has Joe put _____ on the table?

 c. [*Whose mouse*] is the boy looking for _____ ?

The representation in (33) of the sentences of (31) not only isolates the *Wh*-phrase for emphasis, but indicates by means of an arrow and an underlined "gap" where that *Wh*-phrase originated. In these examples, this gap has been placed in the position that would be occupied by an ordinary NP in a corresponding statement. Compare the verb phrases of (31a) and (32a).

34. a. [VP make _____]
    b. [VP make [NP *this cake*]]

What justification is there for representing the question (31a) in this way? Specifically, why must we think of the *Wh*-phrase as linked to that position in the VP, which in the statement (32a) contains the NP *this cake*? Why suppose that there is a rule that in some sense "moves" it from that position?

Intuitively, it seems clear that *which cake* in (31a) is the object of *make*, just as *this cake* is in (32a). There is, in each case, a sentence about some cake that can be made. This alone is not a very clear argument for the precise representation given previously involving movement to the beginning of the sentence from the direct object position. In fact there are clearer indications that the *Wh*-phrase must be regarded as in some sense a part of the verb phrase even though it is not actually inside that phrase in any of these questions. Recall how the verb of a sentence determines what can appear in the VP. The examples of (10–12) are relevant: whereas we can say *The cat slept*, we cannot say **The cat slept the milk*, and similarly, while we can say *My friend likes this puzzle*, *My friend likes is not acceptable. Now look again at the verb phrases of (31). This time, we will represent them as if they had no gap at all corresponding to the *Wh*-phrase:

35. a. Which cake can you [VP make]?
     b. What has Joe [VP put on the table]?
     c. Whose mouse is the boy [VP looking for]?

If we treat each of these verb phrases as a complete VP, as suggested by this last set of representations, then the VPs should be able to occur independently, forming acceptable sentences when they follow NP subjects. But this is simply not so, as illustrated in (36):

36. a. *You [VP made]
     b. *Joe [VP put on the table]
     c. *The boy [VP looked for]

If we try to use just the words *made, put on the table,* or *looked for* in an independent sentence without an initial *Wh*-phrase and *without a direct object,* the result is quite ungrammatical. This is comparable to ungrammatical examples like (11) and (12). It seems clear that in (31b), the verb phrase is not *put on the table* but *put [what] on the table,* and that the word *what* really is acting as the NP object of *put.* This is similar in the other two examples. So, the "real" structure of (31a) is *You can make [which cake].* And this is precisely the structure the sentence might have if it were generated directly by the phrase structure grammar of (21). *Wh*-phrases, at least the ones we will look at here, are simply special kinds of NPs, which generally have to appear at the front of the sentence rather than in their "normal" position, for example, as part of the VP.

One way of analyzing such sentences follows closely the lines suggested by the representation in (32): the normal phrase structure rules (i.e., [21]) derive *Wh*-questions just as if they were ordinary statements, with the *Wh*-phrase in the position it would occupy if it were an ordinary NP. In each of our examples, it would be the object of the verb, inside the VP in the position indicated by the underline in (33). Then a rule of *Wh*-movement moves the phrase to the front of the sentence, as suggested by the arrows in those examples. So, for example, *Which cake can you make* starts out as something like *You can make which cake* and then the phrase *which cake* moves to the front, as in (33)—and the auxiliary moves, too, of course, though we are not concerned with that right now.

═══

EXERCISE 5

1. Use the phrase structure grammar of (21) to draw *basic* trees for each of the following sentences:
   a. What picture will you buy for Henry?

    b. Who was Jane talking about?

    c. Which preacher could Jack have seen in Boston?

    d. Whose father could he be thinking of?

2. Now show, by using arrows and gaps, as in the text, how the two movement rules that we have discussed apply to these basic forms to derive the final forms of the sentences.

(Hint: The first sentence should be in the form *You will buy what picture for Henry* when you use the rules of [21] to construct a basic tree for it. This is similar in the others as well.)

Now, how far should we suppose that a child has to learn specific movement rules of this sort in developing knowledge of English? A child must somehow discover that a *Wh*-phrase belongs in its "real" position in the sentence—and must be interpreted as if it still remained there. Yet there is no audible sign of the gap that we underlined in (33); a child simply has to use his knowledge of the language as a whole (in particular, of the basic sentence structures including the properties of verbs and what complements they permit or require) in order to determine where a gap exists. So far, this might not seem too great a feat. The *Wh*-phrase corresponds to one or other of the places where an NP could appear: the subject of the sentence, or somewhere inside the VP. That is all the learner needs to "discover." However, note that in English, and in many other languages, it is possible for the gap to be virtually any distance away from the *Wh*-phrase.

This comes about because sentences can function as parts of other sentences—which can in turn be parts of other sentences. Look at the example that follows:

37. Sam believes [s1 (that) Bill can ride that horse].

The verb *believe* can appear with an ordinary NP object, as in *Sam believes [the child]*, but it can also appear with a whole sentence as its object, as in (37). There, the sentence *Bill can ride the horse* is the object of *believe*. (In [37] the word *that* may precede the embedded sentence, but it need not. It is shown in parentheses to suggest this. In subsequent examples *that* will often be omitted. This makes the sentences sound more natural to some speakers, though others may prefer to put it back in.)

Now we can repeat the process of embedding, setting (37) within another sentence as the object of yet another verb like *believe*. Let us use *think* in this case.

38. Sue will think [s2 that Sam believes
             [s1 that Bill can ride that horse]].

The process of embedding sentences inside others can go on indefinitely. The following example consists of (38) embedded as the object of the verb *hope*:

39. Your friend hopes [s3 that Sue will think
    [s2 that Sam believes
    [s1 Bill can ride that horse]]].

We could go on to say *I deny that my friend hopes that Sue will think that Sam believes that Bill can ride that horse.* There is no end.

Now look at what happens when we take complex sentences like these and "remove" one of the NPs, inserting a suitable *Wh*-phrase at the very beginning of the whole thing. Two examples will suffice:

40. a. *Which horse* will Sue think [s2 that Sam believes

    [s1 Bill can ride _____]]?

    b. *Which girl* will Sue think   [s2 that Sam believes

    [s1 _____ can ride that horse]]?

The fact that a *Wh*-phrase can appear indefinitely far away from the position in the sentence that it would occupy if it were an ordinary NP results in deviations from the unmarked NP AUX VP structure imposed by the phrase structure rules of (21) (as modified by the addition of AUX). One NP is not overtly present in its normal place, but appears at the beginning of some sentence, not necessarily even the one that it "really" belongs in.

A child learning the language would be better equipped to grasp the structure of such sentences if he did not have to discover from scratch that *Wh*-movement can occur in language—and better still if there were only certain places to which things could move. There is reason to believe that a child starts out with both advantages: the potential for *Wh*-movement is one of the devices that the learner takes for granted (as we have already suggested)—and there are very strict constraints on how phrases can be moved around. It seems very likely that these constraints are also not things a child has to discover but instead are limitations on the structure of human language that a learner can take for granted. These, at any rate, are the tentative results of recent work. We will now take a brief look at some of the limitations that appear to be placed on how a phrase can be moved.

It is striking that the moved *Wh*-phrase always ends up at the edge of a sentence. This is true not only in English but also in other languages, many quite unrelated to English. It would be strange if all languages had developed this constraint by chance, and there is every reason to believe that it results instead from some essential property of the human mind. This is even more true of some of the other constraints, which, although found in language after language in some form, are very complex and may even be in principle unlearnable.

Here is an example of a kind of structure that is excluded in English and many other languages:

41. *Which horse* did Sue ask

[s2 whether Sam believes [S1 Bill can ride____]]?

Any English sentence comparable in relevant ways to (41) will be ungrammatical. What are those "relevant" ways? There is just one difference between (41) and (40)—the latter of which was perfectly grammatical. The word *whether* occurs in the former, where *that* appears in the latter. *Whether* introduces a kind of question, and is in fact a special kind of *Wh*-word. It turns out that, in English, *Wh*-phrases, like *which horse* in (41), cannot be moved over a *Wh*-word. As suggested by the arrow in (41), this is precisely what would have to happen for this example to result from *Wh*-movement.

Now notice a very important implication of this fact. No child can learn that forms like (41) are ungrammatical by listening to the language around him. English speakers simply do not use these forms. There is no way, other than, for example, directly asking an adult, for a child to discover that the reason he never hears them is that they are ungrammatical, not part of the English language. Yet all of us know perfectly well that they are extremely bad: totally ungrammatical. And children have no tendency whatever to produce such forms as "mistakes." It is quite impossible that every child learning English is taught, explicitly, that such forms are not to be used; so the only possible explanation of the fact that we all feel them to be ungrammatical is that they are excluded by reason of some part of the inborn mechanism with which we approach the task of learning language. They reflect something quite deep, not learned but innate, which is part of our linguistic makeup.

As a matter of fact, the position is a little more complicated—and even more interesting. If no language permitted forms corresponding to (41), we might be inclined to say that the reason they are bad and never used by even children learning the language is that they simply make no sense. As speakers of English we are inclined to think that this is so. However, although many languages, including English, exclude forms like (41), there are others (those that form questions without making any use of *Wh*-movement) in which questions like (41) are perfectly well formed. Thus, despite our temptation, as native speakers of English, to think that such questions simply "make no sense," they not only make sense but are perfectly normal in languages that use slightly different constructions to form questions. (We can even approximate in English the meaning that [41] would have if it were grammatical, using a clumsy but grammatical sentence like *Of which horse is it true that Sue asked whether Sam believes Bill can ride it?*)

CONCLUSION

The structure of human languages is determined by the nature of the creatures that construct them: human children. Given this fact, we may hope to learn much of interest about human beings by examining the structure of their languages.

Human language consists of far more than just enormous collections of words; this is especially true if we think of words as limited to their meanings and sounds. Languages, including English, are highly structured, and words themselves are a part of that structure. English consists of sentences, which are built up around verbs, which in turn determine the kinds of phrases that make up the sentences. The structure of the sentences of a language is called the syntax of that language.

Every English sentence has a subject NP, but the verb determines what kinds of phrases must occur as its complement. Those phrases are generally NPs and PPs. The internal structure of NPs is determined (at least in part) by their head nouns—and in fact the structure of PPs is determined by the prepositions that head them, though we have not looked at these phrases in detail.

In English, but not, for example, in Warlpiri, word order largely determines the makeup of phrases. The grouping of words into phrases in basic English sentences can be modeled by a phrase structure grammar. There are, nevertheless, reasons for thinking that we do not store those basic patterns as a phrase structure grammar. Many aspects of language structure do not need to be learned. They are fixed, and a child merely has to determine, for example, the order of the verb and its direct object, or of the preposition/postposition and the NP that goes with it. It is these little language-specific facts about order, and not grammars consisting of rules, that have to be learned, and stored in the mind.

In addition to the basic sentence patterns that can be mimicked by a phrase structure grammar, there are patterns that involve the movement of constituents away from their basic positions. Many of these patterns probably do not have to be learned as separate rules. A child expects to find phenomena like *Wh*-movement in a language, and most of the characteristics of this phenomenon are universally constrained to follow set patterns. On the other hand, phenomena like the movement of the auxiliary in English may well have to be learned, assuming that they turn out not to follow solely from general linguistic principles in the way that *Wh*-movement does. There are idiosyncrasies in individual languages; the systematic study of syntax does not simply ignore them but attempts to set limits on them, at the same time concentrating on the universal principles that govern the structure of human language.

Although much remains to be learned about the syntax of human languages, some very significant facts have already been discovered, and syntactic research continues to throw new light on the nature of the mind.

FOR DISCUSSION AND REVIEW

1. Draw trees like those given in (20a–d) for the following sentences. As far as possible, use the same symbols as those used in the example

trees (i.e., PP, N, NP, VP, and so on), but where you believe that a word does not fall into any of the classes for which symbols have already been given, feel free to invent new ones.

   a. Two beetles crawled over a little leaf.
   b. I can see several old men on the docks.
   c. The goats may eat your straw hat.
   d. Jane drove the new tractor into the barn.
   e. Someone may be asking for assistance.

2. a. Try to give detailed trees for the two interpretations discussed in the text for the string *I watched the prisoner from the tower.* That is, turn the marked sentences (3a and 3b) into proper tree representations. Your two trees should reflect the crucial differences between the two readings that are discussed in the text. (How should you represent *the prisoner from the tower* in [3a]?)

   b. Do the rules given in (21) provide for trees like those you have constructed? If not, how do the rules need to be modified in order to do so? (Concentrate on [3a] and consider rule [21d], which draws NP trees.)

3. Your college library has introductory grammar texts for many languages, as do instructors in foreign-language departments. Look at the grammar of a language unfamiliar to you, preferably one very different from English. Where does the verb occur in statements? (At the end? At the beginning?) What is the structure of the NP? (Where does the N come, the Adj, and so on?) Try to formulate simple phrase structure rules for parts of the language you choose, along the lines of 21a–d) in the text, but with the symbols in the right place to draw appropriate trees for sentences in the language you have chosen. Draw a few trees for this language. Discuss problems that arise in deciding what the rules and trees should be like, and anything about language structure that this attempt has taught you.

4. Consider how information questions are formed in some language with which you are somewhat familiar. Use grammar books if necessary to supplement your knowledge, or ask a speaker of the language to help you find examples of these structures in it. Does the language use *Wh*-movement (as English does) for forming these questions? Give detailed arguments for or against your conclusion. (You will have to consider both the form of the questions and the form of ordinary statements in the language.)

5. Consider how far the development of language in children results from the imitation of what they hear and how far it results from factors that are purely internal to the children. Be as specific as possible in your discussion.

6. Summarize the structure of the grammar that, according to Professor Heny, English-speaking children must have internalized as a representation of their language. What kinds of "rules" does this grammar contain? Comment on aspects of sentence structure that seem to have been left out of this selection and that would need to be added for a complete account.

17

Bad Birds and Better Birds: Prototype Theories

Jean Aitchison

Which of the following colors most closely resembles the color blue: teal blue, peacock blue, sky blue, royal blue, navy blue, or midnight blue? How do we distinguish between such subtle differences in meaning? Semantics is the area of linguistics that analyzes the meaning of individual words and phrases. In this extract from her book Words in the Mind, *Jean Aitchison of the University of Oxford examines a peculiar trait of the English language that allows those who speak it to cope with its ambiguous word-meanings. Speakers of English use many words with slightly different meanings to convey similar messages. For example, the use of the terms "happy," "excited," "jubilant," "delighted," or "elated" expresses a positive, pleasant, personal feeling. Aitchison discusses this ambiguous classification of word-meaning within the framework of "prototype theory." How we choose those words that we believe are best suited to a specific situation is just one of the questions Aitchison attempts to answer in her exploration of the system of word-meanings in English and the way in which words are stored in the brain.*

The Hatter . . . had taken his watch out of his pocket, and was looking at it uneasily, shaking it every now and then, and holding it to his ear . . .

"Two days wrong?" sighed the Hatter. "I told you butter wouldn't suit the works!" . . .

Alice had been looking over his shoulder with some curiosity. "What a funny watch!" she remarked. "It tells the day of the month, and doesn't tell what o'clock it is!"

–Lewis Carroll, *Alice's Adventures in Wonderland*

If words have a hazy area of application, we are faced with a serious problem in relation to the mental lexicon. How do we manage to cope with words at all? The quotation above from *Alice in Wonderland* gives us a clue. Alice appears to have some notion of what constitutes a "proper watch." This enables her to identify the butter-smeared object owned by the Hatter as a watch, and to comment that it is a "funny" one.

A feeling that some examples of words may be more central than others appears to be widespread, as shown by a dialogue between two small girls in a popular cartoon strip:

Reproduced by kind permission of the *London Standard*

Humans, then, appear to find some instances of words more basic than others. Such an observation may shed light on how people understand their meaning. Take birds. Perhaps people have an amalgam of ideal bird characteristics in their minds. Then, if they saw a pterodactyl, they would decide whether it is likely to be a bird by matching it against the features of a bird-like bird, or, in fashionable terminology, a "prototypical" bird. It need not have all the characteristics of the prototype, but if the match was reasonably good, it could be labeled *bird*, though it might not necessarily be a very good example of a bird. This viewpoint is not unlike the checklist viewpoint, but it differs in that, in order to be a bird, the creature in question does not have to have a fixed number of bird characteristics. It simply has to be a reasonable match.

This is an intriguing idea. But, like any intriguing idea, it needs to be tested. How could we find out if people really behave in this way? In fact, psychologists showed quite a long time ago that people treat colors like this (e.g., Lenneberg 1967; Berlin and Kay 1969). However, this type of study has only relatively recently been extended to other types of vocabulary items. Let us consider one of the pioneering papers on the topic.

BIRDY BIRDS AND VEGETABLEY VEGETABLES

About twenty years ago Eleanor Rosch, a psychologist at the University of California at Berkeley, carried out a set of experiments in order to test the idea that people regard some types of birds as "birdier" than other birds, or some vegetables as more vegetable-like or some tools more "tooly."

She devised an experiment which she carried out with more than 200 psychology students: "This study has to do with what we have in mind when we use words which refer to categories," ran the instructions.

> Let's take the word red as an example. Close your eyes and imagine a true red. Now imagine an orangish red . . . imagine a purple red. Although you might still name the orange red or the purple red with the term red, they are not as good examples of red . . . as the clear "true" red. In short, some reds are redder than others. The same is true for other kinds of categories. Think of dogs. You all have some notion of what a "real dog," a "doggy dog" is. To me a retriever or a German shepherd is a very doggy dog while a Pekinese is a less doggy dog. Notice that this kind of judgment has nothing to do with how well you like the thing; you can like a purple red better than a true red but still recognize that the color you like is not a true red. You may prefer to own a Pekinese without thinking that it is the breed that best represents what people mean by dogginess (Rosch 1975, 198).

The questionnaire which followed was ten pages long. On each page was a category name, such as "Furniture," "Fruit," "Vegetable," "Bird," "Carpenter's Tool," "Clothing," and so on. Under each category was a list of fifty or so examples. *Orange, lemon, apple, peach, pear, melon* appeared on the fruit list, and so did most of the other fruits you would be likely to think up easily. The order of the list was varied for different students to ensure that the order of presentation did not bias the results. The students were asked to rate how good an example of the category each member was on a seven-point scale: rating something as "1" meant that it was considered an excellent example; "4" indicated a moderate fit; whereas "7" suggested that it was a very poor example, and probably should not be in the category at all.

The results were surprisingly consistent. Agreement was particularly high for the items rated as very good examples of the category. Almost everybody thought that a *robin* was the best example of a bird, that *pea* was the best example of a vegetable, and *chair* the best example of furniture. On the third list, *sparrow, canary, blackbird, dove,* and *lark* all came out high (figure 17.1). *Parrot, pheasant, albatross, toucan,* and *owl* came somewhat lower. *Flamingo, duck,* and *peacock* were lower still. *Ostrich, emu,* and *penguin* came more than halfway down the seven-point rating, while last of all came *bat,* which probably shouldn't be regarded as a bird at all. Similar results were found for the other categories, that is, *shirts, dresses,* and *skirts* were considered better examples of clothing than *shoes* and *stockings,* which were in turn higher than *aprons* and *earmuffs*. *Guns* and *daggers* were better examples of weapons than *whips* and *axes*, which were better than *pitchforks* and *bricks*. *Saws*, *hammers*, and *screwdrivers* were better examples of carpenters' tools than *crowbars* and *plumblines*.

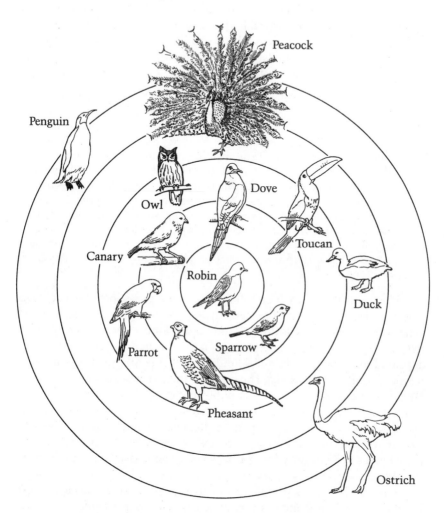

FIGURE 17.1   Birdiness Rankings.

Psychologists on the other side of America obtained very similar results when they repeated the experiment (Armstrong et al. 1983), so the results are not just a peculiar reaction of Californian psychology students. And Rosch carried out other experiments which supported her original results. For example, she checked how long it took students to verify category membership. That is, she said, "Tell me whether the following is true," and then gave the students sentences such as "A penguin is a bird" or "A sparrow is a bird." She found that good exemplars (her name for examples) of a category were verified faster than less good exemplars, so that it took longer to say "Yes" to "A penguin is a bird" than it did to "A sparrow is a bird" (Rosch 1975).

The results of these experiments are fairly impressive. But there is one obvious criticism: were the students just responding faster to more common words? After all, people come across sparrows far more frequently than penguins, and hammers more often than crowbars. Obviously, frequency of usage is likely to have some effect: in California nectarines and boysenberries are commoner than mangoes and kumquats, so it is not surprising that the former were regarded as "better" exemplars of fruit than the latter. However, the results could not be explained away solely on the basis of word frequency. On the furniture list, rare items of furniture such as *love seat, davenport, ottoman,* and *cedar chest* came out much higher than *refrigerator*, which is a standard part of every American household. On the vegetable list, *pea, carrot,* and *cauliflower* came out higher than *onion, potato,* and *mushroom*. And on the clothes list, *pajamas* and *bathing suit* came out higher than *shoe, tie, hat,* and *gloves*. So people genuinely feel that some things are better exemplars of a category than others, a feeling which is not simply due to how often one comes across the word or object in question.

Furthermore, these judgments were not made primarily on the basis of appearance. Peas, according to Rosch, are prototypical vegetables. If people were simply comparing other vegetables to a visual image of a pea, then we would expect carrots to come out near the bottom of the list. In fact, they come very near the top. And if visual characteristics were important, we would also expect vegetables which look similar, such as carrots, parsnips, and radishes, to be clustered together. But they are not. Nor were judgments made purely in terms of use. If this were so, one would expect benches and stools to come out near the top, since they are closest in function to the prototypical piece of furniture, a chair. But in fact bookcases rank higher than either benches or stools. It is not immediately obvious, therefore, how people came to their conclusions. They were making some type of analysis, though its exact basis was unclear, as the criteria used seemed to be heterogeneous.

To summarize, Rosch's work suggests that when people categorize common objects, they do not expect them all to be on an equal footing. They seem to have some idea of the characteristics of an ideal exemplar—in Rosch's words, a "prototype." And they probably decide on the extent to which something else is a member of the same category by matching it against the features of the prototype. It does not have to match exactly, it just has to be sufficiently similar, though not necessarily visually similar.

Prototype theory is useful, then, for explaining how people deal with untypical examples of a category. This is how unbirdy birds such as pelicans and penguins can still be regarded as birds. They are sufficiently like the prototype, even though they do not share all its characteristics. But it has a further advantage: it can explain how people cope with damaged examples. Previously linguists had found it difficult to explain why anyone could still categorize a one-winged robin that couldn't fly as a bird or a three-legged tiger as a quadruped. Now one just assumes that these get matched against the prototype in the same way as an untypical category member. A one-winged robin that can't fly can still be a bird, even though it's not such a typical one.

Furthermore, the prototype effect seems to work for actions as well as objects: people can, it appears, reliably make judgments that *murder* is a better example of killing than *execute* or *commit suicide*, and that *stare* is a better example of looking than *peer* or *squint* (Pulman 1983).

However, so far we have dealt only with assigning objects and actions to larger categories. We now need to consider whether this is the way in which humans cope with individual words.

DEGREES OF LYING

"Can you nominate in order now the degrees of the lie?" asks a character in Shakespeare's play *As You Like It*, and the clown Touchstone responds by listing seven degrees of lying (Shakespeare, *As You Like It*, 5.4). Obviously the idea that some lies are better lies than others has been around for a long time, and still seems to be relevant today.

A "good" lie, it transpires, has several characteristics (Coleman and Kay 1981). First, the speaker has to assert something that is untrue. However, people often utter untruths without being regarded as liars, particularly in cases of genuine mistakes: a child who argued that six and four make eleven would not be thought of as lying. So a second characteristic of a good lie is that a speaker must believe that what he is saying is false. But even this is insufficient, because a person can knowingly tell untruths without being a liar, as in: "You're the cream in my coffee, you're the sugar in my tea" (metaphor), "He stood so still, you could have mistaken him for a doorpost" (exaggeration or hyperbole), "Since you're a world expert on the topic, perhaps you could tell us how to get the cat out of the drainpipe?" (sarcasm). A third characteristic must therefore be added for a good lie: that the speaker must intend to deceive those addressed. In brief, a fully-fledged or prototypical lie occurs when a speaker:

1. asserts something false
2. which they know to be false
3. with the intention of deceiving.

A prototypical lie, therefore, might be when a child denies having eaten a jam tart which it knows full well it has just scoffed. But consider a situation such as the following: "Schmallowitz is invited to dinner at his boss's house. After a dismal evening enjoyed by no one, Schmallowitz says to his hostess, "Thanks, it was a terrific party." Schmallowitz doesn't believe it was a terrific party, and he isn't really trying to convince anyone he had a good time, but is just concerned to say something to his boss's wife, regardless of the fact that he doesn't expect her to believe it (Coleman and Kay 1981, 31).

Did Schmallowitz lie? The seventy-one people asked this question were quite unsure. They had been told to grade a number of situations on a seven-point scale, from 1 (very sure non-lie) to 7 (very sure lie). For many people, Schmallowitz's situation lay just in the middle between these two extremes, at point 4, where they were unable to decide whether it was a lie or not. Another situation which lay in the middle was the case of Superfan, who got tickets for a championship game, and phoned early in the day to tell his boss that he could not come to work as he was sick. Ironically, Superfan doesn't get to the game, because the mild stomachache he had that morning turned out to be quite severe food poisoning.

Both the Schmallowitz and Superfan cases broke one of the conditions of a good lie, though each broke a different condition. Schmallowitz was not trying to deceive his hostess, he was merely trying to be polite. Superfan did not tell an untruth. Lies, then, like birds, can be graded. Lies can still be lies even when they are not prototypical lies, and they shade off into not being "proper" lies at all.

The realization that individual words need not be used in their prototypical sense can explain a number of puzzling problems, especially cases in which people are unsure of whether they are dealing with the "same" word or not. Consider the following sentences (Jackendoff 1983):

I must have seen that a dozen times, but I never noticed it.
I must have looked at that a dozen times, but I never saw it.

Some people have argued that there are two different verbs *see*, one meaning "my gaze went to an object," as in the first sentence, and the other containing in addition the meaning "something entered my awareness," as in the second. But in a prototypical use of the verb *see*, both conditions are present: one's gaze goes to an object *and* the object enters one's awareness. If awareness is missing, one can stare at something without noticing it. Alternatively, something may enter a person's awareness, such as a dream or a hallucination, even though their gaze has not gone anywhere. These are both "ordinary" uses of the word *see*, but not prototypical ones.

To take another example, look at the following sentences:

The janitor goes from top to bottom of the building.
The staircase goes from top to bottom of the building.

The janitor is clearly moving, but the staircase is not. So are these both instances of the same word *go*? A prototype approach allows *go* to be treated as a single word (Aitchison 1985). In its prototypical use, *go* involves movement, with the mover starting at one point, ending at another, and traversing the distance in between. However, *go* can be used untypically, with the "movement" condition omitted, as happens with staircases and roads. This is a better solution than assuming that two different words *go* are involved, because it avoids the need to make difficult decisions as to which use of *go* is found in sentences such as:

The river Ganges goes from the Himalayas to the Indian Ocean.
The power of prayer goes round the world.

The verb *climb* provides a further example (Fillmore 1982; Taylor 1989; Jackendoff 1990). Consider:

Peter climbed a ladder.
The plane climbed to 30,000 feet.
The temperature climbed to 40°C.
The price of petrol climbed daily.
Mavis climbed down the tree.
Brian climbed into his clothes.

These various uses all sound "normal," even though they differ quite considerably from one another. Prototype theory provides a simple explanation. A prototypical or "default" use of *climb* involves upward movement and clambering—effortful use of limbs, as when Peter shinned up the ladder. If one of these conditions is absent, the result is still a normal use of *climb*, though not a prototypical one. Planes, temperature, and the price of petrol can climb because they are moving upward, even though they are not using any limbs. In contrast, Mavis can climb down the tree, and Peter can climb into his clothes because they are effortfully using their limbs, even though they are not going upward.

But when both upward movement and clambering are absent, the result is weird:

The plane climbed down to 20,000 feet.
The temperature climbed down to 10°C.
Marigold climbed down the stairs.
The snail climbed along the drainpipe.

Judging something against a prototype, therefore, and allowing rough matches to suffice, seems to be the way we understand a number of different words. Furthermore, a general realization that this is how humans probably operate could be of considerable use in real-life situations, as in the example below.

MAD, BAD, AND DANGEROUS TO KNOW

Some years ago a man who specialized in brutal murders of women was brought to trial. The Yorkshire Ripper, as he was called, divided public opinion sharply. Some people argued that he was simply bad, and therefore ought to be punished with a long term of imprisonment. Others claimed that he must be mad, in which case he should be admitted to a hospital and treated as someone who was not responsible for his actions.

Was he mad? Or was he bad? According to newspaper reports, the judge asked the jury to consider whether the Ripper had told the truth to the psychiatrists who examined him. The discrepancies and alterations in the Ripper's story made them conclude that he had told a considerable number of lies. This led them to classify him as "guilty"—bad, not mad. This judgment implies, therefore, that anyone who lies cannot be mad, a somewhat strange conclusion. Perhaps the situation would have been less confusing if the terms *mad* and *bad* had been considered in terms of prototypes (Aitchison 1981).

"To define true madness, What is 't to be nothing else but mad?" asks Polonius, on observing the deranged Hamlet (Shakespeare, *Hamlet*, 2.2). But contrary to Polonius's opinion, madness is not an all or nothing state. A prototypical mad person has several different characteristics. A mad person is, first, someone who thinks and acts abnormally. But this is insufficient, as it would categorize as mentally deranged such people as chess champions. Someone truly mad would, in addition, be unaware that he was thinking and acting abnormally, and furthermore, be unable to prevent himself from behaving oddly. A prototypical lunatic, therefore, might be someone who covers his head with tinfoil because he fears that moon men are about to attack, or someone who walks on her hands because God has supposedly told her not to wear out her feet. On this analysis, the Ripper was partially mad, because he acted strangely and seemed unable to prevent himself from doing so. Yet he was not prototypically mad, because he was perfectly aware that his actions were abnormal.

To turn to badness, someone bad commits antisocial acts, is aware that her actions are antisocial and could control her behavior if she wished. So a prototypical villain might be the pirate Captain Hook in *Peter Pan* or Shakespeare's character Iago. On this reasoning, the Ripper was partially bad, in that he acted antisocially and was aware of it, but not entirely bad, since he apparently could not control his actions.

To modify Caroline Lamb's statement about Lord Byron and reapply it to the Ripper, one could say that he is "around two-thirds mad, two-thirds bad, and certainly dangerous to know." No wonder the jury took so long to decide whether he was mad *or* bad, when he was neither prototypically mad nor prototypically bad.

This example shows that the notion of prototype can be extended beyond nouns and verbs—in this case to the adjectives *mad* and *bad*. But it also hides a problem, that the meaning of adjectives may vary, depending on the noun. Our account of *mad* is fine when accompanied by the word *man* or *woman*, but a *mad dog*, a *mad idea*, or a *mad evening* would require an amended analysis. Such examples suggest that the notion of prototype is not always as straightforward as has been suggested so far. Let us go on to consider this issue.

MUZZINESS OF MULTIPLE MEANINGS?

Pig: "Short-legged and typically stout-bodied mammal . . . with a thick bristly skin and long mobile snout"; "shaped mass . . . of cast crude metal." Both these definitions appear under a single entry in a well-known dictionary (LDEL). The dictionary assumes that both are instances of the "same" word *pig*, as opposed to another type of *pig* which is given a separate entry: *pig* "an earthenware vessel; a crock." But how is a plump farmyard animal related to a lump of metal? Above all, how many words are involved?

Ideally, prototype theory allows us to cut down on the multiple meanings found in many dictionaries, and to say that an understanding of the prototype allows other senses to be predicted. But how does anyone distinguish between one word with nonprototypical usages, such as *climb*, and more than one word, as perhaps with *pig* "farmyard animal" and *pig* "lump of metal"? A word such as *fork* provides a further problem. Is a *fork* you eat with the same word as the *fork* you dig with?

Polysemy—"multiple meanings"—is an age-old problem which has been helped by prototype theory, but by no means solved. Ideally, there should be some agreed test to decide whether a word has more than one meaning (polysemy) or is simply muzzy in its coverage (vagueness). But no one can find one which works.

Various suggestions have been put forward (Geeraerts 1992, 1993; Taylor 1992; Kilgarriff 1992), but none of them are foolproof. Dictionaries often rely on history, and combine items in a single entry if they are descended from the same original word—as seems to be true of *pig*. But this is not very helpful when considering how current-day speakers handle words in their minds.

A *so did* test is sometimes used to distinguish items: "The farmer watched the pig feeding its piglets, and so did the foundry foreman" would be very odd if the foundry foreman was looking at a metal pig (Zwicky and Sadock 1975). But used on *fork*, this test gets weird results. Intuitively, a *fork* is a "pronged implement." Yet the *so did* test would split it up into more than one "word": it would be very odd to say "The glutton used a fork to shovel his potatoes, and so did the farmer" if the glutton was shoveling potatoes into his mouth, and the farmer was digging them out of the ground. Similarly, *sad* in "a *sad* book" would probably be regarded as a different word from *sad* in "a *sad* woman." Each case therefore has to be considered on its merits. Let us look at two puzzling words, *over* and *old*.

MULLING OVER *OVER*

Mulling over *over* has taken up a lot of research time recently (e.g., Lakoff 1987; Taylor 1989; Geeraerts 1992). First, it's hard to identify prototypical *over*. Second, it's unclear how many separate meanings *over* has. Consider:

Virginia's picture is over the fireplace.

> The clouds floated over the city.
> Doreen pulled the blanket over her head.

Virginia's picture is stationary, but the clouds are moving. The clouds are unlikely to be touching the city, but the blanket is in contact with Doreen's head. Which of these meanings is basic?

There is no agreed solution. Some people argue that Virginia's static picture represents prototypical *over*, others the moving clouds. Still others suggest that *over* is by nature a muzzy word with vagueness built into it: that it means "above, on top of," versus "under," but does not specify whether the "over" item is stationary or moving, in contact with or separated from what's underneath. In this case, all the sentences quoted could be regarded as prototypical. However, all three uses are clearly instances of the same word, even if the prototype is not obvious.

But now look at:

> The cow jumped over the moon.
> The water flowed over the rim of the bathtub.
> Fenella pushed Bob over the balcony.
> Sam walked over the bridge.

In all these, there is successful movement to a new location. This cannot easily be accommodated in the primary meaning of *over*. But neither is it completely separate. There seem to be at least two overlapping meanings of *over*: a basic one in which location above is specified and an extended one in which successful movement across occurs (figure 17.2).

Over therefore shows that polysemy is a complex affair, in that different senses of a word may overlap. They cannot easily be related to a prototype, nor do they split neatly into different domains. Let us go on to consider another problem of this type.

Old Problems

The word *old* is an old problem (Taylor 1992). Consider:

Pauline was astonished to see
  – an old woman (an aged woman)
  – an old friend (a long-standing friend)
  – her old boyfriend (a former boyfriend)
  – old Fred (Fred whom she knew well).

The old woman is aged, but the others may be young. The old friend is still a friend, but the old boyfriend might now be an enemy. Is there a basic usage which can link the others together?

"Aged" in the sense of "in existence for longer than the norm" is arguably the default meaning of *old*. This sense stays the same when the sentence is switched around: *Old* before the noun—"attributive position"—still means the same when moved to after *is*, "predicative position."

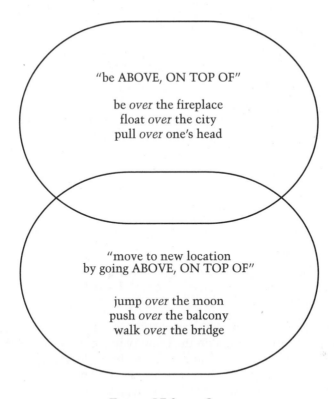

FIGURE 17.2   *Over.*

Pauline saw an old woman: the woman is old.

This meaning also works with various other words, such as *building, tradition*—though a minor complication is that in some cases the opposite of *old* is *young*, as in *young woman*, in others *new*, as in *new building*. The sense "long existence" can also cover *old friend*, though *old* cannot be moved about in the sentence, because the friendship, rather than the friend, is old.

But *old* "former" as in *old boyfriend* does not fit this pattern. Nor does *old Fred*. These have to be regarded as separate, though linked meanings. So how do people know when *old* is used in these funny ways? They have to look for extra clues. A common clue that *old* means "former" is a mark of possession:

Steve's old girlfriend went to Brazil.
An old boyfriend of mine sailed round the world.
Our old house is now divided up into apartments.

In the case of *old Fred*, English speakers have to know that *old* attached to proper names is a mark of friendly affection.

In some cases, then, a basic meaning can be detected by a lack of restrictions on the surrounding syntax, as with *old* "aged." This default meaning can with minor adaptations be extended to other, less prototypical usages, as with *old* "long-standing." But it is impossible to incorporate all meanings under the one prototype. *Old* "former" and *old* "term of affection" need to be recognized as separate words. Their distinctness is signaled by the characteristic nature of the words which accompany them. This situation is shown in figure 17.3.

Old and *over* show that prototypes reduce the polysemy problem, but do not solve it. They also show that prototypes cannot always be handled by looking at words in isolation.

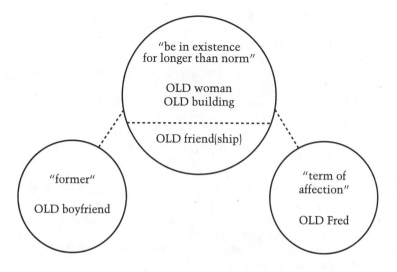

FIGURE 17.3   *Old.*

SUMMARY

We have looked at how people are able to cope with word meaning when it is so fuzzy and fluid. They analyze a prototypical exemplar of a word, and then match any new example against the characteristics of the prototype. It does not have to be a perfect match, merely a reasonable fit. This explains how words can be used with slightly different meanings, and how people can recognize new or damaged examples of a category. It also explains how people can deal with verbs.

However, prototype theory only partially solves the polysemy problem—that of cutting down on the apparent multiple meanings of a word. A full understanding of the meaning of many words requires a knowledge of the words which are found with it or related to it.

BIBLIOGRAPHY

Aitchison, J. 1981. "Mad, Bad and Dangerous to Know." *Literary Review* (July): 81–82.

———. 1985. "Cognitive Clouds and Semantic Shadows." *Language and Communication* 5: 69–93.

Armstrong, S. L., L. R. Gleitman, and H. Gleitman. 1983. "What Concepts Might Not Be." *Cognition* 13, 263–308.

Berlin, B., and P. Kay. 1969. *Basic Color Terms: Their Universality and Evolution*. Berkeley and Los Angeles: University of California Press.

Coleman, L., and P. Kay. 1981. Prototype Semantics: The English Word *lie*. *Language* 57: 26–44.

Fillmore, C. J. 1982. "Frame Semantics." In Linguistic Society of Korea, *Linguistics in the Morning Calm*. Seoul: Hanshin.

Geeraerts, D. 1992. "Polysemy and Prototypicality." *Cognitive Linguistics* 3: 219–31.

———. 1993. "Vagueness's Puzzles, Polysemy's Vagaries." *Cognitive Linguistics* 4: 223–72.

Jackendoff, R. 1983. *Semantics and Cognition*. Cambridge: MIT Press.

———. 1990. *Semantic Structures*. Cambridge: MIT Press.

Kilgarriff, A. 1992. *Polysemy*. Cognitive Science Research Paper 261. Falmer, Sussex: University of Sussex, School of Cognitive and Computing Sciences.

Lakoff, G. 1987. *Women, Fire and Dangerous Things*. Chicago: University of Chicago Press.

Lenneberg, E. 1967. *Biological Foundations of Language*. New York: Wiley.

Pulman, S. G. 1983. *Word Meaning and Belief*. London: Croom Helm.

Rosch, E. 1975. "Cognitive Representations of Semantic Categories." *Journal of Experimental Psychology: General* 104: 192–233.

Taylor, J. R. 1989. *Linguistic Categorization: Prototypes in Linguistic Theory*. Oxford: Clarendon Press.

———. 1992. "Old Problems: Adjectives in Cognitive Grammar." *Cognitive Linguistics* 3: 1–35.

Zwicky, A., and J. Sadock. 1975. "Ambiguity Tests and How to Fail Them. In *Syntax and Semantics*, ed. J. Kimball, Vol. 4. New York: Academic Press.

═══

FOR DISCUSSION AND REVIEW

1. What is a "prototype theory"? In what ways is this theory of word classification useful in our ongoing study of language?

2. How do we qualify the meaning of "lie"? In what instances are untruths not classified as lies? What complications could this "qualification system" present for foreign-language and ESL students?

3. How do verbs such as "see" and "go" adhere to prototype theory? Compare your results with prototypes of other words.

4. How do English speakers learn to judge something against a prototype?

5. What are the differences between *identification criteria* and *stored*

knowledge? How do we communicate successfully if we do not know how identification criteria are interwoven with stored knowledge in speakers' minds?

6. What difficulties exist in defining the characteristics of a prototype?

7. How and where do we place restrictions on the sorting of prototype features? Give examples to support your claims.

8. Why is it important to be aware that we should not deal with words in isolation?

18

The Tower of Babel

Steven Pinker

All humans possess a language, but it is overwhelming to contemplate the vast numbers of languages that are spoken and the differences that make them mutually unintelligible. How did languages evolve? Are they descendants of a single prototypical language, or did they emerge spontaneously in different parts of the world as the result of an innate human instinct? How much of a given language is learned by its speakers, and how much is innate? Is every language unique, or are there certain universal characteristics inherent in all languages? In the following essay, an excerpted chapter from his book The Language Instinct: How the Mind Creates Language, *Steven Pinker, the highly honored professor and director of the Center for Cognitive Neuroscience at the Massachusetts Institute of Technology, examines these and other questions concerning the multiplicity of languages and the structural rules of "Universal Grammar" they share. Using English as the example, Pinker defines the variables that distinguish one language from another and the characteristics that link all languages as a common trait of human nature.*

And the whole earth was of one language, and of one speech. And it came to pass, as they journeyed from the east, that they found a plain in the land of Shinar; and they dwelt there. And they said one to another, Go to, let us make brick, and burn them thoroughly. And they had brick for stone, and slime had they for mortar. And they said, Go to, let us build us a city and a tower, whose top may reach unto heaven; and let us make us a name, lest we be scattered abroad upon the face of the whole earth. And the Lord came down to see the city and the tower, which the children of men builded. And the Lord said, Behold, the people is one, and they have all one language; and this they begin to do: and now nothing will be restrained from them, which they have imagined to do. Go to, let us go down, and there confound their language, that they may not understand one another's speech. So the Lord scattered them abroad from thence upon the face of all the earth: and they left off to build the city. Therefore is the name of it called Babel; because the Lord did there confound the language of all the earth: and from thence did the Lord scatter them abroad upon the face of all the earth. (Genesis 11:1–9)

In the year of our Lord 1957, the linguist Martin Joos reviewed the preceding three decades of research in linguistics and concluded that God had actually gone much farther in confounding the language of Noah's descendants. Whereas the God of Genesis was said to be content with mere mutual unintelligibility, Joos declared that "languages could differ from each other without limit and in unpredictable ways." That same year, the Chomskyan revolution began with the publication of *Syntactic Structures*, and the next three decades took us back to the literal biblical account. According to Chomsky, a visiting Martian scientist would surely conclude that aside from their mutually unintelligible vocabularies, Earthlings speak a single language.

Even by the standards of theological debates, these interpretations are strikingly different. Where did they come from? The 4,000 to 6,000 languages of the planet do look impressively different from English and from one another. Here are the most conspicuous ways in which languages can differ from what we are used to in English:

1. English is an "isolating" language, which builds sentences by rearranging immutable word-sized units, like *Dog bites man* and *Man bites dog*. Other languages express who did what to whom by modifying nouns with case affixes, or by modifying the verb with affixes that agree with its role-players in number, gender, and person. One example is Latin, an "inflecting" language in which each affix contains several pieces of information; another is Kivunjo, an "agglutinating" language in which each affix conveys one piece of information and many affixes are strung together.

2. English is a "fixed-word-order" language where each phrase has a fixed position. "Free-word-order" languages allow phrase order to vary. In an extreme case like the Australian aboriginal language Warlpiri, words from different phrases can be scrambled together: *This man speared a kangaroo* can be expressed as *Man this kangaroo speared*, *Man kangaroo speared this*, and any of the other four orders, all completely synonymous.

3. English is an "accusative" language, where the subject of an intransitive verb, like *she* in *She ran*, is treated identically to the subject of a transitive verb, like *she* in *She kissed Larry*, and different from the object of the transitive verb, like *her* in *Larry kissed her*. "Ergative" languages like Basque and many Australian languages have a different scheme for collapsing these three roles. The subject of an intransitive verb and the *object* of a transitive verb are identical, and the subject of the transitive is the one that behaves differently. It is as if we were to say *Ran her* to mean "She ran."

4. English is a "subject-prominent" language in which all sentences must have a subject (even if there is nothing for the subject to refer to, as in *It is raining* or *There is a unicorn in the garden*). In "topic-prominent" languages like Japanese, sentences have a special position that is filled by the current topic of the conversation, as in *This place, planting wheat is good* or *California, climate is good*.

5. English is an "SVO" language, with the order subject-verb-object (*Dog bites man*). Japanese is subject-object-verb (SOV: *Dog man bites*); Modern Irish (Gaelic) is verb-subject-object (VSO: *Bites dog man*).

6. In English, a noun can name a thing in any construction: *a banana; two bananas; any banana; all the bananas*. In "classifier" languages, nouns fall into gender classes like human, animal, inanimate, one-dimensional, two-dimensional, cluster, tool, food, and so on. In many constructions, the name for the class, not the noun itself, must be used—for example, three hammers would be referred to as *three tools, to wit hammer*.

And, of course, a glance at a grammar for any particular language will reveal dozens or hundreds of idiosyncrasies.

On the other hand, one can also hear striking universals through the babble. In 1963 the linguist Joseph Greenberg examined a sample of thirty far-flung languages from five continents, including Serbian, Italian, Basque, Finnish, Swahili, Nubian, Masaai, Berber, Turkish, Hebrew, Hindi, Japanese, Burmese, Malay, Maori, Mayan, and Quechua (a descendant of the language of the Incas). Greenberg was not working in the Chomskyan school; he just wanted to see if any interesting properties of grammar could be found in all these languages. In his first investigation, which focused on the order of words and morphemes, he found no fewer than forty-five universals.

Since then, many other surveys have been conducted, involving scores of languages from every part of the world, and literally hundreds of universal patterns have been documented. Some hold absolutely. For example, no language forms questions by reversing the order of words within a sentence, like *Built Jack that house the this is?* Some are statistical: subjects normally precede objects in almost all languages, and verbs and their objects tend to be adjacent. Thus most languages have SVO or SOV order; fewer have VSO; VOS and OVS are rare (less than 1%); and OSV may be nonexistent (there are a few candidates, but not all linguists agree that they are OSV). The largest number of universals involves implications: if a language has X, it will also have Y. If the basic order of a language is SOV, it will usually have question words at the end of the sentence, and postpositions; if it is SVO, it will have question words at the beginning, and prepositions. Universal implications are found in all aspects of language, from phonology (for instance, if a language has nasal vowels, it will have non-nasal vowels) to word meanings (if a language has a word for "purple," it will have a word for "red"; if a language has a word for "leg," it will have a word for "arm").

If lists of universals show that languages do not vary freely, do they imply that languages are restricted by the structure of the brain? Not directly. First one must rule out two alternative explanations.

One possibility is that language originated only once, and all existing languages are the descendants of that proto-language and retain some of its features. These features would be similar across the languages for the same reason that alphabetical order is similar across the Hebrew, Greek, Roman, and Cyrillic alphabets. There is nothing special about alphabetical order; it was just the order that the Canaanites invented, and all Western alphabets came from theirs. No linguist accepts this as an explanation for language universals. For one thing, there can be radical breaks in language transmission across the generations, the most extreme being creolization, but universals hold for all languages including creoles. Moreover, simple logic shows that a universal implication, like "If a language has SVO order, then it has prepositions, but if it has SOV order, then it has postpositions," cannot be transmitted from parent to child the way words are. An implication, by its very logic, is not a fact about English: children could learn that English is SVO *and* has prepositions, but nothing could show them that *if* a language is SVO, *then* it must have prepositions. A universal implication is a fact about all languages, visible only from the vantage point of a comparative linguist. If a language changes from SOV to SVO over the course of history and its postpositions flip to prepositions, there has to be some explanation of what keeps these two developments in sync.

Also, if universals were simply what is passed down through the generations, we would expect that the major differences between kinds of language should correlate with the branches of the linguistic family tree, just as the difference between two cultures generally correlates with how long ago they separated. As humanity's original language differentiated over time, some branches might become SOV and others SVO; within each of these branches some might have agglutinated words, others isolated words. But this is not so. Beyond a time depth of about a thousand years, history and typology often do not correlate well at all. Languages can change from grammatical type to type relatively quickly, and can cycle among a few types over and over; aside from vocabulary, they do not progressively differentiate and diverge. For example, English has changed from a free-word-order, highly inflected, topic-prominent language, as its sister German remains to this day, to a fixed-word-order, poorly inflected, subject-prominent language, all in less than a millennium. Many language families contain close to the full gamut of variations seen across the world in particular aspects of grammar. The absence of a strong correlation between the grammatical properties of languages and their place in the family tree of languages suggests that language universals are not just the properties that happen to have survived from the hypothetical mother of all languages.

The second counterexplanation that one must rule out before attributing a universal of language to a universal language instinct is that languages might reflect universals of thought or of mental information processing that are not specific to language. Universals of color vocabulary probably come from universals of color vision. Perhaps subjects precede objects because the subject of an action verb denotes the causal agent (as in *Dog bites man*); putting the subject first mirrors the cause coming before the effect. Perhaps head-first or head-last ordering is consistent across all the phrases in a language because it enforces a consistent branching direction, right or left, in the language's phrase structure trees, avoiding difficult-to-understand onion constructions. For example, Japanese is SOV and has modifiers to the left; this gives it constructions like "modifier-SOV" with the modifier on the outside rather than "S-modifier OV" with the modifier embedded inside.

But these functional explanations are often tenuous, and for many universals they do not work at all. For example, Greenberg noted that if a language has both derivational suffixes (which create new words from old ones) and inflectional suffixes (which modify a word to fit its role in the sentence), then the derivational suffixes are always closer to the stem than the inflectional ones. We see this principle in English in the difference between the grammatical *Darwinisms* and the ungrammatical *Darwinsism*. It is hard to think of how this law could be a consequence of any universal principle of thought or memory: why would the concept of two ideologies based on one Darwin be thinkable, but the concept of one ideology based on two Darwins (say, Charles and Erasmus) not be thinkable (unless one reasons in a circle and declares that the mind must find -*ism* to be more cognitively basic than the plural, because that's the order we see in language)? And keep in mind Peter Gordon's experiments showing that children say *mice-eater* but never *rats-eater*, despite the conceptual similarity of rats and mice and despite the absence of either kind of compound in parents' speech. His results corroborate the suggestion that this particular universal is caused by the way that morphological rules are computed in the brain, with inflection applying to the products of derivation but not vice versa.

In any case, Greenbergisms are not the best place to look for a neurologically given Universal Grammar that existed before Babel. It is the organization of grammar as a whole, not some laundry list of facts, that we should be looking at. Arguing about the possible causes of something like SVO order misses the forest for the trees. What is most striking of all is that we can look at a randomly picked language and find things that can sensibly be called subjects, objects, and verbs to begin with. After all, if we were asked to look for the order of subject, object, and verb in musical notation, or in the computer programming language FORTRAN, or in Morse code, or in arithmetic, we would protest that the very idea is nonsensical. It would be like assembling a representative collection of the world's cultures from the six continents and trying to survey the colors of their hockey team jerseys or the form of their harakiri rituals. We should be impressed, first and foremost, that research on universals of grammar is even possible!

When linguists claim to find the same kinds of linguistic gadgets in language after language, it is not just because they expect languages to have subjects and so they label as a "subject" the first kind of phrase they see that resembles an English subject. Rather, if a linguist examining a language for the first time calls a phrase a "subject" using one criterion based on English subjects—say, denoting the agent role of action verbs—the linguist soon discovers that other criteria, like agreeing with the verb in person and number and occurring before the object, will be true of that phrase as well. It is these *correlations* among the properties of a linguistic thingamabob across languages that make it scientifically meaningful to talk about subjects and objects and nouns and verbs and auxiliaries and inflections—and not just Word Class #2,783 and Word Class #1,491—in languages from Abaza to Zyrian.

Chomsky's claim that from a Martian's-eye-view all humans speak a single language is based on the discovery that the same symbol-manipulating machinery, without exception, underlies the world's languages. Linguists have long known that the basic design features of language are found everywhere. Many were documented in 1960 by the non-Chomskyan linguist C. F. Hockett in a comparison between human languages and animal communication systems (Hockett was not acquainted with Martian). Languages use the mouth-to-ear channel as long as the users have intact hearing (manual and facial gestures, of course, are the substitute channel used by the deaf). A common grammatical code, neutral between production and comprehension, allows speakers to produce any linguistic message they can understand, and vice versa. Words have stable meanings, linked to them by arbitrary convention. Speech sounds are treated discontinuously; a sound that is acoustically halfway between *bat* and *pat* does not mean something halfway between batting and patting. Languages can convey meanings that are abstract and remote in time or space from the speaker. Linguistic forms are infinite in number, because they are created by a discrete combinatorial system. Languages all show a duality of patterning in which one rule system is used to order phonemes within morphemes, independent of meaning, and another is used to order morphemes within words and phrases, specifying their meaning.

Chomskyan linguistics, in combination with Greenbergian surveys, allows us to go well beyond this basic spec sheet. All languages have a vocabulary in the thousands or tens of thousands, sorted into part-of-speech categories including noun and verb. Words are organized into phrases according to the X-bar system (nouns are found inside N-bars, which are found inside noun phrases, and so on). The higher levels of phrase structure include auxiliaries (INFL), which signify tense, modality, aspect, and negation. Nouns are marked for case and assigned semantic roles by the mental dictionary entry of the verb or other predicate. Phrases can be moved from their deep-structure positions, leaving a gap or "trace," by a structure-dependent movement rule, thereby forming questions, relative clauses, passives, and other widespread constructions. New word structures can be created and modified by derivational and inflectional rules. Inflectional rules primarily mark nouns for case and number, and mark verbs for tense, aspect, mood, voice, negation, and agreement with subjects and objects in number, gender, and person. The phonological forms of words are defined by metrical and syllable trees and separate tiers of features like voicing, tone, and manner and place of articulation, and are subsequently adjusted by ordered phonological rules. Though many of these arrangements are in some sense useful, their details, found in language after language but not in any artificial system like FORTRAN or musical notation, give a strong impression that a Universal Grammar, not reducible to history or cognition, underlies the human language instinct.

God did not have to do much to confound the language of Noah's descendants. In addition to vocabulary—whether the word for "mouse" is *mouse* or *souris*—a few properties of language are simply not specified in Universal Grammar and can vary as parameters. For example, it is up to each language to choose whether the order of elements within a phrase is head-first or head-last (*eat sushi* and *to Chicago* versus *sushi eat* and *Chicago to*) and whether a subject is mandatory in all sentences or can be omitted when the speaker desires. Furthermore, a particular grammatical widget often does a great deal of important work in one language and hums away unobtrusively in the corner of another. The overall impression is that Universal Grammar is like an archetypal body plan found across vast numbers of animals in a phylum. For example, among all the amphibians, reptiles, birds, and mammals, there is a common body architecture, with a segmented backbone, four jointed limbs, a tail, a skull, and so on. The various parts can be grotesquely distorted or stunted across animals: a bat's wing is a hand, a horse trots on its middle toes, whales' forelimbs have become flippers and their hindlimbs have shrunken to invisible nubs, and the tiny hammer, anvil, and stirrup of the mammalian middle ear are jaw parts of reptiles. But from newts to elephants, a common topology of the body plan—the shin bone connected to the thigh bone, the thigh bone connected to the hip bone—can be discerned. Many of the differences are caused by minor variations in the relative timing and rate of growth of the parts during embryonic development. Differences among languages are similar. There seems to be a common plan of syntactic, morphological, and phonological rules and principles, with a small set of varying parameters, like a checklist of options. Once set, a parameter can have far-reaching changes on the superficial appearance of the language.

If there is a single plan just beneath the surfaces of the world's languages, then any basic property of one language should be found in all the others. Let's reexamine the six supposedly un-English language traits that opened the chapter. A closer look shows that all of them can be found right here in English, and that the supposedly distinctive traits of English can be found in the other languages.

1. English, like the inflecting languages it supposedly differs from, has an agreement marker, the third person singular *-s* in *He walks*. It also has case distinctions in the pronouns, such as *he* versus *him*. And like agglutinating languages, it has machinery that can glue many bits together into a long word, like the derivational rules and

affixes that create *sensationalization* and *Darwinianisms*. Chinese is supposed to be an even more extreme example of an isolating language than English, but it, too, contains rules that create multipart words such as compounds and derivatives.

2. English, like free-word-order languages, has free ordering in strings of prepositional phrases, where each preposition marks the semantic role of its noun phrase as if it were a case marker: *The package was sent from Chicago to Boston by Mary; The package was sent by Mary to Boston from Chicago; The package was sent to Boston from Chicago by Mary*, and so on. Conversely, in so-called scrambling languages at the other extreme, like Warlpiri, word order is never completely free; auxiliaries, for example, must go in the second position in a sentence, which is rather like their positioning in English.

3. English, like ergative languages, marks a similarity between the objects of transitive verbs and the subjects of intransitive verbs. Just compare *John broke the glass* (glass = object) with *The glass broke* (glass = subject of intransitive), or *Three men arrived* with *There arrived three men*.

4. English, like topic-prominent languages, has a topic constituent in constructions like *As for fish, I eat salmon* and *John I never really liked*.

5. Like SOV languages, not too long ago English availed itself of an SOV order, which is still interpretable in archaic expressions like *Till death do us part* and *With this ring I thee wed*.

6. Like classifier languages, English insists upon classifiers for many nouns: you can't refer to a single square as *a paper* but must say *a sheet of paper*. Similarly, English speakers say *a piece of fruit* (which refers to an apple, not a piece of an apple), *a blade of grass, a stick of wood, fifty head of cattle*, and so on.

If a Martian scientist concludes that humans speak a single language, that scientist might well wonder why Earthspeak has those thousands of mutually unintelligible dialects (assuming that the Martian has not read Genesis 11; perhaps Mars is beyond the reach of the Gideon Society). If the basic plan of language is innate and fixed across the species, why not the whole banana? Why the head-first parameter, the different-sized color vocabularies, the Boston accent?

Terrestrial scientists have no conclusive answer. The theoretical physicist Freeman Dyson proposed that linguistic diversity is here for a reason: "it was nature's way to make it possible for us to evolve rapidly," by creating isolated ethnic groups in which undiluted biological and cultural evolution can proceed swiftly. But Dyson's evolutionary reasoning is defective. Lacking foresight, lineages try to be the best that they can be, *now*; they do not initiate change for change's sake on the chance that one of the changes might come in handy in some ice age ten thousand years in the future. Dyson is not the first to ascribe a purpose to linguistic diversity. A Colombian Bará Indian, a member of an outbreeding set of tribes, when asked by a linguist why there were so many languages, explained, "If we were all Tukano speakers, where would we get our women?"

As a native of Quebec, I can testify that differences in language lead to differences in ethnic identification, with widespread effects, good and bad. But the suggestions of Dyson and the Bará put the causal arrow backwards. Surely head-first parameters and all the rest represent massive overkill in some design to distinguish among ethnic groups, assuming that that was even evolutionarily desirable. Humans are ingenious at sniffing out minor differences to figure out whom they should despise. All it takes is that European/Americans have light skin and African Americans have dark skin, that Hindus make a point of not eating beef and Moslems make a point of not eating pork, or, in the Dr. Seuss story, that the Star-Bellied Sneetches have bellies with stars and the Plain-Bellied Sneetches have none upon "thars." Once there is more than one language, ethnocentrism can do the rest; we need to understand why there is more than one language.

Darwin himself expressed the key insight:

> The formation of different languages and of distinct species, and the proofs that both have been developed through a gradual process, are curiously parallel. . . . We find in distinct languages striking homologies due to community of descent, and analogies due to a similar process of formation. . . . Languages, like organic beings, can be classed in groups under groups; and they can be classed either naturally, according to descent, or artificially by other characters. Dominant languages and dialects spread widely, and lead to the gradual extinction of other tongues. A language, like a species, when extinct, never . . . reappears.

That is, English is similar though not identical to German for the same reason that foxes are similar though not identical to wolves: English and German are modifications of a common ancestor language spoken in the past, and foxes and wolves are modifications of a common ancestor species that lived in the past. Indeed, Darwin claimed to have taken some of his ideas about biological evolution from the linguistics of his time.

Differences among languages, like differences among species, are the effects of three processes acting over long spans of time. One process is variation—mutation, in the case of species; linguistic innovation, in the case of languages. The second is heredity, so that descendants resemble their progenitors in these variations—genetic inheritance, in the case of species; the ability to learn, in the case of languages. The third is isolation—by geography, breeding season, or reproductive anatomy, in the case of species; by migration or social barriers, in the case of languages. In both cases, isolated populations accumulate separate sets of variations and hence diverge over time. To understand why there is more than one language, then, we must understand the effects of innovation, learning, and migration.

Let me begin with the ability to learn, and by convincing you that there is something to explain. Many social scientists believe that learning is some pinnacle of evolution that humans have scaled from the lowlands of instinct, so that our ability to learn can be explained by our exalted braininess. But biology says otherwise. Learning is found in organisms as simple as bacteria, and, as James and Chomsky pointed out, human intelligence may depend on our having *more* innate instincts, not fewer. Learning is an option, like camouflage or horns, that nature gives organisms as needed—when some aspect of the organisms' environmental niche is so unpredictable that anticipation of its contingencies cannot be wired in. For example, birds that nest on small cliff ledges do not learn to recognize their offspring. They do not need to, for any blob of the right size and shape in their nest is sure to be one. Birds that nest in large colonies, in contrast, are in danger of feeding some neighbor's offspring that sneaks in, and they have evolved a mechanism that allows them to learn the particular nuances of their own babies.

Even when a trait starts off as a product of learning, it does not have to remain so. Evolutionary theory, supported by computer simulations, has shown that when an environment is stable, there is a selective pressure for learned abilities to become increasingly innate. That is because if an ability is innate, it can be deployed earlier in the lifespan of the creature, and there is less of a chance that an unlucky creature will miss out on the experiences that would have been necessary to teach it.

Why might it pay for the child to learn parts of a language rather than having the whole system hard-wired? For vocabulary, the benefits are fairly obvious: 60,000 words might be too many to evolve, store, and maintain in a genome comprising only 50,000 to 100,000 genes. And words for new plants, animals, tools, and especially people are needed throughout the lifespan. But what good is it to learn different grammars? No one knows, but here are some plausible hypotheses.

Perhaps some of the things about language that we have to learn are easily learned by simple mechanisms that antedated the evolution of grammar. For example, a simple kind of learning circuit might suffice to record which element comes before which other one, as long as the elements are first defined and identified by some other cognitive module. If a universal grammar module defines a head and a role-player, their relative ordering (head-first or head-last) could thus be recorded easily. If so, evolution, having made the basic computational units of language innate, may have seen no need to replace every bit of learned information with innate wiring. Computer simulations of evolution show that the pressure to replace learned neural connections with innate ones diminishes as more and more of the network becomes innate, because it becomes less and less likely that learning will fail for the rest.

A second reason for language to be partly learned is that language inherently involves sharing a code with other people. An innate grammar is useless if you are the only one possessing it: it is a tango of one, the sound of one hand clapping. But the genomes of other people mutate and drift and recombine when they have children. Rather than selecting for a completely innate grammar, which would soon fall out of register with everyone else's, evolution may have given children an ability to learn the variable parts of language as a way of synchronizing their grammars with that of the community.

The second component of language differentiation is a source of variation. Some person, somewhere, must begin to speak differently from the neighbors, and the innovation must spread and catch on like a contagious disease until it becomes epidemic, at which point children perpetuate it. Change can arise from many sources. Words are coined, borrowed from other languages, stretched in meaning, and forgotten. New jargon or speech styles may sound way cool within some subculture and then infiltrate the mainstream. Specific examples of these borrowings are a subject of fascination to pop language fanciers and fill many books and columns. Personally, I have trouble getting excited. Should we really be astounded to learn that English borrowed *kimono* from Japanese, *banana* from Spanish, *moccasin* from the American Indians, and so on?

Because of the language instinct, there is something much more fascinating about linguistic innovation: each link in the chain of language transmission is a human brain. That brain is equipped with a universal grammar and is always on the lookout for examples in ambient speech of various kinds of rules. Because speech can be sloppy and words and sentences ambiguous, people are occasionally apt to *reanalyze* the speech they hear—they interpret it as having come from a different dictionary entry or rule than the ones that the speaker actually used.

A simple example is the word *orange*. Originally it was *norange*, borrowed from the Spanish *naranjo*. But at some point some unknown creative speaker must have reanalyzed *a norange* as *an orange*. Though the speaker's and hearer's analyses specify identical sounds for that particular phrase, *anorange*, once the hearer uses the rest of grammar creatively, the change becomes audible, as in *those oranges* rather than *those noranges*. (This particular change has been common in English. Shakespeare used *nuncle* as an affectionate name, a recutting of *mine Uncle* to *my nuncle*, and *Ned* came from *Edward* by a similar route. Nowadays many people talk about *a whole nother thing*, and I know of a child who eats *ectarines* and an adult called *Nalice* who refers to people she doesn't care for as *nidiots*.)

Reanalysis, a product of the discrete combinatorial creativity of the language instinct, partly spoils the analogy between language change on the one hand and biological and cultural evolution on the other. Many linguistic innovations are not like random mutation, drift, erosion, or borrowing. They are more like legends or jokes that are embellished or improved or reworked with each retelling. That is why, although grammars change quickly through history, they do not degenerate, for reanalysis is an inexhaustible source of new complexity. Nor must they progressively differentiate, for grammars can hop among the grooves made available by the universal grammar in everyone's mind. Moreover, one change in a language can cause an imbalance that can trigger a cascade of other changes elsewhere, like falling dominoes. Any part of language can change:

• Many phonological rules arose when hearers in some community reanalyzed rapid, coarticulated speech. Imagine a dialect that lacks the rule that converts *t* to a flapped *d* in *utter*. Its speakers generally pronounce the *t* as a *t*, but may not do so when speaking rapidly or affecting a casual "lazy" style. Hearers may then credit them with a flapping rule, and they (or their children) would then pronounce the *t* as a flap even in careful speech. Taken further, even the underlying phonemes can be reanalyzed. This is how we got *v*. Old English didn't have a *v*; our word *starve* was originally *steorfan*. But any *f* between two vowels was pronounced with voicing turned on, so *ofer* was pronounced "over," thanks to a rule similar to the contemporary flapping rule. Listeners eventually analyzed the *v* as a separate phoneme, rather than as a pronunciation of *f*, so now the word actually is *over*, and *v* and *f* are available as separate phonemes. For example, we can now differentiate words like *waver* and *wafer*, but King Arthur could not have.

• The phonological rules governing the *pronunciation* of words can, in turn, be reanalyzed into morphological rules governing the *construction* of them. Germanic languages like Old English had an "umlaut" rule that changed a back vowel to a front vowel if the next syllable contained a high front vowel sound. For example, in *foti*, the plural of "foot," the back *o* was altered by the rule to a front *e*, harmonizing with the front *i*. Subsequently the *i* at the end ceased being pronounced, and because the phonological rule no longer had anything to trigger it, speakers reinterpreted the *o–e* shift as a morphological relationship signaling the plural—resulting in our *foot–feet, mouse–mice, goose–geese, tooth–teeth*, and *louse–lice*.

• Reanalysis can also take two variants of one word, one created from the other by an inflectional rule, and recategorize them as separate words. The speakers of yesteryear might have noticed that an inflectional *oo–ee* rule applies not to all items but only to a few: *tooth–teeth*, but not *booth–beeth*. So *teeth* was interpreted as a separate, irregular word linked to *tooth*, rather than the product of a rule applied to *tooth*. The vowel change no longer acts like a rule—hence Lederer's humorous story "Foxen in the Henhice." Other sets of vaguely related words came into English by this route, like *brother–brethren, half–halve, teeth–teethe, to fall–to fell, to rise–to raise*; even *wrought*, which used to be the past tense of *work*.

• Other morphological rules can be formed when the words that commonly accompany some other word get eroded and then glued onto it. Tense markers may come from auxiliaries; for example, the English *-ed* suffix may have evolved from *did*: *hammer-did → hammered*. Case markers may come from slurred prepositions or from sequences of verbs (for example, in a language that allows the construction *take nail hit it*, *take* might erode into an accusative case marker like *ta-*). Agreement markers can arise from pronouns: in *John, he kissed her*, *he* and *her* can eventually glom onto the verb as agreement affixes.

• Syntactic constructions can arise when a word order that is merely preferred becomes reanalyzed as obligatory. For example, when English had case markers, either *give him a book* or *give a book him* were possible, but the former was more common. When the case markers eroded in casual speech, many sentences would have become ambiguous if order were still allowed to vary. The more common order was thus enshrined as a rule of syntax. Other constructions can arise from multiple reanalyses. The English perfect *I had written a book* originally came from *I had a book written* (meaning "I owned a book that was written"). The reanalysis was inviting because the SOV pattern was alive in English; the participle *written* could be reanalyzed as the main verb of the sentence, and *had* could be reanalyzed as its auxiliary, begetting a new analysis with a related meaning.

The third ingredient for language splitting is separation among groups of speakers, so that successful innovations do not take over everywhere but accumulate separately in the different groups. Though people modify their language every generation, the extent of these changes is slight: vastly more sounds are preserved than mutated, more constructions analyzed properly than reanalyzed. Because of this overall conservatism, some patterns of vocabulary, sound, and grammar survive for millennia. They serve as the fossilized tracks of mass migrations in the remote past, clues to how human beings spread out over the earth to end up where we find them today.

How far back can we trace the language of this book, modern American English? Surprisingly far, perhaps five or even nine thousand years. Our knowledge of where our language has come from is considerably more precise than the recollection of Dave Barry's Mr. Language Person: "The English language is a rich verbal tapestry woven together from the tongues of the Greeks, the Latins, the Angles, the Klaxtons, the Celtics, and many more other ancient peoples, all of whom had severe drinking problems." Let's work our way back.

America and England first came to be divided by a common language, in Wilde's memorable words, when colonists and immigrants isolated themselves from British speech by crossing the Atlantic Ocean. England was already a Babel of regional and class dialects when the first colonists left. What was to become the standard American dialect was seeded by the ambitious or dissatisfied members of lower and middle classes from southeastern England. By the eighteenth century an American accent was noted, and pronunciation in the American South was particularly influenced by the immigration of the Ulster Scots. Westward expansions preserved the layers of dialects of the eastern seaboard, though the farther west the pioneers went, the more their dialects mixed, especially in California, which required leapfrogging of the vast interior desert. Because of immigration, mobility, literacy, and now the mass media, the English of the United States, even with its rich regional differences, is homogeneous compared with the languages in territories of similar size in the rest of the world; the process has been called "Babel in reverse." It is often said that the dialects of the Ozarks and Appalachia are a relict of Elizabethan English, but this is just a quaint myth, coming from the misconception of language as a cultural artifact. We think of the folk ballads, the hand-stitched quilts, and the whiskey aging slowly in oak casks and easily swallow the rumor that in this land that time forgot, the people still speak the traditional tongue lovingly handed down through the generations. But language does not work that way—at all times, in all communities, language changes, though the various parts of a language may change in different ways in different communities. Thus it is true that these dialects preserve some English forms that are rare elsewhere, such as *afeared, yourn, hisn,* and *et, holp,* and *clome* as the past of *eat, help,* and *climb.* But so does *every* variety of American English, including the standard one. Many so-called Americanisms were in fact carried over from England, where they were subsequently lost. For example, the participle *gotten,* the pronunciation of *a* in *path* and *bath* with a front-of-the-mouth "a" rather than the back-of-the-mouth "ah," and the use of *mad* to mean "angry," *fall* to mean "autumn," and *sick* to mean "ill," strike the British ear as all-American, but they are actually holdovers from the English that was spoken in the British Isles at the time of the American colonization.

English has changed on both sides of the Atlantic, and had been changing well before the voyage of the *Mayflower.* What grew into standard contemporary English was simply the dialect spoken around London, the political and economic center of England, in the seventeenth century. In the centuries preceding it, it had undergone a number of major changes, as you can see in these versions of the Lord's Prayer:

CONTEMPORARY ENGLISH: Our Father, who is in heaven, may your name be kept holy. May your kingdom come into being. May your will be followed on earth, just as it is in heaven. Give us this day our food for the day. And forgive us our offenses, just as we forgive those who have offended us. And do not bring us to the test. But free us from evil. For the kingdom, the power, and the glory are yours forever. Amen.

EARLY MODERN ENGLISH (C. 1600): Our father which are in heaven, hallowed be thy Name. Thy kingdom come. Thy will be done, on earth, as it is in heaven. Give us this day our daily bread. And forgive us our trespasses, as we forgive those who trespass against us. And lead us not into temptation, but deliver us from evil. For thine is the kingdom, and the power, and the glory, for ever, amen.

MIDDLE ENGLISH (C. 1400): Our fadir that art in heuenes halowid be thi name, thi kyngdom come to, be thi wille done in erthe es in heuene, yeue to us this day oure bread ouir other substance, & foryeue to us oure dettis, as we forgeuen to oure dettouris, & lede us not in to temptacion: but delyuer us from yuel, amen.

OLD ENGLISH (C. 1000): Faeder ure thu the eart on heofonum, si thin nama gehalgod. Tobecume thin rice. Gewurthe in willa on eorthan swa swa on heofonum. Urne gedaeghwamlican hlaf syle us to daeg. And forgyf us ure gyltas, swa swa we forgyfath urum gyltedum. And ne gelaed thu us on contnungen ac alys us of yfele. Sothlice.

The roots of English are in northern Germany near Denmark, which was inhabited early in the first millennium by pagan tribes called the Angles, the Saxons, and the Jutes. After the armies of the collapsing Roman Empire left Britain in the fifth century, these tribes invaded what was to become England (Angle-land) and displaced the indigenous Celts there into Scotland, Ireland, Wales, and Cornwall. Linguistically, the defeat was total; English has virtually no traces of Celtic. Vikings invaded in the ninth to eleventh centuries, but their language, Old Norse, was similar enough to Anglo-Saxon that aside from many borrowings, the language, Old English, did not change much.

In 1066 William the Conqueror invaded Britain, bringing with him the Norman dialect of French, which became the language of the ruling classes. When King John of the Anglo-Norman kingdom lost Normandy shortly after 1200, English reestablished itself as the exclusive language of England, though with a marked influence of French that lasts to this day in the form of thousands of words and a variety of grammatical quirks that go with them. This "Latinate" vocabulary—including such words as *donate, vibrate,* and *desist*—has a more restricted syntax; for example, you can say *give the museum a painting* but not *donate the museum a painting, shake it up* but not *vibrate it up.* The vocabulary also has its own sound pattern: Latinate words are largely polysyllabic with stress on the second syllable, such as *desist, construct,* and *transmit,* whereas their Anglo-Saxon synonyms *stop, build,* and *send* are single syllables. The Latinate words also trigger many of the sound changes that make English morphology and spelling so idiosyncratic, like *electric–electricity* and *nation–national.* Because Latinate words are longer, and are more formal because of their ancestry in the government, church, and schools of the Norman conquerors, overusing them produces the stuffy prose universally deplored by style manuals, such as *The adolescents who had effectuated forcible entry into the domicile were apprehended* versus *We caught the kids who broke into the house.* Orwell captured the flabbiness of Latinate English in his translation of a passage from Ecclesiastes into modern institutionalese:

> I returned and saw under the sun, that the race is not to the swift, nor the battle to the strong, neither yet bread to the wise, nor yet riches to men of understanding, nor yet favour to men of skill; but time and chance happeneth to them all.

> Objective consideration of contemporary phenomena compels the conclusion that success or failure in competitive activities exhibits no tendency to be commensurate with innate capacity, but that a considerable element of the unpredictable must invariably be taken into account.

English changed noticeably in the Middle English period (1100–1450) in which Chaucer lived. Originally all syllables were enunciated, including those now represented in spelling by "silent" letters. For example, *make* would have been pronounced with two syllables. But the final syllables became reduced to the generic schwa like the *a* in *allow* and in many cases they were eliminated entirely. Since the final syllables contained the case markers, overt case began to vanish, and the word order became fixed to eliminate the resulting ambiguity. For the same reason, prepositions and auxiliaries like *of* and *do* and *will* and *have* were bled of their original meanings and given important grammatical duties. Thus many of the signatures of modern English syntax were the result of a chain of effects beginning with a simple shift in pronunciation.

The period of Early Modern English, the language of Shakespeare and the King James Bible, lasted from 1450 to 1700. It began with the Great Vowel Shift, a revolution in the pronunciation of long vowels whose causes remain mysterious. (Perhaps it was to compensate for the fact that long vowels sounded too similar to short vowels in the monosyllables that were now prevalent; or perhaps it was a way for the upper classes to differentiate themselves from the lower classes once Norman French became obsolete.) Before the vowel shift, *mouse* had been pronounced "mooce"; the old "oo" turned into a diphthong. The gap left by the departed "oo" was filled by raising what used to be an "oh" sound; what we pronounce as *goose* had, before the Great Vowel Shift, been pronounced "goce." That vacuum, in turn, was filled by the "o" vowel (as in *hot*, only drawn out), giving us *broken* from what had previously been pronounced more like "brocken." In a similar rotation, the "ee" vowel turned into a diphthong; *like* had been pronounced "leek." This dragged in the vowel "eh" to replace it; our *geese* was originally pronounced "gace." And that gap was filled when the long version of *ah* was raised, resulting in *name* from what used to be pronounced "nahma." The spelling never bothered to track these shifts, which is why the letter *a* is pronounced one way in *cam* and another way in *came*, where it had formerly been just a longer version of the *a* in *cam*. This is also why vowels are rendered differently in English spelling than in all the other European alphabets and in "phonetic" spelling.

Incidentally, fifteenth-century Englishmen did not wake up one day and suddenly pronounce their vowels differently, like a switch to daylight saving time. To the people living through it, the Great Vowel Shift probably felt like the current trend in the Chicago area to pronounce *hot* like *hat*, or the growing popularity of that strange surfer dialect in which *dude* is pronounced something like "diiihhhooooood."

FOR DISCUSSION AND REVIEW

1. In 1957, Martin Joos and Noam Chomsky wrote "strikingly different" interpretations of the variations in human languages. What

was the argument of each? Which viewpoint prevails in modern linguistics?

2. Pinker identifies the six most conspicuous ways in which languages can differ from English. Review these differences. Some of the terms and concepts Pinker introduces here appear repeatedly throughout this book. What does he mean by an "isolating" as opposed to an "inflecting" language? What is the difference between a "fixed-word-order" and a "free-word-order" language? What does "SVO" mean, and how does it differ from "SOV"?

3. What does Pinker mean by the term "universals" as it relates to languages? Give an example. What does he mean by a "universal implication"? Give an example.

4. By what arguments does Pinker rule out the idea that all existing languages are descended from a single proto-language?

5. How can Chomsky substantiate the claim, in a world where thousands of languages are spoken, that a visiting Martian scientist would conclude that all humans speak a single language?

6. Name three properties of language that are variable within the framework of Universal Grammar. How does Pinker's analogy between Universal Grammar and an archetypal body plan help clarify the constants and variables of language?

7. Using English as the model, how can it be shown that the basic properties of one language exist in all other languages? Cite examples from Pinker's list.

8. Explain Darwin's important insight into the reasons for the existence of multiple languages.

9. According to Pinker, what are the roles of learning and of innate instincts in the acquisition of language by humans?

10. What does the term "reanalysis" mean in relation to language? What are the ways in which reanalysis leads to changes in a language?

11. Why and how does the physical separation of groups of speakers of a common language lead to changes in that language? American English is surprisingly homogeneous, considering the size of the United States and its population; what are the reasons for this relative homogeneity?

Projects for "Syntax and Semantics"

1. Briefly define the term *grammar*. Then ask at least five people, other than those in your class, to define the term. Jot down their definitions. Prepare a brief report in which you summarize your findings.

2. In "What Do Native Speakers Know about Their Language?" Roderick A. Jacobs and Peter S. Rosenbaum give examples of sentences illustrating the ability of native speakers to recognize a grammatical English sentence, to interpret the meaning of a sentence, to perceive ambiguity, and to determine when sentences are synonymous. Using your own native-speaker knowledge, give at least one example of a sentence that illustrates each kind of knowledge, and write a brief explanation of how your example illustrates the knowledge.

3. This exercise is a class activity. Read the following paragraph:

> The hunter crept through the leaves. The leaves had fallen. The leaves were dry. The hunter was tired. The hunter had a gun. The gun was new. The hunter saw a deer. The deer had antlers. A tree partly hid the antlers. The deer was beautiful. The hunter shot at the deer. The hunter missed. The shot frightened the deer. The deer bounded away.

Without changing important words or the meaning, rewrite the paragraph to eliminate the short, choppy sentences. Then compare the revised versions written by the other members of the class. Are the paragraphs alike? If not, describe the differences and explain why passages written so differently can have similar meaning.

4. Prepare and circulate among five to ten people a short questionnaire designed to reveal (a) their experience while studying grammar in school and (b) their attitudes about grammar. Useful information could include the grade(s) in which they were taught grammar, details of what was taught, how much time was devoted to grammar (compared, for example, to literature), and the attitudes of the teachers and students about grammar. Prepare a report summarizing your data. What are your conclusions?

5. Did your previous study of grammar enhance your understanding of English? Of other languages? If so, explain how; if not, explain why not. Be specific.

6. The study of English grammar has a long and interesting history. Write a paper or prepare an oral report on one of the following topics: the first English grammars; changing attitudes toward teaching grammar in schools; "prescriptive" versus "descriptive" grammars; the effect of studying grammar on student writing ability.

7. Based on library research, prepare a report analyzing the differing opinions of Jean Piaget and Noam Chomsky about children's mental development.

8. As a native speaker of English, you have an internalized knowledge of the language—call it a "native-speaker intuition," if you will. For example, you can recognize a grammatical English sentence, you can interpret a sentence, you can perceive ambiguity, and you can determine when strings are synonymous. Examine the following groups of sentences. What can you tell about each group?

   a. 1. The bus station is near the bank.
      2. The soldiers were told to stop marching on the parade ground.
      3. The chicken is ready to eat.
   b. 1. That student continually sleeps in class.
      2. Student in class continually that sleeps.
      3. In class that student continually sleeps.
   c. 1. The Toronto Blue Jays beat the Atlanta Braves in the World Series.
      2. The ones that the Toronto Blue Jays beat in the World Series were the Atlanta Braves.
      3. The Atlanta Braves were beaten by the Toronto Blue Jays in the World Series.
   d. 1. Sam asked the students to build a display.
      2. Sam promised the students to build a display.
      3. Sam told the students to build a display.

Write a short paper describing your conclusions.

9. Study the table "Culinary Semantics" from Dwight Bolinger's *Aspects of Language*, 2nd ed. (New York: Harcourt Brace Jovanovich, 1975, p. 207). Try to develop a similar grid or matrix for another well-defined semantic area.

10. The *semantic differential* was developed originally by psychologists as a method for semantic differentiation and determination of the connotations of words, and was made well known, especially by Charles Osgood. Joseph S. Kess suggests marking your "impressions of a word on the [following] seven-point scale according to whether [you] view [it] as being, for example, extremely good, very good, good, neutral, bad, very bad, or extremely bad. Thus, if [you] had no feeling one way or the other about a word, [you] would mark the middle slot, indicating neutrality. Take, for example, the word *mother*, and mark it according to the way in which the word strikes you as being meaningful on the following sample semantic differential" (*Psycholinguistics: Introductory Perspectives* [New York: Academic Press, 1976], p. 161).

mother

good ___ : ___ : ___ : ___ : ___ : ___ : ___ bad
kind ___ : ___ : ___ : ___ : ___ : ___ : ___ cruel
weak ___ : ___ : ___ : ___ : ___ : ___ : ___ strong
beautiful ___ : ___ : ___ : ___ : ___ : ___ : ___ ugly
nice ___ : ___ : ___ : ___ : ___ : ___ : ___ awful
active ___ : ___ : ___ : ___ : ___ : ___ : ___ passive

Culinary Semantics

	Other Relevant Parameters									Collocates With	
	Nonfat liquid	Fat	Direct heat	Vigorous action	Long cooking time	Large amt. special substance	Kind of utensil	Special ingredient	Additional special purpose	Liquids	Solids
cook3										+	+
boil1	+	−								+	+
boil2	+	−		+						+	+
simmer	+	−		−						+	+
stew	+	−		−	+				+ soften	−	+
poach	+	−		−					+ preserve shape	−	+
braise	+	−		−			+ lid			−	+
parboil	+	−			−					−	+
steam	+	−		+			+ rack, sieve, etc.			−	+
reduce	+	−		+					+ reduce bulk	+	−
fry	−	+					+ frying pan			−	+
sauté	−	+			−					−	+
pan-fry	−	+					+ frying pan			−	+
French-fry	−	+				+				−	+
deep-fry	−	+				+				−	+
broil	−	−	+							−	+
grill	−	−	+				?(griddle)			−	+
barbecue	−	−	+*					+ BarBQ sauce		−	+
charcoal	−	−	+*							−	+
plank	−	−	+				+ wooden board			−	+
bake2	−	−	−							−	+
roast	−	−	±							−	+
shirr	−	−	−		−		+ small dish			−	+
scallop	−	−					+ shell	+ cream sauce		−	+
brown	−								+ brown surface	−	+
burn	−				+					−	+
toast	−	−	+						+ brown	−	+
rissoler	−	+			+				+ brown	−	+
sear	−	+			−				+ brown	−	+
parch	−	−	−						+ brown	−	+
flambé	−	−	+					+ alcohol	+ brown	−	+
steam-bake	+	−	−							−	+
pot-roast	+	−		−			?(lid)			−	+
oven-poach	+	−	−							−	+
pan-broil	−	−	+				+ frying pan			−	+
oven-fry	−	+	−							−	+

Source: Adapted from Adrienne Lehrer, "Semantic Cuisine," *Journal of Linguistics* 5 (1969): 39–55.
*"Hot coals."

| positive ___ : ___ : ___ : ___ : ___ : ___ : ___ negative |
| heavenly ___ : ___ : ___ : ___ : ___ : ___ : ___ hellish |
| reputable ___ : ___ : ___ : ___ : ___ : ___ : ___ disreputable |
| large ___ : ___ : ___ : ___ : ___ : ___ : ___ small |

Different informants will inevitably use different intuitive criteria when making judgments about the same words. It follows, therefore, that a high degree of subjectivity is inherent in the semantic differential, which, paradoxically, is both its principal strength and its major limitation.

Select two words, and ask two people to fill out a rating scale similar to Kess's. After tabulating the results, see what conclusions you can draw. For example, you could compare reactions to the words *sick* and *ill*, or *woman* and *lady*. If this exercise is done as a class project, rather than as an individual project, then the class members should fill out the rating scales. After the results are tabulated, discuss the results and draw conclusions about the meanings of the words that were evaluated.

11. In "Bad Birds and Better Birds," Jean Aitchison examines the trait in the English language in which we qualify lists or groups of words that refer to the same subject or are different types of the same class of words. She uses such examples as distinguishing which birds are most "bird-like," and which vegetables are most "vegetable-like." Create a list of words that you believe are subject to the same judgments Aitchison describes. Organize your list into a questionnaire format and distribute it to the class. Use the questionnaire forms that Aitchison describes in her article as your models. You might include pictures of the items on your list, or you might use pictures only in your results. What do your questionnaires reveal? Does everyone in your class have the same qualification scale? Why might the results differ from one person to the next?

Selected Bibliography

Akmajian, Adrian, Richard A. Demers, and Robert M. Harnish. *Linguistics: An Introduction to Language and Communication*, 2nd ed. Cambridge: MIT Press, 1984. [A thoroughly revised edition of a very good text.]

Akmajian, Adrian, and F. W. Heny. *An Introduction to the Principles of Transformational Syntax*. Cambridge: MIT Press, 1975. [An excellent introductory text.]

Austin, J. L. *How to Do Things with Words*. Cambridge: Harvard University Press, 1962. [One of the classic works.]

Baker, C. L. *Introduction to Generative-Transformational Syntax*. Englewood Cliffs, NJ: Prentice-Hall, 1978. [Another excellent text; very thorough.]

Bierwisch, M. "Semantics." In *New Horizons in Linguistics*, ed. John Lyons. Baltimore: Penguin Books, 1970.

———. "On Classifying Semantic Features." In *Semantics*, ed. D. D. Steinberg and L. A. Jakobovits. Cambridge, England: Cambridge University Press, 1971.

Bolinger, Dwight. *Aspects of Language*, 2nd ed. New York: Harcourt Brace Jovanovich, 1975. [A readable introduction to the study of language.]

Caplan, David, ed. *Biological Studies of Mental Processes*. Cambridge: MIT Press, 1980. [Fifteen difficult but important essays.]

Chomsky, Noam. *Aspects of the Theory of Syntax*. Cambridge: MIT Press, 1965. [The first major revision of TG theory as originally described in *Syntactic Structures*.]

———. *Syntactic Structures*. The Hague: Mouton & Company, 1957. [An essential but difficult study; where it all began.]

Cole, Peter, and Jerry L. Morgan, eds. *Syntax and Semantics*. Vol. 3, *Speech Acts*. New York: Academic Press, 1975. [Excellent articles; see especially "Logic and Conversation" by H. Paul Grice and "Conversational Postulates" by David Gordon and George Lakoff.]

Cole, Ronald A. "Navigating the Slippery Stream of Speech." *Psychology Today* (April 1979): 77–78, 82–94. [A fascinating discussion of how people segment and understand the constantly changing stream of sound that constitutes speech.]

Culicover, Peter W. *Syntax*. New York: Academic Press, 1976. [An excellent introduction to the study of the formal syntax of natural language; presupposes some previous work in linguistics.]

Davidson, D., and G. Harman, eds. *Semantics of Natural Languages*. Dordrecht, The Netherlands: Reidel, 1972. [Another fine collection of essays.]

Ellis, Donald G. *From Language to Communication*. Hillsdale, NJ: Erlbaum, 1992. [An informative book about language and how it relates to human communication.]

Fodor, J. D. *Semantics: Theories of Meaning in Generative Grammar*. New York: Crowell, 1977. [Important but difficult.]

Fromkin, Victoria, and Robert Rodman. *An Introduction to Language*, 5th ed. New York: Holt, Rinehart and Winston, 1993. [An outstandingly readable text for introductory courses in linguistics.]

Goodwin, Marjorie Harness. *He-Said-She-Said: Talk as Social Organization among Black Children*. Indianapolis: Indiana University Press, 1990. [A fascinating look at how speech is used to build social organization within peer groups and how the social lives of children are organized through talk.]

Grinder, John T., and Suzette Haden Elgin. *Guide to Transformational Grammar: History, Theory, Practice.* New York: Holt, Rinehart and Winston, 1973. [Marred by typographical errors, but still a valuable presentation.]

Gumperz, John J., and Dell Hymes, eds. *Directions in Sociolinguistics: The Ethnography of Communication.* New York: Holt, Rinehart and Winston, 1972. [Explores the components of the social context that determine linguistic behavior.]

Halle, Morris, Joan Bresnan, and George A. Miller, eds. *Linguistic Theory and Psychological Reality.* Cambridge: MIT Press, 1978. [With nine main divisions that include material by eleven authors, this is a valuable collection; not for beginners.]

Hatch, Evelyn. *Discourse and Language Education.* Cambridge, England: Cambridge University Press, 1992. [A thought-provoking examination of the ways in which we use language for communication in social contexts.]

Huddleston, Rodney. *An Introduction to English Transformational Syntax.* London: Longman, 1976. [Emphasis on syntax; little about semantics and phonology.]

Jackendoff, R. *Semantic Interpretation in Generative Grammar.* Cambridge: MIT Press, 1972.

Jacobs, Roderick A., and Peter S. Rosenbaum, eds. *Readings in English Transformational Grammar.* Waltham, MA: Ginn and Company, 1970. [An anthology of theoretical and descriptive articles; excellent bibliography.]

Johnson, Nancy Ainsworth. *Current Topics in Language: Introductory Readings.* Cambridge: Winthrop Publishers, 1976. [Essays with a practical orientation.]

Joos, Martin, ed. *Readings in Linguistics.* Chicago: University of Chicago Press, 1966. [Traces the development of linguistics in the U.S. since 1925.]

Katz, J. *Semantic Theory.* New York: Harper & Row, 1972.

———. *Propositional Structure and Illocutionary Force.* Cambridge: Harvard University Press, 1980.

Kayser, Samuel Jay, and Paul M. Postal. *Beginning English Grammar.* New York: Harper & Row, 1976. [Stresses syntactic argumentation, not just assertion.]

Kempson, R. *Semantic Theory.* Cambridge, England: Cambridge University Press, 1977.

Kess, Joseph S. *Psycholinguistics: Introductory Perspectives.* New York: Academic Press, 1976. [Good chapter on the relationship between the semantic differential and simpler versions of learning theory. Draws on the work of Charles Osgood.]

Langacker, Ronald W. *Language and Its Structure: Some Fundamental Linguistic Concepts,* 2nd ed. New York: Harcourt Brace Jovanovich, 1973. [Langacker cogently builds the case for universal principles of language organization in the chapter titled "The Universality of Language Design."]

Leech, Geoffrey N. *Principles of Pragmatics.* New York: Longman, 1983. [Argues that "grammar [in its broadest sense] must be separated from pragmatics"; excellent bibliography.]

Lehrer, Adrienne. *Wine and Conversation.* Bloomington: Indiana University Press, 1983. [Fascinating; excellent bibliography.]

Lenneberg, Eric H. *Biological Foundations of Language.* New York: John Wiley, 1967. [A classic work that every student of linguistics should be familiar with.]

Lester, Mark, ed. *Readings in Applied Transformational Grammar.* New York: Holt, Rinehart and Winston, 1970. [Intended for a nontechnical audience and including articles about psycholinguistic questions and the applications of transformational grammar.]

Lieber, Justin. *Noam Chomsky: A Philosophic Overview.* New York: St. Martin's Press, 1975. [Chomsky says of this book, "It is the book that I would recommend to people who ask me what I'm up to."]

Lightfoot, David. *The Language Lottery: Toward a Biology of Grammars.* Cambridge: MIT Press, 1982. [Highly recommended; not an introduction to the whole field of linguistics, but an exploration of the question "What is the genetic, internally prescribed basis of language structure?" Excellent bibliography.]

Lyons, John. *Semantics.* Cambridge, England: Cambridge University Press, 1977. [An important two-volume work.]

————. *Introduction to Theoretical Linguistics.* Cambridge: Cambridge University Press, 1968. [Still very useful despite its date; unusually complete.]

————. *Noam Chomsky.* Rev. ed. New York: Viking Press, 1978. [Clear and complete account of Chomsky's central ideas. Contains a bibliography of Chomsky's works to 1976.]

Miller, George. "Semantic Relations among Words." In *Linguistic Theory and Psychological Reality,* ed. Morris Halle, Joan Bresnan, and George A. Miller. Cambridge: MIT Press, 1978.

Newmeyer, Frederick J. *Linguistic Theory in America: The First Quarter-Century of Transformational Generative Grammar.* New York: Academic Press, 1980. [An important work; traces chronologically and in detail the evolution of transformational-generative theory from the 1950s through the 1970s.]

Nilsen, Don L. F., and Alleen Pace Nilsen. *Semantic Theory: A Linguistic Perspective.* Rowley, MA: Newbury House Publishers, 1975. [Readable; excellent bibliographies, some of them annotated.]

Palmer, F. R. *Semantics: A New Outline.* Cambridge, England: Cambridge University Press, 1976. [A very good introductory work.]

Piattellini-Palmarini, M., ed. *Language and Learning: The Debate Between Jean Piaget and Noam Chomsky.* London: Routledge and Kegan Paul, 1980. [Fascinating presentation of Piaget's ideas about developmental stages and his belief that the brain develops as a whole contrasted with Chomsky's thesis that various portions of the brain develop independently.]

Postal, Paul M. "Underlying and Superficial Linguistic Structure." *Harvard Educational Review* 34 (1964): 246–66; reprinted in Reibel and Schane, eds. [see below]. [A basic article.]

Pratt, Mary Louise. *Toward a Speech Act Theory of Literary Discourse.* Bloomington: Indiana University Press, 1977. [An essential, synthesizing work.]

Radford, Andrew. *Transformational Syntax: A Student's Guide to Chomsky's Extended Standard Theory.* Cambridge, England: Cambridge University Press, 1981. [One of the most up-to-date specialized texts; useful chapter bibliographies.]

Reibel, David A., and Sanford A. Schane, eds. *Modern Studies in English: Readings in Transformational Grammar.* Englewood Cliffs, NJ: Prentice-Hall, 1969. [An anthology of articles on the transformational analysis of English.]

Rosenberg, Jay F., and Charles Travis, eds. *Readings in the Philosophy of Language.* Englewood Cliffs, NJ: Prentice-Hall, 1971. [Includes sections on "Theories of Meaning," "Semantics," and "Speech Acts."]

Sadock, Jerrold M. *Toward a Linguistic Theory of Speech Acts.* New York: Academic Press, 1974. [A detailed discussion of illocutionary force and performative verbs.]

Saville-Troike, Muriel. "Bilingual Children: A Resource Document." *Bilingual Education.* Series 2. Papers in Applied Linguistics. Washington, DC: Center for Applied Linguistics, 1973. [See pages 9–11 for an interesting discussion of eight components of the social context that affect linguistic behavior.]

Searle, John R. *Speech Acts: An Essay in the Philosophy of Language.* Cambridge: Cambridge University Press, 1969. [A classic work.]

Soames, Scott, and David M. Perlmutter. *Syntactic Argumentation and the Structure of English.* Berkeley: University of California Press, 1979. [Difficult but valuable; focuses on syntactic argumentation and alternative hypothesis testing.]

Steinberg, Danny G., and L. A. Jakobovits, eds. *Semantics: An Interdisciplinary Reader in Philosophy, Linguistics, and Psychology.* New York: Cambridge University Press, 1971. [An excellent but difficult collection of articles.]

Studdert-Kennedy, Michael, ed. *Psychobiology of Language.* Cambridge: MIT Press, 1983. [A collection of twenty essays; difficult but rewarding.]

Templeton, Shane. "New Trends in an Historical Perspective: Old Story, New Resolution—Sound and Meaning in Spelling." *Language Arts* (October 1992): 454–461. [A study of the reawakening of spelling and the ongoing controversy over the entire system, including children's unique spelling systems.]

LANGUAGE VARIATIONS
AND DISCOURSE

This text has been progressing incrementally from consideration of the smallest systematic units of language—phonemes and morphemes—to increasingly larger units—words and their syntax and phrases and sentences and their semantic properties. Part Five discusses discourse, the most comprehensive system of language, which involves the interaction between the speaker and the listener and the dynamics of the context in which the conversation occurs. Linguists have increasingly realized that the context of an utterance plays an important part in determining its meaning, as do the cultural backgrounds and beliefs that are shared by a speaker and a listener. In her book *Language: The Social Mirror*, linguist Elaine Chaika writes, "The dynamics of discourse are most readily understood when observed in the context of distinctive linguistic subcultures." The language spoken in a country, or even in smaller areas—a town or city—varies by region and social class. (It also varies over time, but chronological variation is the subject of Part Seven.) Regional and social dialects differ from one another because of (1) variations in vocabulary (*grinder, submarine, hoagie, hero, sub*); (2) pronunciation (/grisi/ or /grizi/, /krĭk/or krik/, /ant/ or /ænt/); and (3) grammar ("It's quarter [*to, 'til, of*] four," "He is not [*to, at, Ø*] home now"). Some variations are primarily regional; others are primarily social. Still others have more to do with an individual's age, sex, occupation, or particular circumstances. To the trained listener, an individual's speech is personally revealing, and even untrained people often can learn a great deal about people based on how they speak.

The first selection in Part Five, Paul Roberts's "Speech Communities," introduces the concept of language variation. Each of us belongs both successively and simultaneously to a number of different speech communities, some based on age, some on social class and education, and some on the places where we have lived.

The next selection, "Social and Regional Variation," reviews the study of regional and social dialects in the United States. The authors, Albert H. Marckwardt and J. L. Dillard, describe the first dialect research done in this country; it dealt with regional dialects and is best exemplified by works like the *Linguistic Atlas of New England* and the *Linguistic Atlas of the Upper Midwest*. They also identify a number of factors that have contributed to the various regional varieties of American English. Explaining that, in the 1960s, the emphasis in dialect research shifted to the study of social dialects, they discuss some of the pioneering work that was done in this area.

Next, Roger Shuy's "Dialects: How They Differ" focuses on regional dialects and examines examples of American regional variations in pronunciation, vocabulary, and grammar. Shuy also provides extensive questionnaire samples used in regional dialect research.

The final three selections in Part Five address the subject of "nonstandard" English. First, in "The Study of Nonstandard English," William Labov discusses the close relationship between standard American English and nonstandard dialects, making the important point that the latter are rule-governed and not merely corrupt forms of Standard English. In "Pidgins and Creoles," David Crystal discusses the dynamics of what occurs when languages and cultures come into contact with each other. According to Crystal, "a pidgin is a system of communication which has grown up among people who do not share a common language, but who want to talk to each other, for trading or other reasons." He goes on to explain that "a creole is a pidgin language which has become the mother tongue of a community—a definition which emphasizes that pidgins and creoles are two stages in a single process of linguistic development."

In the last selection, "'It Bees Dat Way Sometime': Sounds and Structure of Present-Day Black English," Geneva Smitherman looks at the dialect of African Americans, analyzing its most significant phonological and syntactic features and discussing their relationship to those features of standard American English. Like Labov, she stresses that all varieties of language are rule-governed. It should be understood that, based on linguistic criteria, Black English is one of the many dialects of English used in the United States. Its social and legal histories have been more complicated. As long ago as July, 1979, a federal court ordered the public schools of Ann Arbor, Michigan, to provide opportunities for teachers to learn about Black English so that they could incorporate this knowledge into their teaching methods in order to help children learn to read Standard English. In 1996, in California the Oakland School Board went a step further and caused a furor by decreeing Ebonics a language in its own right, thus entitling its young speakers to receive special language instruction in public schools.

19

Speech Communities

Paul Roberts

The concept of speech communities is basic to an understanding of regional and social variation in language, otherwise known as dialects. In the following excerpt from his book Understanding English, *Professor Paul Roberts introduces this concept and discusses the diverse factors that contribute to the formation of speech communities and to the kinds of variation that occur within those communities. Speech communities, he argues, "are formed by many features: age, geography, education, occupation, social position." He also could have added that an individual's racial or ethnic identity and gender often lead to membership in additional speech communities. In addition to speech variations attributable to membership in speech communities, all speakers of a language use a variety of jargons and a range of styles, the latter varying in terms of levels of formality. (For a discussion of these kinds of variations, see Harvey A. Daniels's "Nine Ideas about Language" in Part Two.) Finally, Professor Roberts emphasizes that language variation is a natural phenomenon that is not necessarily good or bad and that value judgments about language are often value judgments about people.*

Imagine a village of a thousand people all speaking the same language and never hearing any language other than their own. As the decades pass and generation succeeds generation, it will not be very apparent to the speakers of the language that any considerable language change is going on. Oldsters may occasionally be conscious of and annoyed by the speech forms of youngsters. They will notice new words, new expressions, "bad" pronunciations, but will ordinarily put these down to the irresponsibility of youth, and decide piously that the language of the younger generation will revert to decency when the generation grows up.

It doesn't revert, though. The new expressions and the new pronunciations persist, and presently there is another younger generation with its own new expressions and its own pronunciations. And thus the language changes. If members of the village could speak to one another across five hundred years, they would probably find themselves unable to communicate.

Now suppose that the village divides itself and half the people move away. They move across the river or over a mountain and form a new village. Suppose the separation is so complete that the people of New Village have no contact with the people of Old Village. The language of both villages will change, drifting away from the language of their common ancestors. But the drift will not be in the same direction. In both villages there will be new expressions and new pronunciations, but not the same ones. In the course of time the languages of Old Village and New Village will be mutually unintelligible with the language they both started with. They will also be mutually unintelligible with one another.

An interesting thing—and one for which there is no perfectly clear explanation—is that the rate of change will not ordinarily be the same for both villages. The language of Old Village changes faster than the language of New Village. One might expect that the opposite would be true—that the emigrants, placed in new surroundings and new conditions, would undergo more rapid language changes. But history reports otherwise. American English, for example, despite the violence and agony and confusion to which the demands of a new continent have subjected it, is probably essentially closer to the language of Shakespeare than London English is.

Suppose one thing more. Suppose Old Village is divided sharply into an upper class and a lower class. The sons and daughters of the upper class go to preparatory school and then to the university; the children of the lower class go to work. The upper-class people learn to read and write and develop a flowering literature; the lower-class people remain illiterate. Dialects develop, and the speech of the two classes steadily diverges. One might suppose that most of the change would go on among the illiterate, that the upper-class people, conscious of their heritage, would tend to preserve the forms and pronunciations of their ancestors. Not so. The opposite is true. In speech, the educated tend to be radical and the uneducated conservative. In England one finds Elizabethan forms and sounds not among Oxford and Cambridge graduates but among the people of backward villages.

A village is a fairly simple kind of speech community—a group of people steadily in communication with one another, steadily hearing one another's speech. But the village is by no means the basic unit. Within the simplest village there are many smaller units—groupings based on age, class, occupation. All these groups play intricately on one another and against one another, and a language that seems at first a coherent whole will turn out on inspection to be composed of many differing parts. Some forces tend to make these parts diverge; other forces hold them together. Thus the language continues in tension.

THE SPEECH COMMUNITIES OF THE CHILD

The child's first speech community is ordinarily his family. The child learns whatever kind of language the family speaks—or, more precisely, whatever kind of language it speaks to him. The child's language learning, now and later, is governed by two obvious motives: the desire to communicate and the desire to be admired. He imitates what he hears. More or less successful imitations usually bring action and reward and tend to be repeated. Unsuccessful ones usually don't bring action and reward and tend to be discarded.

But since language is a complicated business it is sometimes the unsuccessful imitations that bring the reward. The child, making a stab at the word *mother*, comes out with *muzzer*. The family decides that this is just too cute for anything and beams and repeats *muzzer*, and the child, feeling that he's scored a bull's eye, goes on saying *muzzer* long after he has mastered *other* and *brother*. Baby talk is not so much invented by the child as sponsored by the parent.

Eventually the child moves out of the family and into another speech community—other children of his neighborhood. He goes to kindergarten and immediately encounters speech habits that conflict with those he has learned. If he goes to school and talks about his *muzzer*, it will be borne in on him by his colleagues that the word is not well chosen. Even *mother* may not pass muster, and he may discover that he gets better results and is altogether happier if he refers to his female parent as his ma or even his old lady.

Children coming together in a kindergarten class bring with them language that is different because it is learned in different homes. It is all to some degree unsuccessfully learned, consisting of not quite perfect imitations of the original. In school all this speech coalesces, differences tend to be ironed out, and the result differs from the original parental speech and differs in pretty much the same way.

The pressures on the child to conform to the speech of his age group, his speech community, are enormous. He may admire his teacher and love his mother; he may even—and even consciously—wish to speak as they do. But he *has* to speak like the rest of the class. If he does not, life becomes intolerable.

The speech changes that go on when the child goes to school are often most distressing to parents. Your little Bertram, at home, has never heard anything but the most elegant English. You send him to school, and what happens? He comes home saying things like "I done real good in school today, Mom." But Bertram really has no choice in the matter. If Clarence and Elbert and the rest of the fellows customarily say "I done real good," then Bertram might as well go around with three noses as say things like "I did very nicely."

Individuals differ of course, and not all children react to the speech community in the same way. Some tend to imitate and others tend to force imitation. But all to some degree have their speech modified by forces over which neither they nor their parents nor their teachers have any real control.

Individuals differ too in their sensitivity to language. For some, language is always a rather embarrassing problem. They steadily make boners, saying the right thing in the wrong place or the wrong way. They have a hard time fitting in. Others tend to change their language slowly, sticking stoutly to their way of saying things, even though their way differs from that of the majority. Still others adopt new language habits almost automatically, responding quickly to whatever speech environment they encounter.

Indeed some children of five or six have been observed to speak two or more different dialects without much awareness that they are doing so. Most commonly, they will speak in one way at home and in another on the playground. At home they say, "I did very nicely" and "I haven't any"; these become at school, "I done real good" and "I ain't got none."

THE CLASS AS A
SPEECH COMMUNITY

Throughout the school years, or at least through the American secondary school, the individual's most important speech community is his age group, his class. Here is where the real power lies. The rule is conformity above all things, and the group uses its power ruthlessly on those who do not conform. Language is one of the chief means by which the school group seeks to establish its entity, and in the high school this is done more or less consciously. The obvious feature is high school slang, picked up from the radio, from other schools, sometimes invented, changing with bewildering speed. Nothing is more satisfactory than to speak today's slang; nothing more futile than to use yesterday's.

There can be few tasks more frustrating than that of the secondary school teacher charged with the responsibility of brushing off and polishing up the speech habits of the younger generation. Efforts to make *real* into *really*, *ain't* into *am not*, *I seen him* into *I saw him*, *he don't* into *he doesn't* meet at best with polite indifference, at worst with mischievous counterattack.

The writer can remember from his own high school days when the class, a crashingly witty bunch, took to pronouncing the word *sure* as *sewer*. "Have you prepared your lesson, Arnold?" Miss Driscoll would ask. "Sewer, Miss Driscoll," Arnold would reply. "I think," said Miss Driscoll, who was pretty quick on her feet too, "that you must mean 'sewerly,' since the construction calls for the adverb not the adjective." We were delighted with the suggestion and went about saying "sewerly" until the very blackboards were nauseated. Miss Driscoll must have wished often that she had left it lay.

CONFRONTING THE ADULT WORLD

When the high school class graduates, the speech community disintegrates as the students fit themselves into new ones. For the first time in the experience of most of the students the speech ways of adult communities begin to exercise real force. For some people the adjustment is a relatively simple one. A boy going to work in a garage may have a good deal of new lingo to pick up, and he may find that the speech that seemed so racy and won such approval in the corridors of Springfield High leaves his more adult associates merely bored. But a normal person will adapt himself without trouble.

For others in other situations settling into new speech communities may be more difficult. The person going into college, into the business world, into scrubbed society may find that he has to think about and work on his speech habits in order not to make a fool of himself too often.

College is a particularly complicated problem. Not only does the freshman confront upperclassmen not particularly disposed to find the speech of Springfield High particularly cute, but the adult world, as represented chiefly by the faculty, becomes increasingly more immediate. The problems of success, of earning a living, of marriage, of attaining a satisfactory adult life loom larger, and they all bring language problems with them. Adaptation is necessary, and the student adapts.

The student adapts, but the adult world adapts too. The thousands of boys and girls coming out of the high schools each spring are affected by the speech of the adult communities into which they move, but they also affect that speech. The new pronunciation habits, developing grammatical features, different vocabulary do by no means all give way before the disapproval of elders. Some of them stay. Elders, sometimes to their dismay, find themselves changing their speech habits under the bombardment of those of their juniors. And then of course the juniors eventually become the elders, and there is no one left to disapprove.

THE SPACE DIMENSION

Speech communities are formed by many features besides that of age. Most obvious is geography. Our country was originally settled by people coming from different parts of England. They spoke different dialects to begin with and as a result regional speech differences existed from the start in the different parts of the country. As speakers of other languages came to America and learned English, they left their mark on the speech of the sections in which they settled. With the westward movement, new pioneers streamed out through the mountain passes and down river valleys, taking the different dialects west and modifying them by new mixtures in new environments.

Today we are all more or less conscious of certain dialect differences in our country. We speak of the "southern accent," the "Brooklyn accent," the "New England accent." Until a few years ago it was often said that American English was divided into three dialects: Southern American (south of the Mason-Dixon line); Eastern American (east of the Connecticut River); and Western American. This description suggests certain gross differences all right, but recent research shows that it is a gross oversimplification.

The starting point of American dialects is the original group of colonies. We had a New England settlement, centering in Massachusetts;

a Middle Atlantic settlement, centering in Pennsylvania; a southern settlement, centering in Virginia and the Carolinas. These colonies were different in speech to begin with, since the settlers came from different parts of England. Their differences were increased as the colonies lived for a century and a half or so with only thin communication with either Mother England or each other. By the time of the Revolution the dialects were well established. Within each group there were of course subgroups. Richmond speech differed markedly from that of Savannah. But Savannah and Richmond were more like each other than they were like Philadelphia or Boston.

The Western movement began shortly after the Revolution, and dialects followed geography. The New Englanders moved mostly into upper New York State and the Great Lakes region. The Middle Atlantic colonists went down the Shenandoah Valley and eventually into the heart of the Midwest. The southerners opened up Kentucky and Tennessee, later the lower Mississippi Valley, later still Texas and much of the Southwest. Thus new speech communities were formed, related to the old ones of the seaboard, but each developing new characteristics as lines of settlement crossed.

New complications were added before and after the Revolution by the great waves of immigration of people from countries other than England: Swedes in Delaware, Dutch in New York, Germans and Scots-Irish in Pennsylvania, Irish in New England, Poles and Greeks and Italians and Portuguese. The bringing in of black slaves had an important effect on the speech of the South and later on the whole country. The Spanish in California and the Southwest added their mark. In this century, movement of peoples goes on: the trek of southern blacks to northern and western cities, the migration of people from Arkansas, Oklahoma, and Texas to California. All these have shaped and are shaping American speech.

We speak of America as the melting pot, but the speech communities of this continent are very far from having melted into one. Linguists today can trace very clearly the movements of the early settlers in the still-living speech of their descendants. They can follow an eighteenth century speech community west, showing how it crossed this pass and followed that river, threw out an offshoot here, left a pocket there, merged with another group, halted, split, moved on once more. If all other historical evidence were destroyed, the history of the country could still be reconstructed from the speech of modern America.

SOCIAL DIFFERENCES

The third great shaper of speech communities is social class. This has been, and is, more important in England than in America. In England, class differences have often been more prominent than those of age or place. If you were the blacksmith's boy, you might know the son of the local baronet, but you didn't speak his language. You spoke the language of your social group, and he that of his, and over the centuries these social dialects remained widely separated.

England in the twentieth century has been much democratized, but the language differences are far from having disappeared. One can still tell much about a person's family, his school background, his general position in life by the way he speaks. Social lines are hard to cross, and language is perhaps the greatest barrier. You may make a million pounds and own several cars and a place in the country, but your vowels and consonants and nouns and verbs and sentence patterns will still proclaim to the world that you're not a part of the upper crust.

In America, of course, social distinctions have never been so sharp as they are in England. We find it somewhat easier to rise in the world, to move into social environments unknown to our parents. This is possible, partly, because speech differences are slighter; conversely, speech differences are slighter because this is possible. But speech differences do exist. If you've spent all your life driving a cab in Philly and, having inherited a fortune, move to San Francisco's Nob Hill, you will find that your language is different, perhaps embarrassingly so, from that of your new acquaintances.

Language differences on the social plane in America are likely to correlate with education or occupation rather than with birth—simply because education and occupation in America do not depend so much on birth as they do in other countries. A child without family connection can get himself educated at Harvard, Yale, or Princeton. In doing so, he acquires the speech habits of the Ivy League and gives up those of his parents.

Exceptions abound. But in general there is a clear difference between the speech habits of the college graduate and those of the high-school graduate. The cab driver does not talk like the Standard Oil executive, the college professor like the carnival pitch man, or an Illinois merchant like a sailor shipping out of New Orleans. New York's Madison Avenue and Third Avenue are only a few blocks apart, but they are widely separated in language. And both are different from Broadway.

It should be added that the whole trend of modern life is to reduce rather than to accentuate these differences. In a country where college education becomes increasingly everybody's chance, where executives and refrigerator salesmen and farmers play golf together, where a college professor may drive a cab in the summertime to keep his family alive, it becomes harder and harder to guess a person's education, income, and social status by the way he talks. But it would be absurd to say that language gives no clue at all.

GOOD AND BAD

Speech communities, then, are formed by many features: age, geography, education, occupation, social position. Young people speak differently from old people, Kansans differently from Virginians, Yale graduates differently from Dannemora graduates. Now let us pose a delicate question: aren't some of these speech communities better than others? That is, isn't better language heard in some than in others?

Well, yes, of course. One speech community is always better than all the rest. This is the group in which one happens to find oneself. The writer would answer unhesitatingly that the noblest, loveliest, purest English is that heard in the Men's Faculty Club of San Jose State College, San Jose, California. He would admit, of course, that the speech of some of the younger members leaves something to be desired; that certain recent immigrants from Harvard, Michigan, and other foreign parts need to work on the laughable oddities lingering in their speech; and that members of certain departments tend to introduce a lot of queer terms that can only be described as jargon. But in general the English of the Faculty Club is ennobling and sweet.

As a practical matter, good English is whatever English is spoken by the group in which one moves contentedly and at ease. To the bum on Main Street in Los Angeles, good English is the language of other L.A. bums. Should he wander onto the campus of UCLA, he would find the talk there unpleasant, confusing, and comical. He might agree, if pressed, that the college man speaks "correctly" and he doesn't. But in his heart he knows better. He wouldn't talk like them college jerks if you paid him.

If you admire the language of other speech communities more than you do your own, the reasonable hypothesis is that you are dissatisfied with the community itself. It is not precisely other speech that attracts you but the people who use this speech. Conversely, if some language strikes you as unpleasant or foolish or rough, it is presumably because the speakers themselves seem so.

To many people, the sentence "Where is he at?" sounds bad. It is bad, they would say, in and of itself. The sounds are bad. But this is very hard to prove. If "Where is he at?" is bad because it has bad sound combinations, then presumably "Where is the cat?" or "Where is my hat?" are just as bad, yet no one thinks them so. Well, then, "Where is he at?" is bad because it uses too many words. One gets the same meaning from "Where is he?" so why add the *at*? True. Then "He going with us?" is a better sentence than "Is he going with us?" You don't really need the *is*, so why put it in?

Certainly there are some features of language to which we can apply the terms *good* and *bad*, *better* and worse. Clarity is usually better than obscurity; precision is better than vagueness. But these are not often what we have in mind when we speak of good and bad English. If we like the speech of upper-class Englishmen, the presumption is that we admire upper-class Englishmen—their characters, culture, habits of mind. Their sounds and words simply come to connote the people themselves and become admirable therefore. If we heard the same sounds and words from people who were distasteful to us, we would find the speech ugly.

This is not to say that correctness and incorrectness do not exist in speech. They obviously do, but they are relative to the speech community—or communities—in which one operates. As a practical matter, correct speech is that which sounds normal or natural to one's comrades. Incorrect speech is that which evokes in them discomfort or hostility or disdain. . . .

FOR DISCUSSION AND REVIEW

1. Identify the factors that, according to Roberts, are responsible for the development of speech communities and contribute to internal differences within each community. Trace the changing speech communities of an individual, using age as the only variable.

2. Change has occurred less rapidly in American English than in British English; change also occurs more rapidly in both countries among the educated than among the uneducated. Identify three reasons why this is so.

3. Explain Roberts's statement that "Baby talk is not so much invented by the child as sponsored by the parent." Describe two examples of this phenomenon in your family.

4. Roberts writes of the "pressures on the child" to conform to the speech of his or her age group, class, and speech community. Discuss the pressures that you felt while growing up.

5. Roberts believes that there are marked differences between the speech communities of one generation and the next. Observe and describe speech differences between students and faculty in your school. Compare your findings with those of your instructor. Is age the only factor here? What kinds of differences exist between your speech and that of your parents? Between your speech and that of your grandparents? What, in general, are people's attitudes toward these differences?

6. Explain the geographic basis from which American regional dialects originated. Do you agree with Roberts's statement: "If all other historical evidence were destroyed, the history of the country could still be reconstructed from the speech of modern America"? Why or why not?

7. Roberts writes that "Language differences on the social plane in America are likely to correlate with education or occupation rather than with birth." Discuss the implications of this statement. Do your experiences support it? Explain your answer.
   (Note: Before answering questions 8 through 10, you should review Harvey A. Daniels's "Nine Ideas about Language" in Part Two, pp. 43)

8. Note three distinctive characteristics or functions, or a combination of both, of the consultative style.

9. In what ways does the casual style differ from the consultative?

10. Note five distinctive characteristics of the formal style. To what extent do you think most Americans have learned to speak in this style? Give specific examples—a professor lecturing to a class, for example, or an unrehearsed radio or television interview with a typical American.

20

Social and Regional Variation

Albert H. Marckwardt and J. L. Dillard

In the following chapter from American English *by Albert H. Marckwardt and revised by J. L. Dillard, the authors present an overview of the study of regional and social dialects in the United States. Regional dialects were the first to be studied. The methodology used was based largely on that developed in France by Jules Gilliéron and in Italy, Sicily, Sardinia, and Switzerland by Karl Jaberg and Jakob Jud. Beginning in the late 1920s, under the leadership of Hans Kurath, the original North American project called for a linguistic atlas of the United States and Canada. The first actual research, done in New England in the early 1930s, resulted in the publication of the multivolume* Linguistic Atlas of New England *(LANE) between 1939 and 1943 (reissued in 1972), the* Handbook of the Linguistic Geography of New England *(1939, 1972), and* A Word Geography of the Eastern United States *(1949). Linguistic atlases for other parts of the United States have been published or are in progress.*

In the 1960s, as Marckwardt and Dillard point out, the emphasis shifted to the study of social dialects, the identification and analysis of dialect features that are significant indicators of social class. The authors describe some of the pioneering research in this area carried out by William Labov. Acknowledging the unique problems of working with dialects in the United States, they identify a few of the distinctive differences in the vocabulary, pronunciation, and grammar of various regional and social varieties of American English. As they write, "There is still some faith in the notion that understanding is the key to tolerance."

The English language is spoken natively in America by some two hundred million people, over an area of more than three million square miles, with a large number of minority subcultures offering proof that the "melting pot" was an ideal rather than a reality. For many groups found in all parts of the country, English is by no means the only—or even the first—language. Dialectologists are slowly coming to the realization that both class distribution of language variants and prejudice against the users of "nonstandard" dialects are realities in twentieth-century America. Black

English, the dialect of "disadvantaged" Black children, was recognized legally by a landmark Detroit court decision in July, 1979. Social dialect study was largely the product of the 1960s, but public awareness of social dialects actually came about during the 1980s.

A pioneering sociologist, Glenna Ruth Pickford, began in 1956 to direct our attention to sociological factors like occupation and urban residence rather than to purely geographic factors in a paper published in that year but hardly noticed for ten years or so thereafter. The field of linguistics was, however, branching out into "hyphenated" disciplines like sociolinguistics, and works like William Labov's *Social Stratification of English in New York City* (1965) (though preceded by some important work on caste dialect in India) were perhaps most directly responsible for the new emphasis on social variation. [See figure 20.1.]

Labov's influential work, although it contains much more highly technical data, is best known for its demonstration that certain variables of pronunciation like *that* and *dat* or *fourth floor* "with or without [r]" are socially and contextually distributed. Labov demonstrated that every speaker has some differing pronunciations: to do so, he ranked data collected in casual speech, in the reading of a paragraph, in the reading of lists of unrelated words, and in the reading of paired words with something like minimal contrasts (*guard* and *god*). Not only did everyone pronounce "r" more often in the last context, but floorwalkers at posh Saks' Fifth Avenue put more "r" into *fourth floor* than did those at middle-class Macy's. S. Klein's, the poor man's haberdashery, trailed in the amount of "r" as well as in rank on the social scale.

Even more interesting than relative frequency across class, however, was the greater variability evidenced by the lower-middle class. These sociologically insecure people also indulge extensively, Labov found, in hypercorrection. Insofar as class goes (ignoring, for now, such other factors as the greater likelihood that a new biological generation will make changes), not the highest or the lowest but the class in between is the one most likely to foment linguistic change.

Research by others, as well as by Labov himself, indicates that *Social Stratification* slightly underemphasized social factors like ethnic group membership. Black English, with many of the same features in New York and Detroit as in Shreveport, Louisiana, has become one of the most thoroughly studied dialects of all time. Especially prominent has been work on the so-called zero copula (*He my main man*), and the demonstration that all speakers who use the "zero" also realize the copula in some positions (*Yes, he is*), and that non-use of the verbs *is* and *are* is not categorical with any speaker. Labov's 1969 paper on this feature developed the theory of inherent variability, with variable rules becoming the indispensable new tool of variation studies. Almost overlooked, unfortunately, were the grammatical implications of Black English forms like preverbal *been* (*You been know dat; He been ate de chicken*) marking a stronger past time (longer ago, for example, than *He done ate de chicken*).

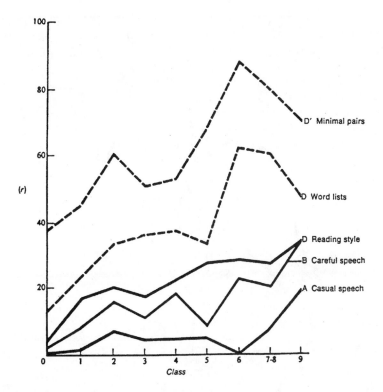

FIGURE 20.1   Detailed style stratification of *(r)*: nine classes. From William Labov's *Social Stratification of English in New York City.* Reprinted by permission of the Center for Applied Linguistics.

Dialectology, before the criticism expressed by sociologist Glenna Ruth Pickford, followed the reconstructive lead of the *Atlas Linguistique de la France* and the *Sprachatlas des Deutschen Reichs.* The approach still dominates publications like the *Journal of English Linguistics* and *American Speech.* The nineteenth century had seen the beginning of the English Dialect Society (and publications like the *English Dialect Dictionary*), and the American Dialect Society was organized in 1889. Beginning in 1928, a group of researchers under the direction of Professor Hans Kurath undertook the compilation of a *Linguistic Atlas of the United States and Canada. The Linguistic Atlas of New England* was published over the period from 1939 to 1943. Considerably more field work has been completed since that time.

Pickford strongly criticized this work for including only three social groups (five in the closely related *Dictionary of American Regional English*) and for limiting, in practice, the interviews almost exclusively to rural informants. In the 1960s, partly in response to Pickford's criticism, dialectologists began to conduct studies in Washington, D.C., Detroit, Chicago, and New York.

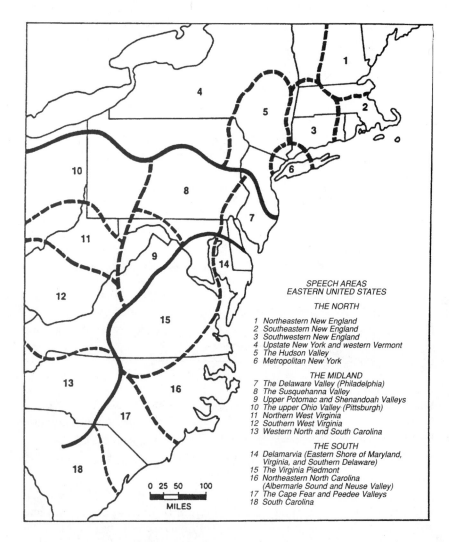

SPEECH AREAS
EASTERN UNITED STATES

THE NORTH

1 Northeastern New England
2 Southeastern New England
3 Southwestern New England
4 Upstate New York and western Vermont
5 The Hudson Valley
6 Metropolitan New York

THE MIDLAND

7 The Delaware Valley (Philadelphia)
8 The Susquehanna Valley
9 Upper Potomac and Shenandoah Valleys
10 The upper Ohio Valley (Pittsburgh)
11 Northern West Virginia
12 Southern West Virginia
13 Western North and South Carolina

THE SOUTH

14 Delamarvia (Eastern Shore of Maryland,
    Virginia, and Southern Delaware)
15 The Virginia Piedmont
16 Northeastern North Carolina
    (Albermarle Sound and Neuse Valley)
17 The Cape Fear and Peedee Valleys
18 South Carolina

0 25 50   100

MILES

FIGURE 20.2

From the *Atlas* research procedures there seemed to emerge three major dialect boundaries, cutting the country into lateral strips and labeled by Kurath: Northern, Midland, and Southern. [See figure 20.2.] This regional distribution had no place for either what Mencken had called the "American Vulgate" or for what others had called General American. Standardizing practices, often associated with the concept of General American, were dismissed as not really part of the informants' "natural" language.

What emerged in the dialect research of the 1960s, however, was something other than a picture of regional distribution. The "neutral" dialect concept of General American was replaced, especially in the research of certain psycholinguists, by that of Network Standard, the speech of television newscasters on the major networks and the kind of English which Americans clearly admired more than any other. They tended, however inaccurately, to form mental pictures of their own speech in terms of that prestige form. This regionally and socially neutral dialect clearly emerged as the ideal, if not the actuality, for most speakers of American English. Television, becoming really important as a medium in the 1960s, would permit relatively "nonstandard" usage from comedians and sportscasters, but anyone else had to disguise his dialect in order to work regularly for the networks. A nationally oriented and highly mobile population substituted this concept of a standard dialect for the older notion of prestige centers.

The older, geographically oriented type of research identified dialect areas for the essentially rural population in terms of predominantly lexical materials. For example, characteristic Northern expressions that were current throughout the area include *pail, swill, whiffletree* or *whippletree, comforter* or *comfortable* for a thick quilt, *brook, co-boss* or *come-boss* as a cow call, *johnny-cake, salt pork,* and *darning needle* for a dragonfly. When one considers how few cattle are called in New York City, or how few Manhattanites see a dragonfly during the course of a day, one realizes how irrelevantly quaint and rustic some of this research came to seem.

In the Midland area one found *blinds* for roller shades, *skillet, spouting* or *spouts* for eaves, a *piece* for food taken between meals, *snake feeder* for dragonfly, *sook* as the call to calves, *armload* for an armful of wood; and one *hulled* beans when he took off the shells. A quarter *till* the hour was a typical Midland expression, as [was] the elliptical *to want off,* or *out,* or *in.* The South had *lightwood* as the term for kindling, a *turn* of wood for an armful; stringbeans were generally *snap beans; low* was used for the sound cows make at feeding time; *hasslet* was the term for the edible inner organs of a pig, and *chittlins* for the small intestines. The last item above has now, of course, achieved nationwide spread in connection with the Black institution of soul food.

Subdialect areas were also found to have their characteristic forms. In coastal New England, for instance, *pigsty* was the normal term for a pigpen, *bonny clapper* for curdled sour milk, *buttonwood* for a sycamore, and *pandowdy* for a cobbler-type of dessert. Some eastern Virginians still have *cuppin* for a cow pen, and *corn house* for a crib. *Lumber room* survives as the term for a storeroom. *Hopper grass* competed with the national term *grasshopper,* and *batter bread* was used for a soft cornbread containing egg.

As far as the domains of the American lexicon which reflect regional differences are concerned, the matter is summarized in Kurath's *Word Geography,* where the author points out first of all that the vocabularies of the arts and sciences, of industries, commercial enterprises, social and political institutions, and even many of the crafts, are national in scope because the activities they reflect are organized on a national basis. He then goes on to say:

Enterprises and activities that are regionally restricted have, on the other hand, a considerable body of regional vocabulary which, to be sure, may be known in other parts of the country, even if it is not in active use. The cotton planter of the South, the tobacco grower, the dairy farmer, the wheat grower, the miner, the lumberman, and the rancher of the West have many words and expressions that are strictly regional and sometimes local in their currency.

Regional and local expressions are most common in the vocabulary of the intimate everyday life of the home and farm—not only among the simple folk and the middle class but also among the cultured. . . . Food, clothing, shelter, health, the day's work, play, mating, social gatherings, the land, the farm buildings, implements, the farm stocks and crops, the weather, the fauna and flora—these are the intimate concern of the common folk in the countryside, and for these things expressions are handed down in the family and the neighborhood that schooling and reading and a familiarity with regional or national usage do not blot out.

In other domains of the lexicon, social differences are more strikingly important. Americans have, from the first, identified themselves much more by occupation than by region, and early commentators made much of the "jargon" of groups like the trappers ("mountain men") and the cowboys. Groups as diverse as hoboes, prostitutes, and advertising men have their own peculiar terminology and phraseology. In particular, American Blacks have had African or Afro-Creole survivals; these survivals came to national attention beginning around 1920, through the vocabulary of jazz and blues musicians. White musicians and then American teenagers made a shibboleth of the use of Black-associated "slang," and British rock groups like the Beatles and the Rolling Stones propagated it among the English youth.

It is not only in the vocabulary that one finds regional differences in American speech; there are pronunciation differences as well. Throughout the Northern area, for example, the distinction between [o] and [ɔ] in such word pairs as *hoarse* and *horse*, *mourning* and *morning*, is generally maintained; [s] regularly occurs in *grease* (verb) and *greasy*, and *root* is pronounced with the vowel of *wood*. Within the Northern area such subdialects as coastal New England and Metropolitan New York also show many characteristic forms, although the extreme amount of variation found in the latter must not be forgotten. The treatment of the vowel of *bird* is only one of these, and words of the *calf, pass, path, dance* group constitute another. In the Midland area speakers fail to distinguish between *hoarse* and *horse* in many contexts. Rounding is characteristic of the vowels of *hog, frog, log, wasp,* and *wash*, and in the last of these words an *r* often intrudes in the speech of the rural and old-fashioned. The vowels of *due* and *new* will resemble that of *food* rather than that of *feud*. In the South and in eastern New England, there is a tendency to "lose" *r* except before vowels; but the former does not have the pronounced *Cuber* (for *Cuba*) and *idear of it* which John F. Kennedy carried from Massachusetts to the presidency. *R* is also "lost" in eastern

New England and in New York City but not in the Northern area generally. Words like *Tuesday*, *due*, and *new* have a *y*-like glide preceding the vowel, and final [z] in *Mrs.* is the normal form. . . .

Regional variation in inflectional forms and syntax at the most superficial level can also be found, especially among older, relatively uneducated groups. *Hadn't ought* is a characteristic Northern double modal; *might could* and *may can* were perhaps exclusively Southern until Black speakers carried them into the Northern cities. Verb forms associated with the North have *been see* as a past tense form, *clim* for "climbed," *wa'n't* for "wasn't," uninflected *be* in such expressions as "How be you?" (much more limited syntactically than the superficially similar Black English form), and the choice of the preposition *to* in *sick to his stomach*. Associated with the Midlands were *clum* for "climbed," *seen* for "saw," *all the further*, and *I'll wait on you*. Characteristic Southern expressions, excluding Black English influence, were *belongs to be*, *heern* for "heard," *seed* as the past tense of "to see," and *holp* for "helped."

However quaint and rustic some of these forms may seem, and however unfamiliar to many other speakers of American English, they have been used, so far unsuccessfully, in attempts to trace the settlement history, particularly of the earliest immigrants. It has been hypothesized that, of ten families of settlers gathered in any one place, two might well have spoken London English, while three or four others spoke one of the southeastern county dialects. There might also have been a couple of families speaking northern English and another two or three employing a western dialect.

What would have happened to this hypothetical dialect mix is another matter. Recent studies emphasize the way in which children are influenced more strongly by the language of their peers than by that of their parents. Even if the parents retained the old regional dialect unchanged—and sociolinguistic research questions whether this is ever completely the case—children of the second generation would level the differences. Whatever compromises between British local dialects were worked out at various points on the Atlantic seaboard would be supplemented by borrowings from the Indians and from other language groups. Other population groups which had extensive contacts with the children of the British immigrants, like the black slaves of the Southern states, would also have strongly influenced their language.

Judging by the reports of observers, these influences became especially noticeable about the beginning of the nineteenth century. At about the same time, other changes occurred which were to have a profound effect upon the language situation in America. First, the industrial revolution resulted in the growth of a number of industrial centers, uprooting a considerable proportion of the farm population and concentrating it in the cities. The development of the railroad and other mechanical means of travel increased greatly the mobility of the average person. The large-scale migrations westward also resulted in some resettlement and shifting, even among those who did not set out on the long trek. All of this would have resulted in a general abandonment of narrowly local speech forms in favor of fewer, more accessible, varieties—even if there had not been prior forces leading toward the same end.

Some local speech forms have remained even to the present day. These are usually known as relics, particularly when they are distributed in isolated spots over an area rather than in concentration. *Open stone peach*, for example, is a relic for "freestone peach," occurring in Maryland. *Smurring up*, "getting foggy," survives as a relic in eastern Maine and more rarely on Cape Cod and Martha's Vineyard.

Even prior to the shifts in population and changes in culture pattern, certain colonial cities such as Boston, Philadelphia, and Charleston had acquired prestige by developing as centers of trade and immigration. They became socially and culturally outstanding, as well as economically powerful, thus dominating the areas surrounding them. As a consequence, local expressions and pronunciations peculiar to the countryside came to be replaced by new forms of speech emanating from these cosmopolitan centers. A fairly recent instance of this is to be found in the New England term *tonic* for soda water, practically coextensive with the area served by Boston wholesalers.

Little if anything of this sort has ever been observed for the influence of New York City on any large surrounding area. Nevertheless, Madison Avenue's influence on the advertising phraseology of the nation, along with the importance of New York City for radio, television, and publication, must have had a general, widely diffused influence. It has been suggested that the "Brooklyn" dialect of popular stereotype, particularly with its pronunciation of *bird, shirt, thirty-third*, etc. (imprecisely believed to be like "oy" of *Floyd*) resembles that of the same working-class people in New Orleans and elsewhere along the Atlantic and Gulf seacoasts because of the trade connections, particularly in cotton, between New Orleans and New York City.

Nor was the general process of dialect formation by any means completed with the settlement of the Atlantic seaboard. As the land to the west came to be taken up in successive stages (for example, western New York, Michigan, Wisconsin in the North; southern Ohio, Indiana and southern Illinois in the Midland area), the same mixtures of speech forms among the settlers were present at first, and the same linguistic compromises had to be worked out. Although virtually every westward-moving group had to work out some way of dealing with the foreign-language groups in its language contact picture, the specific nature of the groups encountered varied at each stage.

The same processes occurred in the interior South, in Texas, and later on in the Far West. The complete linguistic history of the United States depends upon the formulation of what happened in each of those areas. We know, for example, from both surviving forms and historical sources that the Western cowboys used faro and poker terms (*in hock, pass the buck, deal from the bottom of the deck, four-flusher*), and occupational terms (*little dogies*, *break the string*, *hand* for "worker"), many of which moved back toward the East.

Such environmental factors as topography, climate, and plant and animal life also played their part in influencing the dialect of an area, just as they did in the general transplanting of the English language to America. The complexity and size of the network of fresh-water streams affect the distribution and meaning of such terms as *brook*, *creek*, *branch*, and *river*—not to mention *wash* and *bayou*. In parts of Ohio and Pennsylvania, for example, the term *creek* is applied to a much larger body of water than in Michigan. It is even more obvious that in those parts of the country where snow is a rarity or does not fall at all, there will be no necessity for terms to indicate coasting face down on a sled. It is not surprising that those areas of the country where cows can be milked outside, for at least part of the year, will develop a specific term for the place where this is done: witness *milk gap* or *milking gap* current in the Appalachians south of the James River. The wealth of terms for various types of fences throughout the country is again dependent, in part at least, on the material which is available for building them, be it stones, stumps, or wooden rails. It is equally obvious that nationwide technological terms for television, like *commercial*, *station break*, *prime time*, *talk show*, and *situation comedy*, should be the same in all parts of the country. Neither is it surprising that the increasingly nationwide distribution of major sporting events should lead to uniformity in *Super Bowl*, *Number One* ("We're Number One!"), *playoff*, *World Series*, and a host of other terms.

Before the days of radio, television, and national magazine advertising, a new invention or development introduced into several parts of the country at the same time would acquire different names in various places. The baby carriage, for example, seems to have been a development of the 1830s and '40s, and this is the term which developed in New England. Within the Philadelphia trade area, however, the article became known as a *baby coach*. *Baby buggy* was adopted west of the Alleghenies and *baby cab* in other regions throughout the country.

Within the last four decades, the building of large, double-lane, limited-access automobile highways has been undertaken in all parts of the country. In the beginning there were many regional differences: *parkways* in eastern New York, Connecticut, and Rhode Island; *turnpikes* in Pennsylvania, New Jersey, New Hampshire, Maine, Massachusetts, Ohio, and Indiana. (The fanciest highway in Florida, from Miami to Gainesville, is, however, now a turnpike.) In New York *thruway* is used for what are *expressways* in Michigan and *freeways* in California. For a while—in the late 1950s—these seemed like regionalisms in the making, but a generation of car travelers has learned them all and uses them now synonymously, now with some specialization.

It is of interest also to look at the dialect situation from the point of view of various words which are employed for the same concept in different parts of the country. One of the most interesting and instructive distributions is to be found in connection with the terms used for *earthworm*. This word is used by cultivated speakers in the metropolitan centers. *Angleworm* is the regional term in the North, *fishworm* in the Midland area, and *fishing worm* in the coastal South. *Fish bait* and *bait worm* occupy smaller areas within the extensive *fishworm* region, but are also distributed over a wide territory.

In addition, there have been a large number of local terms, many of them used principally by the older and less-educated inhabitants. The Merrimack Valley, in New Hampshire, and Essex County, Massachusetts, have *mud worm*. *Eace worm* is used in Rhode Island. *Angle dog* appears in upper Connecticut, and *ground worm* on the Eastern Shore of Virginia. *Red worm* is used in the mountains of North Carolina, and an area around Toledo, Ohio, uses *dew worm*. Scattered instances of *rainworm* appear on Buzzards Bay in Massachusetts, throughout the Pennsylvania German area, and in German settlements in North Carolina, Maine, and Wisconsin. We have, thus, a wealth of older local terms, three distinct regional words, and the cultivated *earthworm* appearing in addition as a folk word in South Carolina and along the North Carolina and Virginia coasts. Where and how did the various terms originate, and what can be determined about their subsequent history?

Earthworm itself is not an old word; it appears to have been compounded only shortly before the earliest English migrations to America. The earliest *Oxford English Dictionary* citation of the word in its present form is 1591; it appears also as *yearth worm* some thirty years earlier. The three regional terms all seem to have been coined in America; the dictionaries either record no British citations or fail to include the words at all.

The local terms have a varied and interesting history. *Mud worm* seems to occur in standard British English from the beginning of the nineteenth century on. *Eace worm*, as a combined form, goes back at least to Middle English; the first element was a term for "bait" as early as Aelfric; it is used today in a number of southern counties in England from Kent to Gloucester. *Angle dog* is used currently in Devonshire. *Ground worm*, though apparently coined in England, was transferred to North Carolina and Maryland in the eighteenth century. *Red worm* appears first in England in 1450 and continues through to the midnineteenth century, though chiefly in books on fishing, as does *dew worm*, which goes back even farther, to the late Old English period. *Rainworm*, though it appears in Aelfric as *renwyrm*, may be a reformation, even in British English, on the pattern of *Regenwurm* in German, for there is a gap of seven centuries in the citations in the *Oxford English Dictionary* and there is reason to believe that its revival in 1731 was influenced by the German form. Moreover, with but one exception, it has been cited for the United States only in areas settled by Germans.

Thus we have in the standard cultivated term one of relatively recent British formation. Apparently the regional terms were compounded in America, whereas the local terms represent survivals either of dialect usage or anglers' jargon and one loan translation. It is worth noting that the common Old English term, *angle twicce*, surviving as *angle twitch* in Cornwall and Devon, seems not to have found its way to America. There are, furthermore, such other English formations as *tag worm*, *marsh worm*, and *garden worm*, which have not been recorded in America.

At times, too, changes in meaning seem to have entered into the dialect situation, as is illustrated by the development of the regional terms *skillet* and *spider*, the former current in the Midland and the Virginia Piedmont, the latter in the North and the Southern Tidewater area. *Frying pan* is the urban term and is slowly supplanting the others. *Spider*, once a nautical term for "the iron band around the mast to take the lower end of futlock rigging," was then applied to a cast-iron pan with short legs. It was later transferred to the flat-bottomed pan as well. The local term *creeper* is used in Marblehead, Massachusetts. *Skillet*, a term of doubtful etymology, first appears in English in 1403, when it was applied to a long-handled brass or copper vessel used for boiling liquids or stewing meat. It is still so used in dialects throughout England. The shift in meaning to a frying pan took place only in America, but an advertisement of 1790, offering for sale "bakepans, spiders, skillets," would suggest that even as late as this a distinction between the two was recognized.

The examples above have been offered only as a suggestion of the various language processes which have played a part in the distribution and meaning of some of our dialect terms. It is quite obvious that no definite conclusions about such matters can be reached on the basis of rather scant linguistic details. Such evidence as has been accumulated, however, seems to suggest that Kurath's original intuition was correct in that only home and farm terms give much evidence of regional or local distribution in the United States.

The question of social dialects or speech differences is quite another matter, with many scholars seeing much more profound grammatical differences between social—especially ethnic—groups. Black English, of which Gullah is the extreme case, comes immediately to mind; but the English of the Pennsylvania Germans also offers some grammatical constructions that are very strange to mainstream American English speakers.

Frequently, the matter of social dialect has been conceptualized in terms of "standard" and "nonstandard" dialects. H. L. Mencken believed in a so-called "American Vulgate" with reasonably uniform characteristics throughout the country—and with no special stated social distribution. Nonstandard dialects, however, do have many features in common, for whatever reason that may be.

One of the inflectional forms most characteristic of nouns in nonstandard American English is the unchanged plural after numbers: *six mile down the road*, *five foot tall*, and similarly applied to *month*, *year*, and *gallon*. In Black English it resembles the Afro-Creole nonredundant pluralization: *The boys* bears a plural inflection, but either *six boy* or *plenty boy* is plural without the final *s*. Any plural marking in the immediate environment, not just a numeral, may suffice, so that we sometimes find sentences like *Dem chair* for "Those are chairs."

The Mencken-type Vulgate may, in the case of some unmarked plurals, represent a preservation of linguistically older forms than those found in Standard English. It displays the opposite tendency, however, in the possessive pronoun in its so-called absolute form, which in the standard language represents a strange and inconsistent mixture of patterns. *Mine* and the archaic *thine* are derived from the adjectival form by adding -*n*. *Hers, ours, yours,* and *theirs,* on the other hand, add -*s* to the adjectival form. *His* and *its* are indistinguishable so far as their secondary and absolute forms are concerned. In contrast, the "Vulgate" possessive pronouns, *mine, yourn, hisn, hern, ourn, theirn,* present a perfectly regular pattern formed by an analogical extension of *mine* and *thine* to the third person singular and to the plural forms. The fact that Pidgin English probably had absolute *me one, you one, he one,* etc., may have contributed something to the leveling process of the Vulgate.

In the use of absolute possessives, Black English and other nonstandard dialects part company. In the most extreme form, which William Stewart calls *basilect,* Black English has *he book, you friend, they uncle.* In the "exposed" position, *It he book* becomes neither *It he* nor *It hisn.* Instead, basilect *It he own* alternates with a Standard–English influenced *It his.*

The reflexive pronouns give us another instance of a more regular operation of analogy on the nonstandard level than on the standard. In Standard English, *myself, yourself, ourselves,* and *yourselves* are combinations of the genitive pronoun plus the singular or plural of the -*self* form; *himself* and *themselves* employ the object form of the pronoun, whereas *herself* and *itself* could be either. Nonstandard English, in substituting *hisself* and *theirself* in the third person and adhering to the singular of *self* in *ourself* and *yourself* (plural), is not only more consistent but more economical in that the latter combinations signal the plural only once and avoid the redundancy of the plural -*selves*. The only ambiguity is in the second person, but the second personal pronoun has lost its distinctions between singular and plural anyway, except for nonstandard formations like the Southern *you all*—which never figures in the reflexive.

One curious feature of the nonstandard pronoun is the substitution of the object for the subjective form in such sentences as *Us girls went home, John and her was married, Me and him was late.* The use of the object form for the subject is normal in Black English basilect (*Me help you?*) and in Pidgin English. In Cajun English, of Louisiana, it can be used at the end of the sentence for emphasis: *I was late, me.* In the "Vulgate," however, it seems to occur principally when the subject is compound or when the pronoun is syntactically a modifier of the subject, as in *us girls* above. The schools have made such emphatic use of *we girls* and *It is I* (or *he, she*) that the result is a lot of overcorrection on the order of *between you and I* (or even *between he and I*); *She gave it to mother and I; She took all of we children.*

A few typical nonstandard inflectional forms deserve mention. *Them* as a demonstrative adjective (*them* books) probably harks back to the days when the English article and the demonstrative *that* (dative *ðæm*) were one and the same form. *Dem* is the regular demonstrative adjective and noun pluralizer (*dem man* = "men") in Gullah, but postposed use as in Jamaican and other creoles (*man-dem*) is hinted at in the records of early Black English in one speech by newly imported African slaves and remembered by Frederick Douglass. The multiple negative was a regular and accepted feature of older English, but Black English negative concord (*It ain't no cat can't get in no coop*) has no such obvious earlier parallel. The adverb without the *-ly* suffix or other differentiation from the adjective (*He spoke quiet; You did real good*) may reflect very old practices in English.

The standard and nonstandard languages are undoubtedly farthest apart with regard to verb forms. Black English nonpassive preverbal *been* (*He been rub me the wrong way*), and *be* in its negation by *don't*, and in contrast to zero copula are the most extremely different forms outside Gullah *de*. Less significantly, there is a tendency to dispose of the distinctive *-s* inflection for the third person singular, either by eliminating it in such forms as *he want, she write*, etc., or by extending the peculiar form of the third person to the first and second—*I has some good friends; You is in lots of trouble.* Black English makes widespread, often hypercorrective, use of these forms; the records tend to indicate that older varieties used (also hypercorrectively) *he am*, etc.

The overwhelming tendency in English verb development throughout the last seven or eight centuries has been toward an aggrandizement of the regular or weak inflection (*-ed* past tense) at the expense of the older minor conjugations. This is in effect a tendency toward a two-part verb, the infinitive or present stem opposed to an identical past tense and past participle. In general, this has been brought about through analogical processes. It is often impossible to know for certain whether nonstandard forms are the result of retention of an older preterite plural (*writ* as the past tense of *write*; or *begun* and *swum* in that function), or of analogies which have not operated in Standard English. Extension of the regular past inflections to such irregular verbs as *know* and *see* (*knowed, seed*) can only be analogical; as must the amalgamation of the strong preterite or past participle with the complementary form (*I taken, he done* as preterites; *have gave, have wrote, has went* as past participial forms).

The easy transition from one social class to another in the United States has resulted in a very hazy line of demarcation between what is acceptable and what is considered illiterate. According to the most rigorous textbook standard, some of the language employed in American legislative councils and in business life would not pass muster; one could not even be sure that what is spoken in college faculty meetings would always meet those same criteria. The awareness of this, combined with an unrealistic treatment of language in our schools, has resulted at times in a defiance of these questionable standards, in what could be called "dramatic low status assertion." More often it has given people guilt complexes about the language they use. The puristic schoolteacher for whom nothing is good enough has been attacked in linguistics courses and textbooks since the 1940s. Some changes may have been made, but the prescriptive attitude, in one guise or another, lives on in our school systems and in handbooks of usage. On television's Public Broadcasting System, groups consisting of actors, drama critics, newscasters, and occasionally even a linguistics professor meet to discuss the "deplorable" state of the English language in America.

Consequently, many Americans, especially those who are socially mobile, lack confidence and assurance of the essential aptness and correctness of their speech. Fewer members of any class are able to switch comfortably between a nonstandard dialect and the standard—although this is by no means rare in other countries. Those educational programs that have called for use of children's home and peer group dialects in such educational activities as initial or remedial reading have generally met with scorn, even from many dialectologists. The Ann Arbor, Michigan, school district became in July, 1979, the first U.S. school system ordered to take Black children's dialect into account in planning its curriculum. Lawsuits similar to the one that elicited this decision have already been filed in Tampa, Florida, and Houston, Texas, and many others may follow.

Within professional dialectology, new developments like variation theory and inherent variability provide an even more solid foundation for acceptance of and interest in dialect and speech pattern differences. Popularization of the variable rule may be more difficult to achieve than was the case of regional and local differences; but there also seems to be less chance that the popularized knowledge will form the basis for invidious comparisons and linguistic snobbery. There is still some faith in the notion that understanding is the key to tolerance.

=

FOR DISCUSSION AND REVIEW

1. Explain the difference between regional (geographical) and social dialectology. Why has a great deal of work been done in the latter field in the last thirty-five years?

2. Carefully examine figure 20.1 on p. 279. The vertical axis indicates the percentage of respondents using (r); the horizontal axis indicates the frequency of occurrence of (r) by social class; the labels to the right of the chart show the increasing degrees of formality of speech. (The two top lines are broken rather than solid in order to indicate

that these styles do not occur in normal connected speech.) Having studied the figure, explain Marckwardt and Dillard's statement: "Even more interesting than relative frequency across class, however, was the greater variability evidenced by the lower-middle class. These sociologically insecure people also indulge extensively, Labov found, in hypercorrection."

3. Identify the three major geographical dialect boundaries in the United States. How has the identification of these three areas modified earlier ideas about American regional dialects?

4. Explain the concepts of General American (dialect) and Network Standard. Which, if either, is still important? Why or why not?

5. What, according to Marckwardt and Dillard, are the three aspects of American speech in which one finds regional differences? About which aspect do we have the most information? Why? Give three examples of each kind of regional difference.

6. Identify three areas of the lexicon in which regional differences are most important, and explain why this is so.

7. Explain the effects on American regional dialects of (a) the industrial revolution, (b) the development of the railroad, and (c) the large-scale migration westward.

8. List four reasons for the difficulty in doing research on American regional dialects.

9. Using examples not cited by Marckwardt and Dillard, explain how four environmental factors have influenced American regional dialects.

10. Marckwardt and Dillard state that the terms *parkway, turnpike, thruway, expressway,* and *freeway* for a while "seemed like regionalisms in the making, but a generation of car travelers has learned them all and uses them now synonymously, now with some specialization." Do you agree with their conclusion? Identify two other relatively recent inventions or developments that have acquired different names in various places.

11. Marckwardt and Dillard state that "Nonstandard dialects . . . have many features in common, for whatever reason that may be." Identify and describe four such features.

21

≡

Dialects: How They Differ

Roger W. Shuy

We all speak a dialect; a dialect is not a language form spoken by other peo-
ple in other places. One often quoted definition of a dialect is that of Raven
I. McDavid, Jr., who describes a dialect as "simply a habitual variety of a
language, regional or social. It is set off from all other such habitual vari-
eties by a unique combination of language features: words and meanings,
grammatical forms, phrase structures, pronunciations, patterns of stress
and intonation." Professor McDavid then points out that "No dialect is sim-
ply good or bad in itself; its prestige comes from the prestige of those who
use it. But every dialect is in itself a legitimate form of the language, a valid
instrument of human communication, and something worthy of serious
study."* In the following excerpt from Discovering American Dialects,
Roger W. Shuy discusses, using multiple examples, regional variations in
pronunciation, vocabulary, and grammar and provides comprehensive
dialect questionnaire samples. These questionnaires are shortened versions
of those used by field investigators in preparing the Linguistic Atlas of New
England *(LANE) and other regional atlases. The LANE questionnaire, for*
example, contained about 750 items. Shuy also explains the methods used
by fieldworkers to collect dialect data and the importance of the "personal
data sheet," and he warns the would-be investigator that people are usual-
ly more self-conscious about their grammar than they are about their
vocabulary or pronunciation.

Speakers of one dialect may be set off from speakers of a different dialect
by the use of certain pronunciations, words, and grammatical forms. The
frequent first reaction of a person who hears an unfamiliar dialect is that
the strange sounds and words are a chaotic mess. This is similar to the
feeling an American has when he sees British motorists driving "on the
wrong side of the street," or to the bewildered feeling we have upon hearing a foreign language for the first time. Surely, we feel, there is no system in that sort of behavior!

Mankind apparently views all unfamiliar human behavior as suspi-
cious and unsystematic. If you have ever watched a bird build a nest on
a window sill or in a bush within the range of any passing alley cat, you

---

* "Sense and Nonsense About American Dialects" in *Dialects in Culture:*
Essays in General Dialectology by Raven I. McDavid, Jr., edited by William A.
Kretzschmar, Jr. University, AL: University of Alabama Press, 1979, p. 70; originally
published in *PMLA* 81 (1966) 2:7–17.

have probably not questioned the intelligence of the bird. Most people accept even apparently erratic animal behavior and assume that, no matter how foolish the act may seem, it probably makes sense to the animal. But as soon as a human being is seen to behave "differently," he is frequently considered foolish or uncooperative. Language, in this case a dialect, is also a form of behavior. That people speak different dialects in no way stems from their intelligence or judgment. They speak the dialect which enables them to get along with the other members of their social and geographical group.

DIFFERENCES IN PRONUNCIATION

Differences in pronunciation are of two types: totally patterned and partially patterned. A totally patterned difference is one in which the sound behaves consistently in a particular situation. For example, in some parts of the country, particularly in eastern New England, the pronunciation of *r* is lost before consonants and in word-final position. Thus, a Midwesterner's "park the car" becomes the New Englander's "pahk the cah." From the New Englander's point of view, it might be equally valid to say that Midwesterners insert *r*'s before consonants (pa*r*k) and following a vowel at the ends of words (ca*r*). That the words in question have *r*'s in their spellings is really not important here, for spellings remain fixed long after pronunciations change, and letters may have different sound values in different dialects. But whether we say the New Englander *drops* an *r* or the Midwesterner *inserts* one, the fact remains that the difference is totally patterned in most speech styles. Recent dialect research has shown that a person may shift his pattern slightly, depending upon his relationship to his audience and on whether he is reading aloud or speaking impromptu. Professor William Labov of Columbia University has observed, for example, that New York working-class people tend to say *dis* for *this* and *dese* for *these* when they are talking about a bad accident or about a personal brush with death. They say *dis* and *dese* less frequently when talking with teachers and even less frequently when reading aloud.

The second kind of variation in pronunciation, a partially patterned difference, may occur in a few words or even in only one. The partially patterned sound is not consistent throughout the dialect. It was mentioned above that the eastern New Englander "drops" an *r* before consonants and in word-final position in a totally patterned way. Now let us cite the Midwesterner who inserts an *r* in certain words but in no particular phonetic pattern. In most of Ohio, Indiana, and Illinois (except for a few northern counties), *wash* is pronounced "*worsh*" by a large number of speakers, particularly by those with no more than a high school education. If this were totally patterned, these speakers would also say "borsh" instead of *bosh* and "jorsh" instead of *josh* (many of them do say "gorsh" instead of *gosh*).

LANGUAGE VARIATION

FIGURE 21.1

Other examples of partially patterned differences (still sticking with
r problems) include "lozengers" for *lozenges*, "framiliar" for *familiar*,
"quintruplets" for *quintuplets*, and "surpress" for *suppress*. This phenomenon, sometimes referred to as the "intrusive r," is most noticeable
in someone else's dialect. Midwesterners are amused at the Bostonian's
pronunciation of "Cuber" and "Asiar" for *Cuba* and *Asia* before words
beginning with vowels, failing to hear their own intrusive r in *worsh* and
lozengers. Likewise, the Bostonian tends to hear the Midwesterner's
intrusive r's but not his own.

Our standard alphabet cannot record the many sounds in American
English pronunciation. The dialectologist uses a highly detailed phonetic alphabet to record the most minute audible features of speech. The
student can easily learn and use a simpler set of symbols to record the
variations he meets in his dialect studies. [Here the author supplies a
résumé of the phonetic alphabet like that included by Edward Callary in
"Phonetics"(see Part Three). He then suggests that readers practice transcribing how various speakers pronounce certain words.]

Remember that a good ear for sounds is not developed right away.
You may wish to practice with other transcription exercises, or you may
simply write phonetically the words used by teachers, classmates, television performers, or members of your family. If classmates or friends
from a different part of the country are willing to serve as informants,
have them pronounce the following words:

Word	Northern	Midland	Southern
1. cr*ee*k	ɪ and i	ɪ (north Midland) i (south Midland)	i
2. p*e*nny	∈	∈	ɪ–(Southwest)
3. M*a*ry	∈ e (parts of eastern New England)	∈	e
4. m*a*rried	æ (east of Appalachians) ∈ (elsewhere)	∈	∈
5. c*ow*	ɑU	æU	æU or ɑU
6. s*i*ster	ɪ	ɨ (eastern)	ɨ (eastern)
7. f*o*reign	ɔ	ɑ	ɑ
8. *o*range	ɑ (east of Alleghenies) ɔ	ɑ and ɔ	ɑ and ɔ
9. tomat*o*	o	ə	o or ə
10. c*oo*p	u	u (NM), U (SM)	U
11. r*oo*t	U	u and/or U	u
12. b*u*lge	ə	ə or U	ə or U
13. f*a*rm	ɑ	ɑ or ɔ	ɑ or ɔ
14. w*i*re	ɑɪ	ɑɪ or ɑ	ɑ
15. w*o*n't	ə o (urban)	o ɔ	o ɔ
16. f*o*g	ɑ (New England) ɑ and ɔ (Midwest)	ɔ	ɔ
17. h*o*g	ɑ (New England) ɑ and ɔ (Midwest)	ɔ	ɔ
18. *o*n	ɑ	ɔ	ɔ
19. l*o*ng	ɔ	ɔ	ɑ (eastern Virginia) ɔ (elsewhere)
20. car*e*less	ɨ	ə	ɨ
21. stom*a*ch	ə	ɨ	ə

The vowels of these words are pronounced differently in the various parts of our country. The major variants are listed beside the words along with their general distributions.

Consonants sometimes will give clues to the dialect a person speaks. The following generalizations may be helpful:

Word	Northern	Midland	Southern
1. *h*umor	hɪumər	yumər	hɪumər or yumər
2. wa*sh*	waš or wɔš	wɔrš or wɔɪš	wɔš or wɔɪš or waš
3. wi*th*	wið and wiθ (New York, Chicago, Detroit = wɪt working class)	wɪθ	wɪθ
4. grea*sy*	grisɪ	grizɪ	grizɪ
5. *b*arn	bɑrn (Eastern North = bɑn)	bɑrn	bɑrn (East Coast = ban)
6. *th*ese	ðiz (New York, Chicago, Detroit = diz working class)	ðiz	ðiz
7. *wh*ich	hwɪč	wɪč	wɪč
8. mi*ss*	mɪs	mɪs	mɪz
9. Mrs.	mɪsɨz	mɪsɨz	mɪzɨz or mɪz

With the mobility of the American population today, we are bound to discover exceptions to generalizations like these. Also, . . . settlement history has caused some curious mixtures of speech patterns in our country. On the whole, however, the generalizations may be useful in helping you to recognize the dialect of your informant.

One bit of advice as you get your informants to say these words—*try for a natural situation*. One way professional fieldworkers have done this is to ask, for example, for what the person calls a small stream of water that runs through a farm. *Creek* is a likely response. You can easily invent similar questions for other words. It might be interesting, furthermore, to compare a person's response in conversation with his pronunciation when he reads the word in a sentence or in a list of such words. You may discover that your classmates have different pronunciations for different occasions. . . .

DIFFERENCES IN VOCABULARY

Words are interesting to almost everyone. Through his vocabulary a person may reveal facts about his age, his sex, his education, his occupation, and his geographical and cultural origins. Our first reaction may be to imagine that all speakers of English use the same words. Nothing could be further from the truth; our language contains a vast number of synonyms to show different shades of meaning or reveal as much of our inner feelings as we want to. Some of these vocabulary choices are made deliberately. We use other words, however, without really knowing that our vocabulary is influenced by our audience.

Age

Certain words tell how old we are. For example, many people refer to an electric refrigerator as an *ice box* despite the fact that in most parts of our country ice boxes have not been in common use for many years. Older natives of some Northern dialect areas still may call a frying pan a *spider*, a term which remained in the vocabulary of the older generation long after the removal of the four legs which gave the descriptive title. Frying pans no longer look like four-legged spiders, but the name remains fixed in the vocabulary of certain people.

Sex

Our vocabulary may also identify whether we are male or female. Most high school boys, for example, are not likely to use *lovely, peachy, darling,* and many words ending in *-ie*. Adult males are not apt to know or use very many words concerned with fabrics, color shadings, sewing, or women's styles. Women of all ages are not likely to use the specialized vocabulary of sports, automobile repair, or plumbing.*

Education

A person also reveals his educational background through his choice of words. It is no secret that learning the specialized vocabulary of psychology, electronics, or fishing is necessary before one becomes fully accepted as an "insider," and before he can fully participate in these areas. Much of what a student learns about a course in school is shown in his handling of the vocabulary of the subject. It is also true, however, that a person's choice of words is not nearly as revealing of education as his grammar and pronunciations are.

Occupation

The specialized vocabulary of occupational groups also appears in everyday language. Truck drivers, secretaries, tirebuilders, sailors, farmers, and members of many other occupations use such words. Linguists who interview people for *The Linguistic Atlas of the United States and Canada* have found that the calls to certain animals, for example, illustrate what might be called farm vocabulary, particularly for the older generation of farmers (city dwellers obviously have no particular way of calling sheep or cows from pasture). Even within farming areas, furthermore, vocabulary will reveal specialization. Recent Illinois language studies showed that a male sheep was known as a *buck* only to farmers who had at some time raised sheep.

Origins

It is common knowledge that certain words indicate where we are from. Northerners use *pail* for a kind of metal container which Midlanders refer to as a *bucket*. *Pits* are inside cherries and peaches of Northerners; *seeds* are found by some Midlanders. It is amusing to some people, furthermore, that as a general rule horses are said to *whinny* or *whinner* in Northern dialect areas, whereas they *nicker* in some of the Midland parts of our country.

Customs are also revealed in our vocabulary. The *county seat* is relatively unknown in rural New England, where local government is handled at the town meeting.

---

* Editors' note: Writing in 1967, Shuy could not have foreseen the many social changes that have occurred in the United States that necessitate some restriction of his generalizations in this area.

The special names for various ethnic or national groups, whether joking or derogatory, are an indication of the settlement patterns of an area. If a person has the terms *Dago*, *Kraut*, or *Polack* in his active vocabulary, it is likely that he lives among or near Italians, Germans, or Polish people. Sometimes the nickname of a specific immigrant group becomes generalized to include most or all newcomers. Such a case was noted . . . in Summit County, Ohio, where some natives refer to almost all nationality groups as *Hunkies*, regardless of whether or not they come from Hungary. That this practice has been with us for many years is shown in a comment by Theodore Roosevelt that anything foreign was referred to as *Dutch*. One nineteenth-century politician even referred to Italian paintings as "Dutch daubs from Italy."[1]

Vocabulary Fieldwork

To show some of the ways a speaker's vocabulary may reveal his age, sex, occupation, or regional and cultural origins, let us do a dialect vocabulary project as it might be done by a linguist (called a fieldworker in this case) who interviews people (called informants) for *The Linguistic Atlas*.

The *Atlas* fieldworker gathers his information in face-to-face interviews. He may supplement his interview data, however, with questionnaires such as the one which follows. Sometimes these questionnaires are mailed; sometimes the fieldworker distributes them personally. Whatever method of distribution is used, one thing is certain: The questionnaires have been extremely helpful, reliable, and accurate indications of vocabulary in use.

A CHECKLIST OF REGIONAL EXPRESSIONS

Directions

1. Please put a circle around the word or words in each group which you ordinarily use (don't circle words you have heard—just those you actually use).

2. If the word you ordinarily use is not listed in the group, please write it in the space by the item.

3. If you never use any word in the group, because you never need to refer to the thing described, do not mark the word.

   Example:
   Center of a peach: pit, seed, (stone,) kernel, heart

---

[1] H. L. Mencken, *The American Language*, abridged and revised by Raven I. McDavid, Jr. (New York: Knopf, 1963), 371.

Household

1. *to put a single room of the house in order:* clean up, do up, redd up, ridd up, straighten up, tidy up, put to rights, slick up
2. *paper container for groceries, etc.:* bag, poke, sack, toot
3. *device found on outside of the house or in yard or garden:* faucet, spicket, spigot, hydrant, tap
4. *window-covering on rollers:* blinds, curtains, roller shades, shades, window blinds, window shades
5. *large open metal container for scrub water:* pail, bucket
6. *of peas:* to hull, to pod, to shell, to shuck
7. *web hanging from ceiling of a room:* cobweb, dust web, spider's web, web
8. *metal utensil for frying:* creeper, fryer, frying pan, fry pan, skillet, spider
9. *over a sink:* faucet, hydrant, spicket, spigot, tap
10. *overlapping horizontal boards on outside of house:* clapboards, siding, weatherboards, weatherboarding
11. *large porch with roof:* gallery, piazza, porch, portico, stoop, veranda
12. *small porch, often with no roof:* deck, platform, porch, portico, step, steps, stoop, veranda, piazza
13. *devices at edges of roof to carry off rain:* eaves, eaves spouts, eavestroughs, gutters, rain troughs, spouting, spouts, water gutter
14. *rubber or plastic utensil for scraping dough or icing from a mixing bowl:* scraper, spatula, kidcheater, bowl scraper
15. *vehicle for small baby:* baby buggy, baby cab, baby carriage, baby coach
16. *to _____ the baby (in such a vehicle):* ride, roll, wheel, push, walk, stroll
17. *furry stuff which collects under beds and on closet floors:* dust bunnies, dust kittens, lint balls, pussies

Family

18. *family word for father:* dad, daddy, father, pa, papa, pappy, paw, pop
19. *family word for mother:* ma, mama, mammy, maw, mom, mommer, mommy, mother
20. *immediate family:* my family, my folks, my parents, my people, my relatives, my relations, my kin, my kinfolks
21. *others related by blood:* my family, my folks, my kind, my kinfolks, my people, my relation, my relatives, my relations, my kin

22. *of a child:* favors (*his mother*), features, looks like, resembles, takes after, is the spitting image of

23. *of children:* brought up, fetched up, raised, reared

24. *the baby moves on all fours across the floor:* crawls, creeps

Automotive

25. *place in front of driver where instruments are:* dash, dashboard, instrument panel, panel, crash panel

26. *automobile device for making the car go faster:* accelerator, gas, gas pedal, pedal, throttle

27. *place where flashlight and maps may be kept:* glove compartment, compartment, shelf, cabinet

28. *automobile with two doors:* tudor, coupe, two-door

29. *the car needs _____:* a grease job, greased, lubrication, a lube job, to be greased, to be lubed, greasing, servicing, to be serviced

30. *large truck with trailer attached:* truck, truck and trailer, semi, rig, trailer-truck

Urban

31. *new limited access road:* turnpike, toll road, freeway, parkway, pay road, tollway, thruway, expressway

32. *service and eating areas on no. 31:* service stop, service area, oasis, rest area

33. *grass strip in the center of a divided road:* median, center strip, separator, divider, barrier, grass strip, boulevard

34. *place where fire engines are kept:* fire hall, fire house, fire station

35. *place where scheduled airlines operate:* airport, port, terminal, air terminal (by proper name), air field, field

36. *place where train stops:* station, railway station, depot, train stop, train station, railroad station

37. *place where firemen attach hose:* fire hydrant, fire plug, plug, hydrant, water tap

38. *grass strip between sidewalk and street:* berm, boulevard, boulevard strip, parking, parking strip, parkway, sidewalk plot, tree lawn, neutral ground, devil strip, tree bank, city strip

39. *call to hail a taxi:* taxi!, cab!, cabbie!, hack!, hey!, (wave arm), (whistle)

40. *policeman:* cop, policeman, copper, fuzz, dick, officer, bull

41. *the road is:* slick, slippery

42. *place where packaged groceries can be purchased:* grocery store, general store, supermarket, store, delicatessen, grocery, market, food market, food store, supermart

43. *a piece of pavement between two houses on a city block:* gang-way, walk, path, sidewalk
44. *place where you watch technicolor features in a car:* drive-in, drive-in movie, outdoor movie, outdoor theater, open-air movie, open-air theater, passion pit

Nature

45. *animal with strong odor:* polecat, skunk, woodspussy, wood-pussy
46. *small, squirrel-like animal that runs along the ground:* chip-munk, grinnie, ground squirrel
47. *worm used for bait in fishing:* angledog, angleworm, bait worm, eace worm, earthworm, eelworm, fish bait, fishing worm, fish-worm, mudworm, rainworm, redworm
48. *larger worm:* dew worm, night crawler, night walker, (Georgia) wiggler, town worm
49. *dog of no special kind or breed:* common dog, cur, cur dog, fice, feist, mongrel, no-count, scrub, heinz, sooner, mixed dog, mutt
50. *insect that glows at night:* fire bug, firefly, glowworm, june bug, lightning bug, candle bug
51. *large winged insect seen around water:* darning needle, devil's darning needle, dragon fly, ear-sewer, mosquito hawk, sewing needle, snake doctor, snake feeder, sewing bug
52. *freshwater shellfish with claws; swims backward:* crab, craw, crawdad(die), crawfish, crayfish
53. *center of a cherry:* pit, seed, stone, kernel, heart
54. *center of a peach:* pit, seed, stone, kernel, heart
55. *hard inner cover of a walnut:* hull, husk, shell, shuck
56. *green outer cover of a walnut:* hull, husk, shell, shuck
57. *bunch of trees growing in open country (particularly on a hill):* motte, clump, grove, bluff
58. *web found outdoors:* cobweb, dew web, spider nest, spider's nest, spider web, web
59. *tree that produces sugar and syrup:* hard maple, rock maple, sugar maple, sugar tree, maple tree, candy tree, sweet maple

Foods

60. *melon with yellow or orange insides:* muskmelon, melon, mushmelon, lope, cantaloup, mussmellon
61. *a spreadable luncheon meat made of liver:* liver sausage, braun-schweiger, liverwurst
62. *a carbonated drink:* pop, soda, soda pop, tonic, soft drink

63. *a glass containing ice cream and root beer:* a float, a root beer float, a black cow, a Boston cooler
64. *dish of cooked fruit eaten at the end of a meal:* fruit, sauce, dessert, compote
65. *peach whose meat sticks to seed:* cling, cling peach, clingstone, clingstone peach, hard peach, plum-peach, press peach
66. *food eaten between regular meals:* a bite, lunch, a piece, piece meal, a snack, a mug-up, munch, nash, nosh
67. *corn served on cob:* corn-on-the-cob, garden corn, green corn, mutton corn, roasting ears, sugar corn, sweet corn
68. *beans eaten in pods:* green beans, sallet beans, snap beans, snaps, string beans, beans
69. *edible tops of turnips, beets, etc.:* greens, salad, salat
70. *a white lumpy cheese:* clabber cheese, cottage cheese, curd cheese, curd(s), dutch cheese, homemade cheese, pot cheese, smearcase, cream cheese
71. *round, flat confection with hole in center, made with baking powder:* crull, cruller, doughnut, fatcake, fried cake, cake dough-nut, raised doughnut
72. *bread made of cornmeal:* corn bread, corn dodger(s), corn pone, hoecakes, johnnycake, pone bread
73. *cooked meat juices poured over meat, potatoes, or bread:* gravy, sop, sauce, drippings
74. *ground beef in a bun:* hamburg, hamburger, burger
75. *large sandwich designed to be a meal in itself:* hero, submarine, hoagy, grinder, poor boy

Games

76. *children's cry at Halloween time:* trick or treat!, tricks or treats!, beggar's night!, help the poor!, Halloween!, give or receive!
77. *fast-moving amusement park ride (on tracks):* coaster, roller coaster, rolly-coaster, shoot-the chutes, the ride of doom
78. *call to players to return because a new player wants to join:* allie-allie-in-free, allie-allie-oxen free, allie-allie-ocean free, bee-bee bumble bee, everybody in free, newcomer-newcomer!
79. *call to passerby to return a ball to the playground:* little help!, ball!, hey!, yo!, ball up!
80. *to coast on sled lying down flat:* belly-booster, belly-bump, belly-bumper, belly-bunker, belly-bunt, belly-bust, belly-buster, belly-down, belly-flop, belly-flopper, belly-grinder, belly-gut, belly-gutter, belly-kachug, belly-kachuck, belly-whack, belly-whop, belly-whopper, belly-slam, belly-smacker
81. *to hit the water when diving:* belly-flop, belly-flopper, belly-bust, belly-buster
82. *to stop a game you call:* time!, time out!, times!, pax!, fins!

School

83. *to be absent from school:* bag school, bolt, cook jack, lay out, lie out, play hookey, play truant, run out of school, skip class, skip school, slip off from school, ditch, flick, flake school, blow school
84. *where swings and play areas are:* schoolyard, playground, school ground, yard, grounds
85. *holds small objects together:* rubber band, rubber binder, elastic binder, gum band, elastic band
86. *drinking fountain:* cooler, water cooler, bubbler, fountain, drinking fountain
87. *the amount of books you can carry in both arms:* armful, armload, load, turn

Clothing

88. *short knee-length outer garment worn by men:* shorts, bermuda shorts, bermudas, walking shorts, knee (length) pants, pants, knee-knockers
89. *short knee-length outer garment worn by women:* shorts, bermudas, walking shorts, pants
90. *outer garment of a heavy material worn by males as they work:* levis, overalls, dungarees, jeans, blue jeans, pants
91. *garment worn by women at the seashore:* swimsuit, swimming suit, bathing suit
92. *garment worn by men at the seashore:* swimsuit, swimming suit, bathing suit, swimming trunks, trunks, bathing trunks, swimming shorts

Miscellaneous

93. *a time of day:* quarter before eleven, quarter of eleven, quarter till eleven, quarter to eleven, 10:45
94. *someone from the country:* backwoodsman, clodhopper, country gentleman, country jake, countryman, hayseed, hick, hoosier, hillbilly, jackpine savage, mossback, mountain-boomer, pumpkinhusker, railsplitter, cracker, redneck, rube, sharecropper, stump farmer, swamp angel, yahoo, yokel, sodbuster
95. *someone who won't change his mind is:* bull-headed, contrary, headstrong, ornery, otsny, owly, pig-headed, set, sot, stubborn, mulish, muley
96. *when a girl stops seeing a boyfriend she is said to:* give him the air, give him the bounce, give him the cold shoulder, give him the mitten, jilt him, kick him, throw him over, turn him down,

shoot him down, give him the gate, brush him off, turn him off, break up with him

97. *become ill:* be taken sick, get sick, take sick, be taken ill, come down

98. *become ill with a cold:* catch a cold, catch cold, get a cold, take cold, take a cold, come down with a cold

99. *sick _____:* at his stomach, in his stomach, on his stomach, to his stomach, of his stomach, with his stomach

100. *I _____ you're right:* reckon, guess, figger, figure, suspect, imagine

The preceding vocabulary questionnaire, frequently called a checklist, is only suggestive of what might be asked for in a particular community. Of the hundred items in ten general fields, you may find some questions more interesting and useful to study than others. Furthermore, you may add other words to this list, or you may find other answers to questions listed here.

Let us suppose, however, that you wish to make a vocabulary survey of your community using this checklist. If your school has ample facilities and supplies, you could reproduce all or part of this questionnaire, distribute it to various neighbors, let them fill it out at their leisure, and then have them return it to you for tabulation and analysis.

One last matter of data must be included, however, if the checklist is to be meaningful. The dialectologist needs to know certain things about the people who fill out the checklists. The following questions should be answered if the data are to be interpreted meaningfully.

Let us look for a moment at the personal data sheet. We note that dialectologists think it important to keep a record of the informant's age, sex, race, education, mobility, travel, ancestry, language skills, and occupation. People from the same general area may use different words, and this personal data sheet will help us find out why. In parts of Michigan, for example, the older generation may still use the term *spider* for what younger informants may call *frying pan*. This is an indication of current language change. It is never a surprise to us to hear that our parents' generation did things differently. Nor should we be surprised to note that they use different words.

Personal Data Sheet

Sex _____ Race _____

Have you filled out this same   Age _____ Highest grade level
questionnaire before? Yes___ No___ reached in school _____

State _____ County _____ Town _____

How long have you lived here? _____ years

Birthplace _____
                    (town)   (state)

Other towns, states, or nations you have lived in (please give approximate years for each place)

_____

_____

_____

Have you traveled much outside your native state? _____ (Yes or No)
If so, where? _____

_____

Parents' birthplace (state or nation):
Father _____ Grandfather _____
                                Grandmother _____
Mother _____ Grandfather _____
                                Grandmother _____
Do you speak any non-English language? _____ If so, which? _____
                                        (yes or no)
Occupation_____
If retired, former occupation_____
If housewife, husband's occupation_____
Name (optional) _____

There are any number of things you may be able to discover by making a vocabulary survey in your community. What you should remember as you gather your data is the principle of constants and variables, a principle familiar to you, no doubt, from mathematics. You may gather your data in any way you wish, but chances are you will not be able to get a representation of all ages, ethnic groups, religions, and occupations of the people in your area, especially if you live in an urban community. A somewhat narrower approach would be easier and more successful, for example:

1. *Age Contrast:* Collect checklists from three or four people who have lived all their lives in your community. This gives you two constants: the checklist and the native-born residents. The most interesting variables will be their age and education along with, of course, their answers. If you select older people and younger people of roughly the same education and social status, chances are that any vocabulary differences will stem from the contrast in ages.

2. *Education Contrast:* Collect checklists from three or four people who have different educational backgrounds. College graduates, for example, may be contrasted with people who have had less than a high school education. If your informants are of roughly the same age, and if their personal data sheets are otherwise similar, the differences which you note may be attributable to their contrasting educations.

3. *Describe the Local Dialect Area:* Collect checklists from three or four people who have lived all their lives in your community. Try to get older, middle-aged, and younger people who have educational backgrounds characteristic of your community (in some parts of our country, for example, college graduates are simply not frequently found). Then note the responses of these informants to some or all of the following questions: 1, 2, 3, 5, 8, 9, 10, 13, 24, 45, 46, 47, 50, 51, 53, 54, 64, 67, 69, 70, 71, 72, 87, 93, 97, 98, 99. For each of these questions there is a response which research has shown to be characteristic of one side of the dialect map (of course, the term may be used elsewhere, too, but not as

generally). The following chart will indicate some of the words you may expect to find in *certain parts* of the Northern, Midland, and Southern dialect areas:

Word	Northern	Midland	Southern
1. *to put room in order:*		redd up ridd up	
2. *paper container:*	bag	sack	sack
3. *on outside of house:*	faucet	spigot spicket hydrant	spigot spicket hydrant
5. *container:*	pail	bucket	bucket
8. *metal utensil:* (frying pan common everywhere)	spider	skillet	skillet spider
9. *over a sink:*	faucet	spigot spicket	spigot spicket
10. *boards:* (siding common everywhere)	clapboards	weatherboards	
13. *devices at roof:*	gutters (ENE) eaves spouts eavestroughs	gutters spouting spouts	gutters
24. *baby moves:*	creeps	crawls	crawls
45. *animal:*	skunk	skunk polecat woodspussy woodpussy	polecat
46. *animal:* (note: for some people, chipmunk and ground squirrel are two different animals)	chipmunk	ground squirrel	ground squirrel
47. *worm:*	angleworm	fish(ing) worm	fish(ing) worm
50. *insect:*	firefly (urban) lightning buy (rural)	lightning bug fire bug	lightning bug
51. *insect:*	(devil's) darning needle sewing bug dragon fly	snake feeder snake doctor dragon fly	snake feeder snake doctor dragon fly mosquito hawk
53. *cherry:*	pit stone	seed stone	seed stone
54. *peach:*	pit stone	seed stone	seed stone
64. *dish:*	dessert sauce fruit	dessert fruit	dessert fruit
67. *corn:*	corn-on-the-cob green corn sweet corn	corn-on-the-cob sweet corn roasting ears	roasting ears sweet corn
69. *tops:*		greens	greens salad salat

Word	Northern	Midland	Southern
70. *cheese:* (cottage cheese common everywhere)	dutch cheese pot cheese	smearcase	clabber cheese curds
71. *confection:*	doughnut fried cake	doughnut	doughnut
72. *bread:*	johnnycake corn bread	corn bread	corn bread cone pone
87. *to carry:*	armful	armload	armload
93. *quarter——:*	to of	till	till to
97. *become ill:*	get sick	take sick	take sick
98. *with a cold:*	catch a cold	take a cold	take a cold
99. *sick——:* (at his stomach common everywhere)	to his stomach	on his stomach in his stomach	

Many of the suggested checklist items have not been surveyed nationally (the automotive terms, for example), and so we cannot show their regional distributions. This should not prevent you from checking them in your own community to discover what term is characteristic there.

4. *Contrast Regional Dialects:* Have two natives of your area and two newcomers from other parts of the country fill out all or part of the checklist. Note the contrasts which are evidence of geographical differences. Your conclusions will be more certain if your informants are roughly the same age and have roughly the same educational background. This will help rule out age or education as the cause of the vocabulary difference.

DIFFERENCES IN GRAMMAR

In addition to pronunciation and vocabulary differences in dialects, there are differences which involve matters of grammar. In grammar we include such things as past tenses of verbs, plural nouns, and word order (syntax) patterns. For example, many people use *dived* as the past tense of the verb *dive*. Others use *dove*. Still others use both forms. Likewise, some people say *this is as far as I go*. Others habitually say *this is all the farther I go*. These forms are used by educated and respectable people, and their English is considered equally educated and respectable. If one or two of the above examples sound strange or wrong to you, then you are probably living in an area which uses the alternative form. This does not mean that your way is better or worse—only that it is different.

On the other hand, some variants of grammatical items are used by relatively uneducated people. For the past tense of *dive* they might use the forms *duv* or *div*. For the distance statement they might say *this is the furtherest I go* or *this is the fartherest I go*.

Thus we can see that grammatical items may indicate place of origin or social level. Table 21.1 shows how people in two theoretical areas differ internally, because of social class, and externally, because of where they live. Contrary to what some people think, even people of higher social classes do not make the same grammatical choices in different parts of the country. Well-educated natives of Wisconsin tend to say *dove*; their counterparts from Kentucky favor *dived*.

TABLE 21.1

	AREA X		AREA Y	
Speaker	*Grammatical Item Used*		*Speaker*	*Grammatical Item Used*
higher social status	dove		higher social status	dived
middle social status	dove		middle social status	dived
lower social status	dove, duv		lower social status	dived, div

For determining social levels, grammatical choices are as important as pronunciation and vocabulary choices. Regional distributions of grammatical choice, however, are not as clearly marked as other differences. Of particular interest to American fieldworkers are the following items.[2]

1. *Prepositions*
   Trouble comes all _____ once. (to = N, at)
   It's half _____ six. (past, after)
   It's quarter _____ four. (of, to = N, till = M, before, until)
   It's _____ the door. (behind, hindside, in back of, back of)
   He isn't _____. (at home, to home, home)
   It's coming right _____ you. (at, toward, towards)
   Guess who I ran _____. (into, onto, up against, upon, up with, against, again, afoul of = NE, across)
   They named the baby _____ him. (after, for, at, from)
   I fell _____ the horse. (off, off of, offen, off from, from)
   I wonder what he died _____. (of, with, from, for)
   He's sick _____ his stomach. (to = N, at = M, S, of, on = M, in = M, with)
   He came over _____ tell me. (to, for to = SM, S, for = S)
   I want this _____ of that. (instead, stead, in room, in place)
   We're waiting _____ John. (on = M, for)
   The old man passed _____. (away, on, out, φ)
   He did it _____ purpose. (on, a, for, φ)
   I want _____ the bus. (off = M, to get off)

---

[2] Whenever φ appears, it signifies that nothing is added to the statement. N stands for Northern, M for Midland, NM for North Midland, S for Southern, SM for South Midland, and NE for New England.

He was _____ (singing, a-singing) and _____. (laughing, a-laughing)

How big _____ (a, of a) house is it?

2. *Matters of agreement*

Here _____ your pencils. (is, are)

The oats _____ thrashed. (is = M, are = N)

These cabbages _____ (is, are) for sale.

3. *Plural formations*

I have two _____ of shoes. (pair = N, S; pairs = M)

They had forty _____ of apples. (bushel = N, bushels = M)

He has two _____ of butter. (pound = S, pounds = M)

The fence has twenty _____. (posts, post, postis, poss)

He likes to play _____. (horseshoe, horseshoes)

Put your feet in the _____. (stirrup, stirrups)

Let's spray for _____. (moth, moths, mothis)

I bought two _____ of lettuce. (head, heads)

That's a long _____. (way = N, ways = M)

That's a short _____. (way = N, ways = M)

It's nine _____ high. (foot, feet)

We have three _____. (desks, desk, deskis, desses, dess)

4. *Pronouns*

It wasn't _____. (me, I)

This is _____. (yours, yourn)

This is _____. (theirs, theirn)

Are _____ (pl.) coming over? (you, youse, yuz, youns, you-all)

_____ boys are all bad. (Those, Them, Them there)

He's the man _____ owns the car. (that, who, what, which, as, φ)

He's the boy _____ father is rich. (whose, that his, that the, his)

"I'm not going!" "_____." (Me either, Me neither, Neither am I, Nor I either, Nor I neither)

It is _____. (I, me)

It is _____. (he, him)

He's going to do it _____. (himself, hisself)

Let them do it _____. (themselves, themself, theirselves, theirself)

I'll go with _____. (φ, you)

5. *Adjectives*

The oranges are all _____. (φ, gone)

Some berries are _____. (poison, poisonous)

6. *Adverbs*

You can find these almost _____. (anywhere, anywheres, any-place)

This is _____ I go. (as far as, as fur as, all the farther, all the further, the farthest, the furthest, the fartherest, the furtherest)

7. *Conjunctions*

It seems _____ we'll never win. (as though, like, as if)

I won't go _____ he does. (unless, without, lessen, thouten, douten, less, else)

I like him _____ he's funny. (because, cause, on account of, count, owing to)

Do this _____ I eat lunch. (while, whiles, whilst)

This is not _____ long as that one. (as, so)

8. *Articles*

John is _____ university. (in, in the)

She is _____ hospital. (in, in the)

I have _____ apple. (a, an)

John has _____. (flu, the flu)

Do you have _____? (mumps, the mumps)

9. *Verbs*

Past tense forms:	began, begun, begin
	blew, blowed
	climbed, clim (N), clum (M)
	came, come, comed
	could, might could (SM, S)
	dived, dove (N)
	drank, drunk, drinked
	did, done
	drowned, drownded
	ate, et, eat
	gave, give (M)
	grew, growed
	learned, learnt, larnt, larnd
	lay, laid
	rode, rid
	ran, run
	saw, seen (M), seed (M), see (N)
	sat, set
	spoiled, spoilt
	swam, swim
	threw, throwed
	wore, weared
	wrote, writ
Past participles:	tore up, torn up
	wore out, worn out
	rode (M), ridden
	drank, drunk
	bit, bitten
Negative:	hadn't ought (N), ought not, oughtn't, didn't ought

Some of the preceding grammatical choices may seem appropriate to you, others may appear to be undesirable. But in unguarded moments you may find yourself using more than one of the choices. What is particularly interesting to linguists is the fact that many forces contribute to our shift from one variant to another.

Grammar Fieldwork

People tend to be much more self-conscious about their use of verb forms, prepositions, pronouns, and so on, than they are about their vocabulary or pronunciation. Consequently, no simple checklist will be given here. However, you can observe the above items in the casual conversations of your acquaintances, in the speech of television actors (especially those who portray Westerners, hillbillies, blue-collar urbanites, farmers, well-heeled tycoons, and other special "types"), in the dialogue of novels or short stories, and in the speech of out-of-staters who have recently moved to your community. You must remember, however, that people are very sensitive about their grammar. The good fieldworker is tactful and objective. He does not ridicule the grammar of other areas or other social levels; in fact, he does not even seem to be especially interested in the grammar of his subject's responses. Much of the time he contents himself with getting details of grammar in conversation, without direct questioning.

FOR DISCUSSION AND REVIEW

1. As Shuy states, "That people speak different dialects in no way stems from their intelligence or judgment. They speak the dialect which enables them to get along with the other members of their social and geographical group." Despite this fact, many people consider dialects different from their own to sound funny, strange, or even wrong—and these attitudes are often passed on to those who speak different dialects. Drawing on your own experiences and attitudes, discuss the situation described above. For example, what are its implications for a family moving from the South to New England?

2. Shuy describes two types of pronunciation differences. What are they, and how do they differ? Add to his lists of examples.

3. After reviewing the phonetic symbols provided by Callary (in "Phonetics," Part Three), carefully transcribe your pronunciation of each of the following words. Discuss any differences between your transcriptions and those of other members of the class.

   a. calm   f. judgment
   b. water   g. cushion
   c. horse   h. roof
   d. hoarse   i. parking
   e. wharfs   j. scent

4. Discuss, using specific examples from your experience, how vocabulary can reveal facts about a person's age, sex, education, occupation, and geographical and cultural origins.

5. Complete the vocabulary questionnaire. Compare your responses with those of other members of the class and with those provided in the selection. Are the responses patterned? How do you account for any deviations from the patterns?

6. What is the importance of a personal data sheet to a dialectologist?

7. Shuy states that "For determining social levels, grammatical choices are as important as pronunciation and vocabulary choices." Give three examples from your own experience that support or refute his assertion—that is, explain how the grammatical constructions used by people when you first met them affected your opinion of them.

8. Why does Shuy believe that a checklist or questionnaire is inappropriate as the only means for determining the grammatical choices of informants? What are the alternatives to a direct questionnaire?

22

The Study of Nonstandard English

William Labov

William Labov, a research professor at the Center for Urban Ethnography at the University of Pennsylvania, is well known for his many sociolinguistic studies, especially those of New York City speech and of Black English. In this condensed version of "The Study of Nonstandard English," he explains the need, especially for teachers, to study and understand the various nonstandard dialects of English. He also clarifies the relationship between Standard English and non-standard dialects, illustrating the close relationship between a number of their phonological and syntactic rules. Most important, Labov emphasizes that nonstandard dialects of English, like all human languages, are rule-governed; they are not corruptions or inferior versions of Standard English. In other studies, Labov has advocated functional bidialectalism for speakers of a nonstandard dialect and has attempted to show how linguistic knowledge of Black English Vernacular (BEV) can be used to help teachers improve the reading skills of children who speak BEV.

Since language learning does take place outside of the classroom, and the six-year-old child does have great capacity for learning new language forms as he is exposed to them, it may be asked why it should be necessary for the teacher to understand more about the child's own vernacular. First, we can observe that automatic adjustment does *not* take place in all cases. Even the successful middle-class student does not always master the teacher's grammatical forms, and in the urban ghettos we find very little adjustment to school forms. Students continue to write *I have live* after ten or twelve years in school; we will describe below failures in reading the *-ed* suffix, which show no advance with years in school. Second, knowledge of the underlying structure of the nonstandard vernacular will allow the most efficient teaching. If the teacher knows the general difference between standard negative attraction and nonstandard negative concord, he can teach a hundred different standard forms with the simple instruction: *The negative is attracted only to the first indefinite.* Thus by this one rule we can make many corrections.

He don't know nothing . → He doesn't know anything
Nobody don't like him   → Nobody likes him
Nobody hardly goes there → Hardly anybody goes there
Can't nobody do it   → Nobody can do it

Third, the vernacular must be understood because ignorance of it leads to serious conflict between student and teacher. Teachers in ghetto schools who continually insist that *i* and *e* sound different in *pin* and *pen* will only antagonize a great number of their students. The knowledge that *i* and *e* actually sound the same before *m* and *n* for most of their students (and *should* sound the same if they are normal speakers) will help avoid this destructive conflict. Teachers who insist that a child meant to say *He is tired* when he said *He tired* will achieve only bewilderment in the long run. Knowledge that *He tired* is the vernacular equivalent of the contracted form *He's tired* will save teacher and student from this frustration.

Granted that the teacher wishes to learn about the student's language, what methods are available for him to do so? Today, a great many linguists study English through their own intuitions; they operate "out of their own heads" in the sense that they believe they can ask and answer all the relevant questions themselves. But even if a teacher comes from the same background as his students, he will find that his grammar has changed, that he no longer has firm intuitions about whether he can say *Nobody don't know nothing about it* instead of *Nobody knows nothing about it*. He can of course sit down with a student and ask him all kinds of direct questions about his language, and there are linguists who do this. But one cannot draw directly upon the intuitions of the two major groups we are interested in, children and nonstandard speakers. Both are in contact with a superordinate or dominant dialect, and both will provide answers which reflect their awareness of this dialect as much as of their own. One can of course engage in long and indirect conversations with students, hoping that all of the forms of interest will sooner or later occur, and there are linguists who have attempted to study nonstandard dialects in this way. But these conversations usually teach the subject more of the investigator's language than the other way around. In general, one can say that whenever a speaker of a nonstandard dialect is in a subordinate position to a speaker of a standard dialect, the rules of his grammar will shift in an unpredictable manner towards the standard. The longer the contact, the stronger and more lasting is the shift. Thus adolescent speakers of a vernacular make very unreliable informants when they are questioned in a formal framework. The investigator must show considerable sociolinguistic sophistication to cope with such a situation, and indeed the teacher will also need to know a great deal about the social forces which affect linguistic behavior if he is to interpret his students' language.

NONSTANDARD DIALECTS AS "SELF-CONTAINED" SYSTEMS

The traditional view of nonstandard speech as a set of isolated deviations from standard English is often countered by the opposite view: that nonstandard dialect should be studied as an isolated system in its own right, without any reference to standard English. It is argued that the system of grammatical forms of a dialect can only be understood through their internal relations. For example, nonstandard Negro English has one distinction which standard English does not have: there is an invariant form *be* in *He always be foolin' around* which marks habitual, general conditions, as opposed to the unmarked *is, am, are*, etc., which do not have any such special sense. It can be argued that the existence of this distinction changes the value of all other members of the grammatical system and that the entire paradigm of this dialect is therefore different from that of standard English. It is indeed important to find such relations within the meaningful set of grammatical distinctions, if they exist, because we can then *explain* rather than merely describe behavior. There are many concurrence rules which are purely descriptive—the particular dialect just happens to have X' *and* Y' where another has X and Y. We would like to know if a special nonstandard form X' *requires* an equally nonstandard Y' because of the way in which the nonstandard form cuts up the entire field of meaning. This would be a tremendous help in teaching, since we would be able to show what sets of standard rules have to be taught together to avoid confusing the student with a mixed, incoherent grammatical system.

The difficulty here is that linguistics has not made very much progress in the analysis of semantic systems. There is no method or procedure which leads to reliable or reproducible results—not even among those who agree on certain principles of grammatical theory. No one has yet written a complete grammar of a language—or even come close to accounting for all the morphological and syntactic rules of a language. And the situation is much more primitive in semantics; for example, the verbal system of standard English has been studied now for many centuries, yet there is no agreement at all on the meaning of the auxiliaries *have . . . ed* and *be . . . ing*. The meaning of *I have lived here*, as opposed to *I lived here*, has been explained as (a) relevant to the present, (b) past *in* the present, (c) perfective, (d) indefinite, (e) causative, and so on. It is not only that there are many views; it is that in any given discussion no linguist has really found a method by which he can reasonably hope to persuade others that he is right. If this situation prevails where most of the investigators have complete access to the data, since they are native speakers of standard English, we must be more than cautious in claiming to understand the meaning of *I be here* as opposed to *I am here* in nonstandard Black English, and even more cautious in claiming that the meaning of nonstandard *I'm here* therefore differs from standard *I'm here* because of the existence of the other form. Most teachers have learned to be cautious in accepting a grammarian's statement about the meaning of their own native forms, but they have no way of judging statements made about a dialect which they do not speak, and they are naturally prone to accept such statements on the authority of the writer.

There is, however, [much] that we can do to show the internal relations in the nonstandard dialect as a system. There are a great many forms which seem different on the surface but can be explained as expressions of a single rule, or the absence of a single rule. We observe that in nonstandard Black English it is common to say *a apple* rather than *an apple*. This is a standard grammatical fault from the point of view of standard speakers, and the school must teach *an apple* as the written, standard form. There is also a rather low-level, unimportant feature of pronunciation which is common to southern dialects: in *the apple*, the word *the* has the same pronunciation as in *the book* and does not rhyme with *be*. Finally, we can note that, in the South, educated white speakers keep the vocalic schwa which represents *r* in *four*, but nonstandard speakers tend to drop it (registered in dialect writing as *fo' o'clock*). When all these facts are put together, we can begin to explain the nonstandard *a apple* as part of a much broader pattern. There is a general rule of English which states that we do not pronounce two (phonetic) vowels in succession. Some kind of semiconsonantal glide or consonant comes in between: an *n* as in *an apple*, a "y" as in *the apple*, an *r* as in *four apples*. In each of these cases, this rule is not followed for nonstandard Black English. A teacher may have more success in getting students to write *an apple* if he presents this general rule and connects up all of these things into a single rational pattern, even if some are not important in themselves. It will "make sense" to Black speakers, since they do not drop *l* before a vowel, and many rules of their sound system show the effect of a following vowel.

There are many ways in which an understanding of the fundamental rules of the dialect will help to explain surface facts. Some of the rules cited above are also important in explaining why nonstandard Black speakers sometimes delete *is*, in *He is ready*, but almost always delete *are*, in *You are ready*; or why they say *they book* and *you book* but not *we book*. It does not always follow, though, that a grammatical explanation reveals the best method for teaching standard English.

Systematic analysis may also be helpful in connecting up the nonstandard form with the corresponding standard form and in this sense understanding the meaning of the nonstandard form. For example, nonstandard speakers say *Ain't nobody see it*. What is the nearest standard equivalent? We can connect this up with the standard negative foregrounding of *Scarcely did anybody see it* or, even more clearly, the literary expression *Nor did anybody see it*. This foregrounding fits in with the general colloquial southern pattern with indefinite subjects: *Didn't anybody see it*, nonstandard *Didn't nobody see it*. In these cases, the auxiliary *didn't* is brought to the front of the sentence, like the *ain't* in the nonstandard sentence. But there is another possibility. We could connect up *Ain't nobody see it* with the sentence *It ain't nobody see it*, that is, *There isn't anybody who sees it;* the dummy *it* of nonstandard Black English corresponds to standard *there* and, like *there*, it can be dropped in casual speech. Such an explanation is the only one possible in the case of such nonstandard sentences as *Ain't nothin' went down.* This could not be derived from *Nothin' ain't went down,* a sentence type which never occurs. If someone uses one of these forms, it is important for the teacher to know what was intended, so that he can supply the standard equivalent. To do so, one must know a great deal about many underlying rules of the nonstandard dialect, and also a great deal about the rules of English in general.

NONSTANDARD ENGLISH AS A
CLOSE RELATIVE OF STANDARD ENGLISH

Differences between standard and nonstandard English are not as sharp as our first impressions would lead us to think. Consider, for example, the socially stratified marker of "pronominal apposition"—the use of a dependent pronoun in such sentences as

My oldest sister she worked at the bank.

Though most of us recognize this as a nonstandard pattern, it is not always realized that the "nonstandard" aspect is merely a slight difference in intonation. A standard speaker frequently says the same thing, with a slight break after the subject: *My oldest sister—she works at the bank, and she finds it very profitable.* There are many ways in which a greater awareness of the standard colloquial forms would help teachers interpret the nonstandard forms. Not only do standard speakers use pronominal apposition with the break noted above, but in casual speech they can also bring object noun phrases to the front, foregrounding them. For example, one can say

My oldest sister—she worked at the Citizens Bank in Passaic last year.

The Citizens Bank, in Passaic—my oldest sister worked there last year.

Passaic—my oldest sister worked at the Citizens Bank there last year.

Note that if the foregrounded noun phrase represents a *locative*—the "place where"—then its position is held by *there,* just as the persons are represented by pronouns. If we are dealing with a time element, it can be foregrounded without replacement in any dialect: *Last year, my oldest sister worked at the Citizens Bank in Passaic.*

It is most important for the teacher to understand the relation between standard and nonstandard and to recognize that nonstandard

English is a system of rules, different from the standard but not necessarily inferior as a means of communication. All of the teacher's social instincts, past training, and even faith in his own education lead him to believe that other dialects of English are merely "mistakes" without any rhyme or rationale.

In this connection, it will be helpful to examine some of the most general grammatical differences between English dialects spoken in the United States. One could list a very large number of "mistakes," but when they are examined systematically the great majority appear to be examples of a small number of differences in the rules. The clearest analysis of these differences has been made by Edward Klima (1964). He considers first the dialect in which people say sentences like

Who could she see?

Who did he speak with?

He knew who he spoke with.

The leader who I saw left.

The leader who he spoke with left.

What is the difference between this dialect and standard English? The usual schoolbook answer is to say that these are well-known mistakes in the use of *who* for *whom*. But such a general statement does not add any clarity to the situation; nor does it help the student to learn standard English. The student often leaves the classroom with no more than an uneasy feeling that *who* is incorrect and *whom* is correct. This is the state of half-knowledge that leads to hypercorrect forms such as *Whom did you say is calling?* In the more extreme cases, *whom* is seen as the only acceptable, polite form of the pronoun. Thus a certain receptionist at a hospital switchboard regularly answers the telephone: "Whom?"

The nonstandard dialect we see here varies from standard English by one simple difference in the order of rules. The standard language marks the objective case—the difference between *who* and *whom*—in a sentence form which preserves the original subject-object relation:

Q—She could see WH-someone.

The WH-symbol marks the point to be questioned in this sentence. When cases are marked in this sentence, the pronoun before the verb receives the unmarked subjective case and the pronoun after the verb the marked objective case.

Q—She (subjective case)—could—see—WH-someone (objective case).

The combination of WH, indefinite pronoun, and objective case is to be realized later as *whom*. At a later point, a rule of WH-*attraction* is applied which brings the WH-word to the beginning of the sentence:

Q—Whom—she—could—see.

and finally the Q-marker effects a reversal of the pronoun and auxiliary, yielding the final result:

Whom could she see?

Here the objective case of the pronoun refers to the underlying position of the questioned pronoun as object of the verb.

The nonstandard dialect also marks cases: *I, he, she, they* are subjective forms, and *me, him, her, them* are objective. But the case-marking is done after, rather than before, the WH-attraction rule applies. We begin with the same meaningful structure, Q—*She could see* WH-*someone*, but the first rule to consider is WH-*attraction*:

Q—WH-someone—she—could—see.

Now the rule of case-marking applies. Since both pronouns are before the verb, they are both unmarked:

Q—WH-someone (unmarked)—she (unmarked)—could see.

Finally, the question flip-flop applies, and we have

Who could she see?

The same mechanism applies to all of the nonstandard forms given above.

We can briefly consider another nonstandard grammatical rule, that which yields *It's me* rather than *It's I*. The difference here lies again in the rule of case-marking. As noted above, this rule marks pronouns which occur after verbs; but the copula is not included. The nonstandard grammar which gives us *It's me* differs from standard English in only one simple detail—the case-marking rule includes the verb *to be* as well as other verbs. It is certainly not true that this nonstandard grammar neglects the case-marking rule; on the contrary, it applies the rule more generally than standard English here. But the order of the rules is the same as that for the nonstandard grammar just discussed: we get *Who is he?* rather than *Whom is he?* Like the other verbs, the copula marks the pronoun only after WH-attraction has applied.

In all of the examples just given, we can observe a general tendency towards simplification in the nonstandard grammars. There is a strong tendency to simplify the surface subjects—that is, the words which come before the verb. This is most obvious in pronominal apposition. The foregrounded part identifies the person talked about, *my oldest sister*; this person is then "given," and the "new" predication is made with a pronoun subject: *she worked at the Citizens Bank*.

A parallel tendency is seen in the nonstandard grammars which confine the objective marker to positions after the verb. But this tendency to simplify subjects is not confined to standard colloquial English. Sentences such as the following are perfectly grammatical but are seldom if ever found in ordinary speech:

For him to have broken his word so often was a shame.

Most often we find that the rule of *extraposition* has applied, moving the complex subject to the end of the sentence:

It was a shame for him to have broken his word so often.

In general, we find that nonstandard English dialects are not radically different systems from standard English but are instead closely related to it. These dialects show slightly different versions of the same rules, extending and modifying the grammatical processes which are common to all dialects of English.

Any analysis of the nonstandard dialect which pretends to ignore other dialects and the general rules of English will fail (1) because the nonstandard dialect is *not* an isolated system but a part of the sociolinguistic structure of English, and (2) because of the writer's knowledge of standard English. But it would be unrealistic to think that we can write anything but a superficial account of the dialect if we confine our thinking to this one subsystem and ignore whatever progress has been made in the understanding of (standard) English grammar.

FOR DISCUSSION AND REVIEW

1. According to Labov, why is it important for teachers to study "the child's own vernacular" (in this case, the nonstandard vernacular)?

2. Granted that it is desirable for teachers to study the actual vernacular of children, what methods are popular? What, if any, are the problems with these methods? Explain your answer.

3. Labov argues that there is a great deal "that we can do to show the internal relations in the nonstandard dialect *as a system* [italics added]." Give some examples of what he means by this statement, and explain the importance of the phrase "as a system."

4. Labov argues that "nonstandard English is a system of rules, different from the standard but not necessarily inferior as a means of communication." What evidence does he present to support the first part of this claim? In your answer, explain some of the rules of nonstandard English and how they differ from those of standard English. What evidence does he present to support the second part? Do you agree or disagree? Defend your answer.

23

Pidgins and Creoles

David Crystal

In the seventeenth century, a South American trader would have land-ed on the shores of Africa with wares to trade but no common language for communication. In order to conduct business, some means of com-munication had to be developed. A pidgin language incorporates vocab-ulary elements from two languages and simplifies grammatical forms from one or both languages. Typically used by speakers of two or more languages, pidgins are defined as rudimentary languages with simpli-fied grammars and limited lexicons. Because people do not learn pidgins as native speakers, a pidgin language is called an auxiliary language. In contrast, creoles, which develop from pidgins, are learned by native speakers and are considered fully developed languages. In the following selection taken from the Cambridge Encyclopedia of Language, *David Crystal of University College of North Wales examines the differences between pidgin and creole languages and points out that creole lan-guages throughout the world exhibit remarkable structural uniformi-ties. Although the number of creole speakers in the world continually diminishes and several misconceptions surround these languages, cre-ole languages must be observed as valid and, more important, worthy of our attention in the ongoing investigation of human language.*

PIDGIN LANGUAGES

A pidgin is a system of communication which has grown up among people who do not share a common language, but who want to talk to each other, for trading or other reasons. Pidgins have been variously called "makeshift," "marginal," or "mixed" languages. They have a lim-ited vocabulary, a reduced grammatical structure, and a much narrower range of functions, compared to the languages which gave rise to them. They are the native language of no one, but they are nonetheless a main means of communication for millions of people, and a major focus of interest to those who study the way languages change.

It is essential to avoid the stereotype of a pidgin language, as perpe-trated over the years in generations of children's comics and films. The "Me Tarzan, you Jane" image is far from the reality. A pidgin is not a lan-guage which has broken down; nor is it the result of baby talk, laziness, corruption, primitive thought processes, or mental deficiency. On the contrary, pidgins are demonstrably creative adaptations of natural languages, with a structure and rules of their own. Along with creoles, they are evidence of a fundamental process of linguistic change, as languages come into contact with each other, producing new varieties whose structures and uses contract and expand. They provide the clearest evidence of language being created and shaped by society for its own ends, as people adapt to new social circumstances. This emphasis on processes of change is reflected in the terms *pidginization* and *creolization*.

Most pidgins are based on European languages—English, French, Spanish, Dutch, and Portuguese—reflecting the history of colonialism. However, this observation may be the result only of our ignorance of the languages used in parts of Africa, South America, or Southeast Asia, where situations of language contact are frequent. One of the best-known non-European pidgins is Chinook Jargon, once used for trading by American Indians in northwest U.S.A. Another is Sango, a pidginized variety of Ngbandi, spoken widely in west-central Africa.

Because of their limited function, pidgin languages usually do not last for very long—sometimes for only a few years, and rarely for more than a century. They die when the original reason for communication diminishes or disappears, as communities move apart, or one community learns the language of the other. (Alternatively, the pidgin may develop into a creole.) The pidgin French which was used in Vietñam all but disappeared when the French left; similarly, the pidgin English which appeared during the American Vietnam campaign virtually disappeared as soon as the war was over. But there are exceptions. The pidgin known as Mediterranean Lingua Franca, or Sabir, began in the Middle Ages and lasted until the twentieth century.

Some pidgins have become so useful as a means of communication between languages that they have developed a more formal role, as regular auxiliary languages. They may even be given official status by a community, as lingua francas. These cases are known as *expanded pidgins*, because of the way in which they have added extra forms to cope with the needs of their users, and have come to be used in a much wider range of situations than previously. In time, these languages may come to be used on the radio, in the press, and may even develop a literature of their own. Some of the most widely used expanded pidgins are Krio (in Sierra Leone), Nigerian Pidgin English, and Bislama (in Vanuatu). In Papua New Guinea, the local pidgin (Tok Pisin) is the most widely used language in the country.

CREOLE LANGUAGES

A creole is a pidgin language which has become the mother tongue of a community—a definition which emphasizes that pidgins and creoles are two stages in a single process of linguistic development. First, within a community, increasing numbers of people begin to use pidgin as their principal means of communication. As a consequence, their children hear it more than any other language, and gradually it takes on the status of a mother tongue for them. Within a generation or two, native language use becomes consolidated and widespread. The result is a creole, or "creolized" language.

The switch from pidgin to creole involves a major expansion in the structural linguistic resources available—especially in vocabulary, grammar, and style, which now have to cope with the everyday demands made upon a mother tongue by its speakers. There is also a highly significant shift in the overall patterns of language use found in the community. Pidgins are by their nature auxiliary languages, learned alongside vernacular languages which are much more developed in structure and use. Creoles, by contrast, are vernaculars in their own right. When a creole language develops, it is usually at the expense of other languages spoken in the area. But then it too can come under attack.

The main source of conflict is likely to be with the standard form of the language from which it derives, and with which it usually coexists. The standard language has the status which comes with social prestige, education, and wealth; the creole has no such status, its roots lying in a history of subservience and slavery. Inevitably, creole speakers find themselves under great pressure to change their speech in the direction of the standard—a process known as *decreolization*.

One consequence of this is the emergence of a continuum of several varieties of creole speech, at varying degrees of linguistic "distance" from the standard—what has been called the *post-creole continuum*. Another consequence is an aggressive reaction against the standard language on the part of creole speakers, who assert the superior status of their creole, and the need to recognize the ethnic identity of their community. Such a reaction can lead to a marked change in speech habits, as the speakers focus on what they see to be the "pure" form of creole—a process known as *hypercreolization*. This whole movement, from creolization to decreolization to hypercreolization, can be seen at work in the recent history of Black English in the U.S.A.

The term *creole* comes from Portuguese *crioulo*, and originally meant a person of European descent who had been born and brought up in a colonial territory. Later, it came to be applied to other people who were native to these areas, and then to the kind of language they spoke. Creoles are now usually classified as "English based," "French based," and so on— though the genetic relationship of a creole to its dominant linguistic ancestor is never straightforward, as the creole may display the influences of several contact languages in its sounds, vocabulary, and structure.

Today, the study of creole languages, and of the pidgins which gave rise to them, attracts considerable interest among linguists and social historians. To the former, the cycle of linguistic reduction and expansion which they demonstrate, within such a short time-scale, provides fascinating evidence of the nature of language change. To the latter, their development is seen to reflect the process of exploration, trade, and conquest which has played such a major part in European history over the past 400 years.

TABLE 23.1

FRENCH	GUYANESE CRÉOLE	KRIO	ENGLISH
Mangez	Mãʒe	Chɔp	Eat
J'ai mangé	Mo mãʒe	A chɔp	I ate
Il/Elle a mangé	Li mãʒe	I chɔp	He/She ate
Je mange/Je suis en train de manger	Mo ka mãʒe	A de chɔp	I am eating
J'avais mangé	Mo te mãʒe	A bin chɔp	I ate/had eaten
Je mangeais	Mo te ka mãʒe	A bin de chɔp	I was eating
Je mangerai	Mo ke mãʒe	A go chɔp	I shall eat
Il/Elle est plus grand que vous	Li gros pas u	I big pa yu	He/She/It is bigger than you

WHERE DO PIDGINS AND CREOLES COME FROM?

The world's pidgins and creoles display many obvious differences in sounds, grammar, and vocabulary, but they have a remarkable amount in common. Two opposed theories have attempted to explain these differences.

Many Sources?

A long-standing view is that every creole is a unique, independent development, the product of a fortuitous contact between two languages. On the surface, this polygenetic view is quite plausible. It seems unlikely that the pidgins which developed in Southeast Asia should have anything in common with those which developed in the Caribbean. And it is a general experience that these varieties come into use in an apparently spontaneous way—as any tourist knows who has faced a souvenir seller. Would not the restricted features of the contact situations (such as the basic sentence patterns and vocabulary needed in order to trade) be enough to explain the linguistic similarities around the world?

The view is tempting, but there are several grounds for criticism. In particular, it does not explain the *extent* of the similarities between these varieties. Common features such as the reduction of noun and pronoun inflections, the use of particles to replace tenses, and the use of repeated forms to intensify adjectives and adverbs are too great to be the result of coincidence. Why, then, should the pidginized forms of French,

Dutch, German, Italian, and other languages all display the same kind of modifications? Why, for example, should the English-based creoles of the Caribbean have so much in common with the Spanish-based creoles of the Philippines? How could uniformity come from such diversity?

One Source?

The opposite view argues that the similarities between the world's pidgins and creoles can be explained only by postulating that they had a common origin (i.e., are monogenetic), notwithstanding the distance which exists between them. Moreover, a clear candidate for a "protolanguage" has been found—a fifteenth-century Portuguese pidgin, which may in turn have descended from the Mediterranean lingua franca known as Sabir. The Portuguese are thought to have used this pidgin during their explorations in Africa, Asia, and the Americas. Later, it is argued, as other nations came to these areas, the simple grammar of this pidgin came to be retained, but the original Portuguese vocabulary was replaced by words taken from their own languages. This view is known as the *relexification* hypothesis.

There is a great deal of evidence to support the theory, deriving from historical accounts of the Portuguese explorations, and from modern analyses of the languages. For instance, every English-based pidgin and creole has a few Portuguese words, such as *savi* "know," *pikin* "child," and *palava* "trouble." In Saramaccan, an English-based creole of Suriname, 38% of the core vocabulary is from Portuguese. Early accounts of Chinese pidgin refer to a mixed dialect of English and Portuguese. And on general grounds, relexification of a single "proto-pidgin" seems a more plausible hypothesis than one which insists on a radical parallel restructuring of several languages.

The shift in approach, implicit in the relexification theory, is fundamental: it is not the case that English, and the other languages, were creolized, but that an original (Portuguese) creole was anglicized. However, not all the facts can be explained in this way. Pitcairnese creole has no Portuguese influence, and yet has much in common with other varieties. What accounts for those similarities? Then there are several pidgins and creoles which have developed with little or no historical contact with European languages—Sango and Chinook, for instance. And there seem to be many structural differences between European and non-European pidgins and creoles, which the common origin hypothesis finds difficult to explain.

The evidence is mixed. Disentangling the structural similarities and differences between these varieties is a difficult task, and the evidence could be taken to support either a monogenetic or a polygenetic theory. Far more descriptive studies are needed before we rule out one view or the other.

TABLE 23.2   Pidgins Compared

ENGLISH	TOK PISIN	CHINESE PIDGIN	SANGO	CHINOOK JARGON
bell	bɛl	bell	ngbéréná	tíntin
big	bɪgfɛlə	big	kótá	hyás
bird	pɪǧɪn	bird(ee)	ndɛkɛ	kalákala
bite	kajkajɪm	bitee	tɛ	múckamuck
black	blækfɛlə	black	(zo)vɔkɔ́	klale
blood	blʊt	blood	mɛ́nɛ́	pilpil
cold	kilfɛlə	colo	dé	cole, tshis
come	kəm	li	ga	chahko
die	daj	dielo	kúi	mémaloost
dog	dɔg	doggee	mbo	kámooks
drink	drɪŋk	dlinkee, haw	yç	muckamuck
ear	ir	ear	mɛ́	kwolánn
earth	grawn	glound	sése	illahie
eat	kajkaj	chowchow	kóbe, tɛ	múckamuck
fat	gris	fat, glease	mafuta	glease
feather	gras bɪlɔŋ pɪǧɪn	fedder	kɔ́á tí ndɛkɛ	kalákala yaka túpso
fish	fiš	fishee	susu	pish
give	gɪvɪm	pay	fú	pótlatch
green	grinfɛlə	gleen, lu	vɔkɔ́ kété	pechúgh
hair	gras bɪlɔŋ hɛd	hair	kɔ́á	yákso
hand	hæn	hand, sho	mabɔ́kɔ	le mah
head	hɛd	headee	li	la tet
heart	klak	heart	coeur	túmtum
know	save	savvy	hínga	kumtuks
man	mæn	man	kɔ́lĭ	man
no	no	na	non	wake
nose	nos	peedza	hɔ	nose
one	wənfɛlə	one piecee	ɔ́kɔ́	ikt
small	lɪklɪk	likki	kété	ténas
sun	sən	sun	lá	sun, ótelagh
talk	tɔk	talkee	tɛnɛ	wáuwau
two	tufɛlə	two	óse	mokst
warm	hɔtfɛlə	warm	wá	waum

Lexical similarities and differences between pidgins are clearly illustrated in this list of items collected by F. G. Cassidy in the 1960s, taken from the set of "basic words" used in glotto-chronology. The English element predominates in Tok Pisin and Chinese Pidgin; in Sango, the vast majority of the words are African; in Chinook, most words are from Chinook or other Amerindian languages (but note the influence of both French and English). French names for parts of the body have emerged in Sango and Chinook. Though there is no historical connection between the languages, note also the coincidences of thought which have produced the figurative phrases for feather (grass-of-bird [Tok Pisin], hair-of-bird [Sango], and leaf-of-bird [Chinook]), and the words for heart in Tok Pisin and Chinook, both of which stress the notion of heartbeat.

Meanwhile, other theories have been proposed, in an attempt to explain these similarities and differences. Other forms of simplified speech have been noted, such as those used by children, in telegrams and headlines, and in talking to foreigners. It is possible that the processes underlying pidgins and creoles reflect certain basic preferences in human language (such as fixed word order, or the avoidance of inflections). In this connection, these languages provide fresh and intriguing evidence in the search for linguistic universals.

FOR DISCUSSION AND REVIEW

1. How does Crystal define pidgins and creoles?

2. What are the misconceptions that surround the study of pidgins?

3. How do pidgins and creoles develop? When is a pidgin said to become a creole? Which language is more likely to become extinct? How does the size of the population using the language influence the outcome? Give reasons for your explanation.

4. What does Crystal mean by "expanded pidgins"? At what point do pidgins become expanded?

5. How does a creole differ from a pidgin? What conflicts exist between creoles and other language forms?

6. Define the terms *decreolization* and *hypercreolization*. How do these affect language change and tensions among languages? How have such events influenced the growth of languages such as BEV?

7. Crystal says, "The world's pidgins and creoles display many obvious differences in sounds, grammar, and vocabulary, but they have a remarkable amount in common." What are two opposing theories that attempt to explain these differences? Which theory do you favor? Why?

8. Describe the relexification process that sometimes occurs in pidgin languages?

9. Why is it important to study both pidgins and creoles? What is their value in the ongoing study of language?

24

"It Bees Dat Way Sometime": *Sounds and Structure of Present-Day Black English*

Geneva Smitherman

The language of Black Americans is one of the most active areas of current dialectical and sociolinguistic study. This language, after developing quietly since colonial times in tandem with Standard American English, became a center of focus as a result of the civil rights movement of the 1960s. Over the last three decades, a flood of academic books and articles has examined Black English Vernacular (BEV), more recently known as Ebonics. Some of these sources view Black English as a "deficient" type of Standard English, while others, including the following selection, closely explore its grammatical and phonological structures. Disagreement about the nature and validity of Black English has challenged the boundaries of linguistic study and entered the broad arena of American culture. What do we call this language? How can we define it? What role should it play in public education? These are all hot issues of debate. In this chapter from her book Talkin' and Testifyin': The Language of Black America, *Geneva Smitherman defines Black English as a dialect spoken nationwide, with specific, rule-based phonological and syntactical characteristics that distinguish it from regional dialects and Standard American English. By providing examples of common expressions and shifting occasionally into idiomatic Black English, Smitherman emphasizes the wit and vitality of this dialect.*

Black dialect consists of both language and style. In using the term "language" we are referring to sounds and grammatical structure. "Style" refers to the way speakers put sounds and grammatical structure together to communicate meaning in a larger context. Put another way, language is the words, style is what you do with the words.

Let's look first at the language of Black English. As we do so, it is important to keep in mind two facts. One is that, if blacks continue to be accepted into the American mainstream, many of the Africanized features of Black English may be sifted out of the language. Thus we are describing a form of speech which could, in, say, the twenty-first century, be in danger of extinction. (About all I will guarantee is that the patterns I'm describing were in regular and systematic use in the Black com-

328

munity at the time of this writing!) Again, because of the process of decreolization, you should not expect Black English of today to be like that of the seventeenth century. All languages change over time; thus Black English of the twentieth century differs from early Black English just as White English of today is not identical to that of the founding fathers. The main linguistic differences between Black English and White English are cited below. In most other respects, the sounds and structure of the two dialects are generally the same.

The pronunciation system of Black English employs the same number of sounds as White English (ranging from 45–48 sounds, counting stress and intonation patterns) but these sounds exist in a few different patterns of distribution. Of course, the real distinctiveness—and beauty—in the Black sound system lies in those features which do not so readily lend themselves to concrete documentation—its speech rhythms, voice inflections, and tonal patterns. However, here we shall concern ourselves with those features of sound which are concrete and easily identified. For example, the *th* sounds in *then* and *with* are pronounced in Black dialect as *den* and *wif*; that is, *th* [/ð/] may be pronounced as *d* or *f*, depending on position (Of course it would be inaccurate to say that Black language has no *th* sound simply because it's realized differently.) In linguistic environments where the initial *th* sound is voiceless [/θ/], it is pronounced the same way as in White speech, as in *thought*, which is always *thought* (not *dought*), or *thing*, which is *thing*, or more usually *thang* (not *ding* or *dang*). Many times, Black dialect sounds tend to be generally similar to those of White speakers of any given region of the country. That is, some Black speakers in Boston say *pahk the cah* (deleting *r*'s) in the same way as White speakers of that area, and Southern Black speech sounds pretty much the same as Southern White speech. As a matter of fact, when you talk about pronunciation, there is no national standard even among White speakers, since the different regional dialects of the country all have their own individual standards. The following list indicates the few different pronunciations in Black English that are used by large numbers of Black speakers:

Initial /th/ [/ð/] = /d/
  them = dem; then = den

Final /th/ [/θ/] = /f/
  south = souf; mouth = mouf

Deletion of middle and final /r/
  during = doing; more = mow; Paris = pass; star = stah

Deletion of middle and final /l/
  help = hep; will = wi

When the contracted form of *will* is used (/'ll/), you get a kind of /ah/ sound, as: *Iah be dere in a minute* (for *I'll be there in a minute*).

Deletion of most final consonants
hood = *hoo; bed* = *be*
test = *tes; wasp* = *was*

Pluralized forms ending in such double consonants add /es/, thus: *tests* = *tesses; wasps* = *wasses.* (One important exception to this rule involves words ending in /s/, such as the proper name *Wes.* Here the /s/ is *not* deleted.)

Vowel plus /ng/ [/ŋ/] in *thing, ring, sing* rendered as /ang/
thing = *thang; ring* = *rang; sing* = *sang*

Contraction of *going to* rendered as *gon.* Here the *to* is omitted altogether, and the nasal sound at the end is shortened, producing a sound that is somewhat like an abbreviated form of *gone. He was gon tell his momma good-by.*

Primary stress on first syllable and front shifting
police = *PO-lice; Detroit* = *DEE-troit*

Simple vowels
nice = *nahs*
boy = *boah*

While digging on the sights and sounds of the Black community, here are some things you are likely to hear:

"Dem dudes always be doin day thang." (*Those dudes are always doing their thing* . . . Eighth grade student)

"Hur' up, the bell ranging." (*Hurry up, the bell is ringing* . . . Fourth grade student)

"Sang good, now y'all." (*Sing good* . . . Female adult in Baptist church)

"Doin the civil right crisis, we work hard." (*During the civil rights crisis, we worked hard* . . . College student)

"We are aware of the antagonism between the PO-lice and the Black community." (Big city mayor)

Linguistically speaking, the greatest differences between contemporary Black and White English are on the level of grammatical structure. Grammar is the most rigid and fixed aspect of speech, that part of *any* language which is least likely to change over time. Couple this linguistic fact with the historical reality that only in recent years have there been concerted and intense pressures on the Black masses to conform to the language standards of White America. Thus it is logical that the grammatical patterns of Black English have been the last component of Black dialect to change in the direction of White English.

Black idiom speakers throughout the United States have certain grammatical structures in common—despite the region of the country, and in some instances despite the social class level. Middle-class Blacks from Detroit, for example, were found to delete *-ed* in verbs more frequently than middle-class Whites from Detroit.

The most distinctive differences in the structure of Black dialect are patterns using *be* (sometimes written and pronounced as *bees* or *be's*). These forms are mainly used to indicate a condition that occurs habitually. *Be* is omitted if the condition or event is not one that is repeated or recurring. For example, *The coffee bees cold* means *every day the coffee's cold*, which is different from *the coffee cold* which means *today the coffee's cold*. In other words if you the cook and *the coffee cold*, you might only just get talked about that day, but if *the coffee bees cold*, pretty soon you ain't gon have no job! The *be/non-be* rule operates with systematic regularity in the Black-English-speaking community.

Consider another example, this time from a young Black Detroiter commenting on her father: *My father, he work at Ford. He be tired. So he can't never help us with our homework*. The *He be tired* here means *every day my father is tired*. If the speaker had wanted to indicate that that fact applied to one day only, she would have left the *be* out of the sentence; thus, *My father, he work at Ford. He tired*, indicating that although he is tired today, this is generally not the case. (An unlikely situation, however, because if your father work at Ford Motor Company, on that Detroit assembly line where the Brothers bees humpin, he be tired all the time, believe me!) Here are a few examples of *be* used to indicate habitual aspect:

They be slow all the time.

She be late every day.

I see her when I bees on my way to school.

By the time I go get my momma, it be dark.

The kid alway be messing up and everything.

Be is also used in combination with *do* to convey habitual conditions expressed in question form and for emphasis: *Do they be playing all day?* (in White English, *Do they play all day?*) and *Yeah, the boys do be messing around a lot* (in White English, *Yeah, the boys do mess around a lot*).

In addition to the use of *be* for habitual events, there is another important function of *be* that should be noted here. The Black English speaker can use *be* to convey a sense of future time, as in *The boy be here soon* and *They family be gone Friday*. Now keep in mind that these subtle distinctions in the meaning and use of *be* depend heavily on context. Thus the listener has got to heed the contextual cues in order to decode the speaker's meaning properly. For instance:

She be there later. (future *be*)

She be there everyday. (habitual *be*)

I be going home tomorrow. (future *be*)

I be going home all the time. (habitual *be*)

Future *be* may appear in combination with the contracted form of *will* ('ll). (Remember that due to the Black English sound rule of /l/ deletion, we get a kind of /ah/ sound for the letters /'ll/.) Thus you will hear:

He be looking for you next week, as well as *He-ah be looking for you next week*. The explanation for both forms being used can be found in the process of language change (involved in) the transition from a more Africanized Black English to a more Americanized Black English. In the early stages of Black English, probably only *be* by itself was used to denote future time. Then, with the change in time and the collapsing of Black English structures toward those of White English, speakers of Black English began to indicate future time also with the use of *will* (pronounced, of course, according to rules for Black English sounds). However, since the process of language change is still incomplete, we find both ways of expressing future time in the Black community and, indeed, within the speech of any one individual speaker of Black English.

Interestingly enough, forms of *be* (but not *be* itself) appear in places where they are needed for meaning, as in the past tense and in questions tacked on to sentences, so-called "tag" questions. For example, *He was my English teacher last year* rather than something ambiguous like *He my English teacher last year*. And *You ain't sick, is you?* rather than the unintelligible form, *You ain't sick, you?*

When the forms of *be* are used, they are simplified so that *is* and *was* usually serve for all subjects of sentences, whether the subjects are singular or plural, or refer to *I, you, we,* or whatever. For example, as above, we have *You ain't sick, is you?* as well as *She ain't home, is she?* And *He was my English teacher last year*, as above, as well as *They was acting up and going on*. The contracted form ('s) may also be used, as: *We's doing our book work and everythang when she start callin on us.*

As mentioned earlier, the Black English speaker omits *be* when referring to conditions that are fixed in time and to events or realities that do not repeat themselves. Applying the *non-be* rule, you get an absence of *be* before nouns: *He a hippie now;* before adjectives: *He too tall for me;* before adverbs: *They shoes right there;* before prepositional phrases: *My momma in the hospital;* and in auxiliary constructions: *They talking about school now*. Here are some additional examples of the absence of *be* to indicate a nonrecurring event or a fixed, static condition:

He sick today.

This my mother.

That man too tall for her little short self.

They daddy in the house.

The mens playing baseball and the womens cooking today.

Man, your ride really bad.

Black English speakers use *been* to express past action that has recently been completed. "Recently" here depends much more on the particular words in the sentence that express the time, rather than the actual amount of time itself. For example, it is correct Black English to say: *She been tardy twice this semester* (which might have been several weeks or months ago as long as it's what would be called "this semester"). But it is *not* correct Black English to say: *She been tardy twice last semester* (although "last semester" might have just ended at the time the speaker is stating the fact). In order to express the idea of two tardinesses "last semester," the correct Black English statement would be: *She was tardy twice last semester*. If this sounds confusing, remember that White English has similar constraints upon the speaker's expression. Thus White English speakers can say: *I have been to New York this year*, but they *cannot* say: *I have been to New York last year*. As a rule of thumb, you can say that generally where Black English speakers use *been*, White English speakers would use *have*, *has*, or *had* plus *been*.

BLACK ENGLISH: He been there before.
WHITE ENGLISH: He has been there before.

BLACK ENGLISH: They been there before.
WHITE ENGLISH: They have been there before.

BLACK ENGLISH: She been there and left before I even got there.
WHITE ENGLISH: She had been there and left before I even got there.

Note that Black English uses only the verb form *been*, regardless of the form of the subject or whether *have* is present or past tense.

   Been is also used in combination with other verb forms to indicate past action, which might be recently completed, or more distantly completed action (although again, it is structural expression that counts, not the actual semantic reality). For example, *He been gone a year*, but also: *He been gone a day*. The White English equivalents would be a form of *have* plus *been* plus the verb, thus:

BLACK ENGLISH: He been gone a year.
WHITE ENGLISH: He has been gone a year.

BLACK ENGLISH: They been gone a year.
WHITE ENGLISH: They have been gone a year.

BLACK ENGLISH: She been gone a year before anybody know it.
WHITE ENGLISH: She had been gone a year before anybody knew it.

   As mentioned, it is not the time itself that governs the verb choice, but the way the time is expressed. Keeping this in mind will help us distinguish between use of *been* plus the verb and the past tense of *be* plus the verb. Thus, *Tony been seen at her house today*, but not *Tony been seen at her house yesterday*. Instead, this latter statement would be rendered in correct Black English as *Tony was seen at her house yesterday*.

   Now just when you think you got that all straight, I'm gon throw a tricky one in here because sometimes *been* is used to show emphasis, regardless of the time that has elapsed since an action took place. *She BEEN there*, uttered with stress on *BEEN*, means that the speaker wants to emphasize the fact that the individual has been wherever she is for a long enough period of time that it's an established fact. Now, she mighta just got there, or maybe she even been there for days, but the point here is not the amount of time but the intensity and validity of the fact. In other words, she been there long enough for me to be certain bout it, so ain no point in keepin on askin questions bout it!

In similar fashion, *been* patterns with other verb forms to suggest emphatic assertion, *He BEEN gone*, meaning I'm certain of the fact of his leaving (it might have taken place long ago, or the leaving might have just occurred; at any rate, the speaker is not concerned with the precise amount of time, just the real fact of the departure). Note that in both patterns of emphasis, *been* appears in the sentence without any other kind of qualifying expression of time or emphasis. Thus while correct Black English would be *He BEEN gone*, if you added the words *a long time*, it would be incorrect Black English. If there is another word or words that convey the intensity or duration of time in the sentence, then the Black English speaker would not put any special stress on the *been*. Thus we would have simply *He been gone a long time*, not *He BEEN gone a long time*.

Done used by itself indicates past action, either recently completed or completed in the distant past. *I done my homework today* and *I done my homework yesterday* are both correct Black English statements. White English equivalents would be *I did my homework today* and *I did my homework yesterday*. When used in combination with another verb, *done* usually indicates only recently completed action (again "recently" depending on how it's expressed in the sentence). It is correct Black English to say *I done finish my work today*, but it is *not* correct Black English to say *I done finish my work yesterday*. The correct Black English here would be *I finish my work yesterday*. As explained earlier, White English has similar linguistic constraints. Thus White English speakers can say *I have finished my work today*, but they cannot say *I have finished my work yesterday*. The correct White English statement would be *I finished my work yesterday*.

What is important to keep in mind here is the distinction between *done* used by itself and *done* used in combination with other verbs. A Black English statement containing only *done* can usually be understood to mean the White English *did*. However, when it is used with another verb, you cannot substitute the White English form *did*. Instead, the White English equivalent is a form of *have* (*have, has,* or *had*). The Black English *James done seen the show* is NOT White English *James did seen the show*, NOR *James did see the show*, BUT *James has seen the show*. Similarly, the Black English *I done did my hair* is not the White English *I did my hair*, but *I have done my hair*, as in *I have done my hair five times this week*. Note here that the Black English *did* actually translates into the White English *done*. But there are Black English uses of *did*. For example, if the Black English speaker wanted to express emphasis, he or she would use *did* in the same way as White English speakers, thus:

BLACK ENGLISH: I DID do my hair five times this week!
WHITE ENGLISH: I DID do my hair five times this week!

Done can be found in Black English in combination with *been*. In such statements, *done* still functions like White English *have*. He *done been gone all night* (White English: *He has been gone all night*) and *They done been sitting there a hour* (White English: *They have been sitting there an hour*). Sentences like these can also be used without *done* and still be correct Black English. Just as the White English speaker has many different ways of expressing the same thing, so the Black English speaker has many linguistic options. Thus, the speaker of Black English could say any of the following:

He done been gone all night *or* He been gone all night.

They done been sitting there a hour *or* They been sitting there a hour.

She done been tardy twice this semester *or* She been tardy twice this semester.

Now here's a tricky one for you. This Black English use of *done* makes possible a tense that has pretty much gone out of White mainstream usage—that is, the future perfect, also referred to as past future. In White English, you used to get this kind of verb usage in sentences like the following:

He will have left by the time we get there.

I shall have finished before anyone arrives.

If those two expressions sound kinda stuffy, they should. Nowadays, you would more likely hear the following from White English speakers:

He will be gone by the time we get there.

I will be finished before anyone arrives.

Here's how Black English speakers render this future perfect: *be* plus *done* plus verb.

He be done left by the time we get there.

I be done finish before anyone arrive.

This usage is still very popular among Black English speakers and is found in the much-used Black idiom expression "I be done—before you know it." Hip users of this Black English expression simply fill in whatever verb they want to use, according to context. Here are some examples of this use of future perfect from Black English speakers (for White English equivalents, simply substitute *will have* plus verb):

"I *be done did* this lil' spot a hair fo' you know it." ("middle-aged" beautician)

"If you mess wif me, *I be done did* you in fo' you know it." (young male about to git it on)

"The Lord *be done call* me Home fo' you know it." (young church deacon)

"If you ain mighty particular, yo' luck *be done run* out fo' you know it." (senior citizen to young black on the wild)

"Look out, now! Fo' you know it, I *be done caught* you out there bluffin." (doctor at poker game)

Black dialect relies on either the context of the immediate sentence or the context of an entire conversation to signal conditions of time. There is no *-ed* in either past tense or past participle constructions (*I look for him last night* and *This guy I know name Junior* . . .). Using context to signal time, the same verb form serves for both present and past tense, as: *The bus pass me up last week*, but also: *The bus pass me up every day*. The words *last week* and *every day* signal the time of these statements rather than a change in the verb form. Similarly, in the following statement from a Black sermon, the preacher has already established the fact that he's talking about the past since he's talking about the life and sacrifice of Christ: "The man Jesus, He come here, He die to save you from your sins! He walk the earth, He go among the thieves and try to save the unrighteous. The Master say whosoever will, let him come!"

Most Black English verbs are not marked for person. The same verb form serves for all subjects, whether singular or plural. The subject and number of the verb are marked by the context of the sentence or by some word in the sentence. Thus, *She have us say it*. Here the singular subject is indicated by *she*, with no change in the verb *have*. Another example: *He do the same thang they do*. In this sentence, there is no need to alter the verb *do* because the subjects *he* and *they* in the context convey the meaning and notion of two different subjects.

Black dialect obviously has the concepts of plurality and possession, but they are not indicated by the addition of *-s* or apostrophes with *-s*. *Two boys just left*, *two* indicates that *boy* is plural. *That was Mr. Johnson store got burn down*, the position of the noun, *Mr. Johnson*, signals who owns the store.

As a result of trying to conform Africanized patterns to Americanized ones, and doing so without the benefit of formal language instruction, Blacks created in Black English a number of overly correct or hypercorrect forms, such as the addition of *-s* to already pluralized forms, as in *It's three childrens in my family* and *The peoples shouldn't do that*. We also find forms such as *they does*. Such hypercorrections are due to insufficient knowledge and instruction in the erratic rules of White English. For example, in White English, an *s* is added to a singular verb form (as in *He does*) but not to a plural form (as in *They do*). In learning the language without systematic formal instruction, the traditional Africanized English speaker tries to reconcile this paradox and may end up adding an *s* to a lot of forms, so we not only get attempts to be correct producing *They does* but such attempts also produce *I does*.

Black English speakers place stress on the subjects of sentences. In

White English, this might be labeled the "double subject." Rather than being a duplicate subject as such, the repetition of the subject in some other form is used in Black English for emphasis. Two examples: *My son, he have a new car* and *The boy who left, he my friend*. Note that the emphasis is indicated without pronouncing the words in any emphatic way since this is accomplished by the "double subject." This feature of Black English is not a mandatory one, so you may hear it sometimes, other times not at all. As with White English speakers, there are many options open to the speaker of Black English. The repetition of subject is simply another such option.

The personal pronoun system of Black English is not as highly differentiated as that of White English. Thus, for example, with the third person plural pronoun, *they*, the same form serves for subject, possessive, and so-called reflexive as in *The expressway bought they house* and *They should do it theyselves*. In the case of the third person singular pronoun, *he*, we will hear both *He gone* and *Him cool*, and in the reflexive, *He did it all by hisself*. At an earlier stage in the development of Black English, forms like *he book* (for *his book*) and *she house* (for *her house*) were prominent, but these have gradually disappeared. You may hear them in very young preschool children. With many pronouns in White English, you have a somewhat similar rule that allows the same form to be used for subjects, objects, and possessives. Thus, White English speakers say *James hit her* as well as *This is her book*. At one time in the early history of British-American English, there were different forms for all personal pronouns, but as the language changed, the English pronoun system was simplified to a reduced number of forms.

The pronoun *it* is used to refer to things and objects ("itsy" things) as in White English, but Black English adds an additional function for the pronoun. It can be used to introduce statements, and as such, has no real meaning. For example, *It's four boy and two girl in the family* and *It was a man had died*. The patterns of English sentences are such that they may require a "filler" word in some statements, even though the "filler" itself is empty in a semantic sense. Typically, American English uses the word *there* in such sentences. Thus, (White English) *There are four boys and two girls in the family* and *There was a man who had died*. Black English may also use the introductory *it* in question form.

Is it a Longfellow street in this city? (White English: Is there a Longfellow street in this city?)

Is it anybody home? (White English: Is there anybody home?)

As an adverbial demonstrative, *here* or *there* plus *go* is used instead of *here/there* plus *is/are*. For example, *There go my brother in the first row* and *Here go my momma right here*. The speaker also has the option of expressing these two statements with *it* as explained above. Thus, *It's my brother in the first row* and *It's my momma right there*.

As with the deletion of final consonants in many Black English sounds, the dialect omits the final *s* in adverbs, for example, *Sometime they do that* and *He alway be here.*

Whereas the old double negative goes back to Shakespeare and is in abundant use among whites today, triple and quadruple negatives are the sole province of Africanized English. Thus, *Don't nobody never help me do my work, Can't nobody do nothin in Mr. Smith class,* and *Don't nobody pay no attention to no nigguh that ain crazy!* Note that these are statements, not questions, despite the reverse word order. Now the rule for forming negatives in Black English is just a little bit tricky, so check it out closely. If the negative statement is composed of only *one* sentence, then *every* negatable item in the statement *must* be negated. Therefore, *Don't nobody never help me do the work,* which consists of only one sentence, has a negative in every possible place in the sentence. The White English translation is: *No one ever helps me do my work.* If, however, the negative statement involves *two* or more sentences combined together as one, a different rule operates. If every negatable item in the statement is negated, the White English translation would be a statement in the "positive." If, however, the statement contains all negatives plus one positive, the White English translation would be a statement in the "negative." Take the example mentioned above, the line from Lonne Elder's play, *Ceremonies in Dark Old Men: Don't nobody pay no attention to no nigguh that ain crazy!* Here, there are two sentences combined into one statement, and every item in the statement is negated, rendering the White English translation: *If you are a crazy nigger, you will get attention.* Now, suppose you wanted to convey the opposite meaning, that is, the White English, *If you are a crazy nigger, you will not get any attention.* The correct Black English would be expressed as all negatives plus one positive, thus: *Don't nobody pay no attention to no nigguh that's crazy!* (Keep in mind that this rule only applies to statements in which there are two or more sentences combined into one.)

To state the Black English negation rule more succinctly: if the statement consists of only *one* sentence, negate every item; if the statement consists of *two* or *more* sentences combined as one, all negatives indicate "positives," and all negatives *plus one positive* indicate "negatives." Here are some other examples:

It ain nobody I can trust (White English: *I can trust no one.*)

It ain nobody I can't trust. (White English: *I can trust everyone.*)

Wasn't no girls could go with us. (White English: *None of the girls could go with us.*)

Wasn't no girls couldn't go with us. (White English: *All the girls could go with us.*)

Ain't none these dudes can beat me. (White English: *None of these dudes can beat me.*)

Ain't none of these dudes can't beat me. (White English: *All these dudes can beat me.*)

Another distinctive Black dialect negation pattern occurs in statements which are only partly negative. These statements pattern with *but*, as in *Don't but one person go out at a time* and *Don't nobody but God know when that day gon be*.

The foregoing discussion of Black dialect sound and structure patterns should prove useful to teachers and others who wish to understand Black lingo so as to really dig where such speakers are comin from. Obviously this kind of understanding can help bridge the linguistic and cultural gap between Blacks and Whites and thus facilitate communication. However, certain cautions should be observed. First, do not expect *all* Black English speakers to use *all* these patterns *all* the time. The list is intended to be exhaustive of the range of patterns you might encounter in a given situation, but some Black dialect speakers may be more bidialectal than others, preferring to use White English around whites, Black English around Blacks. (For example, among school-age Blacks, one would find a greater degree of bidialectalism among older adolescents than among younger Black children, for adolescents have begun to get hip to the social sensitivities associated with different kinds of languages and dialects.) Second, no speaker of any hue uses the range of patterns in their language one hundred percent of the time. This caution is the more to be exercised in the face of the transition of Africanized English towards the direction of Americanized English. Thus, one may find in any Black English speaker both *he do* and *he does* although the *he do*'s will predominate. You will also find uses of *-ed* in some past tense forms and other features of White English. Again, this is due to dialect mixture and the transition of Black English to White English. . . . However, the Black English forms will prevail most of the time.

And with that, I'm going to close with a statement about "grammar and goodness" from my man, Langston Hughes, who often speaks through his folk hero, Jesse B. Simple—that beer-drinkin, rappin, profound thinkin Harlemite that Hughes first created for the pages of the well-known Black newspaper, the *Chicago Defender*.

> "I have writ a poem," said Simple.
> "Again?" I exclaimed. "The last time you showed me a poem of yours, it was too long, also not too good."
> "This one is better," said Simple. "Joyce had a hand in it, also my friend, Boyd, who is colleged. So I want you to hear it."
> "I know you are determined to read it to me, so go ahead."
> "It is about that minister down in Montgomery who committed a miracle."
> "What miracle?" I asked.
> "Getting Negroes to stick together," declared Simple.
> "I presume you are speaking of Rev. King," I said.
> "I am," said Simple. "He is the man, and this is my poem. Listen fluently now! This poem is writ like a letter. It is addressed to the White Citizens Councilors of Alabama and all their members, and this is how it goes:

Dear Citizens Councilors:
In line of what my folks
Say in Montgomery,
In line of what they
Teaching about love,
When I reach out my hand,
White folks, will you take it?
Or will you cut it off
And make a nub?
Since God put it in
My heart to love you,
If I love you
Like I really could,
If I say, 'Brother,
I forgive you,'
I wonder, would it
Do you any good?
Since slavery-time, long gone,
You been calling me
All kinds of names,
Pushing me down.
I been swimming with my
Head deep under water—
And you wished I would
Stay under till I drowned.
Well, I did not!
I'm still swimming!
Now you mad because
I won't ride in the
Back end of your bus.
When I answer, 'Anyhow,
I'm gonna love you,'
Still and yet, today
You want to make a fuss.

Now, listen, white folks:
In line with Rev. King
Down in Montgomery—
Also because the Bible
Says I must—
In spite of bombs and buses,
I'm gonna love you.
I say, I'm gonna LOVE you—
White folks, OR bust!"

"You never wrote a poem that logical all by yourself in life," I said.

"I know I didn't," admitted Simple. "But I am getting ready to write another one now. This time I am going to write a poem about Jim Crow up North, and it is going to start something like this:

In the North
The Jim Crow line

Ain't clear—
But it's here!
From New York to Chicago,
Points past and
In between,
Jim Crow is mean!
Even though integrated,
With Democracy
Jim Crow is *not* mated.
Up North Jim Crow
Wears an angel's grin—
But still he sin.
I swear he do!
Don't you?

"I agree that the sentiment of your poem is correct," I said. "But I cannot vouch for the grammar."

"If I get the sense right," answered Simple, "the grammar can take care of itself. There are plenty of Jim Crowers who speak grammar, but do evil. I have not had enough schooling to put words together right—but I know some white folks who have went to school forty years and do not do right. I figure it is better to do right than to write right, is it not?"

"You have something there," I said. "So keep on making up your poems, if you want to. At least, they rhyme."

"They make sense, too, don't they?" asked Simple.

"I think they do," I answered.

"They does," said Simple.

"They do," I corrected.

"They sure does," said Simple.

SOME WELL-KNOWN BLACK PROVERBS AND SAYINGS[1]

1. You never miss yo water till yo well run dry.

2. Grits ain't groceries, eggs ain't poultry, and Mona Lisa was a man. (I must be telling the truth since grits *are* groceries, eggs *are* poultry and Mona Lisa sure wasn't a man!)

3. You ain't got a pot to piss in or a window to throw it out of. (you are in poor financial straits)

4. If I'm lying, I'm flying. (proving truth: I must not be lying, if I were, I'd be flying)

5. You so dumb you can't throw rain water out of a boot, and the directions say how.

---

[1] For an outstanding collection and analysis of proverbs, see Jack L. Daniel, "Towards an Ethnography of Afro-American Proverbial Usage," *Black Lines*, Winter 1972, pp. 3–12.

6. The blacker the berry, the sweeter the juice. (he or she must be fine, he or she is so ripe and sweet; also suggestive of sexuality and sensual power)

7. What goes around comes around. (you reap what you sow)

8. If I tell you a hen dip snuff, look under its wing and find a whole box. (proving truth and claim of infallibility by speaker)

9. Study long, you study wrong. (listen to first impulses, because lengthy deliberations are liable to be inaccurate)

10. The eagle flies on Friday. (eagle, symbolizing money; statement commemorates payday)

11. Let the door hit you where the good Lord split you. (nasty command to leave, euphemism of "split you" avoiding profanity)

12. A hard head make a soft behind. (being stubborn, refusing to listen can make you pay a stiff price)

13. If you make yo bed hard, you gon have to lie in it.

14. It was so quiet you could hear a rat piss on cotton.

15. Pretty is as pretty does. (you are known by your actions)

16. Action speak louder than words. (same as above, this proverb is more common among younger Blacks today)

17. You don't believe fat meat is greasy. (signifyin on fools who insist on adhering to certain beliefs or opinions in the face of logical evidence to the contrary)

18. Tight as Dick's hatband. (financially stingy, refusing to share or give)

FOR DISCUSSION AND REVIEW

1. Smitherman begins her chapter by saying that "Black dialect consists of both language and style." Is the word "style," in this case, synonymous with "semantics"? Explain your answer.

2. What two facts about Black English does Smitherman warn the reader to keep in mind? Why are they important in relation to her description of the language?

3. Using the phonetic symbols in Part Three (see "Phonetics" by Edward Callary), transcribe the different ways that speakers of standard American English and speakers of Black dialect pronounce the following words: them, south, more, help, thing, during, tests.

4. In what way does Black English grammar differ from other regional American dialects?

5. Smitherman offers many examples of sentences containing grammatical constructions that follow clearly defined rules but that might be considered incorrect by a speaker of Standard English (e.g., "My father, he work at Ford. He be tired. So he can't never help us with our homework."). Identify three rules that make these sentences correct Black English.

6. Since Black dialect does not add "-ed" to verbs in order to indicate the past tense, how does the speaker distinguish between past and present?

7. In your own words, describe the essence of Langston Hughes' (Jesse B. Simple's) poems and the conversation that follows them.

8. In your opinion, should Black English be treated as a separate language? Is it important for Black Americans to learn Standard English? Why? Is it important for White Americans to learn Black English? Why?

Projects for "Language Variations and Discourse"

1. Prepare a report on the purposes and methods of the *Linguistic Atlas of the United States and Canada* project. Use the library card catalogue, Hans Kurath's *Handbook of the Linguistic Geography of New England*, Lee Pederson's *A Manual for Dialect Research in the Southern States*, and *Newsletter of the American Dialect Society*, the *PMLA Bibliography*, and the *Social Sciences Index* to locate materials for this project.

2. Collection of materials for the *Dictionary of American Regional English (DARE)* began in 1965; the goal was to produce an American dictionary comparable to the *English Dialect Dictionary* by 1976. Prepare a report on the methodology and progress of the *DARE* project. A longer report could examine the similarities and differences in purposes and methods between the *Linguistic Atlas of the United States and Canada* and the *Dictionary of American Regional English*. As a starting point, read Frederic G. Cassidy's "The *Atlas* and *DARE*," in *Lexicography and Dialect Geography*, edited by Harold Sholler and John Reidy (Wiesbaden: F. Steiner, 1973).

3. The names of cities, towns, rivers, and mountains often provide clues to settlement and migration patterns. Using a map of your area, list three local place names and discuss their significance. For example, you may wish to find out the meaning of each name and whether or not any of the names appear elsewhere in the country (and, if so, whether or not they are related). You will find the following references useful: Kelsie B. Hardner's *Illustrated Dictionary of Place Names* (1976) and George R. Stewart's *American Place-Names* (1970).

4. Study the history of your community so that you can write a report in which you discuss the ways in which settlement patterns, population shifts, and physical geography have influenced the speech of the area.

5. Bidialectalism is a highly controversial subject. Write a report (1) presenting opposing views objectively or (2), after explaining the arguments, write a report supporting one particular view. Prepare by rereading Labov, and consult O'Neil (1972), Pixton (1974), Sledd (1969, 1972), and more recent articles. Do you consider the sociologic and economic factors raised by the various authors important? What issues do not appear to be relevant? From an educational point of view, which argument is the strongest? Defend whatever position you take.

6. Prepare a report summarizing the history of Black English in America. (Note: Not all authorities agree on the origin and development of BE.) Consult Smitherman (1977) and Dillard (1972), both of which contain excellent bibliographies on the subject.

7. Roger Shuy's discussion of methodology demonstrates that word geography is a fascinating aspect of dialect study. Read E. Bagby Atwood's "Grease and Greasy: A Study of Geographical Variation," *Texas Studies*

in English 29 (1950), 249–60. Based on this reading, and using Shuy's checklist of regional expressions and personal data sheet, survey your class, your campus (or use a random sample), or your community (or use a random sample). Before you actually collect any data, you will need to consider such matters as the size and nature of the population to be studied, the selection of reliable and representative informants, and the possible significant influences in the history of the college or community. Compile your results. Do any local or regional patterns emerge? Do you find any other patterns (e.g., differences connected with age, sex, educational level, etc.)?

8. In "Sense and Nonsense about American Dialects" (*PMLA*, 81 [1966], 7–17), Raven I. McDavid, Jr., says that "the surest social markers in American English are grammatical forms." Collect examples of grammatical forms used in your community. What social classes are represented?

9. The concept of Standard English has been the source of misunderstanding and debate. For many Americans, "standard" implies that one variety of English is more correct or more functional than other varieties. Investigate the history of the concept of Standard English. How did this concept develop? How do various linguists define it? Is Standard English a social dialect? What is the power or mystique of Standard English?

10. Select the work of an author whose characters speak a social or regional variety of English—e.g., William Dean Howells, *The Rise of Silas Lapham*; Mark Twain, *Roughing It* (particularly "Buck Fanshaw's Funeral"); Bret Harte, *The Luck of Roaring Camp and Other Sketches*; Sarah Orne Jewett, *The Country of the Pointed Firs*; Joel Chandler Harris, *Uncle Remus and Br'er Rabbit*; William Faulkner, *The Sound and the Fury*; Willa Cather, *My Antonia*; John Steinbeck, *The Grapes of Wrath*; or Henry Roth, *Call It Sleep*. Identify the dialect in each and discuss the devices that the author uses to represent dialect. Read a passage aloud; how closely does it approximate actual speech?

11. Dialect differences in pronunciation abound. The following list contains words for which there are distinct regional pronunciations. Compare your pronunciation of these items with those of others in your class:

collar	cot	wash
car	apricot	paw
empty	dog	tomato
door	clientele	marry
garage	mangy	Mary
oil	house	roof
can	very	sorry
greasy	either	fog

lot	caller	water
caught	horse	almond
hurry	class	idea

What pronunciation differences do you note among the members of your class? Are any regional patterns of pronunciation evident? Compare your results with the regional pronunciations discussed by Roger Shuy.

12. In July 1979, the decision regarding Black English and the schools of Ann Arbor, Michigan, received national attention and has been the subject of controversy and misunderstanding (*Martin Luther King Junior Elementary School Children, et al. v Ann Arbor School District Board*, 473 F. Supp. 1371 [1979]). Using your library resources, prepare a report analyzing (a) the causes of the litigation, (b) the findings of the court, or (c) the effects of the decision on the Ann Arbor schools. One useful reference is *Black English: Educational Equity and the Law*, edited by John W. Chambers, Jr. (Ann Arbor, MI: Karoma Publishers, Inc., 1983).

13. The readings in Part Five deal with differences in speech among people of different regions and social classes. Compile a list of "slang" or "popular" terms from the students in your class. Your list may or may not include words such as: "not" (an exclamation), "crunchy" (a type of person), "to dis" (verb), or "choice" (adjective). Using the list of words, create a survey in which you ask whether your subject has heard the term before, whether he or she uses the term, what word, if any, the subject uses in place of a particular term, what other words the subject has heard that have the same meaning as your "slang" term, and where the subject believes the slang term originated. It might be helpful to record the subject's age group and sex for the analysis of your data.

Take your survey to your hometown and prepare a report of your results. Are there any distinct characteristics that you observe? Are there words that are considered masculine or feminine? Which terms are new and which are borrowed? Compare your results with those of others in your class. What does the survey tell you about American dialects or word geographies?

14. Following his selection "Pidgins and Creoles" in *The Cambridge Encyclopedia of Language*, David Crystal lists one hundred different pidgin and creole languages of the world along with a map to illustrate their locations. Some of the most prominent or most widely used of those listed include:

1. Hawaiian Pidgin/Creole, est. 500,000 speakers

2. Gullah, est. 150,000–300,000 speakers

3. Louisiana Creole French

4. Papiamentu (Papiamento), est. 200,000 speakers

5. Haitian French Creole, est. four million speakers

6. Sranan, est. 80,000 speakers

7. Cocoliche

8. Bagot Creole English

9. Australian Pidgin

10. Cameroon Pidgin English, est. two million speakers

11. Tok Pisin (Neo-Malasyian), est. one million speakers

12. Congo Pidgins

Choose one of these pidgin or creole languages, or go to the selection and choose one. After doing library research, prepare a report on the language and share what you have discovered with the class. Where did the pidgin or creole language originate? What other languages or dialects does it influence? What appears to be the future of the language? After your class has shared their reports, create a list of characteristics shared by all pidgins and creoles.

15. William Safire of the *New York Times* called *The Dictionary of American Regional English* "the most exciting linguistic project going on in the United States." To date, three volumes of this dictionary have been published, bringing the project up to the letter *O*. Spend some time familiarizing yourself with this work in preparation for writing a report about it. Questions you may wish to consider include: What is the purpose of the dictionary? What kinds of information does it contain? How was this information collected? How useful is this reference?

Selected Bibliography

The books by J. K. Chambers and Peter Trudgill, Lawrence M. Davis, and W. N. Francis contain excellent general bibliographies. Geneva Smitherman's book contains an excellent bibliography of works on Black English. The journal American Speech *and the monograph series* Publications of the American Dialect Society (PADS) *regularly publish material of interest.*

Allen, Harold B. *The Linguistic Atlas of the Upper Midwest*. Vol. 1, *Regional Speech Distribution*. Minneapolis: University of Minnesota Press, 1973; vol. 2, *Grammar*. Minneapolis: University of Minnesota Press, 1975; vol. 3, *Pronunciation*. Minneapolis: University of Minnesota Press, 1976. [An invaluable reference for study of speech in the Upper Midwest.]

——. "The Linguistic Atlases: Our New Resource." *English Journal* 45 [April 1956]: 188–94. [A discussion of *Linguistic Atlas* data and their applications.]

——. "The Primary Dialect Areas of the Upper Midwest." In *Studies in Language and Linguistics in Honor of Charles C. Fries*, ed. Albert H. Marckwardt. Ann Arbor: The English Language Institute, the University of Michigan, 1964. [A study of the lexical, phonological, and morphological features of the speech in the Upper Midwest region.]

——. "Two Dialects in Contact." *American Speech* 48 (Spring–Summer 1973): 54–66. [A study of dialect boundaries in the Upper Midwest based on *Atlas* materials.]

Allen, Harold B., and Gary N. Underwood, eds. *Readings in American Dialectology*. New York: Appleton-Century-Crofts, 1971. [An anthology of essays dealing with important regional and social aspects of American dialectology.]

"American Tongues" (videorecording, 57 min.). New York: International Production Center, 1986. [An invaluable illustration of various dialects of English in the United States.]

Ann Arbor Decision. Washington, DC: Center for Applied Linguistics, 1979. (Landmark decision requiring the Ann Arbor schools to take Black English into account in planning curricula; Civil Action No. 7–71861, United States District Court, Eastern District of Michigan, Southern Division; *Martin Luther King Junior Elementary School Children, et al., v Ann Arbor School District Board*, 473 F Supp. 1371 [1979].)

Atwood, E. Bagby. *A Survey of Verb Forms in the Eastern United States*. Ann Arbor: University of Michigan Press, 1953. [A fundamental work in linguistic geography.]

Bailey, R. W., and J. L. Robinson, eds. *Varieties of Present-Day English*. New York: Macmillan, 1973 [An excellent collection of articles.]

Bentley, Robert H., and Samuel D. Crawford, eds. *Black Language Reader*. Glenview, IL: Scott, Foresman and Company, 1973. [A good selection of articles that emphasize education.]

Brasch, Ila Wales, and Walter Milton Brasch. *A Comprehensive Annotated Bibliography of American Black English*. Baton Rouge: Louisiana State University, 1974. [An invaluable bibliography on the subject of Black English.]

Burling, Robbins. *English in Black and White*. New York: Holt, Rinehart and Winston, 1973. [A thorough introduction to dialects, with emphasis on Black English; excellent for teachers.]

Carver, Craig M. *American Regional Dialects: A Word Geography*. Ann Arbor: University of Michigan Press, 1987. [A broad, extensive survey of the dialect regions of the United States and their historical and cultural origins.]

Cassidy, Frederic G. *Dictionary of American Regional English*. Cambridge, MA: Belknap Press, Harvard University, forthcoming. [3 volumes now published.]

———. "A Method for Collecting Dialect." *Publication of the American Dialect Society*, no. 20 [November 1953]: 5–96. [The entire issue is devoted to a discussion of field methods and includes a comprehensive dialect questionnaire.]

Chambers, J. K., and Peter Trudgill. *Dialectology*. Cambridge: Cambridge University Press, 1980. [Very complete in its coverage; British orientation; contains excellent bibliography.]

Chambers, John W., Jr., ed. *Black English: Educational Equity and the Law*. Ann Arbor, MI: Karoma Publishers, 1983. [A collection of seven interesting essays plus a foreword, an introduction, and the text of Judge Charles W. Joiner's "Memorandum Opinion and Order."]

Christian, Donna, W. Wolfram, and N. Dube. *Variation and Change in Geographically Isolated Communities*. Tuscaloosa: University of Alabama Press, 1988. [A closer look at language variation and change in America focusing on two specific language communities.]

Crawford, James. *Hold Your Tongue—Bilingualism and the Politics of "English Only."* Reading, MA: Addison-Wesley Publishing, 1992. [This controversial look at the "official language" issue focuses on ethnic intolerance in the United States.]

Cullinan, Bernice E., ed. *Black Dialects & Reading*. Urbana, IL: National Council of Teachers of English, 1974. [Both theoretical and practical; all major positions are presented; includes an excellent fifty-page annotated bibliography.]

Davis, A. L. "English Problems of Spanish Speakers." In *Culture, Class, and Language Variety*, ed. A. L. Davis. Urbana, IL: National Council of Teachers of English, 1972. [A detailed analysis of phonological contrasts between Spanish and English, with some discussion of grammatical contrasts.]

———. "Developing and Testing the Checklist." *American Speech* 46 [Spring–Summer 1971]: 34–37. [A discussion of problems associated with developing a vocabulary questionnaire.]

———. "Dialect Distribution and Settlement Patterns in the Great Lakes Region." *Ohio State Archeological and Historical Quarterly* 60 [January 1951]: 48–56. [A study showing many interesting correlations between linguistic features and settlement patterns in the Great Lakes region.]

Davis, Lawrence M. *English Dialectology: An Introduction*. University, AL: University of Alabama Press, 1983. [Intended as a text for courses in dialectology; surveys regional and social dialect work in the U.S. and Britain; contains excellent bibliography.]

Dillard, J. L. *American Talk*. New York: Random House, 1976. [Popular and interesting treatment of the development of a large variety of American expressions.]

———. *All-American English: A History of the English Language in America*. New York: Random House, 1975. [Stresses Maritime English and its influence on the American colonists.]

———. *Black English: Its History and Usage in the United States*. New York:

Random House, 1972. [An investigation of the ways in which Black English differs from other varieties of American English.]

Drake, James A. "The Effect of Urbanization Upon Regional Vocabulary." *American Speech* 36 (February 1961): 17–33. [A study of regional dialect items and urbanization in Cleveland, Ohio.]

Duckert, Audrey R. "The Second Time Around: Methods in Dialect Revisiting." *American Speech* 46 (Spring–Summer 1971): 66–72. [Methods for studying areas previously surveyed by the *Atlas* project—with an emphasis on New England.]

Fasold, Ralph W. "Distinctive Linguistic Characteristics of Black English." In *Linguistics and Language Study: 20th Roundtable Meeting*, ed. James E. Alatis. Washington, DC: Georgetown University Press, 1970. [An examination of the distinctive differences between the nonstandard speech of poor blacks and the speech of whites.]

Fasold, Ralph W., and Walt Wolfram. *Teaching Standard English in the Inner City*. Washington, DC: Center for Applied Linguistics, 1970. [Discussion of the problems of teaching Standard English—interesting chapter entitled "Some Linguistic Features of Negro Dialect."]

Fishman, Joshua A. *Sociolinguistics: A Brief Introduction*. Rowley, MA: Newbury House Publishers, 1970. [Still a very good brief introduction to the field.]

Francis, W. N. *Dialectology: An Introduction*. New York: Longman, 1983. [An excellent introductory text.]

Grant, Stephen A. "Language Policy in the United States." In *Profession 78*. New York: Modern Language Association of America, 1978. [An examination of both federal and state policies regarding, *inter alia*, foreign language training and use, bilingual education, and cultural pluralism.]

Harder, Kelsie B., ed. *Illustrated Dictionary of Place Names: United States and Canada*. New York: Van Nostrand Reinhold, 1976. [An invaluable reference work for North American place names.]

Haskins, Jim, and Hugh F. Butts, M.D. *The Psychology of Black Language*. New York: Barnes & Noble Books, 1973. [A good, brief overview; extensive notes and bibliography, plus a glossary of Black English words and phrases.]

Hendrickson, Robert. *American Talk: The Words and Ways of American Dialects*. New York: Viking Penguin, 1986. [Excellent for the student curious about American dialects—with plenty of dialect dialogue.]

Hoffman, Charlotte. *An Introduction to Bilingualism*. New York: Longman, 1991. [Focuses on bilingualism in detail using European languages to demonstrate that it is a truly normal and widespread phenomenon.]

Hoffman, Melvin J. "Bi-dialectalism Is Not the Linguistics of White Supremacy: Sense Versus Sensibilities." *English Record* 21 (April 1971): 95–102. [An argument supporting the bidialectal approach to the teaching of Standard English and refuting James Sledd's position.]

Holm, John A. *Pidgins and Creoles*. Vol. 1. New York: Cambridge University Press, 1988. [A comprehensive survey of the field for the general reader and beginning student of linguistics.]

Ives, Sumner. "Dialect Differentiation in the Stories of Joel Chandler Harris." *American Literature* 17 (March 1955): 88–96. [A study of the social implications of Harris's dialects.]

———. "A Theory of Literary Dialect." *Tulane Studies in English* 2 (1950): 137–82. [An essential reference for all students doing work in literary dialects.]

Kenyon, John S. "Cultural Levels and Functional Varieties of English." *College English* 10 (October 1948): 31–36. [A classification of language that recognizes, first, levels having cultural or social associations and, second, levels having formal and familiar varieties of language usage.]

Kretzschmar, William A., Jr., ed. *Dialects in Culture: Essays in General Dialectology by Raven I. McDavid, Jr.* University, AL: University of Alabama Press, 1979. [A collection of sixty essays and reviews by one of America's best-known dialectologists.]

Kurath, Hans. *Studies in Area Linguistics.* Bloomington: Indiana University Press, 1972. [An examination of regional and social dialectology, American and foreign.]

———. *A Word Geography of the Eastern United States.* Ann Arbor: University of Michigan Press, 1949. [A basic book in linguistic geography.]

Kurath, Hans, Miles L. Hanley, Bernard Block, et al. *Linguistic Atlas of New England.* 3 vols. in six parts. Providence, RI: Brown University Press, 1939–1943; reissued New York: AMS Press, 1972. [An indispensable research and reference work for the study of speech in New England and for comparative studies. To be used with companion Handbook.]

Labov, William. *Language in the Inner City: Studies in the Black English Vernacular.* Philadelphia: University of Pennsylvania Press, 1972. [A definitive work; detailed study of Black English and its social setting; bibliography.]

———. "The Logic of Nonstandard English." In *Linguistics and Language Study: 20th Roundtable Meeting,* ed. James E. Alatis. Washington, DC: Georgetown University Press, 1970. [Refutes theories that Black English lacks logic and sophistication, which reveals mental inferiority.]

———. *The Nonstandard Vernacular of the Negro Community: Some Practical Suggestions.* Washington, DC: Education Resources Information Center, 1967. [Some advice to teachers concerning bidialectalism for the speaker of a nonstandard dialect.]

———. *The Social Stratification of English in New York City.* Washington, DC: Center for Applied Linguistics, 1966. [A landmark sociolinguistic study of New York City speech.]

———. "Stages in the Acquisition of Standard English." In *Social Dialects and Language Learning,* ed. Roger W. Shuy. Champaign, IL: NCTE, 1964. [An investigation that examines the acquisition of Standard English by children in New York City.]

Labov, William, Paul Cohen, Clarence Robins, and John Lewis. *A Study of the Non-Standard English of Negro and Puerto Rican Speakers in New York City.* Final Report, Cooperative Research Project no. 3288, vol. 1. Washington, DC: Office of Education, 1968.

Lambert, J. J. "Another Look at Kenyon's Levels." *College English* 24 (November 1969): 141–43. [A reassessment of John S. Kenyon's classification of cultural levels and functional varieties of English.]

McDavid, Raven I., Jr. See Kretzschmar, 1979.

McDowell, Tremaine. "The Use of Negro Dialect by Harriet Beecher Stowe." *American Speech* 6 (June 1931): 322–26. [An early study in literary dialect.]

McMillan, James B. *Annotated Bibliography of Southern American English.* Coral Gables, FL: University of Miami Press, 1971. [A valuable reference work for the study of speech in southern states.]

Mencken, H. L. *The American Language: The Fourth Edition and the Two*

Supplements. Abridged and ed. Raven I. McDavid, Jr. New York: Alfred A. Knopf, 1963. [A classic study of American English.]

Metcalf, Allan A. "Chicano English." *Language and Education: Theory and Practice* 2. Washington, DC: Center for Applied Linguistics, 1979. [Emphasizes that Chicano English is not an imperfect attempt by a native speaker of Spanish to master English.]

O'Neil, Wayne. "The Politics of Bidialectalism." *College English* 33 (1972): 433–38. [Argues that bidialectalism is aimed at maintaining the social status quo—the inequality of blacks in a predominantly white society.]

Pederson, Lee A. "An Approach to Urban Word Geography." *American Speech* 46 (Spring–Summer 1971): 73–86. [A presentation of vocabulary questionnaires suitable for urban testing—specifically, in Chicago.]

———. "Negro Speech in *The Adventures of Huckleberry Finn*." *Mark Twain Journal* 13 (1966): 1–4. [An examination of the literary representation of Negro dialect in Twain's classic novel.]

Pixton, William H. "A Contemporary Dilemma: The Question of Standard English." *College Composition and Communication* Vol. 25, No. 4 (1974): 247–53. [Argues for the use of Standard English by blacks.]

Pyles, Thomas. *Words and Ways of American English*. New York: Random House, 1952. [An introduction to American English from colonial times to the present.]

Reed, Carroll E. *Dialects of American English*, 2nd ed. Amherst: University of Massachusetts Press, 1973. [An introduction to dialect study with units devoted to sectional atlas studies and to urban dialect studies.]

———. "The Pronunciation of English in the Pacific Northwest." *Language* 37 (October–December 1961) No. 4: 559–64. [A description of the pronunciation of vowels and consonants by residents of the Pacific Northwest.]

Schneider, Edgar W. *American Earlier Black English: Morphological and Syntactic Variables*. Tuscaloosa: University of Alabama Press, 1989. [A detailed study of Black English Vernacular (BEV) through its history, terms, and grammatical structures.]

Shopen, Timothy, and Joseph M. Williams, eds. *Style and Variables in English*. Englewood Cliffs, NJ: Winthrop Publishers, 1981. [An excellent collection of essays.]

———. *Standards and Dialects in English*. Englewood Cliffs, NJ: Winthrop Publishers, 1980. [A companion volume to *Style and Variables in English*; tapes for use with the text are available.]

Shores, David L., and Carole P. Hines, eds. *Papers in Language Variation*. University, AL: University of Alabama Press, 1977. [A collection of twenty-nine papers, most originally presented at an ADS or SAMLA meeting.]

Shuy, Roger W. "Detroit Speech: Careless, Awkward, and Inconsistent, or Systematic, Graceful, and Regular?" *Elementary English* 45 (May 1968): 565–69. [A discussion of nonstandard speech in Detroit, Michigan.]

———. "Some Useful Myths in Social Dialectology." *Florida FL Reporter* 11 (Spring–Fall 1973): 17–20, 55. [Identifies several myths that, while they are oversimplifications, are useful to social dialectologists.]

Sledd, James. "Bi-Dialectalism: The Linguistics of White Supremacy." *English Journal* 58 (1969): 1307–15. [Argues against linguists and teachers who advocate bidialectal programs; an opposing view to that of Melvin J. Hoffman.]

———. "Doublespeak: Dialectology in the Service of Big Brother." *College English* 35 (January 1972). [A trenchant argument against bidialectalism; a classic.]

Smith, Riley B. "Research Perspectives on American Black English: A Brief Historical Sketch." *American Speech* 49 (Spring–Summer 1974): 24–39. [A bibliographical essay with a historical perspective.]

Smitherman, Geneva. *Talkin' and Testifyin': The Language of Black America.* Boston: Houghton Mifflin, 1977. [Comprehensive study of Black English; includes an excellent bibliography of works on the subject.]

Spolsky, Bernard, ed. *The Language Education of Minority Children.* Rowley, MA: Newbury House Publishers, 1972. [Fourteen essays; of interest especially to teachers.]

Stewart, George R. *American Place-Names: a Concise and Selective Dictionary for the Continental United States of America.* New York: Oxford University Press, 1970. [Useful compendium by a noteworthy novelist.]

Stockton, Eric. "Poe's Use of Negro Dialect in 'The Gold-Bug.'" In *Studies in Language and Linguistics in Honor of Charles C. Fries,* ed. Albert H. Marckwardt. Ann Arbor: The English Language Institute, the University of Michigan, 1964. [An analysis of Jupiter's speech as an example of literary dialect used by pre-Civil War writers.]

Stoller, Paul, ed. *Black American English: Its Background and Its Usage in the Schools and in Literature.* New York: Dell Publishing, 1975. [An excellent collection of articles on the history and structure of Black English and on Black English and education; also includes three literary excerpts illustrating the use of Black English; bibliography.]

Teschner, Richard V., Garland Bills, and Jerry R. Craddock. *Spanish and English of United States Hispanos: A Critical, Annotated, Linguistic Bibliography.* Washington, DC: Center for Applied Linguistics, 1975. [An invaluable research tool for studies in this area.]

Trudgill, Peter. *The Social Differentiation of English in Norwich.* Cambridge: Cambridge University Press, 1972. [A model study; basic.]

———. *Sociolinguistics: An Introduction.* Penguin Books, 1974. [An excellent introduction by a leader in the field.]

Trudgill, Peter, ed. *Dialects of English: Studies in Grammatical Variation* by J. K. Chambers. New York: Longman, 1991. [A helpful study of the history of American dialects and the British dialectical influences on American speech.]

Underwood, Gary N. "Vocabulary Change in the Upper Midwest." *PADS* 49 (April 1968): 8–28. [An investigation of language change that utilizes four generations of informants.]

Whatley, Elizabeth. "Language Among Black Americans." *Language in the USA.* Cambridge: Cambridge University Press, 1981. [See pp. 92–107 for an excellent treatment of Black English.]

Williamson, Juanita V., and Virginia M. Burke, eds. *A Various Language: Perspectives on American Dialects.* New York: Holt, Rinehart and Winston, 1971. [An anthology of essential articles dealing with American dialects.]

Wolfram, Walt. *A Sociolinguistic Description of Detroit Negro Speech.* Washington, DC: Center for Applied Linguistics, 1969. [Thorough and detailed.]

———. *Sociolinguistic Aspects of Assimilation: Puerto Rican English in New York City.* Washington, DC: Center for Applied Linguistics, 1974. [A thorough study of the language problems encountered by Puerto Ricans in New York City.]

Wolfram, Walt, and Donna Christian. *Sociolinguistic Variables in Appalachian*

Dialects. National Institute of Education Grant no. NIE-G-74-0026, Final Report. Washington, DC: Center for Applied Linguistics, 1975. [Definitive and informative.]

Wolfram, Walt, and Ralph W. Fasold. *The Study of Social Dialects in American English*. Englewood Cliffs, NJ: Prentice-Hall, 1974. [An introduction to the linguist's view of social variation in language—special attention is given to possible educational applications.]

PART SIX

GENDER-BASED
LANGUAGE DIFFERENCES

In the Civil Rights movement of the 1960s, led by Black Americans, one minority culture after another stepped forward to claim both its unique identity and its equality with others by right and by law. Hardly a minority, American women also began to protest the fact that as a group they did not stand on an equal footing with American men. A rapidly burgeoning interest in women's studies (a discipline unheard of in American universities as recently as the 1950s) uncovered sexual inequities deeply embedded in American culture, nowhere more pervasively than in its language. One of the most interesting discoveries in the study of gender and language was that two people from the same culture, conversing in the same language, can be sending and receiving entirely different messages—if one of the speakers is a woman and the other a man.

Nearly everyone is familiar with gender inequities and sexist language in English vocabulary and with the adjustments being made to rectify them. Meetings are no longer led by a *chairman*, but by a *chairperson* or, simply, a *chair*; a *stewardess* is now a *flight attendant*, a *forefather* an *ancestor*. The essays in this section go beyond issues of vocabulary to deal with the cultural inequalities that exist because men and women use the same language for different purposes. It is in relation to gender that linguistics is most closely interwoven with other culture-based disciplines such as sociology and psychology. Three of the authors in this section are not linguists, but writers and journalists whose broad interest in sexual inequalities leads them to explore the role of language.

In "Girl Talk–Boy Talk," John Pfeiffer discusses a number of conversations, each between a man and a woman, in which the following pattern is found: women listen, men interrupt. This difference goes a long way toward explaining male dominance via language.

The next two essays, written by Deborah Tannen, a linguist from Georgetown University, support and extend the discoveries reported by

Pfeiffer. In her article "'I'll Explain It to You': Lecturing and Listening," she determines that when men do interrupt—and it is not only women they interrupt, but other men as well—it is just one of a cluster of conversational strategies to establish status and authority. In her second article, "Ethnic Style in Male–Female Conversation," Tannen explores the role played by ethnic differences between partners in a married couple, one of whom is of Greek descent. She finds that different cultural backgrounds can complicate communication between men and women.

Poet and novelist Louise Erdrich is also concerned with ethnicity in her essay, "The Names of Women." A descendant of the Chippewa tribe, Erdrich meditates on the evocative descriptive names, which are all that survive of the Ikwe, the women of her ancestral tribe. This story of the death and loss of a culture also celebrates the women whose names affirmed their value as individuals and whose immediate descendants were strong survivors.

The final article in this section makes a sharp shift to the cosmopolitan high-tech world of the Internet. In "Men, Women, Computers," journalist Barbara Kantrowitz documents the tremendous inequalities between men and women in the field of computer science. Males dominate every aspect of the industry, including the language of the Internet. Kantrowitz seeks cultural explanations for the discrepancy and identifies a number of areas where women are gaining ground.

25

Girl Talk—Boy Talk

John Pfeiffer

John Pfeiffer is a science writer whose works have appeared in such pop-ular magazines as Science *and* Psychology Today. *Pfeiffer's essay explores the active and rapidly expanding field of gender studies in lan-guage research. Pfeiffer touches on origins of gender-based language and examines differences between male and female speech patterns in con-versation as well as the ways in which these patterns reflect our cul-ture's image of the two sexes. His findings illustrate some of the myths that surround male and female speech patterns. At the same time, Pfeiffer presents new and surprising characteristics of conversations between the sexes and speculates about what these findings mean. That women ask more questions and men do most of the interrupting are two of the traits Pfeiffer discusses. He points out, furthermore, that as our attitudes about men and women change, the way we talk to each other changes, too.*

An investigator, pencil in hand, is transcribing two minutes of an "unob-trusively" recorded coffee-shop conversation between two university students, male and female—listening intently, making out words and pronunciations, noting hesitations, timing utterances. The tape whirs in reverse for a replay and then again, eight replays in all. Part of the final transcript:

> ANDREW: *It's about time uh that my family really went on a vaca-tion (pause) y'know my father goes places all the time* (prolonged syllable) *but he y'know goes on business like he'll go ta' Tokyo for the afternoon 'n he'll get there at* (stammer) *at ten in the morning 'n catch a nine o'clock flight leaving . . .*
> (two-second pause)
> BETSY: *That sounds fantastic (pause) not everybody can jus' spend a day in someplace-* (interruption)
> ANDREW: *Well, we've already established the fact that um y'know he's not just* anyone.
> (eight-second pause)
> BETSY: *Don't you I* (stammer) *well it seems to me you you you prob-ably have such an um interesting background that you must y'know have trouble finding um people uh like to talk to if you-* (interruption)

ANDREW: *Most definitely . . .*

Candace West and Don Zimmerman, the researchers who analyzed these recordings, were particularly interested in the interruptions. The pattern is typical. According to these University of California sociologists, it held for all 11 two-person, cross-sex conversations recorded mainly in public places: Males accounted for some 96 percent of the interruptions. In same-sex conversations males also cut off males and females cut off females, but in 20 recorded encounters, interruptions were equally distributed between the speakers.

This study is part of an active and rapidly expanding field of language research—the role of gender in speech, with the accent primarily on how, under what conditions, and why the sexes talk differently. A 1983 bibliography of relevant publications includes some 800 titles, compared with about 150 titles in a bibliography published eight years before. The boom started little more than a decade ago, inspired by the women's movement. A new generation of investigators began taking hard looks at some of the things that had been written about women's talk by earlier investigators, mainly male. They encountered a number of statements like the following from Otto Jespersen, a Danish linguist who has earned a prominent place in the feminist rogues' gallery: "[W]omen much more often than men break off without finishing their sentences, because they start talking without having thought out what they are going to say."

Such belittlement of female conversation may be somewhat less frequent nowadays. But it lives on in everyday contexts, hardly surprising since it involves attitudes imbedded in thinking that get passed on like bad genes from generation to generation. The latest issue of a women-and-language newsletter notes items involving sexism in everything from the *New England Journal of Medicine* and Maidenform bra ads to campaign speeches and government offices in Japan. Work focused on interruption contributes to understanding who controls conversations and how. To check on their original observations in a more casual context, West and Zimmerman conducted an experiment in which students meeting for the first time were told to "relax and get to know one another," with familiar results. Males again turned out to be the chief culprits, although they made only 75 percent of the interruptions, compared with that 96 percent figure for previously acquainted pairs—perhaps because they were more restrained among new acquaintances.

Men not only do the lion's share of the interrupting (and the talking) but often choose what to talk about. This can be seen in a study conducted by public relations consultant Pamela Fishman. Her subjects were three couples, a social worker and five graduate students, who consented to having tape recorders in their apartments, providing some 52 hours of conversation, 25 of which have been transcribed.

Fishman's first impression: "At times I felt that all the women did was ask questions. . . . I attended to my own speech and discovered the same pattern." In fact, the women asked more than 70 percent of the questions.

Dustin Hoffman put this speech pattern to use in the motion picture *Tootsie*, using the questioning intonation frequently when impersonating a woman and rather less frequently when acting unladylike.

In her study, Fishman discovered that a particular question was used with great frequency: "D'ya know what?" Research by other investigators had described how children frequently use this phrase to communicate with their elders. It serves as a conversation opener, calling for an answer like "What?" or "No, tell me," a go-ahead signal that they may speak up and that what they have to say will be heeded.

Pursuing this lead, Fishman found out why women need such reassurances when she analyzed the 76 efforts in taped conversations to start conversations or keep them going. Men tried 29 times and succeeded 28 times. That is, in all but a single case the outcome was some discussion of the topic broached. Women tried 47 times, sometimes for as long as five minutes, with dead-end results 30 times, an unimpressive .362 batting average. (It could have been worse. Each of the male subjects in this experiment professed sympathy for the women's movement.)

Other actions that control conversation (and often power) are more complicated, less open to statistical analysis. Cheris Kramarae, professor of speech communication at the University of Illinois in Urbana-Champaign, tells what happened when, as the only woman member of an important policy-shaping committee, she tried to communicate with the chairman before the start of a meeting. She suggested that certain items be added to the agenda, apparently to no effect. "He paid no attention to me, and I gave up." Once the meeting got under way, however, he featured her ideas in a review of the agenda and, turning to a male colleague, commented: "I don't remember who suggested these changes. I think it was Dick here."

Kramarae cites such instances of being heard but not listened to, "as if you were speaking behind a glass," as the sort of thing women must cope with every day. Other examples of everyday difficulties include being first-named by people who address males by last names plus "Mr." or "Dr.," hearing men discuss hiring a "qualified" woman, and looking a block ahead to see whether men are around who might make catcalls or pass out unwanted compliments.

These sorts of affronts lead women to a guarded way of life that fosters sensitivity to biases in the King's English. There is the intriguing record of efforts to abolish the generic masculine where *man* means not just males but all humans (as in "Man is among the few mammals in which estrus has disappeared entirely," from *Emergence of Man* by John Pfeiffer, 1978). *Woman* is used only in reference to a female, a rule established by male grammarians some 250 years ago.

At first the move to a more generalized language was widely opposed, mainly on the grounds of triviality and the inviolability of language. Critics included some feminists, the linguistic faculty at Harvard, and *Time* magazine, the latter exhibiting its usual delicate touch in an essay entitled "Sispeak: a Msguided Attempt to Change Herstory." Then a number of psychologists, among them Donald MacKay and Wendy Martyna of the University of California, ran tests showing that, whatever the speaker or writer intended, most people associate *man* and the matching pronoun *he* with a male image and that the generic masculine could hurt the way *boy* hurts blacks. Today it is common practice to edit such references out of textbook manuscripts and other writings.

Meanwhile research continues along a widening front, trying to cope with unconscious attitudes, sexist and otherwise, which distinguish women and men—"two alien cultures, oddly intertwined," in the words of Barrie Thorne of Michigan State University. Recent studies of the American male culture by and large support previous findings. Men spend considerable time playing the dominance game, either at a joking level or for real. The telling of a tall tale, followed by a still taller tale in an I-can-top-that atmosphere, seems to be typically male.

In this game, keeping cool commands the respect of the other players, with an occasional flash of emotion commended, providing it has to do with politics or sports or shop talk—practically anything but personal feelings. Elizabeth Aries of Amherst College, who has recorded 15 hours of conversation among newly acquainted male students, reports that certain males consistently dominated the conversation. Her subjects addressed the entire group rather than individuals at least a third of the time, nearly five times more often than women interacting under similar conditions.

Detailed studies of women's conversations are rare, mainly conducted in the past few years. Aries discovered that leaders in all-female groups tend to assume a low profile and encourage others to speak, while leaders among men tend to resist the contributions of others. Mercilee Jenkins of San Francisco State University studied the conversation of mothers in a discussion group over a five-month period. She was interested in subject matter as well as conversational style. She found that the young mothers discussed a broad range of subjects—much beyond domestic problems.

Storytelling makes up a large proportion of conversational encounters, with narrative styles that reflect other gender differences. "The universe is made of stories, not atoms," said poet Muriel Rukeyser, and linguistic analysis confirms her insight. As a rule, the women in the Jenkins study avoided first-person narratives. In 26 out of 57 transcribed stories, the narrator played no role at all, while men frequently shine in their own stories. The women listening became heavily involved in the incidents recounted and chimed in with stories supporting the narrator, challenging the preceding story in only about five percent of the cases.

Mixing sexes conversationally produces some interesting reactions, at least among newly acquainted Harvard students in the Aries study. The men softened, competing less among themselves and talking more about their personal lives. (This may be a kind of instinctive mating or courting display, an attracting mechanism discarded upon closer acquaintance when the male usually reassumes his impersonal ways.)

Women students responded with a pattern of their own, becoming more competitive. Aries notes that "the social significance of women for one another in a mixed group was low." They maintained a supportive style in talking with men, but it was every woman for herself as they spoke disproportionately more to the men than to each other.

The "music" of conversation may be as meaningful as the words. Women not only have higher voices, but the pitch is notably higher than can be explained solely by the anatomy of the female vocal apparatus. Moreover, Sally McConnell-Ginet of Cornell University finds that women's voices are more colorful—they vary more in pitch and change pitch more frequently than do men's voices. In one experiment, women immediately assumed a monotone style when asked to imitate men's speech. McConnell-Ginet regards speaking tunefully as an effective strategy for getting and holding attention, a strategy used more often by women than men, perhaps because they are more often ignored.

No one has a workable theory that accounts for all these differences. Even the longest running, most thorough searches for the root causes of differences between the sexes raise more questions than they answer. Carol Nagy Jacklin of the University of Southern California and Eleanor Maccoby of Stanford University have been tracking the development of 100 children from birth to age six. These children have been observed at several stages, in various settings. When this group reached 45 months of age, the researchers focused on how 58 of them interacted with their parents during playtime.

A surprising conclusion emerged: Discrimination by gender originates mainly outside the home. "Mothers do little behavior stereotyping," Jacklin summarizes. "They appear to treat [their own] little boys and little girls much the same." (While fathers tend to treat their children in more gender-stereotyped ways during playtimes, they ordinarily have less influence on childrearing and on actually creating the home environment.)

The implication is intriguing. If it is true that outsiders are largely responsible, and since most outsiders are also parents, it follows that parents have gender-based preconceptions more often about other people's children than about their own. In any event, school is one place where highly significant changes take place. In the beginning, teacher is "home base," a surrogate parent to whom children come for reassurance and support, and that holds for all children—until second grade.

At that point boys but not girls begin increasingly to turn away from teacher and toward one another. The stress is more and more on hierarchy, jockeying for position in speech as well as action, in talking as well as playing cowboy, soldier, Star Wars, and so on. All this is part of a constellation of changes. In playgrounds girls tend to go around in pairs, usually near teachers and the school building; boys form groups of half a dozen or so, usually as far away as possible. Boys may get more attention than girls because they are often more disruptive.

In discussing such patterns Thorne cites the classic psychoanalytic theory that boys, being raised mainly by women at home, feel the need at school to assert themselves as "not female." Also, teachers may have biased expectations about boys. But, according to Raphaela Best of the Montgomery County school system in Maryland, a high price may be paid for early male-male competition. She suggests that the resulting tensions may help account for the fact that reading disabilities are at least five times more frequent among boys than among girls.

Though the study of gender-based differences is relatively new, significant steps have been taken. Furthermore—a totally unexpected development—gender-related work has helped spark renewed interest in general language use. The ways in which men talk to men and women talk to women have come under scrutiny, as have the speech differences between people of different cultures and professional backgrounds.

West, for example, is currently interested in exchanges between doctors and patients. This work demands looking as well as listening, analyzing a kind of choreography of nonverbal as well as verbal behavior. Her raw data consist of videotapes complete with sound tracks. So far she has spent more than 550 hours transcribing seven hours of conversation in 21 patient-physician meetings at a family-practice center in the southern United States. Preliminary analysis indicates that doctors out-interrupt their patients, male and female, by a two-to-one margin—except when the doctor is a woman. In that case, the situation is reversed, with patients—both male and female—out-interrupting by the same margin.

Similar studies are tuning in on the finer points of speech and behavior. An outstanding and continuing analysis by Marjorie Harness Goodwin of the University of South Carolina shows that girls as well as boys form social groups, except that the girls tend to form exclusive "coalitions," whereas boys form all-inclusive hierarchies. With the girls not everyone gets to play, while with the boys everyone, even the nerds, can play as long as they respect rank. Girls also are far less direct in arguing with one another, and their debates may simmer for weeks, in contrast to male arguments, which generally end within a few minutes.

These findings are based on taped observations of black children at play in an urban setting. Other observations hint that the same points might apply more widely, a possibility that remains to be probed. What holds true for one culture or society may not for another. Male dominance in speech seems to be a global phenomenon. But the most notable exception cries for analysis: Sexism is probably at a lower level in Bali, where to vote or be otherwise active as a citizen, one must be part of a couple.

While most of the recent research has revealed conflict between the sexes, Carole Edelsky of Arizona State University has discovered a trend worth noting. She has studied five "very informal" meetings of a standing faculty committee consisting of seven women and four men—7.5 hours of taped conversation. It started as a "fishing expedition" project— a search for sexisms, and there were plenty. As usual, men talked longer and interrupted more, appearing to hold the floor longer.

But Edelsky also recognized a second method of holding the floor. She identified short interludes, between the more formal addresses, that featured mutual support and "greater discourse equality." (These episodes were most informal and laughter-filled.) At first Edelsky had the impression that the women were doing most of the talking during these periods. But actual counts of words and time per turn revealed an equal-time situation (thus supporting the observation that a "talkative" woman is one who talks as much as the average man). These episodes made up less than 20 percent of total talk time, but such encounters as these may reflect a change in communication between the sexes.

The future may see great change in our current perception of a conversational gap between the sexes. It may also see a correction of imbalance in present-day research—a shift in the gender composition of the researchers. Today in the United States there are about 200 investigators of language and gender, and all but a dozen of them are women. Many of the researchers believe that as more men enter the field the "two alien cultures" will draw closer together.

FOR DISCUSSION AND REVIEW

1. What new discoveries are being made with regard to women's speech patterns and processes? What myths about women's speech are being disputed as a result of these discoveries?

2. In her study, Pamela Fishman discovered that, in conversation, women asked far more questions than men. What explanations are offered for this trend? What does this say about the differences between men and women in communication?

3. What are conversation-controlling actions? With respect to the research Pfeiffer cites, do men or women use more of these actions?

4. Can you think of any words in our language that are perceived as "feminine," which if used to describe a mixed-sex group are not perceived as an insult? Are there "masculine" terms that are applied to women without insult? What does this trend say about our language? Can you cite examples that suggest that our language might be undergoing change?

5. Pfeiffer explains that men spend considerable time playing the dominance game, either at a joking level or for real. This "I-can-top-that" atmosphere is a seemingly male communication trait. How does this differ from the atmosphere of women communicating? What possible explanations can be offered for these two different styles besides the difference in gender?

6. What are the differences in the vocal patterns of women and men? How do scientists account for these differences?

7. Briefly discuss the differences in the socialization patterns of little boys and girls. In what ways do "play" behaviors differ for the two groups? How might these tendencies contribute to adult speech differences?

26

$$\equiv$$

"I'll Explain It to You": Lecturing and Listening

Deborah Tannen

Gender bias in and via language is a burning issue, not just for linguists, but for English-speaking people in general. Deborah Tannen of Georgetown University crossed the boundary between academic research and popular literature in 1990 with the publication of You Just Don't Understand: Women and Men in Conversation, *a study in socio-linguistics that became a best-selling book. In the following selection from that book, Tannen presents her findings that men and women have different goals when they participate in conversation and that they employ different linguistic strategies to achieve those goals. She concludes that women are more likely to engage in a give-and-take of speaking, questioning, and listening, and men tend to establish author-ity and status by lecturing. This difference bears consequences for the ways in which the sexes communicate and share knowledge. While acknowledging the problems that arise from such differences, Tannen believes that men and women who understand and accommodate each other's goals can achieve enhanced levels of communication.*

At a reception following the publication of one of my books, I noticed a publicist listening attentively to the producer of a popular radio show. He was telling her how the studio had come to be built where it was, and why he would have preferred another site. What caught my attention was the length of time he was speaking while she was listening. He was delivering a monologue that could only be called a lecture, giving her detailed information about the radio reception at the two sites, the archi-tecture of the station, and so on. I later asked the publicist if she had been interested in the information the producer had given her. "Oh, yes," she answered. But then she thought a moment and said, "Well, maybe he did go on a bit." The next day she told me, "I was thinking about what you asked. I couldn't have cared less about what he was say-ing. It's just that I'm so used to listening to men go on about things I don't care about, I didn't even realize how bored I was until you made me think about it."

I was chatting with a man I had just met at a party. In our conversa-tion, it emerged that he had been posted in Greece with the RAF during

1944 an 1945. Since I had lived in Greece for several years, I asked him about his experiences: What had Greece been like then? How had the Greek villagers treated the British soldiers? What had it been *like* to be a British soldier in wartime Greece? I also offered information about how Greece had changed, what it is like now. He did not pick up on my remarks about contemporary Greece, and his replies to my questions quickly changed from accounts of his own experiences, which I found riveting, to facts about Greek history, which interested me in principle but in the actual telling left me profoundly bored. The more impersonal his talk became, the more I felt oppressed by it, pinned involuntarily in the listener position.

At a showing of Judy Chicago's jointly created art work *The Dinner Party*, I was struck by a couple standing in front of one of the displays: The man was earnestly explaining to the woman the meaning of symbols in the tapestry before them, pointing as he spoke. I might not have noticed this unremarkable scene, except that *The Dinner Party* was radically feminist in conception, intended to reflect women's experiences and sensibilities.

While taking a walk in my neighborhood on an early summer evening at twilight, I stopped to chat with a neighbor who was walking his dogs. As we stood, I noticed that the large expanse of yard in front of which we were standing was aglitter with the intermittent flickering of fireflies. I called attention to the sight, remarking on how magical it looked. "It's like the Fourth of July," I said. He agreed, and then told me he had read that the lights of fireflies are mating signals. He then explained to me details of how these signals work—for example, groups of fireflies fly at different elevations and could be seen to cluster in different parts of the yard.

In all these examples, the men had information to impart and they were imparting it. On the surface, there is nothing surprising or strange about that. What is strange is that there are so many situations in which men have factual information requiring lengthy explanations to impart to women, and so few in which women have comparable information to impart to men.

The changing times have altered many aspects of relations between women and men. Now it is unlikely, at least in many circles, for a man to say, "I am better than you because I am a man and you are a woman." But women who do not find men making such statements are nonetheless often frustrated in their dealings with them. One situation that frustrates many women is a conversation that has mysteriously turned into a lecture, with the man delivering the lecture to the woman, who has become an appreciative audience.

Once again, the alignment in which women and men find themselves arrayed is asymmetrical. The lecturer is framed as superior in status and expertise, cast in the role of teacher, and the listener is cast in the role of student. If women and men took turns giving and receiving lectures, there would be nothing disturbing about it. What is disturbing is the imbalance. Women and men fall into this unequal pattern so often because of the differences in their interactional habits. Since women seek to build rapport, they are inclined to play down their expertise rather than display it. Since men value the position of center stage and the feeling of knowing more, they seek opportunities to gather and disseminate factual information.

If men often seem to hold forth because they have the expertise, women are often frustrated and surprised to find that when they have the expertise, they don't necessarily get the floor.

FIRST ME, THEN ME

I was at a dinner with faculty members from other departments in my university. To my right was a woman. As the dinner began, we introduced ourselves. After we told each other what departments we were in and what subjects we taught, she asked what my research was about. We talked about my research for a little while. Then I asked her about her research and she told me about it. Finally, we discussed the ways that our research overlapped. Later, as tends to happen at dinners, we branched out to others at the table. I asked a man across the table from me what department he was in and what he did. During the next half hour, I learned a lot about his job, his research, and his background. Shortly before the dinner ended there was a lull, and he asked me what I did. When I said I was a linguist, he became excited and told me about a research project he had conducted that was related to neurolinguistics. He was still telling me about his research when we all got up to leave the table.

This man and woman were my colleagues in academia. What happens when I talk to people at parties and social events, not fellow researchers? My experience is that if I mention the kind of work I do to women, they usually ask me about it. When I tell them about conversational style or gender differences, they offer their own experiences to support the patterns I describe. This is very pleasant for me. It puts me at center stage without my having to grab the spotlight myself, and I frequently gather anecdotes I can use in the future. But when I announce my line of work to men, many give me a lecture on language—for example, about how people, especially teenagers, misuse language nowadays. Others challenge me, for example questioning me about my research methods. Many others change the subject to something they know more about.

Of course not all men respond in this way, but over the years I have encountered many men, and very few women, who do. It is not that speaking in this way is *the* male way of doing things, but that it is *a* male way. There are women who adopt such styles, but they are perceived as speaking like men.

IF YOU'VE GOT IT, FLAUNT IT—OR HIDE IT

I have been observing this constellation in interaction for more than a dozen years. I did not, however, have any understanding of *why* this happens until fairly recently, when I developed the framework of status and connection. An experimental study that was pivotal in my thinking shows that expertise does not ensure women a place at center stage in conversation with men.

Psychologist H. M. Leet-Pellegrini set out to discover whether gender or expertise determined who would behave in what she terms a "dominant" way—for example, by talking more, interrupting, and controlling the topic. She set up pairs of women, pairs of men, and mixed pairs, and asked them to discuss the effects of television violence on children. In some cases, she made one of the partners an expert by providing relevant factual information and time to read and assimilate it before the videotaped discussion. One might expect that the conversationalist who was the expert would talk more, interrupt more, and spend less time supporting the conversational partner who knew less about the subject. But it wasn't so simple. On the average, those who had expertise did talk more, but men experts talked more than women experts.

Expertise also had a different effect on women and men with regard to supportive behavior. Leet-Pellegrini expected that the one who did not have expertise would spend more time offering agreement and support to the one who did. This turned out to be true—*except* in cases where a woman was the expert and her nonexpert partner was a man. In this situation, the women experts showed support—saying things like "Yeah" and "That's right"—far *more* than the nonexpert men they were talking to. Observers often rated the male nonexpert as more dominant than the female expert. In other words, the women in this experiment not only didn't wield their expertise as power, but tried to play it down and make up for it through extra assenting behavior. They acted as if their expertise were something to hide.

And perhaps it was. When the word *expert* was spoken in these experimental conversations, in all cases but one it was the man in the conversation who used it, saying something like "So, you're the expert." Evidence of the woman's superior knowledge sparked resentment, not respect.

Furthermore, when an expert man talked to an uninformed woman, he took a controlling role in structuring the conversation in the beginning *and* the end. But when an expert man talked to an uninformed man, he dominated in the beginning but not always in the end. In other words, having expertise was enough to keep a man in the controlling position if he was talking to a woman, but not if he was talking to a man. Apparently, when a woman surmised that the man she was talking to had more information on the subject than she did, she simply accepted the reactive role. But another man, despite a lack of information, might still give the expert a run for his money and possibly gain the upper hand by the end.

Reading these results, I suddenly understood what happens to me when I talk to women and men about language. I am assuming that my acknowledged expertise will mean I am automatically accorded authority in the conversation, and with women that is generally the case. But when I talk to men, revealing that I have acknowledged expertise in this area often invites challenges. I *might* maintain my position if I defend myself successfully against the challenges, but if I don't, I may lose ground.

One interpretation of the Leet-Pellegrini study is that women are getting a bum deal. They don't get credit when it's due. And in a way, this is true. But the reason is not—as it seems to many women—that men are bums who seek to deny women authority. The Leet-Pellegrini study shows that many men are inclined to jockey for status, and challenge the authority of others, when they are talking to men too. If this is so, then challenging a woman's authority as they would challenge a man's could be a sign of respect and equal treatment, rather than lack of respect and discrimination. In cases where this is so, the inequality of the treatment results not simply from the men's behavior alone but from the differences in men's and women's styles: Most women lack experience in defending themselves against challenges, which they misinterpret as personal attacks on their credibility.

Even when talking to men who are happy to see them in positions of status, women may have a hard time getting their due because of differences in men's and women's interactional goals. Just as boys in high school are not inclined to repeat information about popular girls because it doesn't get them what they want, women in conversation are not inclined to display their knowledge because it doesn't get them what they are after. Leet-Pellegrini suggests that the men in this study were playing a game of "Have I won?" while the women were playing a game of "Have I been sufficiently helpful?" I am inclined to put this another way: The game women play is "Do you like me?" whereas the men play "Do you respect me?" If men, in seeking respect, are less liked by women, this is an unsought side effect, as is the effect that women, in seeking to be liked, may lose respect. When a woman has a conversation with a man, her efforts to emphasize their similarities and avoid showing off can easily be interpreted, through the lens of status, as relegating her to a one-down position, making her appear either incompetent or insecure.

A SUBTLE DIFFERENCE

Elizabeth Aries, a professor of psychology at Amherst College, set out to show that highly intelligent, highly educated young women are no longer submissive in conversations with male peers. And indeed she found that the college women did talk more than the college men in small groups she set up. But what they said was different. The men tended to set the agenda by offering opinions, suggestions, and information. The women tended to react, offering agreement or disagreement. Furthermore, she found that body language was as different as ever: The men sat with their legs stretched out, while the women gathered themselves in. Noting that research has found that speakers using the open-bodied position are more likely to persuade their listeners, Aries points out that talking more may not ensure that women will be heard.

In another study, Aries found that men in all-male discussion groups spent a lot of time at the beginning finding out "who was best informed about movies, books, current events, politics, and travel" as a means of "sizing up the competition" and negotiating "where they stood in relation to each other." This glimpse of how men talk when there are no women present gives an inkling of why displaying knowledge and expertise is something that men find more worth doing than women. What the women in Aries's study spent time doing was "gaining a closeness through intimate self-revelation."

It is crucial to bear in mind that both the women and the men in these studies were establishing camaraderie, and both were concerned with their relationships to each other. But different aspects of their relationships were of primary concern: their place in a hierarchical order for the men, and their place in a network of intimate connections for the women. The consequence of these disparate concerns was very different ways of speaking.

Thomas Fox is an English professor who was intrigued by the differences between women and men in his freshman writing classes. What he observed corresponds almost precisely to the experimental findings of Aries and Leet-Pellegrini. Fox's method of teaching writing included having all the students read their essays to each other in class and talk to each other in small groups. He also had them write papers reflecting on the essays and the discussion groups. He alone, as the teacher, read these analytical papers.

To exemplify the two styles he found typical of women and men, Fox chose a woman, Ms. M., and a man, Mr. H. In her speaking as well as her writing, Ms. M. held back what she knew, appearing uninformed and uninterested, because she feared offending her classmates. Mr. H. spoke and wrote with authority and apparent confidence because he was eager to persuade his peers. She did not worry about persuading; he did not worry about offending.

In his analytical paper, the young man described his own behavior in the mixed-gender group discussions as if he were describing the young men in Leet-Pellegrini's and Aries's studies:

> In my sub-group I am the leader. I begin every discussion by stating my opinions as facts. The other two members of the sub-group tend to sit back and agree with me. . . . I need people to agree with me.

Fox comments that Mr. H. reveals "a sense of self, one that acts to change himself and other people, that seems entirely distinct from Ms. M.'s sense of self, dependent on and related to others."

Calling Ms. M.'s sense of self "dependent" suggests a negative view of her way of being in the world—and, I think, a view more typical of men. This view reflects the assumption that the alternative to independence is dependence. If this is indeed a male view, it may explain why so many men are cautious about becoming intimately involved with others: It makes sense to avoid humiliating dependence by insisting on independence. But there is another alternative: *inter*dependence.

The main difference between these alternatives is symmetry. Dependence is an asymmetrical involvement: One person needs the other, but not vice versa, so the needy person is one-down. Interdependence is symmetrical: Both parties rely on each other, so neither is one-up or one-down. Moreover, Mr. H.'s sense of self is also dependent on others. He requires others to listen, agree, and allow him to take the lead by stating his opinions first.

Looked at this way, the woman and man in this group are both dependent on each other. Their differing goals are complementary, although neither understands the reasons for the other's behavior. This would be a fine arrangement, except that their differing goals result in alignments that enhance his authority and undercut hers.

DIFFERENT INTERPRETATIONS—AND MISINTERPRETATIONS

Fox also describes differences in the way male and female students in his classes interpreted a story they read. These differences also reflect assumptions about the interdependence or independence of individuals. Fox's students wrote their responses to "The Birthmark" by Nathaniel Hawthorne. In the story, a woman's husband becomes obsessed with a birthmark on her face. Suffering from her husband's revulsion at the sight of her, the wife becomes obsessed with it too and, in a reversal of her initial impulse, agrees to undergo a treatment he has devised to remove the birthmark—a treatment that succeeds in removing the mark, but kills her in the process.

Ms. M. interpreted the wife's complicity as a natural response to the demand of a loved one: The woman went along with her husband's lethal schemes to remove the birthmark because she wanted to please and be appealing to him. Mr. H. blamed the woman's insecurity and vanity for her fate, and he blamed her for voluntarily submitting to her husband's authority. Fox points out that he saw her as individually responsible for her actions, just as he saw himself as individually responsible for his own actions. To him, the issue was independence: The weak wife voluntarily took a submissive role. To Ms. M., the issue was interdependence: The woman was inextricably bound up with her husband, so her behavior could not be separated from his.

Fox observes that Mr. H. saw the writing of the women in the class as spontaneous—they wrote whatever popped into their heads. Nothing could be farther from Ms. M.'s experience as she described it: When she knew her peers would see her writing, she censored everything that popped into her head. In contrast, when she was writing something that only her professor would read, she expressed firm and articulate opinions.

There is a striking but paradoxical complementarity to Ms. M.'s and Mr. H.'s styles, when they are taken together. He needs someone to listen and agree. She listens and agrees. But in another sense, their dovetailing purposes are at cross-purposes. He misinterprets her agreement, intended in a spirit of connection, as a reflection of status and power: He thinks she is "indecisive" and "insecure." Her reasons for refraining from behaving as he does—firmly stating opinions as facts—have nothing to do with her attitudes toward her knowledge, as he thinks they do, but rather result from her attitudes toward her relationships with her peers.

These experimental studies by Leet-Pellegrini and Aries, and the observations by Fox, all indicate that, typically, men are more comfortable than women in giving information and opinions and speaking in an authoritative way to a group, whereas women are more comfortable than men in supporting others. . . .

LISTENER AS UNDERLING

Clearly men are not always talking and women are not always listening. I have asked men whether they ever find themselves in the position of listening to another man giving them a lecture, and how they feel about it. They tell me that this does happen. They may find themselves talking to someone who presses information on them so insistently that they give in and listen. They say they don't mind too much, however, if the information is interesting. They can store it away for future use, like remembering a joke to tell others later. Factual information is of less interest to women because it is of less use to them. They are unlikely to try to pass on the gift of information, more likely to give the gift of being a good audience.

Men as well as women sometimes find themselves on the receiving end of a lecture they would as soon not hear. But men tell me that it is most likely to happen if the other man is in a position of higher status. They know they have to listen to lectures from fathers and bosses.

That men can find themselves in the position of unwilling listener is attested to by a short opinion piece in which A. R. Gurney bemoans being frequently "cornered by some self-styled expert who harangues me with his considered opinion on an interminable agenda of topics." He claims that this tendency bespeaks a peculiarly American inability to "converse"—that is, engage in a balanced give-and-take—and cites as support the French observer of American customs Alexis de Tocqueville, who wrote, "An American . . . speaks to you as if he was addressing a meeting." Gurney credits his own appreciation of conversing to his father, who "was a master at eliciting and responding enthusiastically to the views of others, though this resiliency didn't always extend to his children. Indeed, now I think about it, he spoke to us many times as if he were addressing a meeting."

It is not surprising that Gurney's father lectured his children. The act of giving information by definition frames one in a position of higher status, while the act of listening frames one as lower. Children instinctively sense this—as do most men. But when women listen to men, they are not thinking in terms of status. Unfortunately, their attempts to reinforce connections and establish rapport, when interpreted through the lens of status, can be misinterpreted as casting them in a subordinate position—and are likely to be taken that way by many men.

WHAT'S SO FUNNY?

The economy of exchanging jokes for laughter is a parallel one. In her study of college students' discussions groups, Aries found that the students in all-male groups spent a lot of time telling about times they had played jokes on others, and laughing about it. She refers to a study in which Barbara Miller Newman found that high school boys who were not "quick and clever" became the targets of jokes. Practical joking—playing a joke *on* someone—is clearly a matter of being one-up: in the know and in control. It is less obvious, but no less true, that *telling* jokes can also be a way of negotiating status.

Many women (certainly not all) laugh at jokes but do not later remember them. Since they are not driven to seek and hold center stage in a group, they do not need a store of jokes to whip out for this purpose. A woman I will call Bernice prided herself on her sense of humor. At a cocktail party, she met a man to whom she was drawn because he seemed at first to share this trait. He made many funny remarks, which she spontaneously laughed at. But when she made funny remarks, he seemed not to hear. What had happened to his sense of humor? Though telling jokes and laughing at them are both reflections of a sense of humor, they are very different social activities. Making others laugh gives you a fleeting power over them: As linguist Wallace Chafe points out, at the moment of laughter, a person is temporarily disabled. The man Bernice met was comfortable only when he was making her laugh, not the other way around. When Bernice laughed at his jokes, she thought she was engaging in a symmetrical activity. But he was engaging in an asymmetrical one.

A man told me that sometime around tenth grade he realized that he preferred the company of women to the company of men. He found that his female friends were more supportive and less competitive, whereas his male friends seemed to spend all their time joking. Considering joking an asymmetrical activity makes it clearer why it would fit in with a style he perceived as competitive. . . .

MUTUAL ACCUSATIONS

Considering these dynamics, it is not surprising that many women complain that their partners don't listen to them. But men make the same complaint about women, although less frequently. The accusation "You're not listening" often really means "You don't understand what I said in the way that I meant it," or "I'm not getting the response I wanted." Being listened to can become a metaphor for being understood and being valued.

In my earlier work I emphasized that women may get the impression men aren't listening to them even when the men really are. This happens because men have different habitual ways of showing they're listening. As anthropologists Maltz and Borker explain, women are more inclined to ask questions. They also give more listening responses—little words like *mhm, uh-uh,* and *yeah*—sprinkled throughout someone else's talk, providing a running feedback loop. And they respond more positively and enthusiastically, for example by agreeing and laughing.

All this behavior is doing the work of listening. It also creates rapport-talk by emphasizing connection and encouraging more talk. The corresponding strategies of men—giving fewer listener responses, making statements rather than asking questions, and challenging rather than agreeing—can be understood as moves in a contest by incipient speakers rather than audience members.

Not only do women give more listening signals, according to Maltz and Borker, but the signals they give have different meanings for men and women, consistent with the speaker/audience alignment. Women use "yeah" to mean "I'm with you, I follow," whereas men tend to say "yeah" only when they agree. The opportunity for misunderstanding is clear. When a man is confronted with a woman who has been saying "yeah," "yeah," "yeah," and then turns out not to agree, he may conclude that she has been insincere, or that she was agreeing without really listening. When a woman is confronted with a man who does *not* say "yeah"—or much of anything else—she may conclude that *he* hasn't been listening. The men's style is more literally focused on the message level of talk, while the women's is focused on the relationship or metamessage level.

To a man who expects a listener to be quietly attentive, a woman giving a stream of feedback and support will seem to be talking too much for a listener. To a woman who expects a listener to be active and enthusiastic in showing interest, attention, and support, a man who listens silently will seem not to be listening at all, but rather to have checked out of the conversation, taken his listening marbles, and gone mentally home.

Because of these patterns, women may get the impression that men aren't listening when they really are. But I have come to understand, more recently, that it is also true that men listen to women less frequently than women listen to men, because the act of listening has different meanings for them. Some men really *don't* want to listen at length because they feel it frames them as subordinate. Many women do want to listen, but they expect it to be reciprocal—I listen to you now; you listen to me later. They become frustrated when they do the listening now and now and now, and later never comes.

MUTUAL DISSATISFACTION

If women are dissatisfied with always being in the listening position, the dissatisfaction may be mutual. That a woman feels she has been assigned the role of silently listening audience does not mean that a man feels he has consigned her to that role—or that he necessarily likes the rigid alignment either.

During the time I was working on this book, I found myself at a book party filled with people I hardly knew. I struck up a conversation with a charming young man who turned out to be a painter. I asked him about his work and, in response to his answer, asked whether there has been a return in contemporary art to figurative painting. In response to my question, he told me a lot about the history of art—so much that when he finished and said, "That was a long answer to your question," I had long since forgotten that I had asked a question, let alone what it was. I had not minded this monologue—I had been interested in it—but I realized, with something of a jolt, that I had just experienced the dynamic that I had been writing about.

I decided to risk offending my congenial new acquaintance in order to learn something about his point of view. This was, after all, a book party, so I might rely on his indulgence if I broke the rules of decorum in the interest of writing a book. I asked whether he often found himself talking at length while someone else listened. He thought for a moment and said yes, he did, because he liked to explore ideas in detail. I asked if it happened equally with women and men. He thought again and said, "No, I have more trouble with men." I asked what he meant by trouble. He said, "Men interrupt. *They* want to explain to *me*."

Finally, having found this young man disarmingly willing to talk about the conversation we had just had and his own style, I asked which he preferred: that a woman listen silently and supportively, or that she offer opinions and ideas of her own. He said he thought he liked it better if she volunteered information, making the interchange more interesting.

When men begin to lecture other men, the listeners are experienced at trying to sidetrack the lecture, or match it, or derail it. In this system, making authoritative pronouncements may be a way to begin an *exchange* of information. But women are not used to responding in that way. They see little choice but to listen attentively and wait for their turn to be allotted to them rather than seizing it for themselves. If this is the case, the man may be as bored and frustrated as the woman when his attempt to begin an exchange of information ends in his giving a lecture. From his point of view, she is passively soaking up information, so she must not have any to speak of. One of the reasons men's talk to women frequently turns into lecturing is *because* women listen attentively and do not interrupt with challenges, sidetracks, or matching information.

In the conversations with male and female colleagues that I recounted at the outset of this chapter, this difference may have been crucial. When I talked to the woman, we each told about our own research in response to the other's encouragement. When I talked to the man, I encouraged him to talk about his work, and he obliged, but he did not encourage me to talk about mine. This may mean that he did not want to hear about it—but it also may not. In her study of college students' discussion groups, Aries found that women who did a lot of talking began to feel uncomfortable; they backed off and frequently drew out quieter members of the group. This is perfectly in keeping with women's desire to keep things balanced, so everyone is on an equal footing. Women expect their conversational partners to encourage them to hold forth. Men, who do not typically encourage quieter members to speak up, assume that anyone who has something to say will volunteer it. The men may be equally disappointed in a conversational partner who turns out to have nothing to say.

Similarly, men can be as bored by women's topics as women can be by men's. While I was wishing the former RAFer would tell me about his personal experiences in Greece, he was probably wondering why I was boring him with mine and marveling at my ignorance of the history of a country I had lived in. Perhaps he would have considered our conversation a success if I had challenged or topped his interpretation of Greek history rather than listening dumbly to it. When men, upon hearing the kind of work I do, challenge me about my research methods, they are inviting me to give them information and show them my expertise—something I don't like to do outside of the classroom or lecture hall, but something they themselves would likely be pleased to be provoked to do.

The publicist who listened attentively to information about a radio station explained to me that she wanted to be nice to the manager, to smooth the way for placing her clients on his station. But men who want to ingratiate themselves with women are more likely to try to charm them by offering interesting information than by listening attentively to whatever information the women have to impart. I recall a luncheon preceding a talk I delivered to a college alumni association. My gracious host kept me entertained before my speech by regaling me with information about computers, which I politely showed interest in, while inwardly screaming from boredom and a sense of being weighed down by irrelevant information that I knew I would never remember. Yet I am sure he thought he was being interesting, and it is likely that at least some male guests would have thought that he was. I do not wish to imply that all women hosts have entertained me in the perfect way. I recall a speaking engagement before which I was taken to lunch by a group of women. They were so attentive to my expertise that they plied me with questions, prompting me to exhaust myself by giving my lecture over lunch before the formal lecture began. In comparison to this, perhaps the man who lectured to me about computers was trying to give me a rest.

The imbalance by which men often find themselves in the role of lecturer, and women often find themselves in the role of audience, is not the creation of only one member of an interaction. It is not something that men do to women. Neither is it something that women culpably "allow" or "ask for." The imbalance is created by the difference between women's and men's habitual styles. . . .

HOPE FOR THE FUTURE

What is the hope for the future? Must we play out our assigned parts to the closing act? Although we tend to fall back on habitual ways of talking, repeating old refrains and familiar lines, habits can be broken. Women and men both can gain by understanding the other gender's style, and by learning to use it on occasion.

Women who find themselves unwillingly cast as the listener should practice propelling themselves out of that position rather than waiting patiently for the lecture to end. Perhaps they need to give up the belief that they must wait for the floor to be handed to them. If they have something to say on a subject, they might push themselves to volunteer it. If they are bored with a subject, they can exercise some influence on the conversation and change the topic to something they would rather discuss.

If women are relieved to learn that they don't always have to listen, there may be some relief for men in learning that they don't always have to have interesting information on the tips of their tongues if they want to impress a woman or entertain her. A journalist once interviewed me for an article about how to strike up conversations. She told me that another expert she had interviewed, a man, had suggested that one should come up with an interesting piece of information. I found this amusing, as it seemed to typify a man's idea of a good conversationalist, but not a woman's. How much easier men might find the task of conversation if they realized that all they have to do is listen. As a woman who wrote a letter to the editor of *Psychology Today* put it, "When I find a guy who asks, 'How was your day?' and really wants to know, I'm in heaven."

FOR STUDY AND DISCUSSION

1. Tannen opens her selection by recounting anecdotes that illustrate her thesis. State her thesis in your own words. How does each of her anecdotes support it? Do your own experiences support it?

2. According to Tannen, what do men primarily seek through conversation, and what do women seek? What roles do men and women characteristically adopt as a result, and how do these different roles lead to inequality?

3. Tannen often speaks about her research to both men and women. What are the characteristic responses of each gender?

4. An interpretation of Leet-Pellegrini's study suggests that, in general, men want to be respected and seek status, while women want to be liked and seek rapport. How do these different purposes play out in conversations? Is a man necessarily putting a woman down when he challenges her authority on a subject? Is a woman necessarily agreeing with a man when she doesn't challenge his expertise?

5. In Aries's study, how did the all-female groups seek to establish camaraderie, and how did this differ from the all-male groups?

6. Discuss the characteristics of dependence, independence, and interdependence as expressed in conversation.

7. Why are telling jokes and laughing at them "very different social activities"? In what way is joking an "asymmetrical" activity?

8. According to Maltz and Borker, what characterizes the listening response of women? Of men?

9. What suggestions does Tannen offer to overcome the imbalance between the male "lecturer" and the female "listener"?

27

Ethnic Style in Male–Female Conversation

Deborah Tannen

Having explored the differences between men's and women's conversational expectations in a uniform cultural setting, Tannen sets out to study a second variable: ethnic background. Here she undertakes to define unspoken messages in communication between Greek, American, and Greek-American speakers of English. Tannen studies indirectness as a communication strategy between married partners of different cultural backgrounds. She finds that both ethnicity and gender play roles in the interpretation of a conversation, whether by the partners themselves or by outsiders. She learns also that indirectness as an ethnic conversational strategy perseveres for a generation or more after the language in which it originated is unknown to the user. Her study illustrates the complexity of interpersonal communication; it is tempting to say flatly that women do this with language and men do that. Likewise, it is tempting to generalize about the way in which a particular group expresses itself. The reality is, however, that communication is complicated by many factors.

This chapter focuses on indirectness in male–female discourse, seen as a feature of conversational style. The present analysis investigates social, rather than individual, differences in the context of conversation between married partners; however, the phenomena eludicated operate in individual style as well. Investigation of expectations of indirectness by Greeks, Americans, and Greek-Americans traces the process of adaptation of this conversational strategy as an element of ethnicity.

Misunderstandings due to different uses of indirectness are commonplace among members of what appear to (but may not necessarily) be the same culture. However, such mixups are particularly characteristic of cross-cultural communication. There are individual as well as social differences with respect to what is deemed appropriate to say and how it is deemed appropriate to say it.

It is sharing of conversational strategies that creates the feeling of satisfaction which accompanies and follows successful conversation: the sense of being understood, being "on the same wave length," belonging, and therefore of sharing identity. Conversely, a lack of congruity in conversational strategies creates the opposite feeling: of dissonance, not being understood, not belonging, and therefore of not sharing identity. This is the sense in which conversational style is a major component of what we have come to call ethnicity.

As has been shown in earlier chapters in this volume, conversational control processes operate on an automatic level. While it is commonly understood that different languages or different dialects have different words for the same object, in contrast, ways of signalling intentions and attitudes seem self-evident, natural, and real.

Much recent linguistic research has been concerned with the fact that interpretation of utterances in conversation often differs radically from the meaning that would be derived from the sentences in isolation. Robin Lakoff (1973) observes that sociocultural goals, broadly called *politeness*, lead people to express opinions and preferences in widely varying linguistic forms. Lakoff's (1979) recent work demonstrates that characteristic choices with respect to indirectness give rise to personal style, and that an individual's style is a mixture of strategies which shift in response to shifting situations. Ervin-Tripp (1976) has shown the great variation in surface form which directives may take in American English. Brown and Levinson (1978) argue that the form taken by utterances in actual interaction can be seen as the linguistic means of satisfying the coexisting and often conflicting needs for *negative face* (the need to be left alone) and *positive face* (the need to be approved of by others). As a result, people often prefer to express their wants and opinions *off record*—that is, indirectly.

Indirectness is a necessary means for serving the needs for *rapport* and *defensiveness*, associated respectively with Brown and Levinson's positive and negative face. *Rapport* is the lovely satisfaction of being understood without explaining oneself, of getting what one wants without asking for it. *Defensiveness* is the need to be able to save face by reneging in case one's conversational contribution is not received well— the ability to say, perhaps sincerely, "I never said that," or "That isn't what I meant." The goals of rapport and defensiveness correspond to Lakoff's politeness rules "Maintain camaraderie" and "Don't impose."

An individual learns conversational strategies in previous interactive experience, but chooses certain and rejects other strategies made available in this way. In other words, the range of strategies familiar to a speaker is socially determined, but any individual's set of habitual strategies is unique within that range. For example, research has shown that New Yorkers of Jewish background often use overlap—that is, simultaneous talk—in a cooperative way; many members of this group talk simultaneously in some settings without intending to interrupt (Tannen 1979, 1981). This does not imply that all New Yorkers of Jewish background use overlap cooperatively. However, a speaker of this background is more likely to do so than someone raised in the Midwest. And it is even more unlikely that such simultaneous talk will be used by an Athabaskan raised in Alaska, according to the findings of Scollon, who has shown that Athabaskans highly value silence and devalue what they perceive as excessive talk.

The present analysis and discussion seeks to investigate social differences in expectations of indirectness in certain contexts by Greeks, Americans, and Greek-Americans, tracing the process of adaptation of this conversational strategy as an element of ethnicity. The research design is intended to identify patterns of interpretation, not to predict the styles of individual members of these groups.

A Greek woman of about 65 told me that, before she married, she had to ask her father's permission before doing anything. She noted that of course he never explicitly denied her permission. If she asked, for example, whether she could go to a dance, and he answered,

(1)   An thes, pas. (If you want, you can go.)

she knew that she could not go. If he really meant that she could go, he would say,

(2)   Ne. Na pas. (Yes. You should go.)

The intonation in (1) rises on the conditional clause, creating a tentative effect, while the intonation in (2) falls twice in succession, resulting in an assertive effect. This informant added that her husband responds to her requests in the same way. Thus she agrees to do what he prefers without expecting him to express his preference directly.

This example is of a situation in which interlocutors share expectations about how intentions are to be communicated; their communication is thus successful. To investigate processes of indirectness, however, it is useful to focus on interactions in which communication is not successful (Gumperz and Tannen 1979). Such sequences are the discourse equivalents of starred sentences in syntactic argumentation. They render apparent processes which go unnoticed when communication is successful.

The present chapter focuses on communication between married partners. Interactions between couples reveal the effects of differing uses of indirectness over time. People often think that couples who live together and love each other must come to understand each other's conversational styles. However, research has shown that repeated interaction does not necessarily lead to better understanding. On the contrary, it may reinforce mistaken judgments of the other's intentions and increase expectations that the other will behave as before. If differing styles led to the earlier impression that the partner is stubborn, irrational, or uncooperative, similar behavior is expected to continue. This has been shown for group contact among Greeks and Americans (Vassiliou et al. 1972) and can be seen in personal relations as well. Misjudgment is calcified by the conviction of repeated experience.

Systematic study of comparative communicative strategies was made by asking couples about experiences in which they become aware of differing interpretations of conversations. It became clear that certain types of communication were particularly given to misinterpretation—

requests, excuses, explanation: in short, verbalizations associated with getting one's way. One couple recalled a typical argument in which both maintained that they had not gone to a party because the other had not wanted to go. Each partner denied having expressed any disinclination to go. A misunderstanding such as this might well go undetected between casual acquaintances, but, between couples, ongoing interaction makes it likely that such differences will eventually surface.

In this case, the mixup was traced to the following reconstructed conversations:

(3)   Wife: John's having a party. Wanna go?
       Husband: OK.
       (Later)
       Wife: Are you sure you want to go to the party?
       Husband: OK, let's not go. I'm tired anyway.

In this example the wife was an American native New Yorker of East European Jewish extraction. It is likely that this background influenced her preference for a seemingly direct style. (This phenomenon among speakers of this background is the focus of analysis in Tannen 1979, 1981.) In discussing the misunderstanding, the American wife reported she had merely been asking what her husband wanted to do without considering her own preference. Since she was about to go to this party just for him, she tried to make sure that that was his preference by asking him a second time. She was being solicitous and considerate. The Greek husband said that by bringing up the question of the party, his wife was letting him know that she wanted to go, so he agreed to go. Then when she brought it up again, she was letting him know that she didn't want to go; she had obviously changed her mind. So he came up with a reason not to go, to make her feel all right about getting her way. This is precisely the strategy reported by the Greek woman who did what her father or husband wanted without expecting him to tell her directly what that was. Thus the husband in example (3) was also being solicitous and considerate. All this considerateness, however, only got them what neither wanted, because they were expecting to receive information differently from the way the other was sending it out.

A key to understanding the husband's strategy is his use of "OK." To the wife, "OK" was a positive response, in free variation with other positive responses such as "yes" or "yeah." In addition, his use of *anyway* is an indication that he agrees. Finally, the husband's intonation, tone of voice, and nonverbal signals such as facial expression and kinesics would have contributed to the impact of his message. Nonetheless, the wife asserted that, much as she could see the reasoning behind such interpretations in retrospect, she still missed the significance of these cues at the time. The key, I believe, is that she was not expecting to receive her husband's message through subtle cues; she was assuming he would tell her what he wanted to do directly. To the listener, a misunderstanding is indistinguishable from an understanding; one commits to an interpretation and proceeds to fit succeeding information into that mold. People will put up with a great deal of seemingly inappropriate verbal behavior before questioning the line of interpretation which seems self-evident. Direct questioning about how a comment was meant is likely to be perceived as a challenge or criticism.

This example demonstrates, furthermore, the difficulty of clearing up misunderstandings caused by stylistic differences. In seeking to clarify, each speaker continues to use the very strategy that confused the other in the first place. In this way, interaction often results in increasing divergence rather than convergence of style. That is, each partner's characteristic style leads the other to apply increasingly extreme forms of the conflicting strategy. In example (3), the wife's strategy for clarifying was to go "on record," through a direct question, as inquiring about her husband's preference, and to ask her husband to go on record about his preference. Since the husband did not expect preferences to be directly expressed, his wife's second question seemed to him an even more recondite hint. He responded with an even more subtle use of indirectness: to allow her to get her way and to offer a reason of his own in justification. And so it goes. Expectations about how meaning will be communicated are so compelling that information intended in a different mode is utterly opaque.

A key parameter here is setting. Does a participant define an interaction as one in which it is appropriate to hint? Numerous discussions triggered by the presentation of these findings have suggested possible male–female differences among Americans in this regard. An audience member commented, "When I first started going out with my boyfriend, we never had misunderstandings about where we should go and what we should do. Now that we've been going together for two years, it seems to happen all the time. How come?" My hypothesis is that, at the beginning of their acquaintance, both partners deemed it appropriate to watch out for the other's hints, to give options. However, as the relationship was redefined, the woman expected increased use of indirectness, reasoning, "We know each other so well, you will know what I want without my telling you." The man, on the other hand, expected less indirectness, reasoning, "We know each other so well that we can tell each other what we want." As the context of their relationship changed, they differed in how they expected their communicative strategies to change. In addition, when partners interact over time, they become more rather than less likely to react, perhaps negatively, to each other's subtle cues, as repeated experience leads them to expect such behavior.

Another example of a reported conversation between a married couple follows.

(4)   Husband: Let's go visit my boss tonight.
      Wife: Why?
      Husband: All right, we don't have to go.

Both husband and wife agreed that the husband's initial proposal was an indication that he wanted to visit his boss. However, they disagreed on the meaning of the wife's question, "Why?" The wife explained that she meant it as a request for information. Therefore she was confused and frustrated and couldn't help wondering why she married such an erratic man who suddenly changed his mind only a moment after making a request. The husband, for his part, explained that his wife's question clearly meant that she did not want to go, and he therefore rescinded his request. He was frustrated, however, and resentful of her for refusing. In discussion, the wife, who was American, reported that she systematically confronted this strange reaction to her asking "Why?" Certainly, the use of this question can be either a request for information or an indirect way of stalling or resisting compliance with a perceived request. The key here is which meaning of "why" is likely to be used in this context.

In order to determine to what extent cross-cultural differences are operating in patterns of interpretation of indirectness, further systematic questioning of Greeks, Americans, and Greek-Americans was undertaken. The remainder of this chapter reports results of that research.

The Greek sample was taken from native Greeks living in the Bay Area of California. Most were young men who had come to the United States for graduate study or women contacted through church organizations. Therefore the age and educational levels differed sharply for men and women. In all cases, Greek respondents had been exposed to American communicative systems. That differences emerged nonetheless is a testament to the reality of the effect.

Greek-Americans were contacted in New York City because it was not possible to find California Greek-Americans who had grown up in distinctly Greek communities. The fact that Greek-Americans from New York are compared with Americans from California is now seen as a weakness; subsequent research (Tannen 1979) has indicated that New Yorkers are less likely to expect indirectness than Californians. Again, the fact that differences do emerge is testimony to the effect of ethnicity. Finally, Americans with Greek-born parents and grandparents are lumped together in this study. There is some indication that those with Greek parents show the effect of ethnicity more strongly than do those of Greek grandparents and American-born parents.

A questionnaire was designed to present the Greek, American, and Greek-American respondents with the conversation about going to a party. The questionnaire elicited their interpretations by presenting paraphrase choices and then asked for explanations of those choices in order to identify the interpretive strategies motivating them. The first part of the questionnaire reads:

(5)   A couple had the following conversation:
     Wife: John's having a party. Wanna go?
     Husband: OK.
     Wife: I'll call and tell him we're coming.
     Based on this conversation only, put a check next to the statement which you think explains what the husband really meant when he answered "OK."

[1–I] My wife wants to go to this party, since she asked. I'll go to make her happy.

[1–D] My wife is asking if I want to go to a party. I feel like going, so I'll say yes.

What is it about the way the wife and husband spoke, that gave you that impression?

What would the wife or husband have had to have said differently, in order for you to have checked the other statement?

The first choice, here referred to as 1–I (Indirect), represents roughly what the Greek husband reported he had meant by "OK." 1–D (Direct) represents what the American wife reported she had thought he meant. A comparison of the percentage of respondents in the three groups who opted for Paraphrase 1–I turns out looking much like a continuum, with Greeks the most likely to take the indirect interpretation, Americans the least likely, and Greek-Americans in the middle, somewhat closer to Greeks (see Table 27.1).

TABLE 27.1   **Respondents Choosing 1–I**

GREEKS (27)	GREEK-AMERICANS (30)	AMERICANS (25)
48%	43%	32%
(13)	(13)	(8)

In example (5), and throughout the present discussion, I refer to one interpretation as direct and the other as indirect. These labels reflect the two possible functions of the question: as a request for information (its literal sense) and as an off-record show of resistance (an indirect speech act). This is not to imply, however, that anyone's conversational style is categorically direct. In a sense, all interpretation in context is indirect. What are variable are the modes of indirectness—when and how it is deemed appropriate to hint, that is, to signal unstated contextual and interpersonal information.

It has been suggested (Lakoff 1975) that American women tend to be more indirect than American men. As seen in Tables 27.2 and 27.3, percentages of respondents taking the indirect interpretation are more or less the same for Greek men and women and for Greek-American men and women, while, for Americans, separating male and female respondents yields quite different percentages, with fewer men and more women choosing Paraphrase 1–I. If these samples are representative, they are intriguing in suggesting a stylistic gulf between American men and women which does not exist between Greek men and women.

The second part of the questionnaire presents the second part of the conversation, followed by paraphrase choice and questions about interpretive strategies. It reads:

(6)   Later, the same couple had this conversation:
        Wife: Are you sure you want to go to the party?
        Husband: OK, let's not go. I'm tired anyway.

Based on *both* conversations which you read, put a check next to the statement that you think explains what the husband really meant when he spoke the second time:

    [2–I]   It sounds like my wife doesn't really want to go, since she's asking about it again. I'll say I'm tired, so we don't have to go, and she won't feel bad about preventing me from going.

    [2–D] Now that I think about it again, I don't really feel like going to a party because I'm tired.

What is it about the way the husband or wife spoke that gave you that impression?

What would they have had to have said differently, in order for you to have checked the other statement?

TABLE 27.2   Male Respondents Choosing 1–I

GREEKS (10)	GREEK-AMERICANS (9)	AMERICANS (11)
50% (5)	44% (4)	27% (3)

TABLE 27.3   Female Respondents Choosing 1–I

GREEKS (17)	GREEK-AMERICANS (21)	AMERICANS (14)
47% (8)	43% (9)	36% (5)

The two paraphrases presented in the second part of the questionnaire represent the respective interpretations reported by the Greek husband (the one here labeled 2–I, Indirect) and the American wife (here labeled 2–D, Direct) in the actual interchange. This also highlights an aspect of the questionnaire which is different for male and female respondents. Women and men are both asked to interpret the husband's comments, while it is likely that women identify with the wife and men with the husband. Furthermore, the indirect interpretation is favored by the fact that the husband's response indicates that he took that interpretation.

The choice of both 1–I and 2–I reveals the most indirect interpretive strategy, by which both the wife's questions are taken to indicate her hidden preferences—or at least that the husband's reply is taken to show that he interprets them that way. Again, results fall out on a continuum with Greeks the most likely to take the indirect interpretation, Americans the least likely, and Greek-Americans in between, slightly closer to the Greeks (see Table 27.4).

Quantitative results, then, tended to corroborate the impression that more Greeks than Americans opted for the indirect interpretation of questions, and that Greek-Americans were in between, slightly closer to Greeks. However, the pilot study questionnaire was not designed primarily to yield quantitative data. The main function of the paraphrase choices was to serve as a basis for short answers and extended discussion about the patterns of interpretation which prompted one or the other choice, and the linguistic and contextual factors influencing them. Results of the short answer and interview/discussion components follow.

TABLE 27.4   Respondents Choosing 1–I and 2–I

GREEKS (27)	GREEK-AMERICANS (30)	AMERICANS (25)
26%	20%	12%
(7)	(6)	(3)

Patterns of interpretation emerged from respondents' explanations of their choice of paraphrase and from alternative linguistic forms they reported would have led them to the other choice. Following paraphrase choices, the questionnaire asked, "What is it about the way the wife and the husband spoke, that gave you that impression?" and then, "What would the wife or husband have had to have said differently, in order for you to have checked the other statement?" Differences in explanations of interpretations were systematic in reference to two aspects of the conversation: the wife's asking of questions, and the form of the husband's responses.

Paraphrase 1–I indicates that the wife's question means she wants to go to the party. The reasoning reported by Greeks to explain their choice of 1–I is that if the wife didn't want to go, she would not have brought it up in the first place. Greeks, Americans, and probably members of any cultural group are capable of interpreting a question either as a request for information or as an expression of some unstated meaning. However, members of one culture or another may be more likely to interpret a question in a particular context in one way or another. Much recent research in pragmatics has elaborated on the indirect speech act function of questions as requests for action, or commands. Esther Goody (1978:40) set out to discover why natives of Gonja do not ask questions in teaching and learning situations. She concluded that Gonjans are "trained early on to attend above all to the command function of questioning. The pure information question hasn't got a chance!" Similarly, I suggest, in the context under consideration, natives of Greece are more disposed to attend to the indirect request function of questions.

Respondents' comments explaining why they chose one or the other paraphrase often focused on the husband's choice of OK. Americans who thought the husband really wanted to go to the party explained that "OK" = "yes" (24% of the Americans said this). But if they thought the husband was going along with his wife's preference, the Americans still focused on "OK" as the cue. In this case they explained that "OK" lacks enthusiasm (20% of the Americans said this).

The expectation of enthusiasm was stronger for Greeks than for Americans. Whereas 24% of the Americans pointed to the affirmative nature of "OK," not a single Greek did so. In contrast, fully half of the Greeks who explained their choices referred to the fact that "OK" (in Greek, *endaxi*) was an unenthusiastic response. This is more than double the percentage of Americans (20%) who said this. The *enthusiasm constraint* is in keeping with findings of Vassiliou, Triandis, Vassiliou, and McGuire (1972), who conclude that Greeks place value on enthusiasm and spontaneity (as opposed to American emphasis on planning and organization). Vassiliou et al. observe that such differences in "subjective culture" may contribute to the formation of ethnic stereotypes.

Related to the enthusiasm constraint—perhaps another aspect of it— is the *brevity effect*. Many respondents referred to the brevity of the husband's response when they explained their paraphrase choices. However, if Americans made reference to his brevity, it was in explanation of their choice of paraphrase 1–D, the direct interpretation. Their reasoning was that brevity evidenced informality, casualness, and hence sincerity. This explanation is based on a strategy which assumes that people will express preferences directly in this context. More than a quarter (28%) of the American respondents took this approach. In stark contrast, any Greeks who mentioned the brevity of the husband's answer "OK" (*endaxi*) pointed to it as evidence that he was reluctant to go to the party. To them, brevity is a sign of unwillingness to comply with another's perceived preference. This interpretation presupposes that resistance to another's preference, in this context, will not be verbalized directly; 20% of Greek respondents took this approach.

The explanations given by Greek-Americans for their paraphrase choices were a blend of typical Greek and typical American explanations. They explained that brevity reveals lack of enthusiasm, whereas no Americans did, and they explained that brevity is casual, whereas no Greeks did, in roughly the same proportions (23% and 20%, respectively). Only two (7%) said that "OK" = "yes," whereas no Greeks and 24% of Americans said this. Thus Greek-Americans were closer to Greeks than to Americans in their interpretive style.

Further corroborative results came in the form of comments volunteered by respondents following their completion of the questionnaire; the suggestion that Greeks tend to be more indirect in the context of an intimate relationship "rang true" for respondents.

What are the implications of such differences for cross-cultural communication? It is possible that a good bicultural, like a good bilingual, sees both possibilities and code-switches. For example, an American-born woman of Greek grandparents said that she had to check both paraphrases on the questionnaire. She explained that if she projected herself into the position of the wife, she would take the indirect interpretation, but if she imagined her non-Greek husband asking, she would take the direct paraphrase. In other words, she was aware of both possible strategies. She commented that she tends to be indirect because she picked it up from her mother, who was influenced by her own mother (i.e., the grandmother born in Greece). In the same spirit, another Greek-

American woman laughed when she read paraphrase 2–I, saying, "That sounds just like my grandmother."

It is far from certain, however, that awareness of the existence of differences in communicative strategies makes them less troublesome, since their operation remains unconscious and habitual. Again, a personal testimony is most eloquent: that of a professional man living in New York City, whose grandparents were from Greece. He seemed fully assimilated, did not speak Greek, had not been raised in a Greek neighborhood, and had few Greek friends. In filling out the questionnaire, he chose paraphrase 1–I, the initial indirect interpretation. In later discussion he said that the notion of indirectness "rang such a bell." He commented, ". . . to a great extent being Greek implies a certain feeling of differentness with regard to understanding others which I have some trouble with." He elaborated on what he meant: "I was trying to get at the idea of . . . this very thing that we talked about [indirectness] and I see it as either something heroically different or a real impediment . . . Most of the time I think of it as a problem. And I can't really sort it out from my family and background . . . I don't know if it's Greek. I just know that it's me. And it feels a little better to know that it's Greek."

CONCLUSIONS

These results indicate how respondents report they would interpret a conversation. In actual interaction, intonation, facial expression, past experience with these and other speakers, and a myriad of other factors influence interpretation. Moreover, whenever people communicate, they convey not only the content of their message, but an image of themselves (Goffman 1959). Thus respondents must have referred for their answers not only to their interactive experience but also to their notion of social norms.

Eventually such an approach must be combined with tape-recording and videotaping of actual interaction, to determine not only what speakers expect but what they do.

Conversational style—the ways it seems natural to express and interpret meaning in conversation—is learned through communicative experience and therefore is influenced by family communicative habits. As the Greek-American quoted above put it, one "can't really sort it out from . . . family and background." In other words, conversational style is both a consequence and indicator of ethnicity. Conversational style includes both how meaning is expressed, as seen in patterns of indirectness, and what meaning is expressed, as in how much enthusiasm is expected. All of these conversational strategies create impressions about the speaker—judgments which are made, ultimately, not about how one talks but about what kind of person one is. Conversational style, therefore, has much to do with the formation of ethnic stereotypes.

Conversational style is more resistant to change than more apparent marks of ethnicity such as retention of the parents' or grandparents' language. Seaman (1972:204) demonstrates that the modern Greek language is "practically extinct" among third-generation Greek-Americans and will be "totally extinct in the fourth generation." However, those very third generation Greek-Americans who have lost the Greek language may not have lost, or not lost entirely, Greek communicative strategies. Understanding these strategies, and the patterns of their retention or loss, can offer insight into the process of cultural assimilation at the same time that it provides insight into discourse processes in a heterogeneous society.

WORKS CITED

Brown, P. and Levinson, S. 1978. "Universals in Language Usage: Politeness Phenomena." In *Questions and Politeness*. E. N. Goody, ed. Cambridge: Cambridge University Press.

Ervin-Tripp, S. 1976. "Is Sybil There? The Structure of Some American English Directives." *Language in Society* 5:25–66.

Gumperz, J. J. and Tannen, D. 1979. "Individual and Social Differences in Language Use." In *Individual Differences in Language Ability and Language Behavior*. W. Wang and C. Fillmore, eds. New York: Academic Press.

Lakoff, R. 1973. "The Logic of Politeness; or, Minding Your P's and Q's." *CLS* 10: Chicago Linguistics Society.

Lakoff, R. 1975. *Language and Women's Place*. New York: Harper and Row.

Lakoff, R. 1979. "Stylistic Strategies within a Grammar of Style." In *Language, Sex, and Gender*. J. Orasanu, M. Slater, and L. Loeb Adler, eds. *Annals of the New York Academy of Sciences* 327: 53–78.

Seaman, P.D. 1972. *Modern Greek and American English in Contact*. The Hague: Mouton, 1972.

Tannen, D. 1979. Processes and Consequences of Conversational Style. Ph.D. dissertation. University of California, Berkeley.

Tannen, D. 1981. "New York Jewish Conversational Style." *International Journal of the Sociology of Language* 30:133–49.

Vassiliou, V., Triandis, H., Vassiliou, G., and McGuire, H. 1972. "Interpersonal Contact and Stereotyping." In *The Analysis of Subjective Culture*. H. Triandis, ed. New York: Wiley.

FOR STUDY AND DISCUSSION

1. Tannen implies that at least three dynamics may come into play in conversation between married partners. What are they?

2. What does Tannen mean by *indirectness*? Define the term in your own words, and compare your definition with those of classmates. When a speaker uses indirectness, what needs are likely motivating him or her?

3. What is the role of ethnicity in successful conversation?

4. What characterizes a situation in which successful communication occurs? What may happen when married couples do not understand each other's conversational styles?

5. In Tannen's example, what chief difference characterized the misunderstanding between members of a couple in which one was of Greek heritage and the other was not? How was the cause of this misunderstanding reinforced in a subsequent study of Greek-Americans and their partners? According to the study, are Greeks or Americans more likely to expect indirectness in conversation?

6. Explain the roles of enthusiasm constraint and brevity effect in respondents' interpretations of the misunderstanding.

7. In an American setting, is the male or female more likely to expect indirectness in conversation? On what evidence do you base your response?

8. Comment on Tannen's observation that "conversational style is both a consequence and indicator of ethnicity."

28

The Names of Women

Louise Erdrich

Louise Erdrich is a writer of poetry and fiction, and in 1984 her novel
Love Medicine *won the National Book Critics Circle Award. Erdrich is
fascinated by her Chippewa ancestry, which resonates in the colorful
descriptive names given to the women of the tribe. "These names," she
says, "tell stories, or half stories, if only we listen closely." Using her
imagination and skill with language, she transforms the names of
women into windows that provide tantalizing glimpses of a vanished
culture. Like much Native American history, "The Names of Women"
tells of the loss of a language and a culture, but it also tells of the survival and adaptation of individuals. Erdrich shows how European
invaders destroyed the names but not the spirits of these indomitable
women, who rode their carts through a transient generation from one
culture into another.*

Ikwe is the word for woman in the language of the Anishinabe, my
mother's people, whose descendants, mixed with and married to French
trappers and farmers, are the Michifs of the Turtle Mountain Reservation
in North Dakota. Every Anishinabe *Ikwe*, every mixed-blood descendant
like me, who can trace her way back a generation or two, is the daughter
of a mystery. The history of the woodland Anishinabe—decimated by
disease, fighting Plains Indian tribes to the west and squeezed by
European settlers to the east—is much like most other Native American
stories, a confusion of loss, a tale of absences, of a culture that was blown
apart and changed so radically in such a short time that only the names
survive,

And yet, those names.

The names of the first women whose existence is recorded on the
rolls of the Turtle Mountain Reservation, in 1892, reveal as much as we
can ever recapture of their personalities, complex natures, and relationships. These names tell stories, or half stories, if only we listen closely.

There once were women named *Standing Strong*, *Fish Bones*,
Different Thunder. There once was a girl called *Yellow Straps*. Imagine
what it was like to pick berries with *Sky Coming Down*, to walk through
a storm with *Lightning Proof*. Surely, she was struck and lived, but what
about the person next to her? People always avoided *Steps Over Truth*,
when they wanted a straight answer, and *I Hear*, when they wanted to

392

keep a secret. *Glittering* put coal on her face and watched for enemies at night. The woman named *Standing Across* could see things moving far across the lake. The old ladies gossiped about *Playing Around*, but no one dared say anything to her face. *Ice* was good at gambling. *Shining One Side* loved to sit and talk to *Opposite the Sky*. They both knew *Sounding Feather*, *Exhausted Wind*, and *Green Cloud*, daughter of *Seeing Iron*. *Center of the Sky* was a widow. *Rabbit*, *Prairie Chicken*, and *Daylight* were all little girls. *She Tramp* could make great distance in a day of walking. *Cross Lightning* had a powerful smile. When *Setting Wind* and *Gentle Woman Standing* sang together the whole tribe listened. *Stop the Day* got her name when at her shout the afternoon went still. *Log* was strong, *Cloud Touching Bottom* weak and consumptive. *Mirage* married *Wind*. Everyone loved *Musical Cloud*, but children hid from *Dressed in Stone*. *Lying Down Grass* had such a gentle voice and touch, but no one dared to cross *She Black of Heart*.

We can imagine something of these women from their names. Anishinabe historian Basil Johnston notes that "such was the mystique and force of a name that it was considered presumptuous and unbecoming, even vain, for a person to utter his own name. It was the custom for a third person, if present, to utter the name of the person to be identified. Seldom, if ever, did either husband or wife speak the name of the other in public."

Shortly after the first tribal roll, the practice of renaming became an ecclesiastical exercise, and, as a result, most women in the next two generations bear the names of saints particularly beloved by the French. *She Knows the Bear* became Marie. *Sloping Cloud* was christened Jeanne. *Taking Care of the Day* and *Yellow Day Woman* turned into Catherines. Identities are altogether lost. The daughters of my own ancestors, *Kwayzancheewin—Acts Like a Boy* and *Striped Earth Woman*—go unrecorded, and no hint or reflection of their individual natures comes to light through the scatter-shot records of those times, although they must have been genetically tough in order to survive: there were epidemics of typhoid, flu, measles and other diseases that winnowed the tribe each winter. They had to have grown up sensible, hard-working, undeviating in their attention to their tasks. They had to have been lucky. And if very lucky, they acquired carts.

It is no small thing that both of my great-grandmothers were known as women with carts.

The first was Elise Eliza McCloud, the great-granddaughter of *Striped Earth Woman*. The buggy she owned was somewhat grander than a cart. In her photograph, Elise Eliza gazes straight ahead, intent, elevated in her pride. Perhaps she and her daughter Justine, both wearing reshaped felt fedoras, were on their way to the train that would take them from Rugby, North Dakota, to Grand Forks, and back again. Back and forth across the upper tier of the plains, they peddled their hand-worked tourist items— dangling moccasin brooches and little beaded hats, or, in the summer, the wild berries, plums, and nuts that they had gathered from the wooded hills. Of Elise Eliza's industry there remains in the family only an intricately beaded pair of buffalo horns and a piece of real furniture, a "highboy," an object once regarded with some awe, a prize she won for selling the most merchandise from a manufacturer's catalogue.

The owner of the other cart, Virginia Grandbois, died when I was nine years old: she was a fearsome and fascinating presence, an old woman seated like an icon behind the door of my grandparents' house. Forty years before I was born, she was photographed on her way to fetch drinking water at the reservation well. In the picture she is seated high, the reins in her fingers connected to a couple of shaggy fetlocked draft ponies. The barrel she will fill stands behind her. She wears a man's sweater and an expression of vast self-pleasure. She might have been saying *Kaygoh*, a warning, to calm the horses. She might have been speaking to whomever it was who held the camera, still a novel luxury.

Virginia Grandbois was known to smell of flowers. In spite of the potato picking, water hauling, field and housework, she found the time and will to dust her face with pale powder, in order to look more French. She was the great-great-granddaughter of the daughter of the principal leader of the *A-waus-e*, the Bullhead clan, a woman whose real name was never recorded but who, on marrying a Frenchman, was "recreated" as Madame Cadotte. It was Madame Cadotte who acted as a liaison between her Ojibway relatives and her husband so that, even when French influence waned in the region, Jean-Baptiste Cadotte stayed on as the only trader of importance, the last governor of the fort at Sault St. Marie.

By the time I knew Virginia Grandbois, however, her mind had darkened, and her body deepened, shrunk, turned to bones and leather. She did not live in the present or in any known time at all. Periodically, she would awaken from dim and unknown dreams to find herself seated behind the door in her daughter's house. She then cried out for her cart and her horses. When they did not materialize, Virginia Grandbois rose with great energy and purpose. Then she walked towards her house, taking the straightest line.

That house, long sold and gone, lay over one hundred miles due east and still Virginia Grandbois charged ahead, no matter what lay in her path—fences, sloughs, woods, the yards of other families. She wanted home, to get home, to be home. She wanted her own place back, the place she had made, not her daughter's, not anyone else's. Hers. There was no substitute, no kindness, no reality that would change her mind. She had to be tied to the chair, and the chair to the wall, and still there was no reasoning with Virginia Grandbois. Her entire life, her hard-won personality, boiled down in the end to one stubborn, fixed, desperate idea.

I started with the same idea—this urge to get home, even if I must walk straight across the world. Only, for me, the urge to walk is the urge to write. Like my great-grandmother's house, there is no home for me to get to. A mixed-blood, raised in the Sugarbeet Capital, educated on the

Eastern seaboard, married in a tiny New England village, living now on a ridge directly across from the Swan Range in the Rocky Mountains, my home is a collection of homes, of wells in which the quiet of experience shales away into sweet bedrock.

Elise Eliza pieced the quilt my mother slept under, a patchwork of shirts, pants, other worn-out scraps, bordered with small rinsed and pressed Bull Durham sacks. As if in another time and place, although it is only the dim barrel of a four-year-old's memory, I see myself lying wrapped under smoky quilts and dank green army blankets in the house in which my mother was born. In the fragrance of tobacco, some smoked in home-rolled cigarettes, some offered to the Manitous whose presence still was honored, I dream myself home. Beneath the rafters, shadowed with bunches of plants and torn calendars, in the nest of a sagging bed, I listen to mice rustle and the scratch of an owl's claws as it paces the shingles.

Elise Eliza's daughter-in-law, my grandmother Mary LeFavor, kept that house of hand-hewed and stacked beams, mudded between. She managed to shore it up and keep it standing by stuffing every new crack with disposable diapers. Having used and reused cloth to diaper her own children, my grandmother washed and hung to dry the paper and plastic diapers that her granddaughters bought for her great-grandchildren. When their plastic-paper shredded, she gathered them carefully together and one day, on a summer visit, I woke early to find her tamping the rolled stuff carefully into the cracked walls of that old house.

It is autumn in the Plains, and in the little sloughs ducks land, and mudhens, whose flesh always tastes greasy and charred. Snow is coming soon, and after its first fall there will be a short, false warmth that brings out the sweet-sour odor of highbush cranberries. As a descendent of the women who skinned buffalo and tanned and smoked the hides, of women who pounded berries with the dried meat to make winter food, who made tea from willow bark and rosehips, who gathered snakeroot, I am affected by the change of seasons. Here is a time when plants consolidate their tonic and drop seed, when animals store energy and grow thick fur. As for me, I start keeping longer hours, writing more, working harder, though I am obviously not a creature of a traditional Anishinabe culture. I was not raised speaking the old language, or adhering to the cycle of religious ceremonies that govern the Anishinabe spiritual relationship to the land and the moral order within human configurations. As the wedding of many backgrounds, I am free to do what simply feels right.

My mother knits, sews, cans, dries food and preserves it. She knows how to gather tea, berries, snare rabbits, milk cows, and churn butter. She can grow squash and melons from seeds she gathered the fall before. She is, as were the women who came before me, a repository of all of the homey virtues, and I am the first in a long line who has not saved the autumn's harvest in birch bark *makuks* and skin bags and in a cellar dry and cold with dust. I am the first who scratches the ground for pleasure, not survival, and grows flowers instead of potatoes. I record rather than practice the arts that filled the hands and days of my mother and her mother, and all the mothers going back into the shadows, when women wore names that told us who they were.

===

FOR STUDY AND DISCUSSION

1. The men of Erdrich's Native American ancestry also bore descriptive names. Why, in your opinion, does she focus on the women? Note especially the language of the opening paragraph.

2. Reread the long paragraph in which Erdrich lists Anishinabe names and imagines the women who bore them. What is the impact of listing so many? Of what value are these names to a descendant removed by several generations?

3. Remember that Erdrich is primarily a novelist and poet; how does she use language to explore this lost culture?

4. What happened to the names of Native American women after the arrival of Europeans? What was ironic about the name changes, and what was lost by them? (You might want to refer to Edite Cunha's essay, "Talking in the New Land," in Part One.)

5. Of what significance, both cultural and personal, were the carts that belonged to Erdrich's great-grandmothers?

29

Men, Women, Computers

Barbara Kantrowitz

Computers have affected every aspect of modern life, from our way of gathering and disseminating information to our use of language to the way we think about ourselves and our culture. In the following essay, first published in Newsweek *in May of 1994, editor, author, and journalist Barbara Kantrowitz describes some differences in the ways men and women approach computers, applying linguistic knowledge about men's and women's differing goals and techniques in communication to their use of this communications tool.*

Like other means of communication, the computer is both a reflection and a product of our culture. Here Kantrowitz focuses on the way in which cultural concepts of maleness and femaleness are carried into the world of computers.

As a longtime *Star Trek* devotee, Janis Cortese was eager to be part of the Trekkie discussion group on the Internet. But when she first logged on, Cortese noticed that these fans of the final frontier devoted megabytes to such profound topics as whether Troi or Crusher had bigger breasts. In other words, the purveyors of this "Trek" dreck were all *guys*. Undeterred, Cortese, a physicist at California's Loma Linda University, figured she'd add perspective to the electronic gathering place with her own momentous questions. Why was the male cast racially diverse while almost all the females were young, white, and skinny? Then, she tossed in a few lustful thoughts about the male crew members.

After those seemingly innocuous observations, "I was chased off the net by rabid hounds," recalls Cortese. Before she could say "Fire phasers," the Trekkies had flooded her electronic mailbox with nasty messages—a practice called "flaming." Cortese retreated into her own galaxy by starting the all-female Starfleet Ladies Auxiliary and Embroidery/Baking Society. The private electronic forum, based in Houston, now has more than forty members, including psychologists, physicians, students, and secretaries. They started with Trektalk, but often chose to beam down and go where no man had ever wandered before—into the personal mode. When Julia Kosatka, a Houston computer scientist, got pregnant last year, she shared her thoughts with the group on weight gain, sex while expecting, and everything else on her mind. Says Kosatka: "I'm part of one of the longest-running slumber parties in history."

From the Internet to Silicon Valley to the PC sitting in the family room, men and women often seem like two chips that pass in the night. Sure, there are women who spout techno-speak in their sleep and plenty of men who think a hard drive means four hours on the freeway. But in general, computer culture is created, defined, and controlled by men. Women often feel about as welcome as a system crash.

About a third of American families have at least one computer, but most of those are purchased and used by males. It may be new technology, but the old rules still apply. In part, it's that male-machine bonding thing, reincarnated in the digital age. "Men tend to be seduced by the technology itself," says Oliver Strimpel, executive director of The Computer Museum in Boston. "They tend to get into the faster-race-car syndrome," bragging about the size of their discs or the speed of their microprocessors. To the truly besotted, computers are a virtual religion, complete with icons (on-screen graphics), relics (obsolete programs and machines), and prophets (Microsoft's Bill Gates, outlaw hackers). This is not something to be trifled with by mere . . . females, who seem to think that machines were meant to be *used*, like the microwave oven or the dishwasher. Interesting and convenient on the job but not worthy of obsession. Esther Dyson, editor of *Release 1.0*, an influential software-industry newsletter, has been following the computer field for two decades. Yet when she looks at her own computer, Dyson says she still doesn't "really care about its innards. I just want it to work."

Blame (a) culture, (b) family, (c) schools, (d) all of the above. Little boys are expected to roll around in the dirt and explore. Perfect training for learning to use computers, which often requires hours in front of the screen trying to figure out the messy arcanum of a particular program. Girls get subtle messages—from society if not from their parents—that they should keep their hands clean and play with their dolls. Too often, they're discouraged from taking science and math—not just by their schools but by parents as well (how many mothers have patted their daughters on the head and reassured them: "Oh, I wasn't good at math, either").

The gender gap is real and takes many forms.

BARBIE VERSUS NINTENDO

Girls' technophobia begins early. Last summer, Sarah Douglas, a University of Oregon computer-science professor, took part in a job fair for teenage girls that was supposed to introduce them to nontraditional occupations. With great expectations, she set up her computer and loaded it with interesting programs. Not a single girl stopped by. When she asked why, the girls "told me computers were something their dads and their brothers used," Douglas sadly recalls. "Computer science is a very male profession. . . . When girls get involved in that male world, they are pushed away and belittled. Pretty soon, the girls get frustrated and drop out."

Computer games usually involve lots of shooting and dying. Boy stuff. What's out there for girls? "If you walk down the street and look in the computer store, you will see primarily male people as sales staff and as customers," says Jo Sanders, director of the gender-equity program at the Center for Advanced Study in Education at the City University of New York Graduate Center.

Boys and girls are equally interested in computers until about the fifth grade, says University of Minnesota sociologist Ronald Anderson, who coauthored the recent report "Computers in American Schools." At that point, boys' use rises significantly and girls' use drops, Anderson says, probably because sex-role identification really kicks in. Many girls quickly put computers on the list of not-quite-feminine topics, like car engines and baseball batting averages. It didn't have to be this way. The very first computer programmer was a woman, Ada Lovelace, who worked with Charles Babbage on his mechanical computing machines in the mid-1800s. If she had become a role model, maybe hundreds of thousands of girls would have spent their teenage years locked in their bedrooms staring at screens. Instead, too many are doing their nails or worrying about their hair, says Marcelline Barron, an administrator at the Illinois Mathematics and Science Academy, a publicly funded coed boarding school for gifted students. "You're not thinking about calculus or physics when you're thinking about that," says Barron. "We have these kinds of expectations for young girls. They must be neat, they must be clean, they must be quiet."

Despite great strides by women in other formerly male fields, such as law and medicine, women are turning away from the computer industry. Men earning computer-science degrees outnumber women 3 to 1 and the gap is growing, according to the National Science Foundation. Fifteen years ago, when computers were still new in schools, they hadn't yet been defined as so exclusively male. But now girls have gotten the message. It's not just the technical and cultural barrier. Sherry Turkle, a Massachusetts Institute of Technology sociologist who teaches a course on women and computers, says that computers have come to stand for "a world without emotion," an image that seems to scare off girls more than boys.

In the past decade, videogames have become a gateway to technology for many boys, but game manufacturers say few girls are attracted to these small-screen shoot-'em-ups. It's not surprising that the vast majority of videogame designers are men. They don't call it Game *Boy* for nothing. Now some manufacturers are trying to lure girls. In the next few months, Sega plans to introduce "Berenstein Bears," which will offer players a choice of boy or girl characters. A second game, "Crystal's Pony Tale," involves coloring (there's lots of pink in the background). Neither game requires players to "die," a common videogame device that researchers say girls dislike. Girls also tend to prefer nonlinear games, where there is more than one way to proceed. "There's a whole issue with speaking girls' language," says Michealene Cristini Risley, group director of licensing and character development for Sega. The company would like to hook girls at the age of 4, before they've developed fears of technology.

Girls need freedom to explore and make mistakes. Betsy Zeller, a 37-year-old engineering manager at Silicon Graphics, says that when she discovered computers in college, "I swear I thought I'd seen the face of God." Yet she had to fend off guys who would come into the lab and want to help her work through problems or, worse yet, do them for her. "I would tell them to get lost," she says. "I wanted to do it myself." Most women either asked for or accepted proffered help, just as they are more likely to ask for directions when lost in a strange city. That may be the best way to avoid driving in circles for hours, but it's not the best way to learn technical subjects.

Schools are trying a number of approaches to interest girls in computers. Douglas and her colleagues are participating in a mentorship program where undergraduate girls spend a summer working with female computer scientists. Studies have shown that girls are more attracted to technology if they can work in groups; some schools are experimenting with team projects that require computers but are focused on putting out a product, like a newspaper or pamphlet. At the middle- and high-school level, girls-only computer classes are increasingly popular. Two months ago Roosevelt Middle School in Eugene, Oregon, set up girls-only hours at the computer lab. Games were prohibited and artists were brought in to teach girls how to be more creative with the computer. Students are also learning to use e-mail, which many girls love. Says Debbie Nehl, the computer-lab supervisor: "They see it as high-tech note-passing."

POWER NETWORKS

As a relatively new industry, the leadership of computerdom might be expected to be more gender-diverse. Wrong: few women have advanced beyond middle-management ranks. According to a study conducted last year [1993] by *The San Jose Mercury News*, there are no women CEOs running major computer-manufacturing firms and only a handful running software companies. Even women who have succeeded say they are acutely conscious of the differences between them and their male co-workers. "I don't talk the same as men," says Paula Hawthorn, an executive at Montage Software, in Oakland, California. "I don't get the same credibility." The difference, she says, "is with you all the time."

Women who work in very technical areas, such as programming, are often the loneliest. Anita Borg, a computer-systems researcher, remembers attending a 1987 conference where there were so few women that the only time they ran into each other was in the restroom. Their main topic of discussion: why there were so few women at the conference. That bathroom cabal grew into Systers, an on-line network for women with technical careers. There are now 1,740 women members from 19 countries representing 200 colleges and universities and 150 companies. Systers is part mentoring and part consciousness-raising. One graduate student, for example, talked about how uncomfortable she felt sitting in her shared office when a male graduate student and a professor put a picture of a nude woman on a computer. The problem was resolved when a couple of female faculty members, also on the Systers network, told their offending colleagues that the image was not acceptable.

Women have been more successful in developing software, especially when their focus is products used by children. Jan Davidson, a former teacher, started Davidson & Associates, in Torrance, California, with three programs in 1982. Now it's one of the country's biggest developers of kids' software, with 350 employees and $58.6 million in revenues. Multimedia will bring new opportunities for women. The technology is so specialized that it requires a team—animators, producers, scriptwriters, 3-D modelers—to create state-of-the-art products. It's a far cry from the stereotype of the solitary male programmer, laboring long into the night with only takeout Chinese food for company. At Mary Cron's Rymel Design Group in Palos Verdes, California, most of the software artists and designers are women, Cron says. "It's like a giant puzzle," she adds. "We like stuff we can work on together."

As more women develop software, they may also help create products that will attract women consumers—a huge untapped market. Heidi Roizen, a college English major, cofounded T/Maker Co., in Mountain View, California, a decade ago. She says that because women are often in charge of the family's budget, they are potential consumers of personal-finance programs. Women are also the most likely buyers of education and family-entertainment products, a fast-growing segment of the industry. "Women are more typically the household shopper," Roizen says. "They have tremendous buying power."

WIRED WOMEN

The Infobahn—a.k.a. the Information Superhighway—may be the most hyped phenomenon in history—or it could be the road to the future. In any case, women want to get on. But the sign over the access road says CAUTION, MEN WORKING, WOMEN BEWARE. Despite hundreds of thousands of new users in the last year [1993], men still dominate the Internet and commercial services such as Prodigy or CompuServe. The typical male conversation on line turns off many women. "A lot of the time, to be crude, it's a pissing contest," says Lisa Kimball, a partner in the Meta Network, a Washington, D.C., on-line service that is 40 percent female. Put-downs are an art form. When one woman complained recently in an Internet forum that she didn't like participating because she didn't have time to answer all her e-mail, she was swamped with angry responses, including this one (from a man): "Would you like some cheese with your whine?"

Some men say the on-line hostility comes from resentment over women's slowly entering what has been an almost exclusively male domain. Many male techno-jocks "feel women are intruding into their inner sanctum," says André Bacard, a Silicon Valley, California, technology writer. They're not out to win sensitivity contests. "In the computer world, it's 'Listen, baby, if you don't like it, drop dead,'" says Bacard. "It's the way men talk to guys. Women aren't used to that."

Even under more civilized circumstances, men and women have different conversational styles, says Susan Herring, a University of Texas at Arlington professor who has studied women's participation on computer networks. Herring found that violations of long-established net etiquette—asking too many basic questions, for example—angered men. "The women were much more tolerant of people who didn't know what they were doing," Herring says. "What really annoyed women was the flaming and people boasting. The things that annoy women are things men do all the time."

Like hitting on women. Women have learned to tread their keyboards carefully in chat forums because they often have to fend off sexual advances that would make Bob Packwood blush. When subscribers to America Online enter one of the service's forums, their computer names appear at the top of the screen as a kind of welcome. If they've chosen an obviously female name, chances are they'll soon be bombarded with private messages seeking detailed descriptions of their appearance or sexual preferences. "I couldn't believe it," recalls 55-year-old Eva S. "I said, 'Come on, I'm a grandmother.'"

More and more women are signing on to networks that are either coed and run by women, or are exclusively for women. Stacy Horn started ECHO (for East Coast Hang Out) four years ago because she was frustrated with the hostility on line. About 60 percent of ECHO's 2,000 subscribers are men; among ECHO's 50 forums, only two are strictly for women. "Flaming is nonexistent on ECHO," Horn says. "New women get on line and they see that. And then they're much more likely to jump in." Women's Wire in San Francisco, started in January 1994, has 850 subscribers, only 10 percent of them men—the reverse of most on-line services. "We wanted to design a system in which women would help shape the community and the rules of that community from the floor up," says cofounder Ellen Pack. The official policy is that there is no such thing as a dumb question—and no flaming.

Male subscribers say Women's Wire has been a learning experience for them, too. Maxwell Hoffman, a 41-year-old computer-company manager, says that many men think that only women are overly emotional. But men lose it, too. A typical on-line fight starts with two guys sending "emotionally charged flames going back and forth" through cyberspace (not on Women's Wire). Then it expands and "everybody starts flaming the guy. They scream at each other and they're not listening."

If only men weren't so *emotional*, so *irrational*, could we all get along on the net?

TOYS AND TOOLS

In one intriguing study by the Center for Children and Technology, a New York think tank, men and women in technical fields were asked to dream up machines of the future. Men typically imagined devices that could help them "conquer the universe," says Jan Hawkins, director of the center. She says women wanted machines that met people's needs, "the perfect mother."

Someday, gender-blind education and socialization may render those differences obsolete. But in the meantime, researchers say both visions are useful. If everyone approached technology the way women do now, "we wouldn't be pushing envelopes," says Cornelia Bruner, associate director of the center. "Most women, even those who are technologically sophisticated, think of machines as a means to an end." Men think of the machines as an extension of their own power, as a way to "transcend physical limitations." That may be why they are more likely to come up with great leaps in technology, researchers say. Without that vision, the computer and its attendant industry would not exist.

Ironically, gender differences could help women. "We're at a cultural turning point," says MIT's Turkle. "There's an opportunity to remake the culture around the machine." Practicality is now as valued as invention. If the computer industry wants to put machines in the hands of the masses, that means women—along with the great many men who have no interest in hot-rod computing. An ad campaign for Compaq's popular Presario line emphasizes the machine's utility. After kissing her child good night, the mother in the ad sits down at her Presario to work. As people start to view their machines as creative tools, someday women may be just as comfortable with computers as men are.

FOR STUDY AND DISCUSSION

1. What parallels can be drawn between the observations in this essay and those in Deborah Tannen's article, "'I'll Explain It to You': Lecturing and Listening," about the different conversational goals and techniques used by men and women?

2. How does Kantrowitz explain that men are more likely than women to use, enjoy, and seek careers related to computers? Which of her reasons are primarily cultural? Which have primarily to do with language?

3. Refer to "Literary Metaphors and Other Linguistic Innovations in Computer Language" by Nilsen and Nilsen in Part Three. What words does Kantrowitz add to this vocabulary? How are some of these also used metaphorically?

4. How do electronic forums created and used primarily by women differ from those of men? How do you explain these differences?

5. How do computer games reinforce the gender gap?

6. Why might it be counterproductive for a woman to accept or request help from a man when learning to use a computer?

7. How do men and women generally view the purpose and usefulness of a computer?

8. The world of computers is changing very rapidly. Although this article was written quite recently by literary standards (1994), it cannot reflect the newest thinking in cyberspace. From classes, reading, or your own experience, do you see changes in computer language, gender attitudes, and patterns of use since this article appeared?

Projects for "Gender-Based Language Differences"

1. In his article, John Pfeiffer introduces at least three differences in the communication styles of boys and girls. To observe how girls at different ages communicate, how boys at different ages communicate, and how boys and girls interact in conversation, visit a local school and conduct video sessions. If you don't own video equipment, check with your department or with media services to obtain the use of a video camera.

Select three ages to examine: age five, age ten, and age thirteen. Set up the camera and send your couples into the room with no other instructions than to talk to one another. Show the videotapes to your class. Do you observe any distinct differences in the communication styles of girls and boys? What happened in the mixed groups? What does this tell you about the styles of communication used by men and women?

2. An alternative method to observe the communication styles of men and women is to record conversation groups in your class. Select a topic for debate, and have a tape recorder ready. After the discussion/debate, listen to the tape, record your observations, and analyze your results, keeping in mind such things as length of time talking, interruptions, topics introduced in the conversation, and roles played by members of the group. What do you expect to find? What do you find? Transcribe the tapes. Do you notice anything that went undetected in your initial observations? What do your results tell you about girls and boys, men and women in conversation?

3. A number of popular books have sought to explain and resolve the problems of communication between men and women; prominent among them is John Gray's *Men Are From Mars, Women Are From Venus: A Practical Guide for Improving Communication and Getting What You Want in Your Relationships* (HarperCollins, 1992). Read this or another currently popular book about communication between the sexes. Write an analytical essay in which you explore how the findings of sociologists and linguists are popularized. Are their interpretations valid and/or useful? Why or why not?

4. Visit an elementary school and study the reading textbooks for grades 1 through 3. Analyze these texts for the ratio of (1) male to female characters, (2) male to female pronouns, and (3) male to female characters in proactive roles. Prepare a presentation or write an essay summarizing your findings.

5. Study the distribution of the male and female employees of the college or university you attend. What is the ratio of men to women on the faculty, by position and as a whole? In the administration? On the service staff? How do the salaries differ? Interview a financial officer of the institution to learn how the salary scale is structured. Do inequalities exist between men and women employees?

6. How did the Anishinabe women come by their descriptive names? Did the custom of naming vary from one Native American culture to another? Read and prepare a brief report about Native American practices of naming.

7. If you were to acquire a descriptive name, what would it be, and why? Would the name you choose for yourself bear any similarity to a name someone else might choose for you? Have each member of the class choose a descriptive name and then ask to be named by two other people: a friend and an authority figure from childhood, such as a parent, minister, or teacher. Share your names and the reasons behind them. What did you learn about yourself in the process? This exercise, when done thoughtfully, makes it easier to understand why many Native Americans considered their names to be sacred.

8. The language and cultural imagery of advertisers is extremely sensitive to gender issues. Using recent issues of computer journals (e.g. *InfoWorld*, *PC Magazine*, *Dr. Dobbs Journal*), find several ads with a male bias and several that are gender-neutral. If possible, find ads that clearly are aimed at female consumers. Make copies of these ads and write an essay or prepare a brief illustrated talk discussing the goals and techniques of the advertisers. As an alternative, write two employment ads, one to recruit males for a high-level job in computer technology and one to recruit females. How do the ads differ, and why?

9. Read articles by and about women who have been successful in the field of computers (examples: Esther Dyson, consultant/publisher; Heidi Roizen, founder of T/Maker Co.; Cheryl Currid, consultant/journalist). Why have they been successful; what difficulties have they overcome? Write an essay that defines their trials and explains the reasons for their achievements.

Selected Bibliography

Baron, Dennis. *Grammar and Gender*. Reprint ed. New Haven, CT: Yale University Press, 1987. [Gender differences at the basic levels of language.]

Coates, Jennifer. *Women, Men, and Language: A Sociolinguistic Account of Gender Differences in Language (Studies in Language and Linguistics)*, 2nd ed. New York: Longman Science and Technology, 1993. [Explores history, evidence, causes, and consequences of gender-differentiated language.]

Goodwin, Marjorie Harness. *He-Said-She-Said: Talk as Social Organization among Black Children*, 5th ed. Indianapolis: Indiana University Press, 1990. [A fascinating look at how speech is used to organize within peer groups and how the social lives of children are organized through talk.]

Goueffic, Louise. *Breaking the Patriarchal Code: The Linguistic Basis of Sexual Bias*. Manchester, CT: Knowledge Ideas and Trends, 1996. [Examines language bias in Indo-European languages; lists words showing bias and gives the essentials of explanation.]

Hall, Kira, and Mary Bucholtz, eds. *Gender Articulated: Language and the Socially Constructed Self*. London: Routledge, 1996. [Timely essays related to current cultural power positions.]

Lakoff, Robin T. *Language and Women's Place*. New York: HarperCollins College Division, 1989. [A noted linguist explores sexism in language.]

Lehrer, Adrienne. *Wine and Conversation*, 5th ed. Bloomington: Indiana University Press, 1983. [Fascinating; excellent bibliography.]

Penelope, Julia. *Speaking Freely*. New York: Elsevier Science, 1990. [Argues to reword the English language to help solve gender-based social problems.]

Smith, P.M. *Language, the Sexes, and Society*. Oxford: Blackwell, 1985. [A detailed discussion of sexism in language.]

Tannen, Deborah. *Gender and Discourse*. Oxford: Oxford University Press, 1994. [Scholarly essays on sex-linked and class-linked patterns in language use.]

Thorne, B., C. Kramarae, and N. Henley, eds. *Language, Gender, and Society*. Rowley, MA: Newbury House, 1983. [Essays dealing with aspects of sexism in culture and language.]

Tingley, Judith C. *Genderflex: Men and Women Speaking Each Other's Language at Work*. New York: AMACOM, 1994. [Designed to help men and women in the workplace to be flexible in communication without sacrificing their strengths.]

PART SEVEN

HISTORICAL LINGUISTICS AND LANGUAGE CHANGE

Any living language is in a constant state of change. We are not usually aware of the changes taking place in our language because most of them occur slowly over time. But if we look back at earlier forms of English—Chaucer's *Canterbury Tales*, for example, or the epic poem *Beowulf*—we can see that many significant changes have occurred. The study of the history and development of languages, which often involves comparing different languages, is called *historical* or *comparative linguistics*, and it was the earliest of the diverse areas of linguistics that have developed as fields of study.

The first selection, "Comparative and Historical Linguistics," introduces some basic concepts: the idea that some languages share a common ancestor, and the concepts of reconstruction and the comparative method. Using Grimm's Law as an example, Jeanne H. Herndon illustrates the systematic nature of language change and the key role that phonology plays in understanding such change. The next selection, from the Ohio State University Language Files, discusses theories of the evolution of the Indo-European languages. The two theories complement each other in explaining the relationships among these languages as well as the ways in which these languages changed and spread. In "A Brief History of English," Professor Paul Roberts shows the relationship between historical events and the evolution of English, from the beginnings of Old English around A.D. 600, through Middle English to Early Modern English (1600), outlining the principal characteristics of the language during each of these periods. The first three selections in this part emphasize the gradual, continuous changes that have taken place over the last six or seven thousand years in one language family, Indo-European, and during the last thirteen hundred years in English. In "Language Change: Progress or Decay?" Professor Jean Aitchison concludes that language change is natural, inevitable, and continuous. Aitchison also discusses whether languages, as they change, are progressing or decaying, whether language change is evolutionary, and whether it is socially desirable and/or controllable. In the concluding essay, Professor Julia Falk provides a comprehensive historical overview of the study of language today, all of which increases, as she writes, "the depth of our understanding of what it means to be human."

30

Comparative and Historical Linguistics

Jeanne H. Herndon

Not until the late eighteenth century did language scholars break from traditional Western grammar and begin to look at language in a different way—to study similarities and differences among many languages and to identify patterns of relationships among languages. Their work was entirely descriptive; such objectivity was something new in the Western grammatical tradition. Unfortunately, the work of the great Indian grammarian Pāṇini (fourth century B.C.), who prepared a masterful descriptive grammar of Vedic Sanskrit, was unknown in the West until the beginning of the nineteenth century. In the selection that follows, excerpted from her book A Survey of Modern Grammars, *Professor Jeanne H. Herndon traces the beginnings of comparative and historical linguistics in the eighteenth century and, using Grimm's Law as an example, demonstrates the systematic nature of language change and that these changes can be most clearly traced through comparison of the sound systems of languages.*

In spite of the fact that most [of the early traditional] grammarians relied upon classical grammarians for method and classical languages for criteria of correctness, some new ideas were stirring in the field of language study in the eighteenth century. These new ideas were not to affect the work of school grammarians for several generations. But among these ideas are to be found the roots of a whole new approach to the problem of analyzing and describing language.

Many language scholars had noted similarities between various European languages; some languages had quite clearly developed from one variety or another of provincial Latin. It remained for an Englishman who was not primarily a language scholar to see relationships among the most widely dispersed of those languages that were later to be recognized as the Indo-European family of languages.

Sir William Jones had served in the colonial government of India and while there had studied Sanskrit. In 1786 he wrote of observing similarities between a remarkable number of vocabulary items in Sanskrit and their equivalents in European and Middle Eastern languages. He suggested that all these languages might have "sprung from some common source, which, perhaps, no longer exists."

Investigation of similarities and differences among languages is called *comparative linguistics*. As language scholars began to establish patterns of relationships among languages, their work came to be called *historical linguistics*. (These scholars were interested primarily in relationships among languages; they were concerned with matters of grammar only insofar as these might indicate relationships among languages and not as a matter of establishing rules of correctness.) Their research was simply a matter of gathering data, sorting, and analyzing it. Their view of change was totally objective. They were interested only in what kinds of changes had occurred, not whether these changes were "right" or "wrong," "good" or "bad."

Among the first linguists to make important comparative studies was a Danish scholar named Rasmus Rask, who compared Icelandic and Scandinavian languages and dialects. Another, Jacob Grimm, carried Rask's studies still further and proposed a theory to account for [some of the regular differences in certain sounds which] he found among languages. Out of these and many other similar studies grew the theory that languages not only change gradually, over long periods of time, but that they change systematically and that the changes are best traced through comparison of the sound systems of languages.

The single most sweeping statement of this kind of sound relationship is often referred to as Grimm's Law or the First Germanic Consonant Shift. It is a systematic comparison of the sound systems of Indo-European languages, which both demonstrates the validity of the theory that these languages sprang from a common source and gives a wealth of information about how they are related.

Grimm concentrated, as had his predecessors, on written forms of words. Actually, he had no choice since he dealt with stages of language development long past. The differences he noted and compared were letters and spellings, but the spelling differences came to be recognized as representative of pronunciation or sound differences. Grimm went even further, and in addition to a simple listing and comparing of differences, he proposed an explanation of the orderly nature of the shift.

According to this theory, three whole sets of sounds in an ancestor of the Germanic languages had shifted from their earlier Indo-European pronunciation. [Figure 30.1 shows] the original sounds and how they changed:

1. The sounds *b*, *d*, and *g* became *p*, *t*, and *k*. (There is only one *kind* of change here—three voiced sounds became silent, or voiceless, sounds.)
2. The sounds that began as *p*, *t*, and *k* became *f*, *th*, and *h*. (Again only one kind of change occurred—three "stops" became three "spirants," or sounds where the air is slowed down but not stopped completely.)
3. The history of the third set of sounds is more complex. These had begun as the breathy voiced stops *bh*, *dh*, and *gh* in early stages of Indo-European language development and still remain in Sanskrit. They had developed into similar, but not quite the same, sounds *ph*

or *f, th,* and *h* in later stages of Indo-European language development represented by Latin and Greek. As a part of the Germanic Consonant Shift, this group of sounds shifted to become the voiced stop consonants *b, d,* and *g.* The shift of all three sets of consonant sounds—for speakers of the Germanic parent language only—can be seen as something very like a game of phonetic musical chairs.

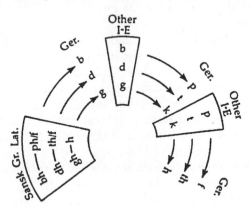

FIGURE 30.1   **Chart of the First Germanic Consonant Shift.**

The boxed letters [in Figure 30.1] represent the sounds that remained in other Indo-European languages; the letters outside the boxes represent the sounds found in Germanic languages as a result of the consonant shift. These correspondences figure prominently in setting the languages derived from the Germanic parent language apart as a distinct branch of the Indo-European family of languages.

These shifts, to repeat, occurred gradually, over very long periods of time. They can be demonstrated by comparing words in a Germanic language, English, which developed after the shift occurred, with items taken from Latin and Greek, languages in which the sounds of these consonants did not shift.

Latin *turba* ⟶ English *thorp*

Latin *dentum* ⟶ English *tooth*

Greek *agros* ⟶ English *acre*

Greek *pous* ⟶ English *foot*

Greek *treis* ⟶ English *three*

Latin *cor* ⟶ English *heart*

Greek *phrater* ⟶ English *brother*

Greek *thygater* ⟶ English *daughter*

Latin *hostis* ⟶ English *guest*

Many words in these languages do not show precisely the same correspondences, but these can be shown to be the result of other shifts or to be related to other factors. Scholars such as Karl Verner noted additional complexities in the nature of the shift and differences resulting from later shifts and proposed theories to explain the apparent "exceptions," until it was possible to trace, in great detail, the development of Indo-European languages over vast stretches of history.

More language samples were gathered, examined, and analyzed; more comparisons were made and new theories proposed. Each new theory could be tested by gathering still more language data and making still more comparisons.

The area of inquiry had been greatly expanded with investigation of Sanskrit and the languages of the Middle East. Sanskrit provided an especially rich body of material for these historical linguists because of the nature of the records open to them. Sanskrit, a literary language of India, had been the subject of grammatical study centuries before Western European scholars had undertaken such investigation of their own languages. As early as the fourth century B.C., an Indian grammarian named Pānini had analyzed Sanskrit and had organized his analysis into a masterful codification of the grammatical units and possible combinations in Sanskrit. For students of historical linguistics, discovery and study of this work were profoundly valuable for two reasons. First, it was a full-fledged grammatical analysis as compared to the fragmentary records of some of the earlier languages they had studied and, second, it represented by far the earliest stage of development of any Indo-European language available to them for study.

Through most of the nineteenth century, linguistic scholarship concentrated primarily on comparative and historical studies. Methods of gathering, classifying, and analyzing data were tested, improved, or discarded, and the improvements tested again.

Comparison of the sound systems of languages was seen to account for only a part of the systematic changes in language. Word forms, inflections, and syntactic differences came to be recognized as important considerations in comparing different stages of the development of languages.

This study of the historical development of a language or languages is sometimes called *diachronic linguistics. Diachronic* is a combination of Greek stems, *dia-* meaning *across*, and *chronos* meaning *time*. For linguists it means that single features of language are traced over long periods of time with changes noted and related to changes in other features of languages over the same periods.

Language researchers gathered data from every nook and cranny of Europe including many dialects peculiar to very small, isolated villages and hamlets. This data led to a major shift of emphasis for some linguists. They moved from the study of historical developments into primary concentration on the similarities and contrasts between contemporary languages and dialects.

After two centuries of enormous amounts of language study, linguists have arrived at some very sweeping theories about the nature of the relationships among the many Indo-European languages. Stated in the simplest possible terms, the important points are these: (1) All these languages developed from a single language which no longer exists. (2) Differences developed when groups of people who spoke this language moved apart and were separated for long periods of time. That is, one group moved into India and their language developed and changed to become Sanskrit; another group moved into southeastern Europe and their language grew into the ancestor of Greek; another group broke off and moved into northern Europe and their language changed in some respects to become the parent language of German, English, Danish, and so on. (3) The fact that all these languages share a common heritage accounts for the fact that some similarities still exist in all of them.

FOR DISCUSSION AND REVIEW

1. What contribution to linguistics did Sir William Jones (1746–1794) make?

2. Describe the attitude of historical (or comparative) linguists toward language change. How does this attitude compare with that held by many popular contemporary writers about language usage (e.g., Edwin Newman and William Safire)?

3. What *kind* of change in language is the most useful to historical linguists? Why?

4. One of the most important characteristics differentiating the Germanic branch of Proto-Indo-European from the languages of all the other branches (see Figure 30.1) is the theory of sound changes called Grimm's Law. Its effects are most easily seen in word-initial sounds. Using the words *tooth, foot,* and *three,* show the effect of Grimm's Law in changing these words from their Latin equivalents.

5. Explain how the following sets of words do or do not illustrate Grimm's Law (note: do not consider *only* initial consonants):

	1	*2*	*3*
Sanskrit	pitar	bhinádmi	bhrátar
Greek	pater	pheídomai	phráter
Latin	pater	findō	fráter
English	father	bite	brother

6. Why was Sanskrit of special importance to early historical linguists?

7. What were the major conclusions of historical linguists concerning the relationships among the many Indo-European languages?

31

The Family Tree and Wave Models

The Ohio State University Language Files

The Indo-European family of languages, of which English is a member, is descended from a prehistoric language, Proto-Indo-European, or Indo-European, which was probably spoken in the fourth millennium B.C. in a region that has not been positively identified. However, we have been able, through the comparative method, to learn a great deal about the phonology, morphology, syntax, and semantics of Indo-European, and— because language is an aspect of culture—about the kind of society that its speakers created. In the following selection, the editors of Language Files *present two popular theories explaining both the relationships among the Indo-European languages and the evolution of their changes and distribution.*

The notion that similar languages are related and descended from an earlier, common language (a protolanguage) goes back to the late eighteenth century when Sir William Jones suggested that the linguistic similarities of Sanskrit to ancient Greek and Latin could best be accounted for by assuming that all three were descended from a common ancestral language. This language was called Proto-Indo-European.

Jones's suggestion was developed in the nineteenth century and gradually came under the influence of Darwin's theory of the evolution of species. Scholars at the time considered language and linguistic development to be analogous in many ways to biological phenomena. Thus, it was suggested that languages, like other living organisms, had "family trees" and "ancestors." A sample "genealogical tree" for the Indo-European (I-E) family of languages appears [in Figure 31.1].

The *family tree theory*, as formulated by August Schleicher in 1871, assumes that languages change in regular, recognizable ways (the *regularity hypothesis*) and that because of this, similarities among languages are due to a "genetic" relationship among those languages (the *relatedness hypothesis*). In order to fill in the particulars of such a relationship, it is necessary to *reconstruct* the hypothetical parent from which the related languages are derived. The principal technique for reconstructing the common ancestor (the protolanguage) of related languages is known as the *comparative method*.

In keeping with the analogy of language relationships to human families, the theory makes use of the terms *mother* (or *parent*), *daughter*,

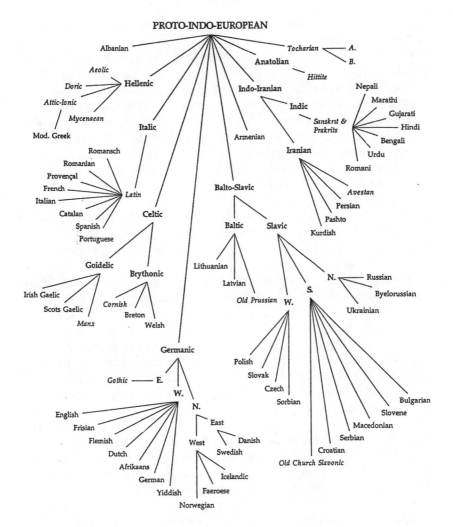

FIGURE 31.1   Indo-European family tree.

Languages that are no longer spoken are italicized (*Cornish*), and language families are in bold-face (**Baltic**). Indo-European Family Tree adapted from Jeffers and Lehiste, *Principles and Methods for Historical Linguistics* (1979), p. 302. © 1979 MIT Press. All rights reserved.

and *sister* languages. In the family tree of I-E, French and Spanish are sisters, both are daughters of Latin; Germanic is the mother of English, and so on. The model clearly shows the direction of change and the relations among languages, the older stages of the languages being located higher in the tree and direct descendants being linked to their ancestors through the straight lines or "branches."

However, a disadvantage exists in that the structure of the family tree may lead people to develop faulty views of two aspects of language change: (1) that each language forms a uniform speech community without internal variation and without contact with its neighbor languages, so that all speakers of Latin, for example, are assumed to have spoken exactly the same way at the time French and Spanish split off; and (2) that the split of a parent language into its daughter languages is a sudden or abrupt occurrence, happening without intermediate stages.

These two views are not supported by the linguistic evidence we have from modern languages. No language is uniform or isolated from others but is always made up of dialects that are still recognized as belonging to the same language, and always shares similarities with other languages in its family, even those belonging to a different subgroup. And as studies of modern language change show, languages do not split apart abruptly but rather drift apart indiscernibly, starting as dialects and ending up as separate languages only after years of gradual change. In fact, the dividing point between two "dialects" and two "languages" is often impossible to locate exactly and is often obscured by nonlinguistic (e.g., political) factors.

To supplement the family tree model and overcome these difficulties, Johannes Schmidt proposed the *wave theory* in 1872. This theory recognizes the gradual spread of change throughout a dialect, language, or a group of languages, much as a wave expands on the surface of a pond from the point where a pebble (i.e., the source of the change) has been tossed in. Dialects are formed by the spread of different changes from different starting points and at different rates; some changes reinforce each other while others only partially overlap or affect only a certain area, much as the waves formed by a scattering of pebbles thrown into a pond may partially overlap. In the wave diagram for I-E [Figure 31.2], the same basic subgroups shown in the family tree are indicated; in addition, however, similarities between various subgroups are also indicated by circles enclosing those languages that share some linguistic feature or set of features, thus cutting across the traditional categories of the family tree. By looking at ever smaller linguistic changes, one can also show the languages within each group and the dialects within each language, indicating clearly how variable languages can be, even though distinct from others. In this way the wave diagram avoids the two faults of the family tree model, though it in turn suffers from disadvantages relating to problems in analyzing the genetic history of the languages displayed.

In fact, neither the family tree model nor the wave model presents entirely adequate or accurate accounts of language change or the relatedness of languages. For example, it is now known that languages can exhibit linguistic similarities without necessarily being related. The similarities may be the result of borrowing from language contact, language drift (that is, independent but identical changes in distinct dialects or languages), similarities in types of morphological structures, syntactic similarities, or other reasons. Nonetheless, the family tree model and the wave model do provide useful frameworks for the discussion of language change.

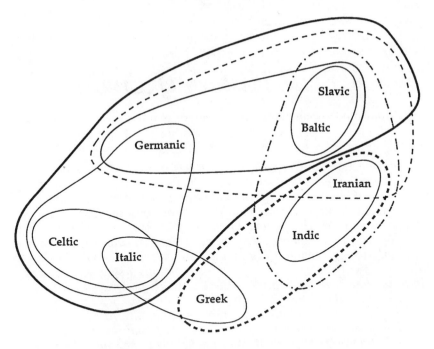

FIGURE 31.2   Indo-European wave diagram.

FOR DISCUSSION AND REVIEW

1. Why is the "family tree theory" so named? What does the family tree theory help to explain?

2. What was found to be inadequate about the family tree theory? How does the wave theory complement the family tree theory?

3. In the wave diagram (Figure 31.2) what is represented by the various lines that enclose languages? Which languages are most closely related, and which are least related?

4. What, if anything, do these two theories leave unexplained about language change?

32

A Brief History of English

Paul Roberts

Earlier selections in this part have discussed how the existence of the Proto-Indo-European language was established through historical reconstuction, and have described the major branches of that language family. In this selection, the late Paul Roberts narrows the focus still more and traces briefly the history of the English language. He places its development in the context of historical events, showing their effects on the language. In general, the grammatical changes from Old English to Modern English have resulted in a change from a synthetic or highly inflected language (like Latin or Russian) to an analytic language, with few inflectional endings and heavy reliance on word order and function words to signal grammatical meaning. Roberts also discusses some of the major changes in pronunciation and vocabulary from Old English through Middle English to Modern English, commenting especially on the effects of the Great Vowel Shift and on the borrowing of large numbers of foreign words that increased the size of the English vocabulary.

No understanding of the English language can be very satisfactory without a notion of the history of the language. But we shall have to make do with just a notion. The history of English is long and complicated, and we can only hit the high spots.

The history of our language begins a little after A.D. 600. Everything before that is pre-history, which means that we can guess at it but can't prove much. For a thousand years or so before the birth of Christ our linguistic ancestors wandered through the forests of northern Europe. Their language was a part of the Germanic branch of the Indo-European Family (see the previous selection).

At the time of the Roman Empire—say, from the beginning of the Christian Era to around A.D. 400—the speakers of what was to become English were scattered along the northern coast of Europe. They spoke a dialect of Low German. More exactly, they spoke several different dialects, since they were several different tribes. The names given to the tribes who got to England are *Angles*, *Saxons*, and *Jutes*. For convenience, we can refer to them as Anglo-Saxons.

Their first contact with civilization was a rather thin acquaintance with the Roman Empire on whose borders they lived. Probably some of the Anglo-Saxons wandered into the Empire occasionally, and certainly

Roman merchants and traders traveled among the tribes. At any rate, this period saw the first of our many borrowings from Latin. Such words as *kettle, wine, cheese, butter, cheap, plum, gem, bishop, church* were borrowed at this time. They show something of the relationship of the Anglo-Saxons with the Romans. The Anglo-Saxons were learning, getting their first taste of civilization.

They still had a long way to go, however, and their first step was to help smash the civilization they were learning from. In the fourth century the Roman power weakened badly. While the Goths were pounding away at the Romans in the Mediterranean countries, their relatives, the Anglo-Saxons, began to attack Britain.

The Romans had been the ruling power in Britain since A.D. 43. They had subjugated the Celts whom they found living there and had succeeded in setting up a Roman administration. The Roman influence did not extend to the outlying parts of the British Isles. In Scotland, Wales, and Ireland the Celts remained free and wild, and they made periodic forays against the Romans in England. Among other defense measures, the Romans built the famous Roman Wall to ward off the tribes in the north.

Even in England the Roman power was thin. Latin did not become the language of the country as it did in Gaul and Spain. The mass of people continued to speak Celtic, with Latin and the Roman civilization it contained in use as a top dressing.

In the fourth century, troubles multiplied for the Romans in Britain. Not only did the untamed tribes of Scotland and Wales grow more and more restive, but the Anglo-Saxons began to make pirate raids on the eastern coast. Furthermore, there was growing difficulty everywhere in the Empire, and the legions in Britain were siphoned off to fight elsewhere. Finally, in A.D. 410, the last Roman ruler in England, bent on becoming emperor, left the islands and took the last of the legions with him. The Celts were left in possession of Britain but almost defenseless against the impending Anglo-Saxon attack.

Not much is surely known about the arrival of the Anglo-Saxons in England. According to the best early source, the eighth-century historian Bede, the Jutes came in 449 in response to a plea from the Celtic king, Vortigern, who wanted their help against the Picts attacking from the north. The Jutes subdued the Picts but then quarreled and fought with Vortigern, and, with reinforcements from the Continent, settled permanently in Kent. Somewhat later the Angles established themselves in eastern England and the Saxons in the south and west. Bede's account is plausible enough, and these were probably the main lines of invasion.

We do know, however, that the Angles, Saxons, and Jutes were a long time securing themselves in England. Fighting went on for as long as a hundred years before the Celts in England were all killed, driven into Wales, or reduced to slavery. This is the period of King Arthur, who was not entirely mythological. He was a Romanized Celt, a general, though probably not a king. He had some success against the Anglo-Saxons, but it was only temporary. By 550 or so the Anglo-Saxons were firmly established. English was in England.

OLD ENGLISH

All this is pre-history, so far as the language is concerned. We have no record of the English language until after 600, when the Anglo-Saxons were converted to Christianity and learned the Latin alphabet. The conversion began, to be precise, in the year 597 and was accomplished within thirty or forty years. The conversion was a great advance for the Anglo-Saxons, not only because of the spiritual benefits but because it reestablished contact with what remained of Roman civilization. This civilization didn't amount to much in the year 600, but it was certainly superior to anything in England up to that time.

It is customary to divide the history of the English language into three periods: Old English, Middle English, and Modern English. Old English runs from the earliest records—i.e., seventh century—to about 1100; Middle English from 1100 to 1450 or 1500; Modern English from 1500 to the present day. Sometimes Modern English is further divided into Early Modern, 1500–1700, and Late Modern, 1700 to the present.

When England came into history, it was divided into several more or less autonomous kingdoms, some of which at times exercised a certain amount of control over the others. In the century after the conversion the most advanced kingdom was Northumbria, the area between the Humber River and the Scottish border. By A.D. 700 the Northumbrians had developed a respectable civilization, the finest in Europe. It is sometimes called the Northumbrian Renaissance, and it was the first of the several renaissances through which Europe struggled upward out of the ruins of the Roman Empire. It was in this period that the best of the Old English literature was written, including the epic poem *Beowulf*.

In the eighth century, Northumbrian power declined, and the center of influence moved southward to Mercia, the kingdom of the Midlands. A century later the center shifted again, and Wessex, the country of the West Saxons, became the leading power. The most famous king of the West Saxons was Alfred the Great, who reigned in the second half of the ninth century, dying in 901. He was famous not only as a military man and administrator but also as a champion of learning. He founded and supported schools and translated or caused to be translated many books from Latin into English. At this time also much of the Northumbrian literature of two centuries earlier was copied in West Saxon. Indeed, the great bulk of Old English writing which has come down to us is in the West Saxon dialect of 900 or later.

In the military sphere, Alfred's great accomplishment was his successful opposition to the Viking invasions. In the ninth and tenth centuries, the Norsemen emerged in their ships from their homelands in Denmark and the Scandinavian peninsula. They traveled far and attacked and plundered at will and almost with impunity. They ravaged Italy and Greece, settled in France, Russia, and Ireland, colonized Iceland and Greenland, and discovered America several centuries before Columbus. Nor did they overlook England.

After many years of hit-and-run raids, the Norsemen landed an army on the east coast of England in the year of 866. There was nothing much to oppose them except the Wessex power led by Alfred. The long struggle ended in 877 with a treaty by which a line was drawn roughly from the northeast of England to the southeast. On the eastern side of the line Norse rule was to prevail. This was called the Danelaw. The western side was to be governed by Wessex.

The linguistic result of all this was a considerable injection of Norse into the English language. Norse was at this time not so different from English as Norwegian or Danish is now. Probably speakers of English could understand, more or less, the language of the newcomers who had moved into eastern England. At any rate, there was considerable interchange and word borrowing. Examples of Norse words in the English language are *sky, give, law, egg, outlaw, leg, ugly, scant, sly, crawl, scowl, take, thrust.* There are hundreds more. We have even borrowed some pronouns from Norse—*they, their,* and *them.* These words were borrowed first by the eastern and northern dialects and then in the course of hundreds of years made their way into English generally.

It is supposed also—indeed, it must be true—that the Norsemen influenced the sound structure and grammar of English. But this is hard to demonstrate in detail.

A Specimen of Old English

We may now have an example of Old English. The favorite illustration is the Lord's Prayer, since it needs no translation. This has come to us in several different versions. Here is one:

> Fæder ure,
> þu þe eart on heofonum,
> si þin nama gehalgod.
> Tobecume þin rice.
> Gewurþe ðin willa on eorðan swa swa on heofonum.
> Urne gedæghwamlican hlaf syle us to dæg.
> And forgyf us ure gyltas, swa swa we forgyfað urum gyltendum.
> And ne gelæd þu us on costnunge,
> ac alys us of yfele. Soþlice.

Some of the differences between this and Modern English are merely differences in orthography. For instance, the sign œ is what Old English writers used for a vowel sound like that in modern *hat* or *and.* The *th* sounds of modern *thin* or *then* are represented in Old English by þ or ð. But of course there are many differences in sound too. *Ure* is the ancestor of modern *our*, but the first vowel was like that in *too* or *ooze*. *Hlaf* is modern *loaf*; we have dropped the *h* sound and changed the vowel, which in *hlaf* was pronounced something like the vowel in *father*. Old English had some sounds which we do not have. The sound represented by *y* does not occur in Modern English. If you pronounce the vowel in *bit* with your lips rounded, you may approach it.

In grammar, Old English was much more highly inflected than Modern English is. That is, there were more case ending for nouns, more person and number endings for verbs, a more complicated pronoun system, various endings for adjectives, and so on. Old English nouns had four cases—nominative, genitive, dative, accusative. Adjectives had five—all these and an instrumental case besides. Present-day English has only two cases for nouns—common case and possessive case. Adjectives now have no case system at all. On the other hand, we now use a more rigid word order and more structure words (prepositions, auxiliaries, and the like) to express relationships than Old English did.

Some of this grammar we can see in the Lord's Prayer. *Heofonum*, for instance, is a dative plural; the nominative singular was *heofon*. *Urne* is an accusative singular; the nominative is *ure*. In *urum gyltendum* both words are dative plural. *Forgyfap* is the first person plural form of the verb. Word order is different: "urne gedæghwamlican hlaf syle us" in place of "Give us our daily bread." And so on.

In vocabulary Old English is quite different from Modern English. Most of the Old English words are what we may call native English: that is, words which have not been borrowed from other languages but which have been part of English ever since English was a part of Indo-European. Old English did certainly contain borrowed words. We have seen that many borrowings were coming in from Norse. Rather large numbers had been borrowed from Latin, too. Some of these were taken while the Anglo-Saxons were still on the Continent (*cheese, butter, bishop, kettle*, etc.); a large number came into English after the conversion (*angel, candle, priest, martyr, radish, oyster, purple, school, spend*, etc.). But the great majority of Old English words were native English.

Now, on the contrary, the majority of words in English are borrowed, taken mostly from Latin and French. Of the words in *The American College Dictionary* only about 14 percent are native. Most of these, to be sure, are common, high-frequency words—*the, of, I, and, because, man, mother, road*, etc.; of the thousand most common words in English, some 62 percent are native English. Even so, the modern vocabulary is very much Latinized and Frenchified. The Old English vocabulary was not.

MIDDLE ENGLISH

Sometime between the years 1000 and 1200 various important changes took place in the structure of English, and Old English became

Middle English. The political event which facilitated these changes was the Norman Conquest. The Normans, as the name shows, came originally from Scandinavia. In the early tenth century they established themselves in northern France, adopted the French language, and developed a vigorous kingdom and a very passable civilization. In the year 1066, led by Duke William, they crossed the Channel and made themselves masters of England. For the next several hundred years, England was ruled by kings whose first language was French.

One might wonder why, after the Norman Conquest, French did not become the national language, replacing English entirely. The reason is that the Conquest was not a national migration, as the earlier Anglo-Saxon invasion had been. Great numbers of Normans came to England, but they came as rulers and landlords. French became the language of the court, the language of the nobility, the language of polite society, the language of literature. But it did not replace English as the language of the people. There must always have been hundreds of towns and villages in which French was never heard except when visitors of high station passed through.

But English, though it survived as the national language, was profoundly changed after the Norman Conquest. Some of the changes—in sound structure and grammar—would no doubt have taken place whether there had been a Conquest or not. Even before 1066 the case system of English nouns and adjectives was becoming simplified; people came to rely more on word order and prepositions than on inflectional endings to communicate their meanings. The process was speeded up by sound changes which caused many of the endings to sound alike. But no doubt the Conquest facilitated the change. German, which didn't experience a Norman Conquest, is today rather highly inflected compared to its cousin English.

But it is in vocabulary that the effects of the Conquest are most obvious. French ceased, after a hundred years or so, to be the native language of very many people in England, but it continued—and continues still—to be a zealously cultivated second language, the mirror of elegance and civilization. When one spoke English, one introduced not only French ideas and French things but also their French names. This was not only easy but socially useful. To pepper one's conversation with French expressions was to show that one was well-bred, elegant, *au courant*. The last sentence shows that the process is not yet dead. By using *au courant* instead of, say, *abreast of things*, the writer indicates that he is no dull clod who knows only English but an elegant person aware of how things are done in *le haut monde*.

Thus French words came into English, all sorts of them. There were words to do with government: *parliament, majesty, treaty, alliance, tax, government*; church words: *parson, sermon, baptism, incense, crucifix, religion*; words for foods: *veal, beef, mutton, bacon, jelly, peach, lemon, cream, biscuit*; colors: *blue, scarlet, vermilion*; household words: *curtain, chair, lamp, towel, blanket, parlor*; play words: *dance, chess,* music, *leisure, conversation*; literary words: *story, romance, poet, literary*; learned words: *study, logic, grammar, noun, surgeon, anatomy, stomach*; just ordinary words of all sorts: *nice, second, very, age, bucket, gentle, final, fault, flower, cry, count, sure, move, surprise, plain.*

All these and thousands more poured into the English vocabulary between 1100 and 1500 until, at the end of that time, many people must have had more French words than English at their command. This is not to say that English became French. English remained English in sound structure and in grammar, though these also felt the ripples of French influence. The very heart of the vocabulary, too, remained English. Most of the high-frequency words—the pronouns, the prepositions, the conjunctions, the auxiliaries, as well as a great many ordinary nouns and verbs and adjectives—were not replaced by borrowings.

Middle English, then, was still a Germanic language, but it differed from Old English in many ways. The sound system and the grammar changed a good deal. Speakers made less use of case systems and other inflectional devices and relied more on word order and structure words to express their meanings. This is often said to be a simplification, but it isn't really. Languages don't become simpler; they merely exchange one kind of complexity for another. Modern English is not a simple language, as any foreign speaker who tries to learn it will hasten to tell you.

For us Middle English is simpler than Old English just because it is closer to Modern English. It takes three or four months at least to learn to read Old English prose and more than that for poetry. But a week of good study should put one in touch with the Middle English poet Chaucer. Indeed, you may be able to make some sense of Chaucer straight off, though you would need instruction in pronunciation to make it sound like poetry. Here is a famous passage from the *General Prologue to the Canterbury Tales*, fourteenth century:

> Ther was also a nonne, a Prioresse,
> That of hir smyling was ful symple and coy,
> Hir gretteste oath was but by Seinte Loy,
> And she was cleped Madame Eglentyne.
> Ful wel she song the service dyvyne,
> Entuned in hir nose ful semely.
> And Frenshe she spak ful faire and fetisly,
> After the scole of Stratford-atte-Bowe,
> For Frenshe of Parys was to hir unknowe.

EARLY MODERN ENGLISH

Sometime between 1400 and 1600 English underwent a couple of sound changes which made the language of Shakespeare quite different from that of Chaucer. Incidentally, these changes contributed much to the chaos in which English spelling now finds itself.

One change was the elimination of a vowel sound in certain unstressed positions at the end of words. For instance, the words *name, stone, wine, dance* were pronounced as two syllables by Chaucer but as just one by Shakespeare. The *e* in these words became, as we say, "silent." But it wasn't silent for Chaucer; it represented a vowel sound. So also the words *laughed, seemed, stored* would have been pronounced by Chaucer as two-syllable words. The change was an important one because it affected thousands of words and gave a different aspect to the whole language.

The other change is what is called the Great Vowel Shift. This was a systematic shifting of half a dozen vowels and diphthongs in stressed syllables. For instance, the word *name* had in Middle English a vowel something like that in the modern word *father; wine* had the vowel of modern *mean; he* was pronounced something like modern *hey; mouse* sounded like *moose; moon* had the vowel of *moan.* Again the shift was thoroughgoing and affected all the words in which these vowel sounds occurred. Since we still keep the Middle English system of spelling these words, the differences between Modern English and Middle English are often more real than apparent.

The vowel shift has meant also that we have come to use an entirely different set of symbols for representing vowel sounds than is used by writers of such languages as French, Italian, or Spanish, in which no such vowel shift occurred. If you come across a strange word—say *bine*—in an English book, you will pronounce it according to the English system, with the vowel of *wine* or *dine.* But if you read *bine* in a French, Italian, or Spanish book, you will pronounce it with the vowel of *mean* or *seen.*

These two changes, then, produced the basic differences between Middle English and Modern English. But there were several other developments that had an effect upon the language. One was the invention of printing, an invention introduced into England by William Caxton in the year 1475. Where before books had been rare and costly, they suddenly became cheap and common. More and more people learned to read and write. This was the first of many advances in communication which have worked to unify languages and to arrest the development of dialect differences, though of course printing affects writing principally rather than speech. Among other things it hastened the standardization of spelling.

The period of Early Modern English—that is, the sixteenth and seventeenth centuries—was also the period of the English Renaissance, when people developed, on the one hand, a keen interest in the past and, on the other hand, a more daring and imaginative view of the future. New ideas multiplied, and new ideas meant new language. The English had grown accustomed to borrowing words from French as a result of the Norman Conquest; now they borrowed from Latin and Greek. As we have seen, English had been raiding Latin from Old English times and before, but now the floodgates really opened, and thousands of words from the classical languages poured in. *Pedestrian, bonus, anatomy, contradict, climax, dictionary, benefit, multiply, exist, paragraph, initiate, scene, inspire* are random examples. Probably the average educated

American today has more words from French in his vocabulary than from native English sources, and more from Latin than from French.

The greatest writer of the Early Modern English period is of course Shakespeare, and the best-known book is the King James Version of the Bible, published in 1611. The Bible (if not Shakespeare) has made many features of Early Modern English perfectly familiar to many people down to present time, even though we do not use these features in present-day speech and writing. For instance, the old pronouns *thou* and *thee* have dropped out of use now, together with their verb forms, but they are still familiar to us in prayer and in Biblical quotations: "Whither thou goest, I will go." Such forms as *hath* and *doth* have been replaced by *has* and *does*; "Goes he hence tonight?" would now be "Is he going away tonight?"; Shakespeare's "Fie, on't, sirrah" would be "Nuts to that, Mac." Still, all these expressions linger with us because of the power of the works in which they occur.

It is not always realized, however, that considerable changes have taken place between Early Modern English and the English of the present day. Shakespearean actors putting on a play speak the words, properly enough, in their modern pronunciation. But it is very doubtful that this pronunciation would be understood at all by Shakespeare. In Shakespeare's time, the word *reason* was pronounced like modern *raisin*; *face* had the sound of modern *glass*; the *l* in *would, should, palm* was pronounced. In these points and a great many others the English language has moved a long way from what it was in 1600.

RECENT DEVELOPMENTS

The history of English since 1700 is filled with many movements and countermovements, of which we can notice only a couple. One of these is the vigorous attempt made in the eighteenth century, and the rather half-hearted attempts made since, to regulate and control the English language. Many people of the eighteenth century, not understanding very well the forces which govern language, proposed to polish and prune and restrict English, which they felt was proliferating too wildly. There was much talk of an academy which would rule on what people could and could not say and write. The academy never came into being, but the eighteenth century did succeed in establishing certain attitudes which, though they haven't had much effect on the development of the language itself, have certainly changed the native speaker's feeling about the language.

In part, a product of the wish to fix and establish the language was the development of the dictionary. The first English dictionary was published in 1603; it was a list of 2,500 words briefly defined. Many others were published with gradual improvements until Samuel Johnson published his *English Dictionary* in 1755. This, steadily revised, dominated the field in England for nearly a hundred years. Meanwhile in America,

Noah Webster published his dictionary in 1828, and before long dictionary publishing was a big business in this country. The last century has seen the publication of one great dictionary: the twelve-volume *Oxford English Dictionary*, compiled in the course of seventy-five years through the labors of many scholars. We have also, of course, numerous commercial dictionaries which are as good as the public wants them to be if not, indeed, rather better.

Another product of the eighteenth century was the invention of "English grammar." As English came to replace Latin as the language of scholarship, it was felt that one should also be able to control and dissect it, parse and analyze it, as one could Latin. What happened in practice was that the grammatical description that applied to Latin was removed and superimposed on English. This was silly, because English is an entirely different kind of language, with its own forms and signals and ways of producing meaning. Nevertheless, English grammars on the Latin model were worked out and taught in the schools. In many schools they are still being taught. This activity is not often popular with schoolchildren, but it is sometimes an interesting and instructive exercise in logic. The principal harm in it is that it has tended to keep people from being interested in English and has obscured the real features of English structure.

But probably the most important force on the development of English in the modern period has been the tremendous expansion of English-speaking peoples. In 1500 English was a minor language, spoken by a few people on a small island. Now it is perhaps the greatest language of the world, spoken natively by over a quarter of a billion people and as a second language by many millions more. When we speak of English now, we must specify whether we mean American English, British English, Australian English, Indian English, or what, since the differences are considerable. The American cannot go to England or the English to America confident that he or she will always understand and be understood. The Alabaman in Iowa or the Iowan in Alabama shows himself or herself a foreigner every time he or she speaks. It is only because communication has become fast and easy that English in this period of its expansion has not broken into a dozen mutually unintelligible languages.

FOR DISCUSSION AND REVIEW

1. Roberts describes in some detail the relationships between historical events in England and the development of the English language. Summarize the most important events and comment on their relationship to or effect on the English language.

2. What are the three major periods in the history of English? What are the approximate dates of each? On what bases do linguists make these distinctions?

3. During what period was the epic poem *Beowulf* written? Does Roberts suggest why this period was propitious for the creation of such a work?

4. How did the pronouns *they*, *their*, and *them* come into English? What is unusual about this occurrence?

5. List four important ways in which the grammar of Old English differed from that of Modern English. What was the principal difference between the vocabulary of Old English and that of Modern English?

6. When the Anglo-Saxons invaded England, their language became the language of the land, almost completely obliterating the Celtic that had been spoken by the earlier inhabitants. Why did French not become the language of England after the Norman Conquest? Explain Roberts's statement that "English . . . was profoundly changed after the Norman Conquest".

7. How would you characterize in social terms the French words that were brought into English by the Norman Conquest? In what areas of life did French have the greatest influence?

8. Describe the changes the English language underwent as a result of the Great Vowel Shift. What is the importance of this linguistic phenomenon for Modern English?

9. Identify two significant effects that the invention of printing had on the English language.

10. Early English grammars—indeed, almost all English grammars published before 1950—were modeled on Latin grammars. Why was this the case? List four of the erroneous assumptions in these Latin-based grammars.

33

*Language Change:
Progress or Decay?*

Jean Aitchison

In this chapter from her book Language Change, *Professor Jean Aitchison of Oxford University asserts that <u>language change is "natural, inevitable, and continuous,</u> and involves interwoven sociolinguistic and psycholinguistic factors which cannot easily be disentangled from one another." It is not, she points out, in any sense "wrong for human language to change." In view of these facts, Professor Aitchison raises three questions: "First, is it still relevant to speak of [language] progress or decay? Second, irrespective of whether the move is a forwards or backwards one, are human languages evolving in any detectable direction? Third, even though language change is not wrong in the moral sense, is it socially undesirable, and, if so, can we control it?" Here Professor Aitchison suggests some reasonable answers: (1) language is constantly changing, but it is neither progressing nor decaying; (2) languages are slowly changing (not "evolving" in the usual sense of the word) in different—indeed, sometimes opposite—directions; (3) language change is not wrong, but it may sometimes lead to situations in which speakers of different dialects of the same language have difficulty understanding one another; and (4) although it is impossible to halt such change by passing laws or establishing monitoring "academies," careful language planning may help.*

> If you can look into the seeds of time,
> And say which grain will grow and which will not . . .
>
> WILLIAM SHAKESPEARE, *Macbeth*

Predicting the future depends on understanding the present. The majority of self-proclaimed "experts" who argue that language is disintegrating have not considered the complexity of the factors involved in language change. They are giving rise to a purely emotional expression of their hopes and fears.

A closer look at language change has indicated that it is natural, inevitable, and continuous, and involves interwoven sociolinguistic and psycholinguistic factors which cannot easily be disentangled from one another. It is triggered by social factors, but these social factors make use of existing cracks and gaps in the language structure. In the circumstances, the true direction of a change is not obvious to a superficial observer. Sometimes alterations are disruptive, as with the increasing loss of *t* in British English, where the utilization of a natural tendency to alter or omit final consonants may end up destroying a previously stable stop system. At other times, modifications can be viewed as therapy, as in the loss of *h* in some types of English, which is wiping out an exception in the otherwise symmetrical organization of fricatives.

However, whether changes disrupt the language system, or repair it, the most important point is this: it is in no sense wrong for human language to change, any more than it is wrong for humpback whales to alter their songs every year (Payne 1979). In fact, there are some surprising parallels between the two species. All the whales sing the same song one year, the next year they all sing a new one. But the yearly differences are not random. The songs seem to be evolving. The songs of consecutive years are more alike than those that are separated by several years. When it was first discovered that the songs of humpbacks changed from year to year, a simple explanation seemed likely. Since the whales only sing during the breeding season, and since their song is complex, it was assumed that they simply forgot the song between seasons, and then tried to reconstruct it the next year from fragments which remained in their memory. But when researchers organized a long-term study of humpbacks off the island of Maui in Hawaii, they got a surprise. The song that the whales were singing at the beginning of the new breeding season turned out to be identical to the one used at the end of the previous one. Between breeding seasons, the song had seemingly been kept in cold storage, without change. The songs were gradually modified as the season proceeded. For example, new sequences were sometimes created by joining the beginning and end of consecutive phrases, and omitting the middle part—a procedure not unlike certain human language changes.

Both whales and humans, then, are constantly changing their communication system, and are the only two species in which this has been proved to happen—though some birds are now thought to alter their song in certain ways. Rather than castigating one of these species for allowing change to occur, it seems best to admit that humans are probably programmed by nature to behave in this way. As a character in John Wyndham's novel *Web* says: "Man is a product of nature. . . . Whatever he does, it must be part of his nature to do—or he could not do it. He is not, and cannot be *un*natural. He, with his capacities, is as much the product of nature as were the dinosaurs with theirs. He is an *instrument* of natural processes."

A consideration of the naturalness and inevitability of change leads us to . . . three final questions which need to be discussed. . . . First, is it still relevant to speak of progress or decay? Second, irrespective of whether the move is a forwards or backwards one, are human languages evolving in any detectable direction? Third, even though language change is not wrong in the moral sense, is it socially undesirable, and, if so, can we control it?

Let us consider these matters.

FORWARDS OR BACKWARDS?

"Once, twice, thrice, upon a time, there lived a jungle. This particular jungle started at the bottom and went upwards till it reached the monkeys, who had been waiting years for the trees to reach them, and as soon as they did, the monkeys invented climbing down." The opening paragraph of Spike Milligan's fable *The Story of the Bald Twit Lion* indicates how easy it is to make facts fit one's preferred theory.

This tendency is particularly apparent in past interpretations of the direction of change, where opinions about progress or decay in language have tended to reflect the religious or philosophical preconceptions of their proponents, rather than a detached analysis of the evidence. Let us briefly deal with these preconceptions before looking at the issue itself.

Many nineteenth-century scholars were imbued with sentimental ideas about the "noble savage," and assumed that the current generation was by comparison a race of decadent sinners. They therefore took it for granted that language had declined from a former state of perfection. Restoring this early perfection was viewed as one of the principal goals of comparative historical linguistics: "A principal goal of this science is to reconstruct the full, pure forms of an original stage from the variously disfigured and mutilated forms which are attested in the individual languages," said one scholar (Curtius 1871, in Kiparsky 1972, 35).

This quasi-religious conviction of gradual decline has never entirely died out. But from the mid-nineteenth century onward, a second, opposing viewpoint came into existence alongside the earlier one. Darwin's doctrine of the survival of the fittest and ensuing belief in inevitable progress gradually grew in popularity: "Progress, therefore, is not an accident, but a necessity. . . . It is a part of nature," claimed one nineteenth-century enthusiast (Herbert Spencer, *Social Statics*, 1850). Darwin himself believed that in language "the better, the shorter, the easier forms are constantly gaining the upper hand, and they owe their success to their inherent virtue" (Darwin 1871, in Labov 1972, 273).

The doctrine of the survival of the fittest, in its crudest version, implies that those forms and languages which survive are inevitably better than those which die out. This is unfortunate, since it confuses the notions of progress and decay in language with expansion and decline. As we have seen, expansion and decline reflect political and social situations, not the intrinsic merit or decadence of a language. Today, it is a historical accident that English is so widely spoken in the world. Throughout history, quite different types of language—Latin, Turkish, Chinese, for example—have spread over wide areas. This popularity reflects the military and political strength of these nations, not the worth of their speech. Similarly, Gaelic is dying out because it is being ousted by English, a language with social and political prestige. It is not collapsing because it has got too complicated or strange for people to speak, as has occasionally been maintained.

In order to assess the possible direction of language, then, we need to put aside both quasi-religious beliefs and Darwinian assumptions. The former lead to an illogical idealization of the past, and the latter to the confusion of progress and decay with expansion and decline.

Leaving aside these false trails, we are left with a crucial question: What might we mean by "progress" within language?

The term *progress* implies a movement towards some desired end-point. What could this be, in terms of linguistic excellence? A number of linguists are in no doubt. They endorse the view of Jespersen, who maintained that "that language ranks highest which goes farthest in the art of accomplishing much with little means, or, in other words, which is able to express the greatest amount of meaning with the simplest mechanism" (Mühlhäusler 1979, 151).

If this criterion were taken seriously, we would be obliged to rank pidgins as the most advanced languages. . . . True simplicity seems to be counterbalanced by ambiguity and cumbersomeness. Darwin's confident belief in the "inherent virtue" of shorter and easier forms must be set beside the realization that such forms often result in confusing homonyms, as in the Tok Pisin *hat* for "hot," "hard," "hat," and "heart."

A straightforward simplicity measure then will not necessarily pinpoint the "best" language. A considerable number of other factors must be taken into account, and it is not yet clear which they are, and how they should be assessed. In brief, linguists have been unable to decide on any clear measure of excellence, even though the majority are of the opinion that a language with numerous irregularities should be less highly ranked than one which is economical and transparent. However, preliminary attempts to rank languages in this way have run into a further problem.

A language which is simple and regular in one respect is likely to be complex and confusing in others. There seems to be a trading relationship between the different parts of the grammar which we do not fully understand. This has come out clearly in the work of one researcher who has compared the progress of Turkish and Yugoslav children as they acquired their respective languages (Slobin 1977). Turkish children find it exceptionally easy to learn the inflections of their language, which are remarkably straightforward, and they master the entire system by the age of two. But the youngsters struggle with relative clauses (the equivalent of English clauses beginning with *who, which, that*) until around the age of five. Yugoslav children, on the other hand, have great problems with the inflectional system of Serbo-Croatian, which is "a classic Indo-European synthetic muddle," and they are not competent at manipulating it until around the age of five. Yet they have no problems with Serbo-Croatian relative clauses, which they can normally cope with by the age of two.

Overall, we cannot yet specify satisfactorily just what we mean by a "perfect" language, except in a very broad sense. The most we can do is to note that a certain part of one language may be simpler and therefore perhaps "better" than that of another.

Meanwhile, even if all agreed that a perfectly regular language was the "best," there is no evidence that languages are progressing towards this ultimate goal. Instead, there is a continuous pull between the disruption and restoration of patterns. In this perpetual ebb and flow, it would be a mistake to regard pattern neatening and regularization as a step forwards. Such an occurrence may be no more progressive than the tidying up of a cluttered office. Reorganization simply restores the room to a workable state. Similarly, it would be misleading to assume that pattern disruption was necessarily a backward step. Structural dislocation may be the result of extending the language in some useful way.

We must conclude therefore that language is ebbing and flowing like the tide, but neither progressing nor decaying, as far as we can tell. Disruptive and therapeutic tendencies vie with one another, with neither one totally winning or losing, resulting in a perpetual stalemate. As the famous Russian linguist Roman Jakobson said fifty years ago: "The spirit of equilibrium and the simultaneous tendency towards its rupture constitute the indispensable properties of that whole that is language" (Jakobson 1949, 336; translation in Keiler 1972).

ARE LANGUAGES EVOLVING?

Leaving aside notions of progress and decay, we need to ask one further question. Is there any evidence that languages as a whole are moving in any particular direction in their intrinsic structure? Are they, for example, moving towards a fixed word order, as has sometimes been claimed?

It is clear that languages, even if they are evolving in some identifiable way, are doing so very slowly—otherwise all languages would be rather more similar than they in fact are. However, unfortunately for those who would like to identify some overall drift, the languages of the world seem to be moving in different, often opposite, directions.

For example, over the past two thousand years or so, most Indo-European languages have moved from being SOV (subject-object-verb) languages, to SVO (subject-verb-object) ones. . . . Certain Niger-Congo languages seem to be following a similar path. Yet we cannot regard this as an overall trend, since Mandarin Chinese may be undergoing a change in the opposite direction, from SVO to SOV (Li & Thompson 1974).

During the same period, English and a number of other Indo-European languages have gradually lost their inflections, and moved over to a fixed word order. However, this direction is not inevitable, since Wappo, a Californian Indian language, appears to be doing the reverse, and moving from a system in which grammatical relationships are expressed by word order to one in which they are marked by case endings (Li & Thompson 1976).

A similar variety is seen in the realm of phonology. For example, English, French, and Hindi had the same common ancestor. Nowadays, Hindi has sixteen stop consonants and ten vowels, according to one count. French, on the other hand, has sixteen vowels and six stops. English, meanwhile, has acquired more fricatives than either of these two languages, some of which speakers of French and Hindi find exceptionally difficult to pronounce. Many more such examples could be found.

Overall, then, we must conclude that "the evolution of language as such has never been demonstrated, and the inherent equality of all languages must be maintained on present evidence" (Greenberg 1963).

IS LANGUAGE CHANGE SOCIALLY DESIRABLE?

Let us now turn to the last question, which has two parts. Is language change undesirable? If so, is it controllable?

Social undesirability and moral turpitude are often confused. Yet the two questions can quite often be kept distinct. For example, it is certainly not "wrong" to sleep out in the open. Nevertheless, it is fairly socially inconvenient to have people bedding down wherever they want to, and therefore laws have been passed forbidding people to camp out in, say, Trafalgar Square or Hyde Park in London.

Language change is, we have seen, in no sense wrong. But is it socially undesirable? It is only undesirable when communication gets disrupted. If different groups change a previously unified language in different directions, or if one group alters its speech more radically than another, mutual intelligibility may be impaired or even destroyed. In Tok Pisin, for example, speakers from rural areas have great difficulty in understanding the urbanized varieties. This is an unhappy and socially inconvenient state of affairs.

In England, on the other hand, the problem is minimal. There are relatively few speakers of British English who cannot understand one another. This is because most people speak the same basic dialect, in the sense that the rules underlying their utterances and vocabulary are fairly much the same. They are likely, however, to speak this single dialect with different accents. There is nothing wrong with this, as long as people can communicate satisfactorily with one another. An accent which differs markedly from those around may be hard for others to comprehend, and is therefore likely to be a disadvantage in job-hunting situations. But a mild degree of regional variation is probably a mark of individuality to be encouraged rather than stamped out.

A number of people censure the variety of regional accents in England, maintaining that the accent that was originally of one particular area, London and the south-east, is "better" than the others. In fact, speakers from this locality sometimes claim that they speak English *without* an accent, something which is actually impossible. It is sometimes socially useful in England to be able to speak the accent of so-called Southern British English, an accent sometimes spoken of as Received Pronunciation (RP), which has spread to the educated classes throughout the country. But there is no logical reason behind the disapproval of regional accents. Moreover, such objections are by no means universal. Some people regard them as a sign of "genuineness." And in America, a regional accent is simply a mark of where you are from, with no stigma attached, for the most part.

Accent differences, then, are not a matter of great concern. More worrying are instances where differing dialects cause unintelligibility, or misunderstandings. In the past, this often used to be the case in England. Caxton, writing in the fifteenth century, notes that "comyn englysshe that is spoken in one shyre varyeth from another" (Caxton, preface to *Erydos*, 1490). To illustrate his point, he narrates an episode concerning a ship which was stranded in the Thames for lack of wind, and put into shore for refreshment. One of the merchants on board went to a nearby house, and asked, in English, for meat and eggs. The lady of the house, much to this gentleman's indignation, replied that she could not speak French! In Caxton's words, the merchant "cam in to an hows and axed for mete and specyally he axyd after eggys. And the good wyf answerde that she coude speke no frenshe. And the merchaunt was angry for he also coude speke no frenshe, but wolde haue hadde egges and she vnderstode hym not." The problem in this case was that a "new" Norse word *egges* "eggs" was in the process of replacing the Old English word *eyren*, but was not yet generally understood.

Unfortunately, such misunderstandings did not disappear with the fifteenth century. Even though, in both America and England, the majority of speakers are mutually intelligible, worrying misunderstandings still occur through dialect differences. Consider the conversation between Samuel, a five-year-old African American boy from West Philadelphia, and Paul, a white psychologist who had been working in Samuel's school for six months:

SAMUEL: I been know your name.
PAUL: What?
SAMUEL: I been know your name.
PAUL: You better know my name?
SAMUEL: I *been* know your name. (Labov 1972a, 62).

Paul failed to realize that in Philadelphia's black community *been* means "for a long time." Samuel meant, "I have known your name for a long time." In some circumstances, this use of *been* can be completely misleading to a white speaker. A black Philadelphian who said *I been married* would in fact mean "I have been married for a long time." But a white speaker would normally interpret her sentence as meaning "I have been married, but I am not married any longer."

Is it possible to do anything about situations where differences caused by language change threaten to disrupt the mutual comprehension and cohesion of a population? Should language change be stopped?

If legislators decide that something is socially inconvenient, then their next task is to decide whether it is possible to take effective action against it. If we attempted to halt language change by law, would the result be as effective as forbidding people to camp in Trafalgar Square? Or would it be as useless as telling the pigeons there not to roost around the fountains? Judging by the experience of the French, who have an academy, the Académie Française, which adjudicates over matters of linguistic usage, and whose findings have been made law in some cases, the result is a waste of time. Even though there may be some limited effect on the written language, spoken French appears not to have responded in any noticeable way.

If legal sanctions are impractical, how can mutual comprehension be brought about or maintained? The answer is not to attempt to limit change, which is probably impossible, but to ensure that all members of the population have at least one common language, and one common variety of that language, which they can mutually use. The standard language may be the only one spoken by certain people. Others will retain their own regional dialect or language alongside the standard one. This is the situation in the British Isles, where some Londoners, for example, speak only standard British English. In Wales, however, there are a number of people who are equally fluent in Welsh and English.

The imposition of a standard language cannot be brought about by force. Sometimes it occurs spontaneously, as has happened in England. At other times, conscious intervention is required. Such social planning requires tact and skill. In order for a policy to achieve acceptance, a population must *want* to speak a particular language or particular variety of it. A branch of sociolinguistics known as "language planning" or, more recently, "language engineering," is attempting to solve the practical and theoretical problems involved in such attempts (Fasold 1984; Lowenberg 1988; Cooper 1982; Milroy & Milroy 1985).

Once standardization has occurred, and a whole population has accepted one particular variety as standard, it becomes a strong unifying force and often a source of national pride and symbol of independence.

GREAT PERMITTERS

Perhaps we need one final comment about "Great Permitters"—a term coined by William Safire, who writes a column about language for the *New York Times* (Safire 1980; Greenbaum 1988, 11-12). "These are intelligent, determined people, often writers, who care about clarity and precision, who detest fuzziness of expression that reveals sloppiness or laziness of thought." They want to give any changes which occur "a shove in the direction of freshness and precision," and are "willing to struggle to preserve the clarity and color in the language." In other words, they are prepared to accept new usages which they regard as advantageous, and are prepared to battle against those which seem sloppy or pointless.

Such an aim is admirable. An influential writer-journalist can clearly make interesting suggestions, and provide models for others to follow. Two points need to be made, however. First, however hard a "linguistic activist" (as Safire calls himself) works, he is unlikely to reverse a strong trend, however much he would like to. Safire has, for example, given up his fight against *hopefully*, and also against *viable*, which, he regretfully admits, "cannot be killed." Second, and perhaps more important, we need to realize how personal and how idiosyncratic are judgments as to what is "good" and what is "bad," even when they are made by a careful and knowledgeable writer, as becomes clear from the often furious letters which follow Safire's pronouncements in the *New York Times*. Even a Safire fan must admit that he holds a number of opinions which are based on nothing more than a subjective feeling about the words in question. Why, for example, did he give up the struggle against *hopefully*, but continue to wage war on *clearly*? As one of his correspondents notes, "Your grudge against *clearly* is unclear to me." Similarly, Safire attacks ex-President Carter's "needless substitution of encrypt for encode," but is sharply reminded by a reader that "the words *encrypt* and *encode* have very distinct meanings for a cryptographer." These, and other similar examples, show that attempts of caring persons to look after a language can mean no more than the preservation of personal preferences which may not agree with the views of others.

Linguistic activists of the Safire type are laudable in one sense, in that they are aware of language and pay attention to it. But, it has been suggested, they may overall be harmful, in that they divert attention away from more important linguistic issues. The manipulation of people's lives by skillful use of language is something which happens in numerous parts of the world. "Nukespeak," language which is used to refer to nuclear devices, is one much publicized example (Aubrey 1982; Chilton 1985; Hilgartner, Bell, & O'Connor 1983). We do not nowadays hear very much about *nuclear bombs* or *nuclear weapons*. Politicians tend to refer to them as *nuclear deterrents* or *nuclear shields*. Recently, other deadly Star Wars weapons have been referred to as *assets* (Ayto, 1989). Whether or not these devices are useful possessions is not the issue here. The important point is that their potential danger is simply not realized by many people because of the soothing language intentionally used to describe them. In the long run, it may be more important to detect manipulation of this type, than to worry about whether the word *media* should be treated as singular or plural.

SUMMARY AND CONCLUSION

Continual language change is natural and inevitable, and is due to a combination of psycholinguistic and sociolinguistic factors.

Once we have stripped away religious and philosophical preconceptions, there is no evidence that language is either progressing or decaying. Disruption and therapy seem to balance one another in a perpetual stalemate. These two opposing pulls are an essential characteristic of language.

Furthermore, there is no evidence that languages are moving in any particular direction from the point of view of language structure—several are moving in contrary directions.

Language change is in no sense wrong, but it may, in certain circumstances, be socially undesirable. Minor variations in pronunciations from region to region are unimportant, but change which disrupts the mutual intelligibility of a community can be socially and politically inconvenient. If this happens, it may be useful to encourage standardization—the adoption of a standard variety of one particular language which everybody will be able to use, alongside the existing regional dialects or languages. Such a situation must be brought about gradually, with tact and care, since a population will only adopt a language or dialect it *wants* to speak.

Finally, it is always possible that language is developing in some mysterious fashion that linguists have not yet identified. Only time and further research will tell. There is much more to be discovered.

But we may finish on a note of optimism. We no longer, like Caxton in the fifteenth century, attribute language change to the domination of man's affairs by the moon:

> And certaynly our langage now vsed varyeth ferre from that which was vsed and spoken whan I was borne. For we englysshe men ben borne vnder the domynacyon of the mone, which is neuer stedfaste but euer wauerynge wexynge one season and waneth and dycreaseth another season (Caxton, preface to *Erydos*, 1490).

Instead, step by step, we are coming to an understanding of the social and psychological factors underlying language change. As the years go by, we hope gradually to increase this knowledge. In the words of the nineteenth-century poet Alfred Lord Tennyson:

> Science moves, but slowly slowly, creeping on from point to point.

BIBLIOGRAPHY

Aubrey, C. *Nukespeak: The Media and the Bomb.* London: Comedia Publishing Group, 1982.

Ayto, J. *The Longman Register of New Words.* London: Longman, 1989.

Bell, R. *Sociolinguistics: Goals, Approaches, and Problems.* London: Batsford, 1976.

Chilton, P., ed. *Language and the Nuclear Arms Debate: Nukespeak Today.* London: Frances Pinter, 1985.

Cooper, R. L. *Language Spread: Studies in Diffusion and Social Change.* Bloomington: Indiana University Press, 1982.

Fasold, R. *The Sociolinguistics of Society.* Oxford: Basil Blackwell, 1984.

Greenbaum, S. *Good English and the Grammarian.* London: Longman, 1988.

Greenberg, J. H. *Essays in Linguistics.* Chicago: University Press; Phoenix Books edition, 1963.

Hilgartner, S., R. C. Bell, and R. O'Connor. *Nukespeak: The Selling of Nuclear Technology in America.* Harmondsworth, Middx: Penguin, 1983.

Keiler, A. R., ed. *A Reader in Historical and Comparative Linguistics.* New York: Holt, Rinehart and Winston, 1972.

Kiparsky, P. "From Paleogrammarians to Neogrammarians." *York Papers in Linguistics* 2 (1972), 33–43.

Labov, W. *Sociolinguistic Patterns.* Philadelphia: University of Pennsylvania Press, 1972.

———. "Where Do Grammars Stop?" Ed. R. W. Shuy. *Sociolinguistics: Current Trends and Prospects,* 23rd Annual Round Table Meeting, Georgetown University School of Languages and Linguistics. Washington, DC: Georgetown University Press, 1972.

Li, C. N., and S. A. Thompson. "Historical Change of Word Order: A Case Study of Chinese and Its Implications." Ed. J. M. Anderson and C. Jones. *Historical Linguistics.* Amsterdam: North Holland, 1974.

———. "Strategies for Signaling Grammatical Relations in Wappo." *Papers from the Twelfth Regional Meeting.* Chicago: Chicago Linguistic Society, 1976.

Lowenberg, P. H., ed. *Language Spread and Language Policy: Issues, Implications and Case Studies.* Washington, DC: Georgetown University Press, 1988.

Milroy, J. and L. Milroy. *Authority in Language: Investigating Language Prescription and Standardisation.* London: Routledge & Kegan Paul, 1985.

Mühlhäusler, P. *Growth and Structure of the Lexicon of New Guinea Pidgin,* Pacific Linguistics C-52. Canberra: Australian National University, 1979.

Payne, R. "Humpbacks: Their Mysterious Songs." *National Geographic* 155, 1 (January 1979), 18–25.

Safire, W. *On Language.* New York: Times Books, 1980.

Slobin, D. I. "Language Change in Childhood and History." *Language Learning and Thought.* Ed. J. MacNamara. New York: Academic Press, 1977.

FOR DISCUSSION AND REVIEW

1. What point about human language does Aitchison make by describing the songs of humpback whales?

2. What was the attitude of the early historical linguists toward language change? How did Darwin's doctrine of survival of the fittest affect linguists' attitudes?

3. Explain three criteria that might be used to measure "progress" in language. Are these criteria completely satisfactory? Why or why not?

4. Describe four of the very slow changes that are occurring in the world's languages, noting especially instances in which languages seem to be evolving in different or opposite directions. In your description, consider such things as word order, inflections, and phonology.

5. Drawing upon you own experience, describe an instance in which "differing dialects cause[d] unintelligibility, or misunderstandings."

6. Summarize Aitchison's conclusions about the "Great Permitters."

34

To Be Human:
A History of the Study
of Language

Julia S. Falk

Julia S. Falk is professor of linguistics at Michigan State University, where she has taught since 1966. The author of many articles on various aspects of language study, Falk is the author of Linguistics and Language: A Survey of Basic Concepts and Implications. *In the following essay, written especially for this book, Falk presents an overview of the history of language study. She investigates the use of language as the quality that separates us from all other creatures and makes us essentially human. She examines the contributing roles played by the Greeks, the Stoics, and the Christian church, as well as the influences of individuals such as Dionysius Thrax and "speculative grammarians" in the growth and development of our understanding of language. She also explores complicated areas of language study in the United States in fields such as dialect study, generative grammar, psycholinguistics, and sociolinguistics. At every point, Falk acknowledges the controversial and continually changing world of knowledge about human language and its study.*

To be human is to be capable of reason, to exercise free will, to have the ability to solve mathematical problems, to possess a visual system that perceives depth, color, and movement in particular ways, but, above all, to be human is to have language.

More than two millennia have passed since the Athenian Isocrates (436–338 B.C.) identified language as the characteristic that distinguishes human beings from other animals: "In most of our abilities we differ not at all from the animals; we are in fact behind many in swiftness and strength and other resources. But because there is born in us the power to persuade each other and to show ourselves whatever we wish, we not only have escaped from living as brutes, but also by coming together have founded cities and set up laws and invented arts, and speech has helped us attain practically all the things we have devised" (Harris and Taylor 1997, xiii). The same theme appears in the seventh-century writings of Isidore of Seville (c. 560–636): "No human beings are so idle as to be ignorant of their own language when they live among their own people. For what else could be thought of such a man or woman, than that he or she is worse than the brute animals?" (adapted from a quotation in Dinneen 1967, 149). A thousand years later, René Descartes (1596–1650) made the point: "It is a very remarkable fact that there are none so depraved and stupid . . . that they cannot arrange different words together, forming of them a statement by which they make known their thoughts; while, on the other hand, there is no other animal, however perfect and fortunately circumstanced it may be, which can do the same" (Chomsky 1966, 4).

It is virtually impossible to imagine a human culture, a human society, that is entirely indifferent to language. We preserve our heritage through language, maintaining libraries and archives for written documents, retelling stories and legends as oral history. In all aspects of our lives, from infancy until death, we interact with other human beings through language. If "intelligent life" exists elsewhere in the universe, we expect to find language there, perhaps not exactly like the languages of Earth, but similar enough so that, with some effort, we might even be able to communicate. When we say that language is universal, we presume that it is literally so.

Language is an integral part of human nature, and, as such, it has been a subject of human study in every part of the world and in every period of recorded history. When we seek knowledge about human language, we seek knowledge about ourselves, as individuals and as members of the human species. What is it that we want to know? Throughout the centuries, recurring themes have included connections between language and the natural world, including questions on the origin of language; the relationship between languages and the cultures in which they are spoken; the uses of language in literature and in speech; the place of language in philosophy; the role of language in science; how to describe a language; how to learn one. Most of all, we want to know what language is. What is the nature of language? What are its properties? How does it work? What is common to all languages? By how much and in what ways do languages differ from one another? Why and how do languages change over time and from one place to another?

To some of these questions, modern linguists believe there are satisfactory answers. With others, we continue the search for understanding, at this point in our own lives and at this point in human history.

LANGUAGE AND NATURE

The formal intellectual history of Europe and the Americas is rooted in ancient Greece with traditions of recorded scholarship beginning there some 2,500 years ago and continuing without pause until our own time. Other cultures and traditions have also influenced the evolution of our understanding of language. The study of language in ancient India, for example, significantly affected European scholarship at the beginning of the nineteenth century, and we will discuss it when we reach that point. But to find the sources of many of our contemporary views and beliefs about language, we must begin with the extensive inquiries conducted by the Greeks. Readers who would like more detailed information on other traditions may wish to consult the volumes edited by Koerner and Asher and by Lepschy listed in the bibliography.

Most consequential of all Greek activity involving language was the development of the alphabet that, in modified form, is now used for the majority of written languages throughout the world. At a time before most of recorded history—obviously so, since written records require writing— the Greeks adopted from the Phoenicians a way of representing language through written symbols that correspond to sounds. Expanding upon earlier writing that recorded only consonants, the Greeks introduced signs for vowels as well, thus creating the kind of alphabet familiar to us today.

As with many other aspects of Greek culture, their alphabet was later adopted, and adapted, by the Romans, who extended this writing system across their domain. The dissemination of the Roman alphabet continues in our own age and, just as in the early days of Christianity, in many regions the work is done by missionaries who modify the alphabet for languages without writing, usually with the goal of translating, printing, and distributing the Bible.

For the Greeks, writing was a fundamental aspect of language. Indeed, our modern word *grammar* comes from Greek *gramma* "letter." But the Greeks did not restrict their consideration of language to writing. The Sophists, in the fifth century B.C., were greatly concerned with rhetoric, the art of convincing verbal argument, and they taught public speaking, as well as prose writing, with as much emphasis on the forms of speech as on the content. This concern for form led to studies of syllable structure and the types of sentences used in successful speeches. It set a foundation for the study of language based on eloquent and effective use.

The Sophists left no written records of their work on language. We learn of them through Plato (c. 427–347 B.C.), writing a century later, and he was not sympathetic. He compares them to his teacher Socrates (469–399 B.C.), recording that the Sophists "profess knowledge of all sorts, [Socrates] professes ignorance; they parade skill in public speaking, he can only ask questions, and rejects the elegant prepared answer; they offer to teach, to make men better, he merely offers to confirm man's ignorance; they charge high fees, his teaching is free" (*The Oxford History of the Classical World* 1986, 229). (The use of *men* and *man* in this quotation, by the way, is historically accurate. Although women sometimes learned to write and to read in classical Greece, few were encouraged to do so; schools were for boys only and, more specifically, for boys whose families could pay for the education.)

It is from Plato, too, that we learn first of a philosophical issue concerning not only language, but all human institutions. The question is: Do human institutions reflect nature (*physis*) or are they matters of convention (*nomos*)? For the Greeks, the choice was between natural rights and permitted behavior, between what is fundamentally just and what is societally legal, between nature as immutable and unchanging as opposed to conventions that are agreed to and therefore subject to change.

Language is a human faculty with which all people are familiar, and therefore it was an area in which the *physis-nomos* issue could be thoroughly discussed. Beginning in the fourth century B.C., some Greek philosophers supported the *physis* position, maintaining that words had a natural connection to reality, that the sounds of a word directly reflected the concept it conveyed. So, in Plato's dialogue *Cratylus*, Socrates discusses the Greek letter *lambda*, representing the sound *l*, and finds it "natural" in a Greek word like *leios*, meaning "slippery," because in making the *l* sound, "the tongue has a gliding movement" (see the chapter "Socrates on Names" in Harris and Taylor 1997, 1–19). It was easy enough for the Greeks of this time to find "evidence" for the *physis* position on language in their own language; all human languages have instances of onomatopoeia and sound symbolism. If you know only English, for example, the *physis* position might seem confirmed by the recurrence of word-initial *sn* in *sneeze-snivel-sniff-snore*. But if you also speak French, you know that the corresponding verbs are *éternuer, pleurnicher, renifler,* and *ronfler.* The key point here is that the specific sounds that seem related to particular concepts differ from one language to another. When we look beyond our own language and survey even a small sample of the 4,000 to 6,000 languages spoken in the world today, we find little evidence of a natural connection between sound and meaning.

The *nomos* position held that the words of language are arbitrary, unrelated to the nature of things, agreed upon by users of the language, and subject to change over time. Human beings, in the normal course of events, create words and these new words are understood and accepted by society. Thus, from the word *photogenic*, "appearing attractive when photographed," English speakers recently created the word *telegenic* to describe those who look good on television. There is nothing remarkable about this new word. Every language contains devices for such creation, and since words are arbitrary, whatever words are created will serve their purpose, so long as the speakers of that language accept and use them. In this sense the *nomos* position is the one that survived the debate. Aristotle (384–322 B.C.) repeatedly affirmed that words exist by convention, and by the time of the major Roman grammarians after the birth of Christ, the issue was so well settled that it no longer required discussion.

Although the question raised by the *physis-nomos* controversy about the basic nature of words in human languages was answered long ago, another aspect of the debate persists into our own time. What was the origin of human language?

In the *nomos* view, humans created language; Socrates and Aristotle mention "those who first assigned the name" when discussing the origin of words. Later scholars, strongly affected by religious beliefs, viewed language as a gift from a higher power, a legendary Great Spirit, God, while others believed that mythical heroes or biblical figures were the source of language. There were also proposals based more directly on nature. Perhaps words somehow evolved from the animal noises made by primal humans. Or maybe the early humans imitated the noises they heard in nature and these imitations became more and more complex, eventually resulting in languages through which everything imaginable could be expressed. The origin of words remained a topic of discussion and debate among Western philosophers for 2,000 years.

Toward the end of the nineteenth century, serious students of language and of history concluded that it was impossible to answer the question about the origin of language. All of our records, no matter how old, reveal human language just as it is today. We have no evidence of "primitive" languages now or in the past. There are no languages with vocabularies limited to a few hundred words, no languages that have verbs and nouns but no modifiers, no languages that use only a half dozen sounds, no languages in which people cannot construct long and complex sentences. All languages that we know of are remarkably complex systems of sounds (or, in sign languages, gestures), words, and grammatical structures. In fact, it is the grammatical systems of human languages that are unique. Noam Chomsky (b. 1928), the most important linguist of the twentieth century, has written: "There is a long history of study of origin of language, asking how it arose from calls of apes and so forth. That investigation in my view is a complete waste of time, because language is based on an entirely different principle than any animal communication system. It's quite possible that human gestures . . . have evolved from animal communication systems, but not human language. It has a totally different principle" (*Language and Problems of Knowledge* 1988, 183). The origin of human language is one of the questions to which we do not, and may never, have an answer, but it continues to intrigue us. Contemporary research in the cognitive sciences on evolution and the human brain may yet provide insights.

We have had more success in answering another fundamental question raised by the Greeks: does nature operate according to laws and principles (the *analogy* position) or is it chaotic and free (the *anomaly* position)? Language, as part of nature, served as a testing ground for both sides of this issue.

Aristotle, as we have seen, held the *nomos* view on the nature of words, and it is not surprising that he also maintained an analogist position. Language, established by human convention, was regular and orderly; as such, it was a suitable vehicle for reasoning and for logic, central concerns in Aristotle's philosophical writings. The Alexandrians also followed this view. The Alexandrians were librarians, literary critics, and teachers of classical literature, centered in Egypt, in the city of Alexandria, founded by Alexander the Great after his conquest there in 331 B.C. The principles of analogy in language were entirely consistent with their work. If language lacked regularity and order, how could the older forms of Greek be taught to the young students who, by this time, spoke a language that differed substantially from that of Homer and the other great literature? The language data used by the Alexandrians in their teachings, unlike those of the earlier Sophists, were drawn from classical literature, and thus we find the beginning of a tradition that was to become very strongly established—the use of literary texts for examples in the study of language.

In order to demonstrate the regularities in language, the Alexandrians prepared summaries of the recurring patterns found in Greek literature for words, their roots, and their prefixes and suffixes. (The patterns, or paradigms, of nouns are known as declensions; for verbs, we refer to conjugations.) This study of words and the patterns by which they are formed is today known as morphology. The summation of work on Greek morphology came in the first century B.C. with a grammar usually attributed to Dionysius Thrax, an Alexandrian scholar about whom almost nothing is known. Translated into Latin in the first century A.D., the *Art of Grammar* was widely used in the schools of Greece and Rome; it became a model for language description for many centuries, surviving even today in the use of paradigms such as those we sometimes encounter when we study another language: Latin *amo, amas, amat* ("I, you, he/she loves"), Spanish *canto, cantas, canta* ("I, you, he/she sings").

But the principles of analogy were not undisputed. The Stoics were philosophers in Greece, rivals of the Alexandrians in Egypt, and they challenged the paradigms of the Alexandrians by citing irregularities in Greek. Since the Stoics dealt with contemporary life and language, it was no problem for them to find anomalies. Actual speech is not as obviously well-ordered as are paradigms. And the Stoics, too, assembled lists by "dividing their data into as many distinguishable parts as they could and assigning a technical term to each division" (Dinneen 1967, 89). It is partly to the Stoics that we owe the classification of words into the parts of speech still widely used in language descriptions today.

Plato had divided the sentence (*logos*) into two parts—the subject or noun (*onoma*) and the predicate or verb (*rhema*). Aristotle added a third category (*syndesmos*), which included such words as prepositions, conjunctions, and pronouns. The Stoics and the Alexandrians made further subdivisions, and by the time of Dionysius Thrax, eight parts of speech had been identified: nouns, verbs, adverbs, participles, prepositions, conjunctions, pronouns, and articles. You may notice that one part of speech is absent. Adjectives were considered part of the class of nouns by the Greeks, as well as by the Romans who adopted this system.

And now we may ask for the answer to the *analogy-anomaly* question. Is language regular or irregular? The answer is that it is both, but the regularities far exceed the irregularities. It is regularity that holds central position in any modern description of a language, and it is the existence of regularity that allows humans to learn languages. Were languages not regular, their complexity would make them extremely difficult, maybe even impossible, to learn, a point forcefully expressed 2,000 years ago by the Roman scholar Marcus Terentius Varro (116–27 B.C).

Varro was one of the few Roman scholars of language who produced original studies, though his work had no detectable influence at the time. Others are important primarily because they adopted and adapted Greek studies, translating Greek works into Latin and transforming descriptions of Greek into descriptions of Latin. In these ways Greek scholarship was preserved and presented to the following generations, along with descriptive data about the Greek and Latin languages and the framework within which these two languages were described. Two grammars of Latin were exceptionally well known to later students of language. These were the works of Aelius Donatus in the fourth century A.D. and of Priscian in the sixth. We know little about these men, not even their dates of birth and death, but their linguistic studies were influential for many centuries. Donatus used as his model a Latin translation of Thrax's grammar, and his study became the teaching grammar of the schools well into the Middle Ages. Priscian, writing in Constantinople after the invasion of the western Roman empire by the Goths, also wrote a teaching grammar based on the Greek model. His work survived in "hundreds of manuscripts, and formed the basis of mediaeval Latin grammar and the foundation of mediaeval linguistic philosophy" (Robins 1990, 70). To survive in so many copies was a sure sign of major influence, for Priscian's work extended to twenty volumes, each of which had to be copied by hand before the invention of modern printing.

FAITH AND REASON

Already in Roman times, the study of language had moved away from the philosophical concerns of the Greeks to descriptivism, and what was described was primarily the language of classical Latin literature, modeled on Alexandrian descriptions of classical Greek literature. As Christianity assumed prominence the Scriptures became more important as written texts, and much of the study of language in the first part of the Middle Ages, from the sixth through the twelfth centuries, consisted of commentaries on the grammars of Priscian and Donatus—commentaries that "corrected" the classical Latin examples by replacing them with forms drawn from religious writing.

Faith overshadowed philosophy for several centuries, and accounts of language became part of encyclopedic works in which medieval scholars attempted to set down in one manuscript all that was known, or believed, about the world. In the seventh century, for example, Isidore of Seville prepared an encyclopedia entitled *Twenty Books of Etymologies or Origins*. Etymology is the study of the historical development of words, tracing their forms and meanings back in time using old texts and citations as evidence. Even today, it is widely practiced, and you will find some etymological information in every major dictionary. For Isidore, however, etymology was based not on evidence drawn from historical documents, but on a combination of faith and fancy. For example, he proposed that the Latin word for "human being," *homo*, had originated with *humo*, "the slime of the earth" (see Dinneen 1967, 148–50, for other examples). Not only had philosophy been displaced for a time by faith, but so had empirical observation, evidence, and the use of data.

It is not surprising that today we find in this period of history little that contributes to our understanding of the nature of language. What we do find, however, is a wealth of examples of language change in progress. There were commentaries on Priscian and Donatus that documented changes that had taken place in the Latin language from the classical period of Cicero, Virgil, and Horace in the first century B.C. to the Vulgate version of the Bible prepared in the fourth century A.D. by Saint Jerome. By the eighth century, Latin had changed even more, in different ways in different places, and we find evidence of what were eventually to be the separate Romance languages—French, Italian, Portuguese, Romanian, and Spanish, as well as Catalan, Provençal, and Sardinian. In 813 a council of bishops was held at Tours and it was agreed that sermons should be given no longer in Latin but in *rustica Romana lingua*, language spoken and understood by the people.

In England, as well, a new language was emerging. Late in the fifth century, members of three Germanic tribes—Angles, Saxons, and Jutes—settled in England and by the end of the seventh century, there are written records of "Englisc"—a language which, from that time until about 1100, shortly after the Norman Conquest, is referred to as Old English by modern scholars.

Throughout Europe, Latin remained the language of the liturgy in the churches, the language of scholarship carried out in large part by members of religious orders, and the language of the educated, but all who used Latin now had to study it as a foreign language. Teaching materials continued to include the grammars of Priscian and Donatus, but new materials were also prepared.

Aelfric (c. 955–1020), an English abbot, composed teaching materials on Latin for English children, including a grammar, a conversation book, and a dictionary. R. H. Robins, a modern historian of the study of language, says of Aelfric: "he told his readers that his book would be equally suitable as an introduction to (Old) English grammar. Though he was aware of differences between the two languages, . . . he did not question or discuss the applicability of the Priscianic system to Old English, and as his was one of the first known grammars specifically directed at English-speaking learners, it may be taken as setting the seal on several centuries of Latin-inspired English grammar" (Robins 1990, 80). Today we still encounter descriptions of English, or foreign language teaching material for another language, with terms originally used for the various forms and functions of Latin nouns (and prior to that, for Greek), such as nominative, genitive, dative, and accusative. We may credit Aelfric for extending this tradition of grammatical description to English and to foreign language teaching.

Classical Greek philosophy regained prominence beginning in the eleventh century. The Crusades brought western Europe into renewed contact with the East; Greek documents, particularly on Aristotelian thought, became widely available, not only through Latin translations begun in Roman times, but also directly in Greek manuscripts transported back to Europe following the entry of the crusaders into Constantinople in 1096. Arab domination of Spain, begun in the eighth century, had continued without interruption until the Christians seized Toledo in 1085; Toledo had been a center of Arab scholarship and Aristotle's work was greatly admired there. And so, from Constantinople in the east and from Toledo in the west, reason and logic once again significantly influenced the study of language. Descriptive work alone was no longer satisfactory; explanation was required.

The most famous of the medieval scientists in this revitalized period was Roger Bacon (c. 1214–1294), an English friar, philosopher, and writer. Responding to a request by Pope Clement IV, Bacon prepared several encyclopedic volumes summarizing his views on all areas of human study. His position on grammar established a major theme that continues without significant interruption to our own time. Bacon maintained that grammar is substantially the same in all languages and that whatever differences might occur among languages were "accidental" and superficial. He suggested that there are universal properties which are present in all human languages. This is not the same as the earlier unquestioned use of the Greek system of grammatical description for Latin, nor is it the same as Aelfric's belief that Latin grammar could be used for English. Rather, it assumes a set of principles and properties common to all human languages. It now became the task of the scholar of language to determine these universal principles and properties and, if possible, to explain their existence. This was a focus of the scholastic philosophers of the thirteenth and fourteenth centuries.

The university system of higher education was formalized in Europe in the thirteenth century, as were opportunities for secondary school education. Teachers at these schools were called *scholastici*, and the scholastic philosophers came from this group. Many such schools were under the control of religious orders, and issues of faith and morality remained important, but the Scholastics, influenced by Aristotelian philosophy, supplemented understanding gained through faith with understanding gained through reason. Although scholars searched for natural laws to explain natural phenomena, science was still a part of philosophy and was considered "speculative." Science was the product of reason, of thinking, of logic. Its results could not be certain because they were not provided by faith. In this sense, the search for universal properties of human language was a science, and the grammars produced were called speculative grammars.

The writers of these speculative grammars attempted to unite their understanding of the world and the properties of the human mind with the principles of language. Such unity of knowledge had its foundation in the encyclopedic works of earlier church scholars, but now it was to be based on thought and reason. The speculative grammarians created a complex system to provide this unified theory, and they often disagreed among themselves. But basic to all of their work was the following line of argument: the nature of the world determines the nature of thought and the nature of thought determines the nature of language; since the world is constant, thought is constant and thereby universal in all humans; since thought is universal, so must be the essential properties of human language. Today we are less certain of such a direct connection between thought and language, but the scholastic philosophers believed that the structure of thought was revealed by the structure of sentences. Petrus Hispanus (c. 1205–1277), later Pope John XXI, argued that sentences should be investigated through their systematic relationship to other sentences. In order to explain the thought behind, and the meaning of, "No animal except man is rational," Hispanus argued that we must consider such related sentences as "No animal other than man is rational," "Man is an animal," and "Man is rational" (see the discussion of Petrus Hispanus in Dinneen 1967, 132–141). This approach goes well beyond the study of morphology carried out so extensively by Greek and Roman scholars; it introduces in some detail the study of syntax, the structure of sentences.

The speculative grammarians broadened the scope of the study of language in important ways. They based argument and analysis on reason; they explored meaning; they considered the relationship between language and the mind; they included extended discussions of syntax; and they sought, although often unsuccessfully, explanations for the properties of language. But their work remained limited to Latin, the language of their faith and of all European scholarship at that time. Theoretically and descriptively, many discoveries about human language remained for the following centuries.

NEW HORIZONS

The greatest advances in the study of language from the fifteenth through the seventeenth centuries occurred as scholars prepared descriptions of an enormous variety of languages. The Reformation and the humanism of the Renaissance, nationalism and the development of modern nation-states, and the Age of Exploration all focused attention on the great diversity of languages used by the peoples of Europe and the many parts of the world that they finally came to know. European scholars no longer limited their linguistic studies to classical languages and the language of religion.

The shift in focus toward the vernacular languages occurred gradually during these centuries. Latin was no longer anyone's first language, but it remained the language of higher education and scholarship in many parts of Europe into the eighteenth century, a liturgical language into the twentieth century, and even a compulsory subject in American high schools until just a few decades ago. On the other hand, people used their native languages for ordinary conversation, for business and commerce, in routine legal matters, in secular songs, and in poetry. The fourteenth century had already produced two of the greatest early vernacular poets, Dante Alighieri (1265–1321) in Italy and Geoffrey Chaucer (c. 1340–1400) in England. Europeans began to write grammars describing modern languages: among the first was an account of Castillian Spanish in the fifteenth century; then Arabic, French, and Hungarian in the sixteenth; Finnish, Turkish, Persian, Russian, Armenian, Chinese, Tamil in the seventeenth. Some of the languages of the Americas were described for interested readers in Europe: from 1555 to 1560 two volumes were published on Mexican languages, and a study of the Quechua language of Peru appeared at the same time.

Many of these early grammars were textbooks intended for foreign language teaching. For trade and commerce, exploration, colonization, and for proselytizing, knowledge of foreign languages became increasingly important not only to members of the ruling elite, but also to an emerging middle class. At the same time, heightened nationalism on the one hand and, on the other, the invention of movable type and the resulting spread of literacy to a growing segment of the population drew attention to the native languages of Europe. Across the continent, language academies were founded by scholars, intellectuals, and even politicians with the goal of "regulating" and "purifying" their national languages. Members of these academies mistakenly believed that the languages of the time were chaotic; they were comparing spoken languages of recent written record to the neatly organized traditional descriptions that had existed for centuries for Greek and Latin. In 1582, the Italian *Accademia della Crusca* was founded; the *Académie française* was established in 1635. No official academy was created in Germany, but in various cities those concerned with "protecting" the German language from "invasion" by foreign words organized language societies; the first was in Weimar in 1617. All of the academies, and even some of the regional societies, proclaimed themselves the final authority on the national language. Dictionaries and grammars were prepared to present a single "correct" spelling for words, to define "hard" words for a new and expanding literate population, to provide words of native origin to replace borrowings from other languages, and to prescribe rules for "proper" grammatical usage. The latter were almost invariably based on formal written style.

England was not immune from this movement to reform the language of its people, although no official academy was ever created. By the beginning of the eighteenth century, however, many British writers had called for one. Jonathan Swift (1667–1745), author of *Gulliver's Travels*, in 1712 wrote *A Proposal for Correcting, Improving and Ascertaining the English Tongue*, arguing that royal officials had a responsibility to establish an academy to oversee the principles of English grammar and to keep the language from changing. Actually, there was no hope of preventing language change since all human languages—indeed all human institutions—change over time, but attempts to codify English in grammars and dictionaries became a major industry of eighteenth-century England. In 1755 Samuel Johnson (1709–1784) published his famous *Dictionary of the English Language*. Americans, opponents of the British not only in the Revolution but also in the War of 1812, saw language as a political instrument in the early years of the republic. Noah Webster (1758–1843) attempted to record uniquely American usage, to propose distinctive American spellings, and to provide an authoritative source on American vocabulary in *The American Dictionary of the English Language*, published in 1828. No corresponding grammar was printed for American English at the time, probably because there were really no significant grammatical differences between British and American speakers.

In England, more than 250 grammars were published during the eighteenth century. Even Joseph Priestley (1733–1804), the British scientist who first produced oxygen in a laboratory, wrote a grammar in 1761, *Rudiments of English Grammar*. Following his scientific training, Priestley observed and described the language of his contemporaries. This objective description of the language, however, was not what his contemporaries wanted. They were looking for a prescriptive grammar, one that would set down rules to be followed for usage that others would consider "correct." With the appearance in 1762 of *Short Introduction to English Grammar* by Robert Lowth (1710–1787), the public's desire for a prescriptive grammar was fulfilled with a vengeance. Lowth did not hesitate to criticize current usage and to suggest "rules," many of which he simply made up, sometimes using his knowledge of Latin. It is from this prescriptive tradition that we encounter the rules still taught in some school grammars: "don't end a sentence with a preposition," "don't split infinitives," "don't say *taller than me*, say *taller than I*." Not until the twentieth century did English grammars return to describing what people actually say and write, rather than what some self-appointed authority thinks they "should" produce.

At the same time that academies, societies, and individuals were engaged in the practical work of writing dictionaries and grammars of the European languages, human language once again became an important topic of philosophical interest. For the most part, the philosophers of the seventeenth and eighteenth centuries belonged to the movement known as the Enlightenment, in which reason replaced faith in the study of natural phenomena and human institutions. When we last considered philosophy, with the speculative grammarians of the thirteenth and fourteenth centuries, reason was used as a supplement to faith. Now there was a major effort to establish science and human reason as the sole bases of all political, social, and educational matters.

In the study of language, the *Port-Royal Grammar* of 1660 marked an important turning point. The original French title of this work begins *Grammaire générale et raisonnée*—"general and rational grammar"—and reveals something of its approach. Here language was viewed as a human invention, rational because it developed from the human mind and general because the basic principles of all languages were assumed to be the same. The authors, Antoine Arnauld (1612–1694) and Claude Lancelot (c. 1615–1695), used examples from French, but since the grammar was general, they also drew on other European languages to illustrate what they believed were universal properties common to all languages. Following the *Port-Royal Grammar*, other French scholars produced works that distinguished between *grammaire générale* (general, universal grammar) and *grammaire particulière* (particular grammar). Grammaire générale was the rational investigation of the unchanging and universal principles common to all languages and to the use of language in all human societies. Grammaire particulière, on the other hand, dealt with the properties of individual languages. It was grammaire générale that these rationalist scholars of the eighteenth century considered important for understanding the human mind, as well as for the more practical goal of serving as a basis for all foreign language study.

Language was considered the creation of the human intellect, and like all human institutions, its development over time could serve as an appropriate object of study. In eighteenth-century France, this prompted a new search for the origin of human language. The search was not based on data or on observation, but on the application of principles of reason. Various points of view were expressed, but there was no evidence to sustain them, and one view was as good (or as bad) as another. Jean-Jacques Rousseau (1712–1778), for example, offered several opinions: language originated in the interaction of mother and child; language resulted from the expression of human passions; language arose when human beings came together in social groups. Although such views on the origin of human language were not based on scientific investigation, the interest in language origin in the eighteenth century set the stage for the development of a science of language in the nineteenth.

LANGUAGE CHANGE

By the end of the eighteenth century, a number of factors had come together in the study of language, and the result was the establishment during the nineteenth century of a specific field of study called *linguistics* in English, *Sprachwissenschaft* in German. The German name clearly specifies the new approach; it translates as "language science." Today linguistics is defined as the scientific study of language, a discipline dealing with a very broad range of topics related to language. In the nineteenth century, however, attention was concentrated on language change.

A strong foundation for the scientific study of language change had been laid in the previous centuries. Some scholars had devoted their lives to the preservation and transmission of classical and religious texts in Greek and Latin. Others, in the spirit of nationalism, sought and published old texts from their own languages. The interest in older texts was supported by a more widespread interest in historical study, and the history of words, texts, and languages was pursued with some vigor. At the same time, explorers and missionaries, emissaries and ambassadors, ordinary travelers and learned teachers had all participated in preparing and collecting descriptions of languages from around the world. By the start of the nineteenth century, the libraries of Europe contained books and manuscripts on every language that Western scholars considered important in human history.

Toward the end of the eighteenth century, some students of language combined information on separate languages into comparative texts, often with parallel lists of words with similar forms and meanings from several languages. For example, in 1786 Peter Simon Pallas (1741–1811), a German scholar serving in the court of Catherine the Great of Russia, edited and published lists of words from more than two hundred languages of Europe and Asia. The data had been collected by members of Catherine's diplomatic corps, and the title of Pallas's work reflected a somewhat naive view of their domain: *A Comparative Vocabulary of the Languages of the Entire World*. From works like this it became possible, and popular, to compare languages, noting similarities and attempting to explain how these similarities had come about.

Earlier scholars had concluded that such similarities among languages were due to development from a single source language (frequently said to be Hebrew), or to the borrowing of words by one language from another, or to universal properties common to all languages. Such conclusions were often reached without the benefit of observable data or objective analysis; they were based on national pride, or religious affiliations, or place of birth, or the supposed use of logic. But with the growing nineteenth-century belief in the importance of scientific inquiry and the extensive data available from many languages, it became widely acknowledged that these early accounts had been inadequate.

Historical and comparative linguistic studies combined in the nineteenth century to provide compelling explanations of how languages change over time and why some languages have many systematic similarities in sounds, words, and grammar while others do not. A major impetus was the "discovery" of Sanskrit by European scholars. An ancient language of India, the oldest form of Sanskrit is found in the Vedic texts, religious rituals composed sometime around 1500 B.C. Sanskrit came to the attention of Europeans as one consequence of the extension of the British empire into India late in the eighteenth century. In 1786 Sir William Jones (1746–1794), serving as chief justice at a British outpost in India, gave a talk in Calcutta that was printed and widely circulated in England. In his talk he compared Sanskrit to Greek and Latin and claimed that its similarities to these well-known European languages were so great that they could not "possibly have been produced by accident." Jones stated that no student of language could examine Sanskrit, Greek, and Latin "without believing them to have sprung from some common source, which, perhaps, no longer exists."

As scholars learned more about the Sanskrit language, they were able to compare it to Greek and Latin, as well as to other European languages. The similarities noted by Sir William were immediately obvious: "mother" is *matar* in Sanskrit, *mater* in Greek, *mater* in Latin; "foot" is *padas* in Sanskrit, *podos* in Greek, *pedis* in Latin; "he/she is" is *asti* in Sanskrit, *esti* in Greek, *est* in Latin. Many such correspondences of basic vocabulary items could be listed. Clearly, this was not an accident. The reasonable explanation was a historical one: at some time in remote history, these different languages had been the same language. Their similarities were due to a common source. Whatever differences could be observed in more recent times were due to changes that had occurred over the centuries in different places.

The linguists of the nineteenth century set about systematically comparing the languages of India and of Europe, attempting to determine what the source language had been like and what changes had occurred over time in each of the modern languages. Rather than taking a great philosophical leap back to prehistory, as scholars of the Enlightenment had done, nineteenth-century linguists attempted to actually trace the development of language back through time, using data from existing languages and records of older languages. As their work progressed, they determined that the source language for much of India and Europe was not the same as any one of the languages for which they had records, and they called it Indo-European. From this hypothesized Indo-European, spoken long before historical records began, changes occurred in different regions, resulting in different languages—still before written records. These languages—including Germanic, Hellenic, Italic, Balto-Slavic, and Indo-Iranian—were in turn the ancestral sources of various more modern languages. Other source languages, similarly reconstructed by comparing modern languages, were proposed for different language groups in other regions of the world.

The success of the nineteenth-century historical-comparative approach to the study of language was so great that linguistics was widely accepted as a science throughout the European and American scholarly communities. Language change was systematic and could be stated by formulas, or rules. Earlier stages of languages could be determined, even in the absence of written records, by comparing more modern stages. Speculation was undesirable; recourse to logic, reason, or philosophy was unnecessary. Empirical data and scientific analysis were sufficient.

In all of this work, much of it conducted in Germany, the focus was on language change, and studies were diachronic (meaning "throughout time"). In 1880 the German scholar Hermann Paul (1846–1921), justifying the title of his book *Principles of the History of Language*, said: "It has been objected that there is another view of language possible besides the historical. I must contradict this." For Paul, only diachronic study of language could be scientific. Although many agreed with him at the time, the times were already changing.

The Sanskrit materials that had attracted Western scholars at the beginning of the century included descriptions of the Sanskrit language written by Indian scholars long before the earliest written descriptions of the Greek language. These accounts were extremely detailed, and included extensive descriptions of Sanskrit pronunciation. Unlike the European history of language study in which letters were considered the smallest units of human language, the Indian scholars had focused on sounds. The seventeenth- and eighteenth-century efforts at spelling reform in England had also called attention to pronunciation, and there were a number of attempts to describe how speech sounds are produced. But a scientific understanding of the nature of speech sounds did not develop fully until advances in physiology were made by nineteenth-century scientists. As more became known about the human vocal tract, the accuracy of the Indian descriptions of Sanskrit pronunciation was more and more appreciated. By the last quarter of the nineteenth century, the field of phonetics (the study of speech sounds) was well established, particularly in England and France. Included in the work on phonetics was the creation of the International Phonetic Alphabet (IPA), a system of letters and marks that can be used to represent the speech sounds of all languages.

These developments in phonetics provided important tools for two major areas of investigation at the end of the nineteenth century and the beginning of the twentieth—the detailed recording of regional variations in pronunciation and the systematic, consistent description of all languages, including those without writing systems.

LINGUISTIC DIVERSITY

Much of the data collected and analyzed by the historical and comparative linguists of the nineteenth century had been drawn from those varieties of languages accepted as "standard" by speakers and scholars alike. These standard varieties typically reflected the language of people from major cultural, educational, and political centers and were often the varieties most widely represented in written documents. Concentrated attention on standard, written varieties of language had simply ignored the large majority of human beings whose language use was different. Virtually no one uses formal literary style in ordinary daily speech. People from different regions speak differently from one another and those in rural areas speak differently from those in cultural centers. These oral and regional varieties of language soon became objects of linguistic study.

Until the end of the nineteenth century, it was not uncommon for the regional forms of a language to be called "dialects" while the standard variety was sometimes assumed to be "the language." Soon, however, the results of dialect study demonstrated conclusively that the regional varieties are linguistically equal to the standard varieties of languages—just as complete, just as complex, just as regular, and just as effective for communication. Today we know that a dialect is simply a variety of a language, standard or not.

Scholarly interest in local, regional dialects in Europe first arose at the start of the nineteenth century along with Romanticism and its emphasis on nature "uncorrupted" by the complexities of modern societies and civilizations. Just as the Grimm brothers at this time collected folktales as reflections of the lives and beliefs of ordinary people, so others began to record aspects of their speech. Dictionaries included regional words, and the first major description of a regional dialect appeared in 1821, *The Dialects of Bavaria* by Johann Schmeller (1785–1852). By the end of the nineteenth century, regional dialectology was thriving in all parts of Europe. Diversity across languages over time had been a center of attention for the historical and comparative linguists; now diversity within languages in the present also became a focus.

Two major projects established approaches to the investigation of regional dialect variation and the presentation of results. During the last quarter of the nineteenth century, Georg Wenker (1852–1911) distributed a questionnaire containing some forty sentences to German school teachers. He asked them to rewrite the sentences to reflect the pronunciation of the people living in their regions, and after he had received the responses, he recorded the different dialect features on maps. The maps formed the basis of a dialect atlas of Germany, a format for presenting the results of regional dialect studies that has been used since that time. But Wenker's use of teachers to collect information, though convenient, was flawed. The teachers varied enormously in how they chose to record their local dialects, and their reports were inconsistent and unreliable, especially in regard to pronunciation. But it was precisely pronunciation that Wenker had set out to investigate, and much of his massive study was later revised by other scholars.

Jules Gilliéron (1854–1926), a Swiss who had long been interested in the French language, was appointed in 1883 to the faculty of l'École des Hautes Études in Paris with a specific assignment to teach about the dialects of French. As part of his work he designed a dialect study of the language, not only in France, but in the neighboring areas where French is spoken—Belgium, Switzerland, and Italy. Gilliéron avoided Wenker's problem by sending an investigator trained in phonetics into the field to collect the data directly from speakers of the dialects. Starting in 1897 Edmond Edmont (1849–1926) visited more than 600 sites, often using his bicycle for transportation, and beginning in 1902 Gilliéron and Edmont started to publish the results as the *Atlas linguistique de la France*. It took a decade to complete publication.

These two major methods of regional dialect study, the use of a field investigator trained in phonetics and the presentation of results by means of maps, were adopted in the United States. In 1930 the American Council of Learned Societies and the Linguistic Society of America announced sponsorship of research on American English dialects. European dialectologists came to the United States the next year to train the investigators who were to collect data for a linguistic atlas of the United States and Canada. At its peak in the 1930s this project resulted in the publication of a linguistic atlas for New England (Kurath et al., 1939–1943) and, later, for the Upper Midwest (Allen 1973–1976); books on pronunciation and word variation for several regions have also been published.

Some dialects of the United States and Canada still have not been investigated, and much of the dialect material that has been gathered remains unpublished. It is available to scholars in archives, though not accessible to more casual readers. The reasons are both logistical and economic. Compared to the dialect situations in Europe described in the German study by Wenker or the French study by Gilliéron and Edmont, for example, the United States and Canada cover enormous expanses of territory. Hundreds of investigators might be required and thousands of people should be interviewed for a thorough study; then the results must be plotted on detailed maps, each map covering an area no larger than a small town. To comprehend the magnitude of the task, recall that it took Gilliéron and Edmont ten years to publish the results obtained from the work of just one field worker covering an area about the size of the state of Texas.

Since a regional dialect is simply the variety of a language spoken in a particular region, we all have a dialect. Do you say *firefly* or *lightning bug*? *Soda* or *pop*? *Quarter to two, quarter of two,* or *quarter till two*? Are *merry, marry,* and *Mary* homonyms in your speech, or do they have different vowels? These are just a few features of various regional dialects of American English. Awareness of our own dialect and other dialects as well enables us to see ourselves as participants in the universal, human experience of linguistic diversity. This is particularly important for those many monolingual Americans who, unlike much of the world's population, are unaccustomed to and uninformed about other languages.

At the same time that regional dialects were engaging the attention of European linguists, a new direction was emerging in the United States, one that revealed yet another type of linguistic diversity. Franz Boas (1859–1942), a German educated in physics and geography, came to North America in 1886 on a field trip intending to study the geography of the region and the cultures of the native peoples. Boas devoted the remaining fifty years of his life to the investigation of native American languages and cultures.

Boas knew about the historical approach to linguistic studies and was familiar with the traditional framework for describing languages based on the Greek and Latin models. He recognized that neither approach was suitable to the languages of native Americans. The written documents of such importance to historical work of the time did not exist for most native American languages, for many did not have writing systems. The labels, categories, and patterns of Greek and Latin, and even of the other Indo-European languages, were inappropriate for native American languages, which differed greatly from the languages of Europe. Not bound to a particular framework for the study of language, Boas forged a new approach. In 1888 he wrote: "If we desire to understand the development of human culture we must try to free ourselves of [the] shackles" imposed by "not only our knowledge, but also our emotions" which "are the result of the form of our social life and of the history of the people to whom we belong" (Jakobson 1944, 190). Through the objective study of native American languages, seeking their patterns and structures, Boas believed that we would learn more about language, culture, and ourselves than could ever be possible with the ethnocentric approach that had dominated European linguistic studies since the time of the Greek Sophists.

PROMINENCE OF DESCRIPTION

The description of native American languages became one of the major goals of twentieth-century American linguists. Two great contributors were Edward Sapir (1884–1939) and Leonard Bloomfield (1887–1949). Both had studied historical and comparative linguistics, and both did research within that framework, enlarging its principles and extending them to native American languages despite the absence of written historical documents. Sapir was primarily interested in the native languages of western America, including the Uto-Aztecan languages of the southwestern United States and Central America; Bloomfield focused on the Algonquian languages around the Great Lakes. Although they continued and expanded upon the diachronic approach developed in nineteenth-century Europe, they are best known today for their synchronic work.

Synchronic study of language involves description of a language at a particular point in time, a snapshot without recourse to historical information. Contrary to the conclusion of Hermann Paul, twentieth-century students of language determined that nonhistorical, synchronic study could be objective and rigorous, that is, scientific, so long as the analysis of a language was based on its structure. Such structural analysis required that all units of the language (sounds, words, sentences) be viewed in relation to one another, as a unified system, independent of other languages, popular assumptions, and other fields of study. Conducted in this way, linguistics is an autonomous science, with its own goals, theories, and methods.

Establishing the autonomy of the discipline can be seen as a major achievement of American linguists in the twentieth century. In the early years, the historical and comparative approach was identified primarily with the study of European languages, modern and classical, while the study of cultures and languages conducted by Boas was considered part of anthropology. Indeed, Sapir, a student of Boas, received his doctoral degree in anthropology; Bloomfield's doctoral dissertation was a historical study of Germanic, and for many years his appointments as a university professor were in German. But as Sapir and Bloomfield, their students, and others studied the native languages of America, they developed field procedures, analytic principles, and a substantial agenda for the autonomous, synchronic, structural description of languages. Many of the concepts and procedures dealt with phonology, the structure of human language sound systems.

Phonetics had developed in the nineteenth century, describing specific speech sounds and explaining how they are produced by the human vocal tract. But in the twentieth century linguists discovered a number of additional important aspects of language sounds. Through phonetics we can describe the particular sound made when someone produces a [p]. But what is the role of that sound within the structure of the language? What similar sounds are perceived by speakers as the same, even though they are physically different? (The [p] in *spin* is not the same as that in *pin*.) Which sounds, when substituted for [p] in a word, produce a different word with a different meaning? (English *gap* and *gab*.) Where does a sound occur in relation to other sounds? ([p] can occur after [s] at the beginning of an English word, but [b] cannot.) Such details differ from one language to another. Spanish uses only the [p] in *spin*, not that of *pin*; German speakers do not use the sound [b] at the end of words; Italian allows words that begin with the spelling *sb* although the actual pronunciation is [zb], another initial sequence that does not occur in English. These facts are as important as the sounds themselves. They are part of the reason that other languages sound different from our own, why other people may speak our language with a foreign accent, and why we tend to do the same when we speak their language. They also explain certain judgments we make about our language, e.g., that *sben* is not a possible English word but *spen* could be one even if it does not happen to be at this time.

The primary descriptive concern of the 1930s in the United States was phonology. The principles developed through the description of the phonology of native American languages were used to describe the phonology of other languages, some not familiar to many Americans of the time (Chinese, Japanese, Korean), others better known (French, German), and most of all, English. Accuracy and completeness in phonetics and phonology enabled the linguist to overcome the ethnocentrism to which Boas had objected and it established a firm empirical base of observable data. The focus on spoken language began in America with Boas; obviously, this continued with the concentration on phonology.

Although Sapir and Bloomfield both played major roles in all these developments, it was Bloomfield who wrote and lectured most about the scientific nature of linguistics. His 1933 textbook *Language* fundamentally altered the way in which American linguists approached the study of human languages. As they became more and more concerned with careful methodology, precise procedures, and clearly defined terms, the focus of mainstream American linguistics began to narrow until it became predominantly descriptive, structural, and synchronic in the 1940s and the early 1950s.

This narrow focus was not what Boas and Sapir had envisaged. In his introductory remarks to the first issue of the *International Journal of American Linguistics*, which Boas founded in 1917 and which was to be, and still is, devoted to the study of native American languages, he wrote:

"The variety of American languages is so great, that they will be of high value for the solution of many fundamental psychological problems. The unconsciously formed categories found in human speech have not been sufficiently exploited for the investigation of the categories into which the whole range of human experience is forced" (p. 5). Boas went on to proclaim the importance not only of describing the sounds, words, and sentences of these languages, but also of recording and studying conversations, tales, literary forms, poetry, and songs. Similarly, Sapir described the broadly encompassing aim of his 1921 book *Language*: "Its main purpose is to show what I conceive language to be, what is its variability in place and time, and what are its relations to other fundamental human interests—the problem of thought, the nature of the historical process, race, culture, art. . . . Knowledge of the wider relations of their science is essential to professional students of language if they are to be saved from a sterile and purely technical attitude" (p. v).

Sapir died in 1939, Boas in 1942, and their generous views of the scope of linguistics were overshadowed for a time in America by the more narrow concerns of scientific synchronic descriptivism. But this restricted view was not shared by the European linguists of this period. The illustrious Danish linguist Otto Jespersen (1860–1943), for example, wrote not only unsurpassed descriptions of English vocabulary and syntax but also major works on such diverse topics as children's language development, international auxiliary languages, foreign language teaching, and language change. Linguistic principles set forth in the 1916 book *Course in General Linguistics*, based on the lectures of the Swiss linguist Ferdinand de Saussure (1857–1913), were extended to anthropology, literary criticism, semiotics (the study of signs), and even psychoanalysis under the general rubric of structuralism. In central Europe an exceptionally talented assembly of scholars known as the Prague School applied structural principles to the analysis of folklore, standard literary languages, poetry, and regional dialects as well as particular languages; they actively sought universals of human language and some were especially interested in the nature of the phonological systems of the languages of the world. Foremost among the latter was Roman Jakobson (1896–1982). Educated in Russia, an intellectual leader in Prague, he escaped World War II in Europe in 1941 by immigrating to the United States. Jakobson brought twentieth-century European views of language to America, but he most influenced linguistics in the United States through his development of distinctive features, the binary component features of sounds. Today our understanding of phonology is the joint legacy of American structuralism and Jakobsonian distinctive features.

SYNTAX, SEMANTICS, AND BEYOND

The principles of observation and description that worked so well in phonology seemed to resist extension to syntax (the study and analysis of sentences), and the American insistence on observable data for a time placed semantics (the study of meaning) beyond the domain of linguistic science. These were serious problems. The primary purpose of human language is to convey meaning from one person to another, and the failure of American structural linguistics to produce a significant account of semantics was a major factor in the development of new approaches to the study of language in the 1950s and beyond. The changes began slowly as a number of linguists sought ways of describing syntax, where a key issue is the infinite number of sentences possible in every human language. Unlike phonological systems in which limited numbers of sounds occur in restricted combinations and patterns, or morphological systems with large but still listable numbers of words and their component roots and affixes, syntactic systems operate according to different principles.

In 1957 Noam Chomsky published *Syntactic Structures*, a slim volume of just over 100 pages that has been called "revolutionary" for the development of modern linguistics. Chomsky proposed a set of finite rules as a way of accounting for the sentences of a language. Basic sentences (e.g., active, affirmative, simple statements) could be produced, or generated, by a set of phrase structure rules, and a different type of rule, the transformation, derived all other sentences (e.g., passives, negatives, questions, complex sentences) from the basic types. This approach became known as transformational generative grammar, and it placed syntax at the center of linguistic investigation in the United States. Within a decade, linguists were struggling with issues of meaning and the relationship between syntax and semantics in a generative grammar.

Chomsky did not restrict his work to the description of language structures; he sought explanations for the principles of human language. As a philosophical basis, he returned to some of the ideas expounded by the rationalist philosophers of the seventeenth and eighteenth centuries. Recalling the rationalist distinction between grammaire générale and grammaire particulière, Chomsky reemphasized the importance of seeking universal properties of human language as a means to understand human nature and the human mind.

Chomsky challenged the narrow characterization of science that had bound so much of American linguistics in the 1940s and early 1950s to the directly observable data of actual samples of speech. He began to raise questions about how language exists in the minds of human beings and about what it is that permits speakers of a language to use it creatively, producing and understanding sentences that they have never before heard or seen. Chomsky maintained that a grammar must account for the creativity that all speakers of a human language possess. Writing such a grammar became a central goal of American linguistics in the second half of the twentieth century; the task has not been easy and the goal has not yet been achieved. As Chomsky said in *Aspects of the Theory of Syntax*: "Any interesting generative grammar will be dealing, for the most part, with mental processes that are far beyond the level of actual or even potential consciousness; furthermore, it is quite apparent that [speakers'] reports and viewpoints about [their] behavior and [their] competence may be in error. Thus a generative grammar attempts to specify what speakers actually [know], not what [they] may report about [their] knowledge" (p. 8).

Early generative grammar, in some ways reminiscent of more traditional grammars of previous centuries, considered the forms, or structures, of the sentences of a language and tried to formulate the rules that had created those structures. This was not unlike grammaire particulière, and the question of grammaire générale soon arose. Was it possible to abstract out of the structures and rules of individual languages a set of general principles that govern all human languages? The search for such universal principles led to consideration of a broader range of languages than had previously been considered by linguists, and it also began to reveal what appear to be a limited set of options according to which human languages can vary one from the other. So, for example, in English the head word in a phrase usually comes first: a verb precedes its object in a verb phrase (ate an apple), a preposition precedes its object in a noun phrase (with a stick). But in Japanese the head word follows (ringo-o tabeta "[an] apple ate"), boo-de "[a] stick with"). English is a "head-initial" language; Japanese is a "head-final" language. Head position is just one of the parameters of variation among languages.

Toward the end of the twentieth century, generative linguists—working within a framework that seeks principles common to all languages and a limited number of parameters—sought to build a theory to explain the universality and the diversity of human languages. But more than that, they also were building a theory that might explain how it is that children are able to acquire their native language with remarkably few mistakes along the way, at a point in their lives when they are as yet unable to tie their shoes or button their shirts.

It is a remarkable characteristic of the human species that its young, without conscious effort or overt teaching, and sometimes despite serious physical or mental disorders, acquire a complete linguistic system. Every human language is so complex that none has ever been completely described, yet somehow all children master the language (or languages) of their environment. How do they accomplish this amazing feat? Not by imitating those around them, although that is a common belief. All children, from their earliest words, produce utterances they have never heard, such as *she hitted me*. It has long been clear that there are properties of the human mind that direct the acquisition of language. Linguistic theory suggests that the universal principles and the parameters of variation are part of our uniquely human inheritance, providing to us as children the genetic material that, in interaction with our environment, allows language to emerge.

And once language does emerge, there are other questions to be answered. How is linguistic knowledge stored in the human brain? How is this knowledge activated to produce or to comprehend speech and writing? How do different contexts and situations affect our use of this knowledge? In Chomsky's words, "What contribution can the study of language make to our understanding of human nature?" (1972, 1). One approach to these questions is through the interdisciplinary field of psycholinguistics where researchers from linguistics and psychology are exploring questions about language acquisition, cognition, language comprehension and processing, and language and the brain. From its beginnings in the 1950s, this field has expanded to the point that in 1990 the *MLA International Bibliography of Linguistics* listed almost 2,000 books and articles on such topics and the number keeps on growing.

During the same time period in which psycholinguistics developed, a different interdisciplinary field called sociolinguistics evolved, which considers language in conjunction with aspects of the society in which it is used. Sociolinguistic studies in the United States have often related directly to broader social concerns. The study of the dialect known as African-American English or Black English, for example, received a major impetus from the American civil rights movement, while the women's movement created interest in issues of language and gender, and population shifts fostered studies of language contact, bilingualism, and language attitudes.

Related to developments in psycholinguistics and in sociolinguistics, but not actually within their domain, have been extensions of linguistic research into the practical arenas of language teaching and language learning. The grammar-translation method of foreign language teaching can be traced to the Middle Ages, even to the Romans who studied the Greek language at the same time that they adopted the Greek form of grammatical description. In the 1940s American linguists had participated actively in the preparation of teaching materials for languages that the U.S. government deemed essential for wartime communication with its allies and its enemies. Consistent with their focus on the structure of spoken language, they created a method of foreign language teaching called the audio-lingual approach, a method widely used in the United States during the 1950s and 1960s. Students memorized samples of spoken language, usually in the form of dialogues, and practiced the structural patterns of sentences. The audio-lingual approach (never accepted in Europe) has been replaced by a variety of teaching methods that focus on using the foreign language for communicative purposes, and contemporary linguists have become interested in the human mental abilities that make second language acquisition possible. The study of foreign- or second-language learning is sometimes referred to as "applied linguistics," although there are certainly other areas to which linguistic research has been applied, including the study and treatment of language loss and speech disorders, the use of language in law and medicine, and the teaching and learning of reading and writing.

Unlike scholars of language in other centuries and in other countries, very few twentieth-century linguists in the United States have worked extensively with literary prose or poetry, although some, like Edward Sapir, have themselves been poets, and a few, like Roman Jakobson, made important contributions in this area. A number of factors may be responsible: the early focus on native American languages without written literatures, the concentration on phonology in the 1930s, the attention to developing objective scientific principles of analysis during the 1940s and early 1950s, and finally, the success of linguistics in the United States in achieving autonomy. With the widespread creation of university linguistics programs and departments independent from the traditional departments of English and foreign languages, many linguists became academically separated from their literary colleagues. Will a renewed interest in interdisciplinary work foster greater connections between linguistics and the literary arts? Perhaps this will become an area of expansion in the scope of modern American linguistics, but at this time we simply do not know what lies ahead in the study of language.

The developments of the past, the changes in emphasis, and the insights achieved in the study of language could not have been predicted. Even with the hindsight of centuries, we cannot explain why the Greeks were intellectually so productive. Nothing that we know about earlier centuries could have foretold the extensive understanding of language change that resulted from nineteenth-century historical and comparative work. The study of the native languages of North and Central America in the twentieth century was not predestined; there are languages that remain uninvestigated. Nor could anyone have predicted that linguistics in the United States would become so narrowly focused on structural description and the methodology of science and then would expand its scope so broadly. Modern American linguistics is no longer isolated from other fields of human inquiry, nor is it internationally located. Linguists from the United States lecture and conduct research in many other countries, and international scholars come to the United States to teach and to do their research. Professional societies, scholarly journals, technical books, and collections of essays extend the study of language around the world. In this sense, language and the study of language unite us all.

Linguistics today encompasses almost every conceivable topic related to human language—description and explanation, universals and properties of particular languages, synchronic and diachronic perspectives, regional and social variation, native-language acquisition and foreign-language learning, language as knowledge and language in use, philosophical questions and practical applications—all increasing the depth of our understanding of what it is to be human.

BIBLIOGRAPHY

Allen, Harold B. *The Linguistic Atlas of the Upper Midwest.* 3 vols. Minneapolis: University of Minnesota Press, 1973–1976.

Andresen, Julie Tetel. *Linguistics in America 1769–1924.* London and New York: Routledge, 1990.

Bacon, Roger. *Opus Majus.* Trans. Robert Belle Burke. 2 vols. New York: Russell and Russell, 1928.

Bloomfield, Leonard. *Language.* New York: Henry Holt, 1933.

Boas, Franz. "Introductory." *International Journal of American Linguistics* 1, 1, (1917), 1–8.

Chomsky, Noam. *Syntactic Structures.* The Hague: Mouton, 1957.

———. *Aspects of the Theory of Syntax.* Cambridge: MIT Press, 1965.

———. *Cartesian Linguistics: A Chapter in the History of Rationalist Thought.* New York: Harper & Row, 1966.

———. *Language and Mind.* Enlarged ed. New York: Harcourt Brace Jovanovich, 1972.

———. *Language and Problems of Knowledge: The Managua Lectures.* Cambridge: MIT Press, 1988.

Culler, Jonathan. *Ferdinand de Saussure.* Rev. ed. Ithaca: Cornell University Press, 1986.

Darnell, Regna. *Edward Sapir: Linguist, Anthropologist, Humanist.* Berkeley: University of California Press, 1990.

Dinneen, Francis P. *An Introduction to General Linguistics.* New York: Holt, Rinehart and Winston, 1967.

Finegan, Edward. *Attitudes toward English Usage: The History of a War of Words.* New York: Teachers College Press, 1980.

Hall, Robert A., Jr. *A Life for Language: A Biographical Memoir of Leonard Bloomfield.* Amsterdam and Philadelphia: John Benjamins, 1990.

———, ed. *Leonard Bloomfield: Essays on His Life and Work.* Amsterdam and Philadelphia: John Benjamins, 1987.

Harris, Roy, and Talbot J. Taylor. *Landmarks in Linguistic Thought: The Western Tradition from Socrates to Saussure,* 2nd ed. London and New York: Routledge, 1997.

Hymes, Dell, and John Fought. *American Structuralism.* The Hague: Mouton, 1981.

Jakobson, Roman. "Franz Boas' Approach to Language." *International Journal of American Linguistics* 10, 4 (1944), 188–195.

———, and Krystyna Pomorska. *Dialogues.* Cambridge: MIT Press, 1983.

Juliard, Pierre. *Philosophies of Language in Eighteenth-Century France.* The Hague: Mouton, 1970.

Juul, Arne, and Hans F. Nielsen, eds. *Otto Jespersen: Facets of His Life and Work.* Philadelphia: John Benjamins, 1989.

Koerner, E.F.K., and R.E. Asher, eds. *Concise History of the Language Sciences.* Tarrytown, NY: Pergamon, 1995.

Kurath, Hans, Miles L. Hanley, Bernard Bloch, et al. *Linguistic Atlas of New England.* 3 vols. Providence: Brown University Press, 1939–1943.

Lepschy, Giulio, ed. *History of Linguistics. I: The Eastern Traditions of Linguistics.* London and New York: Longman, 1994.

Newmeyer, Frederick J. *Linguistic Theory in America,* 2nd ed. Orlando, FL: Academic Press, 1986.

———. *Generative Linguistics: A Historical Perspective.* London and New York: Routledge, 1996.

The Oxford History of the Classical World. Ed. John Boardman, Jasper Griffin, and Oswyn Murray. Oxford: Oxford University Press, 1986.

Paul, Hermann. *Principles of the History of Language.* 2nd ed. Trans. H.A. Strong. London: Swan Sonnenschein, Lowrey, 1888.

Pedersen, Holger. *The Discovery of Language: Linguistic Science in the Nineteenth Century.* Trans. John Webster Spargo. Bloomington: Indiana University Press, 1962.

Robins, R. H. *A Short History of Linguistics,* 3rd ed. London: Longman, 1990.

Rousseau, Jean-Jacques. "Essay on the Origin of Languages." Trans. John H. Moran in *On the Origin of Language.* New York: Frederick Unger, 1966.

Sampson, Geoffrey. *Schools of Linguistics.* Stanford: Stanford University Press, 1980.

Sapir, Edward. *Language: An Introduction to the Study of Speech.* New York: Harcourt, Brace, 1921.

Saussure, Ferdinand de. *Course in General Linguistics.* Trans. Wade Baskin. New York: Philosophical Library, 1959.

Sebeok, Thomas A., ed. *Portraits of Linguists: A Biographical Source Book for the History of Western Linguistics. 1746–1963.* 2 vols. Bloomington: Indiana University Press, 1966.

≡

FOR DISCUSSION AND REVIEW

1. How did the Greeks contribute to the evolution of our understanding of human language? What fundamental questions did the Greeks raise?

2. Falk says: "When we seek knowledge about human language we seek knowledge about ourselves as individuals and as members of the human species." What does Falk mean? Do you agree? Why or why not?

3. Briefly describe the *physis-nomos* debate. Which position has become more powerful? Why is this so?

4. Who was Dionysius Thrax? Who were the Stoics? What role did they play in fostering the growth of our understanding of human language?

5. What does Falk describe as the Christian church's role in language development? What effect did the Crusades have on language in Europe?

6. Who were the speculative grammarians? In what ways did they broaden the scope of language's study?

7. What does Falk credit as "the greatest advances in the study of language from the fifteenth through the seventeenth centuries"? What political events of this time affected language study?

8. Describe the origins of language science, or linguistics, as a field of study. In what ways did this foster our knowledge of languages? What discoveries during the historical-comparative approach to language study encouraged the acceptance of linguistics as a science?

9. What is the earliest recorded language of which we have evidence? How have scientists made connections between this language and our own?

10. Which languages were accepted as standard in the eighteenth-centu-

ry linguistic community? Can you make any connections between this and modern notions of standard language forms?

11. What problems existed and still exist in attempts to study dialects in great detail? What efforts have been made in the United States for dialect study? Have they been successful?

12. What did Edward Sapir and Leonard Bloomfield contribute to the study of native American languages? What is their synchronic approach to language study? Why is the study of native American language so important?

13. In what ways did linguistic study in the United States of the 1950s change its scope and focus? What is transformational generative grammar? Who was responsible for its origins?

14. What is psycholinguistics? How has sociolinguistics played a significant role in this area, especially in the United States? Why is the study of sociolinguistics important?

Projects for "Historical Linguistics and Language Change"

1. The articles in Part Seven have dealt primarily with genetic classification of languages. Another type of classification, typological, was formerly popular and, much refined, is still useful. Prepare a report on typological classification that includes discussion of its earlier problems and its present status. You will want to read "A Quantitative Approach to the Morphological Typology of Language" by Joseph H. Greenberg and consult a text such as *Introduction to Historical Linguistics* by Anthony Arlotto (both are listed in the bibliography).

2. Prepare a report summarizing the development of the English dictionary. One useful source is *Problems in the Origin and Development of the English Language* by John Algeo (listed in the bibliography).

3. *The Oxford English Dictionary (OED)* is probably the finest historical dictionary ever prepared. Prepare a report describing its preparation and explaining the kinds of information that it contains.

4. The following passages are versions of the Lord's Prayer as they were written during different periods in history of the English language. (a) Analyze the forms that the various words have in common, and consider how each word changes from the first to the last version and, also, from one version to the next (e.g. Faeder, fadir, father, Father). (b) Do the same kind of analysis on the various syntactical (i.e., word-order) changes that you discover (e.g., Tōcume þīn rīce; Thy kyngdom cumme to; Let they kingdom come; Thy kingdom come). (c) Write an essay commenting on the changes you have discovered in these excerpts. Give as many examples of the changes as are necessary to support your conclusions. Finally, draw some conclusions about the evolution of the English language as revealed in the passages.

1. Eornostlīce gebiddaþ ēow þus Fæder ūre þū be eart on heofonum, sie þin nama gehālgod.
2. Tōcume þīn rice. Gewurþe þīn willa on eorþan swā swā on heofonum.
3. Ūrne daeghwæmlīcan hlāf syle ūs tōdæg.
4. And forgyf ūs ure gyltas swā swā we forgyfaþ ūrum gyltendum.
5. And ne gelæd þū ūs on costnunge ac ālys us of yfele.
6. Witodlice gyf gē forgyfaþ mannum hyra synna, þonne forgyfþ ēower sē heofonlīca fæder ēow ēowre gyltas.
7. Gyf gē sōþlīce ne forgyfaþ mannum, ne ēower fæder ne forgyfþ ēow ēowre synna.

Old English (ca. 1000)

1. Forsothe thus ȝe shulen preyen, Oure fadir that art in heuenes, halwid be thi name;

470

2. Thy kyngdom cumme to: be thi wille don as in heuen and in erthe;
3. ʒif to vs this day oure breed ouer other substaunce;
4. And forʒeue to vs oure dettis, as we forʒeue to oure dettours;
5. And leede vs nat in to temptacioun, but delyuere vs fro yuel. Amen.
6. Forsothe ʒif ʒee shulen forʒeuve to men her synnys, and ʒoure heuenly fadir shal forʒeue to ʒou ʒoure trespassis.
7. Sothely ʒif ʒee shulen forʒeue not to men, neither ʒoure fadir shal forzʒue to ʒou ʒoure synnes.

Middle English (Wycliffe, 1389)

1. After thys maner there fore praye ye, O oure father which arte in heven, halowed be thy name;
2. Let thy kingdom come; they wyll be fulfilled as well in erth as hit ys in heven;
3. Geve vs this daye oure dayly breade;
4. And forgeve vs oure treaspases, even as we forgeve them which trespas vs;
5. Leede vs not into temptacion, but delyvre vs ffrom yvell. Amen.
6. For and yff ye shall forgeve other men there trespases, youre father in heven shal also forgeve you.
7. But and ye wyll not forgeve men there trespases, no more shall youre father forgeve youre trespases.

Early Modern English (Tyndale, 1526)

1. Pray then like this: Our Father who art in heaven, Hallowed be thy name.
2. Thy kingdom come, Thy will be done, On Earth as it is in heaven.
3. Give us this day our daily bread;
4. And forgive us our debts, As we also have forgiven our debtors;
5. And lead us not into temptation, But deliver us from evil.
6. For if you forgive men their trespasses, your heavenly Father also will forgive you;
7. But if you do not forgive men their trespasses, neither will your father forgive your trespasses.

Modern English (1952)

5. Roberts mentions that there was at one time interest in establishing an "academy" to monitor and purify the English language. One of those interested was Jonathan Swift (1667–1745). Prepare a report on the history of interest in the arguments for and against the establishment of such an academy.

6. A number of artificial languages have been developed with the aim of providing a universal language that would be acceptable to everyone and easily learned. The best known of these languages are Volapük, Esperanto, and Interlingua. Basic English is also sometimes included in this group. Prepare a report on one of these languages; be sure to include samples of it, and argue for or against the concept of a universal language. The following

works will be helpful: (1) Connor, George Alan, D.T. Connor, and William Solzbacher. *Esperanto: The World Inter-Language*. New York: Bechhurst Press, 1948. (2) Pei, Mario. *One Language for the World*. New York: Devin-Adair, 1961. (3) White, Ralph G. "Toward the Construction of a Lingua Humana." *Current Anthropology* 13 (1972), 113–23. (4) Hayes, Curtis W., Jacob Ornstein, and William W. Gage. *ABC's of Languages and Linguistics*. Silver Spring, MD: Institute of Modern Languages, 1977, especially Chapter X, "One Language for the World?"

7. The following words have interesting etymologies: *algebra, anesthetic, assassin, caucus, crocodile, tawdry,* and *zest*. Look at their entries in the *Oxford English Dictionary* and then write a brief statement about each. If you have difficulty understanding the abbreviations and designations in the *OED*, consult the frontmatter.

8. Aitchison mentions the importance of "language planning." A great deal has been written about this subject in recent years, and the material deals with a number of different countries (e.g., India, the Sudan, various African countries, Haiti, Papua-New Guinea, and the Scandinavian countries). Using the resources in your college library, investigate the particular problems faced in one country and the kinds of "language planning" that have been done. Evaluate the success (or lack of success) of the planning.

9. Modern English developed from the East Midland dialect of Middle English (1100–1500). Chaucer wrote in this dialect, which is one reason that his poetry is relatively easy to read. But *why* did Modern English develop from the East Midland dialect? Based on library research, write a brief paper explaining the various reasons for this development.

10. After briefly discussing the "Great Permitters," Aitchison concludes that "attempts of caring persons to look after a language can mean no more than the preservation of personal preferences which may not agree with the views of others." Read at least three articles or book chapters by such "Great Permitters" as William Safire, Edwin Newman, and John Simon, and then write a short paper in which you analyze the validity of Aitchison's statement. You may find two books particularly helpful: (a) Harvey A. Daniels, *Famous Last Words: The American Language Crisis Reconsidered* (Carbondale: Southern Illinois University Press, 1983) and (b) Jim Quinn, *American Tongue and Cheek* (New York: Pantheon, 1981).

11. In "To Be Human: A History of the Study of Language," Falk examines historical events, people, and groups that have contributed significantly to the growth and development of our language. Among them are:

Individuals	Groups	Events
Dionysius Thrax	The Sophists	Invasion of England
Donatus	Greek philosophers	The Crusades
Priscian	Alexandrians	Invention of movable
Roger Bacon	Angles, Saxons, Jutes	type

Jonathan Swift   Speculative
Samuel Johnson   grammarians

Prepare a report on one of these individuals, groups, or events demonstrating the contributions made by your selection to the development of language. Feel free to select a topic not included in the lists. You may find helpful resources in the bibliography at the end of this section. You may also consult encyclopedias or history books. Compare reports in class in order to get an idea of the complications historical linguists face in their study of our language's history.

12. As we have seen, English is a member of the Germanic branch of the Indo-European language family. Prepare a report on either the Indo-Iranian, Balto-Slavic, or Italic branch, indicating what contemporary languages have developed from it, where they are spoken, and, if possible, by how many people.

13. Of the world's approximately five thousand living languages, only seventy are Indo-European. Some of the major non–Indo-European language families are the Afro-Asiatic, Altaic, Dravidian, Malayo-Polynesian, Niger-Congo, and Sino-Tibetan. Each of these families contains a number of languages, each of which has more than a million native speakers. Choose one of these six language families and prepare a report describing it. For example, does the language family have subfamilies? What are they? What languages belong to each subfamily? Where are they spoken? By how many people? What features characterize these languages?

Selected Bibliography

Aitchison, Jean. *Language Change: Progress or Decay?* 2nd ed. New York: Cambridge University Press, 1991. [Explores the process of language change without confusing technical terms and attempts to answer all questions on the subject.]

Algeo, John. *Problems in the Origin and Development of the English Language*, 3rd ed. New York: Harcourt Brace Jovanovich, 1982. [An outstanding workbook; interesting and thoughtful exercises.]

Anttila, Raimo. *An Introduction to Historical and Comparative Linguistics.* New York: Macmillan, 1972. [An excellent text; many examples; difficult but comprehensive.]

Arlotto, Anthony. *Introduction to Historical Linguistics.* Boston: Houghton Mifflin, 1972. [Very clear, readable, brief (243 pp.) introductory text.]

Baron, Dennis. *Declining Grammar and Other Essays on the English Vocabulary.* Urbana, IL: National Council of Teachers of English, 1989. [An accessible book about where the English language has been, where it is now, and speculations on where it is going.]

Baugh, Albert C., and Thomas Cable. *A History of the English Language*, 3rd ed. Englewood Cliffs, NJ: Prentice-Hall, 1978. [Long a standard, nontechnical text, the third edition is largely unchanged from the second.]

Bender, Harold H. *The Home of the Indo-Europeans.* Princeton, NJ: Princeton University Press, 1922. [The standard work on the subject.}

Bolton, W. F. *A Living Language: The History and Structure of English.* New York: Random House, 1982. [An excellent text; uncommon linking of the history of the language and the development of its literature.]

Breivik, Leiv Egil, E. H. Taylor, eds. *Trends in Linguistics: Language Change—Contributions to the Study of Its Causes.* New York: Mouton de Gruyter, 1989. [An accessible collection of short essays on the subject of language change.]

Dillard, J. L. *All-American English: A History of the English Language in America.* New York: Random House, 1975. [Emphasizes influence of maritime English on American colonists and the later imports of Yiddish, Pennsylvania Dutch, and "Spanish."]

Gordon, James D. *The English Language: An Historical Introduction.* New York: Thomas Y. Crowell, 1972. [A good text; useful bibliography.]

Greenberg, Joseph H. "A Quantitative Approach to the Morphological Typology of Language." *International Journal of American Linguistics* 26 (1960), 178–194. [Presents a number of criteria for typological classification of languages; an important article.]

Greenough, James B., and George L. Kittredge. *Words and Their Ways in English Speech.* New York: Crowell-Collier and Macmillan, 1901; paperback by Beacon Press, 1962. [An older book but still valuable especially on meaning changes and slang.]

Haas, Mary. *The Prehistory of Languages.* The Hague: Mouton, 1969. [The title of an earlier version describes the contents: "Historical Linguistics and the Genetic Relationship of Languages."]

Jeffers, Robert J., and Ilse Lehiste. *Principles and Methods for Historical Linguistics.* Cambridge: MIT Press, 1979. [An excellent advanced text; numerous examples.]

Keiler, Alan R., ed. *A Reader in Historical and Comparative Linguistics*. New York: Holt, Rinehart and Winston, 1972. [Twenty essays, from 1902 on.]

King, Robert D. *Historical Linguistics and Generative Grammar*. Englewood Cliffs, NJ: Prentice-Hall, 1969 [A pioneering work; not for the beginner.]

Krapp, George Philip. *Modern English: Its Growth and Present Status*. Rev. Albert H. Marckwardt. New York: Charles Scribner's Sons, 1969. [First published in 1909, it became a classic; updated by the late Professor Marckwardt.]

Lamb, Sidney M., and E. D. Mitchel, eds. *Sprung from Some Common Source*. Stanford, CA: Stanford University Press, 1991. [An in-depth look at the origins of language with a short history of Indo-European languages.]

Lass, Roger, ed. *Approaches to English Historical Linguistics: An Anthology*. New York: Holt, Rinehart and Winston, 1969. [Thirty articles of general interest.]

Lehmann, Winfred P. *Historical Linguistics: An Introduction*, 2nd ed. New York: Holt, Rinehart and Winston, 1973. [An excellent standard text; annotated bibliography.]

Lloyd, Donald J., and Harry R. Warfel. *American English in Its Cultural Setting*. New York: Alfred A. Knopf, 1956. [Includes an excellent short history of the American dictionary plus sections ("Our Land and Our People" and "Our Language") interesting for the history of American English.]

Lodwig, Richard R., and Eugene F. Barrett. *The Dictionary and the Language*. New York: Hayden Book Companies, 1967. [A good section on the making of a modern dictionary.]

Markman, Alan M., and Erwin R. Steinberg, eds. *English Then and Now: Readings and Essays*. New York: Random House, 1970. [A collection of essays and excerpts arranged by language period.]

Marckwardt, Albert H. *American English*, 2nd ed. Rev. J. L. Dillard. New York: Oxford University Press, 1980. [A fine revision and updating of a classic work.]

Myers, L. M. *The Roots of Modern English*. Boston: Little, Brown, 1966. [See especially Myers's specimens of OE.]

Nunberg, Geoffrey. "The Decline of Grammar." *The Atlantic* (December 1983), 31–46. [An excellent and entertaining essay about attitudes toward change in the English language.]

Pedersen, Holger. *The Discovery of Language: Linguistic Science in the Nineteenth Century*. Trans. John Webster Spargo. Bloomington: Indiana University Press, 1962. [A readable discussion of the principles of historical linguistics; many examples; originally published in Copenhagen in 1924.]

Pyles, Thomas. *Words and Ways of American English*. New York: Random House, 1952. [An introduction to American English from colonial times to the present.]

Pyles, Thomas, and John Algeo. *The Origins and Development of the English Language*, 3rd ed. New York: Harcourt Brace Jovanovich, 1982. [An outstanding revision of an already fine text; the Algeo workbook (*supra*) accompanies this text.]

Renfrew, Colin. *Archaeology and Language: The Puzzle of Indo-European Origins*. New York: Cambridge University Press, 1987. [An excellent text on the origins of languages used in the world today.]

Roberts, Paul. "How to Find Fault with a Dictionary." *Understanding English*. New York: Harper & Row, 1958. [Useful on both the history of dictionaries and how to use them.]

Sledd, James, and Wilma R. Ebbitt. *Dictionaries and THAT Dictionary*. Glenview, IL: Scott, Foresman, 1962. [A casebook on the controversy concerning the publication of *Webster's Third New International Dictionary, Unabridged;* introductory section on the history of dictionaries.]

Thieme, Paul. "The Indo-European Language." *Scientific American* (October, 1958). [Discusses the comparative method for reconstructing the Indo-European language and the insights it provides about Indo-European culture.]

Watkins, Calvert. "The Indo-European Origin of English," "Indo-European and the Indo-Europeans," "Indo-European Roots," *The American Heritage Dictionary of the English Language.* Ed. William Morris. Boston: American Heritage Publishing Co. and Houghton Mifflin, 1969. [The first two items are somewhat technical essays; the third item is an Indo-European root dictionary to which items in the dictionary proper are cross-referenced.]

Weinreich, Uriel. *Languages in Contact: Findings and Problems.* The Hague: Mouton, 1967. [A classic work; a revision of the original 1953 edition.]

Whitehall, Harold. "The Development of the English Dictionary," in *Webster's New World Dictionary of the English Language.* New York: The World Publishing Company, 1958. [A basic historical survey.]

William, Joseph M. *Origins of the English Language: A Social and Linguistic History.* New York: The Free Press, 1975. [Contains especially fine and numerous problems.]

Wilson, Kenneth G., R. H. Hendrickson, and Peter Alan Taylor. *Harbrace Guide to Dictionaries.* New York: Harcourt, Brace & World, 1963. [Thorough, but does not treat recently published dictionaries; good historical section.]

PART EIGHT

LANGUAGE VARIETY
AND CULTURE

It is an accident of history that the people of the United States speak English instead of French or Spanish, even Dutch or Portuguese. All of those countries sent their explorers and claimed their own pieces of the new world; but it was the English who established a fragile line of settlements along the eastern shore and a government forged of new ideals in an old language. Their adopted country was vast. Over the next century and a half it absorbed wave after wave of immigrants from other cultures and languages, each contributing some of their own flavor to the emergent nation; but the English foundations endured and dominated.

Around the middle of the twentieth century came the dawn of an uncomfortable new awareness. Not only had the apparently limitless opportunities of America reached their final frontier, but there was the growing realization that those opportunities had been grasped at the expense of others—not "savages," as the colonists saw them, but Africans and Native Americans, people whose ancient oral cultures were in their own ways as rich as those of the literate Europeans who subjugated them. The Civil Rights movement of the 1960s saw the resurgence of pride and identity in ethnic groups who survived, some just barely, on the fringes of modern American life. Cultures and languages that had long appeared subsumed by English-speaking America reappeared as colorful bits in a homogeneous blend. And the English language, already one of the world's most complex tongues after centuries of mutation, integration, and adaptation, is again facing the forces of change.

The six essays in this section examine two sides of the current linguistic upheaval in the United States. The first three—"Bilingual Education: Outdated and Unrealistic" by Richard Rodriguez, "It's the Talk of Nueva York: The Hybrid Called Spanglish" by Lizette Alvarez, and "Not White, Just Right" by Rachel L. Jones—deal with the relationships between "standard" English and the languages spoken by ethnic minority groups. Rodriguez and Jones are concerned primarily with the impact of bilingual education in Spanish and in dialects such as Ebonics. They defend the idea that Americans of ethnic minority groups must master standard English if they are to achieve success in their own country. Alvarez breaks in with a light-hearted exploration of "Spanglish," a Spanish-English hybrid. It is widely spoken in Hispanic communities throughout the United States and is spreading into the mainstream popular culture through TV, radio, magazines, and music.

The next two essays—"Saving California Languages" by Katharine Whittemore and "How Do You Say Computer in Hawaiian?" by Constance Hale—concern the efforts of Native Americans to bring moribund languages back to life. Whittemore observes a Master-Apprentice Language Program in which one (sometimes the only) speaker of a California Native American language teaches the language and culture to one adult student, with the hope that this apprentice will go on to teach it to many more children. Hale revisits her native Hawaii to observe a computer-linked group of total-immersion Hawaiian schools dedicated to reclaiming the ancient, poetic language and culture of the islands.

In the final essay, "Rearing Bilingual Children in a Monolingual Culture: A Louisiana Experience," Stephen J. Caldas and Suzanne Caron-Caldas face head-on the challenges posed by both the hazards of bilingual education and the desire to preserve and perpetuate a valued culture. To raise children who are fluent in both French and English, they call on the resources of a proud but dying heritage in their Louisiana community and on the wisdom of linguistic scholarship.

35

≡

Bilingual Education: Outdated and Unrealistic

Richard Rodriguez

In 1982, Richard Rodriguez wrote Hunger of Memory, *an autobiographical account of his experiences as a Spanish-speaking Mexican American child in an English-speaking American public school. Rodriguez embraced and became proficient in English, achieving a distinguished academic career; but he has never lost his deep interest in the conflicts faced by children whose first language is different from that they must use in school. In the following article, he examines the premise that bilingual education is not simply an issue of pedagogy, but also of politics and socioeconomic class. And he offers anecdotal evidence of the psychological and emotional realities of this issue. Beyond the rhetoric, what is it like for the children of bilingual education?*

How shall we teach the dark-eyed child *ingles?* The debate continues much as it did two decades ago.

Bilingual education belongs to the 1960s, the years of the black Civil Rights movement. Bilingual education became the official Hispanic demand; as a symbol, the English-only classroom was intended to be analogous to the segregated lunch counter; the locked school door. Bilingual education was endorsed by judges and, of course, by politicians well before anyone knew the answer to the question: Does bilingual education work?

Who knows? *¿Quien sabe?*

The official drone over bilingual education is conducted by educationalists with numbers and charts. Because bilingual education was never simply a matter of pedagogy, it is too much to expect educators to resolve the matter. Proclamations concerning bilingual education are weighted at bottom with Hispanic political grievances and, too, with middle-class romanticism.

No one will say it in public; in private, Hispanics argue with me about bilingual education and every time it comes down to memory. Everyone remembers going to that grammar school where students were slapped for speaking Spanish. Childhood memory is offered as parable; the memory is meant to compress the gringo's long history of offenses against Spanish, Hispanic culture, Hispanics.

It is no coincidence that, although all of America's ethnic groups are implicated in the policy of bilingual education, Hispanics, particularly Mexican Americans, have been its chief advocates. The English words used by Hispanics in support of bilingual education are words such as "dignity," "heritage," "culture." Bilingualism becomes a way of exacting from gringos a grudging admission of contrition—for the nineteenth century theft of the Southwest, the relegation of Spanish to a foreign tongue, the injustice of history. At the extreme, Hispanic bilingual enthusiasts demand that public schools "maintain" a student's sense of separateness.

Hispanics may be among the last groups of Americans who still believe in the 1960s. Bilingual-education proposals still serve the romance of that decade, especially of the late 60s, when the heroic black Civil Rights movement grew paradoxically wedded to its opposite—the ethnic revival movement. Integration and separatism merged into twin, possible goals.

With integration, the black movement inspired middle-class Americans to imitations—the Hispanic movement; the Gray Panthers; feminism; gay rights. Then there was withdrawal, with black glamor leading a romantic retreat from the anonymous crowd.

Americans came to want it both ways. They wanted in and they wanted out. Hispanics took to celebrating their diversity, joined other Americans in dancing rings around the melting pot.

MYTHIC METAPHORS

More intently than most, Hispanics wanted the romance of their dual cultural allegiance backed up by law. Bilingualism became proof that one could have it both ways, could be a full member of public America and yet also separate, privately Hispanic. "Spanish" and "English" became mythic metaphors like country and city, describing separate islands of private and public life.

Ballots, billboards, and, of course, classrooms in Spanish. For nearly two decades now, middle-class Hispanics have had it their way: They have foisted a neat ideological scheme on working-class children. What they want to believe about themselves, they wait for the child to prove, that it is possible to be two, that one can assume the public language (the public life) of America, even while remaining what one was, existentially separate.

Adulthood is not so neatly balanced. The tension between public and private life is intrinsic to adulthood—certainly middle-class adulthood. Usually the city wins because the city pays. We are mass people for more of the day than we are with our intimates. No Congressional mandate or Supreme Court decision can diminish the loss.

I was talking the other day to a carpenter from Riga, in the Soviet Republic of Latvia. He has been here six years. He told me of his having to force himself to relinquish the "luxury" of reading books in Russian or Latvian so he could begin to read books in English. And the books he was able to read in English were not of a complexity to satisfy him. But he was not going back to Riga.

Beyond any question of pedagogy there is the simple fact that a language gets learned as it gets used, fills one's mouth, one's mind, with the new names for things.

The Civil Rights movement of the 1960s taught Americans to deal with forms of discrimination other than economic—racial, sexual. We forget class. We talk about bilingual education as an ethnic issue; we forget to notice that the program mainly touches the lives of working-class immigrant children. Foreign-language acquisition is one thing for the upper-class child in a convent school learning to curtsy. Language acquisition can only seem a loss for the ghetto child, for the new language is psychologically awesome, being, as it is, the language of the bus driver and Papa's employer. The child's difficulty will turn out to be psychological more than linguistic because what he gives up are symbols of home.

PAIN AND GUILT

I was that child! I faced the stranger's English with pain and guilt and fear. Baptized to English in school, at first I felt myself drowning—the ugly sounds forced down my throat—until slowly, slowly (held in the tender grip of my teachers), suddenly the conviction took; English was my language to use.

What I yearn for is some candor from those who speak about bilingual education. Which of its supporters dares speak of the price a child pays—the price of adulthood—to make the journey from a working-class home into a middle-class schoolroom? The real story, the silent story of the immigrant child's journey is one of embarrassments in public; betrayal of all that is private; silence at home; and at school the hand tentatively raised.

Bilingual enthusiasts bespeak an easier world. They seek a linguistic solution to a social dilemma. They seem to want to believe that there is an easy way for the child to balance private and public, in order to believe that there is some easy way for themselves.

Ten years ago, I started writing about the ideological implications of bilingual education. Ten years from now some newspaper may well invite me to contribute another Sunday supplement essay on the subject. The debate is going to continue. The bilingual establishment is now inside the door. Jobs are at stake. Politicians can only count heads; growing numbers of Hispanics will insure the compliance of politicians.

Publicly, we will continue the fiction. We will solemnly address this issue as an educational question, a matter of pedagogy. But privately, Hispanics will still seek from bilingual education an admission from the gringo that Spanish has value and presence. Hispanics of middle class will continue to seek the romantic assurance of separateness. Experts will argue. Dark-eyed children will sit in the classroom. Mute.

———

FOR DISCUSSION AND REVIEW

1. Rodriguez asks, "Does bilingual education work?" and then brushes aside his own question by saying: "Who knows? ¿*Quien sabe?*" Since whether it "works" would seem to be a primary consideration in evaluating any educational policy, why does the author dismiss it?

2. In Rodriguez's opinion, why have Hispanics been so much more insistent than other ethnic groups in pursuing the legal right to bilingual education?

3. What opposing movements grew out of the original Civil Rights movement of the 1960s? How, according to Rodriguez, did bilingualism come to symbolize the best of both worlds to Hispanics?

4. What does Rodriguez mean when he refers to bilingual education as a "romantic" notion?

5. Why is bilingual education a class issue as much as or more than an ethnic issue? Do you agree that this is the case?

6. What does a working-class Hispanic child lose when taught entirely in English? When taught in Spanish in a bilingual program? Does Rodriguez imply that the child will have anything to gain from either approach? (You might want to refer to the essays by Edite Cunha and Maxine Hong Kingston in Part One. How do their childhood experiences of home and school echo Rodriguez's? In what particulars would they agree with him?)

7. Why does Rodriguez interrupt his discussion of bilingual education for Hispanic children with a story about a Latvian carpenter?

36

It's the Talk of Nueva York: The Hybrid Called Spanglish

Lizette Alvarez

*In various Hispanic American communities a hybrid language is emerg-
ing—a flexible, colloquial mixture of Spanish and English variously
called "Cubonics," "Tex-Mex," and "Spanglish." More and more,
through TV, the popular press, and literature written by Hispanic
authors, this language is entering mainstream American culture. In her
article "It's the Talk of Nueva York," Hispanic American journalist
Lizette Alvarez brings the force and flavor of Spanglish to one of
America's leading newspapers, the* New York Times. *Decried by traditionalists who deplore a loss of purity in both English and Spanish,
speakers of Spanglish take pride in being fully bilingual; they claim for
themselves the best of both languages.*

Nely Galan, guest host for a day, and the television actress Liz Torres
plop down onto the plump, oversized chairs that dominate the late-night
talk show set, and without missing a beat, slip into the language that
comes most naturally to both of them.

"Oye, oye, check out those red lips, girlfriend," Ms. Galan says.

"Madonna Red," Ms. Torres replies, pouting her full lips.

"Madonna Red, una belleza," Ms. Galan says. "You look beautiful."

"Sí, gracias," Ms. Torres remarks, returning the compliment. "Y tú
te ves tan linda."

Ms. Galan tells her late-night audience: "It's a Latina girlfest. We
love makeup."

Never mind that the talk show, "Later," appears on NBC and is geared
to an English-speaking audience. Ms. Galan, born in Cuba and reared in
New Jersey, and Ms. Torres, Puerto Rican and raised in Hell's Kitchen in
Manhattan, were speaking the hybrid lingo known as Spanglish—the language of choice for a growing number of Hispanic-Americans who view
the hyphen in their heritage as a metaphor for two coexisting worlds.

"I think Spanglish is the future," said Ms. Galan, 32, the president of
Galan Entertainment, a Los Angeles television and film production company that focuses on the Latino market. "It's a phenomenon of being
from two cultures. It's perfectly wonderful. I speak English perfectly. I

speak Spanish perfectly, and I choose to speak both simultaneously. How cool is that?"

Immigrants struggling to learn a new tongue have long relied on a verbal patchwork to communicate in their adopted land. But Spanglish today is far from the awkward pidgin of a newcomer. As millions of Hispanic-Americans, first, second and third generation, take on more prominent roles in business, media, and the arts, Spanglish is traveling right along with them.

The headlines of a glossy new magazine aimed at young Hispanic women spout a hip, irreverent Spanglish. Young Hispanic rappers use the dialect in recordings, and poets and novelists are adapting it to serious literary endeavors. Spanglish has few rules and many variations, but at its most vivid and exuberant, it is an effortless dance between English and Spanish, with the two languages clutched so closely together that at times they actually converge. Phrases and sentences veer back and forth almost unconsciously, as the speaker's intuition grabs the best expressions from either language to sum up a thought. Sometimes, words are coined.

Some Spanish-language purists still denounce Spanglish as a debasement of their native tongue. And many Latinos, wary of the Ebonics controversy that flared over the suggestion that black English should be considered a separate language, are unsure just how far they want to push their own hybrid. Many see it as a purely colloquial form of communication best suited to popular culture, and there is little talk of introducing a Spanglish curriculum in schools or demanding that Spanglish be accepted in the workplace.

Most speakers fall into Spanglish only among other bilingual Latinos, and when they do, it is often with a sense of humor.

"If in addition to, quote, 'taking all those good fruit-picking jobs' we then begin bastardizing the language, we are really going to catch it," said Christy Haubegger, publisher of *Latina* magazine. "We don't need another strike against us."

But those reservations have not limited Spanglish's popularity. Ms. Haubegger, a Mexican-American lawyer, began Spanglish's most successful foray into the magazine world last June when she started *Latina* magazine, a bilingual glossy in New York for young Hispanic women. The magazine peppers its stories and headlines with Spanglish. "When He Says Me Voy . . . What Does He Really Mean?" one headline reads. ("Me voy" is "I'm leaving.") "Mi padre's infidelity. Are cuernos genetic?" another reads. ("Cuernos" are horns.) The magazine, published six times a year, is so successful that it will go monthly.

In Miami, *generation ñ*, another bilingual magazine, found an audience in part because of a regular humor column by Bill Cruz called "Cubanamericanisms." Nothing more than a list of Webster-style definitions of Spanglish words, now dubbed Cubonics in Miami, it had Miami's Cuban community guffawing over their own expressions. In January, the magazine printed 4,000 novelty books featuring excerpts from the column, and they sold faster than a maicrogüey (microwave) can cook up a Weigüache (Weight Watchers) meal.

The much-praised Hispanic writers Sandra Cisneros, Julia Alvarez, and Roberto G. Fernandez routinely drop Spanglish into their novels and poetry, believing it to be a legitimate, creative form of communication.

"Language is not a little, airtight, clean, finished container of something," said Ms. Alvarez, a Dominican-American author (who is not related to this writer). "It's permeable, alive. It moves."

The language has also picked up momentum in music. Jellybean Benitez, a New York–based record producer and the founder of Hola, a recording company whose name stands for Home of Latino Artists, said a new wave of popular artists, most of them young rappers, are using Spanglish in their lyrics.

When Reign, a young Latino singer, warns "danger, danger, cuidado" as he slides in and out of the two languages on the title track of his recording, "Indestructible," he is doing it to connect to his audience, but also to show Latino pride, Mr. Benitez said.

And in Texas, where some say a Spanish-English hybrid has been around as long as Texas has been Texas, Spanglish—or Tex-Mex as they call it—has reached unrivaled levels of acceptance. Towns close to the border resonate with the language.

Those who tune into KXTN-FM in San Antonio, which has been No. 1 in the ratings for four years running, hear deejays saying things like, "Recuérdales que hoy, esta tarde, vamos a estar en vivo in Dillards, broadcasting live from 3 to 5, with your chance to win some cool KXTN prizes. Acompañen a sus amigos." Translation: Remember that today, this afternoon, we are going to go live from Dillards, broadcasting live from 3 to 5. Come with your friends."

Even the station's advertisers have requested that their commercials be broadcast in Spanglish, recognizing that the language can tap into the listener's bicultural world.

Ms. Haubegger, 28, the publisher of *Latina* magazine, also believes that Spanglish is good business.

"If we were an English magazine, we would just be general market," she said. "If we were a Spanish-language magazine, we would be Latin American. We are the intersection of the two, and we reflect a life between two languages and two cultures that our readers live in."

There are two basic approaches to Spanglish, with countless variations: switching and borrowing. Borrowing words from English and Spanishizing them has typically been the creation of immigrants, who contort English words for everyday survival. This method makes new words by pronouncing an English word "Spanish style" (dropping final consonants, softening others, replacing M's with N's and V's with B's), and spelled by transliterating the result using Spanish spelling conventions.

Thus, a grandfather suffering from a chest cold in Miami will walk into a drugstore and ask for "Bibaporrú," ordinarily called Vick's

VapoRub. A teenager will buy a pair of "chores"—"shorts"—for the gym. A housekeeper will plug in the "bacuncliner" to vacuum the rug. And, since regional differences exist in Spanglish, Latinos in New York might complain about "el estín" during winter if the steam shuts off or warn you late at night about "los joldoperos," robbers who hold you up.

Sometimes, an English word is borrowed for reasons of efficiency, since Spanish is famously multisyllabic. Instead of saying, "estacionamiento" for "parking," Spanglish speakers opt for "parquin." Instead of "escribir a máquina" for "to type," they say "taipear." Swiftly advancing technology has also added the verbs "bipiar" (from the noun "beeper") and "i-meiliar" ("to E-mail") to the vocabulary.

"Dame un bipeo later," said Mike Robles, a stand-up comic from the Bronx who does a whole riff on Spanglish. Give me a beep. "There are whole generations out there that speak exactly that," he said.

The children of immigrants, who grow up speaking or hearing Spanish at home, and English everywhere else, use these borrowed words, but they take Spanglish one step further. Ask them what they speak among themselves or at home and the answer is inevitably the same: Hablo un mix de los dos languagés, a mix of the two.

Traditionalists have sometimes deplored this "code-switching" between languages, often calling it a product of laziness and ignorance. And it is true that as Spanish gets fuzzier to American-born Hispanics, they come to rely on English words to fill the gap. But a new school of thought has recently emerged that says that Spanglish illustrates a high degree of fluency in both languages.

"It's a sign of linguistic dexterity," said Ana Celia Zentella, a linguist at Hunter College and at the CUNY Graduate Center who has written a book on bilingualism in New York. "It's like a complex juggling act or a train car able to run on two tracks at the same time, shifting from one to the other at the appropriate time. It's a skill that is often misunderstood."

Luz de Armas, chief creative officer and managing partner of Conill Advertisers in New York, who said she and her co-workers speak mostly Spanglish among themselves, agreed. She often switches into Spanglish, she said, to convey anger, joy, love, or embarrassment, because Spanish is a more descriptive, emotional language than English—not because she doesn't know the word.

That is also true for Ms. Alvarez, the novelist. "For me, Spanish is my childhood language," she said. "I came to this country when I was 10. It's the language of sensations and emotions, of the day to day."

As with other foreign languages, some Spanish words simply cannot be translated.

"English is very concise and efficient," said Gustavo Perez Firmat, a Duke University professor and poet who has written a collection of poems called *Bilingual Blues*. "Spanish has sabrosura, flavor."

It is also a statement of identity. "The reality is, because you do have a constant influx, we don't assimilate, we acculturate," said Ms. de

Armas, whose parents are from Spain. "I'm not turning my back on what I came from. You pick and choose and accommodate, and that's what Spanglish is."

GLOSSARY

Talking the Talk

Of the two basic forms of Spanglish, borrowing—saying English words "Spanish style" and spelling them accordingly—is more common among first-generation speakers; later generations tend to switch back and forth. Here are examples of the hybrid language—often spoken with a sense of humor—that has vaulted from streets to talk shows to the pages of magazines like *Latina* and *generation ñ*.

bacuncliner vacuum cleaner

biper beeper, pager

boyla boiler

chileando chilling out

choping shopping

fafu fast food

jangear hang out

joldoperos muggers, holdup artists

liqueo leak

maicrogüey microwave oven

pulóver T-shirt

roofo roof

sangüiche sandwich

tensén 10-cent store, like Kmart or Woolworth's

SPANGLISH

EL Oye, me estoy frisando y el estin está broken—close the door. ¿Vamos a lonchar, or what? I need to eat before I go to my new job as a chiroquero.

ELLA ¿Quieres que te cocine some rice en la jitachi, or should I just get you some confley con leche? By the way, you embarkated me el otro díia. ¿What did you do, pick up some fafu en vez de ir al restaurante where I was waiting? Eres tan chipero.

TRANSLATION

HE Hey, I'm freezing and the steam [or heat] is broken—close the door. Are we going to have lunch or what? I need to eat before I go to my new job as a Sheetrocker.

SHE Do you want me to cook you some rice in the Hitachi [catchall term for all steam cookers], or should I just get you some cornflakes [ditto for any kind of cereal] with milk? By the way, you stood me up the other day. What did you do, pick up some fast food instead of going to the restaurant where I was waiting? You're so cheap.

FOR DISCUSSION AND REVIEW

1. What is Spanglish? Having read the article, define it in your own words, being sure to include both linguistic and cultural considerations.

2. What do proponents of Spanglish see as its strengths? What do detractors see as its weakness? Why don't speakers of Spanglish try to make it accepted in the schools or the workplace?

3. Alvarez cites many examples of the use of Spanglish by public figures. What elements do they have in common? What, in your opinion, are the linguistic implications of these common characteristics?

4. Author Julia Alvarez says, "Language is not a little, airtight, clean, finished container of something. It's permeable, alive. It moves." With this quote in mind, refer back to "Language Change" by Jean Aitchison. In what ways do Alvarez and Aitchison reflect each other's ideas of language? How might Aitchison view the advent of Spanglish? Cite her work to support your opinion.

5. What are the "two basic approaches to Spanglish" as defined by Lizette Alvarez? How does each work?

6. Traditional and nontraditional linguists hold different views of the techniques by which Spanglish is derived. What are these views?

7. Under what circumstances are Spanglish speakers most likely to revert to Spanish words? To English? Why?

8. In your opinion, does Spanglish solve the dilemma raised by Richard Rodriguez in the preceding essay ("Bilingual Education: Outdated and Unrealistic")? Can Spanglish speakers sustain a hybrid culture that truly represents both their public and private lives? Where do working-class Hispanic children fit in a Spanglish-speaking culture?

37

Not White, Just Right

Rachel L. Jones

When, in 1982, Newsweek *magazine published Rachel Jones's essay "What's Wrong with Black English," a writer's career was launched, and a nation's assumptions about language were challenged. Like Richard Rodriguez, the Hispanic author whose autobiography* Hunger of Memory *was published in the same year (see "Bilingual Education: Outdated and Unrealistic"), Jones argued that the key to success for minority children in the United States is a good education in standard English. Jones identifies some drawbacks for black Americans in claiming a subset of language (i.e., Ebonics), including reinforcing the history of inequity and lack of access to equal educational opportunities.*

In December of 1982, *Newsweek* published a My Turn column that launched my professional writing career and changed the course of my life. In that essay, entitled "What's Wrong With Black English," I argued that black youngsters need to become proficient in standard English. While the dialect known as Black English is a valid part of our cultural history, I wrote, success in America requires a mastery of communications skills.

Fourteen years later, watching the increasingly heated debate over the use of Black English in struggling minority urban school districts, I can't help but offer my own experience as proof that the premise is greatly flawed. My skill with standard English propelled me from a life of poverty and dead ends to a future I could have scarcely imagined. It has opened doors for me that might never have budged an inch for a poor black girl from Cairo, Illinois. It has empowered me in ways I can't begin to explain.

That empowerment still amazes me. The column, one that Ralph Waldo Emerson might have described as "a frank and hearty expression of what force and meaning is in me," has assumed an identity of its own, far beyond what I envisioned. It has been reprinted in at least 50 college English texts, anthologies, and writing course books. I still have a scrapbook of some of the letters that poured in from around the country, from blacks and whites, overwhelmingly applauding my opinion. An editor in Detroit said he recognized my name on a job-application letter because he'd clipped the column and used it in a class he'd taught.

Recently, a professor from Brigham Young University requested permission to record the material on a tape used for blind students. But perhaps the most humbling experience of all occurred in 1991, when I was on fellowship in Chicago and received a phone call from a 20-year-old college student. He had just read the essay in one of his textbooks and, on impulse, dialed directory assistance, seeking my name. Because the column was written in 1982 when I'd been a student in Carbondale—and Chicago wasn't my hometown—there was no reason for him to have found me; I could have been anywhere in the world.

We talked for about an hour that night. He thanked me profusely for writing that column. He was biracial, and said that all his life his peers had teased him for "talking proper, for wishing [he] was *all* white." He said he was frustrated that so many black kids believed that speaking articulately was a white characteristic.

He thanked me so often it was almost unnerving. I hung up the phone in a sort of daze. Something I had written, communicated from my heart, had touched him so deeply he had to reach out to me. It brings tears to my eyes remembering it; I related to him so well.

I, too, had been ridiculed as a youth for my proper speech. But I had lots of support at home, and many poor urban black youths today may not share my advantages. Every afternoon my eight older brothers and sisters left their schoolbooks piled on every available surface, so I was poking through "The Canterbury Tales" by age 8. My sister Julie corrected me every time I used "ain't" or "nope." My brother Peter was a star on the high-school debate team. And my mother, Eloise, has one of the clearest, most resonant speaking voices I've ever known. Though she was a poor housekeeper when I was growing up, she was articulate and plain-spoken.

Knowing the price that was paid for me to develop my abilities, it's infuriating to hear that some young blacks still perceive clear speech as a Caucasian trait. Whether they know it or not, they're succumbing to a dangerous form of self-abnegation that rejects success as a "white thing." In an age of backlash against affirmative action, that's a truly frightening thought.

To me, this "whitewashing" is the crux of the problem. Don't tell me that calling Ebonics a "bridge" or an "attempt to reach children where they are" will not deepen this perception in the minds of disadvantaged young blacks. And though Oakland, California, school administrators have amended their original position on Ebonics, it still feels like a very pointed political statement to me, one rooted in the ongoing discussions about socioeconomic justice and educational equity for blacks. As much as I respect the cultural foundations of Ebonics, I think Oakland trivializes these discussions and stokes the fires of racial misunderstanding. Sen. Lauch Faircloth may have been too hasty in calling the Oakland school board's plan to introduce Ebonics "political correctness gone out of control," but he's hardly to be condemned for raising the flag of concern.

When immigrants worldwide fight to come to the United States, many seeking to gain even the most basic English skills, claiming a subset of language for black Americans is a damning commentary on our history of inequity and lack of access to equal educational opportunities in this country. Frankly, I'm still longing for a day when more young blacks born in poverty will subscribe to my personal philosophy. After a lifetime of hard work to achieve my goal of being a writer, of battling racism and forging my own path, I've decided that I really don't care if people like me or not. But I demand that they *understand* me, clearly, on my own terms. My mastery of standard English gave me a power that no one can take away from me, and it is important for any group of people hoping to succeed in America. As a great-granddaughter of slaves, I believe success is my birthright.

As I said back in December of 1982, I don't think I "talk white, I think I talk right." That's not quite grammatically correct, but it's a blessing to know the difference.

———

FOR DISCUSSION AND REVIEW

1. What are the hazards for a black or biracial student who speaks and writes correct "standard" English? What are the eventual potential rewards?

2. What dangers lie in store for the black or biracial student who does not speak or write correct "standard" English?

3. Why do many young black Americans reject "standard" English? Why does Jones find this a "truly frightening thought" in "an age of backlash against affirmative action"?

4. What is the appeal of Ebonics to black students and parents? To politicians and school boards? Why, in Jones's view, is this appeal unrealistic?

5. What contrasting views does Jones hold of the cultural value and the political status of Black English?

38

Saving California Languages

Katharine Whittemore

Katharine Whittemore, a journalist whose work has been published in many of the country's leading magazines, became interested in vanishing languages when she edited the American Retrospective Series, *anthologies of articles written for* Harper's Magazine *that focused on the broad history of life in the United States. Part of that history recounts the loss of Native American cultures and of their languages. Whittemore finds the rapid disappearance in this century of indigenous languages, not just in America but worldwide, sad and alarming. She warns that some 90 percent of the world's languages will be extinct by the century's close. She goes on to observe, "We work feverishly to save endangered species, yet we let these exquisite products of human culture disappear." In "Saving California Languages," Whittemore details in narrative form the grass-roots efforts of California's Advocates for Indigenous California Language Survival. This group sponsors the Master-Apprentice Language Learning Program, which brings together a few dedicated academicians (advocates), surviving speakers of scattered, nearly extinct tribal languages (mentors), and students wishing to learn the languages (apprentices). The emphasis of participants in this program is not to record and analyze a language, but to learn, absorb, preserve, and pass it on, along with whatever remnants of culture still adhere.*

They leave Berkeley for Porterville at dusk, driving five hours southeast with the windows down, smelling California instead of seeing it: garlic fields, they guess, then orange groves, truck-crushed tomatoes, oil refineries. It's August and hot. In a thatch of tape recorders, notebooks, and video cameras, five passengers sit talking or asleep. Four are Yurok, from a Native American tribe up north in Humboldt County: Carol Korb, her husband Vernon, and their two small sons. The other is Anglo, a linguistics professor at the University of California at Berkeley named Leanne Hinton.

Carol and Leanne belong to a group with the bulky title of the Advocates for Indigenous California Language Survival. The Advocates sponsor something called the Master-Apprentice Language Learning Program, which pursues a nearly desperate mission: to save Native Californian languages on the rim of extinction. It does this not through some sophisticated methodology, but by simply pairing speakers and non-speakers. The Advocates then help those pairs with a steady pulse of workshops, materials, and house calls. It's less bureaucratic than personal.

"The Master-Apprentice program is almost antilinguistic," explains Leanne. "True-blue linguists are taught to analyze a language. Apprentices just want to absorb it." In other words, the program isn't committed to saving these languages for Science, but for the tribes themselves. Carol and Leanne will spend the next few days visiting three Master-Apprentice teams here in vast central California, to see how they're faring.

Masters are usually elder members of a tribe, often one of a handful of speakers left. The apprentices are mostly younger adults. Today's middle generation wasn't taught the language; most of their parents were stigmatized, even beaten, for speaking their own words at Indian boarding schools. The hope is that the apprentice will now learn the language (it takes about 500 hours of intense instruction) then teach it, in turn, to groups of tribal children. Those children will grow up and hand down their knowledge to the next generation. The words—and not just the words, but words as aquifers of values and culture—will thus flow on.

Since 1993, the Advocates have scratched together twenty Master-Apprentice teams, blowing on the embers of Mojave, of Hupa, of Chemehuevi, of as many tribal dialects as humanly possible. Their idea is starting to be applied throughout the world, and none too soon. We're living in an age where languages are dying off at appalling rates. Indeed, 90 percent of all the world's languages are considered threatened, *90 percent*, including most Australian aboriginal dialects, and even those laced through larger populations, like Basque and Breton, since they aren't officially taught in local school systems.

Blame it on the "cultural nerve gas" of television, as University of Alaska linguist Michael Krauss calls it, or on marching globalization, or on government policy. Whatever the reasons, languages are being trampled at a faster clip than at any other time in history. Ironically, one of the culprits is increased literacy. Most governments can't afford to print textbooks in multiple languages, thus the linguistic mainstream floods any tributaries of minority dialects. Languages have always eroded throughout history. But in the past, normal attrition was outstripped by growing diversity, as languages mutated and recombined over time. Now, though, they're not so much evolving as dying out.

The issue hasn't drawn much concern outside the linguistic community, which mourns the likely decimation of 90 percent of its knowledge base, plus, of course, the affected populations themselves. In America, where a vast majority of us speak English only, it's hard to stoke up much passion for saving strings of unintelligible sound. Yet diversity—the byword of our era—is as fundamental to human development, linguists argue, as it is to the natural world. Even so, endangered languages spark much less attention than endangered species. They lack cachet. "Should we mourn the loss of Eyak or Ubykh (two Alaskan tongues) any less than the loss of the panda or California condor?" asked

Krauss at a conference on language loss, held at Dartmouth College in February 1995.

Or Yowlumni and Wukchumne, a couple of near-moribund languages now depending on Master-Apprentice matches for their survival, here in central California. Carol and Leanne will visit both these teams. They're a good team themselves. Carol is a graduate of Humboldt State, and is an Apprentice in Yurok. She is a strong-shouldered woman, with crow-black hair and the confident bearing of someone used to shuttling between the Anglo and Indian worlds. She relishes the poetry of her own language, how the word for sun translates into "daytime traveller," for moon "nighttime traveller," or how the Yurok have no terms for north, south, east, or west. Their Oregon border country is too sinuous with streams and mountains; the terms don't apply. The door of a house stands not on its "western" but "downstream" corner. One looks "upstream," rather than to his or her left.

Leanne is a pivotal figure in the world of language rescue. Aside from her teaching duties at Berkeley, she also writes an intriguing column on language for the Berkeley-based journal *News from Native California*, since collected into the 1994 book *Flutes of Fire: Essays on California Indian Languages*. The book has stirred things up. "Leanne is why you hear about this program," explains Carol matter-of-factly. "Not us." She says this without rancor; she and Leanne are friends. But Carol has few illusions about how interest in her cause is generated.

Leanne is 53, has worried brown eyes and a warm, almost therapeutic buzz. Her interests spill all over the place. She teaches linguistic theory, has illustrated children's books on Indian tales, written the *Oakland Tribune* editorials in favor of language rescue, reviewed an Arapaho version of *Bambi*, and done a dissertation on the songs of the Havasupai, with whom she lived for several years, in Arizona. She is a nonacademic academic who once wrote, in a letter to the president of Berkeley, that her work with Californian native speakers has been "pure joy."

After spending the night at the Porterville Motel 6, then, Carol and Leanne and the others set out for the Tule River Reservation. It abuts Sequoia National Park and enfolds about 700 Yowlumni, Wukchumne, Mono, and Chukchansi. This is hill country, buff-colored and bright. The radio says it's 103 degrees out. They drive past two whitewashed stone teepees, then the Wooden Nickel General Store, and after a few miles turn off at a neat brown ranch house. The Master-Apprentice team of Agnes Vera, in her 60s, and her son Matt, in his 30s, live within. They are Yowlumni. One of Matt's brothers resides here, too, plus Agnes's husband, whom she calls, affectionately, "The Last of the Chichanzis." (There are only a hundred or so left.)

Everyone is greeted at the door with hugs; Carol has only met them once before, but Leanne has known them for some time, and is in regular phone contact. Agnes draws Leanne aside to give her a small beaded pocketbook. Matt thanks her for sending the Yowlumni-English dictionary a few months back, compiled by anthropologist Stanley Newman in 1944. Fans whirr against the heat. The shades are drawn. Before the assessment gets under way, Matt tells Vernon Korb how to find a nearby rock with impressive pictographs, then where to take the boys swimming.

Last year at this time, Matt couldn't hold a rudimentary conversation in Yowlumni; it's a remarkably difficult language, famed among linguists for its dozens of verb-suffixes which alter the verb's meaning. "There are four or five ways to say the verb 'burn,' depending on what's being burned," explains Matt, as everyone arranges themselves in the living room. "If it's paper, wood, food, your skin, a hillside, you use a different suffix." He is an intense, almost brooding person, whose paintbrush hair falls into a long ponytail. "I could spend the rest of my life just working on verbs," says Matt. "Sometimes I just throw the paper on the floor and shout 'I give up!'"

But Agnes doesn't let him; she's a formidable Master. Leanne lets on that, at Advocates-sponsored language immersion camps, everyone quickly learns not to sit by Agnes at meals. She won't lapse into English to make things easier, ever. A staunch woman with a sun-creased face and polished nails, she drives Matt pretty hard. "Some teams quit because they get mad at each other," Leanne admits later on. "But if you're really close anyway, you've spent a lifetime working things out, and you have a commitment that goes way beyond any kind of anger."

Still, it can't be easy for a grown man to move back home. Matt had been working in Bakersfield, about 100 miles away, trying to do lessons over the phone. But it just didn't sink in as well as the immersion he was seeking. The job was sacrificed. It's not too much to say that the health of the language rides squarely on Matt, for besides Agnes, there's only about half a dozen speakers fluent in Yowlumni, and they're all at least in their sixties. Learning Yowlumni is now his occupation.

Leanne sets out a pile of color photocopies, mostly of Native American paintings. Matt lights a cigarette and forgets about it, the smoke curling over ceremonial bowls and a copy of the Fresno *Bee*. Horses whinny in the distance. He peers at the top one and Agnes begins pointing to figures within, asking him questions in Yowlumni. He answers haltingly, also in Yowlumni. Leanne crouches on the carpet to get a good shot of mother and son conversing. Later, the Veras will watch the video together, to see where they need more work. The tape will also act as a morale-boosting time capsule; next year at this time, they'll theoretically be doing much better.

Leanne and Carol can't speak Yowlumni, so after Matt's done, Agnes translates a bit of what he's said about the picture: "Two Indian ladies, they are going to cut up the cow, the cow is dead, it is cloudy, there is lightning, the lady wears a white dress, she looks tired." Agnes nods approvingly. "I understood what he was telling me," she says, "even if it was in broken Indian." Matt sighs audibly, quashes his cigarette. Leanne says, "Matt, if it's not hard for you, you're not learning." He half-smiles.

Matt decided to devote himself to learning his language, at root, for what can only be called spiritual reasons. He conducts beginning

Yowlumni classes on the reservation and in town, and is renowned for his ability to summon the tribal past through meditation and dreams. He and Agnes lead most of the rituals and sweatlodge ceremonies here. "I wanted to pray to my ancestors, but they didn't know English," Matt explains. As to why he was driven to become an Apprentice, "They knew Yowlumni. Maybe they understood me anyway, but I was unsatisfied with my level of prayer. I want to be *eloquent*."

The Veras have a grant for all of $3,000 for sustaining this ancient tongue. It's supposed to hold them for four months, but they need much more than a third of a year to take hold of Yowlumni. The language is too demanding. "You have to have a really intense need to learn because there's any reason in the world to quit," says Leanne. Like the need to make money, for one. Or the considerable frustration of taking on a complicated language. "Everyday life gets in the way of being Indian," admits Carol, laughing slightly. Matt and Agnes call their knottiest lessons "The Indian Comedy Hour."

The rest of the afternoon is taken up with loosely testing Matt from a questionnaire Leanne has brought along, to gauge his competency. But mostly Leanne and Carol watch, tape, and offer a little advice. They let Agnes and Matt ramble. Matt's mistakes sometimes trigger Agnes's memory of a long-forgotten word; they've learned not to discount anything that surfaces. There are other techniques to language rescue, like writing down or recording the words of those speakers still left, then working off the notes and tapes. But nothing, the Advocates believe, can replace the give and take of teacher and student, master and apprentice.

"There are lots of reasons to like this program," writes Leanne in one of her *Flutes of Fire* essays. "It is simple, and based on common sense; it has a direct and easily observable effect in increasing fluency; and it doesn't take a ton of money, equipment, or expertise to implement."

Every morning, Matt sits on the grass outside and quizzes himself. "I try to make up sentences," he says. "Yesterday I saw buds in the two little trees my Mom planted. I tried to say 'Mom planted the trees' but it came out 'The trees planted Mom.'" He will stay until he can say something in Yowlumni about everything he sees—the trees, the hawks, the hot blue sky. Then he'll come inside, and the next lesson begins.

When Christopher Columbus scraped upon New World sands in 1492, there were 10,000,000 Native Americans scattered from coast to coast. By 1910, after four centuries of disease, displacement, and violence, there were 300,000. Scholars believe that some 350 native languages were in active use as Columbus came ashore, and about 200 of those 350 survive today.

Of those 200, nearly 80 percent are no longer passed down to the children of each tribe. California both conforms to and deviates from this scenario. It boasts the most native languages of any state in the union, some eighty in existence when the first European settlers arrived, and fifty today. Fifty languages seems like a pretty healthy figure, until you realize that all of those fifty lie in a critical state. Another 30 or so languages now have no living speakers.

Such verbal abundance arose from California's history and topography; because the area is so enormous, fertile, and climatically enticing, it was peopled early on. In theory, unlike early white settlers, Native Americans moved across North America from west to east, migrating first over a thin blade of land that later slipped under the waves of the Bering Strait. In California, there was plenty of room (and time) for tribes to develop languages astonishingly disparate from one another.

"Hupa and Yurok are as different as Chinese and English," explains Leanne, referring to two northern California tribal languages. That's the kind of thing one learns paging through *Flutes of Fire*, the title of which comes from a myth of Maidu origin. The essays tender much insight into Indian culture and language, but more lastingly, they lend a feel for the wordmusic of the languages, the power of the concepts jeweled within.

In Karuk, for instance, there is no word for "apology." That's because redress must always be made through concrete action—talk will not suffice. The concept of the integrity of the individual is paramount in many Indian languages, especially in Wintu, which has none of the linguistic possessives we regularly bandy about in English. Where we would say "I took my son to the river," for instance, the Wintu would employ something like "I went with the child to the river." The coercive implications of English verbiage ("I took") are softened into the repeatedly stressed cooperation of Wintu ("I went with," freely). Indeed, one can't even say "my son" in Wintu; "I am sonned" is the closest equivalent.

"One really important motivation to learn a language is the idea that it may contain values superior to the values of mainstream mass society," Leanne explains. This is precisely the way Matt and Agnes Vera see it. Knowing the language can resurrect a value system dessicated by outside incursions. It's not just the words, it's what they mean, the nourishment they impart. "There was an emptiness before," Matt says. "Now I feel spiritually good." In *Flutes of Fire*, Hinton quotes a female elder of the Atchumawi-Atsugewi tribe: "Yes, we must know the white man language to survive in *this* world. But we must know our language to survive *forever*."

Not surprisingly, Californian Indians have just barely survived in this world. The state's tribes have worked down the same weary roster of privations and broken promises afforded other Native Americans across the country. But it's also been much worse here. First, the tribes contended with Spanish missionaries, who carried in enough disease to reduce their numbers by half, from 300,000 in the sixteenth century to 150,000 by the nineteenth.

Then came the Gold Rush. From 1848 to the close of the 1850s, that 150,000 had dropped a cataclysmic 80 percent, to about 30,000. "It was out and out genocide," says Leanne. Indeed, actual bounties were placed on Indians who lived on land deemed desirable for mining. Each Indian killed brought $5 to the hunter. In one year in the 1850s, the federal government paid out $1 million in claims. "If the Gold Rush hadn't happened, you'd probably still see tenacious Indian cultures in California," Leanne says.

Californian Indians can't mimic the language-sustaining tactics of more well-known tribes like the Navaho or Sioux. Such bigger populations are now seeing that their language is taught pervasively, usually in a school setting. "We have none of those resources," admits Leanne. Californian Indians also live differently. After the twenties or so, they were encouraged to move into white society (hence the lack of colorful Indian names for most native Californians). Also, unlike the Great Plains and southwestern tribes, they had been previously herded onto small patches of land called "rancherias," owned by whites, with Indians as tenants, rather than onto broad reservations. Tule River is one of only three official reservations in the state. (There's a Native American rap group, based in San Francisco, that bears unwitting testament to this setup. It's called "Without Reservation.")

At the end of our own century, then, Californian Indians find themselves in linguistic crisis for basically two reasons. First, the population as a whole was tragically decimated, mostly from Gold Rush atrocities, and second, the vast cornucopia of tribes precluded cohesiveness. Any power in numbers was lost. But this catastrophic situation—some tribes were actually eliminated, others now have no living speakers at all—created, perversely, an appealing arena for scholarship. It's this horrible twist that helps make today's Master-Apprentice program possible; practitioners from an exciting new field called anthropology flocked to the state in the early 1900s, and made meticulous, invaluable records of languages they believed would soon vanish.

Indeed, California provided the underpinnings of American anthropology: the Hearst Museum of Anthropology was founded in San Francisco in 1911 (it's now located at Berkeley). Anthropologists at the time were keenly aware that civilization had eclipsed the last of the frontier. Yet out here, as west as you could get, there were still some relatively isolated Indians, more conversant with their traditions than Indians to the east of them, who'd been in Anglo contact longer.

The most famous object of scholarly interest was a Yahi Indian named Ishi, who walked out of the woods in Tehama County in 1911, having hid for forty years with the few members of his tribe not killed in a series of Gold Rush massacres. Anthropologist Alfred L. Kroeber brought Ishi to the Museum, and with the help of other linguists, captured as much of the Yahi language on tape and paper as he could. The story became the subject of a 1994 documentary; mention native languages to a Californian, and if he or she knows anything, it's probably Ishi's name. When Ishi died in 1916, the Yahi culture passed with him.

Kroeber and anthropologist John Peabody Harrington—the most famous and obsessive of the bunch—and their colleagues performed a great service. But they did the work not so much for the Indians themselves, as for the grail of linguistic data. Actually, California's early anthropologists would be shocked to know that their notes are used by their subject's descendants; they thought there wouldn't be any descendants, that most tribes would go the way of the Yahi. "The time will come and *soon* when there won't be an Indian language left in California," as Harrington wrote in an emphatic letter to his assistant. "All the languages developed for thousands of years will be *ashes*, the house is *afire*, it's *burning*."

Eddie Sartuche is handing out peaches. He's high-spirited about the task, as he is about nearly everything, making little jokes, his voice too loud by half. With his new blue jeans, cowboy boots, and wrinkle-free skin—from being dipped in a boiled bark solution as a baby, he claims—one forgets he's a 68-year-old with a hearing aid. Eddie is Wukchumne. He's very fit. He was a trucker for many years, and before that a merchant marine, and before that a zoot-suited gang member in San Francisco in the forties. He still has a tiny blue-green tattoo between his eyes, marking him as a gang leader.

It's another blast-furnace August afternoon, and Leanne and Carol are drinking ice water and munching plump *philasna* (Wukchumne for peaches). They finished up with Matt and Agnes yesterday. Today they're doing a sort of roundup of assessments, here at Eddie's daughter Yolanda Clavenger's home, in the hills between Lemoncove and Three Rivers. Yolanda is apprenticed to her father. So are two of the Tapleras sisters, Susan Weese and Darlene Franco, plus Weese's grown daughter, Debra Weese Fierro. Then there's Agnes Vera's sister Jane Flippo, who is teaching Yowlumni to another Tapleras sister, Cindy Tapleras. (The Taplerases grew up in the nearby city of Visalia; they are both Wukchumne and Yowlumni.) Some women sit inside, the rest talk out on the porch, gazing through rafter garlic skeins to Lake Keweah.

If one views the ultimate objective of the Master-Apprentice program as instilling the language in tribal children, one of these women particularly stands out. Darlene Franco supports her family as a dental claims processor at CIGNA, while her husband, Lalo (Chumash and Wukchumne), home-schools their three kids. The Anglo schools in Visalia, where they live, had little to teach about native culture. The Francos are fiercely committed to saving the Wukchumne language and its traditions.

They try to weave them through their life. They won't utter the name of a deceased relative for a year after his death. Darlene often carries a pouch of tobacco, as her grandmother did, giving a small snuff offering to the land in exchange for its gifts—a little sage for incense, a few acorns for traditional Wukchumne soup. In the house, everyone speaks as much Wukchumne as possible. The children know many Wukchumne stories, and perform dances and skits at tribal meetings.

Darlene is an engaging woman of 35, with the pretty burnished features of her Wukchumne mother and Filipino father. Once, when she was a girl, her public school teacher blithely told the class that most area tribes, including the Wukchumne, had been completely wiped out. Darlene raised her hand, and explained otherwise. These days, she is on the board of the Advocates, as well as serving as Eddie's apprentice.

When their children were born, Darlene and her husband Lalo asked her mother, Martha Tapleras, to name each in a traditional Wukchumne ceremony. Martha decided upon Lahoci—"happiness" in Wukchumne— for their oldest boy, Yaynicut, which means sage blossom, for their little girl, and Kowonash, for their younger son. He was born during an August meteor shower, and so christened after a shooting star.

These children are among about 300 Wukchumne left in the world; the tribe was hit especially hard in the Gold Rush. It's not that the Wukchumne women at Yolanda's house today don't ever feel bitter about this; it's more that they don't have the time. There's too much work to be done. While Matt Vera pursues Yowlumni for spiritual reasons, they concentrate on passing everything they know to their children, who take it in more easily. The motivation is spiritual, too, but with a deep maternal overlay.

Indeed, Susan Weese brought along her eleven-year-old granddaughter, Monique, this afternoon to get a load of Eddie firsthand, and watch her mother and aunts learn too. She wants her to see that this is important. Monique's a little shy in the din of adults, but at a ceremony a while back, she led the tribe in a Wukchumne sing-along of (really) "Ten Little Indians." Monique (her Indian name is Tushamoy, Wukchumne for "spring") and her cousins Lahoci, Yaynicut, and Kowonash Franco have put on other skits. They are steadily learning more Wukchumne as their mothers keep at it. "They're little sponges!" as Eddie says jovially. "Sponges!"

Back inside the house, it's time to get under way. Leanne passes out more of her conversation-piece photocopies, and she and Carol walk around listening to each team. It's too easy to describe it thus, but the scene is Babel. A rush of throaty vowels and percussive consonants clatter forth, as each apprentice struggles to describe what he or she sees in the pictures. The smell of burritos fills the air, and split peaches. A fleet of tape recorders is going, which makes Leanne frown; she knows how easy it is to slack off on memorization if the crutch of the tape is there for later reference. At one point, a tape is rewound and played. It fouls, the voices speeding up abnormally, and everyone laughs, saying it sounds like "chipmunk Wukchumne."

Most nights, Eddie falls asleep listening to anthropologists' Wukchumne tapes, honing the language he hasn't spoken consistently since he was a boy. Or he works from the 1928 notes of anthropologist Frank Latta, who acted as a stenographer to Martha Tapleras's "Grandma and Grandpa Icho," a couple who'd lived next door to her natural grandparents. Or he flips through the rudimentary Wukchumne-English dictionary compiled by Martha's nephew who has "time on his hands," as she politely put it in her Master application. (He's in prison.)

One senses Eddie's motivation for being an apprentice is that it brings him the past as well as allows him to shape the future. "My grandma wouldn't talk to you unless you spoke Indian," Eddie remembers. "She was mean, but sweet, you know? It makes me cry thinking of her. When I teach, I hear my grandma."

Aside from Eddie, there are three very elderly men (his uncles) who speak Wukchumne, plus Martha Tapleras—who had signed up to be a Master, then had a stroke that took away most of her speech. That's how delicate it is in some tribes. Just months ago, the "last speaker" of Northern Pomo, who was one of the Masters, died in her sleep. (A few months later, though, another speaker was discovered. No one has exact counts on who knows these languages. "We're used to surprises," says Leanne.)

As adults, we look for props when it comes to learning a language. Leanne explains that we should try to learn as children do, through sound, not relying on the medium of the written word, or tapes, or translations from English. She sees a lot that's heartening in this pack of masters and apprentices today—the will is there—but feels they need some tactical help. "Use pantomime instead of English," she says, after everyone settles down from the assessment. "If you want someone to say 'water' in Wukchumne or Yowlumni, don't say water in English. Point to a faucet."

Cindy Tapleras throws up her hands. "I'm getting brain fade," she sighs. In *Flutes of Fire*, Hinton writes: "You are doing a heroic task; forgive mistakes." They break for burritos and more ice water, and some aspirins are passed around. Headaches are routine during lessons; it's from all that concentration. The talk is in English now, with a few morsels of Wukchumne and Yowlumni tossed in for spice. Eddie tells a few tales of his boyhood, his voice rising. He brags about Lahoci Franco, and how much Wukchumne he can speak. "Sponges," he says again.

"I will carry on teaching, as long as I'm on this earth!" Eddie adds robustly, between bites. Everyone laughs; they trade glances. He's practically shouting now. "If I go, I don't want [Wukchumne] to go with me. I want to give it away! We're not *trying* to save our language," he continues, looking straight at Leanne and Carol. "We're doing it."

═══

FOR DISCUSSION AND REVIEW

1. Why does Leanne Hinton say that the Master-Apprentice program is "almost antilinguistic"? Why does the program nonetheless occupy an important place in a linguistics text?

2. Unlike most of the essays in this book, "Saving California Languages" is structured primarily as a narrative. Why is this form appropriate to the piece's subject?

3. Throughout human history, languages have continually evolved, mutated, recombined, eroded. How has this pattern changed in the twentieth century, and what, according to Whittemore, are the causes of change?

4. We think of schools and literacy—the ability to produce and read

printed words—as powerful positive forces in the preservation of language. How can they also cause the suppression and destruction of language?

5. Refer to "Native Tongues" by Nancy Lord in Part One. What do the Dena'ina and Yurok languages have in common? What unique qualities of indigenous language do Lord and Whittemore fear to lose?

6. Why did so many separate indigenous languages develop in California? Why is it so much more of a challenge to save these languages than those of larger tribes such as the Navajo or Sioux?

7. What effect did the Gold Rush have on the indigenous cultures of California? Why?

8. It is extremely difficult to be an apprentice. For what reasons do the apprentices introduced in this essay choose to take on the task? Do these reasons seem valid to you? Why or why not?

39

How Do You Say Computer in Hawaiian?

Constance Hale

Constance Hale, the author of Wired Style: Principles of English Usage in the Digital Age, *has often written about the impact of technology on language. In this article, editor/journalist Hale considers the intersection of computer technology and the culture and language of her homeland, Hawaii. When missionaries, businessmen, and politicians converged on the Hawaiian Islands throughout the 1800s, they paid scant heed to the local culture. Both the ancient Polynesian culture and its beautiful poetic language, which had flourished untouched by outside influences for many centuries, nearly disappeared. A renewed interest in Native Hawaiian language and culture has led to vigorous efforts to save them from extinction. Hale examines the computerized Hawaiian-language BBS (bulletin board system), which connects schoolchildren and adult speakers of Hawaiian with each other and the world at large.*

It is 1823 in Honolulu, and the Reverend Hiram Bingham is sitting down to his writing table. Not one to let tropical humidity dampen his sense of propriety, Bingham is wearing a black frock coat and high-necked white blouse. His countenance: austerity in the extreme. Bingham is leader of a group of New England Calvinist missionaries who have come to the Polynesian chain with one expressed purpose: to stamp out paganism.

To this end, Bingham is bracing for a formidable task, one that will take him and his seven accomplices 16 years to achieve: translating the Bible into Hawaiian. Bingham's Bible project will be no cakewalk: Hawaiian—a poetic Polynesian tongue with few parallels to English—has never been consigned to letters. Only one printing press even exists West of the Rockies—an aging Ramage iron-and-mahogany model Bingham hauled around Cape Horn. But no matter: Bingham is determined to hoist the pre-literate, ancient Hawaiian culture into a new medium and a new age.

Now, fast-forward. A trio of unlikely geeks is huddled around a computer rammed into the corner of a tiny office at University of Hawai'i in Hilo, a modern campus whose blocky concrete buildings defy the lush surroundings. The three are Keao NeSmith, a 29-year-old hunk of a

Hawaiian wearing a white WordPerfect T-shirt, blue-and-black plaid shorts, and black zoris; Keiki Kawai'ae'a, a 38-year-old perky mom dressed in tapa-print culottes and gold cloisonné bracelets (whose black lettering spells out her full name, Keikilani, or "child of the heavens"); and Keola Donaghy, 35, the full-bellied son of an electrician from Philly, sporting jeans, a UMEN T-shirt, and aviator glasses.

The year? 1994. The mission? To undo much of what Hiram Bingham set in motion a century and a half earlier. The means? A Mac IIfx with 8 megs of RAM and a 175-Mbyte hard drive. This is the central nervous system of *Leokī* (the powerful voice), a Hawaiian-language bulletin board system [BBS] that is one of the first BBSes set up to teach a Native American language. In addition to e-mail, it features a newspaper, chat lines, a tailor-made Hawaiian-English dictionary, user feedback, and a voting booth.

The trio's purpose is every bit as religious as was Bingham's: they want to save their ancient culture. They, too, are using language—what their University of Hawai'i colleague Professor Larry Kimura describes as "the bearer of a people's culture, history, and traditions." Unlike Bingham, they are attempting to retrieve something that had almost slipped away. But can technology bring a lost legacy back from the brink?

When the Hawaiian Islands were "discovered" by the British Captain James Cook in 1778, about 350,000 Hawaiians inhabited them. These Polynesians cultivated plantations of bananas, coconuts, sugar cane, and taro. They cooked pigs and harvested the sea. Living in villages of thatched huts, they were guided by concepts of *mana* (spiritual power) and *kapu* (human laws or taboos). Chiefs and priests held sway over commoners. Tradition and heritage were expressed primarily through chant and dance.

Needless to say, when the missionaries arrived in 1820, they were less than thrilled by *this* version of paradise. Their attitude was aptly summed up by the nineteenth-century evangelical A. F. Judd: "Darkness still brooked over the land, and there still continued idolatry, the taboos of the priests, wars, famines and death. . . ." The language, too, seemed primitive and deficient in the missionaries' eyes: not only had it never been written down, but it lacked a whole host of words the missionaries deemed critical. (*Jesus*, for starters.)

But there were dissenters. Reverend Lorenzo Lyons, for one, praised the native tongue as "grand, old, sonorous, and poetical." Lyons wrote: "I've studied Hawaiian for 46 years but am by no means perfect . . . it is an interminable language . . . one of the oldest living languages of the earth, as some conjecture, and may well be classed among the best."

And while there had been no writing in Hawaiian before Bingham— no Bible, no books, no newspapers—there *were* stories. There were stories about Maui, the Hawaiian Apollo, who wove a rope out of his sister's hair, snared the sun as soon as it rose one day, and negotiated for longer hours to fish, farm, and dry bark cloth. There were stories about Pele, the goddess of the volcano, who expressed her wrath with molten lava and orange fire. And there were ancient chants that related the spiritual, familial, historical, and cultural vitality of Hawaiians; among them was the *Kumulipo,* a creation myth that has often been compared with *Beowulf.*

But the Hawaiians' belief in chants and the power of the *spoken* word didn't necessarily translate to a belief in the *written* word. When Liholiho, the young son of the conqueror Kamehemeha I, asked missionary Asa Thurston to write his name, Thurston spelled it out: "li-ho-li-ho." Liholiho looked at it "long and steady," according to a missionary account, then announced to Thurston: "This does not look like me, nor any other man."

Written or not, Hawaiian *was* an incredibly precise language—especially when it came to things that really mattered to Hawaiians. No fewer than seventeen names exist for the various winds of tiny Hālawa Valley on Moloka'i. And each of the different permutations of just one kind of fish has its own term: *pua'ama* is a "mullet under a finger length"; *kahaha* a "mullet about eight inches long"; and *'ama'ama* a "mullet about twelve inches long."

But, for all its richness, the language still struck the missionaries as lacking: there were no words for such New Testament necessaries as *faith, holiness, throne,* and *demoniac.* "The natives call an angel either an *akua,* a god, or a *kanaka lele,* flying man," lamented one missionary. Another pointed out that the Hawaiian *aloha* had to be used in the Bible for everything from *salutation,* to *love, charity,* and *merry.*

But the missionaries made do. They devised an alphabet, settling on twelve Roman letters for Hawaiian words, plus a few more letters for foreign words. When a Hawaiian synonym didn't exist, they just transliterated: "Christ" begat *Kristo,* "David" begat *Kāwika,* "school" begat *kula.*

Ultimately, Bingham's Bible did help bring literacy to the Hawaiians—by the turn of the century, 125 newspapers were being printed in the Hawaiian language. But what began as an assault on Hawaiian spirituality soon widened to an assault on the entire culture. The missionaries suppressed bawdy chants and the salacious hula; American and European immigrants wrested lands from Hawaiian chiefs; *haole* (white) businessmen, seeking to improve agricultural profits and backed by US Marines, overthrew Hawai'i's monarchy. And, by 1900, the Hawaiian tongue—the culture's linchpin—was officially banished from government offices and could only be taught in public schools as a foreign language. This prohibition on speaking Hawaiian ushered in a century of linguistic decline.

"I didn't realize Hawaiian was a dying language until I went to Honolulu," says Keao NeSmith. "My friends would speak to me in Hawaiian; I answered in English. No big deal." As a child, NeSmith was steeped in Hawaiian tradition: he grew up among Hawaiian-speaking families in Kekaha, a rural town on the western shore of Kaua'i, and his mother is a master of the hula. A Mormon, NeSmith attended the Brigham Young University on O'ahu's North Shore, then followed friends to Provo, Utah, where he worked as a customer-support operator at WordPerfect.

It was in Provo that NeSmith's nostalgia kicked in. "I got shanghaied into being a teacher for a local Hawaiian language class," he remembers. By day he was answering questions about WordPerfect; by night he was fielding questions about his native tongue. It wasn't long before he started thinking about putting computers and Hawaiian together.

NeSmith came home to Hawai'i for good in 1992, four days after Hurricane Iniki had devastated his island and hometown. He returned to help clean up the yard and "pick up whatever was left of the roof." But however much his home had been destroyed, other cultural forces had wreaked even greater devastation on Hawai'i as a whole. "Seeing Honolulu was really depressing, really sad," he says, referring to the development and overcrowding that had turned the capital into a "concrete jungle." The Hawaiian language, too, needed rescue.

NeSmith's timing was perfect. By 1992, two decades of Native Hawaiian activism were coming to fruition. The civil rights and antiwar movements of the '60s and early '70s had sparked anger and stirred ethnic pride among Native Hawaiians, who moved to reclaim their land, their language, and their heritage. If there was one watershed moment for the dying Hawaiian language, it must have come in 1983, when a study showed that only 32 students under 18 (most of them concentrated in remote hamlets of Kaua'i and Ni'ihau) were able to speak Hawaiian. (At the time, experts estimated that fewer than 3,000 adults spoke the language—most of them over 60, scattered across seven islands, and speaking mostly English day to day.)

Immediately after the study, a dedicated group of professors and activists—many of them now at the University of Hawai'i in Hilo—gathered in Honolulu to start plotting the great Hawaiian-language comeback. Step One: repeal the century-old law prohibiting the teaching of Hawaiian in public schools. Step Two: establish a system of public schools with Hawaiian-language immersion programs.

Today, students attend eight Hawaiian-language elementary schools on five different islands. One middle school has opened its doors, and last January, state agencies approved (to the tune of US$2.1 million) the first Hawaiian-language high school to open its doors in a century. Classes will start there this September.

Once the schools started opening, it came time to hoist the Hawaiian language into the techno age—hook, line, and SLIP* connection. That's when NeSmith joined forces with Keiki Kawai'ae'a and Keola Donaghy. In computer networks the three found a new medium that used the oral *and* the textual as its currency, a medium perhaps better suited to an oral tradition than the book ever was.

The BBS idea started when Keiki Kawai'ae'a became one of the first teachers for the Hawaiian-immersion schools, known as Kula Kaiapuni. Like the children she coaches, Kawai'ae'a reflects the ethnic soup that is

---

*SLIP (Serial Line Internet Protocol). A standard method for connecting to the Internet via telephone lines.

Hawai'i and the Pacific Rim. A mix of Hawaiian, Chinese, and Okinawan ancestry, she was raised on Maui and in Los Angeles. Her foundation in the Hawaiian language came from her family, where she was the eldest of eighteen grandchildren at the family ranch. She credits her Hawaiian grandfather for instilling in her a sense of tradition. Her first fishing lesson: Never catch a fish and think it's your pet.

At the University of Hawai'i in Honolulu, Kawai'ae'a was inspired by Professor Larry Kimura, well known among Hawaiians as a Hawaiian-language scholar and songwriter. Before long she was a Hawaiian-studies teacher at a Honolulu private school. And after 10 years, she moved to Pā'ia on Maui, to launch the Kula Kaiapuni there.

Computers were an essential part of her plan: she wanted to instill students with a sense of pride in both their language and its utility. "We want everything available to children who speak Hawaiian that is available to children who speak English," she says. "We want children to know that Hawaiian is not just good enough for sitting at a party and talking story. Hawaiian is good enough for every part of life. That is the sign of a healthy, living language."

But during time with her students in the computer lab, which was stocked with Apple II and IIe computers, Kawai'ae'a was faced with a new dilemma: how to make her pupils as computer-literate as any other students while using all-Hawaiian instructions. "They were *so* excited about computers," she remembers, "but the only thing we had to teach them with was in English."

Soon, Kawai'ae'a latched onto the promise of telecomputing and the hope that in corresponding with *each other*, students would get more of the pure Hawaiian they'd need: "Our members are small at each immersion site, and in many ways the groups are isolated. Could we hook them up to the students at other sites?"

It was at this juncture that Kawai'ae'a crossed paths with NeSmith, enlisted to translate computer-menu options into Hawaiian, and Donaghy, a computer jock learning Hawaiian on his own. Donaghy's Irish surname reflects his ethnic identity: he is the son of mainlanders, though born and raised on Maui. After a stint as a cop, then music school in LA and some studio work as a jazz and rock electric-guitarist, he settled into a job at Nadine's Music in Kahului, Maui. From there he freelanced with Steely Dan ("taking care of the group's Macs and making sure everything was working"); before long he had started a Macintosh BBS called MauiLink.

By 1990, he was also nurturing contacts in the Hawaiian community, and through the "coconut wireless" (Hawaii's grapevine), he hooked up with Kawai'ae'a. The big kahuna of MauiLink found a new calling—as the big sysop* of *Leokī*.

By March '94, Donaghy had *Leokī* up and running. Six months later, the Kula Kaiapuni were on the Net; soon after they were homesteading on the World Wide Web. Today, a dozen years after the original study (and

---

*System operator.

wake-up call) showing that only thirty-two Hawaiian children spoke their native tongue, the number is 1,000 and climbing. And that's just the kids.

"I'm mother dreamer," says Kawai'ae'a, adding: "Keola is father doer. We can't make our dreams happen without technology. It's taken thousands of hours to figure out how to make technology work for us."

Beginning with the terminals in the various computer labs, Donaghy and Kawai'ae'a linked the sites with a Macintosh IIfx server (donated by Apple Library of Tomorrow) and FirstClass software (bought with a $5,000 grant from the Bank of Hawai'i). They connected the server to a statewide electronic services gateway that gives islanders toll-free access from anywhere in six of the state's seven inhabited islands. (The seventh and smallest inhabited island, Ni'ihau, has no phones.) They named their brainchild *Leokī*.

As it turned out, the mechanical obstacle—getting the computers and setting up the BBS—was the *easiest* part of Donaghy's job. Other hurdles were far greater—ones Hiram Bingham would have found all too familiar. Donaghy had to devise a means to word process two diacritical language marks, without which Hawaiian would be much tougher to decipher. For instance, take out the diacriticals in the word *pā'ū* (pah-ooo) and you get *pau* (pow). It's the difference between the term for a Victorian riding skirt and the word for "finished."

He had to be inventive. What hardware and software combination could accommodate such idiosyncrasies as the ubiquitous glottal stop (denoted by a single open quote before vowels and equivalent to a consonant) and the macron (a bar over vowels that changes their sound)? He modified screen fonts, created a new keyboard layout, and made sure that once logged on, a child didn't see a single word of English.

This accomplished, Donaghy found he could translate programs like ClarisWorks and Kid Pix into Hawaiian. And he imported the entire text of the immersion program's working dictionary into Claris Dictionary—after all, nothing would be complete without the ability to have kids spell check their assignments. Having created new characters, Donaghy customized the keyboard and modified the initial login screen to read entirely in Hawaiian.

Kawai'ae'a, Donaghy, and NeSmith managed to get computers that spewed Hawaiian throughout the classrooms of the Kula Kaiapuni. But once the computers are there, what on earth do you call them? Do you transliterate (as Bingham did to settle on *Kristo* for Christ), and call the computer *kamepiula*? Or do you make up a term from components that already exist in Hawaiian—say *lolouila*, or "electric brain"?

As the curriculum of the Kula Kaiapuni expanded, teachers found themselves needing terms unimaginable a century ago, when the language had, in effect, become frozen in time. (What is the Hawaiian word for an adventure story? How do you say "floppy disk"?) Before long, Kawai'ae'a and NeSmith turned to a lexicon committee—comprised of professors and native speakers—that now gathers seven times a year to grow the language. Searching for a Hawaiian term for "upload," the committee settled on *ho'ouka*, "to load or put up on." *Ho'ouka* describes how you would put a saddle on a horse. *Ho'ouka* also gets a suitcase into a trunk. Now it also gets a file onto the Net. In other cases, the committee members resorted to Bingham's transliteration methods: they took an English term and made it Hawaiian sounding. "Line" became *laina*. "Telephone" became *kelepona*. "Beep" became *pīpa*.

In the transition from an oral to a more textual tradition, curious resonances crop up. Over and over again each day, a child computing in Hawaiian selects *Mālama*, from the pull-down File menu. Meaning "to save," *mālama* has become a kind of rallying cry in contemporary Hawai'i: *mālama pono* means "take proper care," *mālama 'āina* means "save the land," and *mālama 'ōlelo* means "save the language." Perhaps unwittingly, the children are "saving the language" every day.

The Pā'ia School sprawls across the lower slope of Haleakalā, Maui's enormous dormant volcano and "house of the sun." The main building is a gracious, turn-of-the-century hall that lords over a sweeping grassy lawn shaded by banyan and monkeypod trees.

At Pā'ia School, the Hawaiian-immersion classes open each day with an *oli*, a call-and-response chant between teacher and students. In the chant, students—fresh off the lawn from running and playing—as permission to come into the class and seek knowledge.

The children gather and chant:

> *Ka uka o Kaukini* (from the uplands of Kaukini)
> *Ka nahele 'o Waiho'i ē* (to the forest of Waiho'i)
> *Komo ē, e komo ma loko nei* (may we enter, do we have an invitation)
> *Ma loko aku ho'i au ē.* (we acknowledge your welcome and shall now
> enter).

The teacher having granted permission, they enter a generous high-ceilinged room with louvered windows and hardwood floors. In one half, the walls are azure blue, decorated with posters of Hawaiian kings and queens and kids' block prints in the style of Polynesian petroglyphs. In the other half—a computer lab jammed with twenty-five terminals—walls are covered with a hand-drawn cartoon character, kind of a Casper the Friendly Computer. He speaks in Hawaiian: *Leo nahenahe* (speak in a sweet, gentle voice), *Mai ku'i i nā pihi* (don't pound on the keys), *Ho'iho'i i kāu pā malule* (return your floppy disk).

Of the school's 250 students, roughly half are in the Hawaiian-immersion program. I visit the "lead class"—seventeen fifth- and sixth-graders, most of them of an ethnic mix favoring Hawaiian.

As I sit and try (unsuccessfully) to blend in, four children—with deep mahogany-colored skin, black hair, and dark, alert eyes—cluster around an L-shaped table. Today, they are tackling long division—in Hawaiian! Their sense of identity is evident: one boy's T-shirt reads *Pūko'a kani 'ā ina/Waihe'e Maui* (an ancient Hawaiian proverb describing how a coral reef grows into Waihe'e Maui), emblazoned above a drawing of a Hawaiian warrior in a field, a giant volcano looming behind him. The slogan is straight from a land battle Hawaiians recently won against a Japanese developer planning to lay a golf course over an ancient burial site.

But leave the politics to the adults; these are still kids, struggling with math. *"Kumu!"* (teacher) they call, whenever they're stuck. When it's time for a live chat with Kumu Keiki, in Hilo, the entire class sits on the floor in front of a projection screen. Students take turns typing messages. One boy, named Keawe, types gingerly, then loses all self-consciousness when Keiki Kawai'ae'a sends him a reply: "Wait," he begs in Hawaiian, "Can I answer her?" Everyone helps him spell out: *'o kinipopo pōpeku ko'a hāuki punahele* ("football is my favorite sport"—with a couple of spelling errors thrown in).

"Computers lend a lot to their literacy in Hawaiian," says teacher Mālia Melemai, adding that reinforcing literacy is critical in what is otherwise an oral tradition. Even more than longhand, computers heighten the children's consciousness of spelling and expression as they write, edit, and revise.

"The urgency and value of computers is higher here than in conventional schools," Melemai says. These kids really hunger for connections and look forward to the day when the BBS will link them with kids on the mainland and around the Pacific. *"Leokī* opens a door for them, to friends who speak Hawaiian and who are not teachers, who are their own age but far away."

"It's fun," says 11-year-old Lē'ahi Hall, who says *Leokī* is her favorite application. "You can talk to friends on other islands that you miss a lot—and you don't have to use the telephone."

The articulate, balletic sixth-grader, daughter of an attorney and an activist, plans to use Hawaiian throughout her life. Her ambition? To become a teacher "like Kumu Keiki and Kumu Mālia, because the language needs to go on."

Talk to kids like Lē'ahi—or to Keola Donaghy, who is organizing Hawaiian lessons via the Internet—and it all seems so simple: get Hawaiian online, spread the word, revive the language. But is it?

The best way to learn languages is through immersion—not just in the language, but in the culture. The same is true for Hawaiian, perhaps even more so, since it has always been largely aural and highly esoteric. Mary Kawena Pukui, the late expert in Hawaiian, warned that the language has more words with multiple meanings than almost any other. She told the story of some eager business folks who wanted to give a new hotel a Hawaiian name. They chose Hale Le'a, or "joyous house." Little did they know that *le'a* also means "orgasm." And what about the Hawaiian language's sheer musicality? (Hawaiians were so taken aback by the consonant-laden harshness of English, writes Larry Kimura, that in slang they called it *namu,* "grumbling," and *hiohio,* "of a flatulence-like whistling.")

Can a computer BBS—or, for that matter, can the Net —ever do justice to a language so full of melody and nuance?

Or, on the other hand, is the Net a fertile ground for languages like Hawaiian? After all, computer networks—home of the "live chat"—

bridge the spoken and the written. But who knows yet whether the global village promises a flourishing of indigenous tongues, or whether the Net will become, linguistically, The Great Homogenizer?

Maybe the language of the online world will be enriched by projects like *Leokī*. Certainly, NeSmith, Kawaiʻaeʻa, and Donaghy envision the day when islanders are linked with Hawaiian-speaking emigrés on the mainland. Ultimately, they plan to link up Hawaiians with their Polynesian cousins throughout the Pacific.

Perhaps the Hawaiian experiment with technology will be mirrored by other projects in indigenous languages—ones that have been all but subsumed by a more widespread national language. Imagine BBSes spreading Catalan, Welsh, Breton, or Maori, the indigenous language of New Zealand, whose 850 native "language nest" schools have been an inspiration for the Kula Kaiapuni. (Unlike the Hawaiian schools, which suffered a devastating blow in January 1995 when the new Republican House threw the future of the Native Hawaiian Education Act into political jeopardy, the Maoris have enjoyed full government support—including a cabinet-level language minister for Maori affairs—that Hawaiians have, so far, been denied.)

For some, like *Leokī* supporter Steve Cisler of Apple Library of Tomorrow, such BBSes represent the kind of community building that is the essence of telecomputing. The task, he says, is to get more people to talk to each other, and that will happen as more people hear—usually by word of mouth—about the real benefits of being in touch with others across the globe and of having access to useful information. He compares telecomputing to Amish barn-raisings where a community bands together to fill a need. Telecomputing, he adds, achieves the same thing and can be delivered in the same spirit.

A vestige of plantation Hawaiʻi, Pāʻia School reminds me—in its architecture, grace, verdancy, and those umbrella-like trees—of the elementary school I attended in another plantation town on Oʻahu. But at Waialua Elementary in the '60s, despite a large native Hawaiian population, Hawaiian culture was only present in traces. We did learn one hula each year, but that was for an annual festival of oddly European origins: May Day. We spoke pidgin English (a creole that mixed influences from each of the islands' main ethnic groups—Hawaiian, Caucasian, Chinese, Japanese, Filipino). No one spoke Hawaiian—not the teachers, not the kids who were by blood pure Hawaiian, not the *haoles* like me.

What a thrill to visit the UH-Hilo campus and to hear everyone speaking exclusively in the beautiful language that so nearly perished. And it's not just the language they are bringing back, it's the culture. Every child I meet there greets me not in the mainland way, by shaking hands, but in the Hawaiian way, with "*aloha*" and a kiss on the cheek. "*A hui ho!*" they call after me as I leave: Until we meet again!

Born and raised in Hawaiʻi, the islands are indisputably, deeply, *my home*. Yet, ironically, I have never felt so much an outsider as when wandering the halls of UH-Hilo, listening helplessly to so many voices chattering in Hawaiian. More profoundly than at any other time in my life, I am reduced to a *haole* in the most original sense of the word: because I don't speak the Hawaiian language, I have become "a stranger."

But the revival of Hawaiian isn't about estrangement; it's about bridges. One image, in particular, has stayed with me from UH-Hilo: As I am leaving Edith Kanaka'ole Hall (named after "Auntie" Edith, an educator, advocate, and cultural scholar), I walk down a long, gently sloping ramp. It leads away from the maze of *lānai* that connect the campus' utilitarian concrete buildings, to wide, sloping lawns sheltered by abundant, ancient trees—banyan, norfolk pine, *hala*, coconut palm.

Ahead of me is a young man we might, in pidgin, call a "moke": He's a strapping native Hawaiian, dressed in a local version of the '90s protest outfit—worn black T-shirt and low-slung shorts, black zoris, ponytailed dreadlocks that reach all the way to his *okole*, and a squarish, straggly beard. He's big, beefy, and imposing.

Approaching us from the direction of the lawn is an older, fragile Hawaiian woman whom we'd affectionately call a *tūtū* (a grandmother, auntie, or elder). She displays a headful of neatly combed white hair and wears a sky-blue polyester blouse and white slacks; she carries a very '50s pocketbook.

"*Aloha!*" she calls out to her opposite, and they launch into a spirited, enthusiastic conversation. They are "talkeen story" as we would say in that bastard local lingo. But for their heart-to-heart they choose Hawaiian, not pidgin. In the melody of their exchange a message is clear: Hawaiian, that elegant language once thought dead, is reclaiming its home.

FOR DISCUSSION AND REVIEW

1. In the beginning of her essay, Hale carefully contrasts the Reverend Hiram Bingham and the "trio of unlikely geeks . . . huddled around a computer," yet these people so far removed from each other in time and purpose had linguistic problems in common. What were these difficulties, and how were they resolved in 1823 and in 1994?

2. What are some characteristics of the Hawaiian language that are very different from English?

3. What linguistic, cultural, and political pressures caused the near-disappearance of the Hawaiian language? If these pressures have such a negative effect on cultures and languages, why do they remain so powerful in today's world?

4. Even though the Hawaiians are using computers to reclaim their language, many people see modern technology (TV as well as computers) primarily as a threat to oral languages. Why? (You may want to refer to the preceding essay, "Saving California Languages" by Katharine Whittemore.)

5. Why do the teachers of Kula Kaiapuni consider the computer indispensable to total immersion education in Hawaiian? What is *Leokī*, and what role does it play in the Kula Kaiapuni?

6. When Hispanic children attending American schools receive their instruction in Spanish, it is called "bilingual education." Hale does not use this term to refer to Kula Kaiapuni, even though Hawaii is a state of the union whose dominant language is English. Is there a difference, and if so, what is it?

7. Hale says, perhaps optimistically, that "the revival of Hawaiian isn't about estrangement; it's about bridges." In your opinion, will children educated by immersion in the Hawaiian language and culture thrive as adult citizens in the English-speaking United States, or will they struggle with isolation and separatism?

40

≡

Rearing Bilingual Children in a Monolingual Culture: A Louisiana Experience

Stephen J. Caldas
Suzanne Caron-Caldas

When the authors of this study married, they brought together in their heritages the two most persistent French-language subcultures on the North American continent, those of Quebec and southern Louisiana. Ironically, Caldas, descended directly from the French-speaking Acadians (Cajuns), spoke only English when he met the French-speaking Quebec woman who was to become his wife. The difficulty these two educators experienced in attempting to become proficient in each other's languages prompted them to raise their children to be bilingual. This essay is an account of their largely successful efforts to instill both French and English into the lives of their children from birth to school age. Using their experience and extensive research in linguistics, and taking advantage of a nostalgia for the historic French language and culture of their Louisiana community, Caldas and Caron-Caldas carefully monitored their children's exposure to both languages. They found that the children made equal gains in French at home and in English in their preschool and neighborhood.

Rearing children to be bilingual in a culture which is overwhelmingly monolingual is a formidable task. There are a multitude of obstacles to achieving this goal which arise from the constant invasion on all sides of the dominant culture's language. These obstacles seem to be particularly magnified in North America, where there has been a long history of intolerance to any language but English. According to one linguist, the dominant attitude seems to be, "It would be so much simpler if we all spoke the same language, namely English" (Darbelnet, 1976, 5).

This article is a descriptive ethnography of a genre similar to Heath's study (1983) of language acquisition and usage in two small Carolina piedmont communities. We attempt to describe a particular family's experience in a specific social milieu. Though we feel as though there are certain universal principals of language acquisition, we caution against the generalizibility of our study experiences.

514

Our story begins in 1980 with our marriage, and Stephen's exposure for the first time to French Canada. Stephen stepped off an airplane in Québec City and into the middle of the "separatist" movement. Though never taking sides in this heated issue, the experience sensitized him to the threatened French culture and language of his own state and planted the seed for our family project.

The French-speaking Acadians (Cajuns) of South Louisiana, originally exiled from Nova Scotia in the mid-eighteenth century, successfully resisted linguistic assimilation for almost two centuries. However, even this exceptionally close-knit culture has not been able to withstand the onslaught of American English. As a testament to this fact, though Stephen is the son of an Acadian woman, he spoke no French before marrying his Québecoise co-author. Suzanne likewise spoke no English. Our initial attempts to communicate were centered around a French-English paperback dictionary which was quickly reduced to tatters by our romantically inspired efforts to understand each other. In this work we outline our efforts to achieve bilingualism ourselves, and our subsequent project to raise our three children to be French/English bilinguals in the increasingly monolingual culture of South Louisiana.

The decline of French in Louisiana dates to the early 1920s, when a wave of isolationist anti-foreign sentiment swept across the United States. This mood resulted in the passage of legislation by several states restricting the language of instruction to English (Alexander, 1980). The state legislature of Louisiana passed a law which made utilizing French as the language of instruction in Louisiana's schools illegal (Mazel, 1979). Acadian children who spoke French while at school were often harshly disciplined. Though anti-French-speaking sentiment has all but disappeared in Louisiana, so has the French language among this generation of Cajuns. Remarking on the current situation, one historian laments, "It is monstrous that people who speak English with an unmistakable French accent should have to be taught French" (Taylor, 1976, 184).

But this was exactly Suzanne's mission when she was hired by COD-OFIL (Council for the Development of French in Louisiana) in 1980: to help in the revival of the French language in Louisiana. She was soon teaching French in the first elementary-school immersion program in the state.

Suzanne was as anxious to improve her English as Stephen was to improve his French. Since she was now immersed in an English-speaking culture, it was agreed that we should speak as much French as possible at home. Though the tendency to speak English was strong, Stephen daily forced himself to communicate with his new wife in her native tongue. Since we were both educators, we had the opportunity to spend several of our summer and winter vacations in Québec, where Stephen had no choice but to speak French.

By 1983 Stephen felt confident enough to minor in French as he worked on his master's degree at Louisiana State University, eventually becoming certified to teach French at the primary and secondary levels. Still, bilingualism seemed an elusive goal to both of us. We adopted

Darbelnet's definition (1976, 4) of *bilingual* "being equally at home and equally effective in two languages," though among scholars there is little consensus as to precisely how the term is to be defined (Fraser and Mougeon, 1990). Our mutual efforts notwithstanding, as we struggled to master each other's language, it was becoming clear to both of us that the goal of bilingualism was truly difficult to achieve.

Or so we thought. Our perception of bilingualism changed as a result of two factors. The first was a scene we witnessed while crossing the English Channel during a summer trip to Europe in 1982. Seated across from us on the ferry was a couple with a three-year-old child. The father spoke to him in French, and the mother spoke to him in English. The child not only understood both of his parents, but he replied to both of them in their respective tongues and without an accent! The second factor was Suzanne's experience as an elementary French immersion teacher. In short, her fourth graders, in their first year of French, progressed rapidly enough to hold a conversation in French after only a few months. We resolved to spare our future offspring all of the effort we were expending to acquire a second language—we were going to *rear* our children bilingually from birth.

Suzanne became pregnant in 1984. We had already devised our strategy—Suzanne was to address our first-born only in French, while Stephen was to speak to our child only in English. We implemented our plan with the birth of John in May of 1985.

One of our first instinctual concerns was that we would confuse our newborn son. We countered this fear by continually reminding ourselves of the Channel-crossing episode as well as of the fact that a majority of the world's population is, after all, multilingual (Lambert et al., 1981). Secondly, we were initially very self-conscious of the fact that among our family, friends, and acquaintances, we were the only parents who spoke to their child in two different languages. However, we realized soon enough that there was no basis for concern on either count. As John grew, his capacity to understand our French and English seemed perfectly normal for a child his age. Also, rather than being regarded strangely by our fellow Louisianians, we were often encouraged and praised by the many Cajuns we encountered who wished that their French-speaking parents and grandparents had raised them bilingually. Stephen's mother, herself of Acadian descent, regretted that her French-speaking mother had never spoken to her in French. Members of Suzanne's Québecois family, who were particularly sensitive to the importance of speaking both French and English, were clearly pleased by our efforts to raise John bilingually.

John spent about eight hours a day, five days a week, in English-speaking day care from the time he was three months old until we enrolled him in preschool at age four. As he grew, we slowly became aware that Suzanne's French communication represented a fraction of the English John was exposed to in his environment (via day care, TV, relatives, neighbors, etc.). Thus when John was 18 months old, we resolved that both of us had to speak to him only in French to more equally balance his exposure to the two languages. Also, given that our home communications had grown a bit sloppy over the preceding years, with our communicating to each other in a mixture of French and English, or "Franglais," we fervently resolved to speak to each other only in French. Thus French became the exclusive language of our home from the time John was 18 months old.

Though he understood both languages equally well, John had still barely begun to speak by the time he was 21 months old. We were aware that bilingual children might begin speaking later than monolingual children (Saunders, 1984), so we were hoping that this was the case with John. It was. By his second birthday, to our great relief and astonishment, John exploded in language! He initially mixed French and English words together (e.g., "Look at the maison"), referred to as *code switching* (Commins and Miramontes, 1989), but within several months he could clearly differentiate between the two languages. He rarely mixed French and English thereafter.

In May of 1987, just as John turned two, Suzanne gave birth to a set of identical twin girls. Given the success we were having with John, we extended our practice of only speaking French to Valérie and Stéphanie as well. Consequently, unlike John, they were never addressed in English at home.

In the meantime, John's French and English vocabulary continued to expand, though he seemed to have a preference for English. Research emphasizes the importance of exposing children to the culture of their second language to facilitate their acquisition of it (Harding and Riley, 1986). Thus, in order to show him that his parents were not the only people in the world speaking French, John spent two weeks in Québec with Suzanne not long after his third birthday.

Upon their return from Québec we noted a decided preference for and improvement in our son's French. This preference lasted several months until he returned to day care in the fall, at which time English again became his dominant mode of communication. In fact throughout his third year, the bulk of his utterances to both us, and his twin sisters, were in English. We doggedly continued our practice of speaking only French to each other, and to the children. The twins, like John, understood our French, and everyone else's English, with equal facility. However, they were even slower to speak than John had been. We were somewhat encouraged to discover through research that twins, on average, speak later than do singletons (Savić, 1980). We were also concerned with John's practice of speaking to his sisters only in English. By their second birthday, the twins were beginning to imitate John's speech.

We concluded that another trip to Québec was necessary. During the summer of 1989, when John was four and the twins two, we left on our two-week summer vacation to Lac Trois Saumons, a resort lake community northeast of Québec city. Upon arriving, John's aunt offered to keep John with her and his nine-year-old French-speaking cousin during the entire two-week period. John would have no recourse to English. This proved to be a watershed event in our bilingual family experiment.

Following this two weeks of total immersion in French, our son completely abandoned his use of English in the home. In the fall of 1989, we enrolled John in a university preschool in Baton Rouge, where all communication was in English. During the first parent/teacher conference in November, where Stephen assumed that the teacher already knew that John spoke only French at home, he casually mentioned this fact to her. To our mutual surprise, John had never mentioned his bilingualism to her. He spoke English, the teacher informed Stephen, as well as any other four-year-old in his class.

In May of 1990 at the conclusion of his preschool year, and as John turned five years old, his teacher administered the Houghton Mifflin Reading Program Readiness Test to each student in the class. The test is widely used to determine a child's readiness for kindergarten. John scored above the readiness level in all 10 subtests. The absence of English at home clearly had not impaired his performance in an English-speaking preschool.

Following the example of their brother upon returning from Québec, the twins quickly abandoned the few English utterances they were capable of articulating and began speaking only French words at home. In day care, however, where they spent 8 hours a day five days a week, their developing language was English. Interestingly enough they spoke not only to others but also to each other mostly in English while at day care, but switched to French as their interpersonal language upon returning home.

In May of 1990 when they turned three years old, we took Valérie and Stéphanie for a speech screening test provided by our local school district. In order to get as objective an assessment as possible, we did not inform the speech pathologist that only French was spoken in the home. Both girls were individually screened. We were informed that except for their pronunciation of the /ɹ/ phoneme, their speech was developing normally for children their age. Our speculation is that their constant exposure to the French uvular [ʀ] may be slowing their acquisition of the English /ɹ/ sound.

In conclusion, it seems that our efforts to raise our children bilingually, guided by research, determination, and a desire to preserve Louisiana's unique French heritage, are succeeding. Nevertheless, it must be emphasized that the process is ongoing, and consequently the verdict is in a sense still out. John scored well on an English measure of his kindergarten readiness, but he was not administered a parallel test in French. Though our subjective impression is that he speaks French as well as he speaks English, at this time we lack objective evidence to confirm this.

We anticipate continuing challenges in our struggle. First, as the children become more aware of their unique linguistic status, it's conceivable that their current spontaneous French communication with us in public will be replaced by a self-conscious reluctance to speak differently from everyone else (Commins and Miramontes, 1989). Thus we deem it important not only to educate them to speak French, but to be proud of their French-speaking heritage as well. Second, there is the equally challenging task of ensuring that they learn to read and write French as well as speak it. We may be able to accomplish this by enrolling them in a French immersion program, teaching them at home, or some combination of the two. Frequent trips to Québec could help out on both counts.

We caution against the generalizibility of our particular experience. Our setting is somewhat unique in that the negative stereotype once associated with French-speaking Louisianians has been largely replaced by nostalgia for the disappearing French language. In many other parts of the United States, minority language speakers are still negatively stereotyped, resulting in a reluctance by the bilingual child to speak in his or her minority tongue (Commins and Miramontes, 1989). We find this unfortunate, to say the least, especially in light of research which indicates that bilingual students score higher on both verbal and nonverbal measures of intelligence than do their monolingual classmates (Lambert, 1972).

Based on our experience and the experience of Louisiana, however particularistic, the current xenophobic mood among some in the United States who insist on making English the "official" language for fear it may decline in importance seems completely unfounded. We have made virtually no attempt to teach English to our children, yet they are obtaining fluency in it like any other American child. We concur with Melendez (1989, 71) who notes that ". . . learning English—developing a common [national] language does not require unlearning or not learning other languages."

BIBLIOGRAPHY

Alexander, Kern. S*chool Law*. St. Paul: West, 1980.

Commins, Nancy L., and Ofelia B. Miramontes. "Perceived and Actual Linguistic Competence: A Descriptive Study of Four Low-Achieving Hispanic Bilingual Students." *American Educational Research Journal*, 26 (1989), 443–72.

Darbelnet, Jean. *Le Français en contact avec l'Anglais en Amérique du Nord*. Québec: Les Presses de L'Université Laval, 1976.

Fraser, Carol A., and François Mougeon. "Developing a Test of Advanced Bilingualism: The Glendon Experience." *The Canadian Modern Language Review/La Revue canadienne des langues vivantes*, 46 (1990), 779–93.

Harding, Edith, and Philip Riley. *The Bilingual Family: A Handbook for Parents*. Cambridge: Cambridge University Press, 1986.

Heath, Shirley Brice. *Ways with Words: Language, Life, and Work in Communities and Classrooms*. Cambridge: Cambridge University Press, 1983.

Lambert, Wallace E. *Bilingual Education of Children: The St. Lambert Experiment*. Rowley, MA: Newbury, 1972.

Lambert, Wallace E., Catherine E. Snow, Beverly A. Goldfield, Anna Uhl Chamot, and Stephen R. Cahir. *Faces and Facets of Bilingualism*. Bilingual Education Series 10. Washington: National Clearinghouse for Bilingual Education, 1981.

Mazel, Jean. *Louisiane: Terre d'aventure*. Paris: Laffont, 1979.

Melendez, Sarah F. "A Nation of Monolinguals, a Bilingual World." *NEA Today* 7, 6 (1989), 70–74.

Saunders, George. *Bilingual Education: Guidance for the Family*. Avon, England: Multilingual Matters, 1984.

Savić, Svenka. *How Twins Learn to Talk*. Trans. Vladislava Felbabov. New York: Academic, 1980.

Taylor, Joe Gray. *Louisiana: A Bicentennial History*. New York: Norton, 1976.

FOR DISCUSSION AND REVIEW

1. Caldas and Caron-Caldas warn the reader against generalizing from their experience. Of what value to a broad field like linguistics is such a particular first-person account as theirs?

2. How would you compare Caldas, Caron-Caldas, and their children to the mentors and apprentices of Katharine Whittemore's study (see "Saving California Languages")? What advantages do Caldas and Caron-Caldas have over the Native American teachers and learners?

3. What prompted the authors to raise their children to be bilingual?

4. What were the two primary concerns the parents faced in attempting to raise a bilingual child? How were they resolved? What characteristics of the authors' particular situation were helpful? Might parents attempting to raise bilingual children in different circumstances face more difficult problems; if so, how might they be overcome?

5. Why did the parents resolve to speak only French at home when John became 18 months old? Why did they feel it was important to take him for visits to Quebec?

6. According to the authors, what are the advantages of growing up bilingual?

7. What challenges do the parents anticipate as the children grow older? Which of these challenges is primarily linguistic? Which cultural?

8. In what ways is the situation of the Caron-Caldas children different from that of bilingual Hispanic American children? In what ways is it similar?

9. Is it likely that the Caron-Caldas children will eventually face the problem poignantly set forth by Richard Rodriguez (see "Bilingual Education: Outdated and Unrealistic") in the need to leave behind their private French-speaking lives?

Projects for "Language Variety and Culture"

1. The concept of "standard English" has caused much misunderstanding and debate. For many Americans, "standard" implies that one variety of English is more correct or more functional than others. Investigate the history of the concept of "standard English." How did the concept develop? How do various linguists define it? Is "standard English" a social dialect? What exactly is the power or mystique of "standard English"?

2. Note the definition of *bilingual* quoted in the essay by Caldas and Caron-Caldas: "being equally at home and equally effective in two languages." What other definitions of the term *bilingual* can you find and infer from the essays in this section and from other sources, including linguistics texts? How has the term been used since the 1960s by ethnic groups, educators, politicians? Write an essay defining the various meanings and applications of the term *bilingual* used in this century in the United States.

3. Constance Hale mentions the Maori "language nest" schools of New Zealand, which served as a model for the Hawaiian-immersion schools. Read about the history, legal status, and educational goals and techniques of the Maori "language nest" schools and write a report of your findings.

4. Hawaii has a particularly varied and interesting linguistic history in the twentieth century. Constance Hale mentions that as a schoolgirl she spoke "pidgin English (a creole that mixed influences from each of the islands' main ethnic groups—Hawaiian, Caucasian, Chinese, Japanese, Filipino)." Read about the history of Hawaii since about 1880. Under what circumstances did various ethnic groups converge upon the islands, and how did the creole language develop? (Maxine Hong Kingston's book *China Men* sheds interesting light on this history, as does the work of linguist Derek Bickerton.)

5. How and why did French survive for so long as the dominant language in southern Louisiana? Read and report on the history of the Acadian (Cajun) culture there, paying particular attention to issues of language.

6. College and university communities are likely to attract people who are fluent in more than one language. Interview two or more bilingual speakers in your community. If possible, interview at least one person who was bilingual from birth and one who acquired a second language later in life. Determine at what age he or she began to learn a second language, and the difficulties and rewards of the learning process. What do they find to be the advantages, disadvantages, and uses of bilingualism in a monolingual culture? Report your findings to the class.

7. Journalist Lizette Alvarez presents the emergence of "Spanglish" in a positive light; in his *New York Times* essay "Kay Possa?! Is

'Spanglish' a Language?" scholar Robert Gonzalez Echevarría, professor of Hispanic and comparative literatures at Yale, heaps scorn upon it. Spanglish, he claims, "poses a grave danger to Hispanic culture and to the advancement of Hispanics in mainstream America. Those who condone and even promote it do not realize that this is hardly a relationship based on equality. Spanglish is an invasion of Spanish by English. . . . If, as with so many of the trends of American Hispanics, Spanglish were to spread to Latin America, it would constitute the ultimate imperialistic takeover, the final imposition of a way of life that is economically dominant but not culturally superior in any sense."

Echevarría goes on to observe, "I suppose my Medievalist colleagues will say that without the contamination of Latin by local languages, there would be no Spanish (or French or Italian). We are no longer in the Middle Ages, however, and it is naïve to think that we could create a new language that would be functional and culturally rich." Therefore, he concludes, "I think that people should learn languages well and that learning English should be the first priority for Hispanics if they aspire, as they should, to influential positions."

What is the issue here? Is Spanglish a contaminant of English, Spanish, both, or neither? How does language relate to cultural richness? To economic wealth? To "influential positions"? Identify and choose an issue raised by Alvarez, Rodriguez, and/or Echevarría. Write a persuasive essay, citing these and other current authorities to support your views.

8. In the introduction, "'They Done Taken My Blues and Gone': Black Talk Crosses Over," from her book *Black Talk: Words and Phrases from the Hood to the Amen Corner*, Geneva Smitherman documents many instances of the absorption of black speech into American English. Read this and other contemporary sources documenting the influence of Black English vernacular on mainstream American English. Report your findings to the class.

Selected Bibliography

Note: The reader should consult the articles contained in Part One, "Language and Personal Identity"

Abraham, Roberta G., and Roberta J. Vann. "Strategies of Two Language Learners: A Case Study." *Learner Strategies in Language Learning.* Ed. Anita Wenden and Joan Rubin. Englewood Cliffs, NJ: Prentice-Hall, 1987. [Provides a model for students interested in doing a case study.]

Angelou, Maya. *I Know Why the Caged Bird Sings.* New York: Random House: 1970. [Language repression and language recovery in a classic African American woman's autobiography.]

Anzaldua, Gloria. *Borderlands/La Frontera: The New Mestiza.* San Francisco: Aunt Lute Books, 1987. [Recounts the Mexican-Anglo language conflicts of this Chicana writer.]

Castro, Janice. "Spanglish Spoken Here." *Time.* 11 July 1988. [Discusses the emergence of Spanglish as a blended language.]

Cummins, Jim. "Bilingualism, Language Proficiency, and Metalinguistic Development." *Childhood Bilingualism: Aspects of Linguistic, Cognitive, and Social Development.* Ed. Peter Homel et al. Hillsdale, NJ: Lawrence Erlbaum, 1987. [Discusses the significantly better linguistic performance of bilingual children.]

Diamond, Jared. "Speaking with a Single Tongue." *Discover* (February 1993), 78, 81–82, 84–85. [Discusses the inseparability of language and culture and argues that as languages around the world are threatened with extinction, so are the indigenous cultures.]

Edwards, J. *Language, Society, and Identity.* Oxford: Blackwell, 1985. [Explores issues in language planning, i.e., choosing and promulgating an official language in a particular social setting.]

Freeman, David E., and Yvonne S. Freeman. *Between Worlds: Access to Second Language Acquisition.* Portsmouth, NH: Heinemann, 1994. [Issues in teaching and learning a second language.]

Fromkin, Victoria, Stephen Krashen, Susan Curtiss, Davis Rigler, and Marilyn Rigler. "The Development of Language in Genie: A Case of Language Acquisition beyond the 'Critical Period.'" *Brain and Language,* Vol. 1, No. 1. New York: Academic Press, 1974. [This article appears, along with a postscript by Maya Pines, in Part Nine.]

Hakuta, Kenji. *Mirror of Language: The Debate on Bilingualism.* New York: Basic Books, 1986. [An overview of the controversy surrounding bilingual education.]

Hatch, Evelyn. *Psycholinguistics: A Second Language Perspective.* Rowley, MA: Newbury House, 1983. [Useful citations to second-language research.]

Heny, Jeannine. "Learning and Using a Second Language." *Language: Introductory Readings,* 5th ed. Ed. Virginia Clark, Paul Eschholz, and Alfred Rosa. New York: St. Martin's Press, 1994, 160–189. [A clear illustration of the important and somewhat controversial impact of bilingualism on the modern world of linguistics and education.]

Hoffman, Eva. *Lost in Translation: A Life in a New Language.* New York:

Penguin, 1989. [Experiences of a Polish-speaking Jew in English-only Canadian schools.]

Kando, Dorinne K. *Crafting Selves: Power, Gender, and Discourses of Identity in a Japanese Workplace.* Chicago: University of Chicago Press, 1990. [Insightful commentary by a woman caught between Japanese and American cultures.]

Lorde, Audre. *Zami: A New Spelling of My Name.* Freedom, CA: Crossing Press, 1982. [Narrates her early experiences in school; see especially chapter 3.]

Mandelbaum, D. G., ed. *Selected Writings in Language, Culture, and Personality.* Berkeley and Los Angeles: University of California Press, 1949. [An exploration of the work of Edward Sapir.]

McKay, Sandra Lee, and Nancy Hornberger, eds. *Sociolinguistics and Language Teaching.* Cambridge: Cambridge University Press, 1996. [Highly recommended general text in sociolinguistics.]

Ortiz, Simon. "The Language We Know." *I Tell You Now: Autobiographical Essays by Native American Writers.* Ed. Brian Swann and Arnold Krupat. Lincoln: University of Nebraska Press, 1987. [Account of attempts to Americanize Ortiz by teaching him English.]

Rodriguez, Richard. *Hunger of Memory.* Boston: Godine, 1982. [Raises serious questions about the effectiveness of bilingual education.]

Romaine, Suzanne. *Language in Society: An Introduction to Sociolinguistics.* New York: Oxford University Press, 1994. [A good contemporary basic text.]

Rose, Mike. *Lives on the Boundary: The Struggles and Achievements of America's Underprepared.* New York: 1989. [A highly readable account of Rose's many years of teaching disadvantaged students.]

Sapir, Edward. *Language: An Introduction to the Study of Speech.* New York: Harcourt Brace & World, 1921; reprint, 1949. [Explores the relationship between speech and culture.]

Silko, Leslie Marmon. "Language and Literature from a Pueblo Indian Perspective." *English Literature: Opening Up the Canon.* Ed. Leslie A. Fiedler and Houston A. Baker Jr. Baltimore: Johns Hopkins University Press, 1979. [Draws a sharp cultural contrast to American language and literature.]

Tan, Amy. "The Language of Discretion." *The State of the Language.* Ed. Leonard Michaels and Christopher Ricks. Berkeley: University of California Press, 1990. [Provocative self-reflection on a bilingual past.]

Wardhaugh, Ronald. *An Introduction to Sociolinguistics*, 2nd ed. Oxford: Blackwell, 1986. [A recommended introductory text.]

Whittemore, Katharine. "Endangered Languages," *The Boston Globe Magazine*, 7 May 1995. [Argues that a way of looking at the world is lost when we lose a language.]

Whorf, Benjamin Lee. *Language, Thought, and Reality.* Ed. John B. Carroll. Cambridge: MIT Press, 1956. [A classic work on the relationship between language and culture.]

PART NINE

CHILDREN AND LANGUAGE

A child is born, and grows, and learns to speak and to understand others when they speak. What could be more ordinary, more easily taken for granted? But that children—all children—master a large part of their native language(s) at as early an age as five is astonishing. We still do not fully understand how children learn language. However, once linguists and psychologists realized how extraordinary an accomplishment language acquisition is, they began to investigate. What they have discovered in recent years about language acquisition is the subject of the articles in this section.

In "The Acquisition of Language," Breyne Arlene Moskowitz provides an overview of the language acquisition process. She shows how children, in learning all the systems of grammar—phonology, syntax, lexicon, and pragmatics—use the same basic technique of developing a general rule, testing it, modifying and narrowing its scope gradually, until near-mastery is achieved. Following this discussion, Eric H. Lenneberg juxtaposes, in chart format, a description of motor skills and language development for children aged twelve weeks to four years. Broadening the focus, Jean Aitchison, in "Predestinate Grooves," argues explicitly that language acquisition is a biologically triggered behavior that must occur during a specific critical period if it is to occur normally. She discusses the characteristics of biologically triggered behaviors—walking, for example—and explains in what ways speech shares these features.

According to George A. Miller and Patricia M. Gildea, "the average child learns at the rate of 5,000 words per year, or about thirteen per day." Surprisingly, linguists know very little about how children learn words, but Miller and Gildea believe, on the basis of their research, that computers can help children increase their vocabulary.

Much can be learned about the language acquisition process from the study of a normal child who, for whatever reasons, has lived in a severely deficient linguistic environment, and Aitchison briefly describes several such cases. In the next article, "The Development of Language in

Genie: A Case of Language Acquisition beyond the 'Critical Period,'" Victoria Fromkin and her colleagues report in detail on the linguistic development of Genie, a thirteen-year-old girl found in 1970 who had suffered extreme isolation. Genie's case is particularly interesting because of its relevance to the idea that there is a "critical period" for language acquisition and because of the unusual amount of information that is available about Genie's linguistic development.

Early in her career ethnographer Shirley Brice Heath worked for ten years in two towns, a white working-class community and a black working-class community, in the southeast, which she referred to as "Roadville" and "Trackton," respectively. There she carefully observed the ways in which children acquire language. In the final article in this section, Heath describes how young children learned how to ask and answer questions through their interaction with siblings, parents, and other adults in Roadville.

We have learned a great deal in recent years about the language acquisition process, but we still do not fully understand it. The selections in Part Nine suggest that future research will significantly increase our understanding of the unique phenomenon that most people take for granted—learning their language.

41

The Acquisition of Language

Breyne Arlene Moskowitz

The image of proud parents leaning over their young baby's crib, urging the infant to repeat such words as "mama" and "dada," is an American stereotype. The acquisition of language, however, follows quite a different path than such a picture suggests. Language acquisition occurs in all children in the same succession of stages, as linguistics professor Breyne Arlene Moskowitz describes in the following selection. Professor Moskowitz explores the prerequisites for language learning, the one-word stage utterances, the two-word stage, the telegraphic stage, the acquisition of function words, the process of rule formation, semantic processes, and the phonology and actual articulation of utterances. She shows that in all areas of language acquisition, children are active learners and follow the same basic procedure: hypothesizing rules, trying them, and modifying them. Children formulate the most general rules first and apply them across the board; narrower rules are added later, with exceptions and highly irregular forms. Although the examples discussed in this selection concern children who are learning English, the same process has been observed in children learning other languages. While reading the selection, reflect on the language development of any young children you know to see if you can identify the stages described by Moskowitz.

An adult who finds herself in a group of people speaking an unfamiliar foreign language may feel quite uncomfortable. The strange language sounds like gibberish: mysterious strings of sound, rising and falling in unpredictable patterns. Each person speaking the language knows when to speak, how to construct the strings, and how to interpret other people's strings, but the individual who does not know anything about the language cannot pick out separate words or sounds, let alone discern meanings. She may feel overwhelmed, ignorant, and even childlike. It is possible that she is returning to a vague memory from her very early childhood, because the experience of an adult listening to a foreign language comes close to duplicating the experience of an infant listening to the "foreign" language spoken by everyone around her. Like the adult, the child is confronted with the task of learning a language about which she knows nothing.

The task of acquiring language is one for which the adult has lost most of her aptitude but one the child will perform with remarkable skill. Within a short span of time and with almost no direct instruction the child will analyze the language completely. In fact, although many subtle refinements are added between the ages of five and ten, most children have completed the greater part of the basic language-acquisition process by the age of five. By that time a child will have dissected the language into its minimal separable units of sound and meaning; she will have discovered the rules for recombining sounds into words, the meanings of individual words, and the rules for recombining words into meaningful sentences, and she will have internalized the intricate patterns of taking turns in dialogue. All in all she will have established herself linguistically as a full-fledged member of a social community, informed about the most subtle details of her native language as it is spoken in a wide variety of situations.

The speed with which children accomplish the complex process of language acquisition is particularly impressive. Ten linguists working full time for ten years to analyze the structure of the English language could not program a computer with the ability for language acquired by an average child in the first ten or even five years of life. In spite of the scale of the task and even in spite of adverse conditions—emotional instability, physical disability, and so on—children learn to speak. How do they go about it? By what process does a child learn language?

WHAT IS LANGUAGE?

In order to understand how language is learned it is necessary to understand what language is. The issue is confused by two factors. First, language is learned in early childhood, and adults have few memories of the intense effort that went into the learning process, just as they do not remember the process of learning to walk. Second, adults do have conscious memories of being taught the few grammatical rules that are prescribed as "correct" usage, or the norms of "standard" language. It is difficult for adults to dissociate their memories of school lessons from those of true language learning, but the rules learned in school are only the conventions of an educated society. They are arbitrary finishing touches of embroidery on a thick fabric of language that each child weaves for herself before arriving in the English teacher's classroom. The fabric is grammar: the set of rules that describe how to structure language.

The grammar of language includes rules of phonology, which describe how to put sounds together to form words; rules of syntax, which describe how to put words together to form sentences; rules of semantics, which describe how to interpret the meaning of words and sentences; and rules of pragmatics, which describe how to participate in a conversation, how to sequence sentences, and how to anticipate the information needed by an interlocutor. The internal grammar each adult has constructed is identical with that of every other adult in all but a few superficial details. Therefore each adult can create or understand an infinite number of sentences she has never heard before. She knows what is acceptable as a word or a sentence and what is not acceptable, and her judgments on these issues concur with those of other adults. For example, speakers of English generally agree that the sentence "Ideas green sleep colorless furiously" is ungrammatical and that the sentence "Colorless green ideas sleep furiously" is grammatical but makes no sense semantically. There is similar agreement on the grammatical relations represented by word order. For example, it is clear that the sentences "John hit Mary" and "Mary hit John" have different meanings although they consist of the same words, and that the sentence "Flying planes can be dangerous" has two possible meanings. At the level of individual words all adult speakers can agree that "brick" is an English word, that "blick" is not an English word but could be one (that is, there is an accidental gap in the adult lexicon, or internal vocabulary), and that "bnick" is not an English word and could not be one.

How children go about learning the grammar that makes communication possible has always fascinated adults, particularly parents, psychologists, and investigators of language. Until recently diary keeping was the primary method of study in this area. For example, in 1877 Charles Darwin published an account of his son's development that includes notes on language learning. Unfortunately most of the diarists used inconsistent or incomplete notations to record what they heard (or what they thought they heard), and most of the diaries were only partial listings of emerging types of sentences with inadequate information on developing word meanings. Although the very best of them, such as W. F. Leopold's classic *Speech Development of a Bilingual Child*, continue to be a rich resource of contemporary investigators, advances in audio and video recording equipment have made modern diaries generally much more valuable. In the 1960s, however, new discoveries inspired linguists and psychologists to approach the study of language acquisition in a new, systematic way, oriented less toward long-term diary keeping and more toward a search for patterns in a child's speech at any given time.

An event that revolutionized linguists was the publication in 1957 of Noam Chomsky's *Syntactic Structures*. Chomsky's investigation of the structure of grammars revealed that language systems were far deeper and more complex than had been suspected. And of course if linguistics was more complicated, then language learning had to be more complicated. In the . . . years since the publication of *Syntactic Structures* the disciplines of linguistics and child language have come of age. The study of the acquisition of language has benefited not only from the increasingly sophisticated understanding of linguistics but also from the improved understanding of cognitive development as it is related to language. The improvements in recording technology have made experimentation in this area more reliable and more detailed, so that investigators framing new and deeper questions are able to accurately capture both rare occurrences and developing structures.

The picture that is emerging from the more sophisticated investigations reveals the child as an active language learner, continually analyzing what she hears and proceeding in a methodical, predictable way to put together the jigsaw puzzle of language. Different children learn language in similar ways. It is not known how many processes are involved in language learning, but the few that have been observed appear repeatedly, from child to child and from language to language. All the examples I shall discuss here concern children who are learning English, but identical processes have been observed in children learning French, Russian, Finnish, Chinese, Zulu, and many other languages.

Children learn the systems of grammar—phonology, syntax, semantics, lexicon, and pragmatics—by breaking each system down into its smallest combinable parts and then developing rules for combining the parts. In the first two years of life a child spends much time working on one part of the task, disassembling the language to find the separate sounds that can be put together to form words and the separate words that can be put together to form sentences. After the age of two the basic process continues to be refined, and many more sounds and words are produced. The other part of language acquisition—developing rules for combining the basic elements of language—is carried out in a very methodical way: the most general rules are hypothesized first, and as time passes they are successively narrowed down by the addition of more precise rules applying to a more restricted set of sentences. The procedure is the same in any area of language learning, whether the child is acquiring syntax or phonology or semantics. For example, at the earliest stage of acquiring negatives a child does not have at her command the same range of negative structures that an adult does. She has constructed only a single very general rule: Attach "no" to the beginning of any sentence constructed by the other rules of grammar. At this stage all negative sentences will be formed according to that rule.

Throughout the acquisition process a child continually revises and refines the rules of her internal grammar, learning increasingly detailed subrules until she achieves a set of rules that enable her to create the full array of complex, adult sentences. The process of refinement continues at least until the age of ten and probably considerably longer for most children. By the time a child is six or seven, however, the changes in her grammar may be so subtle and sophisticated that they go unnoticed. In general children approach language learning economically, devoting their energy to broad issues before dealing with specific ones. They cope with clear-cut questions first and sort out the details later, and they may adopt any one of a variety of methods for circumventing details of a language system that they have not yet dealt with.

PREREQUISITES FOR LANGUAGE

Although some children verbalize much more than others and some increase the length of their utterances much faster than others, all chil-

(1)	(2)	(3)	(4)	(5)	(6)
boy		boys	boysəz	boys	boys
cat		cats	catsəz	cats	cats
			catəz		
man	men	mans	mansəz	mans	men
			menəz		
house		house	housəz	houses	houses
foot		foots	footsəz	feets	feet
feet		feets	feetsəz		

Table 41.1 Sorting out of competing pronunciations that result in the correct plural forms of nouns takes place in the six stages shown in this table. Children usually learn the singular forms of nouns first (1), although in some cases an irregular plural form such as "feet" may be learned as a singular or as a free variant of a singular. Other irregular plurals may appear for a brief period (2), but soon they are replaced by plurals made according to the most general rule possible: To make a noun plural add the sound "s" or "z" to it (3). Words such as "house" or "rose," which already end in an "s"- or "z"-like sound, are usually left in their singular forms at this stage. When words of this type do not have irregular plural forms, adults make them plural by adding an "əz" sound. (The vowel "ə" is pronounced like the unstressed word "a.") Some children demonstrate their mastery of this usage by tacking "əz" endings indiscriminately onto nouns (4). That stage is brief and use of the ending is quickly narrowed down (5). At this point only irregular plurals remain to be learned, and since no new rule-making is needed, children may go on to harder problems and leave final stage (6) for later.

dren overgeneralize a single rule before learning to apply it more narrowly and before constructing other less widely applicable rules, and all children speak in one-word sentences before they speak in two-word sentences. The similarities in language learning for different children and different languages are so great that many linguists have believed at one time or another that the human brain is preprogrammed for language learning. Some linguists continue to believe language is innate and only the surface details of the particular language spoken in a child's environment need to be learned. The speed with which children learn language gives this view much appeal. As more parallels between language and other areas of cognition are revealed, however, there is greater reason to believe any language specialization that exists in the child is only one aspect of more general cognitive abilities of the brain.

Whatever the built-in properties the brain brings to the task of language learning may be, it is now known that a child who hears no language learns no language, and that a child learns only the language spoken in her environment. Most infants coo and babble during the first six months of life, but congenitally deaf children have been observed to cease babbling after six months, whereas normal infants continue to babble. A child does not learn language, however, simply by hearing it spoken. A boy with normal hearing but with deaf parents who communicated by the American Sign Language was exposed to television every day so that he would learn English. Because the child was asthmatic and was confined to his home he interacted only with people at home, where his family and all their visitors communicated in sign language. By the age of three he was fluent in sign language but neither understood nor spoke English. It appears that in order to learn a language a child must also be able to interact with real people in that language. A television set does not suffice as the sole medium for language learning because, even though it can ask questions, it cannot respond to a child's answers. A child, then, can develop language only if there is language in her environment and if she can employ that language to communicate with other people in her immediate environment.

CARETAKER SPEECH

In constructing a grammar children have only a limited amount of information available to them, namely the language they hear spoken around them. (Until about the age of three a child models her language on that of her parents; afterward the language of her peer group tends to become more important.) There is no question, however, that the language environments children inhabit are restructured, usually unintentionally, by the adults who take care of them. Recent studies show that there are several ways caretakers systematically modify the child's environment, making the task of language acquisition simpler.

Caretaker speech is a distinct speech register that differs from others in its simplified vocabulary, the systematic phonological simplification of some words, higher pitch, exaggerated intonation, short, simple sentences, and a high proportion of questions (among mothers) or imperatives (among fathers). Speech with the first two characteristics is formally designated Baby Talk. Baby Talk is a subsystem of caretaker speech that has been studied over a wide range of languages and cultures. Its characteristics appear to be universal: in languages as diverse as English, Arabic, Comanche, and Gilyak (a Paleo-Siberian language) there are simplified vocabulary items for terms relating to food, toys, animals, and body functions. Some words are phonologically simplified, frequently by the duplication of syllables, as in "wawa" for "water" and "choo-choo" for "train," or by the reduction of consonant clusters, as in "tummy" for "stomach," and "scambled eggs" for "scrambled eggs." (Many types of phonological simplification seem to mimic the phonological structure of an infant's own early vocabulary.)

Perhaps the most pervasive characteristic of caretaker speech is its syntactic simplification. While a child is still babbling, adults may address long, complex sentences to her, but as soon as she begins to utter meaningful, identifiable words they almost invariably speak to her in very simple sentences. Over the next few years of the child's language development the speech addressed to her by her caretakers may well be describable by a grammar only six months in advance of her own.

The functions of the various language modifications in caretaker speech are not equally apparent. It is possible that higher pitch and exaggerated intonation serve to alert a child to pay attention to what she is hearing. As for Baby Talk, there is no reason to believe the use of phonologically simplified words in any way affects a child's learning of pronunciation. Baby Talk may have only a psychological function, marking speech as being affectionate. On the other hand, syntactic simplification has a clear function. Consider the speech adults address to other adults; it is full of false starts and long, rambling, highly complex sentences. It is not surprising that elaborate theories of innate language ability arose during the years when linguists examined the speech adults addressed to adults and assumed that the speech addressed to children was similar. Indeed, it is hard to imagine how a child could derive the rules of language from such input. The wide study of caretaker speech conducted over the past eight years has shown that children do not face this problem. Rather it appears they construct their initial grammars on the basis of the short, simple, grammatical sentences that are addressed to them in the first year or two they speak.

(1)	(2)	(3)	(4)	(5)	(6)
walk		walked	walkedəd	walked	walked
play		played	playedəd	played	played
need		need	needəd	needed	needed
			camedəd		
come	came	comed	comedəd	comed	came
			goed		
go	went	goed	wentəd	goed	went

TABLE 41.2 Development of past-tense forms of verbs also takes place in six stages. After the present-tense forms are learned (1) irregular past-tense forms may appear briefly (2). The first and most general rule that is postulated is: To put a verb into the past tense, add a "t" or "d" sound (3). In adult speech, verbs such as "want" or "need," which already end in a "t" or "d" sound, are put into the past tense by adding an "əd" sound. Many children go through a brief stage in which they add "əd" endings to any existing verb forms (4). Once the use of the "əd" ending has been narrowed down (5), only irregular past-tense forms remain to be learned (6).

CORRECTING LANGUAGE

Caretakers simplify children's language-analysis task in other ways. For example, adults talk with other adults about complex ideas, but they talk with children about the here and now, minimizing discussion of feelings, displaced events, and so on. Adults accept children's syntactic and phonological "errors," which are a normal part of the acquisition process. It is important to understand that when children make such errors, they are not producing flawed or incomplete replicas of adult sentences; they are producing sentences that are correct and grammatical with respect to their own current internalized grammar. Indeed, children's errors are essential data for students of child language because it is the consistent departures from the adult model that indicate the nature of a child's current hypotheses about the grammar of language. There are a number of memorized, unanalyzed sentences in any child's output of language. If a child says, "Nobody likes me," there is no way of knowing whether she has memorized the sentence intact or has figured out the rules for constructing the sentence. On the other hand, a sentence such as "Nobody don't like me" is clearly not a memorized form but one that reflects an intermediate stage of a developing grammar.

Since each child's utterances at a particular stage are from her own point of view grammatically correct, it is not surprising that children are fairly impervious to the correction of their language by adults, indeed to any attempts to teach them language. Consider the boy who lamented to his mother, "Nobody don't like me." His mother seized the opportunity to correct him, replying, "Nobody likes me." The child repeated his original version and the mother her modified one a total of eight times until in desperation the mother said, "Now listen carefully! Nobody likes me." Finally her son got the idea and dutifully replied "Oh! Nobody don't likes me." As the example demonstrates, children do not always understand exactly what it is the adult is correcting. The information the adult is trying to impart may be at odds with the information in the child's head, namely the rules the child is postulating for producing language. The surface correction of a sentence does not give the child a clue about how to revise the rule that produced the sentence.

It seems to be virtually impossible to speed up the language-learning process. Experiments conducted by Russian investigators show that it is extremely difficult to teach children a detail of language more than a few days before they would learn it themselves. Adults sometimes do, of course, attempt to teach children rules of language, expecting them to learn by imitation, but Courtney B. Cazden of Harvard University found that children benefit less from frequent adult correction of their errors than from true conversational interaction. Indeed, correcting errors can interrupt that interaction, which is, after all, the function of language. (One way children may try to secure such interaction is by asking "Why?" Children go through a stage of asking a question repeatedly. It serves to keep the conversation going, which may be the child's real aim. For example, a two-and-a-half-year-old named Stanford asked "Why?" and was given the nonsense answer: "Because the moon is made of green cheese." Although the response was not at all germane to the conversation, Stanford was happy with it and again asked "Why?" Many silly answers later the adult had tired of the conversation but Stanford had not. He was clearly not seeking information. What he needed was to practice the form of social conversation before dealing with its function. Asking "Why?" served that purpose well.)

In point of fact adults rarely correct children's ungrammatical sentences. For example, one mother, on hearing "Tommy fall my truck down," turned to Tommy with "Did you fall Stevie's truck down?" Since imitation seems to have little role in the language-acquisition process, however, it is probably just as well that most adults are either too charmed by children's errors or too busy to correct them.

Practice does appear to have an important function in the child's language learning process. Many children have been observed purposefully practicing language when they are alone, for example in a crib or a playpen. Ruth H. Weir of Stanford University hid a tape recorder in her son's bedroom and recorded his talk after he was put to bed. She found that he played with words and phrases, stringing together sequences of similar sounds and of variations on a phrase or on the use of a word: "What color . . . what color blanket . . . what color mop . . . what color glass . . . what color TV . . . red ant . . . fire . . . like lipstick . . . blanket . . . now the blue blanket . . . what color TV . . . what color horse . . . then what color table . . . then what color fire . . . here yellow spoon." Children who do not have much opportunity to be alone may use dialogue in a similar fashion. When Weir tried to record the bedtime monologues of her second child, whose room adjoined that of the first, she obtained through-the-wall conversations instead.

THE ONE-WORD STAGE

The first stage of child language is one in which the maximum sentence length is one word; it is followed by a stage in which the maximum sentence length is two words. Early in the one-word stage there are only a few words in a child's vocabulary, but as months go by her lexicon expands with increasing rapidity. The early words are primarily concrete nouns and verbs; more abstract words such as adjectives are acquired later. By the time the child is uttering two-word sentences with some regularity, her lexicon may include hundreds of words.

When a child can say only one word at a time and knows only five words in all, choosing which one to say may not be a complex task. But how does she decide which word to say when she knows 100 words or more? Patricia M. Greenfield of the University of California at Los Angeles and Joshua H. Smith of Stanford have suggested that an important criterion is informativeness, that is, the child selects a word reflecting what is new in a particular situation. Greenfield and Smith also found that a newly acquired word is first used for naming and only later for asking for something.

Superficially the one-word stage seems easy to understand: a child says one word at a time, and so each word is a complete sentence with its own sentence intonation. Ten years ago a child in the one-word stage was thought to be learning word meanings but not syntax. Recently, however, students of child language have seen less of a distinction between the one-word stage as a period of word learning and the subsequent period, beginning with the two-word stage, as one of syntax acquisition. It now seems clear that the infant is engaged in an enormous amount of syntactic analysis in the one-word stage, and indeed that her syntactic abilities are reflected in her utterances and in her accurate perception of multiword sentences addressed to her.

Ronald Scollon of the University of Hawaii and Lois Bloom of Columbia University have pointed out independently that important patterns in word choice in the one-word stage can be found by examining larger segments of children's speech. Scollon observed that a nineteen-month-old named Brenda was able to use a vertical construction (a series of one-word sentences) to express what an adult might say with a horizontal construction (a multiword sentence). Brenda's pronunciation, which is represented phonetically below, was imperfect and Scollon did not understand her words at the time. Later, when he transcribed the tape of their conversation, he heard the sound of a passing car immediately preceding the conversation and was able to identify Brenda's words as follows:

BRENDA: "Car [pronounced 'ka']. Car. Car. Car."
SCOLLON: "What?"
BRENDA: "Go. Go."
SCOLLON: [Undecipherable.]
BRENDA: "Bus [pronounced 'baish']. Bus. Bus. Bus. Bus. Bus. Bus. Bus. Bus."
SCOLLON: "What? Oh, bicycle? Is that what you said?"
BRENDA: "Not ['na']."
SCOLLON: "No?"
BRENDA: "Not."
SCOLLON: "No. I got it wrong."

Brenda was not yet able to combine two words syntactically to express "Hearing that car reminds me that we went on the bus yesterday. No, not on a bicycle." She could express that concept, however, by combining words sequentially. Thus the one-word stage is not just a time for learning the meaning of words. In that period a child is developing hypotheses about putting words together in sentences, and she is already putting sentences together in meaningful groups. The next step will be to put two words together to form a single sentence.

THE TWO-WORD STAGE

The two-word stage is a time for experimenting with many binary semantic-syntactic relations such as possessor-possessed ("Mommy sock"), actor-action ("Cat sleeping"), and action-object ("Drink soup"). When two-word sentences first began to appear in Brenda's speech, they were primarily of the following forms: subject noun and verb (as in "Monster go"), verb and object (as in "Read it"), and verb or noun and location (as in "Bring home" and "Tree down"). She also continued to use vertical constructions in the two-word stage, providing herself with a means of expressing ideas that were still too advanced for her syntax. Therefore once again a description of Brenda's isolated sentences does not show her full abilities at this point in her linguistic development. Consider a later conversation Scollon had with Brenda:

> BRENDA: "Tape corder. Use it. Use it."
> SCOLLON: "Use it for what?"
> BRENDA: "Talk. Corder talk. Brenda talk."

Brenda's use of vertical constructions to express concepts she is still unable to encode syntactically is just one example of a strategy employed by children in all areas of cognitive development. As Jean Piaget of the University of Geneva and Dan I. Slobin of the University of California at Berkeley put it, new forms are used for old functions and new functions are expressed by old forms. Long before Brenda acquired the complex syntactic form "Use the tape recorder to record me talking" she was able to use her old forms—two-word sentences and vertical construction—to express the new function. Later, when that function was old, she would develop new forms to express it. The controlled dovetailing of form and function can be observed in all areas of language acquisition. For example, before children acquire the past tense they may employ adverbs of time such as "yesterday" with present-tense verbs to express past time, saying "I do it yesterday" before "I dood it."

Bloom has provided a rare view of an intermediate stage between the one-word and the two-word stages in which the two-word construction—a new form—served only an old function. For several weeks Bloom's daughter Alison uttered two-word sentences all of which included the word "wida." Bloom tried hard to find the meaning of "wida" before realizing that it had no meaning. It was, she concluded, simply a placeholder. This case is the clearest ever reported of a new form preceding new functions. The two-word stage is an important time for practicing functions that will later have expanded forms and practicing forms that will later expand their functions.

TELEGRAPHIC SPEECH

There is no three-word stage in child language. For a few years after the end of the two-word stage children do produce rather short sentences, but the almost inviolable length constraints that characterized the first two stages have disappeared. The absence of a three-word stage has not been satisfactorily explained as yet; the answer may have to do with the fact that many basic semantic relations are binary and few are ternary. In any case a great deal is known about the sequential development in the language of the period following the two-word stage. Roger Brown of Harvard has named that language telegraphic speech. (It should be noted that there is no specific age at which a child enters any of these stages of language acquisition and further that there is no particular correlation between intelligence and speed of acquisition.)

Early telegraphic speech is characterized by short, simple sentences made up primarily of content words: words that are rich in semantic content, usually nouns and verbs. The speech is called telegraphic because the sentences lack function "words": tense endings on verbs and plural endings on nouns, prepositions, conjunctions, articles, and so on. As the telegraphic-speech stage progresses, function words are gradually added to sentences. This process has possibly been studied more thoroughly than any other in language acquisition, and a fairly predictable order in the addition of function words has been observed. The same principles that govern the order of acquisition of function words in English have been shown to operate in many other languages, including some such as Finnish and Russian, that express the same grammatical relations with particularly rich systems of noun and verb suffixes.

In English many grammatical relations are represented by a fixed word order. For example, in the sentence "The dog followed Jamie to school" it is clear it is the dog that did the following. Normal word order in English requires that the subject come before the verb, and so people who speak English recognize "the dog" as the subject of the sentence. In other languages a noun may be marked as a subject not by its position with respect to the other words in the sentence but by a noun suffix, so that in adult sentences word order may be quite flexible. Until children begin to acquire suffixes and other function words, however, they employ fixed word order to express grammatical relations no matter how flexible adult word order may be. In English the strong propensity to follow word order rigidly shows up in children's interpretations of passive sentences such as "Jamie was followed by the dog." At an early age children may interpret some passive sentences correctly, but by age three they begin to ignore the function words such as "was" and "by" in passive sentences and adopt the fixed word-order interpretation. In other words, since "Jamie" appears before the verb, Jamie is assumed to be the actor, or the noun doing the following.

FUNCTION WORDS

In spite of its grammatical dependence on word order, the English language makes use of enough function words to illustrate the basic principles that determine the order in which such words are acquired. The progressive tense ending "-ing," as in "He going," is acquired first, long before the present-tense third-person singular ending "-s," as in "He goes." The

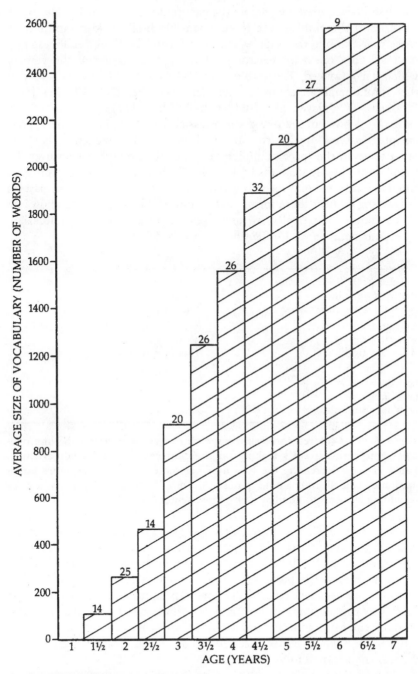

FIGURE 41.1   Children's average vocabulary size increases rapidly between the ages of one-and-a-half and six-and-a-half. The numbers over the first ten columns indicate the number of children tested in each sample age group. Data are based on work by Madorah E. Smith of the University of Hawaii.

"-s" itself is acquired long before the past tense endings, as in "He goed." Once again the child proves to be a sensible linguist, learning first the tense that exhibits the least variation in form. The "-ing" ending is pronounced only one way, regardless of the pronunciation of the verb to which it is attached. The verb endings "-s" and "-ed," however, vary in their pronunciation: compare "cuts (s)," "cuddles (z)," "crushes (əz)," "walked (t)," "played (d)," and "halted (əd)." (The vowel "ə," called "schwa," is pronounced like the unstressed word "a.") Furthermore, present progressive ("-ing") forms are used with greater frequency than any other tense in the speech children hear. Finally, no verb has an irregular "-ing" form, but some verbs do have irregular third-person present-tense singular forms and may have irregular past-tense forms. (The same pattern of learning earliest those forms that exhibit the least variation shows up much more dramatically in languages such as Finnish and Russian, where the paradigms of inflection are much richer.)

---

(1) Laura (2:2)	(4) Andrew (2:0)
Her want some more.	Put that on.
Her want some more candy.	Andrew put that on.
(2) Laura (2:2)	(5) Andrew (2:1)
Where my tiger?	All wet.
Where my tiger book?	This shoe all wet.
(3) Laura (2:2)	(6) Benjy (2:3)
Let's dooz this.	Broke it.
Let's do this.	Broke it.
Let's do this puzzle.	Broke it I did.

TABLE 41.3　Children correct their speech in ways that reflect the improvements they are currently making on their internal grammar. For example, Laura (1–3) is increasing the length of her sentences, encoding more information by embellishing a noun phrase. Andrew (4, 5) and Benjy (6) appear to be adding subjects to familiar verb-phrase sentences.

The past tense is acquired after the progressive and present tenses, because the relative time it represents is conceptually more difficult. The future tense ("will" and a verb) is formed regularly in English and is as predictable as the progressive tense, but it is a much more abstract concept than the past tense. Therefore it is acquired much later. In the same way the prepositions "in" and "on" appear earlier than any others, at about the same time as "-ing," but prepositions such as "behind" and "in front of," whose correct usage depends on the speaker's frame of reference, are acquired much later.

It is particularly interesting to note that there are three English morphemes that are pronounced identically but are acquired at different times. They are the plural "-s," the possessive "-s," and the third-person singular tense ending "-s," and they are acquired in the order of listing. Roman Jakobson of Harvard has suggested that the explanation of this

(7) Jamie (6:0)
Jamie: Why are you doing that?
Mother: What?
Jamie: Why are you writing what I say down?
Mother: What?
Jamie: Why are you writing down what I say?

(8) Jamie (6:3)
Jamie: Who do you think is the importantest kid in the world except me?
Mother: What did you say, Jamie?
Jamie: Who do you think is the specialest kid in the world not counting me?

(9) Jamie (6:6)
Jamie: Who are you versing?
Mother: What?
Jamie: I wanted to know who he was playing against.

(10) Jamie (6:10)
Jamie: I figured something you might like out.
Mother: What did you say?
Jamie: I figured out something you might like.

TABLE 41.4.   Jamie (7–10) seems to be working on much more subtle refinements such as the placement of verb particles, for example the "down" of "writing down." (Each child's age at time of correction is given in years and months.) Corrections shown here were recorded by Judy S. Reilly of University of California at Los Angeles.

phenomenon has to do with the complexity of the different relations the morphemes signal: the singular-plural distinction is at the word level, the possessive relates two nouns at the phrase level, and the tense ending relates a noun and a verb at the clause level.

The forms of the verb "to be"—"is," "are," and so on—are among the last of the function words to be acquired, particularly in their present-tense forms. Past- and future-tense forms of "to be" carry tense information, of course, but present-tense forms are essentially meaningless, and omitting them is a very sensible strategy for a child who must maximize the information content of a sentence and place priorities on linguistic structures still to be tackled.

PLURALS

When there are competing pronunciations available, as in the case of the plural and past tenses, the process of sorting them out also follows a predictable pattern. Consider the acquisition of the English plural, in which six distinct stages can be observed. In English, as in many other (but not all) languages, nouns have both singular and plural forms. Children usually use the singular forms first, both in situations where the singular form would be appropriate and in situations where the plural form would be appropriate. In instances where the plural form is irregular in the adult model, however, a child may not recognize it as such and may use it in place of the singular or as a free variant of the singular. Thus in the first stage of acquisition, before either the concept of a plural or the linguistic devices for expressing a plural are acquired, a child may say "two cat" or point to "one feet."

When plurals begin to appear regularly, the child forms them according to the most general rule of English plural formation. At this point it is the child's overgeneralization of the rule, resulting in words such as "mans," "foots," or "feets," that shows she has hypothesized the rule: Add the sound /s/ or /z/ to the end of a word to make it plural. (The slashes indicate pronounced sounds, which are not to be confused with the letters used in spelling.)

For many children the overgeneralized forms of the irregular nouns are actually the earliest /s/ and /z/ plurals to appear, preceding "boys," "cats," and other regular forms by hours or days. The period of overgeneralization is considered to be the third stage in the acquisition of plurals because for many children there is an intermediate second stage in which irregular plurals such as "men" actually do appear. Concerned parents may regard the change from the second-stage "men" to the third-stage "mans" as a regression, but in reality it demonstrates progress from an individual memorized item to the application of a general rule.

In the third stage the small number of words that already end in a sound resembling /s/ or /z/, such as "house," "rose," and "bush," are used without any plural ending. Adults normally make such words plural by adding the suffix /əz/. Children usually relegate this detail to the remainder pile, to be dealt with at a later time. When they return to the problem, there is often a short fourth stage of perhaps a day, in which the child delightedly demonstrates her solution by tacking /əz/ endings indiscriminately onto nouns no matter what sound they end in and no matter how many other plural markings they may already have. A child may wake up one morning and throw herself into this stage with all the zeal of a kitten playing with its first ball of string.

Within a few days the novelty wears off and the child enters a less flamboyant fifth stage, in which only irregular plurals still deviate from the model forms. The rapid progression through the fourth stage does not mean that she suddenly focused her attention on the problem of /əz/ plurals. It is more likely that she had the problem at the back of her mind throughout the third stage. She was probably silently formulating hypotheses about the occurrence of /əz/ and testing them against the plurals she was hearing. Finding the right rule required discovering the phonological specification of the class of nouns that take /əz/ plurals.

Arriving at the sixth and final stage in the acquisition of plurals does not require the formulation of any new rules. All that is needed is the simple memorizing of irregular forms. Being rational, the child relegates such minor details to the lowest-priority remainder pile and turns her attention to more interesting linguistic questions. Hence a five-year-old may still not have entered the last stage. In fact, a child in the penultimate stage may not be at all receptive to being taught irregular plurals. For example, a child named Erica pointed to a picture of some "mouses," and her mother corrected her by saying "mice." Erica and her mother each repeated her own version two more times, and then Erica resolved the standoff by turning to a picture of "ducks." She avoided the picture of the mice for several days. Two years later, of course, Erica was perfectly able to say "mice."

NEGATIVE SENTENCES

One of the pioneering language-acquisition studies of the 1960s was undertaken at Harvard by a research group headed by Brown. The group studied the development in the language of three children over a period of several years. Two members of the group, Ursula Bellugi and Edward S. Klima, looked specifically at the changes in the children's negative sentences over the course of the project. They found that negative structures, like other subsystems of the syntactic component of grammar, are acquired in an orderly, rule-governed way.

When the project began, the forms of negative sentences the children employed were quite simple. It appeared that they had incorporated the following rule into their grammar: To make a sentence negative attach "no" or "not" to the beginning of it. On rare occasions, possibly when a child had forgotten to anticipate the negative, "no" could be attached to the end of a sentence, but negative words could not appear inside a sentence.

In the next stage the children continued to follow this rule, but they had also hypothesized and incorporated into their grammars more complex rules that allowed them to generate sentences in which the negatives "no," "not," "can't," and "don't" appeared after the subject and before the verb. These rules constituted quite an advance over attaching a negative word externally to a sentence. Furthermore, some of the primitive imperative sentences constructed at this stage began with "don't" rather than "no." On the other hand, "can't" never appeared at the beginning of a sentence, and neither "can" nor "do" appeared as an auxiliary, as they do in adult speech: "I can do it." These facts suggest that at this point "can't" and "don't" were unanalyzed negative forms rather than contractions of "cannot" and "do not," but that although "can't" and "don't" each seemed to be interchangeable with "no," they were no longer interchangeable with each other.

In the third stage of acquiring negatives many more details of the negative system had appeared in the children's speech. The main feature of the system that still remained to be worked out was the use of pronouns in negative sentences. At this stage the children said "I didn't see something" and "I don't want somebody to wake me up." The pronouns "somebody" and "something" were later replaced with "nobody" and "nothing" and ultimately with the properly concorded forms "anybody" and "anything."

Many features of telegraphic speech were still evident in the third stage. The form "is" of the verb "to be" was frequently omitted, as in "This no good." In adult speech the auxiliary "do" often functions as a dummy verb to carry tense and other markings; for example, in "I didn't see it," "do" carries the tense and the negative. In the children's speech at this stage "do" appeared occasionally, but the children had not yet figured out its entire function. Therefore in some sentences the auxiliary "do" was omitted and the negative "not" appeared alone, as in "I not hurt him." In other sentences, such as "I didn't did it," the negative auxiliary form of "do" appears to be correct but is actually an unanalyzed, memorized item; at this stage the tense is regularly marked on the main verb, which in this example happens also to be "do."

Many children acquire negatives in the same way that the children in the Harvard study did, but subsequent investigations have shown that there is more than one way to learn a language. Carol B. Lord of U.C.L.A. identified a quite different strategy employed by a two-year-old named Jennifer. From twenty-four to twenty-eight months Jennifer used "no" only as a single-word utterance. In order to produce a negative sentence she simply spoke an ordinary sentence with a higher pitch. For example, "I want put it on" spoken in a high pitch meant "I don't want to put it on." Lord noticed that many of the negative sentences adults addressed to Jennifer were spoken with an elevated pitch. Children tend to pay more attention to the beginning and ending of sentences, and in adult speech negative words usually appear in the middle of sentences. With good reason, then, Jennifer seemed to have hypothesized that one makes a sentence negative by uttering it with a higher pitch. Other children have been found to follow the same strategy. There are clearly variations in the hypotheses children make in the process of constructing grammar.

SEMANTICS

Up to this point I have mainly discussed the acquisition of syntactic rules, in part because in the years following the publication of Chomsky's *Syntactic Structures* child-language research in this area flourished. Syntactic rules, which govern the ordering of words in a sentence, are not all a child needs to know about language, however, and after the first flush of excitement over Chomsky's work investigators began to ask questions about other areas of language acquisition. Consider the development of the rules of semantics, which govern the way words are interpreted. Eve V. Clark of Stanford reexamined old diary studies and noticed that the development in the meaning of words during the first several months of the one-word stage seemed to follow a basic pattern.

The first time children in the studies used a word, Clark noted, it seemed to be as a proper noun, as the name of a specific object. Almost immediately, however, the children generalized the word based on some feature of the original object and used it to refer to many other objects.

STAGE 1	STAGE 2	STAGE 3
No . . . wipe finger.	I can't catch you.	We can't make another broom.
No a boy bed.	I can't see you.	I don't want cover on it.
No singing song.	We can't talk.	I gave him some so he won't cry.
No the sun shining.	You can't dance.	No, I don't have a book.
No money.	I don't want it.	I am not a doctor.
No sit there.	I don't like him.	It's not cold.
No play that.	I don't know his name.	Don't put the two wings on.
No fall.	No pinch me.	**A**
Not . . . fit.	Book say no.	I didn't did it.
Not a teddy bear.	Touch the snow no.	You didn't caught me.
More . . . no.	This a radiator no.	I not hurt him.
Wear mitten no.	No square . . . is clown.	Ask me if I not made mistake.
	Don't bite me yet.	
	Don't leave me.	**B**
	Don't wake me up . . . again.	Because I don't want somebody to wake me up.
	He not little, he big.	I didn't see something.
	That no fish school.	**C**
	That no Mommy.	I isn't . . . I not sad.
	There no squirrels.	This not ice cream.
	He no bite you.	This no good.
	I no want envelope.	I not crying.
	I no taste them.	That not turning.
		He not taking the walls down.

TABLE 41.5   Three stages in acquisition of negative sentences were studied by Ursula Bellugi of the Salk Institute for Biological Studies and Edward S. Klima of the University of California at San Diego. They observed that in the first stage almost all negative sentences appear to be formulated according to the rule: Attach "no" or "not" to the beginning of a sentence to make it negative. In the second stage additional rules are postulated that allow the formation of sentences in which: "no," "not," "can't," and "don't" appear after the subject and before the verb. In the third stage several issues remain to be worked out, in particular the agreement of pronouns in negative sentences (B), the inclusion of the forms of the verb "to be" (C), and the correct use of the auxiliary "do" (A). In adult speech the auxiliary "do" often carries tense and other functional markings such as the negative; children in the third stage may replace it by "not" or use it redundantly to mark tense that is already marked on the main verb.

For example, a child named Hildegard first used "tick-tock" as the name for her father's watch, but she quickly broadened the meaning of the word, first to include all clocks, then all watches, then a gas meter, then a firehose wound on a spool, and then a bathroom scale with a round dial. Her generalizations appear to be based on her observation of common features of shape: roundness, dials, and so on. In general the children in the diary studies overextended meanings based on similarities of movement, texture, size, and, most frequently, shape.

As the children progressed, the meanings of words were narrowed down until eventually they more or less coincided with the meanings accepted by adult speakers of the language. The narrowing-down process has not been studied intensively, but it seems likely that the process has no fixed end point. Rather it appears that the meanings of words continue to expand and contract through adulthood, long after other types of language acquisition have ceased.

One of the problems encountered in trying to understand the acquisition of semantics is that it is often difficult to determine the precise meaning a child has constructed for a word. Some interesting observations have been made, however, concerning the development of the meanings of the pairs of words that function as opposites in adult language. Margaret Donaldson and George Balfour of the University of Edinburgh asked children from three to five years old which one of two cardboard trees had "more" apples on it. They asked other children of the same age which tree had "less" apples. (Each child was interviewed individually.) Almost all the children in both groups responded by pointing to the tree with more apples on it. Moreover, the children who had been asked to point to the tree with "less" apples showed no hesitation in choosing the tree with more apples. They did not act as though they did not know the meaning of "less"; rather they acted as if they did know the meaning and "less" meant "more."

Subsequent studies have revealed similar systematic error making in the acquisition of other pairs of opposites such as "same" and "different," "big" and "little," "wide" and "narrow," and "tall" and "short." In every case the pattern of learning is the same: one word of the pair is learned first and its meaning is overextended to apply to the other word in the pair. The first word learned is always the unmarked word of the pair, that is, the word adults use when they do not want to indicate either one of the opposites. (For example, in the case of "wide" and "narrow," "wide" is the unmarked word: asking "How wide is the road?" does not suggest that the road is wide, but asking "How narrow is the road?" does suggest that the road is narrow.)

Clark observed a more intricate pattern of error production in the acquisition of the words "before" and "after." Consider the four different types of sentence represented by (1) "He jumped the gate before he patted the dog," (2) "Before he patted the dog he jumped the gate," (3) "He patted the dog after he jumped the gate," and (4) "After he jumped the gate he patted the dog." Clark found that the way the children she observed interpreted sentences such as these could be divided into four stages.

In the first stage the children disregarded the words "before" and "after" in all four of these sentence types and assumed that the event of the first clause took place before the event of the second clause. With this order-of-

CHILD'S LEXICAL ITEM	FIRST REFERENTS	OTHER REFERENTS IN ORDER OF OCCURRENCE	GENERAL AREA OF SEMANTIC EXTENSION
mooi	moon	cake round marks on windows writing on windows and in books round shapes in books tooling on leather book covers round postmarks letter "o"	shape
bow-wow	dog	fur piece with glass eyes father's cufflinks pearl buttons on dress bath thermometer	shape
kotibaiz	bars of cot	large toy abacus toast rack with parallel bars picture of building with columns	shape
bébé	reflection of child (self) in mirror	photograph of self all photographs all pictures all books with pictures all books	shape
vov-vov	dog	kittens hens all animals at a zoo picture of pigs dancing	shape
ass	goat with rough hide on wheels	things that move: animals, sister, wagon . . . all moving things all things with a rough surface	movement texture
tutu	train	engine moving train journey	movement
fly	fly	specks of dirt dust all small insects child's own toes crumbs of bread a toad	size
quack	ducks on water	all birds and insects all coins (after seeing an eagle on the face of a coin)	size
koko	cockerel's crowing	tunes played on a violin tunes played on a piano tunes played on an accordion tunes played on a phonograph all music merry-go-round	sound
dany	sounds of a bell	clock telephone doorbells	sound

TABLE 41.6 Children overgeneralize word meanings, using words they acquire early in place of words they have not yet acquired. Eve V. Clark of Stanford University has observed that when a word first appears in a child's lexicon, it refers to a specific object but the child quickly extends semantic domain of the word, using it to refer to many other things. Eventually meaning of the word is narrowed down until it coincides with adult usage. Clark found that children most frequently base the semantic extension of a word on the shape of its first referent.

mention strategy the first and fourth sentence types were interpreted correctly but the second and third sentence types were not. In the second stage sentences using "before" were interpreted correctly, but an order-of-mention strategy was still adopted for sentences that used "after." Hence sentences of the fourth type were interpreted correctly, but sentences of the third type were not. In the next stage both the third and the fourth sentence types were interpreted incorrectly, suggesting that the children had adopted the strategy that "after" actually meant "before." Finally, in the fourth stage both "before" and "after" were interpreted appropriately.

It appears, then, that in learning the meaning of a pair of words such as "more" and "less" or "before" and "after" children acquire first the part of the meaning that is common to both words and only later the part of the meaning that distinguishes the two. Linguists have not yet developed satisfactory ways of separating the components of meaning that make up a single word, but it seems clear that when such components can be identified, it will be established that, for example, "more" and "less" have a large number of components in common and differ only in a single component specifying the pole of the dimension. Beyond the studies of opposites there has been little investigation of the period of semantic acquisition that follows the early period of rampant overgeneralization. How children past the early stage learn the meanings of other kinds of words is still not well understood.

PHONOLOGY

Just as children overgeneralize word meanings and sentence structures, so do they overgeneralize sounds, using sounds they have learned in place of sounds they have not yet acquired. Just as a child may use the word "not" correctly in one sentence but instead of another negative word in a second sentence, so may she correctly contrast /p/ and /b/ at the beginnings of words but employ /p/ at the ends of words, regardless of whether the adult models end with /p/ or /b/. Children also acquire the details of the phonological system in very regular ways. The ways in which they acquire individual sounds, however, are highly idiosyncratic, and so for many years the patterns eluded diarists, who tended to look only at the order in which sounds were acquired. Jakobson made a major advance in this area by suggesting that it was not individual sounds children acquire in an orderly way but the distinctive features of sound, that is, the minimal differences, or contrasts, between sounds. In other words, when a child begins to contrast /p/ and /b/, she also begins to contrast all the other pairs of sounds that, like /p/ and /b/, differ only in the absence or presence of vocal-cord vibration. In English these pairs include /t/ and /d/, and /k/ and the hard /g/. It is the acquisition of this contrast and not of the six individual sounds that is predictable. Jakobson's extensive examination of the diary data for a wide variety of languages supported this theory. Almost all current work in phonological theory rests on the theory of distinctive features that grew out of his work.

My own recent work suggests that phonological units even more basic than the distinctive features play an important part in the early acquisition process. At an early stage, when there are relatively few words in a child's repertory, unanalyzed syllables appear to be the basic unit of the sound system. By designating these syllables as unanalyzed I mean that the child is not able to separate them into their component consonants and vowels. Only later in the acquisition process does such division into smaller units become possible. The gradual discovery of successively smaller units that can form the basis of the phonological system is an important part of the process.

At an even earlier stage, before a child has uttered any words, she is accomplishing a great deal of linguistic learning, working with a unit of phonological organization even more primitive than the syllable. That unit can be defined in terms of pitch contours. By the late babbling period children already control the intonation, or pitch modulation, contours of the language they are learning. At that stage the child sounds as if she is uttering reasonably long sentences, and adult listeners may have the impression they are not quite catching the child's words. There are no words to catch, only random strings of babbled sounds with recognizable, correctly produced question or statement intonation contours. The sounds may accidentally be similar to some of those found in adult English. These sentence-length utterances are called sentence units, and in the phonological system of the child at this stage they are comparable to the consonant-and-vowel segments, syllables, and distinctive features that appear in the phonological systems of later stages. The syllables and segments that appear when the period of word learning begins are in no way related to the vast repertory of babbling sounds. Only the intonation contours are carried over from the babbling stage into the later period.

No matter what language environment a child grows up in, the intonation contours characteristic of adult speech in that environment are the linguistic information learned earliest. Some recent studies suggest that it is possible to identify the language environment of a child from her babbling intonation during the second year of life. Other studies suggest that children can be distinguished at an even earlier age on the basis of whether or not their language environment is a tone language, that is, a language in which words spoken with different pitches are identifiable as different words, even though they may have the same sequence of consonants and vowels. To put it another way, "ma" spoken with a high pitch and "ma" spoken with a low pitch can be as different to someone speaking a tone language as "ma" and "pa" are to someone speaking English. (Many African and Asian languages are tone languages.) Tones are learned very early, and entire tone systems are mastered long before other areas of phonology. The extremely early acquisition of pitch patterns may help to explain the difficulty adults have in learning the intonation of a second language.

PHONETICS

There is one significant way in which the acquisition of phonology differs from the acquisition of other language systems. As a child is acquiring the phonological system she must also learn the phonetic realization of the system: the actual details of physiological and acoustic phonetics, which call for the coordination of a complex set of muscle movements. Some children complete the process of learning how to pronounce things earlier than others, but differences of this kind are usually not related to the learning of the phonological system. Brown had what has become a classic conversation with a child who referred to a "fis." Brown repeated "fis," and the child indignantly corrected him, saying "fis." After several such exchanges Brown tried "fish," and the child, finally satisfied, replied, "Yes, fis." It is clear that although the child was still not able to pronounce the distinction between the sounds "s" and "sh," he knew such a systematic phonological distinction existed. Such phonetic muddying of the phonological waters complicates the study of this area of acquisition. Since the child's knowledge of the phonological system may not show up in her speech, it is not easy to determine what a child knows about the system without engaging in complex experimentation and creative hypothesizing.

Children whose phonological system produces only simple words such as "mama" and "papa" actually have a greater phonetic repertory than their utterances suggest. Evidence of that repertory is found in the late babbling stage, when children are working with sentence units and are making a large array of sounds. They do not lose their phonetic ability overnight, but they must constrain it systematically. Going on to the next-higher stage of language learning, the phonological system, is more important to the child than the details of facile pronunciation. Much later, after the phonological system has been acquired, the details of pronunciation receive more attention.

In the period following the babbling period the persisting phonetic facility gets less and less exercise. The vast majority of a child's utterances fail to reflect her real ability to pronounce things accurately; they do, however, reflect her growing ability to pronounce things systematically. (For a child who grows up learning only one language the movements of the muscles of the vocal tract ultimately become so overpracticed that it is difficult to learn new pronunciations during adulthood. On the other hand, people who learn at least two languages in early childhood appear to retain a greater flexibility of the vocal musculature and are more likely to learn to speak an additional language in their adult years without the "accent" of their native language.)

In learning to pronounce, then, a child must acquire a sound system that includes the divergent systems of phonology and phonetics. The acquisition of phonology differs from that of phonetics in requiring the creation of a representation of language in the mind of the child. This representation is necessary because of the abstract nature of the units of phonological structure. From only the acoustic signal of adult language the child must derive successively more abstract phonological units: first intonations, then syllables, then distinctive features, and finally consonant-vowel segments. There are, for example, few clear segment boundaries in the acoustic signal the child receives, and so the consonant-and-vowel units could hardly be derived if the child had no internal representation of language.

At the same time that a child is building a phonological representation of language she is learning to manipulate all the phonetic variations of language, learning to produce each one precisely and automatically. The dual process of phonetics and phonology acquisition is one of the most difficult in all of language learning. Indeed, although a great deal of syntactic and semantic acquisition has yet to take place, it is usually at the completion of the process of learning to pronounce that adults consider a child to be a full-fledged language speaker and stop using any form of caretaker speech.

ABNORMAL LANGUAGE DEVELOPMENT

There seems to be little question that the human brain is best suited to language learning before puberty. Foreign languages are certainly learned most easily at that time. Furthermore, it has been observed that people who learn more than one language in childhood have an easier time learning additional languages in later years. It seems to be extremely important for a child to exercise the language-learning faculty. Children who are not exposed to any learnable language during the crucial years, for example children who are deaf before they can speak, generally grow up with the handicap of having little or no language. The handicap is unnecessary: deaf children of deaf parents who communicate by means of the American Sign Language do not grow up without language. They live in an environment where they can make full use of their language-learning abilities, and they are reasonably fluent in sign language by age three, right on the developmental schedule. Deaf children who grow up communicating by means of sign language have a much easier time learning English as a second language than deaf children in oral-speech programs learning English as a first language.

The study of child language acquisition has made important contributions to the study of abnormal speech development. Some investigators of child language have looked at children whose language development is abnormal in the hope of finding the conditions that are necessary and sufficient for normal development; others have looked at the development of language in normal children in the hope of helping children whose language development is abnormal. It now appears that many of the severe language abnormalities found in children can in some way be traced to interruptions of the normal acquisition process. The improved understanding of the normal process is being exploited to create treatment programs for children with such problems. In the past therapeutic methods for children with language problems have emphasized the memorizing of language routines, but methods now being developed would allow a child to work with her own language-learning abilities. For example, the American Sign Language has been taught successfully to several autistic children. Many of these nonverbal and antisocial children have learned in this way to communicate with therapists, in some cases becoming more socially responsive. (Why sign language should be so successful with some autistic children is unclear; it may have to do with the fact that a sign lasts longer than an auditory signal.)

There are still many questions to be answered in the various areas I have discussed, but in general a great deal of progress has been made in understanding child language over the past 20 years. The study of the acquisition of language has come of age. It is now a genuinely interdisciplinary field where psychologists, neurosurgeons, and linguists work together to penetrate the mechanisms of perception and cognition as well as the mechanisms of language.

BIBLIOGRAPHY

Bloom, Lois. *One Word at a Time*. The Hague: Mouton, 1975.

Brown, Roger. *A First Language: The Early Stages*. Cambridge: Harvard University Press, 1973.

Dil, Anwar S., ed. *Language Structure and Language Use: Essays by Charles A. Ferguson*. Stanford: Stanford University Press, 1971.

McNeill, David. *The Acquisition of Language: The Study of Developmental Psycholinguistics*. New York: Harper & Row, 1970.

FOR DISCUSSION AND REVIEW

1. Explain how the tables showing the development of correct noun plural forms and of correct past-tense forms of verbs illustrate and support the claim that "children approach language learning economically, devoting their energy to broad issues before dealing with specific ones."

2. What are the characteristics of "caretaker speech"? Why is its use important to children in their acquisition of language? How has the recognition of caretaker speech modified linguists' thinking about the process of language acquisition?

3. Explain how and why children in the one-word and two-word stages of language acquisition use vertical constructions. In what sense is this linguistic strategy an example of a technique that children use in all areas of cognitive development?

4. Children's acquisition of function words (including inflectional affixes such as noun plurals and the -*ing* and past-tense forms of verbs) in English and in other languages follows a very predictable

order. Using examples from English, explain what principles govern the sequence of function-word acquisition.

5. Discuss how children expand their semantic understanding and use of a word. What features of the referent are most important? Although less is known about the narrowing-down process, consider what might be the results of semantic overgeneralization and subsequent narrowing-down in the communication process—among both older children and adults, especially since "the meanings of words continue to expand and contract through adulthood."

6. With regard to the manner in which children learn to understand pairs of words with opposite meanings (e.g., *more* vs. *less*), explain the statement that "children acquire first the part of the meaning that is common to both words and only later the part that distinguishes the two."

7. What part of the language system do children learn first? What are some implications of this very early learning for adults who are trying to learn a new language?

8. Explain the statement that "learning to pronounce . . . , a child must acquire a sound system that includes the divergent systems of phonology and phonetics."

42

Developmental Milestones in Motor and Language Development

Eric H. Lenneberg

All normal children, whatever their native language, go through the same stages of language acquisition in nearly the same order, although not all progress at the same rate. All normal children also move through the same stages of motor development—though again at different rates. However, the relationship between language acquisition and sensorimotor development is not clear. Some researchers believe that some level of sensorimotor knowledge must be present in order for language acquisition to proceed; others argue that it is cortical maturation itself that is the essential prerequisite for both language and sensorimotor development. The issue is whether language is an autonomous cognitive system or whether it is only one way of many in which development of general cognitive ability is manifested. A further question is whether and to what extent children possess an innate capacity specifically for language acquisition. The following chart juxtaposes the stages of motor and language development typically reached by children from twelve weeks through four years of age.

AT THE COMPLETION OF:	MOTOR DEVELOPMENT	VOCALIZATION AND LANGUAGE
12 weeks	Supports head when in prone position; weight is on elbows; hands mostly open; no grasp reflex	Markedly less crying than at 8 weeks; when talked to and nodded at, smiles, followed by squealing-gurgling sounds usually called *cooing*, which is vowel-like in character and pitch-modulated; sustains cooing for 15–20 seconds
16 weeks	Plays with rattle placed in his hands (by shaking it and staring at it), head self-supported; tonic neck reflex subsiding	Responds to human sounds more definitely; turns head; eyes seem to search for speaker; occasionally some chuckling sounds

(continued)

AT THE COMPLETION OF:	MOTOR DEVELOPMENT	VOCALIZATION AND LANGUAGE
20 weeks	Sits with props	The vowel-like cooing sounds begin to be interspersed with more consonantal sounds; labial fricatives, spirants, and nasals are common; acoustically, all vocalizations are very different from the sounds of the mature language of the environment
6 months	Sitting: bends forward and uses hands for support; can bear weight when put into standing position, but cannot yet stand with holding on; reaching: unilateral; grasp: no thumb apposition yet; releases cube when given another	Cooing changing into babbling resembling one-syllable utterances; neither vowels nor consonants have very fixed recurrences; most common utterances sound somewhat like *ma, mu, da,* or *di*
8 months	Stands holding on; grasps with thumb apposition; picks up pellet with thumb and fingertips	Reduplication (or more continuous repetitions) becomes frequent; intonation patterns become distinct; utterances can signal emphasis and emotions
10 months	Creeps efficiently; takes side steps, holding on; pulls to standing position	Vocalizations are mixed with sound-play such as gurgling or bubble-blowing; appears to wish to imitate sounds, but the imitations are never quite successful; beginning to differentiate between words heard by making differential adjustment
12 months	Walks when held by one hand; walks on feet and hands—knees in air; mouthing of objects almost stopped; seats self on floor	Identical sound sequences are replicated with higher relative frequency of occurrence and words (*mamma* or *dadda*) are emerging; definite signs of understanding some words and simple commands (show me your eyes)
18 months	Grasp, prehension, and release fully developed; gait stiff, propulsive, and precipitated; sits on child's chair with only fair aim; creeps downstairs backward; has difficulty building tower of three cubes	Has a definite repertoire of words—more than three, but fewer than fifty; still much babbling but now of several syllables with intricate intonation pattern; no attempt at communicating information and no frustration for not being understood; words may include items such as *thank you* or *come here,* but there is little ability to join any of the lexical items into spontaneous two-item phrases; understanding is progressing rapidly

(continued)

AT THE COMPLETION OF:	MOTOR DEVELOPMENT	VOCALIZATION AND LANGUAGE
24 months	Runs, but falls in sudden turns; can quickly alternate between sitting and stance; walks stairs up or down, one foot forward only	Vocabulary of more than 50 items (some children seem to be able to name everything in the environment); begins spontaneously to join vocabulary items into two-word phrases; all phrases appear to be own creations; definite increase in communicative behavior and interest in language
30 months	Jumps up into air with both feet; stands on one foot for about two seconds; takes few steps on tiptoe; jumps from chair; good hand and finger coordination; can move digits independently; manipulation of objects much improved; builds tower of six cubes	Fastest increase in vocabulary with many additions every day; no babbling at all; utterances have communicative intent; frustrated if not understood by adults; utterances consist of at least two words, many have three or even five words; sentences and phrases have characteristic child grammar, that is, they are rarely verbatim repetitions of an adult utterance; intelligibility is not very good yet, though there is great variation among children; seems to understand everything that is said to him
3 years	Tiptoes three yards; runs smoothly with acceleration and deceleration; negotiates sharp and fast curves without difficulty; walks stairs by alternating feet; jumps 12 inches; can operate tricycle	Vocabulary of some 1000 words; about 80% of utterances are intelligible even to strangers; grammatical complexity of utterances is roughly that of colloquial adult language, although mistakes still occur
4 years	Jumps over rope; hops on dominant foot; catches ball in arms; walks line	Language is well-established; deviations from adult norm tend to be more in style than in grammar

FOR DISCUSSION AND REVIEW

1. According to Lenneberg's table, do motor and language development seem to progress at similar rates—that is, do children develop more rapidly in one area than in the other?

2. Jean Piaget has argued that children acquire meanings as an extension of sensorimotor intelligence and that the development of vocabulary categories, for example, depends on motor development (things can be "graspable" or "suckable"). Thus, abilities in different areas

(e.g., motor skills and language) that appear at the same age should be similar because they are based on the same cognitive knowledge. Can you support or refute this argument on the basis of Lenneberg's table? If you need additional information, describe the kind(s) of data that you would want to have.

43

*Predestinate Grooves:
Is There a Preordained
Language "Program"?*

Jean Aitchison

*A biological trigger is one possible and increasingly accepted explanation
for why all children go through the same stages of language acquisition in
the same order but at different rates. In the following chapter from her
book* The Articulate Mammal, *Jean Aitchison, a British linguist, describes
the characteristics of biologically determined behaviors and considers
whether and to what extent language acquisition fits this model. She also
describes a "critical period" for language acquisition. In addition, using
examples of specific children, Aitchison discusses certain aspects of language acquisition, such as crying, cooing, babbling, the acquisition order
of various grammatical forms, and the significance of the mean length of
utterance (MLU) measure.*

> There once was a man who said, "Damn!"
> It is born in upon me I am
> An engine that moves
> In predestinate grooves,
> I'm not even a bus, I'm a tram.
>   –MAURICE EVAN HARE

Language emerges at about the same time in children all over the world.
"Why do children normally begin to speak between their eighteenth and
twenty-eighth month?" asks one researcher. "Surely it is not because all
mothers on earth initiate language training at that time. There is, in fact,
no evidence that any conscious and systematic teaching of language
takes place, just as there is no special training for stance or gait"
(Lenneberg 1967, 125).

This regularity of onset suggests that language may be set in motion
by a biological time-clock, similar to the one that causes kittens to open
their eyes when they are a few days old, chrysalises to change into but-
terflies after several weeks, and humans to become sexually mature at
around 13 years of age. However, until relatively recently, few people had
considered language within the framework of biological maturation.

But in 1967 E. H. Lenneberg, then a biologist at the Harvard Medical School, published an important book, entitled *The Biological Foundations of Language.* Much of what is said in this chapter is based on his pioneering work.

THE CHARACTERISTICS OF BIOLOGICALLY TRIGGERED BEHAVIOR

Behavior that is triggered off biologically has a number of special characteristics. In the following pages we shall list these features, and see to what extent they are present in language. If it can be shown that speech, like sexual activities and the ability to walk, falls into the category of biologically scheduled behavior, then we shall be rather clearer about what is meant by the claim that language is "innate."

Exactly how many "hallmarks" of biologically controlled behavior we should itemize is not clear. Lenneberg lists four. The six listed below were obtained mainly by subdividing Lenneberg's four:

1. The behavior emerges before it is necessary.
2. Its appearance is not the result of a conscious decision.
3. Its emergence is not triggered by external events (though the surrounding environment must be sufficiently "rich" for it to develop adequately).
4. There is likely to be a "critical period" for the acquisition of the behavior.
5. Direct teaching and intensive practice have relatively little effect.
6. There is a regular sequence of "milestones" as the behavior develops, and these can usually be correlated with age and other aspects of development.

Let us discuss these features in turn. Some of them seem fairly obvious. We hardly need to set about testing the first one, that "the behavior emerges before it is necessary"—a phenomenon sometimes pompously labeled the "law of anticipatory maturation." Language develops long before children need to communicate in order to survive. Their parents still feed them, clothe them, and look after them. Without some type of inborn mechanism, language might develop only when parents left children to fend for themselves. It would emerge at different times in different cultures, and this would lead to vastly different levels of language skills. Although children differ enormously in their ability to knit or play the violin, their language proficiency varies to a much lesser extent.

Again, little explanation is needed for the second characteristic of biologically triggered behavior: "Its appearance is not the result of a conscious decision." Clearly, a child does not suddenly think to himself, "Tomorrow I am going to start to learn to talk." Children acquire language without making any conscious decision about it. This is quite unlike a decision to learn to jump a four-foot height, or hit a tennis ball, when a child sets himself a target, then organizes strenuous practice sessions as he strives toward his goal.

The first part of feature 3 also seems straightforward: "The emergence of the behavior is not triggered by external events." Children start to talk even when their surroundings remain unchanged. Most of them live in the same house, eat the same food, have the same parents, and follow the same routine. No specific event or feature in the child's surroundings suddenly sets him off talking. However, we must here digress briefly in order to point out an aspect of biologically scheduled behavior that is sometimes misunderstood; although no external event *causes* the behavior, the surrounding environment must be sufficiently "rich" for it to develop adequately. Biologically programmed behavior does not develop properly in impoverished or unnatural surroundings. We have the apparent paradox that some types of "natural" behavior require careful "nurturing." Just as Chris and Susie, two gorillas reared away from other gorillas in Sacramento Zoo, are unable to mate satisfactorily (according to an item in the *Evening Standard*)—so an impoverished linguistic environment is likely to retard language acquisition. Children brought up in institutions, for example, tend to be backward in speech development. Lenneberg notes that a child raised in an orphanage will begin to talk at the same time as other noninstitutionalized children. But his speech will gradually lag behind the norm, being less intelligible, and showing less variety of construction. . . .

Rather more discussion is needed to justify the existence in language of a fourth characteristic of biologically controlled behavior: "There is likely to be a critical period for the acquisition of the behavior." It is clear that there is a biologically scheduled starting point for language acquisition, but far less clear that there is a biologically scheduled finishing point.

We know for certain that language cannot emerge before it is programmed to emerge. Nobody has ever taught a young baby to talk—though it seems that there is nothing much wrong with the vocal cords of a newborn infant, and from five or six months onwards it can "babble" a number of the sounds needed in speech. Yet children utter few words before the age of eighteen months. It is clear that they have to wait for some biological trigger. The "trigger" appears to be connected with brain growth. Two-word utterances, which are usually regarded as the beginning of "true language," begin just as a massive spurt in brain growth slows down. Children do not manufacture any new brain cells after birth. They are born with millions, perhaps billions. At first the cells are not all interconnected, and the brain is relatively light (about 300 g). From birth to around two years, many more cells interconnect, and brain weight increases rapidly. By the age of two, it weighs nearly 1000 g (Lenneberg 1967).

It is not nearly so easy to tell when a child has finished acquiring a language. Nevertheless, there are a number of indications that, after the onset of adolescence, humans can acquire a new language only after a considerable struggle.

First of all, almost everybody can remember how difficult it was to learn French at school. Even the best pupils had a slightly odd accent, and made numerous grammatical mistakes. The difficulty was not that one was learning a second language, since children who are brought up speaking French and English as equal "mother tongues" do not experience similar problems. Nor is there much difficulty for children who emigrate to France around the age of five or six, when they already speak fluent English. Moreover, the failure to learn perfect French cannot be due simply to lack of exposure to the language. There are numerous people who have emigrated to France as adults, and converse only in French—yet few, if any acquire a mastery of the new language equivalent to that of their native tongue. It seems that the brain loses its "plasticity" for language learning after a certain age.

However, evidence concerning difficulties with French at school is mainly anecdotal. Perhaps the most impressive evidence for the existence of a critical period comes from comparing the case histories of two socially isolated children, Isabelle and Genie. Both these children were cut off from language until long after the time they would have acquired it, had they been brought up in normal circumstances.

Isabelle was the illegitimate child of a deaf mute. She had no speech, and made only a croaking sound when she was found in Ohio in the 1930s at the age of six and a half. Mother and child had spent most of the time alone in a darkened room. But once found, Isabelle's progress was remarkable: "Isabelle passed through the usual stages of linguistic development at a greatly accelerated rate. She covered in two years the learning that ordinarily occupies six years. By the age of eight and one half Isabelle was not easily distinguishable from ordinary children of her age" (Brown 1958, 192).

Genie, however, was not born so lucky. She was not found until she was nearly fourteen. Born in April 1957, she had lived most of her life in bizarre and inhuman conditions. "From the age of twenty months, Genie had been confined to a small room. . . . She was physically punished by her father if she made any sounds. Most of the time she was kept harnessed into an infant's potty chair; otherwise she was confined in a homemade sleeping bag in an infant's crib covered with wire mesh" (Curtiss et al. 1974, 529). When found, she was totally without language. She began acquiring speech well after the onset of adolescence—after the apparent "critical period."

Although she learned to speak in a rudimentary fashion, she progressed more slowly than normal children (Curtiss 1977). For example, ordinary children go through a stage in which they utter two words at a time ("want milk," "Mummy play"), which normally lasts a matter of weeks.

Genie's two-word stage lasted for more than five months. Again, ordinary children briefly pass through a phase in which they form negative sentences by putting the word *no* in front of the rest of the utterance, as in "no Mummy go," "no want apple." Genie used this primitive form of negation for over two years. Normal children start asking questions beginning with words such as *where, what,* at the two-word stage ("where Teddy?"). Genie finds this kind of question impossible to grasp, occasionally making inappropriate attempts such as "where is stop spitting?" The only aspect of speech in which Genie outstripped normal children was her ability to learn vocabulary. She knew many more words than ordinary children at a comparable stage of grammatical development. However, the ability to memorize lists of items is not evidence of language capacity—even the chimps Washoe and Sarah found this relatively easy. It is the rules of grammar that are the important part, and this is what Genie finds difficult. Her slow progress compared with that of Isabelle seems to provide evidence in favor of there being a "cutoff" point for language acquisition. We must be cautious however. Two individual cases cannot provide firm proof, especially as each is problematical. Isabelle was not studied by linguists, so her speech may have been more deficient than was reported. Genie, on the other hand, shows some evidence of brain damage. Tests suggest that her left hemisphere is atrophied, which means that she may be functioning with only one half of her brain, the half not usually associated with language (Curtiss 1977; Curtiss et al. 1974).

According to Lenneberg, further evidence in favor of a critical period is provided by mentally handicapped children, such as "mongols" (Down's syndrome cases) (Lenneberg 1967). These follow the same general path of development as normal children, but much more slowly. Lenneberg claims that they never catch up because their ability to learn language slows down dramatically at puberty. But some researchers have disputed this claim, arguing that the children's language ceases to develop through lack of stimulation, not lack of ability.

The recovery possibilities of brain-damaged patients give further support and, in addition indicate that the critical period coincides with the period of lateralization—the gradual specialization of language to one side of the brain. Lenneberg suggests that this process occurs between the ages of 2 and 14, though others have suggested that its completion occurs around the age of 5 or 6. If a child under the age of 2 sustains severe damage to the left (language) hemisphere of the brain, his speech will develop normally, though it will be controlled by the right hemisphere. But as the child gets older, the likelihood of left hemisphere damage causing permanent impairment gets progressively greater. At the age of 7 or 8, the damage is usually long-lasting, whereas in an adolescent or adult it often results in lifelong speech disturbance. When lateralization is complete, the brain seems to have lost a natural "bent" for learning languages.

We have now considered several pieces of indirect evidence for the existence of a "critical period." They all suggest (though do not conclusively prove) that toddler time to adolescence is a time set aside by nature for the acquisition of language. Lenneberg notes:

> Between the ages of two and three years language emerges by an interaction of maturation and self-programmed learning. Between the ages of three and the early teens the possibility for primary language acquisition continues to be good; the individual appears to be most sensitive to stimuli at this time and to preserve some innate flexibility for the organization of brain functions to carry out the complete integration of subprocesses necessary for the smooth elaboration of speech and language. After puberty, the ability for self-organization and adjustment to the physiological demands of verbal behavior quickly declines. The brain behaves as if it had become set in its ways and primary, basic skills not acquired by that time usually remain deficient for life [Lenneberg 1967 158]

A similar critical period is found for the acquisition of their song by some species of birds. A chaffinch's song, for example, becomes fixed and unalterable when it is around fifteen months old. If the chaffinch has not been exposed to chaffinch song before that time, it never learns to sing normally (Thorpe 1972).

Let us now turn to the fifth characteristic of biologically triggered behavior, "Direct teaching and intensive practice have relatively little effect." In activities such as typing or playing tennis, a person's achievement is often directly related to the amount of teaching he receives and the hours of practice he puts in. Even people who are not "naturally" superb athletes can sometimes win tennis tournaments through sheer hard work and good coaching. But the same is not true of language, where direct teaching seems to be a failure. Let us consider the evidence for this.

When one says that "direct teaching is a failure," people smile and say, "Of course—whoever tries to *teach* a child to speak?" Yet many parents, often without realizing it, try to persuade their children to imitate them. They do this in two ways: first, by means of overt correction, second, by means of unconscious "expansions."

The pointlessness of overt correction has been noted by numerous researchers. One psychologist attempted over a period of several weeks to persuade his daughter to say *other* + noun instead of *other one* + noun. The interchanges went somewhat as follows:

CHILD: Want other one spoon, Daddy.
FATHER: You mean, you want the other spoon.
CHILD: Yes, I want the other one spoon, please Daddy.
FATHER: Can you say "the other spoon"?
CHILD: Other . . . one . . . spoon.
FATHER: Say "other."
CHILD: Other.
FATHER: "Spoon."
CHILD: Spoon.
FATHER: "Other spoon."
CHILD: Other . . . spoon. Now give me other one spoon?

[Braine 1971, 161]

Another researcher tried vainly to coax a child into saying the past tense form *held*:

CHILD: My teacher holded the baby rabbits and we patted them.
ADULT: Did you say your teacher held the baby rabbits?
CHILD: Yes.
ADULT: What did you say she did?
CHILD: She holded the baby rabbits and we patted them.
ADULT: Did you say she held them tightly?
CHILD: No, she holded them loosely.

[Cazden 1972, 92]

In fact, repeated corrections are not merely pointless: they may even hinder a child's progress. The mother of seventeen-month-old Paul had high expectations, and repeatedly corrected his attempts at speech. He lacked confidence, and his progress was slow. But the mother of four-teen-month-old Jane was an accepting person who responded uncritical-ly to everything Jane said. Jane made exceptionally fast progress, and knew eighty words by the age of fifteen months (Nelson 1973, 105).

So forcing children to imitate is a dismal failure. Children cannot be trained like parrots. Equally unsuccessful is the second type of coaching often unconsciously adopted by parents—the use of "expansions." When talking to a child an adult continuously "expands" the youngster's utter-ances. If the child says, "There go one," a mother is likely to expand this to "Yes, there goes one." "Mommy eggnog" becomes "Mommy had her eggnog," and "Throw Daddy" is expanded to "Throw it to Daddy." Children are exposed to an enormous number of these expansions. They account for perhaps a third of parental responses. Brown and Bellugi note:

The mothers of Adam and Eve responded to the speech of their children with expansions about 30 percent of the time. We did it ourselves when we talked with the children. Indeed, we found it very difficult to with-hold expansions. A reduced or incomplete English sentence seems to constrain the English-speaking adult to expand it into the nearest prop-erly formed complete sentence. [Brown and Bellugi 1964, 144]

At first researchers were uncertain about the role of expansions. Then Courtney Cazden carried out an ingenious experiment using two groups of children, all under three and a half (Cazden 1972). She exposed one group to extensive and deliberate expansions, and the other group to well-formed sentences which were *not* expansions. For example, if a child said "Dog bark," an expanding adult would say, "Yes, the dog is barking." An adult who replied with a nonexpanded sentence might say, "Yes, he's trying to frighten the cat" or "Yes, but he won't bite," or "Yes, tell him to be quiet." After three months the rate of progress of each group was measured. Amazingly, the expansion group were *less advanced* than the other group, both in average length of utterance and grammatical complexity.

Several explanations of this unexpected result have been put forward. Perhaps adults misinterpret the child's intended meaning when they expand. Erroneous expansions could hinder his learning. Several "wrong" expansions have been noted. For example:

CHILD: What time it is?
ADULT: Uh huh, it tells what time it is.

Alternatively, a certain degree of novelty may be needed in order to capture a child's attention, since he may not listen to apparent repetitions of his own utterances. Or it may be that expansions overrestrict the data the child hears. His speech may be impoverished because of an insufficiently rich verbal environment. As we noted earlier, the child *needs* copious and varied samples of speech.

The last two explanations seem to be supported by a Russian experiment (Slobin 1966, 144). One group of infants was shown a doll and three phrases were repeatedly uttered, "Here is a doll . . . Take the doll. . . Give me the doll." Another group of infants was shown the doll, but instead, *thirty* different phrases were uttered, such as "Rock the doll . . . Look for the doll." The total number of words heard by both groups was the same, only the composition differed. Then the experimenters showed the children a selection of toys, and asked them to pick out the dolls. To their surprise, the children in the second group, the ones who had heard a richer variety of speech, were considerably better at this task.

We may conclude then that parents who consciously try to "coach" their children by simplifying and repeating may be actually *interfering* with their progress. It does not pay to talk to children as if one were telling a foreign tourist how to get to the zoo. Language that is impoverished is harder to learn, not simpler. Children appear to be naturally "set" to extract a grammar for themselves, provided they have sufficient data at their disposal. Direct teaching is irrelevant, and those who get on best are those who are exposed to a rich variety of language—in other words, those whose parents talk to them in a normal way.

But what does "talk in a normal way" mean? Before we go on to discuss the role of practice, this is perhaps the best place to clear up a misunderstanding which seems to have originated with Chomsky. He claims that what children hear "consists to a large extent of utterances that break rules, since a good deal of normal speech consists of false starts, disconnected phrases and other deviations" (Chomsky 1967, 441). Certainly, children are likely to hear *some* deviant sentences. But recent research indicates that the speech children are exposed to is not particularly substandard. Adults tend to speak in shorter sentences and make fewer mistakes when they address children. There is considerable difference between the way a mother talks to another adult, and the way she talks to her child. One researcher recorded a mother talking to an adult friend. Her sentences were an average fourteen to fifteen words long, and she used several polysyllabic medical terms:

I was on a inhalation series routine. We wen' aroun' from ward to ward. People, are, y'know, that get all this mucus in their chest, and it's very important to breathe properly an' to be able to cough this mucus up and out an' through your chest, y'know as soon as possible. And we couldn't sterilize the instruments 'cause they were plastic.

But when she spoke to her child the same mother used five- or six-word sentences. The words were shorter, and referred to things the child could see or do:

Come look at Momma's colorin' book.
You wanna see my coloring book?
Look at my coloring book.
Lookit, that's an Indian, huh?
Is that an Indian?
Talk to me.
   [Drach, quoted in Ervin-Tripp 1971]

It seems that parents automatically simplify both the content and syntax when they talk to children. This is not particularly surprising—after all, we do not address bus conductors and boyfriends in the same way. The use of language appropriate to the circumstances is a normal part of a human's language ability. "Motherese," as it is sometimes called, consists of short, well-formed sentences spoken slowly and clearly. . . . Direct teaching, in the sense of correction and [expansion], does not accelerate the speed of learning and might even be a hindrance.

Let us now return to the question of practice. What is being claimed here is that practice alone cannot account for language acquisition. Children do not learn language simply by repetition and imitation. Two types of evidence support this view.

The first concerns the development of "inflections" or word endings. English has a number of very common verbs which have an "irregular" past tense (e.g., *came, saw, went*) as opposed to the "regular" forms such as *loved, worked, played*. It also has a number of irregular plurals such as *feet* and *mice*, as well as the far more numerous plurals ending in *-s* such as *cats, giraffes,* and *pythons*. Quite early on, children learn correct past tense and plural forms for common words such as *came, saw,* and *feet*. Later, they abandon these correct forms and replace them with over-generalized "regular" forms such as *comed, seed,* and *foots* (Ervin 1964). The significance of this apparent regression is immense. It means that language acquisition cannot possibly be a straightforward case of "practice makes perfect" or of simple imitation. If it were, children would never replace common forms such as *came, saw,* and *feet*, which they hear and use all the time, with odd forms such as *comed, seed,* and *foots*, which they are unlikely to have come across.

The second type of practice which turns out to be unimportant for language acquisition is spontaneous imitation. Just as adults subconsciously imitate and expand their children's utterances, so children appear to imitate and "reduce" sentences uttered by their parents. If an adult says

"I shall take an umbrella," a child is likely to say "Take rella." Or "Put the strap under her chin" is likely to be repeated and reduced to "Strap chin." At first sight, it looks as if this might be an important mechanism in the development of language. But Susan Ervin of the University of California at Berkeley came to the opposite conclusion when she recorded the spontaneous utterances of a small group of toddlers (Ervin 1964). To her surprise she found that when a child spontaneously imitates an adult, her imitations are not any more advanced than her normal speech. She shortens the adult utterance to fit in with her current average length of sentence and includes the same number of endings and "little" words as in her nonimitated utterances. Not a single child produced imitations which were more advanced. And one child, Holly, actually produced imitations that were less complex than her spontaneous sentences! Susan Ervin notes: "There is not a shred of evidence supporting a view that progress toward adult norms of grammar arises merely from practice in overt imitation of adult sentences" (Ervin 1964, 172).

We may conclude, then, that mere practice—in the sense of direct repetition and imitation—does not affect the acquisition of language in a significant way. However, we must be careful that such a statement does not lead to misunderstandings. What is being said is that practice alone cannot account for language acquisition: children do not learn merely by constant repetition of items. In another sense, they do need to "practice" talking but even this requirement is not as extensive as might be expected. They can learn a surprising amount by just listening. It has been shown that the amount of talking a child needs to do in order to learn language varies considerably. Some children seem to speak very little. Others are constantly chattering, and playing with words. One researcher wrote a whole book on the presleep monologues of her first child, Anthony, who murmured paradigms to himself as he prepared for sleep:

> Go for glasses
> Go for them
> Go to the top
> Go throw
> Go for blouse
> Pants
> Go for shoes
>   (Weir 1962)

To her disappointment, her second child, David, was nowhere near as talkative although he eventually learned to speak just as well. These repetitious murmurs do not seem to be essential for all children.

So far, then, we have considered five of the six characteristics of biologically triggered behavior which we listed at the beginning of this chapter. All these features seem to be present in language. We now come to the sixth and final feature, "There is a regular sequence of 'milestones' as the behavior develops, and these can usually be correlated with age and other aspects of development." We shall deal with this in a section by itself.

THE PREORDAINED PROGRAM

All children seem to pass through a series of more or less fixed "stages" as they acquire language. The age at which different children reach each stage or "milestone" varies considerably, but the relative chronology remains the same. The milestones are normally reached in the same order, though they may be nearer together for some children and farther apart for others.

Consequently, we can divide language development into a number of approximate phases. Table 43.1 is highly oversimplified. The stages overlap, and the ages given are only a very rough guide—but it does give some idea of a child's likely progress.

In order to illustrate this progression we shall describe the successive phases which a typical (and nonexistent) English child is likely to go through as she learns to speak. Let us call this child *Barbara*—a name derived from the Greek word "foreigner" and meaning literally "someone who says bar-bar, who talks gibberish."

Barbara's first recognizable vocal activity was *crying*. During the first four weeks of her life, she was truly:

> An infant crying in the night:
> An infant crying for the light:
> And with no language but a cry.
> —TENNYSON

TABLE 43.1

LANGUAGE STAGE	BEGINNING AGE
Crying	birth
Cooing	6 weeks
Babbling	6 months
Intonation patterns	8 months
One-word utterances	1 year
Two-word utterances	18 months
Word inflections	2 years
Questions, negatives	2¼ years
Rare or complex constructions	5 years
Mature speech	10 years

A number of different types of cry could be detected. She cried with hunger when she wanted to be fed. She cried with pain when she had a tummyache, and she cried with pleasure when she was fed, comfortable, and lying in her mother's arms. However, strictly speaking, it is perhaps inaccurate to speak of crying as a "language phase," because crying seems to be instinctive communication and may be more like an animal call system than a true language. This seems to be confirmed by some research which suggests that the different "messages" contained in the crying of babies may be universal, since English parents could identify the "messages" of a foreign baby as easily as those of English babies (Ricks 1975). So although crying may help to strengthen the lungs and vocal cords (both of which are needed for speech), crying itself perhaps should not be regarded as part of true language development.

Barbara then passed through two reasonably distinct prelanguage phases, a *cooing* phase and a *babbling* phase. Early researchers confused these stages and sometimes likened them to bird song. . . .

The first of these two phases, *cooing*, began when Barbara was approximately six weeks old. To a casual observer, she sounded as if she was saying, "goo goo." But cooing is difficult to describe. Some textbooks call it "gurgling" or "mewing." The sound is superficially vowel-like, but the tracing produced on a sound spectogram show that it is quite unlike the vowels produced by adults. Cooing seems to be universal. It may be the vocal equivalent to arm and leg waving. That is, just as babies automatically strengthen their muscles by kicking their legs and moving their arms about, so cooing may help them to gain control over their vocal apparatus.

Gradually, consonant-type sounds become interspersed in the cooing. By around six months, Barbara had reached the *babbling* stage. She gave the impression of uttering consonants and vowels together, at first as single syllables—but later strung together. The consonants were often made with the lips, or the teeth, so that the sequences sounded like *mama*, *dididi*, or *papapa*. On hearing these sounds, Barbara's parents confidently but wrongly assumed that she was addressing them. Such wishful thinking accounts for the fact that *mama*, *papa*, and *dada* are found as nursery words for mother and father all over the world (Jakobson 1962). Barbara soon learned that a cry of *mama* meant immediate attention—though she often used it to mean, "I am hungry" rather than to refer to a parent. This phenomenon has been noted by numerous researchers.

Throughout the babbling period Barbara seemed to enjoy experimenting with her mouth and tongue. She not only babbled, she blew bubbles, gurgled, and spluttered. Superficially, she appeared to be uttering an enormous variety of exotic sounds. At one time, researchers wrongly assumed that children are naturally capable of producing every possible speech sound. . . . More recent investigators have noted that the variety of sounds used in babbling is not particularly great. But because the child does not yet have complete control over his vocal organs, the noises are often unlike adult sounds, and seem exotic to an untrained observer. In general, babbling seems to be a period when a child experiments and gradually gains muscular control over his vocal organs. Many people claim that babbling is universal. But there are a few puzzling records of children who did not babble, which provide problems for this point of view. All we can say at the moment is that babbling is sufficiently widespread to be regarded as a normal stage of development.

Some investigators have tried to compare babbling babies who have been exposed to different languages. It has been reported that Chinese babbles are distinguishable from American, Russian, and Arabic ones

(Weir 1966). Because Chinese is a language which distinguishes words by means of a change in "tone" or "pitch," Chinese babies tend to produce monosyllabic utterances with much tonal variation. American babies produce polysyllabic babbles with intonation spread over the whole sequence. The nontone babies sound superficially similar—though American mothers could often pick out the American baby, Russians the Russian baby, and Arabs the Arab baby. But the mothers could not distinguish between babies babbling the other two languages. This research supports the notion of a "babbling drift," in which a child's babbling gradually moves in the direction of the sounds he hears around him. In this respect babbling is clearly distinct from crying, which has no discernible relationship with any one language.

A question which perhaps should be asked at this stage is the following: how much can children actually distinguish of their parents' speech? It is sometimes assumed that babies hear merely a general mishmash of sound and only gradually notice the difference between say *p* and *b*. However, recent research indicates that infants are capable of discriminating a lot more than we realize. Eimas and his colleagues (1971), for example, have shown that babies between one and four months old *can* distinguish between *p* and *b*. They started by playing a repeated *b* sound to selected infants. They then switched to *p*. A clear change in the babies' sucking behavior showed that they had noticed the alteration. So even though infants may not listen carefully to everything their parents say, they may well be capable of hearing a considerable amount from a very young age. Somewhat surprisingly, these results of Eimas have been replicated with rhesus and chinchilla monkeys (Kuhl and Miller 1974, 1975; Morse 1976), and so may be due to the hearing mechanisms in certain types of mammals, and not just humans alone. In brief, a child's perception may be much sharper than had previously been supposed, even though it may not be equivalent to an adult's for some time (Fourcin 1978).

Simultaneously with babbling, and from around eight or nine months, Barbara began to imitate *intonation patterns*. These made her output sound so like speech that her mother sometimes said, "I'm sure she's talking, I just can't catch what she's saying. . . ." English mothers have noted that their children often use a "question" intonation, with a rise in tone at the end of the sentence. This may be due to a normal parent's tendency to bend over the child, asking, "What are you trying to say then?" "Do you want some milk?" "Do you know who this is?" and so on.

Somewhere between one year and eighteen months Barbara began to utter *single words*. She continued to babble as well, though her babbling gradually diminished as true language developed. The number of single words acquired at around this time varies from child to child. Some have only four or five, others have around fifty. As an average child Barbara acquired about fifteen. Many of them were names of people and things, such as *uf* (woof) "dog," *daba* "grandma, *da* "doll." Then as she neared her second birthday, she reached the more impressive *two-word stage*.

From the time Barbara started to put words together she seemed to be in a state of "language readiness," and mopped up language like a sponge. The most noticeable feature of this process was a dramatic increase in her vocabulary. By the time she was two and one half years old, she knew several hundred words. Meanwhile, there was a gradual but steady increase in her average or mean length of utterance—usually abbreviated to MLU. MLU is calculated in terms of grammatical items or "morphemes": plural *-s* and past tense *-d*, for example, each count as one item and so do ordinary words such as *mummy* and *bath*. Compound words such as *birthday* and *quack-quack* also count as a single item (Brown 1973, 54). Many (but not all) researchers accept this as a useful gauge of progress—though the child with the longest utterances does not necessarily have the most grammatically advanced, or even the most grammatically correct utterances (Garman 1979).

The fact that a steady increase in MLU occurs from the age of around two onwards has been shown by Roger Brown of Harvard University, who carried out a detailed study of the speech development of three unacquainted children, Adam, Eve, and Sarah—though he found that the chronological age at which different children reached an MLU stage differed considerably (Brown, Cazden, Bellugi 1968; Brown 1973). A comparison of Adam and Eve showed that Eve outstripped Adam by far. Eve's MLU was two items at around twenty months, three at twenty-two months, and four at twenty-eight months. Adam was over twenty-six months old before he achieved an MLU of two items. He was nearly three years old before his MLU reached three items and three and one half before it reached four items—a whole year behind Eve. [See Figure 43.1.]

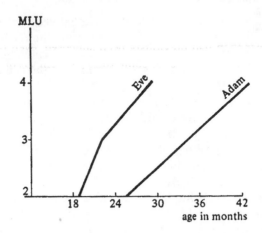

FIGURE 43.1

If we assume that Barbara is not as advanced as Eve, but ahead of Adam, she possibly had an MLU of two items a little before her second birthday, an MLU of three items at two and one half, and four items around her third birthday.

In the early part of the two-word stage, when she was around two years old, Barbara's speech was "telegraphic." She sounded as if she was sending urgent telegrams to her mother: "Want milk," "Where duck?" As in a real telegram, she tended to preserve the nouns and verbs in the correct order, but omitted the "little" words such as *the, a, has, his, and.* She also left out word endings, such as the plural *-s* or past tense *-d* as in *two shoe* and *milk spill.*

Then, gradually, the "little" words and *inflections* were added. "All these, like an intricate work of ivy began to grow up between and upon the major construction blocks, the nouns and verbs" (Brown 1973, 249).

In this aspect of language, Barbara is following the same path of development as the Harvard child Adam, but at a slightly earlier age (Brown 1973, 271). Between the ages of two and three and one half, Barbara acquired the following grammatical forms:

Age Two

Progressive *-ing*	I singing
Plural *-s*	Blue shoes
Copula *am, is, are*	He is asleep
Articles *a, the*	He is a doctor

Age Three

Third person singular *-s*	He wants an apple
Past tense *-d*	I helped Mummy
Full progressive *am, is, are* + *-ing*	I am singing
Shortened copula	He's a doctor
Shortened progressive	I'm singing

Note that it is important to distinguish between the *emergence* or first appearance of an ending, and its *acquisition*, its reliable use in the places where an adult would expect to find it. An ending can be considered acquired if it occurs in at least 90 percent of the contexts where it is needed (Brown 1973, 258).

The actual age at which Barbara acquired each form is not significant because it varies widely from child to child. What is important and interesting is the *order* of acquisition. The sequence seems surprisingly similar among English-speaking children. Roger Brown notes that in the unacquainted Harvard children, the developmental order of these grammatical forms was "amazingly consistent." There were one or two minor variations: Sarah, for example, acquired the progressive *-ing* after the plural, whereas Adam and Eve acquired it before. But in all the children, both the progressive *-ing* and the plural *-s* occurred before the past tense, the third person singular *-s*, and the copula *am, is, are.*

Perhaps even more surprising, is the fact that in all the Harvard children the copula *am, is, are* as in *I am a doctor* developed before *am, is, are* when it was part of the progressive construction, for example, *I am singing.* And the shortened copula as in *He's a bear* came before the shortened progressive, for example, *He's walking.* This is really quite an astonishing discovery. Although we might expect children to go through similar general lines of development, there seems to be no obvious reason why a variety of English children should correspond so closely in their acquisition of specific items.

A similar consistency of order is found in the acquisition of more complicated constructions, such as *questions* and *negatives*. For example, in the acquisition of *wh-* questions (questions beginning with *what, why, where, who,* etc.), we can safely assume that Barbara, like Adam, Eve, and Sarah, went through three intermediate stages before she acquired them perfectly (Klima and Bellugi 1966). First of all, soon after her second birthday, she placed the *wh-* word in front of the rest of the sentence:

What	Mummy doing?
Why	you singing?
Where	Daddy go?

A second stage occurred three or four months later when she added an auxiliary verb such as *can* or *will* to the main verb:

Where	you	will go?
Why	kitty	can't see?
Why	you	don't know?

Finally, before she was three, she realized that the subject noun must change places with the auxiliary and produced correct sentences such as:

Where	will you	go?
Why	can't kitty	see?
Why	don't you	know?

Once again [we have] the rather surprising finding that all English children tend to follow the same pattern. . . . As already noted, the actual *age* at which each stage is reached is irrelevant. It is the order that matters.

By the age of three and one half, Barbara, like most children, was able to form most grammatical constructions—and her speech was reasonably intelligible to strangers. Her constructions were, however, less varied than those of an adult. For example, she tended not to use the "full" passive such as *The man was hit by a bus.* But she was able to converse quite adequately on most topics.

By five, she gave the superficial impression of having acquired language more or less perfectly. But this was an illusion. Language acquisition was still continuing, though more slowly. The grammar of a child of five differs to a surprising degree from adult grammar. But the five-year-old is not usually aware of his shortcomings. In comprehension tests, children readily assign interpretations to the structures presented to them—but they are often the wrong ones. "They do not, as they see it, fail to understand our sentences. They understand them, but they understand them wrongly" (Carol Chomsky 1969, 2). To demonstrate this point, the researcher (Noam Chomsky's wife) showed a group of five- to eight-year-olds a blindfolded doll, and said: "Is this doll hard to see or easy to see?" All the five-and six-year-olds said *hard to see*, and so did some of the seven- and eight-year-olds. The response of six-year-old Lisa was typical:

CHOMSKY: Is this doll easy to see or hard to see?
LISA: Hard to see.
CHOMSKY: Will you make her easy to see?
LISA: If I can get this untied.
CHOMSKY: Will you explain why she was hard to see?
LISA: (to doll): Because you had a blindfold over your eyes.

Some psychologists have criticized this particular test. A child sometimes believes, ostrich-fashion, that if his own eyes are covered, others will not be able to see him. And he may be partly switching to the doll's viewpoint when he says a blindfolded doll is hard to see. But a rerun of this experiment using wolf and duck puppets, and sentences such as:

The wolf is hard to bite.
The duck is anxious to bite.

confirmed the original results (Cromer 1970). Children of five and six just do not realize that pairs of sentences such as *The rabbit is nice to eat* and *The rabbit is eager to eat* have completely different underlying meanings.

In fact, the gap between child and adult speech lasts longer than was once realized. More recently, detailed experiments on French children's understanding and use of the articles *le/la* "the" and *un/une* "a" have shown quite surprising differences between child and adult usage, which remained in some cases up till the age of twelve (Karmiloff-Smith 1979).

But the discrepancies between Barbara's speech and that of the adults around her gradually disappeared over the next few years. By the age of about eleven, Barbara exhibited a command of the structure of her language comparable to that of an adult. At the age of puberty, her language development was essentially complete. She would continue to add individual vocabulary items all her life, but her grammatical rules were unlikely to change except in trivial respects. The "critical period" set by nature for the acquisition of language was over.

Note, incidentally, that language milestones tend to run parallel with physical development. Clearly, there is no essential correlation between language and motor development, since there are numerous examples of children who learn to talk, but never walk, and vice versa. However, researchers are agreed that in normal children the two often go together. Language milestones are often loosely linked to physical milestones. For example, the gradual change of cooing to babbling occurs around the time an infant begins to sit up. A child utters single words just before he starts to walk. Grammar becomes complex as hand and finger coordination develops.

Let us now summarize our conclusions. . . . [We] have shown that language seems to have all the characteristics of biologically programmed behavior. It emerges before it is necessary, and its emergence cannot be accounted for either by an external event, or by a sudden decision taken by the child. There seems to be a "critical period" set aside by nature for its acquisition, and direct teaching and intensive practice have relatively little effect. Language acquisition follows a regular sequence of milestones in its development, which can be loosely correlated with other aspects of the child's development. In other words, there is an internal mechanism both to trigger it off and to regulate it.

However, it would be wrong to think of language as something that is governed *only* by internal mechanisms. These mechanisms require external stimulation in order to work properly. The child needs a rich verbal environment during the critical acquisition period.

This suggests that the so-called nature-nurture controversy . . . may be misconceived. Both sides are right: nature triggers off the behavior, and lays down the framework, but careful nurture is needed for it to reach its full potential. The dividing line between "natural" and "nurtured" behavior is by no means as clear-cut as was once thought. In other words, language is "natural" behavior—but it still has to be carefully "nurtured" in order to reach its full potential. . . .

BIBLIOGRAPHY

Bernstein, B. "Social class, language, and socialization." In *Language and Social Context.* ed. P. P. Giglioli. Harmondsworth: Penguin, 1972.

Braine, M. D. S. "The acquisition of language In infant and child." In *The Learning of Language.* ed. C. E. Reed. New York: Appleton-Century-Crofts, 1971.

Brown, R. *Words and Things.* New York: The Free Press, 1958.

———. *A First Language.* London: Allen & Unwin, 1973.

Brown, R., and U. Bellugi. "Three processes in the child's acquisition of syntax." In *New Directions in the Study of Language.* ed. E. H. Lenneberg. Cambridge: MIT Press, 1964. Also in *Psycholinguistics: Selected Papers.* R. Brown ed. New York: The Free Press, 1964.

Brown, R., C. Cazden, and U. Bellugi. "The child's grammar from I to III." In *Minnesota Symposium on Child Psychology,* vol. 2. ed. J. P. Hill. Minneapolis: University of Minnesota Press, 1968.

Cazden, C. *Child Language and Education.* New York: Holt, Rinehart and Winston, 1972.

Chomsky, C. *The Acquisition of Syntax in Children from 5 to 10.* Cambridge: MIT Press, 1969.

Chomsky, N. "The formal nature of language." In *Biological Foundations of Language.* E. H. Lenneberg. New York: Wiley, 1967.

Curtiss, S. *Genie: A Psycholinguistic Study of a Modern-Day "Wild Child."* New York: Academic Press, 1977.

Curtiss, S., V. Fromkin, S. Krashen, D. Rigler, and M. Rigler. "The linguistic development of Genie." *Language* 50 (1974), 528–554.

Eimas, P., E. Siqueland, P. Juszyk, and J. Vigorito. "Speech perception in infants." *Science* 171 (1971), 303–306.

Ervin, S. M. "Imitation and structural change in children's language." In *New*

Directions in the Study of Language. ed. E. H Lenneberg. Cambridge: MIT Press, 1964.

Ervin-Tripp, S. "An overview of theories of grammatical development." In *The Ontogenesis of Grammar.* ed. D. I. Slobin. New York: Academic Press, 1971.

Fourcin, A. J. "Acoustic Patterns and speech acquisition." In *The Development of Communication.* eds. N. Waterson and C. Snow. Chichester: John Wiley & Sons, 1978.

Garman, M. "Early grammatical development." In *Language Acquisition.* ed. P. Fletcher and M. Garman. Cambridge: Cambridge University Press, 1979.

Jakobson, R. "Why 'Mama' and 'Papa'?" In *Child Language: A Book of Readings.* ed. A. Bar-Adon and W. F. Leopold. Englewood Cliffs, NJ: Prentice-Hall, 1971.

Karmiloff-Smith, A. *A Functional Approach to Child Language: A Study of Determiners and Reference.* Cambridge: Cambridge University Press, 1979.

Klima, E., and U. Bellugi. "Syntactic regularities in the speech of children." In *Psycholinguistics Papers.* ed. J. Lyons and R. J. Wales. Edinburgh: Edinburgh University Press, 1966. Revised version in A. Bar-Adon and W. F. Leopold, eds. *Child Language: A Book of Readings.* Englewood Cliffs, NJ: Prentice-Hall, 1971.

Kuhl, P., and J. D. Miller. "Discrimination of speech sounds by the chinchilla: /t/(vs)/d/ in CV syllables." *Journal of the Acoustical Society of America* 57 (1974), series 41 (abstract).

———. "Speech perception by the chinchilla: phonetic boundaries for synthetic VOT stimuli." *Journal of the Acoustical Society of America* 57 (1975), series 49 (abstract).

Lenneberg, E. H., *The Biological Foundations of Language.* New York: Wiley, 1967.

Morse, P. A. "Speech perception in the human infant and rhesus monkey." In *Origins and Evolution of Language and Speech.* eds. S. Harnad, H. Steklis, and J. Lancaster. *Annals of the New York Academy of Sciences,* vol. 280, 1976.

Nelson, K. "Structure and strategy in learning to talk." *Monograph of the Society for Research in Child Development* 38 (1973), 1–2.

Ricks, D. M. "Vocal communication in pre-verbal normal and autistic children." In *Language, Cognitive Deficits, and Retardation.* ed. N. O'Connor. London: Butterworth, 1975.

Slobin, D. I. "The acquisition of Russian as a native language." In *The Genesis of Language.* eds. F. Smith and G. A. Miller. Cambridge: MIT Press, 1966.

Thorpe, W. H. "Vocal communication in birds." In *Non-Verbal Communication.* ed. R. A. Hinde. Cambridge: Cambridge University Press, 1972.

Weir, R. H. *Language in the Crib.* The Hague: Mouton, 1962.

———. "Some questions on the child's learning of phonology." In *The Genesis of Language.* ed. F. Smith and G. A. Miller. Cambridge: MIT Press, 1966.

≡

FOR DISCUSSION AND REVIEW

1. What does Aitchison mean by "a biological time-clock"? Give four examples of its effects in animals that Aitchison does not mention.

2. Aitchison discusses six features of biologically scheduled behavior in addition to its one predominant characteristic. To what extent is each of these seven actually a characteristic of human language? Are there any qualifications or caveats? What are they?

3. Discuss the importance of a child's environment and his or her biological predisposition for language acquisition. What conclusions, if any, can you draw concerning the function of day care centers, nursery schools, and kindergartens?

4. Explain the term *critical period*. Summarize the arguments for both a biologically controlled starting point and a similarly controlled finishing point for language acquisition.

5. Reread the two examples of parent–child dialogue and the paragraph that follows them. How do the dialogues support the concept of language acquisition as biologically determined behavior? Consider outright correction, attempts to force imitation, and adult expansions of children's utterances.

6. Compare and contrast Aitchison's description of the way that parents talk to young children with Moskowitz's description of "caretaker speech." What similarities do you find? What differences?

7. What is the significance, in terms of theories of language acquisition, of the fact that children learn and use correct plural forms of some irregular nouns and correct past-tense forms of some irregular verbs, but then seem to "regress"—i.e., cease using the correct irregular forms, replacing, for example, *went* with *goed* or *feet* with *foots*?

8. Explain the apparent paradox that practice is in one sense unimportant for language acquisition, but in another sense children need to practice.

9. Moskowitz and Aitchison discuss the stages of normal language acquisition, although they do so in different ways. (For example, Moskowitz deals in generalizations, whereas Aitchison discusses specific children, both real and imaginary.) Compare and contrast the two discussions, looking especially for similarities and differences. Summarize your conclusions in a chart or table.

10. Review Lenneberg's "Developmental Milestones in Motor and Language Development" in light of Aitchison's discussion and examples of the fact that "Language milestones are often closely linked to physical milestones." Are her examples persuasive? What about the link between cognitive development and language milestones?

44

≡

How Children Learn Words

George A. Miller and Patricia M. Gildea

The only surprise that surfaces in detailed examinations of the word-learning process in children is that we may not in fact teach them as much about words and speech as we think we do. In this selection scientists George A. Miller of Purdue University and Patricia H. Gildea of Rutgers University examine the complicated word-learning process of children. The authors discuss the two stages of the word-learning process: how and in what manner words are learned, and the remarkable ability of children to learn much more than they are actually taught. Miller and Gildea demonstrate children's tendency toward "overextension" of meaning as new words are acquired. The authors discuss computers as new and helpful tools for teaching new words, along with the more traditional uses of definitions and sentence contexts. Miller and Gildea examine these teaching techniques with the hope that they will discover the most efficient method of facilitating the complicated process of word learning.

Listening to a child who is just learning to talk, one is most aware of the child's limited command of the language. What one tends to overlook is the sheer magnitude of the child's achievement. Simply learning the vocabulary is an enormous undertaking. The fact is that for many years after starting to talk a child learns new words at a rate of more than ten per day! Yet little is known about how children do it. Certainly they do not do it by memorizing dictionary entries. Our findings and those of other workers suggest that formal efforts to build vocabulary by sending children to the dictionary are less effective than most parents and teachers believe. We are exploring the possibility that a computer program providing lexical information about new words encountered in the context of a story might be more effective.

When adults set out to learn a new language, they know what is in store. They realize they will have to learn a new pronunciation, a new grammar, a new vocabulary, and a new style of using language. They know they will have to spend many hours every day for years before they can call themselves fluent in the new language. They also know, however, that they will be able to rely on teachers to explain, in their first language, everything they need to learn about the second language.

How different it is for infants. Having no language, they cannot be told what they need to learn. Yet by the age of three they will have mastered the basic structure of their native language and will be well on their way to communicative competence. Acquiring their first language is the most impressive intellectual feat many people will ever perform.

Students of how children learn language generally agree that the most remarkable aspect of this feat is the rapid acquisition of grammar. Nevertheless, the ability of children to conform to grammatical rules is only slightly more wonderful than their ability to learn new words.

How many words must one know in order to use English effectively? The answer depends on several variables, including the definition of "word." For the purpose of counting, a word can be defined as the kind of lexical unit a person has to learn; all the derivative and compound forms that are merely morphological variations on the conceptual theme would not be counted as separate words. For example, *write* is a word and its morphological variants (*writes, writ, wrote, written, writing, writer,* and so on) are relatives in the same family. If such a family is counted as a single word and knowing a word is defined as being able to recognize which of four definitions is closest to the meaning, the reading vocabulary of the average high school graduate should consist of about 40,000 words. If all the proper names of people and places and all the idiomatic expressions are also counted as words, that estimate would have to be doubled.

This figure says something about the ability of children to learn words. If the average high school graduate is 17 years old, the 80,000 words must have been learned over a period of 16 years. Hence the average child learns at the rate of 5,000 words per year, or about 13 per day. Children with large vocabularies probably pick up new words at twice that rate. Clearly, a learning process of great complexity goes on at a rapid rate in every normal child.

No one teaches children 13 or more words a day. Children must have a special talent for this kind of learning. Some valuable hints as to how they do it were uncovered a decade ago by Susan Carey and Elsa J. Bartlett, who were then at Rockefeller University. They worked with the names of colors. First they established that a group of three-year-olds did not know the color olive. Most of the children called it green and some of them called it brown.

Carey and Bartlett taught the children a nonsense name for olive—a name they would not have heard anywhere else. They took two cafeteria trays and painted one tray olive and the other blue. Each child was then told casually, "Hand me the chromium tray. Not the blue one, the chromium one." The child would pause and perhaps point to the olive tray. "This one?" "Yes, that one. Thank you."

A week later, with no further guidance, the children were again asked to name the colors. When olive was presented, they paused. They did not remember *chromium*, but now they knew that this color was not called green or brown. A single exposure was enough to begin a reorganization of their color lexicon.

This simple experiment demonstrated some important points about how children learn words. First, in order to learn a word a child must be able to associate its sound with its meaning. Mastering the mechanics of uttering and recognizing a word and mastering the concept that it expresses are separate learning processes. After their experience with the trays the children knew that olive has a special name—that it is not called green or brown—but they did not remember the particular spoken sound associated with that perceived color. Many repetitions may be necessary before the sound of a new word becomes familiar.

Second, a child's appreciation of the meaning of a word seems to grow in two stages, one rapid and the other much slower. Children are quick to notice new words and to assign them to broad semantic categories. After hearing *chromium* just once the three-year-olds assigned it to the semantic field of color names. Children are able to keep such fields separate even before they know what the individual words mean. Asked the color of something, they may respond with almost any color term at random, but they never answer *round* or *five* or *lunch*.

The slow stage entails working out the distinctions among words within a semantic category. A child who has correctly assigned *red*, *green*, *yellow*, and *blue* to the semantic field of color terms still has to learn the differences between and relations among those words. This stage ordinarily takes much longer than the first and may never be completely finished; some adults, for example, correctly assign *delphinium* and *calceolaria* to the semantic field of flowering-plant names but have not learned what plants the words denote and cannot identify the flowers on sight. At any given time many words will be in this intermediate state in which they are known and categorized but still not distinguished from one another.

A related aspect of word learning by preschoolers that has attracted wide attention is called overextension. For example, a small child learning the word *apple* may apply it to a tomato. *Apple* is thought to mean, say, round, red, and of a certain size; without further qualification those attributes define ripe tomatoes as well as ripe apples. Overextension can occur when a child's conception of a word's meaning is incomplete.

The opposite error also occurs, but it is revealed only by special questioning. For example, a child who thinks that being round, red, and of a certain size defines *apple* might fail to use *apple* to refer to green or yellow apples. The only way to identify such an underextension is to show the child green or yellow apples and ask what they are called.

The ability of preschoolers to soak up words has attracted increasing attention in recent years. Much more is known about it than was known when Carey and Bartlett did their pioneering study with color names. The word-learning process becomes even more complex, however, during the school years.

In the early grades schoolchildren are expected to learn to read and write. At first they read and write familiar words they have already learned by means of conversation. In about the fourth grade they begin to see written words they have not heard in conversation. At this point it is generally assumed that something special must be done to teach children these unfamiliar words.

This educational assumption runs into serious problems. Although children can recognize that they have not seen a word before, learning it well enough to use it correctly and to recognize it automatically is a slow process. Indeed, learning a new word entails so much conceptual clarification and phonological drill that there simply is not enough classroom time to teach more than 100 or 200 words a year in this way. Since learning runs so far ahead of teaching—some 5,000 words learned in a year compared with 200 taught—it is hard to avoid the question: How do schoolchildren learn so much more than they are taught?

Many words are acquired through reading. Children learn words at school in the same way as they do at home: by observing how the words are used in intelligible contexts. The difference is that the academic environment depends more on written contexts. Both public opinion and scientific evidence are converging on the view that the best way to facilitate vocabulary growth in schoolchildren is to have them read as much as possible.

Learning words by reading them in context is effective but not efficient. Some contexts are uninformative, others misleading. If the word in question expresses an unfamiliar concept, a single context of use will seldom support more than one hypothesis about the word's meaning. In order for reading to have any substantial effect on vocabulary a great deal of reading must be done.

How much? A child who spent fifty minutes of every school day reading at, say, 200 words per minute would read one million words in a 100-day school year. A million running words of English prose would typically contain no more than 50,000 distinct word types, representing roughly 10,000 word families. Schoolbooks would probably contain fewer different words. Even among 10,000 different words, it is unlikely that more than 1,000 would be totally new lexical items. Since multiple encounters are required in order to learn a new word, it is clear that reading one million words per year is not enough. In order to account for a growth rate of 5,000 words in a year it seems necessary to think about continued learning from conversational interactions supplemented by reading several million words per year. Indeed, children who read little outside the classroom generally do poorly on vocabulary tests.

The fact that children learn many more words than anyone has time to teach them also carries implications for the role of teachers in this learning process. Learning new words from purely literary contexts of use—from the contexts provided on the printed page—is harder than learning them through interaction with a person. In conversation it is usually possible to ask the speaker what an unfamiliar word means. Moreover, in most conversations visual information supplements the linguistic information. Such help is missing from the printed page.

Given this additional difficulty, it seems reasonable to ask teachers to help children to be more efficient in learning new words from context. If they cannot teach all the words children need to know, perhaps teachers could help their students learn how to work out such things for themselves.

One way to figure out what an unfamiliar word means is to use a dictionary. In about the fourth grade, therefore, most schools begin to teach dictionary skills: spelling, alphabetizing, pronunciation, parts of speech, and a little morphology and etymology. The idea, which is perfectly reasonable, is that children should learn how to find unfamiliar words in a dictionary and how to understand what they read there.

One trouble with this approach is that most healthy, right-minded children have a strong aversion to dictionaries. There may be good reason. We have looked at some of the tasks teachers assign in order to get students to use dictionaries. In our opinion these exercises do not merit the faith that teachers and parents have in them.

Two tasks are often assigned when children are being taught how to use a dictionary. One task entails disambiguation: the child is given a sentence that contains an ambiguous word—a word with two or more senses—and told to find it in the dictionary and to decide which sense the author of the sentence had in mind. The other task calls for production: the child is given a word and told to look it up in the dictionary and to write a sentence incorporating it. On the face of it both tasks look as though they should be instructive. It is therefore surprising to discover how ineffectual they are.

Learning from a dictionary requires considerable sophistication. Interrupting your reading to find an unfamiliar word in an alphabetical list, all the while keeping the original context in mind so that you can compare it with the alternative senses given in the dictionary, then selecting the sense that is most appropriate in the original context—that is a high-level cognitive task. It should not be surprising that children are not good at it. Even when most of the complications are removed, children are still not good at it. On a simplified disambiguation task, in which fourth-grade students were given just two senses and asked to choose the one that was intended in a particular sentence, the students did little better than chance.

The second task, producing a sentence incorporating a new word, has the virtue of requiring the student to use the word and so, presumably, to think about its meaning. We have studied this production task extensively. After reading several thousand sentences that were written by children in the fifth and sixth grades we have concluded that it too is a waste of time.

Typical of the curious sentences we encountered was "Mrs. Morrow stimulated the soup." It illustrates the most frequent kind of error made by children in that age range. If they already know the word, their sentences are usually all right. If the word is unfamiliar, however, the results are often mystifying. In order to understand what the child did, you have to read carefully the same dictionary definitions the child read. The child who looked up *stimulate* found *stir up* among the definitions.

The example provides a key to what happens when children consult a dictionary. They find the unfamiliar word and then look for a familiar word or phrase among the definitions. Next they compose a sentence using the familiar word or phrase and substitute the new word for it. One of our favorite examples came from a fifth-grader who looked up the unfamiliar word *erode*, found the familiar phrases *eat out* and *eat away* in the definition, and thought of the sentence "Our family eats out a lot." She then substituted *erode* for *eats out*; the resulting sentence was "Our family erodes a lot."

If children are so good at learning new words when they hear or see them used in context, why do they have trouble learning new words when they see them in a dictionary? We decided to look more closely at what goes on when an unfamiliar word is encountered in the context of a typical sentence. A preliminary study indicated that children can write better sentences when they are given a model sentence employing the word than when they are given a definition of the word. Since many of the sentences they wrote were patterned on the models, this result could not be interpreted to mean that the children learned more about the meaning of a word from illustrative sentences than they learned from definitions. Nevertheless, the observation was encouraging, and we pressed on.

The next step was simple: if one example is good, three should be better. When we made this comparison, however, we found that the number of examples made little difference. The acceptability ratings of sentences written after seeing one model sentence were the same as the ratings of sentences written on the basis of three examples.

That observation made us think again about what was going on. Apparently three unrelated sentences are hard for children to integrate, and so they simply focus on one of three examples and ignore the others. This behavior resembles what children do in reading dictionary definitions.

We were surprised by one result, although perhaps in retrospect we should have expected it. Mistakes resembling simple substitutions appeared even when model sentences were given instead of dictionary definitions. For example, given the model sentence "The king's brother tried to usurp the throne" to define the unfamiliar word *usurp*, the children wrote such sentences as "The blue chair was usurped from the room," "Don't try to usurp that tape from the store," "The thief tried to usurp the money from the safe," and so on. They had gathered from the model sentence that *usurp* means *take*, and so they composed sentences using *take* and then substituted *usurp* for it.

Children can appreciate at least part of the meaning of an unfamiliar word from its context, as in the case of *take* as one component of the meaning of *usurp*. Just as younger children may overextend *apple* because they know only part of its meaning, so this partial definition of *usurp* resulted in its being overextended. That is to say, if *usurp* is incompletely defined as *take*, it can be said of anything takable: chairs, tape, money, or whatever. When it is seen from this perspective, the behavior of these children in the fifth and sixth grades is merely a later stage in the development of a word-learning process employed by preschool children.

The substitution strategy therefore seems to be quite general. In the context of a model sentence, however, something more than a simple substitution error appears. The children cannot search through an illustrative sentence for a familiar word as they could in a dictionary definition. First they must abstract a familiar concept from the context of the unfamiliar word. Only then can they apply the substitution rule.

Might there be a better way to foster the growth of vocabulary? What we and others have found out about the word-learning process will support some plausible suggestions. Put at the front of your mind the idea that a teacher's best friend in this endeavor is the student's motivation to discover meaning in linguistic messages. Then the problems with the traditional modes of instruction will begin to make sense. Drill on arbitrarily preselected lists of words seldom takes place at a time when the student feels a need to know those words; it fails to draw on the natural motivation for learning the associations between word and meaning. Learning through reading faces the opposite problem; not enough information about the word is available at the moment the student is motivated to learn its meaning.

What is needed is reading, which can make students curious about unfamiliar words, supplemented by immediate information about the meaning and use of those words. The important thing is to provide the information while the reader still wants it. Dictionaries are too slow. Recourse to a dictionary may help a mature and well-motivated student, but for the average child in the elementary grades it is likely to compound interruption with misunderstood information. A human tutor—someone immediately available to detect and resolve lexical misunderstandings—would be much better than a dictionary.

Given the shortage of attentive tutors to sit at every young reader's elbow, it is natural to wonder how much of the tutoring task might be carried out by a suitably programmed computer. For example, suppose reading material was presented to the student by a computer that had been programmed to answer questions about the meanings of all the words in the material. No alphabetical search would be needed: the student would simply point to a word and information about it would appear. No sophisticated disambiguation would be necessary: the computer would know in advance which particular sense of a word was appropriate in the context. Indeed, no definition would be necessary: the phrase or sentence containing the word could be rephrased to show what the word meant in the context.

As a case in point, imagine what such a computer might do with *erode* and *usurp*. It might present a text containing the sentence "The president's popularity was eroded by his bad relations with Congress." If the student asked for information about *erode*, the computer might state: "Things can erode; when soil is eroded by rain or wind, it breaks up and so is slowly destroyed and removed. Someone's power or authority can erode too, being slowly destroyed or removed by unfavorable developments. That kind of erosion is meant in the sentence about the president."

Suppose that for *usurp* the computer presented a text containing the sentence "The king's brother failed in his effort to usurp the throne." Asked for information, the computer might say: "When you usurp a title, job, or position from someone else, you seize it or take it away even though you have no right to it. In the sentence about the king's brother, *throne* means not just the piece of furniture the king sits on; it also stands as a symbol of the king's authority."

Providing such explanations almost instantly is well within the range of currently available computer technology. It is even possible to add a voice that pronounces the target word and explains it, or to show pictures indicating what the word denotes in the context.

We are exploring some of these possibilities with a setup in which children in the fifth and sixth grades interact with a video display. They are asked to read a text that describes an episode from a motion picture they have just seen. Included in the text are certain marked words the reader is expected to learn. When one of them comes up, the child can ask for information about its meaning in any or all of three forms: definitions, sentences, and pictures.

For some children illustrative sentences are more informative than definitions or pictures. When such children are given a definition, they read it and quickly return to the story. When they are given a sentence that is relevant to the story and uses the word in the same context, they interpret it as a puzzle to be solved. They spend more time thinking about the meaning of the word and remember it better a week later.

We found that providing information when it is wanted can significantly improve the children's grasp of unfamiliar words, as is demonstrated by their ability to recognize the meanings and to write acceptable sentences incorporating the words. The results reinforce our belief that much can be done with computers to make learning words easier.

FOR DISCUSSION AND REVIEW

1. The first two paragraphs suggest that readers compare how they learned or were taught new words as a child with how they learn new words now. Try to recall your earliest memories and make some comparisons. Compare your results with classmates.
2. How do Miller and Gildea describe the early processes children use in their acquisition of language?
3. As children learn new words, there are two stages through which they must pass. What are these two stages and what characterizes each? Do you pass through any similar stages today when you learn new words?
4. What is meant by the term "overextension"? Describe some instances in which you have heard a child "overextend" the meaning of a word.
5. Miller and Gildea propose the question: "How do children learn so much more than they are taught?" What explanations can be offered as a solution? How might an answer to this question support the work of Noam Chomsky?
6. Miller and Gildea suggest that children can learn new words in textual context, through interaction, as well as through the use of dictionaries. "If children are so good at learning new words when they hear or see them in context, why do they have trouble learning new words when they see them in a dictionary?" What difficulties are associated with the use of dictionaries?
7. We have observed how "overextension" is apparent in the speech of young children. Miller and Gildea demonstrate several instances in which older grade-school children employ this "overextension" technique as well. What are some suggestions for the continued use of such a technique?
8. What do the authors suggest as a means to foster the growth of vocabulary in children? Can you think of any other methods to aid in this complicated process?

45

The Development of Language in Genie: A Case of Language Acquisition beyond the "Critical Period"

Victoria Fromkin, Stephen Krashen, Susan Curtiss, David Rigler, and Marilyn Rigler

Genie's story is tragic, involving, as it does, the irretrievable loss of human potential. For most of the first fourteen years of her life, Genie was isolated in a small, dark room, where she suffered extreme physical and emotional neglect. Out of this tragedy, linguists, psychologists, neurologists, and others have learned a great deal from careful study of Genie's development. Beginning almost immediately after she was discovered in 1970 and continuing until 1979, she was evaluated regularly, and as a result, our understanding of many aspects of language acquisition, cognitive development, the critical age theory, and brain lateralization and function has advanced enormously.

In this selection the development of Genie's linguistic abilities is examined in detail. As you read, keep in mind the normal stages of language acquisition described in earlier selections in Part Nine. When the following article first appeared, the authors were guardedly optimistic about the possibility of Genie's further linguistic development. Unfortunately, by 1979 it had become clear that her progress in language development had slowed dramatically and that a 1974 prediction of permanent dysphasia had been correct. However, Genie continued to be far more advanced cognitively than linguistically, and she could communicate effectively using a variety of nonverbal techniques, including her own drawings. In 1977, Susan Curtiss published a study, Genie: A Psycholinguistic Study of a Modern-Day "Wild Child" *(New York: Academic Press), which presented background material on Genie's personality, especially her interactions with Curtiss, and*

Notes: The research reported on in this paper was supported in part by a grant from the National Institutes of Mental Health, U.S. Department of Health, Education and Welfare, No. MH-21191-03.

This is a combined and expanded version of a number of papers presented before the American Psychological Association, the Linguistic Society of America, the Acoustical Society of America, and the American Speech and Hearing Association, including S. Curtiss (1972); Curtiss et al. (1972, 1973); Krashen et al. (1972a, 1972b); Fromkin (1972); D. Rigler (1972).

detailed her linguistic development and the ways in which she was evaluated.

According to Maya Pines, "within a few months of [Genie's] arrival at Children's Hospital [in 1970] she began going to nursery classes for normal children. She soon transferred to a special elementary school for handicapped children. Next, she spent several years in a city high school for the mentally retarded. Outside school, a speech therapist worked with her consistently for many years" (Psychology Today, September 1981, p. 31).

Genie, the subject of this study, is an adolescent girl who for most of her life underwent a degree of social isolation and experiential deprivation not previously reported in contemporary scientific history. It is a unique case because the other children reported on in contemporary literature were isolated for much shorter periods and emerged from their isolation at much younger ages than did Genie. The only studies of children isolated for periods of time somewhat comparable to that of this case are those of Victor (Itard 1962) and Kaspar Hauser (Singh and Zingg 1966).

All cases of such children reveal that experiential deprivation results in a retarded state of development. An important question for scientists of many disciplines is whether a child so deprived can "catch up" wholly or in part. The answer to this question depends on many factors including the developmental state achieved prior to deprivation, the duration, quality, and intensity of the deprivation, and the early biological adequacy of the isolated child. In addition, the ability of such "recuperation" is closely tied to whether there is a "critical period" beyond which learning cannot take place. The concept of a "critical period" during which certain innately determined faculties can develop derived from experimental embryology. It is hypothesized that should the necessary internal or external conditions be absent during this period, certain developmental abilities will be impossible.

Lenneberg (1967) presents the most specific statement about critical periods in humans as it concerns the acquisition of language. He starts with the assumption that language is innately determined, that its acquisition is dependent upon both necessary neurological events and some unspecified minimal exposure to language. He suggests that this critical period lasts from about age two to puberty: language acquisition is impossible before two due to maturational factors, and after puberty because of the loss of "cerebral plasticity" caused by the completion of the development of cerebral dominance, or lateralized specialization of the language function.

The case of Genie is directly related to this question, since Genie was already pubescent at the time of her discovery, and it is to this question that the discussion is primarily directed. The case also has relevance for other linguistic questions such as those concerning distinctions between the comprehension and production of language, between linguistic competence and performance, and between cognition and language.

There are many questions for which we still have no answers. Some we may never have. Others must await the future developments of this remarkable child. The case history as presented is therefore an interim report.

CASE HISTORY

Genie was first encountered when she was thirteen years, nine months. At the time of her discovery and hospitalization she was an unsocialized, primitive human being, emotionally disturbed, unlearned, and without language. She had been taken into protective custody by the police and, on November 4, 1970, was admitted into the Children's Hospital of Los Angeles for evaluation with a tentative diagnosis of severe malnutrition. She remained in the Rehabilitation Center of the hospital until August 13, 1971. At that time she entered a foster home, where she has been living ever since as a member of the family.

When admitted to the hospital, Genie was a painfully thin child with a distended abdomen who appeared to be six or seven years younger than her age. She was 54.5 inches tall and weighed 62.25 pounds. She was unable to stand erect, could not chew solid or even semisolid foods, had great difficulty in swallowing, was incontinent of feces and urine, and was mute.

The tragic and bizarre story which was uncovered revealed that for most of her life Genie had suffered physical and social restriction, nutritional neglect, and extreme experiential deprivation. There is evidence that from about the age of twenty months until shortly before admission to the hospital Genie had been isolated in a small closed room, tied into a potty chair where she remained most or all hours of the day, sometimes overnight. A cloth harness, constructed to keep her from handling her feces, was her only apparel of wear. When not strapped into the chair she was kept in a covered infant crib, also confined from the waist down. The door to the room was kept closed and the windows were curtained. She was hurriedly fed (only cereal and baby food) and minimally cared for by her mother, who was almost blind during most of the years of Genie's isolation. There was no radio or TV in the house and the father's intolerance of noise of any kind kept any acoustic stimuli which she received behind the closed door to a minimum. (The first child born to this family died from pneumonia when three months old after being put in the garage because of noisy crying.) Genie was physically punished by the father if she made any sounds. According to the mother, the father and older brother never spoke to Genie although they barked at her like dogs. The mother was forbidden to spend more than a few minutes with Genie during feeding.

It is not the purpose of this paper to attempt to explain the psychotic behavior of the parents which created this tragic life for Genie, not to relate the circumstances which led to the discovery. (See Hansen 1972; D. Rigler 1972.) It is reported that Genie's father regarded her as a hopelessly retarded child who was destined to die at a young age and convinced the mother of this. His prediction was based at least in part on Genie's failure to walk at a normal age. Genie was born with a congenital dislocation of the hips which was treated in the first year by the application of a Frejka pillow splint to hold both legs in abduction, and the father placed the blame for her "retardation" on this device.

On the basis of what is known about the early history, and what has been observed so far, it appears that Genie was normal at the time of birth and that the retardation observed at the time of discovery was due principally to the extreme isolation to which she was subjected, with its accompanying social, perceptual, and sensory deprivation. Very little evidence exists to support a diagnosis of early brain damage, primary mental deficiency, or infantile autism. On the other hand, there is abundant evidence of gross environmental impoverishment and of psychopathological behavior on the part of the parents. This is revealed to some extent in Genie's history and equally by the dramatic changes that have occurred since her emergence. (See D. Rigler 1972; M. Rigler 1972.)

Genie's birth was relatively normal. She was born in April 1957, delivered by Caesarian section. Her birth problems included an Rh negative incompatibility for which she was exchange transfused (no sequelae were noted), and the hip dislocation spoken of above. Genie's development was otherwise initially normal. At birth she weighed 7 pounds, 7.5 ounces. By three months she had gained 4.5 pounds. According to the pediatrician's report, at six months she was doing well and taking food well. At eleven months she was still within normal limits. At fourteen months Genie developed an acute illness and was seen by another pediatrician. The only other medical visit occurred when Genie was just over 3.5 years of age.

From the meager medical records at our disposal, then, there is no indication of early retardation. After admission to the hospital, Genie underwent a number of medical diagnostic tests. Radiology reported a "moderate coxa valga deformity of both hips and a narrow rib cage" but no abnormality of the skull. The bone age was reported as approximately eleven years. Simple metabolic disorders were ruled out. The neurologist found no evidence of neurological disease. The electroencephalographic records reported a "normal waking record." A chromosomal analysis was summarized as being "apparently normal."

During the first few months of her hospitalization additional consultations were undertaken. The conclusion from among all of these evaluative efforts may be summarized briefly. Functionally Genie was an extremely retarded child, but her behavior was unlike that of other mentally defective children. Neither, apparently, was she autistic. Although emotionally disturbed behavior was evident there was no discernible evidence of physical or mental disease that would otherwise account for her retarded behavior. It therefore seems plausible to explain her retardation as due to the intensity and duration of her psychosocial and physical deprivation.

The dramatic changes that have occurred since Genie's emergence reinforce this conclusion. Approximately four weeks after her admission to the hospital a consultant described a contrast between her admission status and what he later observed (Shurley, personal communication). He wrote that on admission Genie

> was pale, thin, ghost-like, apathetic, mute, and socially unresponsive. But now she had become alert, bright-eyed, engaged readily in simple social play with balloons, flashlight, and toys, with familiar and unfamiliar adults. . . . She exhibits a lively curiosity, good eye–hand coordination, adequate hearing and vision, and emotional responsivity. . . . She reveals much stimulus hunger . . . . Despite her muteness . . . Genie does not otherwise use autistic defenses, but has ample latent affect and responses. There is no obvious evidence of cerebral damage or intellectual stenosis—only severe (extreme) and prolonged experiential, social, and sensory isolation and deprivation during her infancy and childhood . . . Genie may be regarded as one of the most extreme and prolonged cases of such deprivation to come to light in this century, and as such she is an "experiment in nature."

GENIE'S LINGUISTIC DEVELOPMENT

Important elements in Genie's history are still unknown and may never be known. We have no reliable information about early linguistic developments or even the extent of language input. One version has it that Genie began to speak words prior to her isolation and then ceased. Another is that she simply never acquired language at all beyond the level observed on hospital entry. One thing is definite: when Genie was discovered she did not speak. On the day after admission to the hospital she was seen by Dr. James Kent who reports (Kent 1972):

> Throughout this period she retained saliva and frequently spit it out into a paper towel or into her pajama top. *She made no other sounds except for a kind of throaty whimper.* . . . (Later in the session) . . . she imitated "back" several times, as well as "fall" when I said "The puppet will fall." . . . She could communicate (her) needs nonverbally, at least to a limited extent. . . . Apart from a peculiar laugh, frustration was the only other clear affective behavior we could discern. . . . When very angry she would scratch at her own face, blow her nose violently into her clothes and often void urine. During these tantrums *there was no vocalization.* . . . We felt that the eerie silence that accompanied these reactions was probably due to the fact that she had been whipped by her father when she made noise.

At the outset of our linguistic observations, it was not clear whether

Genie's inability to talk was the result solely of physiological and/or emotional factors. We were unable to determine the extent of her language comprehension during the early periods. Within a few days she began to respond to the speech of others and also to imitate single words. Her responses did not however reveal how heavily she was dependent on non-verbal, extralinguistic cues such as "tone of voice, gestures, hints, guidance, facial and bodily expressions" (Bellugi and Klima 1971). To determine the extent of her language comprehension it was necessary to devise tests in which all extralinguistic cues were eliminated.[1] If the comprehension tests administered showed that Genie did comprehend what was said to her, using linguistic information alone, we could assume that she had some knowledge of English, or had acquired some linguistic "competence." In that case, the task facing Genie would not be one of language learning but of learning how to use that knowledge—adding a performance modality—to produce speech. If the tests, on the other hand, in addition to her inability to speak, showed that she had little ability to understand what was said to her when all extralinguistic cues were eliminated, she would be faced with true first-language acquisition.

LINGUISTIC COMPREHENSION

The administration of the comprehension tests which we constructed had to wait until Genie was willing and able to cooperate. It was necessary to develop tests which would not require verbal responses since it was her comprehension not her active production of speech to be tested at this stage. The first controlled test was administered in September 1971, almost eleven months after Genie's emergence. Prior to these tests Genie revealed a growing ability to understand and produce individual words and names. This ability was a necessary precursor to an investigation of her comprehension of grammatical structure, but did not in itself reveal how much language she knew since the ability to relate the sounds and meanings of individual lexical items, while necessary, is not a sufficient criterion for language competence.

It was quite evident that at the beginning of the testing period Genie could understand individual words which she did not utter herself, but, except for such words, she had little if any comprehension of grammatical structures. Genie was thus faced with the complex task of primary language acquisition with a postpubescent brain. There was no way that a prediction could be made as to whether she could or would accomplish this task. Furthermore, if she did not learn language it would be impossible to determine the reasons. One cannot draw conclusions about children of this kind who fail to develop. One can, however, draw at least some conclusions from the fact that Genie has been acquiring language at this late age. The evidence for this fact is revealed in the results of the

---

[1] The tests were designed, administered, and analyzed by S. Curtiss.

seventeen different comprehension tests which have been administered almost weekly over the last two years. A slow but steady development is taking place. We are still, of course, unable to predict how much of the adult grammar she will acquire.

Among the grammatical structures that Genie now comprehends are singular-plural contrasts of nouns, negative-affirmative sentence distinctions, possessive constructions, modifications, a number of prepositions (including *under, next to, beside, over,* and probably *on* and *in*), conjunction with *and,* and the comparative and superlative forms of adjectives. (For further details on the comprehension tests, see Curtiss et al. 1973.)

The comprehension tests which are now regularly administered were designed by Susan Curtiss, who has been most directly involved in the research of Genie's linguistic development. (New tests are constantly being added.) The nouns, verbs, and adjectives used in all of the tests are used by Genie in her own utterances (see below for discussion on Genie's spontaneous speech production). The response required was primarily a "pointing" response. Genie was familiar with this gesture prior to the onset of testing. One example can illustrate the kinds of tests and the procedures used.

To test Genie's singular/plural distinction in nouns, pairs of pictures are used—a single object on one picture, three of the identical objects on the other. The test sentences differ only by absence or presence of plural markers on the nouns. Genie is asked to point to the appropriate picture. The words used are: balloon(s), pail(s), turtle(s), nose(s), horse(s), dish(es), pot(s), boat(s). Until July 1972, the responses were no better than chance. Since July 1972, Genie gives 100 percent correct responses. It is important to note that at the time when she was not responding correctly to the linguistically marked distinction, she could appropriately use and understand utterances including numbers ("one," "two," "three," etc.) and "many," "more," and "lots of."

SPEECH PRODUCTION AND PHONOLOGICAL DEVELOPMENT

Genie's ability to comprehend spoken language is a better indication of her linguistic competence than is her production of speech because of the physical difficulties Genie has in speaking. At the age when normal children are learning the necessary neuromuscular controls over their vocal organs to enable them to produce the sounds of language, Genie was learning to repress any and all sounds because of the physical punishment which accompanied any sounds produced. This can explain why her earliest imitative and spontaneous utterances were often produced as silent articulations or whispered. Her inability to control the laryngeal mechanisms involved in speech resulted in monotonic speech. Her whole body tensed as she struggled to speak, revealing the difficulties she had in the control of air volume and air flow. The intensity of the acoustic signal produced was very low. The strange voice quality of her vocalized utterances is at least partially explainable in reference to these problems.

Because of her speech difficulties, one cannot assess her language competence by her productive utterances alone. But despite the problems which still remain, there has been dramatic improvement in Genie's speech production. Her supraglottal articulations have been more or less normal, and her phonological development does not deviate sharply from that observed in normal children. In addition, she is beginning, both in imitations and in spontaneous utterances, to show some intonation and her speech is now being produced with greater intensity.

Like normal children, Genie's first one-word utterances consisted of Consonant-Vowel (CV) monosyllables. These soon expanded into a more complex syllable structure which can be diagrammed as (C) (L/G) V (C), where L stands for liquid, G, glide, and the parenthesized elements optional.

Words of two and three syllables entered into her productive vocabulary and in these words stress was correctly marked by intensity and/or duration of the vowel as well as vowel quality (with the unstressed vowel being ə). To date, all of the consonants of Standard American English are included in her utterances (with the interdental fricatives occurring only in imitations, and the affricates occurring inconsistently). She still deletes final consonants more often than not. Their correct sporadic presence, however, shows them to be part of her stored representation of the words in which they occur. Consonant clusters were first simplified by the deletion of the /s/ in initial /sp/ /sk/ /st/ clusters; at the present time, in addition to this method of preserving the CV syllable structure, she sometimes adds an epenthetic schwa between the two consonants.

Other changes in Genie's phonological system continue to be observed. At an earlier stage a regular substitution of /t/ for /k/, /n/, and /s/ occurred in all word positions: this now occurs only word medially. /s/ plus nasal clusters are now being produced.

What is of particular interest is that in imitation Genie can produce any English sound and many sound sequences not found in her spontaneous speech. It has been noted by many researchers on child language that children have greater phonetic abilities than are revealed in their utterances. This is also true of Genie; her output reflects phonological constraints rather than her inability to articulate sounds and sound sequences.

Neither Genie nor a normal child learns the sound system of a language totally independent from the syntactic and semantic systems. In fact, the analysis of the syntactic and semantic development of Genie's spontaneous utterances reveals that her performance on the expressive side is paralleling (although lagging behind) her comprehension.

As stated above, within a few weeks after admission to the hospital Genie began to imitate words used to her, and her comprehension of individual words and names increased dramatically. She began to produce single words spontaneously after about five months.

SENTENCE STRUCTURE

For normal children perception or comprehension of syntactic structures exceeds production; this is even more true in Genie's case possibly for the reasons given above. But even in production it is clear that Genie is acquiring language. Eight months after her emergence Genie began to produce utterances, two words (or morphemes) in length. The structures of her earliest two-word "sentences" were Modifier + Noun and Noun + Noun genitive constructions. These included sentences like "more soup," "yellow car," "Genie purse," and "Mark mouth." After about two months she began to produce strings with verbs—both Noun (subject) + Verb, and Verb + Noun (object), e.g., "Mark paint" (N + V), "Curtiss cough" (N + V), "want milk" (V + N), and "wash car" (V + N). Sentences with a noun followed by a predicate adjective soon followed, e.g., "Dave sick."

In November 1971, Genie began to produce three- and four-word strings, including subject + verb + object strings, like "Tori chew glove," modified noun phrases like "little white clear box," subject-object strings, like "big elephant long trunk," and four-word predications like "Marilyn car red car." Some of these longer strings are of interest because the syntactic relations which were only assumed to be present in her two-word utterances were now overtly expressed. For example, many of Genie's two-word strings did not contain any expressed subject, but the three-word sentences included both the subject and object: "Love Marilyn" became "Genie love Marilyn." In addition, Modifier-noun Noun Phrases and possessive phrases which were complete utterances at the two-word sentence stage are now used as constituents of her longer strings, e.g., "more soup" occurred in "want more soup" and "Mark mouth" became a constituent in "Mark mouth hurt."

In February 1972, Genie began to produce negative sentences. The comprehension test involving negative/affirmative distinctions showed that such a distinction was understood many months earlier. (In the tests she had no difficulty in pointing to the correct picture when asked to "show me 'The girl is wearing shoes'" or "Show me the bunny that has a carrot" vs. "Show me the bunny that does not/doesn't have a carrot.") The first negative morpheme used by Genie was "no more." Later she began to use "no" and "not." To date, Genie continues to negate a sentence by attaching the negative morpheme to the beginning of the string. She has not yet acquired the "negative movement transformation" which inserts the negative morpheme inside the sentence in English.

About the same time that the negative sentences were produced, Genie began to produce strings with locative-nouns, such as "cereal kitchen" and "play gym." In recent months prepositions are occurring in her utterances. In answer to the question "Where is your toy radio?" she answered "On chair." She has also produced sentences such as "Like horse behind fence" and "Like good Harry at hospital."

In July 1972, Verb plus Verb-phrase strings were produced: "Want go shopping," "Like chew meat." Such complex VPs began to emerge in sentences that included both a complex Noun-phrase and a complex Verb-phrase, e.g., "Want buy toy refrigerator" and "Want go walk (to) Ralph." Genie has also begun to add the progressive aspect marker "ing" to verbs, always appropriately to denote ongoing action: "Genie laughing," "Tori eating bone."

Grammatical morphemes that are phonologically marked are now used, e.g., plurals as in "bears," "noses," "swings," and possessives such as "Joe's room," "I like Dave's car."

While no definite-indefinite distinction has appeared, Genie now produces the definite article in imitation, and uses the determiner "another" spontaneously, as in "Another house have dog."

At an earlier stage, possession was marked solely by word order; Genie now also expresses possession by the verb "have," as in "bears have sharp claw," "bathroom have big mirror."

A most important syntactic development is revealed by Genie's use of compound NPs. Prior to December 1971, she would only name one thing at a time, and would produce two sentences such as: "Cat hurt" followed by "dog hurt." More recently she produced these two strings, and then said "Cat dog hurt." This use of a "recursive" element is also shown by the sentence "Curtiss, Genie, swimming pool" in describing a snapshot.

Genie's ability to combine a finite set of linguistic elements to form new combinations, and the ability to produce sentences consisting of conjoined sentences, shows that she has acquired two essential elements of language that permit the generation of an infinite set of sentences.

This is of course an overly sketchy view of the syntactic development evidence in Genie's utterances. (For further details see Curtiss et al. 1972.) It is clear even from this summary that Genie is learning language. Her speech is rule-governed—she has fixed word-order of basic sentence elements and constituents, and systematic ways of expressing syntactic and semantic relations.

LINGUISTIC DEVELOPMENT IN RELATION TO NORMALS

Furthermore it is obvious that her development in many ways parallels that of normal first-language acquisition. There are, however, interesting differences between Genie's emerging language and that of normal children. Her vocabulary is much larger than that of normal children whose language exhibits syntactic complexity parallel to Genie's. She has less difficulty in storing lists than she does learning the rules of the grammar. This illustrates very sharply that language acquisition is not simply the ability to store a large number of items in memory.

Genie's performance on the active/passive comprehension test also appears to deviate from that of normal children. Bever (1970) reports on experiments aimed at testing the capacity in young children "to recognize explicitly the concept of predication as exemplified in the appreciation of the difference between subject-action and action-object relations." The children in these experiments were requested to act out using both simple active sentences and reversible passive sentences, such as "The cow kisses the horse" and simple passives such as "The horse is kissed by the cow." He reports that "children from 2.0 to 3.0 act out simple active sentences 95 percent correctly, (and) . . . do far better than 5 percent on simple passives." He concludes that "since they perform almost randomly on passives . . . they can at least distinguish sentences they can understand from sentences they cannot understand. Thus, the basic linguistic capacity evidenced by the two-year-old child includes the notion of reference for objects and actions, the notion of basic functional internal relations, and at least a primitive notion of different sentence structures." Genie was similarly tested but with the "point to" response rather than the "acting out" response. That is she was asked to point to "The boy pulls/is pulling the girl" or "The girl is pulled by the boy." For each such test sentence she was presented with two pictures, one depicting the boy as agent, the other with the girl as agent. Unlike the children tested by Bever, Genie's responses to both active and passive sentences have been random, with no better than a chance level of correct responses for either the active or the passive sentences. This is particularly strange when compared with Genie's own utterances which show a consistent word order to indicate Subject Verb Object relations. While she never produces passive constructions, her active sentences always place the object after the verb and the subject before the verb (when they are expressed).

Another difference between Genie and normal children is in the area of linguistic performance. Genie's linguistic competence (her grammar, if we can speak of a grammar at such an early stage of development) is in many ways on a par with a two- or two-and-a-half-year-old child. Her performance—particularly as related to expressive speech—is much poorer than normal children at this level. Because of her particular difficulties in producing speech, however, a number of relatively successful efforts have been directed to teaching her written language. At this point she recognizes, names, and can print the letters of the alphabet, can read a large number of printed words, can assemble printed words into grammatically correct sentences, and can understand sentences (and questions) constructed of these printed words. On this level of performance, then, she seems to exceed normal children at a similar stage of language development.

Genie's progress is much slower than that of normals. Few syntactic markers occur in her utterances; there are no question words, no demonstratives, no particles, no rejoinders. In addition, no movement transformations are revealed. Such rules exist in the adult grammar and in normal children's grammars as early as two years. Transformational rules are those which, for example, would move a negative element from the beginning of the sentence to the position after an auxiliary verb. Such a transformational rule would change *I can go* in its negative form from *Neg + I + can + go* to *I + can + neg* (can't) *+ go*. As stated above, Genie continues to produce negative sentences only by the addition of the negative element to the beginning of the sentence, e.g., *No more ear hurt, No stay hospital, No can go.*

Cognitively, however, she seems to be in advance of what would be expected at this syntactic stage. Her earliest productive vocabulary included words cognitively more sophisticated than one usually finds in the descriptions of first vocabulary words. Color words and numbers, for example, were used which usually enter a child's vocabulary at a much later grammatical stage (Castner 1940; Denckla 1972).

At the time that Genie began to produce utterances of two words (June 1971) she had an active vocabulary of 200 words, which far exceeds the size of the normal children's lexicon at this stage (about fifty words). This development seems to parallel that found in aphasic children (Eisenson and Ingram 1972). She comprehends all the *wh-* questions; normal children ordinarily learn *how, why,* and *when* questions later than *who, what,* and *where* (Brown 1968), although syntactically such questions are similar. Her comprehension of the comparative and superlative, and the differences between *more* and *less* also indicate cognitive sophistication not revealed by her syntax, suggesting at least a partial independence of cognition and language.

COGNITIVE DEVELOPMENT

The attempt to assess Genie's cognitive development is extremely difficult. All tests purported to measure cognitive abilities, in fact, measure knowledge that has been acquired through experience. In addition, many tests are substantially dependent on verbal response and comprehension. The distinction between cognition and language development is therefore not always possible. A number of tests have, however, been utilized.

Genie could not easily be psychologically tested by standard instruments at the time of her admission. It is still difficult to administer many of the standard tests. On the Vineland Social Maturity Scale, however, she averaged about fifteen months at the time of admission, and on a Gesell Developmental Evaluation, a month and a half later, scores ranged from about one to about three years of age. There was a very high degree of scatter when compared to normal developmental patterns. Consistently, language-related behavior was observed to occur at the lower end of the range of her performance and was judged (by the psychologists at the hospital) to be at about the fifteen months level.

Her cognitive growth, however, seemed to be quite rapid. In a seven-month span her score had increased from fifteen to forty-two months, and six months after admission, on the Leiter International Performance Scale (which depends relatively little on culturally based, specific knowledge, and requires no speech) she passed all the items at the four year level, two at the five year level, and two out of four at the seven year level. In May 1973 her score on this test was on the six to eight year level. At the same time, the Stanford Binet Intelligence Scale elicited a mental age of five to eight. In all the tests, the subsets which involved language were considerably lower than those assessing other abilities.

From this brief summary of Genie's linguistic development we can conclude the following: (1) When she first emerged from isolation, Genie, a child of thirteen years, nine months had not acquired language; (2) Since there is no evidence of any biological deficiencies, one may assume this was due to the social and linguistic isolation which occurred during eleven years of her life; (3) Since her emergence she has been acquiring her first language primarily by "exposure" alone (this is revealed both by her own speech and by her comprehension of spoken language); (4) Her cognitive development has exceeded her linguistic development.

THE "CRITICAL AGE" HYPOTHESIS AND LANGUAGE LATERALIZATION

As mentioned above, Genie's ongoing language acquisition is the most direct test of Lenneberg's critical age hypothesis seen thus far. Lenneberg (1967) has presented the view that the ability to acquire primary language (and the acquisition of second languages "by mere exposure") terminates with the completion of the development of cerebral dominance, or lateralization, an event which he argues occurs at around puberty. As we have demonstrated above, however, while Genie's language acquisition differs to some extent from that of normal children, she is in fact in the process of learning language, as shown by the results of tests and by the observations of her spontaneous and elicited speech. Thus, at least some degree of first-language acquisition seems to be possible beyond the critical period.

Genie also affords us the opportunity to study the relationship of the development of lateralization and language acquisition.

Lateralization refers to the fact that each hemisphere appears to be specialized for different cognitive functions; that is, some functions seem to be "localized" primarily on one side of the brain. . . . [The various monaural and dichotic listening tests given to Genie suggested a pronounced right-hemisphere dominance for language as well as for environmental sounds.]

In trying to assess this unusual situation it is important to note that Genie seems very proficient in what are considered right-hemisphere functions. . . . [In] psychological tests her development can be comprehended more meaningfully when performances on two kinds of test tasks are distinguished: those that require analytic or sequential use of symbols, such as language and number; and those that involve perception of spatial configurations or Gestalts. On the first group of tasks Genie's performance is consistently in the low range, presently approximating an age of two-and-a-half to three years, approximately the age level of her linguistic performance using comparative linguistic criteria. On configurational tests, however, her performance ranges upwards, lying somewhere between eight years and the adult level, depending on the test. . . . The rate of growth on these tests has been very rapid. . . .

It would appear then that Genie is lateralized to the right for both language and nonlanguage functions. This assumes that these nonlinguistic abilities, which have been shown to be right-hemisphere lateralized, are indeed functions of Genie's right hemisphere. We are now in the process of designing tests involving other modalities which will hopefully provide more conclusive evidence on this question.

If this proves to be the case, one tentative hypothesis to explain how this developed is as follows: At the time of her isolation, Genie was a "normal" right-handed child with potential left-hemisphere dominance. The inadequate language stimulation during her early life inhibited or interfered with language aspects of left hemisphere development. This would be tantamount to a kind of functional atrophy of the usual language centers, brought about by disuse or suppression. Apparently, what meager stimulation she did receive was sufficient for normal right-hemisphere development. (One can imagine her sitting, day after day, week after week, year after year, absorbing every visual stimulus, every crack in the paint, every nuance of color and form.) This is consistent with the suggestion (Carmon et al. 1972) that the right hemisphere is the first to develop since it is more involved with the perception of the environment. Genie's current achievements in language acquisition, according to this reasoning, are occurring in that hemisphere which somehow did mature more normally.

The hypothesis that Genie is using a developed right hemisphere for language also predicts the dichotic listening results. The undeveloped language areas in the left hemisphere prevent the flow of (just language) impulses from the left primary auditory receiving areas to the right hemisphere. This explains why Genie's scores are so similar to split-brain and hemispherectomized subjects; the only auditory pathways that are functional for *verbal* stimuli are the right ipsilateral and left contralateral. The low right score is due to the suppression that occurs under the dichotic condition. Her perfect monotic scores are predicted, since suppression only takes place dichotically.

If this hypothesis is true it modifies the theory of the critical period: while the normal development of lateralization may not play a role in the critical period, lateralization may be involved in a different way; the left hemisphere must perhaps be linguistically stimulated during a specific period of time for it to participate in normal language acquisition. If such stimulation does not take place during this time, normal language acquisition must depend on other cortical areas and will proceed less efficiently due to the previous specialization of these areas for other functions.

A comparison of Genie's with the other instances of right (minor) hemisphere speech in adults implies that Genie's capacity for language acquisition is limited and will cease at some time in the near future. Such cases are rare and not well described from a linguistic point of view. A. Smith's (1966) description of a left hemispherectomized man is the best of these. This man could not speak at all after his left hemisphere was removed but did begin to communicate in "propositional language" ten weeks later. The patient continued to make linguistic progress but remained severely aphasic eight months after surgery (see also Bogen 1969). Similarly, Hillier (1954) reported a left hemispherectomy performed on a fourteen-year-old boy for a tumor whose onset was one year previous to surgery. Again, there was early progress in language learning but after nineteen months progress ceased and the deficit became stable.

It is unfortunate that there is no information concerning cerebral dominance for other cases of isolated children—those that acquired language as well as those that didn't. Itard suggests that Victor was about twelve years of age when he was found in the woods of Aveyron, and that "It is . . . almost proved that he had been abandoned at the age of four or five years" (Itard 1962). If, in those first years he was not genetically deficient, lateralization should have been complete and language should have been acquired. Itard states further that "if, at this time, he already owed some ideas and some words to the beginning of an education, this would all have been effaced from his memory in consequence of his isolation." How, why, and if such "memory effacement" occurs are questions open to speculation. Despite this "effacement," Victor "did acquire a very considerable reading vocabulary, learning, by means of printed phrases, to execute such simple commands as to pick up a key" (Itard 1962, xii), but he never learned to speak. The scar "which (was) visible on his throat" may have damaged his larynx. It is impossible to tell from Itard's reports the exact extent of Victor's comprehension of spoken language.

Another case, similar to some extent to that of Genie, is that of a child who was not exposed to language until she was six-and-a-half years old because of her imprisonment with a mute and totally uneducated aphasic mother (Mason 1942). Within twenty-two months, she progressed from her first spoken words ("ball," "car," "bye," "baby") to asking such questions as "Why does the paste come out if one upsets the jar?" The rapidity with which she acquired the complex grammar of English provides some support for the hypothesis that the language learning mechanism is more specific than general.

This case is also consistent with a two-to-puberty critical period theory. The language learning capacity of the right hemisphere, then, may be limited either in time or amount of learning. Because we have no grammatical descriptions of right-hemisphere speech, we cannot predict how far Genie will progress from comparisons with such cases. On the other hand, Genie's progress in language acquisition impressionistically seems to have far exceeded that of the other reported cases. We intend to continue administering dichotic listening tests to see if the left hemisphere begins to show increasing language function. If this occurs, one plausible conclusion would be that language acquisition and use are a precondition for such lateralization to occur. We note, of course, that this would be contrary to the Krashen and Harshman position that lateralization *precedes* language acquisition. There is also some evidence of laterality differences in neonates (Wada, quoted in Geschwind 1970; Molfese 1972).

It is clear from this report that we have more questions than answers. We are hopeful that Genie's development will provide some of these answers.

As humanists we are hopeful that our tentative prognosis of a slowing down of language and permanent dysphasia will prove to be wrong. For despite the predictions of our hypothesis, Genie continues to make modest but steady progress in language acquisition and is providing us with data in an unexplored area, first-language acquisition beyond the "critical period." After all, a discarded hypothesis is a small price to pay for confirmation of the astonishing capabilities and adaptability of the human mind. (See the postscript by Maya Pines on page 605.)

BIBLIOGRAPHY

Bellugi, U., and E. Klima. Consultation Report, March, 1971.

Bever, T. G. "The cognitive basis for linguistic structures." In *Cognition and the Development of Language.* ed. J. R. Hayes. New York: John Wiley, 1970, 279–362.

Bogen, J. E. "The other side of the brain I: Dysgraphia and dyscopia following cerebral commissurotomy." *Bulletin of the Los Angeles Neurological Societies* 34 (July 1969), 73–105.

Brown, R. "The development of WH questions in child speech." *Journal of Verbal Learning and Verbal Behavior* 7 (1968), 279–290.

Carmon, A., Y. Harishanu, R. Lowinger, and S. Levy. "Asymmetries in hemispheric blood volume and cerebral dominance." *Behavioral Biology*, 1972.

Castner, B. M. *Language Development in the First Five Years of Life.* ed. A. Gesell. New York: Harper & Row, 1940.

Chomsky, N. "Explanatory models in linguistics." In *Logic, Methodology, and the Philosophy of Science.* ed. E. Nagel, P. Suppes, and A. Taiski. Stanford: Stanford University Press, 1962.

Clarke, A. D. B., and A. M. Clarke. "Some recent advances in the study of early deprivation." *Child Psychology and Psychiatry* 1, 1960.

Curtiss, S. "The development of language in Genie." Paper presented to the 1972 Annual Convention of the American Speech and Hearing Association, San Francisco, November 1972, 18–20.

Curtiss, S., V. Fromkin, and S. Krashen. "The syntactic development of Genie." Paper presented to the annual meeting of the Linguistic Society of America, Atlanta, Georgia, December 1972.

Davis, K. "Extreme social isolation of a child." *American Journal of Sociology* 45 (1940), 554–565.

———. "Final note on a case of extreme isolation." *American Journal of Sociology* 52 (1947), 432–437.

Denckla, M. B. "Performance on color tasks in kindergarten children." *Cortex* 8 (1972), 177–190.

Dennis, W., and P. Najarian. "Infant development under developmental handicap." *Psychological Monographs* 71, no. 7 (1957).

Eisenson, J., and D. Ingram. "Childhood aphasia—an updated concept based on recent research." *Papers and Reports on Child Language Development.* Stanford University (1972), 103–120.

Fraiberg, S., and D. A. Freedman. "Studies in the ego development of the congenitally blind child." *The Psychoanalytic Study of the Child* 19 (1964), 113–169.

Fromkin, V. "The development of language in Genie." Paper presented at the 80th Annual Convention of the American Psychological Association, Honolulu, Hawaii, September 1–8, 1972.

Geschwind, N. "The organization of language and the brain." *Science* 170 (1970), 940–944.

Haggard, M., and A. Parkinson. "Stimulus and task factors as determinants of ear advantage." *Quarterly Journal of Experimental Psychology* 23 (1971), 168–177.

Hansen, H. "The first experiences and the emergence of 'Genie.'" Paper presented at the 80th Annual Convention of the American Psychological Association, Honolulu, Hawaii, September 1–8, 1972.

Hillier, F. "Total left hemispherectomy for malignant glaucoma." *Neurology* 4 (1954), 718–721.

Howe, M., and F. G. Hall. *Laura Bridgeman.* Boston: Little, Brown, 1903.

Itard, J. *The Wild Boy of Aveyron.* New York: Appleton-Century-Crofts, 1962.

Kent, J. "Eight months in the hospital." Paper presented at the 80th Annual Convention of the American Psychological Association, Honolulu, Hawaii, September 1–8, 1972.

Koluchova, J. "Severe deprivation in twins." *Child Psychology and Psychiatry* 13 (1972).

Krashen, S. "Language and the left hemisphere." *Working Papers in Phonetics* 24 (1972), UCLA.

———. "Lateralization, language learning, and the critical period: Some new evidence." *Language Learning* 23 (1973a), 63–74.

———. "Mental abilities underlying linguistic and non-linguistic functions." *Linguistics* (1973b).

Krashen, S., V. Fromkin, S. Curtiss, D. Rigler, and S. Spitz. "Language lateralization in a case of extreme psychological deprivation." Paper presented to the 84th meeting of the Acoustical Society of America, 1972a.

Krashen, S., V. Fromkin, and S. Curtiss. "A neurolinguistic investigation of language acquisition in the case of an isolated child." Paper presented to the Linguistic Society of America. Winter meeting, Atlanta, Georgia, December 27–29, 1972b.

Krashen, S., and R. Harshman. "Lateralization and the critical period." *Working Papers in Phonetics* 23 (1972), 13–21. UCLA (Abstract in *Journal of the Acoustical Society of America* 52, 174).

Lenneberg, E. H. *Biological Foundations of Language.* New York: Wiley, 1967.

Mason, M. K. "Learning to speak after six and one-half years." *Journal of Speech Disorders* 7 (1942), 295–304.

Milner, B., L. Taylor, and R. Sperry. "Lateralized suppression of dichotically presented digits after commissural section in man." *Science* 161 (1968), 184–186.

Molfese, D. L. "Cerebral asymmetry in infants, children and adults: Auditory evoked responses to speech and musical stimuli." *Journal of the Acoustical Society of America* 53 (1972), 363 (A).

Rigler, D. "The Case of Genie." Paper presented to the 1972 Annual Convention of the American Speech and Hearing Association, San Francisco, California. November 18–20, 1972.

Rigler, M. "Adventure: At home with Genie." Paper presented at the 80th Annual Convention of the American Psychological Association, Honolulu, Hawaii, September 1–8, 1972.

Singh, J. A. L., and R. M. Zingg. *Wolf-Children and Feral Man.* Archon Books, 1966.

Skinner, B. F. *Verbal Behavior.* New York: Appleton-Century-Crofts, 1957.

Smith, A. "Speech and other functions after left (dominant) hemispherectomy." *Journal of Neurology, Neurosurgery and Psychiatry* 29 (1957), 467–471.

Spitz., R. A. "The role of ecological factors in emotional development." *Child Development* 20 (1949), 145–155.

Von Feuerbach, A. *Kasper Hauser.* (Translated from the German) London: Simpkin and Marshall, 1833.

Zurif, E. B., and M. Mendelsohn. "Hemispheric specialization for the perception of speech sounds: The influences of intonation and structure." *Perception and Psychophysics* 11 (1972), 329–332.

Genie: A Postscript

Maya Pines

In 1978, Genie's mother became her legal guardian. During all the years of Genie's rehabilitation, her mother had also received help. An eye operation restored her sight, and a social worker tried to improve her behavior toward Genie. Genie's mother had never been held legally responsible for the child's inhuman treatment. Charges of child abuse were dismissed in 1970, when her lawyer argued that she "was, herself, a victim of the same psychotic individual"—her husband. There was "nothing to show purposeful or willful cruelty," he said.

Nevertheless, for many years the court assigned a guardian for Genie. Shortly after Genie's mother was named guardian, she astounded the therapists and researchers who had worked with Genie by filing a suit against Curtiss and the Children's Hospital among others—on behalf of herself and her daughter—in which she charged that they had disclosed private and confidential information concerning Genie and her mother for "prestige and profit" and had subjected Genie to "unreasonable and outrageous" testing, not for treatment, but to exploit Genie for personal and economic benefits. According to the *Los Angeles Times*, the lawyer who represents Genie's mother estimated that the actual damages could have totaled $500,000. [*Editor's note:* The case was settled out of court, with no damages awarded.]

[In the years since the case] was filed, Genie has been completely cut off from the professionals at Children's Hospital and UCLA. Since she is too old to be in a foster home, she apparently is living in a board-and-care home for adults who cannot live alone. The *Los Angeles Times* reported that as of 1979 her mother was working as a domestic servant. All research on Genie's language and intellectual development has come to a halt. However, the research Genie stimulated goes on. Much of it concerns the relationship between linguistic ability and cognitive development, a subject to which Genie has made a significant contribution.

Apart from Chomsky and his followers, who believe that fundamental language ability is innate and unrelated to intelligence, most psychologists assume that the development of language is tied to—and emerges from—the development of nonverbal intelligence, as described by Piaget. However, Genie's obvious nonverbal intelligence—her use of tools, her drawings, her knowledge of causality, her mental maps of space—did not lead her to an equivalent competence in the grammar normal children acquire by the age of five.

Puzzled by the discrepancy between Genie's cognitive abilities and her language deficits, Curtiss and Fromkin wondered whether they could find people with the opposite pattern—who have normal language ability despite cognitive deficits. That would be further evidence of the independence of language from certain aspects of cognition.

In recent months, they have found several such persons among the mentally retarded, as well as among victims of Turner's syndrome, a chromosomal defect that produces short stature, cardiac problems, infertility, and specific learning difficulties in females. With help from the National Science Foundation (which had also funded some of Curtiss's research on Genie), Fromkin and Curtiss have identified and started working with some children and adolescents who combine normal grammatical ability with serious defects in logical reasoning, sequential ability, or other areas of thinking.

"You can't explain their unimpaired syntax on the basis of their impaired cognitive development," says Curtiss, who is greatly excited by this new developmental profile. She points out that in the youngsters studied, the purely grammatical aspect of language—which reflects Chomsky's language universals—seems to be isolated from the semantic aspect of language, which is more tied to cognition. "Language no longer looks like a uniform package," she declares. "This is the first experimental data on the subject." Thus the ordeal of an abused child may help us understand some of the most puzzling but important aspects of our humanity.

FOR DISCUSSION AND REVIEW

1. Noting that all children who suffer serious experiential deprivation show retarded development, Fromkin and colleagues state that "An important question for scientists of many disciplines is whether a child so deprived can 'catch up' wholly or in part." List the various factors to consider in answering this question.

2. Describe as fully as you can the condition (physical, developmental, etc.) of Genie at the time she was discovered and hospitalized. Summarize the conditions under which she had lived and consider the possible effect on her of each.

3. On what basis do the authors conclude that although "functionally, Genie was an extremely retarded child," the most plausible explanation of this retardation was "the intensity and duration of her psychosocial and physical deprivation"?

4. Explain the importance of devising at the outset tests to use with Genie to ascertain the extent (if any) of her language comprehension.

5. Explain the following statement: "The ability to relate the sounds and meanings of individual lexical items, while necessary, is not a sufficient criterion for language competence."

6. The authors state, "Genie's ability to comprehend spoken language is a better indication of her linguistic competence than is her production of speech because of the physical difficulties Genie has in speaking." What does this fact suggest about the importance of such early stages of language discussed by Aitchison as crying, cooing, babbling, and intonation patterns, and of practice?

7. After stating that Genie is learning language, the authors point out differences in her linguistic development from that of "normals." What are these differences, and what is their significance? What stage has Genie reached in the acquisition of negative sentences? What are the implications of this fact?

8. Review the earlier discussions in this section of the relationship between cognitive development and language acquisition. What is the significance of the fact that "cognitively, . . . she [Genie] seems to be in advance of what would be expected at this syntactic stage"? Note, too, that the *rate* of Genie's cognitive growth exceeded that of her language acquisition.

9. Explain how Genie's linguistic development has been a test of Lenneberg's critical age hypothesis (pp. 600–603). Discuss the results of this test.

10. What has Genie taught us about the relationship between language

acquisition and brain lateralization? How do these findings relate to the critical age hypothesis?

11. Explain the tentative hypothesis developed by the authors to account for Genie's being "lateralized to the right for both language and nonlanguage functions." How does this hypothesis, if correct, modify the critical period theory?

46

Teaching How to Talk in
Roadville: The First Words

Shirley Brice Heath

Shirley Brice Heath is currently a professor of anthropology and linguistics in the School of Education at Stanford University. From 1969 to 1978, she "lived, worked, and played," in Roadville and Trackton, two very different communities in the Carolina piedmont. Her research in Roadville involved the study of children learning to use language at home and school, and it "raises fundamental questions about the nature of language development, the effects of literacy on the oral habits, and the sources of communication problems in school and workplaces." This research resulted in the landmark ethnographic book Ways with Words: Language, Life and Work in Communities and Classrooms. *Prior to its publication no in-depth, long-range language study had been conducted to examine children's language in the context of the community in which it was spoken.*

In this selection from Ways with Words, *Heath meticulously describes what she observed of language acquisition in Roadville. Her observations offer invaluable insights into the nature of baby talk, how young children learn to ask and answer questions, and how and when children are trained in their communities' accepted linguistic behaviors.*

Relatives especially caution young mothers not to spoil their babies by picking them up and holding them too much, yet they are also not to let their babies lie and cry. A distinction of noises from the baby is the guideline for when the baby should be picked up. If he is "jus' makin' noise, talkin' to himself," he should be left alone; if, on the other hand, he is "cryin' a li'l bit," he is to be listened to, but not picked up. Only to a loud cry sustained for several moments is the mother to respond by picking up the baby. Those giving advice to young mothers urge that a baby be left to himself some, to explore, to move about, to make noise. The babbling and cooing of babies before and after they go to sleep is recognized as part of this exploring, and mothers happily report to their female relatives when their babies begin to coo, smile, and babble. Young mothers often take the first "da, da, da, da" sounds from the crib as "daddy" and report the "word" proudly to the father. Whenever the baby is then picked up the father or by anyone to whom the story had been reported, "daddy" becomes a favorite word for use in talking to the baby.

Young mothers home alone, with their first child in particular, often have many hours with no one around to talk to. They talk to their babies, strapped in an infant seat after a feeding, and placed on the kitchen table while the mother sews or irons. When her hands are not busy with household chores, she carries the baby about, telling him to "see" certain things, such as his own image in the mirror or the nursery rhyme plaques on his room's walls, or to touch the family pet. As soon as babies begin to smile, mothers impute motives to the smile: "You like that, don't you?" "You're all happy today, 'cause you know we're goin' for a ride." Young mothers often take their babies out in the stroller to visit relatives or friends or to walk downtown. Adults and older children along the way stop and stoop down to talk to the baby. They tickle toes or "tummy," hold a hand, or straighten a cap while addressing the child. For a woman friend not to stop and talk to a baby is considered the gravest of rebuffs. Men acquaintances who do not do so are considered awkward or "ignorant 'bout babies." Young boys are the only ones who rarely stop to talk to babies. Young girls ask to hold the baby, and once the baby begins being taken to church, young girls take the baby around and show him off. All those who talk to babies and toddlers use baby talk; especially short, simplified sentences, special lexical items, a high pitch and exaggerated intonation, and a punctuation of talk with tickling, manipulation of the baby's chin, and most often with direct face-to-face contact. If a baby is sleepy and closes its eyes while someone is talking to him, the speaker stops talking. If the baby does not seem sleepy but is, for example, being held so the sun is in his eyes and he is squinting, the talker suggests turning the baby to get the sun out of his eyes and then begins talking again once the baby's eyes are open. Baby talk during the first two years of a Roadville child's life is a normal part of the baby's daily interactions.

Alone during the day, each young mother uses the reporting of her child's new accomplishments as an excuse for visiting with neighbor women either in person or by phone. When, by the age of seven or eight months, babies vigorously avoid certain foods by turning their heads away from a proffered spoon or by lashing at the air with their arms, the mother reports to a neighbor: "He doesn't like that new cereal, and he knows how to tell me so." Eye movements to follow mobiles, family pets, or siblings are noted and reported, and mothers comment on these movements and their "meanings" to the baby and to any other available audience.

When the baby begins to respond verbally, to make sounds which adults can link to items in the environment, questions and statements are addressed to the baby, repeating or incorporating his "word." This practice is carried out with not only first children, but also subsequent children, and when adults are not around to do it, older children take up the game of repeating children's sounds as words and pointing out new items in the environment and asking babies to "say _____." When Sally, Aunt Sue's youngest child, began saying "ju, ju, ju" from her infant seat and high chair, Lisa, her older sister, said "Juice, juice, mamma, she wants some of my juice, can I give it to her?" Lisa also named other items for Sally: "Milk, say milk," and when Sally discovered a sesame seed on the tray of her high chair and tried to pick it up, Lisa said "Seed, see:d, that's a seed, can you say see::d?" There is verbal reinforcement and smiles and cuddling when the baby repeats.

If the baby renders the "word" with a peculiar pronunciation or over-extends its meaning, the family may even take up the baby's version. For several weeks, after Lisa introduced Sally to "tissue" at age twenty months, Sally called everything that was soft and crushable in her hand and could be used to wipe her face a "tita." The family began to use "tita" occasionally as the conventional signal for not only tissues, but also diapers, baby wash-cloths, and Sally's bib. *Tita* for *tissue, diaper,* or *bib* was used on occasion by all the family members for a period of three months. Sally, after a month or so, began using *tita* for all soft cuddly things made of fabric: her stuffed lamb, tissues, diapers, towels, et cetera, and then began sorting out terms for each of these. Only gradually did the original term *tita* pass out of use for other members of the family. Sally's game of picking up cuddly things and wiping them across her face or the tray of her high chair was replaced by other games exploring how her communicative behavior could produce adult reactions and partici-patory responses.

Certain lexical items referring to excrement develop in each house-hold and tend to continue throughout the preschool period for use by all the young children of the family. Bobby, at fourteen months, was playing with Danny, his cousin, whose mother, Peggy, had put him in Bobby's playpen while she visited with Betty. Danny dirtied his diapers, and when his mother picked him up saying "Poooo, you stink, boy." Danny responded "Poo, kee, poo, kee." Later in the afternoon, the boys managed to puncture a jelly-filled teething ring in the playpen, and the thick pecu-liar-smelling substance oozed out on the plastic pad covering the playpen floor, Bobby got his fingers in it, and Danny began sliding toys through it, squealing "Poo::kee, poo::kee." Both boys continued their play until Danny's mother came in to find the mess. A day or so later, Bobby was given a new food for lunch, and after the first approach of the spoon, he drew away and said "poo:kee." His mother, unfamiliar with the use of the word in connection with something which had an unusual smell, reported the incident as one which had produced a new word referring to the specific food item. She persisted in trying to get Bobby to eat the food, but he slapped at the spoon, getting the food on his hand and smear-ing it on the highchair tray. Later, that afternoon when Bobby woke from a nap and had a particularly messy and smelly diaper, he monologued in his crib: "Poo kee, noo kee, nee, nee, nee, poo kee, nee, neekeenee, neemee, neemee, mama, mama." His mother came in to hear this and as she changed the diaper, said "You're pookee yourself." Bobby laughed, and his mother repeated the word, making contorted faces, laughing, and squeezing Bobby's chubby legs. Thereafter, *pookee* became generalized as a family word to refer to a general category of smelly, messy substances, and its meaning was extended to refer to having a bowel movement.

During Bobby's toilet training period, his mother would ask "Let's go pookee now." Once when Danny and Bobby were playing, when both were beyond two years of age, Bobby began saying "Pookee, pookee" to Danny. Bobby's mother shushed him, scolding, saying "No, Bobby, we don't use that word, that's not nice," and giving them both a cookie to stop the language play with that word.

Children's language play alone or with siblings or other playmates is encouraged, and adults often intervene to offer reinforcement unless the words are dirty or the children are making too much "racket." When children are left to play in their rooms, parents put records on for them or turn on their music boxes or toys that talk. Martha's daughter, Wendy, at thirty-two months was playing with Kim Macken (thirty-six months); the girls were setting up a "tea party," and their mothers were having iced tea at the kitchen table nearby. As the girls prepared tea and hand-ed each other cups and "cookies," Wendy handed a cookie to Kim saying "here." Wendy's mother broke in and said, "Wendy, that's no way to talk, 'Have a cookie.' Now say it right." Kim held the cookie and waited. Wendy repeated "Have a cookie," and Kim began munching happily. Mrs. Macken said, "Kim, what do you say?" Kim responded "It's good, good." Her mother said "No uh yes, it's good, but how about 'Thank you'?" Kim said "Thank you, good."

A baby will often repeat parts of a mother-child dialogue in mono-logue when he is alone. If his mother overhears him, she repeats and extends these phrases as she changes and feeds him. Bobby at eighteen months often talked to himself in his crib before and after a nap:

> wanna, wanna a cookie wanna a cookcook now? cook, cook, book, book
> ah, ah a a a ta ta [thank you] ta ta cook cook nudder cook book cook-
> book, book cook cook, all gone.

This monologue contains parts of a dialogue he and his mother had carried out earlier in the afternoon, when after lunch, she had offered Bobby a cookie, forced him to say "ta ta," and after he had done so and eaten the first cookie, she had offered him another cookie. Children who are too young to engage in cooperative play are often put together in playpens, and there they babble and monologue to themselves in parallel play. Their mothers often intervene and try to get the two children to talk to each other, for example, to talk about the sharing of a toy rather than to squeal and tug.

When Roadville children begin combining words, usually between the ages of eighteen and twenty-two months, adults respond by expan-sions, that is, by repeating the combined items in a well-formed adult utterance which reflects the adult interpretation of what the child has said. Sally, banging on the backdoor, screamed "Go kool," and Aunt Sue responded, "No, Sally, you can't go to *school* yet, Lisa will be back, come on, help mamma put the pans away." Aunt Sue assumed Sally both wanted to *go to school* and was commenting on the fact that Lisa had just *gone to school*. This phenomenon of expansions, taking a minimal phrase such as "Go kool" and interpreting and expanding it, character-izes much of the talk adults address to young children. Adults seize upon a noun used by the child, adopt this as a topic, and build a discourse around it. The topic is then accepted as known to the child, and the adult utterances which follow use definite articles, deictic pronouns (those which locate something in space and time, such as *this* and *that*), and anaphoric pronouns (those which substitute for an expression already used by either the child and/or the adult). The habit of picking up a topic from a noun used by a child either in spontaneous utterance or in response to an adult's question which asks for the name of something is illustrated in the following exchange.

Mrs. Macken and two-year-old Kim were making cookies in the kitchen. They were using cookie cutters in the shape of Christmas items. Kim especially liked the snowman, and she was allowed to put the "red hots" (small pieces of red candy) on the cookies to mark the snowman's nose. Kim picked up a freshly baked snowman and bit the head off, saying "noman all gone." Mrs. Macken, in the next three min-utes, used eleven utterances which either restated the label *snowman* or assumed it as a given topic in the discourse. Talk about the snowman continued in spite of the fact that Kim and her mother were using cook-ie cutters in the shape of a Christmas tree, a reindeer, a Santa, and a bell—and not the snowman cutter—as they talked.

> Did you eat the snowman? Do you want to give daddy a snowman? That snowman's smile is all gone. He's lost an eye. He has a nose too. Did the snowman fill you up? We can make some more like him. 'member the snowman song? Can we build one? There's a snowman in your book. We can take Gran'ma one.

Kim did not collaborate with her mother on the snowman topic, but went on chattering about the red hots, the green sugar for the Christmas trees, and the broken cookie in the shape of a bell. Mother and daughter seemingly engaged in parallel talk, and not a cooperative dialogue, once Kim introduced the topic of *snowman* for her mother. Mrs. Macken talked on about the snowman, as though she thought Kim had intended this as the topic of discussion.

The use of a child's label for an item, as the topic of an extended dia-logue constructed primarily by adults, is a habit which is especially evi-dent on certain occasions. When a child and adult interact over a book, or on occasions when the child has himself shown an interest in some item or event in which the adult wishes him to maintain an interest, adults almost always adopt the label as the focus of the dialogue. Wendy and her mother Martha were looking through Wendy's baby book one day when Wendy was just over two years old. Wendy had been sick, and the doctor had told Martha to keep her quiet for twenty-four hours, so the uninterrupted exchange between mother and child over a specific item was particularly extended. Martha had explained to Wendy that she had to be "doctored" for a while, and that meant she had to stay in bed and be quiet. Martha was trying to keep Wendy entertained until she fell asleep. An excerpt from the ten-minute exchange follows.

Roadville Text I

MARTHA: /*pointing to a picture of Wendy's dog in the baby book*/
Who's that?

WENDY: Nuf [the dog's name was Snuffy]

MARTHA: Let's see if we can find another picture of Nuffie.
//*Wendy points to the same picture*//
/*pointing to another picture*/ Here he is, he's had a bath with daddy. There he is, this is Nuffie.

WENDY: All wet.

MARTHA: Nuffie got daddy all wet too.

WENDY: Where's daddy?

MARTHA: Daddy's gone to work. /*seeing Wendy look at the picture*/
Oh, he's not in the picture.

WENDY: Where Nuf

MARTHA: Nuffie's over to gran'ma's, he dug under the fence again.

WENDY: Bad dog, Nuf, bad dog.

MARTHA: That's right. Nuffie *is* a bad dog, now let's find another picture of Nuffie /*turns pages of book*/

WENDY: Nana, nana /*pointing to a picture of Mrs. Dee*/

MARTHA: Yes, that's nana, where's Nuffie?

WENDY: I don't wanna /*pushes book away*/

MARTHA: But, look, there's daddy fixin' to give Nuffie a bath.

WENDY: No. /*trying to get down off her bed*/

MARTHA: No, let's stay up here. /*holding Wendy around her waist*/
we'll find another Nuffie
See, look here, who's that with Nuffie?
//*Wendy struggles and begins to cry*//

Here, Martha, in spite of Wendy's wandering interest and struggles to change first the topic and then the activity, persists in looking for pictures of Snuffy. Once Wendy responded to her request for that label, Martha continued it as a topic, and did not take up Wendy's possible suggestion of Nana (or the finding of pictures of other persons) as a new topic. Thus throughout the conversation, Nuffie is the topic, both with reference to the pictures in the book and to the here and now. Martha lets the topic drop only once—when Wendy asks the question "Where's daddy?" Initially, Martha thinks Wendy is referring to daddy's whereabouts at the present moment, but she then realizes Wendy is referring to the fact that daddy is not in the photograph they have been discussing. Martha remembered the incident surrounding the picture, but daddy's getting wet was not recorded in the picture, and Wendy called attention to the dissonance between what Martha said was in the picture and what was actually in the photograph.

Adults help children focus their attention on the names and features of particular items or events. They believe that if adults teach children to "pay attention, listen, and behave," children learn not only how to talk, but also how to learn. Roadville adults believe young children have two major types of communicative abilities to develop during their preschool years. First, they must learn to communicate their own needs and desires, so that if mothers stay attuned to children's communications, they can determine what these are. Second, children must learn to be communicative partners in a certain mold. Preschool children do not go to playschool or nursery schools before the age of four; thus they must play alone much of the time. Parents believe that the mother must therefore talk to her child and give him [or her] adequate opportunities to communicate. As adults talk to their children, they teach them how to talk and how to learn about the world. They sort out parts of the world for them, calling attention to these, and focusing the children's attention. Children learn the names of things; they then learn to talk about these "right." Peggy, describing her own thoughts about how Danny learned to talk, said:

> I figure it's up to me to give 'im a good start. I reckon there's just some things I know he's gotta learn, you know, what things are, and all that. 'n you just don't happen onto doin' all that right. Now, you take Danny 'n Bobby, we, Betty 'n me, we talk to them kids all the time, like they was grown-up or something, 'n we try to tell 'em 'bout things, 'n books, 'n we buy those educational toys for 'em.

Peggy acknowledges here her feeling that her guidance is necessary for Danny to learn what to say, how to say it, and what to know.

This guidance comes through conversations in which adults force children to accept the role of both information-giver and information-receiver. Adults ask for the names of items; if the child gives an unsuitable name, the adult proposes another and then follows with a series of questions to test the child's reception of this term. On future occasions, adults use the same term again and again, making a conscious effort to be consistent in the information they give, and often one member of the family insists that his term for an item or for an animal sound be used with the child and not an alternative term.

Sally had a woolly lamb which she kept in her crib and later in her playpen. Her family heard her begin to associate her sound of "wa wa" with the lamb, but rejected this as the "right" label and began asking Sally "What does the lamb say?" and answering their own question with "The lamb says baaaa." This sequence for giving an item the "right" name is continued and elaborated on as adults read early picture books to the preschoolers. Adults point to the item on the page, name it, provide a simple sentence such as "That's a lamb." "Sally's got a lamb like that." "What does the lamb say?" "Where's Sally's lamb?" Sally was asked to point to the lamb in the earliest stage of "book-reading," and later to answer questions such as "What's that?"

Children are believed to progress in stages—to crawl, take their first step, walk, and run, to respond nonverbally; to babble, to say words, to put them together, and then to ask and answer questions. Mothers keep "baby books" on their children's progress, and such records are kept not only for the first child, but often for the second and third child as well. Mothers with children of the same age compare their developmental stages: "Is he walking yet?" "How many words does he say?" and they report and evaluate their children's behavior in accordance with what they believe to be the ideal stages. The particular time schedules and co-occurrences of action in these sequences are, however, highly varied; some mothers believe a child always talks before he walks; others believe a child does not talk until he can walk. Therefore, though there is a general consensus on the fact that children follow a sequence of behaviors and certain activities occur with others, there is no consensus on when the sequence begins or which stage in the sequence follows another stage.

Adults see themselves as the child's teacher at the preschool stage, and teachers ask and answer questions. Aunt Sue described herself: "I'd have been a good teacher, if I could have got some real school education. I can make children listen, an' I'm all time askin' questions and thinkin' up things they oughta know. I ask Sally all kindsa questions, so she'll learn about this world." Questions were of the type indicated in Table 46.1.

Question-statements are used predominantly with children in the first eight months and often carry a message not to the baby, but to others present. Young mothers and the older female relatives or friends most intimately involved with the baby begin asking questions of babies within their first few weeks home from the hospital. As noted earlier, older women often do this to give an indirect message to the young mother, saying to the baby, "You're too warm, aren't you?" "That shirt's too big for you, isn't it?" These question-statements serve another function, however; they often express the needs and desires of the child. Adults speak for the child, and since adults believe that the first type of communicative ability children must develop is the expression of their needs, they perhaps unwittingly model this function of communication in the earliest stage of the baby's development. They make statements about the baby's state of affairs, wants, likes, dislikes, et cetera. The high pitch, marked intonation, slow pace, and direct face-to-face contact with the baby mark this as baby talk though it does not consistently have all the simplifying and clarifying features of talk addressed solely to the baby. Because the message serves the secondary purpose of telling the young mother what the baby needs, there are often fully formed adult sentences in the midst of this talk to babies.

Young mothers themselves begin to use question-statements in their talk with their baby, usually within the first month for the first child and almost immediately with subsequent children. Betty, within the first month of bringing Bobby home from the hospital, commented on her own uneasiness with the practice, seemingly so easily engaged in by older women:

I guess hit's 'cause I'm here by myself so much. I talk to this baby all the time. I feel foolish, but Aunt Sue says, talkin' like that's only natural, and it shows I care, uh, I guess I mean, it shows I'm payin' attention to Bobby. 'Bout the only time I don't talk to 'im is when my soaps [television soap operas] are on, and even then, I find myself, oh, well, ya know.

Questions in which the questioner knows the answer (Q-1), indeed often has a specific answer in mind, are frequent throughout the preschool years, but are most frequent when the child is between two and four years of age. When Bobby was twenty-eight months old and again when he was forty-three months old, Betty taped her talk with Bobby every day for a week in the period before his morning nap (about two hours each day). The tapes indicated that out of an average daily total of 110 sentence-like utterances directed to Bobby, 54 percent were

TABLE **46.1**   **Types of Questions Asked of Preschool Children in Roadville**

TYPE	*RESPONSE CALLED FOR*	*EXAMPLES QUESTION*	*RESPONSE*
Question-statement	No verbal response. Used primarily in baby talk addressed to young infants; carries a content message to nearby adult listener who is expected to interpret the message as a mild directive or as a statement about the baby	Mamma's got to get some softer bedsheets, don't she? Bobby's gettin' a rash	(None)
Q-1 (Questioner has information)	Specific piece of information known to both questioner and addressee. Used often to initiate ritualistic rote performances	What's that? (pointing to a picture in a book)	Nuffie
Question-directive	Realignment of behavior and or utterance of a politeness formula. Often carries secondary message to listeners other than the child	Don't you know I just wiped that off? (said to a child dropping crumbs on the table)	I'm sorry (brushing crumbs off)
A-1 (Answerer has information)	Specific information known to addressee, but not to questioner	Do you want chocolate or vanilla?	'nilla

Note. These types are *not* listed in approximate order of frequency, because the frequency of each varies greatly in accordance with the age of the children and who is around as audience.

in question form in his second year and only 32 percent in his fourth year. In his second year, most of the questions were in ritualistic attention-focusing routines such as those discussed earlier in this chapter. In the fourth year, Bobby not only talked more (of a total of 230 utterances, only 90 were made by Bobby's mother), but a high percentage (56 percent) of *his* talk was given over to questions. Though Betty was exasperated by his questions to her (she now had a newborn baby to care for), she looked on his talkativeness and curiosity as signs that he would "run the teacher crazy," and bragged about the child's inquisitiveness, which she believed would have good positive transfer to school.

In their earliest talk to babies, Roadville parents use *Question-directives*, utterances in the form of questions which function as directives or commands: "What'd you do that for?" "Oh, Bobby, won't you ever sit still?" They use many of these in the presence of others to exclaim over their own dismay at a disobedient child or the general fatigue they feel in dealing with a child. Betty, pregnant with her second child by the time Bobby was three, often asked such questions of Bobby in the presence of her husband and relatives who she thought might help her out. Bobby was a very active and persistent child, and Betty easily became exasperated with his antics which others tended to think cute. One Sunday afternoon, several family members were sitting in the backyard visiting, and Bobby had disappeared around the house. He came out the back door, carrying a sand bucket full of water. Betty looked up and yelled at him "Bobby, what are you doing?" Everyone stopped talking and laughed as they watched Bobby carefully walk down the back steps, while explaining he was "makin' cookies." Betty, in her sixth month of pregnancy, got up to go in the house to survey the damage and found sand tracked from the front door across the living room and into the bathroom, where a trail of water began and led out the back door. Betty began a series of scolding questions, designed as much to inform the adults and elicit a response from them as to scold Bobby: "Will you look at this mess?" "Bobby, won't you ever learn?" "Why on earth did you do that?" "Don't you know I just mopped this floor? What am I going to do with you?"

These questions are used as scoldings and as directives. Betty's "What are you doing?" was intended to be interpreted as "Don't do that" as well as an exclamation over Bobby's unusual action of going through the house to get water for sandbox play. Other questions used as directives are those issued by parents requesting a specific politeness formula or the recounting of a previous scolding or a story. As early as six months, children are asked "Can you wave bye-bye?" as their hands are manipulated for them in a suitable gesture. The pattern of "Can you say _____?" continues through the preschool years requesting children to say "ta-ta [thank you]," "more, please," and on through a hierarchy of politeness formulae ranging from these baby talk items to such responses as "Pleased to meet you" on being introduced to someone and "Come again" to guests as they prepare to leave. Such occasions are prefaced by a particular look in the child's direction from a parent or intimate relative, and if the child does not respond to the nonverbal cue, the parent asks: "Can you say _____?" or "What do you say?" or "Don't you have anything to say?"

Other types of questions addressed by adults to Roadville children are those which ask them about their state of affairs, or their feelings and desires (A-1). These questions often ask children their food preferences when choices are feasible. Children are also asked to explain where they hurt and how they feel when they seem feverish, cry, or are whiny. When they are toddlers and have occasions to play with other children, they are often asked to give an accounting of what led to a sand-throwing, wet clothes, or [a] broken toy.

=

FOR DISCUSSION AND REVIEW

1. According to Heath, what are the key stages of baby talk for the children of Roadville?

2. As an ethnographer, Shirley Brice Heath is supposed to report objectively what she observes. Is it possible for her to be objective? Is she objective? Support your opinion by referring to specific passages in the text.

3. As you read Heath's description of adults "teaching" children "to talk right," did you remember how parents, teachers, or other adults helped you "to talk right"? Share several examples of the types of your speech acts that they corrected.

4. On the basis of research Heath describes in her article, what conclusions could you make regarding the following statements:

   a. Parents, other adults, and siblings actually teach a child to speak.

   b. Correctness, or the ability "to talk right," can be taught to a child.

   c. A child's use of language is creative.

   d. Babies "not only learn to speak but teach" those in their environment to speak.

5. As a student of language, what do you learn from Heath's "poo kee" and "snowman" examples?

6. Review Table 46.1. What insights into the nature of question-asking does this chart give you? What types of questions do you and your friends use in conversation?

7. In what ways is Heath's approach and tone in this article different from that of the other articles in this book? Explain.

Projects for "Children and Language"

1. Examine the following conversation (from Bellugi 1970) between Eve, a twenty-four-month-old child, and her mother:

EVE: Have that?
MOTHER: No, you may not have it.
EVE: Mom, where my tapioca?
MOTHER: It's getting cool. You'll have it in just a minute.
EVE: Let me have it.
MOTHER: Would you like to have your lunch right now?
EVE: Yeah. My tapioca cool?
MOTHER: Yes, it's cool.
EVE: You gonna watch me eat my lunch?
MOTHER: Yeah, I'm gonna watch you eat your lunch.
EVE: I eating it.
MOTHER: I know you are.
EVE: It time Sarah take a nap.
MOTHER: It's time for Sarah to have some milk, yeah. And then she's gonna take a nap and you're gonna take a nap.
EVE: And you?
MOTHER: And me too, yeah.

Compare the grammar of Eve's speech with that of her mother. What elements are systematically missing from the child's speech? Now, look at Eve's speech in a conversation (from Bellugi 1970) with her mother that was taped three months later:

MOTHER: Come and sit over here.
EVE: You can sit down by me. That will make me happy. Ready to turn it.
MOTHER: We're not quite ready to turn the page.
EVE: Yep, we are.
MOTHER: Shut the door, we won't hear her then.
EVE: Then Fraser won't hear her too. Where he's going? Did you make a great big hole there?
MOTHER: Yes, we made a great big hole in here; we have to get a new one.
EVE: Could I get some other piece of paper?
MOTHER: You ask Fraser.
EVE: Could I use this one?
MOTHER: I suppose so.
EVE: Is Fraser goin take his pencil home when he goes?
MOTHER: Yes, he is.

What changes do you note in Eve's speech? Try to describe the "grammatical rules" that govern her speech in each passage. Although

Eve could not tell us of the rules she learned during the three-month interval, what rules, as evidenced by her speech, has she internalized? What conclusions can you draw about the process of language learning among children? Write a short paper dealing with these questions.

2. Read Noam Chomsky's well-known article "Review of B. F. Skinner's *Verbal Behavior*" (*Language* 35 [1959], 26–58). Prepare a report explaining the objections of Chomsky, a linguist, to the views of Skinner, a behaviorist psychologist, about language acquisition.

3. Prepare a report on how children acquire social skills in the use of language simultaneously with their acquisition of other language skills. Use as one source Susan Ervin-Tripp's "Social Backgrounds and Verbal Skills" in *Language Acquisition: Models and Methods*, ed. Renira Huxley and Elisabeth Ingram (New York: Academic Press, 1971).

4. One of the best texts on language acquisition is Jill G. de Villiers and Peter A. de Villiers, *Language Acquisition* (Cambridge: Harvard University Press, 1978). Any single chapter in the book would provide enough material for a more detailed look at some stage or aspect of language acquisition than we could provide in this anthology, and the extensive bibliography will suggest additional topics. Write a report in which you discuss one or more of the de Villierses encounters with children and what these encounters reveal about the language acquisition process.

5. Using the selected bibliography on pp. 623–625, prepare a report on feral or isolated children. Comparing the various cases with your classmates should clarify some of the problems earlier investigators have encountered.

6. We know that young children who are learning two or more languages at the same time use similar strategies to acquire the different languages. But it is not clear what effect, if any, being bilingual has on people. Using library resources, prepare a report in which you summarize opinions about the advantages or disadvantages of being bilingual.

7. The process of learning a second language is usually different for adults (and older children) than it is for young children, if only because the former group is likely to learn in a classroom. Using library resources, prepare a report in which you describe the difficulties that adult second-language learners encounter and the learning strategies they employ.

8. Throughout much of the world, people need to speak at least two languages in order to function in their societies. In the United States, however, only about 10 percent of Americans speak a language in addition to English. Proposals for curriculum reform in U.S. schools often call for an increase in the teaching of foreign languages. As a group project, hold a debate on the subject, "American high-school graduates should be fluent in at least one language besides English."

9. As noted in "Genie: A Postscript," Susan Curtiss and Victoria Fromkin's research has focused on "people with the opposite pattern [from Genie]—who have normal language ability despite cognitive deficits." Using the resources in your college library, especially journals, prepare a report describing what they have learned.

10. Read Lenneberg's article on the stages of sensorimotor and

speech development in a young child. Do the language activities of the preschoolers that Heath describes correspond to those stages?

11. Do some ethnographic research and study of your own. Tape record up to five minutes of a live conversation between two people or a segment of a radio or television talk show. Using Table 46.1, analyze your tape for the kinds of questions asked most often. What effect, if any, did the questions asked have on the conversation or the show?

Selected Bibliography

Note: Three of the six articles in this section include bibliographies (Moskowitz, Aitchison, and Fromkin et al.). The reader should consult these for a more exhaustive list of sources.

Anderson, Elaine S. *Speaking with Style: The Sociolinguistic Skills of Children.* New York: Routledge, 1990. [Describes the linguistic competence of children in conjunction with Chomsky's views.]

Bain, Bruce, ed. *The Sociogenesis of Language and Human Conduct.* New York: Plenum Press, 1983. [A large and eclectic collection of interesting essays.]

Baron, Naomi S. *Growing Up with Language: How Children Learn to Talk.* Reading, MA: Addison-Wesley Publishing Company, 1992. [A look at the whys and hows of language development with a helpful reference section of more specific sources.]

Bates, Elizabeth. *Language and Context: The Acquisition of Pragmatics.* New York: Academic Press, 1976. [Describes the development in children of knowledge of pragmatics.]

Bellugi, Ursula. "Learning the Language." *Psychology Today* 4 (December 1970), 32–35, 66. [A nontechnical description of language acquisition and the grammar of children.]

Bickerton, Derek. *Roots of Language.* Ann Arbor: Karoma Publishers, 1981. [Develops the argument that Creole languages provide the key to understanding the nature of all human languages.]

Brown, Roger. *A First Language.* Cambridge: Harvard University Press, 1973. [An important and classic work.]

————. "How Shall a Thing Be Called?" *Psychological Review* 85 (1958), 145–154. [A discussion of how adults teach children the names of objects.]

Cox, Maureen V. "Children's Over-Regularization of Nouns and Verbs." *Journal of Child Language* 16 (1989), 203–206. [A short and informative look at some patterns of child language development.]

Curtiss, Susan. *Genie: A Psycholinguistic Study of a Modern-Day "Wild Child."* New York: Academic Press, 1977. [A detailed analysis of Genie's linguistic and cognitive development.]

————. "Genie: Language and Cognition." *UCLA Working Papers in Cognitive Linguistics* 1 (1979), 15–62. [Genie's cognitive development and its relationship to her linguistic ability.]

————. "The Critical Period and Feral Children." *UCLA Working Papers in Cognitive Linguistics,* 2 (1980), 21–36. [A complete description of known cases of feral children; argues for the existence of a specific language faculty.]

de Villiers, Jill G., and Peter A. de Villiers. *Language Acquisition.* Cambridge: Harvard University Press, 1978. [If you read only one book about language acquisition, choose this one. Thorough, complete, balanced; includes discussion of the language problems of deaf, retarded, dysphasic, and autistic children.]

Dromi, Esther. *Early Lexical Development.* New York: Cambridge University Press, 1987. [An excellent guide to the study of language acquisition including helpful chapter outlines and summaries.]

Ferguson, Charles A., and Daniel I. Slobin, eds. *Studies of Child Language Development.* New York: Holt, Rinehart and Winston, 1973. [A valuable collection of hard-to-find papers; covers the acquisition by children of a number of languages.]

Ferguson, Charles A., and Catherine E. Snow, eds. *Talking to Children: Language Input and Acquisition.* Cambridge: Cambridge University Press, 1977. [Focuses on the importance of mothers' speech to children; covers a number of languages.]

Foster, Susan H. *The Communicative Competence of Young Children.* New York: Longman, 1990. [An important source on language and communication that attempts to answer the question of how almost all children are able to learn a native language.]

Heath, Shirley Brice. *Ways with Words: Language, Life, and Work in Communities and Classroom.* Cambridge: Cambridge University Press, 1983. [Classic ethnographic study; contains an excellent bibliography.]

Heatherington, Madelon E. *How Language Works.* Cambridge, MA: Winthrop Publishers, 1980. [Excellent introduction to the study of language; see Chapter 2 about language acquisition.]

Kagan, Jerome. "Do Infants Think?" *Scientific American* 226 (1972), 74–82. [Argues that cognitive development is under way as early as nine months of age.]

Kess, Joseph, F. *Psycholinguistics: Introductory Perspectives.* New York: Academic Press, 1976. [See Chapter 3 for a detailed description of language acquisition.]

Larsen-Freeman, Diane, and M. H. Long. *An Introduction to Second Language Acquisition Research.* New York: Longman, 1991. [A detailed study for anyone pursuing research in the field.]

Lenneberg, Eric H. *Biological Foundations of Language.* New York: John Wiley & Sons, 1967. [A seminal and now classic work; technical investigation of the biological aspects of language.]

Levy, Yonata, and I. M. Schlesinger. *Categories and Processes in Language Acquisition.* Hillsdale, NJ: Lawrence Erlbaum, 1988. [A thorough study that explores a variety of theories for language acquisition.]

"Love's Labors" (videotape). New York: Ambrose Video Publishing, 1991. (57 min.) [Explores the period between six months and three years to demonstrate how babies and infants are active participants in their linguistic worlds.]

Marcus, Gary F., S. Pinker, M. Ullman, M. Hollander, T. J. Rosen, and F. Xu. *Overregularization in Language Acquisition.* Chicago: University of Chicago Press, vol. 57, no. 4, 1992. [An excellent source of study for child language development with an interesting commentary on a comparative study of English and German.]

McNeill, David. *The Acquisition of Language: The Study of Developmental Psycholinguistics.* New York: Harper & Row, 1970. [A brief but technical discussion of language acquisition.]

Meier, Richard P. "Language Acquisition by Deaf Children." *American Scientist,* January/February 1991, 60. [An intriguing article that explores how deaf children acquire linguistic skill in a manner similar to children who hear.]

Morehead, Donald M., and Ann E. Morehead, eds. *Normal and Deficient Language.* Baltimore: University Park Press, 1976. [Excellent studies of language acquisition by normal, deaf, dysphasic, and retarded children.]

Nilsen, Don L. F., and Alleen Pace Nilsen. *Language Play: An Introduction to Linguistics*. Rowley, MA: Newbury House Publishers, 1978. [A thoroughly readable book; see especially Chapters 2 and 4 for discussions of the behaviorist and innatist hypotheses of language acquisition and of the important role of playing with language.]

Owens, Robert E., Jr. *Language Development: An Introduction*, 3rd ed. New York: Macmillan, 1992. [Excellent chapter entitled "Preschool Language Development: Brown's Stages of Development."]

Pinker, Steven. *The Language Instinct: How the Mind Creates Language*. New York: Morrow, 1994. [See especially Chapters 3 "Mentalese" and 9 "Baby Born Talking—Describes Heaven."]

Radford, Andrew. *Syntactic Theory and the Acquisition of English Syntax*. Cambridge: Basil Blackwell, 1990. [A helpful study meant for students with little familiarity in the field; devoid of unnecessary technical language.]

Schiefelbusch, Richard L., and Lyle L. Lloyd, eds. *Language Perspectives: Acquisition, Retardation and Intervention*. Baltimore: University Park Press, 1974. [An important collection; deals with a number of aspects of language acquisition by normal, deaf, retarded, and autistic children.]

Shipley, Elizabeth F., Carlota S. Smith, and Lila R. Gleitman. "A Study in the Acquisition of Language: Free Responses to Commands." *Language* 45 (1969), 322–342. [Comprehension of speech exceeds ability to produce speech in children who are at certain stages of language development.]

Slobin, Dan I. *Psycholinguistics*. Glenview, IL: Scott, Foresman, 1971. [Still a good, brief introduction, especially helpful concerning language acquisition in children.]

————. "Children and Language: They Learn the Same Way All around the World." *Psychology Today* 6 (July 1972), 71–74, 82. [A nontechnical description of language acquisition by children of different cultures.]

Smith, Frank, and George A. Miller, eds. *The Genesis of Language: A Psycholinguistic Approach*. Cambridge: MIT Press, 1966. [Essays dealing with language development in children.]

Steinberg, Danny D. *Psycholinguistics: Language, Mind, and World*. New York: Longman, 1982. [Focuses on reading and second-language teaching; see especially Chapters 8 and 9.]

Teller, Virginia, and Sheila J. White, eds. "Studies in Child Language and Multilingualism." *Annals of the New York Academy of Sciences* 365 (1980). [Contains four interesting articles on language acquisition.]

Walker, Edward, ed. *Explorations in the Biology of Language*. Montgomery, VT: Bradford Books, 1978. [Six difficult but important essays focusing on language as a biological manifestation of universal cognitive structure.]

Wood, David. *How Children Think and Learn*. New York: Basil Blackwell, 1988. [A psychologist's account of the stages of children's language development.]

PART TEN

LANGUAGE, THOUGHT, AND THE BRAIN

Stimulated by what was learned from the split-brain operations of the 1960s, interest in and research about brain lateralization have increased dramatically. Many popular books have appeared, most of them enthusiastic but not all of them entirely accurate. And, the field has attracted specialists from a variety of disciplines—psychology, philosophy, neurology, history, art, education, and most important from our point of view, linguistics. By the early 1980s, it had become clear that earlier ideas about the total dominance of the left hemisphere for language functions were major oversimplifications. The situation is far more complicated than early researchers believed, and we now know that the right hemisphere plays an important role in language processing.

No discussion of language and the brain can ignore the notion of thinking and its relationship to language. In the opening article, "Language and Thought," David Crystal identifies the major kinds of human thinking before addressing the question of whether there is identity between language and thought. Crystal puts the possibilities directly before us: "First, there is the hypothesis that language and thought are totally separate entities, with one being dependent on the other. At the opposite extreme, there is the hypothesis that language and thought are identical—that it is not possible to engage in any rational thinking without using language. The truth seems to lie somewhere between these two positions." Crystal concludes his discussion of language and thought with an overview of the Sapir-Whorf hypothesis, one of the most popular and controversial theories of the middle decades of the twentieth century.

In "Brain and Language," Jeannine Heny traces the development of research on the relationship of the brain to language and explores probable reasons for the development of brain lateralization. She then describes a variety of methods for measuring which hemisphere does what, and identifies the limitations of each method. The right hemisphere, Professor Heny explains, has a number of important functions, including some that are crucial to normal language processing. In addition, she notes that linguistic tasks are not assigned identically in terms of hemispheres in all people, a point she makes clear in her discussion of bilinguals, deaf users of American Sign Language, literate people, speakers of certain languages, left-handers, and women.

In the third selection, "Signals, Signs, and Words: From Animal Communication to Language," William Kemp and Roy Smith turn to a fascinating topic: the differences between animal communication and human language. Animal communication systems are interesting in themselves; in addition, by studying them we may learn more about how human language evolved. But of more immediate interest to many readers will be the question of human attempts to communicate with various animals, especially chimpanzees. The early 1970s brought what many people, scientists and nonscientists alike, believed was a real breakthrough: a number of chimpanzees had apparently learned forms of human language, ranging from American Sign Language, to a keyboard linked to a computer and used to make requests and respond to questions, to the rearrangement of plastic symbols so as to produce meaningful utterances. By the 1980s, however, some skeptics suggested that the problem of uncontaminated human-animal experiments designed to teach some form of human language to animals might be insoluble. Kemp and Smith survey the evidence thoroughly and objectively, concluding that the chimpanzee research achieved less than its extreme advocates claim but more than its severest critics allow.

Finally, in "The Continuity Paradox," Derek Bickerton explores the role evolution has played in the development of human language. If humans are the result of an evolutionary process, what then is the origin of language? According to Bickerton, "Language must have evolved out of some prior system, and yet there does not seem to be any such system out of which it could have evolved" and therein lies the central paradox that Bickerton discusses in this chapter from his book *Language and Species*.

There are still a great many questions about the relationships among the human brain, language, and cognition. It is clear, however, that research will continue and that, as it does, we will learn more about the functioning of the brain.

47

Language and Thought

David Crystal

In the following selection from the Cambridge Encyclopedia *of the English* Language, *David Crystal of the University of North Wales explores the complex relationship between language and thought that leads to the classic question: Can we think without language? Or does language actually determine the ways in which we think? Crystal identifies the major kinds of thinking before addressing the question of whether there is identity between language and thought. He then sketches the range of possibilities from total separation or independence to inseparability or identity. According to Crystal, "The truth seems to lie somewhere between these two positions." Crystal concludes his discussion with an overview of the Sapir-Whorf hypothesis, and explains why this popular and controversial theory held sway during the thirties, forties, and fifties.*

It seems evident that there is the closest of relationships between language and thought: everyday experience suggests that much of our thinking is facilitated by language. But is there identity between the two? Is it possible to think without language? Or does our language dictate the ways in which we are able to think? Such matters have exercised generations of philosophers, psychologists, and linguists, who have uncovered layers of complexity in these apparently straightforward questions. A simple answer is certainly not possible; but at least we can be clear about the main factors which give rise to the complications.

KINDS OF THINKING

Many kinds of behavior have been referred to as "thinking," but not all of them require us to posit a relationship with language. Most obviously, there is no suggestion that language is involved in our emotional response to some object or event, such as when we react to a beautiful painting or an unpleasant incident: we may use language to explain our reaction to others, but the emotion itself is "beyond words." Nor do people engaged in the creative arts find it essential to think using language: composers, for example, often report that they "hear" the music they wish to write. Also, our everyday fantasies, daydreams, and other free associations can all proceed without language.

629

The thinking which seems to involve language is of a different kind: this is the reasoned thinking which takes place as we work out problems, tell stories, plan strategies, and so on. It has been called "rational," "directed," "logical," or "propositional" thinking. It involves elements that are both deductive (when we solve problems by using a given set of rules, as in an arithmetical task) and inductive (when we solve problems on the basis of data placed before us, as in working out a travel route). Language seems to be very important for this kind of thinking. The formal properties of language, such as word order and sentence sequencing, constitute the medium in which our connected thoughts can be presented and organized.

INDEPENDENCE OR IDENTITY?

But how close is this relationship between language and thought? It is usual to see this question in terms of two extremes. First, there is the hypothesis that language and thought are totally separate entities, with one being dependent on the other. At the opposite extreme, there is the hypothesis that language and thought are identical—that it is not possible to engage in any rational thinking without using language. The truth seems to lie somewhere between these two positions.

Within the first position, there are plainly two possibilities: language might be dependent upon thought, or thought might be dependent upon language. The traditional view, which is widely held at a popular level, adopts the first of these: people have thoughts, and then they put these thoughts into words. It is summarized in such metaphorical views of language as the "dress" or "tool" of thought. The view is well represented in the field of child language acquisition, where children are seen to develop a range of cognitive abilities which precede the learning of language.

The second possibility has also been widely held: the way people use language dictates the lines along which they can think. An expressive summary of this is Shelley's "He gave men speech, and speech created thought, /Which is the measure of the universe" (*Prometheus Unbound*). This view is also represented in the language acquisition field, in the argument that the child's earliest encounters with language are the main influence on the way concepts are learned. The most influential expression of this position, however, is found in the Sapir-Whorf hypothesis.

A third possibility, which is also widely held these days, is that language and thought are interdependent—but this is not to say that they are identical. The identity view (for example, that thought is no more than an internalized vocalization) is no longer common. There are too many exceptions for such a strong position to be maintained: we need think only of the various kinds of mental operations which we can perform without language, such as recalling a sequence of movements in a game or sport, or visualizing the route from home to work. It is also widely recognized that pictorial images and physical models are helpful in problem solving, and may at times be more efficient than purely verbal representations of a problem.

On the other hand, these cases are far outnumbered by those where language does seem to be the main means whereby successful thinking can proceed. To see language and thought as interdependent, then, is to recognize that language is a regular part of the process of thinking, at the same time recognizing that we have to think in order to understand language. It is not a question of one notion taking precedence over the other, but of both notions being essential, if we are to explain behavior. Once again, people have searched for metaphors to express their views. Language has been likened to the arch of a tunnel; thought, to the tunnel itself. But the complex structure and function of language defy such simple analogies.

The Sapir-Whorf Hypothesis

The romantic idealism of the late eighteenth century, as encountered in the views of Johann Herder (1744–1803) and Wilhelm von Humboldt (1762–1835), placed great value on the diversity of the world's languages and cultures. The tradition was taken up by the American linguist and anthropologist Edward Sapir (1884–1939) and his pupil Benjamin Lee Whorf (1897–1941), and resulted in a view about the relation between language and thought which was widely influential in the middle decades of this century.

The "Sapir-Whorf hypothesis," as it came to be called, combines two principles. The first is known as *linguistic determinism*: it states that language determines the way we think. The second follows from this, and is known as *linguistic relativity*: it states that the distinctions encoded in one language are not found in any other language. In a much-quoted paragraph, Whorf propounds the view as follows:

> We dissect nature along lines laid down by our native languages. The categories and types that we isolate from the world of phenomena we do not find there because they stare every observer in the face; on the contrary, the world is presented in a kaleidoscopic flux of impressions which has to be organized by our minds—and this means largely by the linguistic systems in our minds. We cut nature up, organize it into concepts, and ascribe significances as we do, largely because we are parties to an agreement to organize it in this way—an agreement that holds throughout our speech community and is codified in the patterns of our language. The agreement is, of course, an implicit and unstated one, *but its terms are absolutely obligatory*; we cannot talk at all except by subscribing to the organization and classification of data which the agreement decrees.

Whorf illustrated his view by taking examples from several languages, and in particular from Hopi, an Amerindian language. In Hopi, there is one word (*masa'ytaka*) for everything that flies except birds—

which would include insects, airplanes, and pilots. This seems alien to someone used to thinking in English, but, Whorf argues, it is no stranger than English-speakers having one word for many kinds of snow, in contrast to Eskimo, where there are different words for falling snow, snow on the ground, snow packed hard like ice, slushy snow (cf. English *slush*), and so on. In Aztec, a single word (with different endings) covers an even greater range of English notions—snow, cold, and ice. When more abstract notions are considered (such as time, duration, velocity), the differences become yet more complex: Hopi, for instance, lacks a concept of time seen as a dimension; there are no forms corresponding to English tenses, but there are a series of forms which make it possible to talk about various durations, from the speaker's point of view. It would be very difficult, Whorf argues, for a Hopi and an English physicist to understand each other's thinking, given the major differences between the languages.

Examples such as these made the Sapir-Whorf hypothesis very plausible; but in its strongest form it is unlikely to have any adherents now. The fact that successful translations between languages can be made is a major argument against it, as is the fact that the conceptual uniqueness of a language such as Hopi can nonetheless be explained using English. That there are some conceptual differences between cultures due to language is undeniable, but this is not to say that the differences are so great that mutual comprehension is impossible. One language may take many words to say what another language says in a single word, but in the end the circumlocution can make the point.

Similarly, it does not follow that, because a language lacks a word, its speakers therefore cannot grasp the concept. Several languages have few words for numerals: Australian aboriginal languages, for example, are often restricted to a few general words (such as "all," "many," "few," "one," and "two." In such cases, it is sometimes said that the people lack the concept of number—that aborigines "haven't the intelligence to count," as it was once put. But this is not so, as is shown when these speakers learn English as a second language: their ability to count and calculate is quite comparable to that of English native speakers.

However, a weaker version of the Sapir-Whorf hypothesis is generally accepted. Language may not determine the way we think, but it does influence the way we perceive and remember, and it affects the ease with which we perform mental tasks. Several experiments have shown that people recall things more easily if the things correspond to readily available words or phrases. And people certainly find it easier to make a conceptual distinction if it neatly corresponds to words available in their language. Some salvation for the Sapir-Whorf hypothesis can therefore be found in these studies, which are carried out within the developing field of psycholinguistics.

FOR DISCUSSION AND REVIEW

1. What are the major kinds of thinking that Crystal describes? Using examples from your own experience, discuss the differences among them.

2. Which position on the issue of independence or identity between language and thought do you support? Explain your reasons.

3. What is the Sapir-Whorf hypothesis? Explain the two principles upon which it is founded: linguistic determinism and linguistic relativity. What is your reaction to the hypothesis?

4. According to Crystal, what is the status of the Sapir-Whorf hypothesis today?

48

Brain and Language

Jeannine Heny

In the following selection, Jeannine Heny, professor of English at Indiana University of Pennsylvania, examines the evolution of the human brain and some possible causes of brain lateralization. She traces the sometimes halting progress of early research involving aphasia and the attempts to "map out" the language functions of the cortex. Describing the many contemporary methods of measuring hemispheric activity, Professor Heny demonstrates that both the left and right hemispheres of the brain are important in language processing, and that it is probably the type of processing, rather than the material being processed, that differentiates the two hemispheres. Curiously, though, people do not all use the same hemisphere for language tasks; in fact, the same person may process identical material differently at different times. As Professor Heny points out, our understanding of the complex relationship between language and the brain has increased enormously in recent years, but it is still tantalizingly incomplete.

About five million years ago, early hominid brain size began to increase dramatically. After about ten million years of relatively stable weight, the human brain was embarking on a growth phase that would see it more than triple its volume to reach today's proportions. Five million years may seem very long; but, as Figure 48.1 shows, it can represent a phenomenal rate of growth on an evolutionary scale.

At the same time, other changes were taking place as well: our forebears became predominantly right-handed, made use of increasingly sophisticated tools, and organized their culture in ever more complex ways. The result of this evolution, *homo sapiens*, looked rather unimpressive: a puny, almost hairless animal, with a bent windpipe that reduced breathing efficiency to nearly half of its original capacity. The creature's teeth were practically useless for chewing; it had nothing to match the sharp incisors of rats or the long canine teeth of wolves, lions, and other primates. Even inside the nervous system, the human species had taken risks, giving up a potentially useful insurance policy: the two halves of the brain were no longer identical, as in many lower species; thus, there was little chance of "backup" from one half of the brain if the other suffered damage. But the animal did have at least one feature that

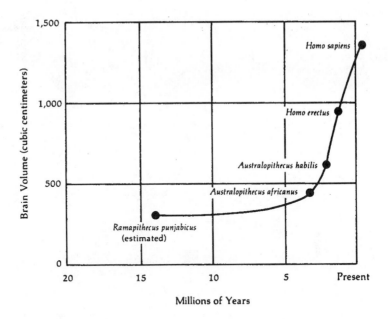

FIGURE **48.1**   Human evolution: brain size.

more than compensated for all it had lost: the most highly developed communication system on Earth—human language.

In fact, human brain evolution involved much more than increased size, as Figure 48.2 reveals. In lower mammals such as the rat, the brain is almost wholly taken up with sensory and motor functions. In contrast, the primate brain has a greatly enlarged outer layer or *cortex*, resulting in a dramatic increase in "uncommitted" cortical tissue not needed for basic functions. A high degree of asymmetry, or hemispheric specialization, nearly doubles this available space in humans (by the way, one estimate suggests that the human cortex contains more nerve connections than there are people on Earth!).[1] This essay focuses on the way in which the brain's powerful outer layer handles language.

DISCOVERING THE BRAIN

The Classical Language Areas

For centuries, the nature of the brain was shrouded in mystery. Aristotle is said to have thought it was a cold sponge, whose main task

---

[1] Trevarthen (1983, 60).

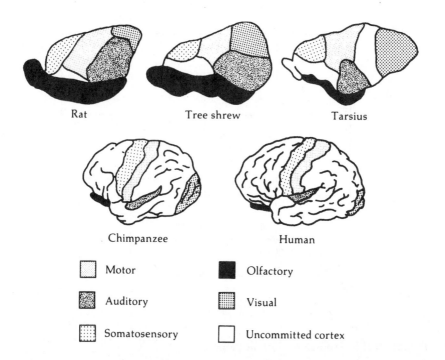

Rat   Tree shrew   Tarsius

Chimpanzee   Human

☐ Motor   ■ Olfactory

▨ Auditory   ▦ Visual

▤ Somatosensory   ☐ Uncommitted cortex

FIGURE 48.2   Human evolution: brain function. These figures show the approximate space devoted to sensory and motor functions in various mammalian brains. The white areas, called *association cortex*, represent neural tissue not committed to basic functions. As shown, the increase in brain size is accompanied by a dramatic increase in the proportion of association cortex in humans.

was to cool the blood.[2] Later, Leonardo da Vinci represented the brain as a curious void filled by three tiny bulbous structures arranged in a straight line behind the eyeball, whose functions he defined according to commonly held assumptions of his time.[3]

Not all early theories were quite so misguided, however. From the first studies on language deficits in the Greco-Roman era, it was suspected that the brain played some direct part in language use. Still, modern scholarship on this question dates only to the early nineteenth century. At that stage, scientific opinion was divided; some believed that language resided in the frontal lobes, while Franz Gall, the founder of phrenology, drew language in Area XV on his now famous map of the brain. Neither theory contained any hint that language might be handled more actively in one hemisphere than the other.

In 1836 an obscure French country doctor, Marc Dax, attended a

---

[2] Comment (cited from work by Clarke and O'Mally) in Arbib, Caplan, and Marshall (1982, 6); this article provides an interesting overview of neurolinguistic history.

[3] Harth (1982, 37–42).

medical conference in Montpelier, France, and presented the only scientific paper of his life. Dax claimed that, in forty aphasic patients he had seen in his practice, loss of language ability always correlated with damage to the left half of the brain. The paper went unnoticed at the time, and its remarkable insight was soon forgotten.

It was the French surgeon Paul Broca who, in 1864, dramatically proved Dax's original claim (about which, by the way, he knew nothing). Broca described his patient "Tan," named after the only word he could say. Tan could write normally, and seemed to understand everything said to him; he could move his lips or tongue in any direction when asked to do so, but he was totally incapable of meaningful speech. Broca hypothesized that his patient suffered from a pure disturbance of language, resulting from left-hemisphere injury. Soon, his claim was proven: at autopsy, patients like Tan were found to have brain damage in the rear portion of the left frontal lobe, just above the left ear. Equivalent damage to the right hemisphere seemed to have little effect on speech. The area Broca isolated, and the aphasia associated with it, now bear his name: the term *Broca's aphasia* (also called *nonfluent* or *motor* aphasia) has come to stand for a complex of symptoms, ranging from extreme difficulty in articulation to *agrammatic* speech, where a patient produces halting strings of words without grammatical markers (e.g., inflections on verbs) or function words (such as articles and prepositions). The passage below gives an example of speech by a patient with Broca's aphasia. The patient is trying to describe a picture showing a little boy stealing cookies from a cookie jar while his chair is tipping over; a little girl is helping him. Their mother stands at the window staring into space while the sink in front of her overflows.

> Cookie jar . . . fall over . . . chair . . . water . . . empty . . . ov . . . ov . . . [Examiner: "overflow?"] Yeah.[4]

Another agrammatic patient, asked to tell the story of Cinderella, responded as follows:

> Cinderella . . . poor . . . um 'dopted her . . . scrubbed floor, um, tidy . . . poor, um . . . 'dopted . . . si-sisters and mother . . . ball. Ball, prince um, shoe.[5]

Ten years after Broca's discovery, Karl Wernicke, a twenty-six-year-old researcher in Germany, made yet another startling breakthrough. The patients who especially attracted his interest had no damage to Broca's area. Nor did they have obvious physical difficulty producing speech: in some cases, they could produce a stream of speech with no trouble in pronunciation and no significant loss of grammatical morphemes. But the content of their utterances ranged from puzzling to meaningless.

The Wernicke's aphasic who produced the following passage was

---

[4] Cited from earlier work by Goodglass and Kaplan, in Blumstein (1982, 205).
[5] Schwartz, Linebarger, and Saffran (1985, 84).

also trying to describe the cookie theft picture described above. His flowing speech contrasts sharply with the hesitant, ungrammatical answer of the first patient. Yet, despite his fluency, he seems to make very little sense of the situation he sees:

> Well, this is . . . mother is away here working out o'here to get her better, but when she's working, the two boys looking in the other part. One their small tile into her time here. She's working another time because she's getting, too.[6]

The symptoms of Wernicke's aphasia are diverse and complex: a particularly striking form, called *jargon aphasia*, is marked by super-fluent speech and *neologisms*, that is, nonwords whose origin is unknown. The excerpt below is taken from a long spontaneous monologue:

> And I say, this is wrong, I'm going out and doing things and getting ukeleles taken every time and I think I'm doing wrong because I'm supposed to take everything from the top so that we do four flashes of four volumes before we get down low . . . Face of everything. This guy has got to this thing, this thing made out in order to slash immediately to all of the windpails . . . This is going right over me from there, that's up to five station stuff form manatime, and with that put it all in and build it all up so it will all be spent with him conversing his condessing . . .[7]

Wernicke's aphasics typically have great problems finding the simplest, everyday words, especially names for things. One patient, shown a knife, tried to tell what it was:

> That's a resh. Sometimes I get one around here that I can cut a couple regs. There's no rugs around here and nothing cut right. But that's a rug, and I had some nice rekebz. I wish I had one now. Say how Wishi idaw, uh windy, look how windy. It's really window, isn't it?[8]

As a result of studying such patients, the young Wernicke managed not only to isolate a new area, but also to present the first coherent model of language processing in the brain. According to Wernicke, a speaker first draws the words from Wernicke's area where meanings are stored, located near the primary auditory cortex (just above and behind the left ear). A bundle of nerves called the *arcuate fasciculus* then transmits the idea to Broca's area, where it picks up sound structure before being sent to the motor cortex. There, the message is encoded into commands to the tongue, lips, and other articulators, and emerges as speech. Wernicke's model, illustrated in Figure 48.3, still stands at the center of current research.

---

[6] Blumstein (1982, 205).

[7] Brown (1981, 170–171).

[8] Adapted from Buckingham (1981, 59).

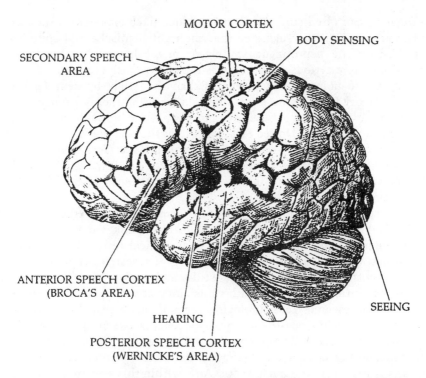

MOTOR CORTEX

BODY SENSING

SECONDARY SPEECH
AREA

ANTERIOR SPEECH CORTEX
(BROCA'S AREA)

SEEING

HEARING

POSTERIOR SPEECH CORTEX
(WERNICKE'S AREA)

FIGURE **48.3** The classical language areas of the brain. Note the proximity of Broca's area to the "motor cortex," where instructions to speech articulators originate. The proximity of Wernicke's area to neural centers for sight and hearing is also important, because this arrangement seems to allow the spoken and written word to be available for semantic processing in Wernicke's area as soon as they are perceived.

The discovery of Broca's and Wernicke's areas in the left hemisphere soon inspired others to seek the remaining pieces of the neurolinguistic puzzle. Scientists reasoned that all brain function must follow a clear, if complex, mapping system. Indeed, a few striking cases turned up to fuel the prevailing enthusiasm, where highly circumscribed damage caused specific, clearly identifiable symptoms. In 1892, for example, the French neurologist Dejerine observed a patient who could not read, although his visual skills, writing, and speech were normal. On autopsy, it was found that his left visual area was destroyed, along with the nerves connecting visual regions in the two hemispheres. Thus, only the right, nonverbal hemisphere could "see"—and it could not perceive what it saw as *language.* Hence, of course, it could not "read" what it saw. Nor could it transmit the image it received to the language centers on the left for interpretation.

But the diagram-makers ran into problems from the outset. For one thing, it had long been known that severe aphasics, with extensive left-hemisphere lesions and with no ability to produce a normal spontaneous utterance, can often sing, curse, and produce fixed expressions such as "How are you?" This suggested that the right hemisphere (despite its absence on the neurolinguistic "map") might have some linguistic potential. More serious, however, was the elusive task of pinning down symptoms to points on the cortex. Exhaustive study by neurologists such as Henry Head in the 1920s showed that, at best, only a rough correlation could be found between symptom types and broad cortical areas. (Imagine a map of the United States in which the best one could do was place Boston "somewhere in the New England–New York State area." One could indeed capture the distinction between San Francisco and Boston with such a picture, but it could hardly be termed a useful guide for getting to Boston!)

These problems led many to abandon mapmaking altogether, on the grounds that language may be too complex to be broken down into discrete subprocesses, each assigned its own cortical territory. Now, the trend has again partially reversed, with recent research combining the spirit of both approaches. Scientists still search for the locus of specific verbal capacities, sometimes with painstaking accuracy, as in electrical stimulation research. Yet neurologists generally agree that this search is not likely to yield a one-to-one correspondence between units of grammatical knowledge and points on the brain's surface. The cortical areas that handle higher cognitive activity are too closely intertwined to be clearly teased apart and mapped out. And, within this system, linguistic and nonlinguistic capacity must be linked: a patient with a general impairment affecting, for example, memory or the ability to carry out purposeful actions, will have trouble speaking normally—but not because his grammatical knowledge is impaired.

Linguistics and Aphasia

When Broca and Wernicke made their discoveries about the brain, modern cognitive linguistics was unknown, and the terminology used to describe the functions of the language areas was vague; neurologists spoke of "sensory images" and "motor images" of words as being stored in Wernicke's and Broca's areas, respectively. Only now, after a century of brain research, has linguistic theory become rich enough to make a significant contribution to the understanding of aphasic syndromes. Three examples will help illustrate how this is happening.

First, consider the concept of "agrammatism." On the surface, it seems simple to describe. Take a sentence, like *A girl is playing in the yard*, and remove all the little particles, function words, and verb endings (*a, is, -ing*, etc.), and you have a plausible agrammatic sentence, right? (In this case, *girl . . . play . . . yard*.) Unfortunately, the answer is no. Broca's aphasics do not produce perfect language with a few predictable parts missing. For one thing, it may not be accurate to say that parts are *missing* at all: note that, in English, where both the bare stem *play* and the past tense *played* are fully acceptable forms, one *could* say that the aphasic simply chooses one form over another in saying *play* and not *played*. As it turns out, in languages where there is no "bare verb stem" form, such as *play*, this does seem to be what happens. In these languages, agrammatic speakers produce fully acceptable verb forms, but they use them in the wrong places. This suggests that the original "missing parts" description was prejudiced by the form of English, where the simple, unsuffixed verb form (e.g., *like*) happens to be the one agrammatics overuse most. This makes a critical difference in the linguistic interpretation of agrammatism. The earlier description implied that Broca's aphasics cannot form words properly; their *morphological*, or word-formation, rules for language do not function as they should. But under this new view things look very different: the rules that put elements like *play* and *-ed* together might be quite intact; it could be the *choice* of word forms, not their construction, that fails in these patients.

In fact, Broca's aphasic symptoms are not limited to word formation. Broca's aphasics produce too many nouns (recall the aforementioned sentence of *ball, prince um, shoe*). They often omit the verb altogether in a sentence, or use a related noun (e.g., *discussion* instead of *discuss*). Sentence patterns seem generally disrupted, as can be easily seen from agrammatic sentences cited in the literature, such as *the girl is flower the woman* and *the boy and the girl is valentine*. Researchers are now focusing on this question, trying to learn just how sensitive Broca's aphasics are to syntactic patterns, and where their attempts to put words together in the right order might be failing.

Other related work tries to interpret the classical description itself in linguistic terms. The trick is to characterize neatly the cluster of little elements lost: prepositions, articles, the *-ed* ending of the verb *walked*, the *'s* of *John's here*. What do all these have in common? Some represent whole words, and some represent parts of words. The preposition plays a major part in grammar, but articles don't. Just what part of linguistic *knowledge* would be missing in a patient whose only deficit was the omission of these elements? Mary-Louise Kean (1977) first proposed that these elements are all *unstressed*; hence, the agrammatic's problem, claimed Kean, is phonological (i.e., related to the sound system of the language). Since then, equally interesting suggestions have linked agrammatism to syntax, morphology, and language processing.[9] Although the final answer remains to be found, it is exciting that careful work on aphasic speech is finally able to yield such clear proposals.

A second line of research suggests that Wernicke's aphasia, too, may have been described in overly simplistic terms: it has been assumed that a Broca's aphasic has access to the meaning of words, while a Wernicke's aphasic does not. One recent study challenges this notion, emphasizing the case of a Wernicke's aphasic who could neither read words nor iden-

---

[9] A detailed discussion and references to these theories can be found in Caplan (1987).

tify pictures of an object, but could nevertheless say what category the object belongs to (girl's name, tool, animal, etc.). This suggests that a more careful view of "meaning" must be identified if Wernicke's aphasia is to be fully understood.[10] A similar note of caution comes from a recent study on meaning. When normal subjects are given series of letter-strings and asked to say whether they are real words, most respond more quickly if the current word is semantically related to one they have just heard. So, if the subject has just heard the word *barn*, he will react faster to, say, *horse* than to an unrelated word like *fry*. Amazingly enough, it is *Wernicke's* aphasics, and not Broca's, who react as normal subjects in this so-called semantic priming experiment,[11] suggesting that some kind of semantic access functions normally in these patients. Again, this kind of study can lead to important results, not only in defining aphasic types, but in understanding the nature of meaning itself.

A third exciting question being raised is this: is there a common denominator, some factor or cluster of factors that all aphasia types share? Goodglass and Menn (1985) found that *all* aphasics, regardless of type, had difficulty with sorting out the proper relationships between the underlined pairs of words in these sentences:

Point to the spoon with the pencil.
Point to the pencil with the spoon.

The trainer's dog is here
The dog's trainer is here.[12]

Others have suggested that certain sentence patterns or even word forms may cause difficulty for virtually all aphasics. If such a common denominator can be found, it will obviously contribute a great deal to the task of defining classical aphasia types. And, again, it will help flesh out Wernicke's model of how the brain processes language.

TWO BRAINS OR ONE: HEMISPHERIC ASYMMETRIES AND THEIR ORIGIN

The realization that one important mental faculty seemed to belong to one side of the brain raised a host of intriguing questions from the start. Does a human being have two consciousnesses or one? Is the mute right hemisphere teeming with unsatisfied desires and ideas that will never be expressed due to its dominant, talkative left twin? If the connections between the two halves were severed, would the result be a creature with two quite distinct personalities, each having its own thoughts, worldview, and feelings? The famous nineteenth-century psy-

---

[10] Warrington and Shallice (1979), and later ongoing research cited in Caplan (1987).

[11] Milberg et al. (1987).

[12] Goodglass and Menn (1985, 22).

chologist William McDougall thought not. In fact, so deep was his conviction that he offered to have his brain anatomically split should he develop a terminal illness. He never did, and the experiment was left undone in his lifetime.[13]

To the more prosaic, however, other questions arose: what else does the left hemisphere do? And what, if anything, is the special domain of the right hemisphere? Hypotheses meant to capture the brain's left-right dichotomy have sprung up in abundance, especially in the past fifteen years. These include the short list given in Table 48.1.

At its most fanciful, the contrast implied in the last pair of terms has led to global claims about "Eastern" and "Western" modes of thought, which, fascinating as they may be, are unsubstantiated. This speculation often comes uncomfortably close in spirit to the now-discounted claims of phrenologists in the early nineteenth century that bumps on each person's skull mirror "bumps on the brain," which in turn reveal personality traits.

But serious scientific questions arise from Table 48.1 as well. First, what counts as "language"? Most would agree that the word *cow*, printed on a card, should be perceived as language, but what about the single letter *c*? Or, for that matter, what about groups of letters that don't spell a word? There is some evidence that we perceive sequences like *kug*, *zeb*, or *bem* as language while sequences like *nku*, *lke*, and *okl* are perceived more as though they were simply geometric shapes (Young et al. 1984). Pronounceability seems to be the cue here; one could imagine Dr. Seuss creating a character called a *Zeb*, if he hasn't already done so, but a name like *Lke* would take some getting used to, even for the most imaginative child.

More puzzling still, the very same linguistic material presented in two forms may be handled differently. Subjects seem to use the left hemisphere to read text in standard print such as this, but the right hemisphere is called upon to handle elaborate lettering styles, which presumably require more visual skill (Bryden and Allard 1976). Likewise, mirror-image writing, or blurred or incomplete text, seems to be processed on the right.

In fact, subtleties of this sort abound. Japanese readers show some tendency for right-hemisphere activity when reading in the *kanji* script,

TABLE 48.1   The Two Brains and What They Do

LEFT BRAIN	*RIGHT BRAIN*
Analytic processing	Holistic processing (dealing with overall patterns, or "gestalt" forms)
Temporal relations	Spatial relations
Speech sounds	Nonspeech sounds
Mathematics	Music
Intellectual	Emotional

---

[13] Springer and Deutsch (1985, 26).

where each character represents a word. But in the phonetically based *kana* script, where a letter usually stands for a syllable, the expected left-hemisphere dominance reemerges. Aphasia types distinguish between the two writing systems as well. Japanese aphasics often seem to retain some ability to read *kanji* script, while no longer able to comprehend the sound-based *kana* system. This again suggests that the processing of *kanji* characters can be mediated by areas outside the normal language centers, possibly in the right hemisphere.

Thus, some seemingly verbal tasks may be handled by the right hemisphere. And the converse seems also to be true: some spatial work seems to be done on the left, especially if it involves comparison or association between pairs of shapes. To further complicate matters, in an interesting study done in 1980, Gur and Reivich found no hemispheric advantage for a spatial (gestalt completion) test, suggesting that it can be handled equally well by either hemisphere. But there was a significant difference in how well the job was done: subjects who "chose" to use the right, spatially adept, hemisphere performed with significantly greater efficiency. But those who used the left hemisphere also achieved reasonable results; this suggests that, in some cases, the unspecialized hemisphere may be like an untrained worker who manages to succeed at a job although he may not be the ideal person to do it.

In the light of these and similar findings, researchers now believe that it is the type of processing, not the type of material processed, that distinguishes the two hemispheres; in other words, the first entry in Table 48.1 can be thought of as the only true difference. The left hemisphere is called upon whenever detailed analysis is in order, whereas the right hemisphere goes into action if holistic processing is needed. Language and mathematics typically involve sequential analysis or other kinds of analytical thinking, whereas pictures and faces are usually taken in all at once, as are musical patterns.

Under this more subtle view of lateralization, the Gur and Reivich results can be more plausibly explained. If, for some reason, a task does not clearly identify itself as requiring a right- or left-hemisphere approach, the job might be shunted off to different halves of the brain in different people—or even in the same person at different times, depending on which hemisphere happens to be more active. But it is quite reasonable to expect that the hemisphere with a more appropriate approach to the task will get better results.

Interesting support for the "processing strategy" approach comes from several experiments showing that trained musicians (who analyze as they listen) actually process music in the *left* hemisphere. Only the musically unsophisticated layperson, who hears music as holistic patterns, shows the expected right-hemisphere dominance. Layperson and musician hear the same patterns, but their reaction, their *way of listening*, differs.

Finally, once lateralization is seen in this more abstract way, another seemingly unrelated fact may tie in as well: the ability for fine, sequenced hand movements, called *manual praxis*, is also linked to the left hemisphere. Although hand movement and language seem very different on the surface, it is reasonable to suppose that a similar type of neural mechanism might be needed to orchestrate fine hand movements and to fashion complex sentence patterns.

This last point brings us back to the opening theme of this article: where did brain asymmetry come from? Was language the first activity to move into the analytical left hemisphere? Some think not. As a species, they argue, we must have developed fine manual coordination before language as we now know it. The need to make a rock into a sharp arrowhead or scraping tool calls for complex techniques involving fingers, wrist, and hand; this, many believe, is the left hemisphere's original specialty. If so, language may have been drawn to the left hemisphere simply because the neural circuitry available there for complex tool use was somehow suited to take on linguistic calculations.

This hypothesis remains open for debate. But tantalizing pieces of evidence seem to support it. For instance, in aphasia, fine hand coordination is often impaired along with language. Furthermore, the human species has been overwhelmingly right-handed for a long time, suggesting that asymmetry for handedness came early in human evolution. Cro-Magnon hand tracings were virtually always of the left hand; thus, the artists must have been drawing with the right. The skulls of prehistoric animals provide mute evidence as well; archeologists tell us that the earliest hunting hominids must have used tools held in the right hand to slay game, judging from the position of fractures and marks on the skulls of ancient animals.

Other hints scattered along our evolutionary trail lead to a quite different view. Brain asymmetry has been found elsewhere in the animal kingdom—in rodents, in other primates, and especially in birds. Even the most imaginative of scientists has yet to suspect a song sparrow of being an effective tool user, yet sparrows and chaffiniches have song strongly lateralized in the left hemisphere. Looking at such species makes it seem plausible to some scientists that tool use is not necessarily the answer. In fact, it may have been the right brain, not the left, that first specialized. In the struggle for survival, even a rat can use an acute eye and a quick emotional response to avoid becoming dinner for a hungry hawk. Some would argue that, for humans too, the demands of survival and the hunt preceded the impulse toward language. If so, the right hemisphere's visual and emotional roles may have taken their place *before* left-hemisphere functions. Language may have simply migrated to the left hemisphere by default, as it were.

TESTING THE BRAIN

The careful reader will by now wonder how all the claims in Table 48.1 can be made with certainty. How do we know what a single hemisphere is doing? There are, of course, the aphasia studies, but studies of brain malfunction are not ideally reliable. Suppose you wanted to find out what a specific transformer does in a radio: would you remove the transistor or break it, turn the radio on, and see what happens? Relying on aphasia as an indicator of localized function comes remarkably close to this intuitively unsatisfactory method. In fact, matters are even worse than a simple analogy would suggest. It is well known that brain tissue (unlike radio components) can "reorganize." That is, if one area of the brain is damaged, especially at an early age, other areas may take over the original tissue's function. Clearly, information from aphasia must be treated with caution.

The "Split Brain"

A surgical technique known as *commissurotomy*, used to treat severe cases of epilepsy, seems at first sight to provide perfect subjects for studying brain lateralization. Commissurotomy involves severing the corpus callosum, the main bundle of fibers connecting the brain's two hemispheres, as shown in Figure 48.4. With patients who have undergone this operation, neurologists can communicate with each cerebral hemisphere separately. Thus, using specialized techniques, one can show a picture or a written text to a single hemisphere and see how it responds.

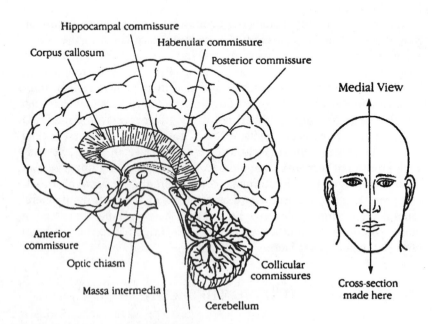

FIGURE 48.4   The corpus callosum.

These patients have been studied intensely, and with interesting results; but the general implications of these studies are controversial. Epilepsy is clearly accompanied by abnormal brain activity, often from an early age. Thus, as with aphasics, the brain tissue of split-brain patients may have reorganized in ways that make them atypical. For decades, researchers have grappled with these problems by searching for tests that can be used with normal subjects.

Behavioral Tests

A widely used technique called *tachistoscopic presentation* represents one attempt to learn what one hemisphere does more efficiently or more accurately than the other. A subject is asked to fix her gaze on a central point directly in front of her. An image is then flashed to her right or left visual field. The subject does not know which side will display the image, and the flash is too brief (less than one-fifth of a second) to allow eye movement to one side or the other. Because of the human nervous system's organization, the image is perceived primarily by one side of the brain—the one *opposite* the visual field involved. If a subject handles stimuli presented on the right side of the screen better, she is assumed to be using the left hemisphere more actively.

Doreen Kimura at the Montreal Neurological Institute has adapted this principle to auditory stimuli in the *dichotic listening test*. The ear, like the eye, conveys messages most effectively via the so-called contralateral nerve pathway to the opposite hemisphere of the brain. Thus, if two different words are played to a subject's two ears, the left hemisphere will hear the word played to the right ear, and vice versa. As it turns out, many subjects consistently hear words more accurately with their right ear, but identify tunes played to the left ear more accurately. As with tachistoscopic data, dichotic listening results have played an important role in confirming the assumptions underlying Table 48.1.

The lateral eye movement (or LEM) provides a more indirect, and more controversial, way to look at brain activity via behavior. When answering a question, we tend to look left or right, rather than directly into the eyes of the asker. This sideways glance is said to show which hemisphere is providing the answer: activity on one side of the brain is said to trigger an automatic response to eye movement, in the opposite direction from the locus of mental activity. So, an emotional question should trigger an automatic eye shift leftwards; a verbal or intellectual question should cause the eyes to drift toward the right, while the analytical left hemisphere computes the necessary answer.

Unfortunately, behavioral tests have their drawbacks. A single subject tested twice with one week intervening may show different results. Furthermore, hemispheric activation at any given moment is fickle enough to be disrupted by seemingly minor factors, as in the phenomenon called *priming*. Subjects are asked to memorize a list of words, thus

presumably "turning on" the left hemisphere's circuits. If asked immediately afterwards to perform some spatial task that normally yields
right-hemisphere dominance, they will often fail to show the expected
result. Instead, they will perform the spatial task with the left hemisphere, presumably using the "wrong" processing strategy. To use a
rough analogy, people seem to use the calculator which is already turned
on, rather than the one specialized for the task at hand. Obviously, the
success of lateralization tests demands control of such outside factors,
which is no simple matter.

Physiological Measures

The cerebral cortex is highly asymmetrical, even to the naked eye.
The Sylvian fissure, a deep cleft running through the cortex, rises more
sharply on the right, and is longer on the left. Its rear inner surface (called
the *planum temporale*), which includes Wernicke's area, is usually larger on the left, even in fetal brains. In fact, the human skull, the brain's
outer casing, protrudes noticeably in the left rear area, pushed out by the
bulging left hemisphere. But despite a long and heated debate in the nineteenth century about the relationship between brain size and intelligence (Broca believed a large brain meant high intelligence), no detailed
conclusions have resulted from gross measurement of brain tissue. More
subtle methods are needed to deal with the brain in physiological terms.

Scientists have learned to observe chemical and electrical activity in
different regions of the brain. Sophisticated devices for accomplishing
this include computerized axial tomography (CT or CAT) scan, positron
emission tomography (PET) scan, electroencephalogram (EEG), and measures of regional cerebral bloodflow (rCBF). Also useful is the famous
Wada test, named after its developer, Juhn Wada.

In the Wada test, the powerful barbiturate sodium amytal is injected
into the carotid artery leading to one hemisphere in patients about to
undergo brain surgery, to determine whether language is affected. When
the drug enters the language hemisphere, the patient's speech is arrested
within seconds; thus, the surgeon can be sure which hemisphere should
be protected during the operation. Yet another surgical technique
involves direct stimulation of the brain. Pioneered in the 1950s by the
surgeon Wilder Penfield, this method has recently attracted renewed
interest with the advent of improved techniques.

ARE WE ALL ALIKE?

What, the reader may ask, about *my* brain? Where do I store math,
physics, music, or for that matter, language? Can one make a reliable
guess for any individual brain as to how closely it approximates the classical model? The answer is yes—but only if you are a healthy monolin-

gual, English-speaking, right-handed, hearing, adult male who can read. Beyond this class, caution is in order: some believe that the ideal classical pattern may apply to only about one person in four. The following sections show how populations may diverge from the picture given so far.

Babies

Babies, and even unborn fetuses, have physically enlarged language areas in their left hemispheres. Behaviorally, too, the very young show signs of asymmetry: by monitoring factors such as sucking response and changed heartbeat, one can determine the responses of infants to stimuli around them. Studies using such measures have found clear lateralization for speech sounds in the left hemisphere of infant brains, as opposed to chirps or nonspeech sounds, which the babies seem to process in the right hemisphere—this exists even in preterm babies born in about the thirty-sixth week of gestation.

However, until about age ten, child aphasia cases differ markedly from adult ones. Most young children show symptoms of something like Broca's aphasia regardless of where brain injury occurs within the left hemisphere. Thus, although language may be situated on the left by age five, localization within the left hemisphere may come later; hence, the classical diagram in Figure 48.3 may be only partially spelled out in children.

The question of infant asymmetry raises interesting questions. How can a brain that has no language be "specialized" for language? What kind of processing is the infant brain doing, and how does it assign a stimulus to a given hemisphere? Research on this intriguing topic may ultimately show which prelinguistic faculties lead to the development of language in children.

Bilinguals

A child's brain may in fact be like an electronic board with only some minimal (albeit highly significant) circuits provided at the outset. The details of the remaining circuitry may be up to the user to determine—in this case, the child, whose experiences in growing up "reconfigure" the brain's circuits. If so, different people may wire their neural boards in quite different ways, provided, that is, that they stay within the bounds imposed by the initial connections (which, in this case, ensure that some variant of wiring for human language emerges, and not binary code or birdsong).

Seen via this analogy, a bilingual speaker might be like a computer buff trying to do with one central processing unit the job normally done by two. Hence, one would expect the details of his processing machinery to be quite different. In fact, for some time, it has been noted that polyglot speakers (people with more than one language) produce unexpected aphasia types, perhaps because their experiences have led to special neural patterns. In about half the reported cases of polyglot aphasia, any recovery that takes place affects both (or all) languages at the same rate. Still, many patients recover one language earlier or more perfectly than others, and about one-fourth never regain one or more of their languages.[14] Physicians cannot predict which language will be recovered first or more fully, although some generalization is possible. The language best recovered is likely to be the last one used before injury, or the best known, or the one that is heard most during the recovery period.

Some rare cases pose especially perplexing challenges. One such case reported in 1980 involved a French-Arabic bilingual nun in Morocco who had a moped accident and became severely aphasic, losing speech altogether. Four days later, she could speak a few words of Arabic, but no French. After two weeks, she could speak French again fluently, but in the space of one day, her French fluency quite disappeared. She astounded observers by being able to converse fluently only in Arabic.[15]

The occurrence of bilingual aphasia suggests quite clearly that bilinguals have more right-hemisphere linguistic activity than monolinguals. Aphasia is about five times more likely to result from right-hemisphere damage in a polyglot speaker than in a monolingual. This can only be explained if some of a bilingual's linguistic ability is stored on the right side of the brain, or at least in areas not affected by damage to the classical language areas on the left. Research involving electrical stimulation of brain sites also gives some support for differential storage of two languages in a single brain: When the brain is stimulated at a given point, a patient may have trouble naming familiar objects. For bilinguals, naming difficulties in the two languages arise from stimulation at *different* points. Furthermore, electrical stimulation disturbs a patient's ability to name things in the less proficient language over a broader range of sites, suggesting that the second or nondominant language takes up more neural space than the first language.

Finally, some believe that the right hemisphere plays a major role in second-language learning, especially in the early stages when memory for stock phrases is essential to the learner. Can the very experience of learning a second language alter cerebral patterns in unexpected ways? Some early research suggests that bilingual children think differently— more independently and more creatively—and that this may extend to nonverbal areas. The significance of such intriguing findings has yet to be fully worked out.

The fact that languages can be stored, learned, or lost in different areas of the brain suggests strongly that the neural anatomy for two languages within a single brain can be different. Unfortunately, the relationship between gross anatomy and brain function remains mysterious. At best, we can turn to another analogy: Multilingual speakers may be

---

[14] Grosjean (1982, 259).
[15] Op. cit., 260.

telling us that the cerebral cortex is like a computer in some respects—highly complex, rigid in its basic setup, yet also versatile and subject to "programming" (here, unconscious) by the user.

Speakers versus Signers

Users of American Sign Language (ASL or Ameslan) depend on manual activity, not speech, to encode basic meanings. If experience molds neural patterns, then the very nature of ASL raises some fascinating questions. Do the deaf generate and process signs in the left hemisphere? Can Broca's area, with its ability to interface with commands to the tongue and lips, also handle a system based on hand signals?

Early lateralization studies for ASL showed inconsistent results; some seemed to indicate right-hemisphere language processing, which could be explained by the visual nature of signing. Others concluded that signers had no cerebral asymmetry at all. The key may lie in the researchers' conception of signing: most early studies used static photographs to test asymmetry. But ASL signers do not communicate by flashing pictures at one another. In normal situations, signers deal with a number of dimensions at once: hand position, orientation, and crucially, movement. It makes intuitive sense to claim, as some have done, that signers in action do indeed make crucial use of the traditional left-brain language centers; we simply need more sophisticated techniques to verify this hypothesis.

Recent studies of impaired signers (see Bellugi 1983) yield important evidence for the claim that signers may process language as oral speakers do: injury to the classical language areas on the left has been found to produce strikingly similar aphasia types in ASL and oral languages.

Here, too, experience may be crucial. Deaf people whose schools used different training methods show consistently different patterns in the usual asymmetry tests. In fact, one startling finding about signers suggests that experience may be an even more potent force on the brain's map than previously suspected. Neville (1977) reported that he observed evoked potential (that is, electrical activity) in the *auditory* cortex of native signers in response to flashes of light. For oral speakers, the auditory cortex is the center, near Wernicke's area, where sound is first perceived. If Neville's claim is substantiated, the term *auditory cortex* may prove quite inappropriate for signers.

Readers, Japanese, and Others

The theme of experience leads neatly to the next point, which has implications for anyone reading this article. Where signing and multiple languages may cause a person's brain to diverge from the classical pattern, some believe that the experience of literacy may have a significant effect in *reinforcing* left-hemisphere dominance for language. Some studies report that illiterates show a much lower incidence of aphasia following left-hemisphere brain damage, and may even develop aphasia from right-hemisphere injury. If this is true, it suggests that language ability is more symmetrical in this group. Dealing with the written word may involve the left hemisphere's analytical techniques in such an intense way as to strengthen the ties between language and the left brain. This claim, however, has been controversial (it is challenged in Caplan 1987), and the aphasia data have proven difficult to confirm.

Yet another suggestion about early experience comes from Japanese. Normally, Americans tend to treat pure vowel sounds as "nonlanguage" in dichotic listening tests (sounds like "ah" and "ooooh" are likely to be interpreted as emotional utterances rather than as words). Japanese speakers, in contrast, seem to process single-vowel sounds on the left, as normal linguistic material. Professor Tadanoku Tsunoda of Tokyo's Medical and Dental University blames this on the "vowel dominant" nature of his language, which may influence the way Japanese children perceive the boundary between language and other sounds.[16]

This recalls a widely accepted claim about tone languages, based on lateralization for tone in Thai. Native speakers of Thai, who must make use of the pitch levels in a word to understand its meaning, tend to perceive tone as linguistic material. To most English speakers, the complex pitch patterns of a tone language like Thai or Vietnamese simply sound like some kind of puzzling singsong effect overlayed on speech; hence, they are likely to filter out the tone and send it off to the right hemisphere. Given this, it is not surprising that English speakers have substantial difficulty in learning tone languages!

Left-Handers and Women

Two more groups stand out as neurologically different: left-handers and women. This time, the difference obviously cannot be linked to experience: genetics must play an important role.

This history of left-handers is fraught with myths and misleading ideas. In some societies, left-handed people have been viewed as clumsy and awkward, *gauche* if not downright *sinister*, to cite two words owing their origin to French and Latin forms meaning "left." In China, India, and in Arab countries, left-handers are said to have been banned from the dinner table. To many, however, reversed hand preference is seen as a sign of eminence: Michelangelo, Benjamin Franklin, Alexander the Great, and Einstein are cited as examples.

In their widely read book *Left Brain, Right Brain*, Sally Springer and Georg Deutsch include one chapter entitled "The Puzzle of the Left-Hander." They point out that it is difficult to even identify a left-hander

---

[16] Brabyn (1982, 11).

for sure since many people use the left hand for some activities and the right for others. Even supposedly unconscious tests for handedness (e.g., how a person crosses his arms, or draws a horse in profile, etc.) invariably yield mixed results.

Springer and Deutsch go on to trace opposing claims on the cause of handedness (genetic versus environmental), and many claims of smaller scope, such as the notion that the characteristic "inverted" writing position found in some left-handers may indicate left-hemisphere language, and that this may be part of a more general pattern for detecting "like-hemisphere" language and handedness. Supporters point to one isolated right-handed "inverter" who showed right-hemisphere language dominance.

But the puzzles of handedness remain. Scientists no longer believe that the left-handed person is simply a mirror image of a right-hander, with speech on the right and spatial abilities on the left. As many as 70 percent of left-handers have a dominant left hemisphere for language, just as do right-handers. Of the rest, half are thought to have bilateral language representation, with no clearly dominant hemisphere. This leaves a mere 15 percent of left-handers with language dominant on the right. Even this picture may not be accurate; one recent study reanalyzes data from aphasia and concludes that bilateral speech representation may be more common than previously believed, perhaps occurring in as high as 40 percent of all left-handed people (cited in Segalowitz and Bryden 1983, 348).

Aphasia tends to be less severe and to last a shorter time for left-handers, and even for right-handers in families with left-handed members. Moreover, left-handed speakers are eight times more likely than right-handers to suffer from aphasia after damage to the right hemisphere only. This must mean that they store more linguistic knowledge in the non-dominant hemisphere than do right-handers. Since there is no clear evidence for bilateral speech in right-handed monolinguals, this points to handedness as a clear indication of cerebral difference.

On women, our last interesting population, in 1879 the then-eminent social psychologist Gustave LeBon wrote:

> In the most intelligent races, as among the Parisians, there are a large number of women whose brains are closer in size to those of gorillas than to the most developed male brains . . . All psychologists who have studied the intelligence of women . . . recognize that they . . . represent the most inferior form of human evolution and that they are closer to children and savages than to an adult, civilized man.[17]

LeBon, following Broca, felt that bigger meant better in cerebral terms, and thus justified his sexist views by biological argument.

None but the most irrational antifeminist would today accept LeBon's comments. But we do know that women's brains are distinctive.

---

[17] Gould (1980, 155).

For one thing, the gross physiological differences noted between the hemispheres are less obvious in women than in men. And other strong indicators of cerebral asymmetry are equally hard to confirm in women. Like left-handers, women may tend toward more asymmetrical, evenly balanced, language capacities in the two hemispheres. Again, the aphasia statistics are revealing: women are less likely than men to become aphasic from unilateral damage to the left hemisphere. This suggests that, at the very least, the right hemisphere in women can take over language functions readily if the language centers on the left become disabled. More likely, the right hemisphere in women takes a more active role in language processing even in the absence of injury.

Behavioral tests yield supporting evidence. In dichotic listening tests, men outnumber women nearly 2 to 1 in showing right-ear advantage for verbal material. In fact, some early attempts to find cerebral asymmetries seem to have failed simply because they included too many female subjects! It is clear that neurological lateralization patterns must be considered in understanding the biological distinction between the sexes. Hopefully, further research will clarify and explain these differences.

WHERE DO WE GO FROM HERE?

The human brain still shelters the fundamental mystery of our existence: what does it mean to be human? Clearly, language must be an important part of the answer, and we have come a long way from the Egyptian physicians who attributed language disorders to the "breath of an outside god."[18] As this essay shows, much progress has been made in finding the answers to an ancient and fundamental question: how does the *homo sapiens* in Figure 48.1 differ from his Australopithecine ancestors? How does this creature manage to handle such a highly complex communication system in the three pounds or so of gray matter lodged in the human skull?

To fully understand the neurology of language, researchers will have to answer the questions raised above, and many more not yet even hinted at. How is language related to other cognitive skills? What goes on behind the scenes, in the subcortical tissue beneath the language areas? It is clear that the thalamus, for instance, plays an important role in language. The complexity of the issues involved, and the way they touch on many disciplines at once, is clearly reflected in recent publications. The coming years are sure to see an ever-increasing crop of journals and books devoted to the mysteries of language, brain, and cognition.

---

[18] Arbib et al. (1982).

BIBLIOGRAPHY

Arbib, M. A., D. Caplan, and J. C. Marshall. "Neurolinguistics in Historical Perspective." In *Neural Models of Language Processes,* eds. M. Arbib, D. Caplan, and J. Marshall. New York: Academic Press, 1982.

Bellugi, U. "Language Structure and Language Breakdown in American Sign Language." In *Psychobiology of Language,* ed. M. Studdert-Kennedy. Cambridge: MIT Press, 1983.

Blumstein, S. E. "Language Dissolution in Aphasia: Evidence for Linguistic Theory." In *Exceptional Language and Linguistics,* eds. L. Obler and L. Menn. New York: Academic Press, 1982.

Brabyn, H. "Mother Tongue and the Brain." *UNESCO Courier* (February 1982), 10–13.

Brown, J. W. "Case Reports of Semantic Jargon." In J. W. Brown, ed., 1981.

———, ed. *Jargonaphasia.* New York: Academic Press, 1981.

Bryden, M. P., and F. Allard. "Visual Hemifield Differences Depend on Typeface." *Brain and Language* 3 (1976), 41–46.

Buckingham, H. "Where Do Neologisms Come From?" In J. W. Brown, ed., 1981.

Caplan, D. *Neurolinguistics and Linguistic Aphasiology: An Introduction.* New York: Cambridge University Press, 1987.

Caramazza, A., J. Gordon, E. G. Zurif, and D. De Luca. "Right Hemisphere Damage and Verbal Problem Solving Behavior." *Brain and Language* 3 (1976), 41–46.

Dennis, M. "Language Acquisition in a Single Hemisphere: Semantic Organization." In *Biological Studies of Mental Processes,* ed. D. Caplan. Cambridge: MIT Press, 1980.

Gardner, H., J. Silverman, W. Wapner, and E. Zurif. "The Appreciation of Antonymic Contrasts in Aphasia." *Brain and Language* 6 (1978), 301–317.

Goodglass, H., and L. Menn. "Is Agrammatism a Unitary Phenomenon?" In M. L. Kean, ed. 1985.

Gould, S. J. *The Panda's Thumb: More Reflections in Natural History.* New York: Norton, 1980.

Grosjean, F. *Life with Two Languages.* Cambridge: Harvard University Press, 1982.

Gur, R. C., and N. Reivich. "Cognitive Task Effects on Hemispheric Blood Flow in Humans: Evidence for Individual Differences in Hemispheric Activation." *Brain and Language* 9 (1980), 78–92.

Harth, E. *Windows on the Mind: Reflections on the Physical Basis of Consciousness.* New York: Morrow, 1982.

Kean, M.-L. "The Linguistic Interpretation of Aphasic Syndromes: Agrammatism in Broca's Aphasia, an Example." *Cognition* 5 (1977), 9–46.

———., ed. *Agrammatism.* New York: Academic Press, 1985, 1977.

Milberg, W., S. Blumstein, and B. Dworetzky. "Processing of Lexical Ambiguities in Aphasia." *Brain and Language* 31 (1987), 138–150.

Neville, H. J. "Electroencephalographic Testing of Cerebral Specialization in Normal and Congenitally Deaf Children: A Preliminary Report." In *Language Development and Neurological Theory,* eds. S. Segalowitz and F. Gruber. New York: Academic Press, 1977.

Schwartz, M., M. Linebarger, and E. Saffran. "The Status of the Syntactic Theory of Agrammatism." In ed. M.-L. Kean. 1985.

Segalowitz, S., and M. Bryden. "Individual Differences in Hemispheric Representation of Language." In *Language Functions and Brain Organization*, ed. S. Segalowitz. New York: Academic Press, 1983.

Springer, S. P., and G. Deutsch. *Left Brain, Right Brain*, rev. ed. San Francisco: W. H. Freeman and Company, 1985.

Trevarthen, C. "Development of the Cerebral Mechanisms for Language." In *Neuropsychology of Language, Reading, and Spelling*. New York: Academic Press, 1983.

Wapner, W., S. Hamby, and H. Gardner. "The Role of the Right Hemisphere in the Apprehension of Complex Linguistic Materials." *Brain and Language* 14 (1981), 15–33.

Warrington, E. K., and T. Shallice. "Semantic Access Dyslexia." *Brain* 102 (1979), 43–63.

Winner, E., and H. Gardner. "The Comprehension of Metaphor in Brain-Damaged Patients." *Brain* 100 (1977), 719–727.

Young, A. W., A. W. Ellis, and P. L. Birn. "Left Hemisphere Superiority for Pronounceable Nonwords, But Not for Unpronounceable Letter Strings." *Brain and Language* 22 (1984), 14–23.

FOR DISCUSSION AND REVIEW

1. What is the difference between Broca's area and Wernicke's area? How does each area seem to contribute to language production or understanding? How do relationships between these areas and cortical centers for sight, hearing, and motor function play an important role in Wernicke's overall model of how the brain works in terms of language?

2. Why might studies done on aphasics and split-brain subjects yield misleading information on brain lateralization?

3. Why is it difficult to clearly label a person as left- or right-handed? Do you know people who use different hands for different tasks? If so, which hand is used for which specific tasks? What pattern(s), if any, can you suggest?

4. Divide the following activities into two columns (left and right), according to which hemisphere you think is likely to be dominant for performing each. In cases where you are unsure, explain the aspects of the task that led you to list it tentatively on one side rather than the other:

   a. distinguishing between the syllables *ba* and *pa*
   b. choosing the right answer in a multiplication problem
   c. defining the word *independence*
   d. recognizing a friend's face
   e. singing the "Star Spangled Banner"
   f. deciding whether your employer is in a good mood
   g. recognizing the string of letters *ZBQ*

    h. playing the guitar

    i. recognizing a grasshopper's chirp

    j. understanding the utterance: "The girl was bitten by the dog."

    k. finding a word to rhyme with *inch*

5. There is some uncertainty about how blind people process Braille characters. In tests, it seems that subjects with good vision, when they first encounter the raised characters, can make them out best with the left hand. But it is very difficult to get clear-cut results for experienced Braille readers. How do you explain this? How might this situation be comparable to how trained and untrained people process music? What is the relationship to Heny's discussion of sign language? How would nonsigners be likely to process signs?

6. Would you expect a measure of electrical impulses from the brain of a sleeping person during an active dreaming session to reveal left- or right-hemispheric activity? Why? What kind of mental activity seems to be going on when a person dreams?

7. How do dichotic listening and tachistoscopic tests work? If a subject sees or hears more accurately on the left, which cerebral hemisphere must be involved? Why?

8. In general terms, how do women and left-handers seem to differ from other individuals in terms of brain asymmetry?

9. Suppose you constructed an experiment in which you asked people to choose a picture that matches the sentence: "He's really gotten himself into a nice pickle now!" Their choices include illustrations of:

    a. A man who has just dug his way into a giant pickle.

    b. A man with a bewildered look on his face standing near a disabled car on an isolated road. His clothes are covered with grease, and strewn around him on the ground are what appear to be the parts of his engine.

    c. A man sitting in an armchair reading a book.

10. What performance would you expect on this test from each of the following groups, and why?

    a. Broca's aphasics

    b. Wernicke's aphasics

    c. right-hemisphere–damaged patients

    d. normal "control" subjects

49

Signals, Signs, and Words: From Animal Communication to Language

William Kemp and Roy Smith

For many years, and for many reasons, human beings have studied a variety of animal communication systems. Just as the possibility of life somewhere in space has long fascinated people, so too has the possibility of finding that some animal here on earth can learn a form of language. People have studied "talking" horses, dolphins, bees, whales, monkeys, and chimpanzees, all in an effort to discover if only humans possess language. Other researchers, especially ethologists, have studied animal communication systems because of their intrinsic interest and because such study helps us to understand both the similarities and differences between animal communication and human language. This research has revealed a great deal about the complexity of animal communication systems; it has also shown that human beings "share with other species an impressive degree of nonlingual communication." In the following selection, Professors William Kemp and Roy Smith, both of Mary Washington College, survey the research on animal communication. They explain the difficulties of such research, as well as its importance. They also describe the elaborate communication systems of bees, birds, and mammals, especially the nonhuman primates. Discussing the extensive work with chimpanzees and gorillas that was done in the 1970s, 1980s, and 1990s, they argue convincingly that these experiments have demonstrated that apes can learn to use semantically a large number of arbitrary symbols. That achievement is more than the most hostile critics will allow. But it is also considerably less than human semantic abilities.

> The sound of the waterfall
> has for a long time
> ceased,
> yet with its name
> we can hear it still.
> –FUJIWARO NO KINTO, d. 1041

Haiku is human language at its peak: stunning images from a few carefully chosen syllables. Despite claims for remarkable communication and even language among the many animals around us, no one has offered an example of haiku by a humpback whale or a chimpanzee. This is not to say that animals do not communicate effectively; they certainly do. Still, most humans use language as something qualitatively different from other forms of communication, at least some of the time.

Because language is so important to the experience of being human, most who study language reserve to humans the ability to use and understand language. As a result, the possibility of animal language has become a challenge to our unique position in the natural world. But evolutionary theory, the organizing framework of the biological and social sciences, warns that we must examine any behavior in its context. Behaviors develop from the interaction over many generations of subtle and not-so-subtle alterations in the physical and physiological conformation of an organism. If these changes allow their bearers to develop behaviors to exploit better the world they live in, they are more fit than other individuals and reproduce more successfully. The new behaviors then become the baseline for further changes. These adaptive changes cumulatively alter the nature of a group of organisms and the way it fits into the environment.

Given the essential dependence of human personal, social, and cultural experience on language, its mastery clearly changes the way we deal with our world. And most linguists agree that language is based on just the sorts of inherited physical capacities that an evolutionary understanding of language requires. But then where are the precursors of human language? Can we recognize in the communication systems of other animals analogies to the pieces that gave birth to human language? Do other animals have communication systems with characteristics parallel to our own? Are there examples of animal language?

An easy answer might be that humans use language to communicate while nonhumans use animal signaling. Unfortunately, this view implies that a loving glance from your mother is part of language while a loving glance from your dog is not. Humans use language layered atop other forms of communication, such as body language, and the nonlanguage signals often contain the more important messages. At the very least, we share with other species an impressive degree of nonlingual communication. Examining animal communication reveals important ways in which language differs from communication in other animals. It also suggests that language is not an aberration that appeared suddenly, without evolutionary precursors.

Ethologists treat animal communication under three headings. The first is *form*. For an animal's behavior to have value as a signal, it must be in a constant form that others can recognize and connect reliably to some future behavior by the signaler. Ethologists call such stereotyped behavior a *display*. The second part of animal communication is *context*; it includes the general environment in which an animal is displaying as well as simultaneous displays it sends through sensory modes or channels. Thus, a dog's bark may convey one message about future behavior when its tail is wagging, another when its tail is stiff. Context usually resolves such ambiguities. The third part of animal communication is the *response* to the signal. Communication is valuable because it increases the likelihood of one animal's choosing behavior that fits with the behavior of others. The choice by the receiving animal must be clear to be sure it has actually communicated. Otherwise, we can't tell the difference between ruffling feathers to get them straight and ruffling feathers to signal an impending conflict.

Consider one of the elaborate prairie dog cities on the western plains. Alarm calls announce a stranger's approach and send nearby animals scurrying to holes from which they cautiously peer. Can there be any doubt that sentries are telling their comrades about the intruder? Patient observation and careful analysis suggest that this alarm, like other prairie-dog vocalizations, is a display. Prairie dogs apparently give this signal whenever they become aroused enough to stop what they are doing and scan the environment, but not scared enough to run for cover immediately. They give the same call during territorial disputes when the caller is unsure whether to attack or retreat. Other prairie dogs, upset by the signaler, give their own version of the display, spreading agitation through the colony. The alarm system works very effectively; knowing that your neighbor is aroused is important. But the prairie dog's display contains information about the caller, not about the source of the alarm. Each prairie dog must sit up and look for himself.

Distinctive behavior that reliably indicates what an animal will do promotes cooperation and reduces conflict, because it allows neighbors to adjust their actions according to what the display predicts. Few animals seriously injure one another in disputes over territory, food, or mates, because displays allow rivals to establish which one is dominant without resorting to combat. Crudely put, the meaning of an agonistic display is, "I feel like attacking you ferociously very soon." The individual whose display is more convincing usually wins. We need not imagine animals computing the combat odds or planning their displays. Sending and comprehending displays are parts of each animal's (and human's) automatic behavior. In human interactions, smiling usually elicits a responding smile and a frown prompts a frown, without any planning by anyone.

In discussing human language, linguists use concepts similar to the ethologist's form, context, and response. Linguists work with *syntax*, which emphasizes form; *semantics*, which emphasizes meaning (defined partly by context); and *pragmatics*, which emphasizes how context modifies or replaces the meaning of an utterance. Linguists also analyze human speech into meaning units called *morphemes* and sound units called *phonemes*—units that seem unique to spoken language. But particular manifestations of phonemes (called *allophones*) share with displays an invariant surface form guided by a stable program in the central nervous system. Both allophones and displays are examples of unvarying sets of motor movements that ethologists call *fixed action patterns*.

As displays become language, several things change. The form of communication shifts from a limited number of lengthy, stereotyped displays to a very large number of very short displays (allophones) that can be combined in many ways according to hierarchical rules. The importance of context also changes. Displays begin as indications of an animal's response to its environment; they are more about the animal itself than about the world. In contrast, humans frequently use language to describe environment(s), while their displays signal much of the accompanying affective content. Although the context of a sentence usually colors its meaning, the sentence has meaning independent of context. Displays have only contextual meaning.

While the response to a display is how we know its meaning, the response of others to language may be unimportant. Although Fujiwaro wrote his haiku for others to read, and probably would be delighted to know that people appreciate it nine hundred years after his death, he must have written it partly or perhaps chiefly for the delight of capturing his experience in words. We have no clear evidence that nonhumans play with their communication systems simply to revel in the workings of the system itself.

Language is also capable of abstraction, a power that seems to have few natural parallels in animal communication. Of course, many animals can create general concepts; some dogs understand that *all* cars are to be chased. And some higher primates, having learned artificial sign systems from humans, clearly use and understand some abstract signs. But even in the cleverest animals, natural displays have no way of presenting abstract propositions about either the animal or its world. The human abilities conferred by language to plan for the future and control our environment are without parallel in other species. Language is far removed from the simple fixed action patterns of affective displays. A hierarchy of rule systems, from phonetics to semantics, transforms language from a set of environmental responses to a self-contained, generative symbol system operating simultaneously on several independently structured levels. Thus our thoughts are at least partly dissociated from our feelings.

Despite clear differences, animal communication systems have a lot to tell us about language. For one thing, displays have evolved in every species out of environmental demands and adaptations to meet those demands. The more carefully we study how other animals exchange signals, the more clearly we see how closely communication systems connect to other elements of behavior. We also find that many creatures are a good deal more clever than we suppose.

For example, we usually regard insects as just barely sentient, doing their business by instinct and incapable of significant mental activity, yet we marvel at the architectural achievements of social insects (ants, bees, termites, and wasps). In fact, the architecture of a termite mound or an ant nest is genetically designed. Each insect responds to the chemical and tactile signals around it with a set of fixed action patterns programmed into its simple brain. In a real sense no member of this miniature corps of engineers has any plan at all; the genetic repository of the whole community contains the blueprint for building the nest, and for other activity besides. More marvelous still are the systems of communication by which social insects manage their collective lives, using emitted chemicals (called *pheromones*), sound, and physical activity to exchange information and coordinate their behavior.

The best understood insect communication system is the dance of the honeybee (*Apis mellifera*). Humans have been interested for centuries in honeybees, but until the 1920s no one noticed that bees returning from a successful foray convey to hivemates important information, which concentrates hive activity on the best sources of nectar. In 1919 Karl von Frisch set out to discover how hundreds of foraging bees could arrive as if by magic at a rich food source recently discovered by a single bee. The result of his experiment was striking:

> I attracted a few bees to a dish of sugar water, marked them with red paint and then stopped feeding for a while. As soon as all was quiet, I filled the dish again and watched a scout which had drunk from it . . . after her return to the hive. I could scarcely believe my eyes. She performed a round dance on the honeycomb which greatly excited the marked foragers around her and caused them to fly back to the feeding place.
>
> (von Frisch 1967, 72–73)

In a series of elegant experiments over the next twenty years, von Frisch established that the round dance conveys three pieces of information: the presence of a food source, its richness, and the type of food available (see Figure 49.1). The scent clinging to the dancer's body, along with droplets of nectar regurgitated from her honey stomach, tell nearby bees of her find. If she dances vigorously, other recruits follow her dance, then promptly leave the hive and search busily for the odors she carries, completely ignoring all other food sources. They may also be guided by a "Here it is!" pheromone the scout releases as she visits the source a second time. Returning to the hive, the recruits will also dance vigorously and spread the odor. Soon, hundreds of hivemates will be exploiting the recently discovered trove.

In 1944 von Frisch began exploring how honeybees deal with food sources far from their hive. He discovered that bees use a "tail-wagging" dance to communicate the distance and direction of remote food sources (see Figure 49.2). "In the tail-wagging dance," he reported (1967), "they run in a straight line wagging their abdomen to and fro, then return to the starting point in a semicircle, repeat the tail-wagging run, return in a semicircle on the other side, and so on." Bees responding to this dance would completely ignore food sources near the hive—even those with identical odors—in their flight to the distant goal.

Von Frisch also discovered that the tail-wagging dance tells the recruit bees which direction to fly and how far to go before starting their search. The scout bee does her dance on a vertical comb inside the dark hive. The angle between an imaginary vertical line running up the comb

FIGURE 49.1   Round dance.

surface and the tail-wagging run of her dance corresponds to the angle between the sun and the food source (see Figure 49.3). So if the food source is twenty degrees to the left or right of the sun as seen from the opening of the hive, her waggle run will be offset twenty degrees to the left or right of the vertical. If the food source is directly away from the sun, she will start at the top of the comb, dancing straight down, and so on. Later experiments established that this directional information is extremely accurate. In a typical trial lasting fifty minutes, 42 of 54 bees (78%) found the target food source, 7 missed by an angle of fifteen degrees to the right or left, 4 by thirty degrees, and 1 directionally challenged bee by forty-five degrees. The scout bees also compensate for detours, directing hivemates to fly straight toward the goal. Having reasonably accurate internal clocks, they can even adjust their waggle dance for the sun's movement across the sky. While the angle of the waggle run indicates the direction of the goal, its tempo indicates the distance; the farther the source, the more waggle runs the dancer makes per unit of time.

Not all honeybees use exactly the same set of dances. Von Frisch's students have established that different honeybee strains set the boundaries between the round and tail-wagging dances at different distances, and encode like distances by different tempos. For example, Italian bees (*Apis m. ligustica*) dance slower for any given distance than did von Frisch's Austrian bees (*Apis m. carnica*). When Boch, a student of von Frisch, put both kinds of bees into one hive, miscommunication ran ram-

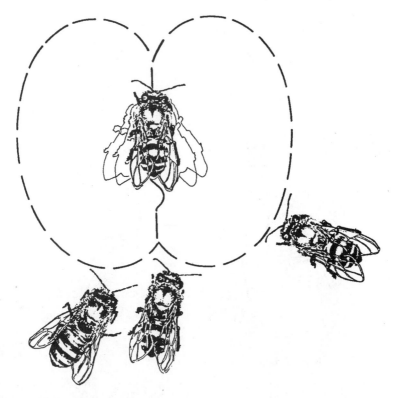

FIGURE 49.2   Tail-wagging dance.

pant. In response to Italian bees, the Austrians flew too far; in response to the Austrian scouts, Italians did not fly far enough. One can accurately say that the bee "language" has genetic dialects.

But is the bee dance really language? It certainly conveys information in an arbitrary code about parts of the world outside the bee herself and remote from where she dances. The dance thus satisfies several of the design features by which Hockett and Altmann (see page 64) attempted to distinguish between animal communication and human language. But von Frisch himself found significant limits to the bee's communication system. He put a hive beneath a radio tower, placed a very rich sugar-water solution high up in the tower, and showed several scouts where it was. After they returned to the hive and danced heroically, their mates searched busily all around the hive—but not up the tower. Evolved for foraging across horizontal landscapes, the powerful communication system of honeybees has no way of indicating up or down. Unlike human language, bee displays are not productive; they do not recombine bits of the code to produce novel messages. Bee messages are essentially the same message, differing only in a few details, uttered almost mechanically, over and over again in response to a narrow band of stimuli. This rigidity prevents the bees in mixed hives from learning each others' dialects, despite repeated attempts to communicate.

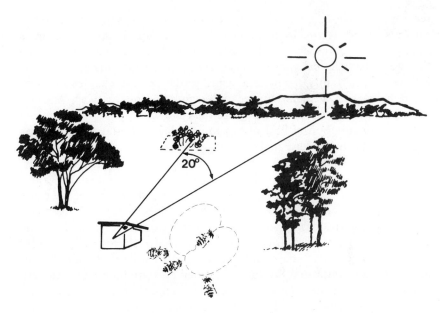

Figure 49.3   Angle of wagging dance showing the sun's position.

Because birds are larger than bees and interact over longer distances, one might suppose they use even more complicated communication systems. Their behavior certainly seems more varied than that of insects, and more vocal. Calls and songs are embedded in a rich context of elaborate visual displays. Their messages to mates, rivals, or neighbors arise from a coordinated package of activities, not any single element within the package. Still, to linguists the sounds birds make are the most interesting part of their behavior because, like humans, birds are physiologically and behaviorally specialized to produce and respond to streams of meaningful sound.

Ornithologists divide bird vocalizations into two categories: *calls* and *songs*. Calls tend to be brief, simple in structure, and confined to a particular context. As a result, some calls elicit sharp reactions from nearly every bird hearing them. The contrasting *alarm* and *mobbing* calls that many birds produce when they spot a predator are often shared across species; many birds make similar acoustic distinctions between the two calls. Alarms, given when the predator is airborne and thus able to strike promptly, have acoustic properties that make it difficult for the predator to find the bird emitting them. In contrast, mobbing calls, which summon neighbors to attack a stationary predator, have acoustic features that make the sound easy to locate, so that every bird responding will know where to attack. The survival value of differing calls is obvious.

But only a predator, rival, or prospective mate shows interest in the information contained in birdsong. Song is usually loud, sustained, complex in structure, seasonal, confined to males, and prompted by mating or territorial concerns. Some species, of course, sing no songs at all, using calls instead for territorial and breeding information; in strictest terms a song is simply an especially elaborate call. Still, the distinction between the two has a practical value to us because song seems musical to us and calls do not. Certainly, if a male songbird is to breed, he must learn to sing the right tune: it attracts females and keeps rival males away. And if a female is to breed, she must recognize the tune of an appropriate male.

A major function of birdsong is to establish and maintain breeding territories. Each resident male spends much of his time patrolling his boundaries and declaring his presence in song. The "message" of the song indicates the singer's probable behavior. Roughly translated, a territorial song says that the singer will attack any adult male of the same species who enters his territory. But as the singer's probable behavior changes across the spring, so does the meaning of the song. Early in the season, when pairs are still forming, a male chaffinch (*Fringilla coelebs*) will not attack adult females entering his territory. At that time of year, his song is all invitation. But later on, when eggs are incubating, he will attack strange females. The song does not change, but its meaning does. Other birds know the meaning from the time of year.

Of even greater interest to linguists than the purpose of birdsong is that they learn to repeat sometimes long and complex songs with great precision. In fact, most do not *learn* their songs in the strict meaning of the word. Only four of the twenty-nine avian orders have complex song repertoires or dialects and clearly must acquire their songs after birth. In the other twenty-five orders, the appropriate calls or songs appear to be part of each bird's genetic heritage.

Even within the largest family of songbirds, learning strategies differ sharply from one species to the next. Young song sparrows (*Melospiza melodia*), for example, must hear themselves sing to produce their full repertoire; song sparrows deafened when young fail to develop normal song, unlike individuals merely isolated when young. In contrast, young finches of several species learn the song of the adult male who helps care for them, even if he is of another species. White-crowned sparrows (*Zonotrichia leucophyrs*) and chaffinches must hear adults of their own species sing during the first spring of their lives; white-crowned sparrows raised in isolation until their second spring never perform properly, even after hearing adult song. In such species, it appears that each male is born with a generalized template for his species song. The length and timing of his critical learning period differ according to species, but the pattern is similar. The point of crystallization, when the template has become rich enough to support full adult song during the coming year, varies with the species, but the necessity of a passive learning period does not. This template is analogous to Chomsky's hypothesis of a genetic template supporting universal grammar in humans.

Although genetics establishes dialects of bees, learning appears to produce regional dialects in birds, as it does in human speech. In many species, birds of one area develop shared variations of the species song.

These variations persist for several generations at least, and are clearly differences in learning rather than in the genetic template; fledglings from one area transported to another sing the new dialect, not that of their parents.

Because birds are more like humans than bees, are they closer in communicative ability as well? Probably not. Insect communication and behavior are in many ways as complex as our own. The impressive achievements of insect communities depend on reliable communication systems to coordinate the behavior of thousands, even millions. In contrast, bird vocalizations seem ambiguous. It may even be useful to see birdsong as a simpler form of communication than either the stereotyped, meaning-packed movements and chemical signals of bees or the more variable multichannel displays of some mammals.

But the complexity and variability of mammalian signaling may disguise the rather limited range of subjects of their signal. If most mammals communicate about the same limited set of subjects, and if those subjects are part of an environment shared by humans, it is not surprising that humans understand their mammalian pets—or that the pets appear to understand humans.

Four activities account for almost all the displays of mammals: mating, rearing young, resolving conflict, and maintaining group organization. In many species, from insects to birds, elaborate courtship rituals supplement the basic chemical signals of sexual readiness. Still, the rituals give only redundant information about the sexual condition and identity of the displaying animal. Mammals are no different, although their sexual displays are rather ordinary compared to the courtship of other animals. In contrast, the other three display categories show extensive expansion, reflecting specific mammalian adaptations.

Communication between mother and offspring is unimportant in sea turtles, which abandon their newly laid eggs and return to the sea. Even birds, many of which are good and faithful parents, communicate with their young through a simple set of calls and several kinds of specialized physical contact until the young are ready to fly. Then the fledgling is on its own to find food, avoid predators, and maybe migrate. Young turtles are genetically programmed to run for the sea as soon as they hatch. In ways we do not fully understand, migratory birds are programmed to find their way accurately across immense distances. Neither turtles nor birds learn much from their parents. So it is hardly surprising that all turtles and most birds produce multiple offspring as insurance that the species will continue. Although the casualty rate may be high, some offspring are bound to survive and keep the species going.

In contrast, most mammalian parents invest a remarkable amount of energy and time in a few offspring. Maternal care over a long period involves elaborate and sustained interaction between mothers and their young. The displays guiding this interaction are no more complex than those controlling mating. In fact, to a casual human observer they may not seem to be displays at all, because we behave very similarly in caring for our own infants: feeding, cleaning, restraining, warning, punishing, and petting.

Still, the fundamental feature of animal communication persists in even the most social mammals: the value of displays does not depend on a desire to tell another animal something. And even the most highly social mammals send messages with great redundancy. Such redundancy, together with a fairly limited number of messages, perhaps only a couple of dozen, is important because it means that pulling one sensory channel from the display for some other purpose need not seriously disrupt the message. In developing language, humans appear to have reserved the acoustic channel for complex spoken language. But the original display system still functions in human behavior, as the expanding literature on kinesics testifies.

Representatives of another group of mammals, the cetaceans, have also adapted the auditory channel for special communication. Water as a medium for chemical, visual, or acoustic signals is considerably different from air. Because a liquid veil shields the individual and social lives of water-based vertebrates from casual observation, we lack much of the behavioral context to understand their communication systems. For years scientists studied the sonar signals of dolphins as a model for artificial sonar systems. Various explanations for dolphin sonar have included stunning or killing prey, forming acoustic images of their surroundings, identifying individuals, and, according to one author, deliberately communicating with each other and with humans. A decade of intensive work with captive dolphins showed both the refinement of dolphin sonar and the flexibility with which the animals apply it to solving problems. Early behavioral studies using trained animals also suggested that dolphin problem-solving ability stems from a high level of intelligence but failed to find a useful way of measuring their cognitive skills.

More recently, Louis Herman and his colleagues have shown that dolphins are capable of responding to unique sequences of learned signals that identify various objects and actions; his subjects can execute accurately an interesting range of instructions. While the resulting claims for dolphin syntax and sentence comprehension are based on linguistically questionable definitions, this carefully described work illustrates again the remarkable cognitive capacities of the animals.

The humpback whales, another group of cetaceans (*Megaptera novaeangliae*), have been extensively studied in their breeding grounds off Hawaii and Baja California, and in their Alaskan hunting grounds. The animals seem to live in social aggregations without discernible structure. During their summer feeding season off Alaska, stable groups (most often chiefly female) sometimes hunt together in clearly coordinated ways, and even in the same areas from one year to the next. But during the winter breeding season, when the animals do little if any hunting, the only stable social groups are pairs of cows and calves, often followed by an interested adult male or three.

Like other cetaceans, humpback whales make a variety of sounds, but they are famous for singing. (Shortly after the discovery of this behavior in the 1960s, an album of whale songs was briefly popular.) In several ways whale and birdsongs are similar: males do the singing only during the breeding season, and the whale song is learned. Each song consists of several discrete *themes*, usually sung in the same sequence. The themes in turn contain *phrases*, the phrases contain *subphrases*, and the subphrases contain *units*. Complex birdsong can be analyzed using the same concepts. Whale song is also dialectical; Atlantic and Pacific humpbacks sing clearly different songs.

The most interesting feature of whale song is that within a given breeding population it changes rapidly over time. Analyzing the singing of Pacific whales for two breeding seasons, Payne, Tyack, and Payne (1983) found "dramatic monthly evolution following set rules of change. Substitution, omission, and addition occur at different rates in different times, but at any one time all songs are similar." We know almost nothing about what constitutes "good" whale singing; since no one has been able to identify the offspring of any male humpback, we cannot correlate a specific performance of a whale song with success at breeding. But it appears that a singing male must do two things simultaneously: produce the complex song and listen to the songs of his competitors. Nothing else can explain the fact that although the song changes steadily, nearly all males sing the same song all the time. The acoustic transactions among humpback whales exemplify a special kind of reciprocity in which the singing of each animal simultaneously shapes and is shaped by the singing of his neighbors.

Unfortunately, we do not know the meaning of this behavior. Since nearly all males seem to be singing the same song, females may choose mates on the basis of their troubadorial gifts. Possibly the songs are addressed entirely to other males as a way of spacing out individuals in the breeding territory. Given our ignorance about how aquatic creatures spend their time, we might construct several models to explain whale singing, based on the behavior of various land creatures.

To understand the basis of human language in animal communication, it seems wise to study our closest surviving biological relatives, the other primates. Although the similarities hold obvious promise for advancing understanding of humans, they make valid, objective research with primates difficult. Anne Premack writes:

> Aside from a human baby, I can think of no creature which can arouse stronger feelings of tenderness than an infant chimpanzee. It has huge round eyes and a delicate head and is far more alert than a human infant of the same age. When you pick up a young chimp, it encircles your body with its long, trembling arms and legs, and the effect is devastating—you want to take it home! (1967, 17).

Early studies, some using human infants as controls, investigated whether raising chimpanzees in a completely human environment (*cross-fostering*) would produce humanlike behavior, including spoken language. Although the chimps learned rapidly to respond to a variety of spoken commands, none acquired speech or even clearly intelligible word sounds. This result is hardly surprising; other primates do not share the subtle genetic adaptations of the human vocal track that enable speech. So, beginning in the mid sixties, several research teams began exploring other means of communicating with the animals.

Although these studies used different methodologies, they had two important goals in common. First, they focused on teaching the animals to produce symbols. Whether making signs, placing plastic tokens, or pushing computer keys, the animals were to create recognizable utterances to obtain reinforcement from their human trainers. Second, researchers hoped that the animals would produce strings of signs that would show meaning not only in the individual symbols but also in the order of the signs. Linguists have always emphasized the importance of syntax in human language, and sequence, or word order, is certainly important in the grammars of many languages—including English, the native language of these researchers. So ape language projects followed the lead of linguists.

Allen and Beatrice Gardner (1969) chose American Sign Language (ASL) and began teaching it to a female chimp whom they named Washoe. ASL is a complex, flexible system of hand signs developed for the deaf. A language in its own right rather than a facsimile of English, ASL uses the shape of the hand(s), their relative position, and their movement to convey ideas. Since home-raised chimps had shown excellent motor control at an earlier age than human infants, the Gardners felt confident that chimps could master ASL. Certain that a chimpanzee could readily learn arbitrary signs to obtain food, drink, and other things, they set a larger goal: "We wanted Washoe not only to ask for objects but to answer questions about them and also to ask us questions. We wanted to develop behavior that could be described as conversation" (Gardner and Gardner 1969). Just under two years into the project, Washoe had acquired 34 signs. By the end of the third year, she knew 85 signs. Her mature vocabulary reached approximately 180 signs (see Figure 49.4).

In later years the Gardners acquired other animals and offered them similar training, with similar results. Changes in funding transported this small colony of signing chimpanzees from Nevada to the University of Oklahoma for several years and finally to Central Washington University, where Roger Fouts, who began working with the animals as a graduate student of the Gardners, presides over a number of chimps living in a laboratory approximation of a social group. In the seventies, Herbert Terrace directed a Gardner-like program with one animal, Nim Chimsky. Penny Patterson carries on a similar project with two gorillas, Koko and Michael, and Lynn Miles did similar work with an orangutan named Chantek.

FIGURE 49.4 Washoe signing "tickle."

Not all investigators used adaptations of ASL. Even before the Gardners' first reports, Anne and David Premack (1983) had begun training a chimp named Sarah to answer simple questions using plastic tokens affixed to a sticky board, and their first publications nearly coincided with the Gardners'. Sarah's tokens were completely arbitrary shapes and colors (a blue triangle meant "apple," for instance), and the Premacks gave her very elaborate, step-by-step training in both definitions and sequence of tokens within a statement (see Figure 49.5).

Inspired by both the Gardners and the Premacks, Duane Rumbaugh developed an arbitrary language called Yerkish (after the Yerkes Primate Center in Atlanta) to communicate first with a female chimp named Lana, then with two males named Sherman and Austin. Its symbols, called lexigrams, are arbitrary designs displayed on the backlit keys of a large computer-controlled keyboard (see Figure 49.6). They are moved randomly from key to key so the animals will learn to select the designs rather than locations on the board. The lexigrams of the current message appear on a screen above the board, and the computer records all input.

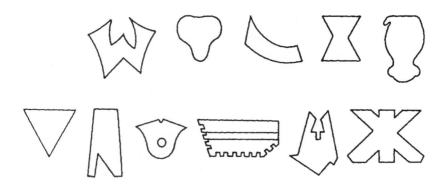

FIGURE 49.5   Sarah's symbols.

The Gardners themselves no longer work with chimps. The Premacks' project continued, focusing on the cognitive rather than linguistic abilities of their animals. Rumbaugh and his wife Sue Savage-Rumbaugh have extended their lexigram system to work with profoundly retarded humans and with bonobos, another species of ape. Fouts and Patterson continue their ASL research programs. Fouts has given Washoe an adopted son, Loulis, and studies the transfer of signing from one generation to the next.

Through the seventies and eighties, these projects attracted some popular attention—Washoe, for example, appeared in two different programs of the PBS science series *NOVA*. The projects also provoked considerable controversy about methodology, the nature of the animals' capabilities, and what it means to be "human." Thirty years ago, humans were often defined as "the tool-making animal." But then Jane Goodall (1986) and other field scientists demonstrated that wild chimpanzees make and use a variety of tools, which constitutes a kind of protoculture for particular groups of animals. Not all groups make or use the same tools, and within a given group toolmaking and use are passed from one generation to the next. By the early seventies, only language conspicuously separated humans from other higher primates. However, the images of Washoe, Sarah, and Lana apparently engaging in communicative transactions with humans through arbitrary symbolic signs called into question even that distinction. No one denied that the animals were performing arbitrary and "unnatural" behavior. At issue was the mean-

FIGURE 49.6   Yerkish: sample lexigrams.

ing of that behavior. What was going on in the animals' minds? Was it language? Was it a kind of protolanguage, which could give a shadowy glimpse into our own evolutionary past? Or were the primate communication researchers overinterpreting their data? Criticism took two main forms: attacks on the accuracy of data, and alternative analyses of what the accumulating data means.

The most severe critics charged that the researchers were either dishonest or unable to avoid providing behavioral cues to their animals, which could explain away any instance of symbol use. Led by Thomas Sebeok, these critics campaigned to discredit all the ape language projects and deny funding to the investigators. Interestingly, even the first studies by the Gardners had used a standard technique to avoid just the sort of cuing their critics attributed to them. They used the double-blind design developed by social psychologists to control the influence of extraneous information on the behavior of human subjects in experiments.

In a double-blind design, no one in the direct contact with the subjects knows which experimental condition is in effect at any time. Consider, for example, a study to test for the effects of hypnosis on suggestibility. The chief experimenter decides on the design of the experiment but does not interact with the subjects. In turn, the hypnotist, having been told perhaps that the experiment is about pain perception, is blind to the hypotheses, so neither the hypnotized nor the control subjects can gather relevant cues from the person they actually work with. The experimenter gathering data, not knowing which of the subjects have been hypnotized and which are in the control group, is blind to the experimental manipulation and cannot provide distorting cues either.

The Gardners early established a reliable double-blind system for testing Washoe's vocabulary. They report that in a typical double-blind testing session Washoe correctly named 91 or 92 of 128 items. The obvious meaning of these experiments, confirmed by the Premacks and Rumbaughs using different symbol systems, is that chimpanzees can learn to use arbitrary signs within the problem/reward structure of a behavioral experiment. The animals earned their treats honestly, by learning the symbols the experimenters asked them to learn.

Still, critics have rejected the significance of this achievement, offering a limited interpretation of the data: that the animals are simply using a learned maneuver—whether making a gesture, selecting a plastic token, or punching a computer key—to get something they want. The claim, in other words, is that the animals are not performing a cognitive function even vaguely analogous to naming familiar objects and actions; they are simply doing tricks for reward, just as a pet mynah bird will say "come in" when it hears a knock on the door. This area of controversy developed into a discussion of whether strings of symbols produced by the animals constitute syntax. To demonstrate the point, pigeons were trained to peck four colors in rigid sequence to obtain food. Labeling the four colors with words to produce English sentences like "please give me corn," "start give corn stop," or "dammit, where's the corn" does not mean that pigeons have learned language. The "messages" they produce are artifacts of the experimental apparatus, not constructions of the pigeons' minds. Although the process is laborious, careful conditioning of sequenced responses can produce such behavior in a variety of animals.

In the late eighties, Sue Savage-Rumbaugh realized that a fundamental feature in the design of all the projects had simultaneously fed the controversy and made it unresolvable: all projects had concentrated on training animals to produce signs, using their comprehension of signs only as evidence of reliable mastery of production. This emphasis gave all the projects similar features:

- long training periods before significant results appeared
- communicative transactions that interested the experimenters more than the animals

Emphasis on positive reinforcement—getting a treat for the right answer—meant that critics could always claim the animals were simply doing tricks to get rewards. Transactions interesting chiefly to the experimenters meant that the animals sometimes performed erratically, throwing the reliability of their mastery into question. It also meant that the animals' interests were not the focus of using signs.

Benefitting from the results and problems of earlier ape studies, Savage-Rumbaugh has carefully built a program of research into the basic language capacities of chimps and their cousins, bonobos. These two species certainly are the most closely related to humans genetically, and an evolutionary understanding of human nature suggests studying them for insight into the underpinnings of human language. Based on work in parallel programs for encouraging language development in apes and mentally retarded individuals, Savage-Rumbaugh has presented important and challenging results on just how both groups acquire the use of signs.

Starting with the program for teaching Lana to use Yerkish for acquiring rewards, Savage-Rumbaugh began a series of experiments with Sherman and Austin designed to make symbolic communication functional for them as well as for her. In one experiment, for example, she required Sherman and Austin to exchange information through lexigrams so they could use appropriate tools to extricate food from various containers. The animals were placed in different rooms, and one was allowed to watch a human put food into one of six kinds of container. After the human left, whichever animal knew where the food was hidden could use the keyboard to ask his comrade for the appropriate tool. If they completed the transaction successfully, they could share the prize. Allowed to use lexigrams, each would readily ask for or provide the appropriate tool; deprived of lexigrams, each would present the available tools in random order, or persistently offer the same tool. Having or not having access to the arbitrary symbols of Yerkish completely changed how they solved their problem. Having reframed the problem to be studied from production of syntactic utterances to comprehension of symbols for objects of value and use to a chimp, Savage-Rumbaugh clearly demonstrated that chimps and bonobos both possess cognitive capacities to comprehend and use arbitrary symbols for communication.

This new orientation, combined with access to another species of ape, has led to the most interesting results from ape language research. Kanzi, a bonobo raised from infancy in a symbol-rich environment, spontaneously acquired a small set of symbols. Constantly present in tutoring sessions with his mother, the young bonobo was never the focus of training; he acquired his first symbols through observation, much as a young human learns early words through constant exposure and observation. Kanzi's ability became obvious only when he started using the Yerkish keyboards to get desired objects (food or toys) and initiate desired play activities. Thereafter, Kanzi learned a large set of symbols quite rapidly.

Savage-Rumbaugh has shown convincingly that after intensive language exposure Kanzi can also understand spoken words and has the ability to respond to at least some aspects of word order. As she notes: "Such an ape can also understand the intentions of others as expressed through language, though the nonlinguistic expression of intent must match the linguistic one or the words will be ignored" (1994, xi–xii). Analysis by a developmental linguist, Patricia Greenfield, suggests that Kanzi may well be using Yerkish lexigram combinations in a systematic way—one similar to the simple grammar that governs the two-word stage in young humans. Further, the replication of these results with two other bonobos and a common chimpanzee imply that this basic ability is generally available to both species, though bonobos seem more proficient at this kind of learning.

These results justify Savage-Rumbaugh's shift in experimental focus from production to comprehension. Certainly neither Kanzi nor any other ape has *produced* utterances or sign strings that match the complexities of human grammar. And although Kanzi responds appropriately to requests, commands, and even embedded identifiers, verb modifiers and conditionals leave him completely confused. Still, the basic ability to comprehend ordered symbol strings and extract the information about the world they convey appears in nonhuman as well as human primates. Chimps, bonobos, and possibly gorillas and orangutans have the basic cognitive ability that humans use in language comprehension. The unique ability is the control humans exert over modified vocal, breathing, and swallowing structures.

Although primate studies have not uncovered systems that closely parallel human language, they have certainly provided insight into the variety of ways that animals exchange meaningful and useful information about their environments and their actions and intentions in relation to them. Attempts to elicit ordered communication by signs in apes may have failed in their original objective, but they have given us evidence of cognitive capacities in apes that are far beyond our expectations. And we are closer to understanding the basic abilities from which our ancestors developed the language capacity that shapes the world we inhabit.

What are we to take away from a quarter century of ape language work? A combination of classic experimental research, informed observation, and quasi-ethological research on the relationship between symbol use and environmental consequences reveals that apes comprehend even when their spontaneous production of signs is limited. But of course this is also true for young children. Indeed, examined objectively, the corpus of evidence for early language usage in Kanzi is more convincing than that in many linguistic development studies of children. Like young humans, apes are capable of using arbitrary symbol systems to manipulate their environment and relationships with others. Unlike bees and most birds, apes are not limited to a neurologically programmed set of behavioral signals.

What does this tell us about apes and about ourselves? The basic cognitive and neurological abilities that underlie language exist in our closest biological relatives. But full comprehension of syntax and the production of syntactic utterances appear limited to humans. This difference correlates interestingly with human brain lateralization. Among all nonhuman higher primates, handedness is evenly distributed—approximately fifty percent of chimpanzees are right-handed and fifty percent left-handed. In contrast, something like ninety percent of human beings are right-handed—that is, left hemisphere dominant. It begins to seem increasingly significant that the brain areas most concerned with the intricate processes of speech and syntax production are typically located in the left hemisphere. If this level of syntactic competence is beyond the mastery of nonhuman primates, then syntax production becomes a promising candidate for one dimension of language capability that only humans as a species have developed.

The expanding body of information on animal communication in general and the acquisition of symbol systems by primates in particular is valuable to students of human language in several ways. First, it helps us to understand, however vaguely, the mental worlds of animals we often consider mindless if not senseless. And for linguists particularly, the study of ape communication provides a rare contrast to normal human language competence. Parallels between teaching the Yerkish lexigram system to severely mentally retarded humans as well as chimps and bonobos have already proved instructive. Last, because language does not leave fossils, we are unlikely to resolve all our questions about its evolution. We might resolve some of them by examining the closest thing to language fossils: the communicative and cognitive capacities of our nearest biological relatives. Although the other higher primates are not in any sense our linguistic ancestors, their evolutionary history may have conserved the cognitive abilities shared by our common prelingual ancestors.

Careful study has shown the degree of human communication that takes place on the level of affective displays using fixed action patterns. The same studies, however, have shown how great a gap separates animal and human use of symbols. Human language is an additional symbolic layer, extremely rich in hierarchical rule systems, superimposed on an existing pattern of communication that we share with other animals. This new layer has led to rapid alteration of every facet of human social structure and even to changes in human perception of the world.

To continue to acquire information about communication systems in a broad range of animals, investigators need to rethink older data, integrate new studies, and reexamine some operating assumptions. Communication within social groups is a fundamental part of animal life, and particular features of a species' communication system have long been seen as defining that species' unique social and even biological nature. The human capacity to appreciate multiple levels of meaning in a set of auditory or written signals clearly separates the cognitive worlds of humans and other primates. Advances in fields such as neurophysiology, linguistics, cognitive science, and comparative psychology seem to be converging on new and exciting conceptions that will challenge much of our understanding of the role language plays in human cognition and behavior. While current information does not show that any other animals have even a close approximation of formal language systems, such formal language (as opposed to other verbal and nonverbal communication systems) plays a relatively small role in the majority of our everyday lives.

By changing the focus of primate research from the study of formal language skills to cognitive strategies, several investigators have shown that chimps have cognitive mapping skills very similar to those of humans. The differences in the basic perceptual skills of higher primates may be slight indeed; genetic data suggest that the physical differences are minimal. The similarity of the cognitive world of great apes and humans, in contrast to their seemingly absolute difference in syntactic ability, suggests the decisiveness of the world-constructing power of language. The linguistic differences between human and animal may, in the case of higher primates, represent only small cognitive differences. Yet the power of language, once unleashed, has magnified them into an unbridgeable gulf.

WORKS CITED

Gardner, B. T., and R. A. Gardner. "Teaching Sign Language to a Chimpanzee." *Science* 165 (1969), 664–672.

Hockett, C. F., and S. A. Altmann. "A Note on Design Features." In *Animal Communication*, ed. T. A. Sebeok. Bloomington: University of Indiana Press, 1968.

Payne, K., P. Tyack, and R. Payne. "Progressive Changes in the Songs of Humpback Whales (*Megaptera novaeangliae*): A Detailed Analysis of Two Seasons in Hawaii." In *Communication and Behavior of Whales*, ed. R. Payne. AAAS Selected Symposia Series. Boulder: Westview Press, 1983.

Premack, Anne. *Why Chimps Can Read.* New York: Harper & Row, 1976.

Savage-Rumbaugh, E. Sue, and Roger Lewin. *Kanzi: The Ape at the Brink of the Human Mind.* New York: John Wiley and Sons, 1994.

Von Frisch, Karl. *A Biologist Remembers.* Trans. Lisbeth Gombrich. Oxford: Pergamon Press, 1967.

SUGGESTED READINGS

General

Griffin, D. R. *The Question of Animal Awareness: Evolutionary Continuity of Mental Experience.* Los Altos, CA: William Kaufmann, 1981. [In this important book Griffin opened the way to a reconsideration of cognitive capacities and functions in animals.]

Peters, R. *Mammalian Communication: A Behavioral Analysis of Meaning.* Monterey, CA: Brooks/Cole, 1980. [A well-written, clearly organized analysis of nonverbal communication from moles to man.]

Smith, W. John. *The Behavior of Communicating.* Cambridge: Harvard University Press, 1977. [A good general introduction to communication as a kind of behavior that fits into other behavior and environment.]

Bees

Gould, J. L., and C. G. Gould. "Can a Bee Behave Intelligently?" *New Scientist* 98 (1983), 84–87. [An interesting update on bee language research.]

Von Frisch, K. *Bees: Their Vision, Chemical Senses, and Language.* Rev. ed. Ithaca, NY: Cornell University Press, 1971. [The classic story of von Frisch's seminal work on honeybee communication.]

Whales

Payne, R., ed. *Communication and Behavior of Whales.* AAAS Selected Symposia Series. Boulder: Westview Press, 1983. [A compendium of papers that explore the communicative behavior of whales.]

Schusterman, R. J., J. A. Thomas, and F. G. Wood, eds. *Dolphin Cognition and Behavior: A Comparative Approach.* Hillsdale, NJ: Lawrence Erlbaum Associates, 1986. [The editors collected an array of reports on dolphin communication and placed it in the larger context of communicative behavior in other species.]

Birds

Catchpole, C. K., and P. J. B. Slater. *Bird Song: Biological Themes and Variations.* Cambridge: Cambridge University Press, 1995. [A comprehensive survey of research on birdsong.]

Apes

de Luce, J., and H. T. Wilder, eds. *Language in Primates: Perspectives and Implications.* New York: Springer-Verlag, 1983. [This third compendium is somewhat more balanced, definitely more philosophical, and less polemic than the first two.]

Goodall, J. *The Chimpanzees of the Gombi: Patterns of Behavior.* Cambridge: Belknap, 1986. [Among the observations in this summary of decades of meticulous work are several on the nature of chimp vocalization and its role in their social organization.]

Premack, D., and A. Premack. *The Mind of an Ape*. New York: W. W. Norton, 1983. [An entertaining and informative summary of a more cognition-oriented line of research with chimps.]

Savage-Rumbaugh, E. Sue, and Roger Lewin. *Kanzi: The Ape at the Brink of the Human Mind*. New York: John Wiley and Sons, 1994. [The most recent book on the subject, it offers a clear overview and details the shift in emphasis from language production to cognitive capacities of primates.]

Sebeok, T. A., and J. Umiker-Sebeok, eds. *Speaking of Apes: A Critical Anthology of Two-Way Communication with Man*. New York: Plenum Press, 1980. [This anthology is largely an outgrowth of a conference spearheaded by Sebeok and Terrace to publicize their doubts about ape language research.]

Sebeok, T. A., and R. Rosenthal, eds. *The Clever Hans Phenomenon: Communication with Horses, Whales, Apes, and People*. Annals of the New York Academy of Sciences, vol. 364. New York: New York Academy of Sciences, 1981. [A second anthology covers areas and commentators left out of the first volume, but with the same intent and purpose.]

Terrace, H. *Nim: A Chimp Who Learned Sign Language*. New York: Alfred Knopf, 1979. [Terrace presents in detail his work with Nim and the basis for his reinterpretation of his results.

≡

FOR DISCUSSION AND REVIEW

1. Explain why ethologists and linguists believe that studying different kinds of animal communication is important.

2. In analyzing animal communication, ethologists use the terms *form, context,* and *response*. Define and give an original example of each term.

3. Kemp and Smith state that "distinctive behavior that reliably indicates what an animal will do promotes cooperation and reduces conflict, because it allows neighbors to adjust their actions according to what the display predicts." Drawing on your own experience, write brief descriptions of three situations involving animals that illustrate this principle.

4. Explain the relationship between the *allophones* of human speech and animal *displays*.

5. Review Hockett's "design features" discussed by W. F. Bolton (pp. 61–72) in "Language: An Introduction." To what extent does animal communication embody these features? Be specific; you may wish to consider only bees, or birds, or mammals.

6. Explain the differences between bird calls and songs; be sure to consider the functions of each.

7. Explain the implications for comparisons of human language and animal communication of Kemp and Smith's statement that "the

fundamental feature of animal communication persists in even the most social mammals: the value of displays does not depend on a desire to tell another animal something."

8. Why are specialists from many disciplines interested in studying nonhuman primate communication?

9. In all human languages, sentences have both hierarchical and linear structure. What is the significance of this fact in research with non-human primates?

10. What did Savage-Rumbaugh do to change the orientation of primate research? What impact has this change had?

11. What have researchers learned from working with Kanzi, a bonobo primate?

12. How do Kemp and Smith answer their own question: "What are we to take away from a quarter century of ape language work?"

50

The Continuity Paradox

Derek Bickerton

Where and how did humans acquire language? What events took place among people that stimulated the development of language? What role has language played in the development of our species? Scientists and linguists have long been trying to answer these questions. In this selection from his book Language and Species, *Derek Bickerton, professor of linguistics at the University of Hawaii, examines what he refers to as a "paradox" in the evolution of and examination of human language: the Paradox of Continuity. Bickerton asserts that if the theory of evolution is accepted, then language must be no more than an evolutionary adaptation. The paradox exists because language is far too complicated to have been the result of a genetic mutation or shift. Bickerton discusses innate differences between human and animal communication systems as he focuses on such specifics as "creativity" and the differences between "calls" and "words." He also examines "formalist" versus "antiformalist" views in his attempt to solve the paradox of the evolution of language. In his search for solutions, Bickerton clearly demonstrates how our ability to use language distinguishes us from all other species, and how language is an invaluable asset to human beings.*

Anyone who sets out to describe the role played by language in the development of our species is at once confronted by an apparent paradox, the Paradox of Continuity. If such a person accepts the theory of evolution, that person must accept also that language is no more than an evolutionary adaptation—one of an unusual kind, perhaps, yet formed by the same processes that have formed countless other adaptations. If that is the case, then language cannot be as novel as it seems, for evolutionary adaptations do not emerge out of the blue.

There are two other ways in which evolution can produce novel elements: by the recombination of existing genes in the course of normal breeding, or by mutations that affect genes directly. Even in the second case, absolute novelties are impossible. What happens in mutation is that the instructions for producing part of a particular type of creature are altered. Instructions for producing a new part cannot simply be added to the old recipe. There must already exist specific instructions that are capable of being altered, to a greater or lesser extent. What this means is that language cannot be wholly without antecedents of some kind.

But what kind of antecedents could language have? Since language is so widely regarded as a means of communication, the answer seems obvious: earlier systems of animal communication. It has long been known that many species communicate with one another. Some, like fireflies, have blinking lights, others, like crickets, rub legs or wingcases together, while many exude chemical signals known as pheromones. Of course, such means are limited in their range of potential meaning and may signal nothing more complex than the presence of a potential mate. But the more sophisticated the creature, the more sophisticated the means—from the dances of honeybees, through the posturing of sea gulls, to the sonar of dolphins—hence, the more complex the information that can be conveyed. Could not human language be just a super-sophisticated variant of these?

The trouble is that the differences between language and the most sophisticated systems of animal communication that we are so far aware of are qualitative rather than quantitative. All such systems have a fixed and finite number of topics on which information can be exchanged, whereas in language the list is open-ended, indeed infinite. All such systems have a finite and indeed strictly limited number of ways in which message components can be combined, if they can be combined at all. In language the possibilities of combination, while governed by strict principles, are (potentially at least) infinite, limited for practical purposes only by the finiteness of the immediate memory store. You do not get from a finite number to infinity merely by adding numbers. And there are subtler but equally far-reaching differences between language and animal communication that make it impossible to regard the one as antecedent to the other.

But the net result of all this is the Paradox of Continuity: language must have evolved out of some prior system, and yet there does not seem to be any such system out of which it could have evolved. Until now, arguments about the nature, origin, and function of language have remained inextricably mired in this paradox. Let us see if there is any way in which they can be released from it.

A WORD ABOUT FORMALISM

We can at least clean a little of the mud from our wheels if we begin by tackling what might seem at first an unpromising and unrelated issue: the role that formal structure plays in language. Some linguists will tell you that the formal structure of language is very important. Others will tell you that it is relatively unimportant. Who is right?

There are two very odd imbalances between the formalist and antiformalist groups. The first imbalance is in what they believe. No formalist believes that a purely formal approach is the only way to study language. Any formalist would agree that there are many aspects of language—meaning, use, interaction with other social and psychological domains—that are all worthy of study. If you ask formalists why they insist on studying formal structure in isolation from all these other factors, they will probably tell you that significant advances in knowledge have always involved focusing on particular aspects of things and abstracting away from other aspects. They can see no reason for the study of our own species to reverse this sensible procedure.

But if you ask antiformalists why they ignore the formal structure of language, you will sometimes hear a much less tolerant story. They may tell you that it is quite senseless to study the formal aspects of language in isolation from its mode of functioning in society. Quite possibly they will go on to say that since those aspects are merely uninteresting mechanisms, or superficial trimmings, or even artifacts of the method of inquiry, they can be relegated to an inferior position, if not dismissed altogether.

The second imbalance between formalists and antiformalists is that since formalists have ignored all issues involving the evolution of language, that field has been yielded without a blow to the enemies of formalism. Subsequently there has been no significant interchange between the two sides, indeed they are barely on speaking terms. This has left the antiformalists alone to grapple with the Continuity Paradox.

Now to tackle a paradox, or indeed any research issue, from a one-sided position is not the best recipe for success. In large part, failure to resolve the Continuity Paradox has resulted precisely from what one might call the "naive continuism" of the antiformalists, who have tried in a variety of ways to establish a direct line of development from animal communication to human language. Although all their efforts have signally failed to produce a convincing "origins" story, their rejection of more formal approaches has left them without any viable alternative.

Accordingly the present work tackles the Paradox from a rather different viewpoint. This viewpoint takes as basic the assumption that formal properties of language do exist and do matter, and that without the very specific types of formal structure that language exhibits, it could not perform the social and communicative functions that it does perform, and could not convey the wealth of peculiarly human meaning that it does convey.

Those functions and that meaning should not—and, indeed, in a work of this nature literally cannot—be ignored or even minimized. However, it seems reasonable to stand the antiformalist position on its head and say that it is quite senseless to study the origins and functions of language without at the same time studying the formal structures that underlie those functions. For these formal structures, abstract though they may appear, are exactly what enable language to communicate so efficiently. Nothing else that we know of (or can imagine) could have given language the unprecedented power that it proved to have: power that gave to a single primate line the mastery of the physical world and the first, and perhaps only, entry into the world of consciousness.

THE GULF BETWEEN LANGUAGE AND ANIMAL COMMUNICATION

Having established this perspective, we can now look a little more closely at the ways in which animal communication differs from language. Perhaps the most obvious is that of productivity. The calls or signs of other creatures usually occur in isolation from one another. There are as yet few, if any, clear cases where they can be combined to form longer utterances whose meaning differs from the sum of their meanings in isolation, in the way in which "look out," for instance, differs from the sum of the meanings of *look* and *out*.

It is not impossible that future research will uncover such cases. But then, if we were to parallel language, we would have to look for cases where the same calls in a different order can mean different things, like "Dog bites man" versus "Man bites dog." Even this far from exhausts the possibilities of human syntax, which can also place similar words in different orders to mean the same thing ("John gave Mary the book," "Mary was given the book by John") or the same words in almost the same order to mean quite different things ("The woman that saw the man kicked the dog," "The woman saw the man that kicked the dog").

Note however that to achieve such effects we have to use elements like *-en, by, that*. Later on we shall look at such elements in more detail. For the moment it is sufficient to note that they differ from elements like *John* or *woman* in that the latter refer (if only indirectly) to some entity or class of entities in the real world, whereas the former do not really refer at all, but rather serve to express structural relations between items that do refer. The first class of elements can be described as *grammatical items* and the second, the class that refers, as *lexical items*. To which class of items do animal calls and signs belong?

Certainly there seems to be nothing in any animal communication system that corresponds even vaguely to grammatical items. But it is also questionable, in at least a large majority of cases, whether there is any true correspondence with lexical items either. We may find, for example, a particular facial expression, accompanied perhaps by a bristling of hair, that we might want to translate as "I am very angry with you," or a peculiar cry that perhaps we would translate as, "Look out, folks, something dangerous is coming." In other words, most elements in animal communication systems might seem to correspond, in a very rough and ready sense, with complete human utterances, rather than with single words per se. But note that the true correspondence is with utterance rather than sentence, because oftentimes a single-word utterance like "Help!" or "Danger!" would serve as well. The category *complete utterance*, however, is not a structural category in language, precisely because it can cover anything from a complex sentence (or even a series of such sentences) to a one-word exclamation.

It follows that, for the most part, the units in animal communication systems do not correspond with any of the units that compose human language. There is a good reason why this is so. Animal communication is *holistic*, that is to say it is concerned with communicating *whole situations*. Language, on the other hand, talks mainly about *entities* (whether other creatures, objects, or ideas) and *things predicated of entities* (whether actions, events, states, or processes).

The units of animal communication convey whole chunks of information (rough equivalents of "I am angry," "You may mate with me," "A predator just appeared"). Language breaks up those chunks in a way that, to the best of our knowledge, no animal communication system has ever done. In order to convey our anger, we must, as an absolute minimum, specify ourselves by a particular sign and the state in which we find ourselves by another sign (in English and numerous other languages we have, in addition, to use an almost meaningless verb in order to link ourselves with our current state, while in another set of languages, we would have to add a particle to indicate that our state was indeed current, not a past or future one).

If we think about it, this way of doing things may seem somewhat less natural than the animal way. Suppose that the situation we want to convey is one in which we have just seen a predator approaching. From a functional point of view, it might seem a lot quicker to let out a single call with that meaning, rather than "Look out! A lion's coming!" But the oddity is not just functional. In the real situation, it is simply not the case that we would see two things: an entity (the lion) and something predicated of that entity ("coming"). If we actually were in that situation, what we would perceive would be the frontal presentation of a lion getting rapidly larger. That is, we would experience a single intact cluster of ongoing perceptions. So the animal's representation of this would seem to be not merely more expeditious, but more in accord with reality than ours.

But there are, even in this limited example, compensating features. A generalized predator warning call, or even a specific lion warning call, could not be modified so as to become "A lion was coming" (as in the context of a story), "A lion may come" (to propose caution in advance), "No lions are coming" (to convey reassurance), "Many lions are coming!" (to prompt still more vigorous evasive measures), and so on. To achieve this kind of flexibility, any utterance has to be composed of a number of different units each of which may be modified or replaced so as to transmit a wide range of different messages. And after all, if we want a rapid response, the possession of language in no way inhibits use of the human call system. In a tight corner, we can still just yell.

Still, you might argue, language had to begin somewhere, and where is it most likely to have begun than in some particular call whose meaning was progressively narrowed until it now covers about the same semantic range as does some noun in a language? Once the species had acquired a short list of entities—lions, snakes, or whatever—it needed only to attribute states or actions to those entities and it would then already have the essential subject-predicate core of language, to which all other properties could subsequently have been added.

You might then point to creatures such as the vervet monkey which have highly developed alarm calls. The vervet, a species that lives in East Africa, has at least three distinct alarm calls that might seem to refer to three species that are likely to prey upon vervets: pythons, martial eagles, and leopards. That it is the calls themselves that have this reference, and not any other behavioral or environmental feature, has been experimentally established by playing recordings of the calls to troops of vervets in the absence of any of the predators concerned. On hearing these recordings, most vervets within earshot respond just as they would to a natural, predator-stimulated call. They look at the ground around them on hearing the snake warning, run up trees on hearing the leopard warning, and descend from trees to hide among bushes on hearing the eagle warning.

We might therefore think that these calls were, in embryo at least, the vervet "words" for the species concerned. But in fact, a warning call about pythons differs from a word like *python* in a variety of ways. Even though *python* is only a single word, it can be modified, just as we saw the sentence "A lion is coming!" could be modified. It can, for instance, be given at least four intonations, each of which has a distinct meaning. With a rising intonation it can mean "Is that a python there?" or "Did you just say python?" With a neutral intonation, it merely names a particular variety of snake, as in a list of snake species, for example. With a sustained high-pitch intonation it can mean that there's a python right there, right now. With an intonation that starts high and ends low, especially if delivered in a sneering, sarcastic tone, it can mean "How ridiculous to suppose that there's a python there!"

Assuming that all these are used without intent to deceive, only in the third case is a python there for sure. But with the vervet call, there is always a python. At least, with one rare exception, the vervet involved genuinely believes there is a python there. (Just like human children, young vervets have to learn the semantic range of their calls, and again like children they tend to overgeneralize and sometimes give calls in inappropriate circumstances.)

In order to understand further differences between humans and vervets, certain aspects of meaning must first be clarified. We might suppose that any relation between events in the world and meaningful utterances could be characterized as a mapping relation, that is to say, an operation that matches features of the environment with features of a (more or less arbitrary) representational system. We might begin by saying that a python in the real world is matched with a particular call in the vervet system and a particular noun in a given human language. This would be not very far from Bertrand Russell's theory of meaning and reference, for Russell believed, and got into terrible difficulties through believing, that nouns referred directly to entities in the real world.

Linguists, at least since Russell's contemporary de Saussure, have known that this is not so for human language. As noted above, grammatical items do not refer at all, and lexical items refer to real-world entities only indirectly. This is because not one, but at least two mapping operations lie between the real world and language. First our sense perceptions of the world are mapped onto a conceptual representation, and then this conceptual representation is mapped onto a linguistic representation.

Indeed, even in the animal case there cannot be a direct relationship between external object and call. Every now and then, even adult vervets will use, say, an eagle call for something that is not an eagle. It is no help to say that the vervet merely made a mistake. Why did it make that mistake? Because it thought that what it saw really was an eagle. In other words, if the vervet is wrong, it is wrong because it is responding to its own act of identification, rather than to the object itself. But are we then to say that the vervet responds to its own identification when it happens to be wrong and to the real object when it happens to be right? Obviously not. Vervets respond to their own identifications under all circumstances. But in that case there cannot be a direct link between call and object. The call labels an act of identification: the placing of some phenomenon in a particular category. In some sense, vervets too must have concepts.

That the things words refer to are not external entities is even clearer in our own case. One piece of evidence is the very existence of expressions like *a unicorn* or *the golden mountain* that gave Russell so much trouble. Since such expressions cannot refer to real-world entities, they must refer to a level of representation that is to some extent independent of the real world.

Indeed, it is sometimes inescapable that linguistic expressions are referring not to real-world entities but to our conceptions of these. It is surprising that Russell never discussed sentences like "The Bill Bailey I love and respect is very different from the drunken monster you depict him as being." Here, obviously, two concepts of the same person are in conflict. Nor can we escape the situation by pointing to the indisputable fact that one does not normally preface proper names with the definite article, and claim therefore that while "the Bill Bailey I love and respect" may refer to a concept of Bill Bailey, "Bill Bailey" alone can only refer to Bill Bailey the real-world individual.

Suppose I say "Bill Bailey is honest" and you say "Bill Bailey is a rascal." Since both qualities cannot be simultaneously predicated of the same person, the referent for the first use can only be my concept of Bill Bailey while that for the second can only be yours. But what about "Bill Bailey left early"? If we say that the name here refers to a real-world entity, we are in the uncomfortable position of claiming that names sometimes refer to real entities and sometimes to concepts. It seems safer to say that they refer to concepts all the time.

Yet even though both calls and words refer indirectly, there is evidence that they do not do so in the same way. For instance, it's a safe bet that no animal system has calls for unicorns or golden mountains or anything else of which there is no sensory evidence.

Another way in which calls and words differ is that words can be, and usually are, used in the physical absence of the objects they refer to, whereas calls hardly ever are so used. There is one exception: numerous observers have reported, for vervets and other primate species, what look like deliberate uses of alarm calls in the absence of any predator, designed to distract other monkeys from aggressive intentions or to remove potential competitors for some item of food.

If these can be proven to be genuine cases of deception, would they serve to undermine the distinction between words and calls? The answer is no, for two reasons. First, the strategy would not work unless all the other vervets believed, and behaved as if, there was a predator there. That is, it would work only if the deceiving monkey could rely on other monkeys to respond in the appropriate fashion. Second, in such observed instances the deceiving monkey itself failed to respond appropriately to its own call, even when it was in plain view of other monkeys. This suggests that the animal is not truly "using a call in the absence of its referent" but simply exploiting one consequence of alarm calls (the disappearance of other animals from the vicinity) for its own personal ends.

Closely linked to these issues is the question of evolutionary utility. If human words were no more than the equivalents of animal calls, referring in the same way that animal calls referred, it would be remarkable that we have all the words we do. Vervets can "name" pythons, leopards, and martial eagles. They cannot "name" vultures, elephants, antelopes, and a variety of other creatures that do not have a significant impact on the lives of vervets. Why, in that case, is the human insect repertoire not limited to *fly*, *mosquito*, *locust*, and *cockroach* (plus any other insects that may significantly affect the lives of humans), and why is it that we have words—like *cockchafer*, *ladybird*, *earwig*, and *dung beetle*—for countless species that affect us minimally, if at all?

Here we differ from other creatures along a rather interesting dimension. All other creatures can communicate only about things that have evolutionary significance for them, but human beings can communicate about anything. In other words, what is adaptive for other species is a particular set of highly specific referential capacities. What is adaptive for our species is the *system* of reference *as a whole*, the fact that any manifestation of the physical world can (potentially at least) be matched with some form of expression. The fact that this difference is qualitative rather than quantitative (vervets could increase their repertoire by many orders of magnitude without even approximating the global scope of human reference) suggests again that quite different mechanisms are involved.

We should take account, too, of the fact that while animal calls and signs are structurally holistic, the units of human language are componential in nature. What this means is that animal calls and signs cannot be broken down into component parts, as language can. Words are, on one level, simply combinations of sounds. These sounds are finite and, indeed, small in number, not exceeding seventy or so in any known language.

Though in themselves the sounds of a language are meaningless, they can be recombined in different ways to yield thousands of words, each distinct in meaning. A word like *pat*, for example, can be broken down into three distinct sounds: /p/, /a/, and /t/. Those same sounds can be recombined to form *tap* and *apt*, two words of entirely different meaning. In just the same way, a finite stock of words (usually some tens of thousands, probably not much more than half a million even in the most "developed" language) can be combined to produce an infinite number of sentences. Nothing remotely like this is found in animal communication.

To those already convinced that human language and animal communication are wholly unconnected, the foregoing paragraphs may seem like overkill. Yet contrasting animal communication and language has a purpose beyond merely convincing continuists that naive continuism won't work. It has the purpose of clarifying exactly what it is that makes language look like an evolutionary novelty. For if we don't do at least this, our prospects of explaining the evolutionary origins of language are dim. After all, anticontinuists have failed even more dismally than continuists at providing a convincing history of language and mind. Until we cease to regard language as primarily communicative and begin to treat it as primarily representational, we cannot hope to escape from the Continuity Paradox.

THE NATURE OF REPRESENTATION

It may be advisable to begin by clarifying some aspects of the general nature of representations. What do we mean when we say that *X* represents *Y*? Normally that *Y*, an event or an entity in the real world, bears some kind of correspondence relation to *X*, such that *X* somehow recalls or expresses *Y*, but not necessarily vice versa. This definition is informal and crude, and there may be several things about it that are questionable, but it will do as a starting point.

The first point to note is that in fact everything that we or any other creatures perceive is a representation, and not in any sense naked reality itself. That is to say, no creature apprehends its environment except by means of sensory mechanisms whose mode of functioning is everywhere the same. Particular facets of the environment excite responses (in terms of variations from their unstimulated firing rate) from particular cells that are specialized to respond to just those facets and no others. These neural responses in themselves constitute a level of representation. The firing of such-and-such a collection of neurons at such-and-such frequencies corresponds to the presence, in the immediate environment, of such-and-such set of features. Almost simultaneously, in all vertebrates and many invertebrates, the original responses are synthesized and their synthesis, if functionally relevant to the creature concerned, is assigned to its appropriate category. This can be regarded as a further level of representation, in which the category assignment corresponds to a particular set of neuronal responses.

We do not, for example, directly see our surroundings. What happens is that sets of cells in our retinas programmed to react to specific features of the environment (lines at various angles, motions of varying kinds, different qualities of light, and so on) respond to those features on an individual basis, and this information is then relayed electrochemically to the visual areas of the cortex, where it is automatically reconstituted to provide a fairly, but not always completely, accurate simulacrum of what there is around us.

If this were not so, if our visual system merely presented us with a direct image of reality in the way that a mirror reflects whatever is before it, there would be no optical illusions. Optical illusions arise when properties of the visual system are imposed on the raw data of the physical world. Nor can we dismiss such illusions as marginal phenomena. When we look around us we see an entirely colored world, but color is simply a property of the perceiving mechanism. All of us have seen mountains, gray or brown in the light of midday, turn to blue as the sun descends, then perhaps to pink or crimson as the last rays touch them, then finally to black as night falls. Of course the mountains have not really changed color, only the light reflected by them has changed, and these changes in turn interact with our means of perceiving and categorizing differences in wavelengths. But in that case, what are the mountains' *real* colors? Clearly they cannot have any.

We can now return to an earlier remark that may have seemed problematic at the time. In the previous section, it was stated that expressions such as *the golden mountain* must refer not to the real world but to "a level of representation that is to some extent independent of the real world." How can we, one might ask, have a level that represents the real world but contains entities that do not exist in that world? If we treat "representation" as meaning simply "re-presentation"—a wholly faithful one-to-one mapping from one medium to another—this seems absurd. But in fact, representation can never have such a meaning.

Consider the most basic facts about what a representation is and does. Although what follows applies to representations generally, let us, for the sake of concreteness, take as a particular example a painting of the Battle of Lepanto; and let us for ease of exposition ignore for the present any intervening layer(s) of representation (sensory, conceptual, or other) that may come between the actual Battle of Lepanto and the painting with that title. It should immediately be clear that there are many properties of the Battle of Lepanto that the painting cannot represent. It cannot enable us, for instance, to smell the gunpowder smoke, or the sea spray, or the stench of blood below decks. The time that passed for an observer of the battle was determined by the length of the battle, but the time that passes for an observer of the picture is determined only by the observer's will. And there are many more properties of the actual Battle of Lepanto that are not, and indeed cannot be, represented in "The Battle of Lepanto."

But the converse is equally the case: there are many properties of the painting that never belonged to its original. "The Battle of Lepanto," unlike the Battle of Lepanto, is made of paint and canvas, hangs on a wall, can be bought and sold, has properties of proportion that can be discussed by art critics, and so on. Yet even though "The Battle of Lepanto" lacks much that the Battle of Lepanto possessed, and possesses much that the Battle of Lepanto lacked, we do not balk or express our derision when we read its title; instead we are perfectly prepared to accept it as a representation. Indeed someone who was actually present at the battle might have realized what the painting was meant to represent even without its title, by virtue of those features (names, types, and positions of ships, flags displayed, actual incidents depicted, and so forth) that the battle and the painting did share.

The relationship between a real-world event and a painting may look like an extreme kind of example to choose, since the level of real events and the level of pictorial representations might seem excessively remote from one another. However, it is hard to see how they are more remote than the level of real events is from the level of processing units in the brain, or than the level of processing units in the brain is from the level of spoken or written utterance. Moreover, remote or not, similar principles must apply wherever representation exists.

Both the properties of the Battle of Lepanto that must be excluded from the picture and the nonproperties of battle that a picture must impose will be determined by the properties of static (as opposed to dynamic) representations, the properties of two-dimensional (as opposed to three-dimensional) objects, the properties of paint (as opposed to other media), and so on. In the same way, wherever representation exists, the properties of the medium in which the representation is made (or, to put it another way, the formal structures onto which the things to be represented are mapped) must both select from and add to the properties of the original.

In particular, the properties of neural systems, some of which are general but some of which are highly species-specific, and the properties of language, almost all of which are species-specific, must both add to and subtract from anything that they represent. Indeed, since everything we seem to perceive is in fact only a representation, these principles must apply universally. For there is not, and cannot in the nature of things ever be, a representation without a medium to represent in, any more than there can be a medium that lacks properties of its own.

Perhaps the only way in which pictorial representation might mislead us about the nature of representations in general is by suggesting that if any representation exists there must also exist someone to perceive it. Thus if we talk of nervous systems "representing" reality in the brain, it seems natural to think of someone or something—ourselves, a little person, or the soul—who sits inside our head and looks at the representation. Such beliefs have been the cause of endless pseudoproblems. For the moment, all we have to do is note that a representation does not have to be perceived by any kind of discrete or conscious agent. If the particular set of neurons in a rabbit's brain that are triggered by the appearance of a fox should happen to fire, thereby representing a fox to a particular rabbit, that representation has only to be read by the motor neurons that control the rabbit's legs. If, under similar circumstances, we are somehow conscious of ourselves seeing the fox, that only appears to be a different story. . . .

How veridical are representations? How much difference does it make that we can only perceive through a series of representations rather than somehow perceiving directly? One might argue, with some justice, that representation at a lower level—what our brain derives from immediate sensory input—cannot stray too far from the reality it represents. If it did, the result would surely be dysfunctional from an evolutionary point of view. We would be continually colliding with obstacles, falling from high places, consuming poisonous substances, and performing a variety of other behaviors calculated to shorten our lifespan or even extinguish ourselves as a species. Indeed, you might argue that evolution must actively select for more veridical representations by eliminating those creatures that have less veridical ones.

But this line of reasoning cannot be taken too far. There is no indication that color blindness, astigmatism, or tone deafness are being bred out of us, nor that the range of our hearing is gradually extending, over succeeding generations, so that it will eventually approximate that of the dog or the bat. The sense of smell has not improved but has steadily deteriorated throughout the development of primates. Moreover, creatures like frogs or cockroaches with sensoria far poorer than ours have survived for tens of millions of years without apparent problems. Evolution does not hone and fine-tune representation to some point of near perfection. Rather it provides creatures with representational systems that are just about good enough for their immediate evolutionary needs. So long as a species can get by on what it has, there will be no selective pressure to improve.

What was said in the previous paragraph applies with even greater force to representation at the second level—the mapping from concepts to language. It was noted in the previous section that what gave our species its evolutionary advantage was not a capacity to represent in language just those things that had evolutionary significance for us, but a capacity (potential, at least) to represent *anything at all* in language, whether it was significant or not. The advantage this gave us was so enormous that members of our species can produce a great deal of dysfunctional behavior and still survive. Thus we would expect that the series of representational mappings from sense data to concepts and from concepts to language might carry us some distance from the world of reality, even to the point of representing entities that do not exist in that world.

We could even predict that a representational medium with the particular properties that language has would inevitably contain entities of the type of *the golden mountain*. [One property] . . . is that, subject to the constraints of a Sommers-Keil predictability tree, any adjective can apply to any noun. This means that if there is an adjective, *golden*, it can apply without limit to any noun that represents the concept of a concrete object. If a mountain is such an object, *the golden mountain* becomes inescapable, regardless of the fact that there is no mountain made of gold anywhere in nature.

The remarkable thing is that the relationship between concepts and language is a two-way street. Normally we assume that a linguistic expression refers to a preexisting concept, but this is by no means necessarily the case. Linguistic expressions can equally well create concepts. Once we have heard of *the golden mountain*, we can imagine such a thing, and even what it might look like if it did exist. A friend once remarked, "To evaluate that speech you'd really need your oxometer." On being asked what an oxometer was, he replied, "It measures the percentage of bullshit." There is, alas, as yet no oxometer in the real world. But you can imagine what it would be like, and maybe wish that you had one, too.

REPRESENTATION AND CONTINUITY

Having reviewed some of the ways in which representational systems work, we can return to the issue with which this chapter began. We have seen that between language and animal communication there exist qualitative differences, differences so marked as to indicate that no plausible ancestry for language can be found in prior communication systems. Yet evolution still requires that language have an ancestry of some sort. Thus if there is to be continuity, it must lie in some domain other than that of communication.

Communication is, after all, not what language is, but (a part of) what it does. Countless problems have arisen from a failure to distinguish between language and the use of language. Before language can be used communicatively, it has to establish what there is to communicate about.

If we perceived the world directly, this might not be so. Language might then indeed involve no more than the slapping of labels on preexisting categories and the immediate use of those labels for communicative ends. But, as the last section showed, no creature perceives the world directly. The categories a creature can distinguish are determined not by the general nature of reality but by what that creature's nervous system is capable of representing. The capacities of that nervous system are, in part at least, determined by what the creature minimally needs in order to survive and reproduce. (They may also be influenced by what the creature's ancestors needed—but unneeded sensory powers tend to decay, witness the eyeless fish in subterranean caverns.) The categories distinguished by frogs, it would seem, do not extend very far beyond bugs they can snap at, ponds they can jump into, and other frogs they can mate with. The categories distinguished by vervets are more numerous, and those distinguished by our own species more numerous still, but the same principles apply.

Note that it is immaterial, for our purposes, how such categories are derived. They may be innate, they may be learned, or they may be acquired by the process of experience fine-tuning an innate propensity. There is good reason to believe, for instance, that some primates have an innate representation of snakes; when members of these species, raised in isolation, are first confronted by a stuffed snake, or by anything that looks like a snake, they show signs of alarm or avoidance (in contrast to the high curiosity they exhibit towards certain other kinds of objects). At the opposite extreme, our representations of automobiles and airplanes are obviously learned.

Vervet categories seem to occupy an intermediate position. They cannot be wholly learned, for there are certain mistakes that young vervets seldom if ever make. They may generalize the martial-eagle call to owls or vultures, but they very seldom, if ever, use the eagle-call for snakes, or the python-call for leopards. In other words, they seem innately capable of distinguishing things that creep, things that walk, and things that fly. Experience is needed only to narrow those categories—of creeping, walking, and flying things—to just those species that prey upon vervets.

Perhaps a word should be said about innateness, since many people still find the term objectionable. It may seem less so when one considers that all representations, whether innate, learned, or of mixed origins, share a common infrastructure. The medium onto which representations are mapped consists of sets of interconnected neurons, such that when enough of these respond to external phenomena, a particular behavioral response is triggered (the monkey's avoidance, the vervet's alarm call). Almost all creatures possess sensory cells that substantially vary their firing rate when particular features of the environment are presented to them, and they do so without benefit of experience. Let us suppose that in monkeys one set of cells responds to wavy lines, another set to rounded objects, a third set to the quality of light reflected from very smooth objects, a fourth to motions, and so on. It follows that most, if not all, of those sets of cells will vary their firing rates simultaneously when presented with a snake or similar object.

So far, there is nothing in the least marvelous about this. No one supposes that neurons are acquired through experience, or that we learn, in the traditional sense of learning, the difference between straight and wavy lines or between shiny and dull surfaces. The capacity to make such distinctions is simply part of our genetic inheritance, and it appears, if not actually at birth, at least early on in the development cycle (provided of course that those distinctions are observable in the environment). Nor does anyone express surprise if, as a result of particular experiences, the firing of all the relevant sets of neurons should eventually trigger a particular response. Anyone would then be content to say that a learned response had developed.

Now it is true that learned responses cannot be transmitted to offspring. However, if, by sheer chance, one out of countless billions of monkeys should happen to be born with a mutation that directly linked the sets of snake-responding cells to the cells that activated avoidance behavior, then that monkey would enjoy a selective advantage over its fellows. That monkey alone could be guaranteed to react appropriately to its very first encounter with a snake, while a small proportion of its unmutated fellows in each generation might fail to survive that experience. Clearly, the genes that conveyed such an advantage would produce more offspring than those that did not. Thus, gradually, over time, the strain that lacked an automatic snake reaction would die out, leaving that reaction as a truly species-specific innate response.

On this analysis, it is hard to see what there could be to object to in the notion that there are innate concepts. Indeed, the issue would hardly need to be treated at such length were it not a fact that resistance to what are often rather oddly termed "innate ideas" tends to grow stronger as one approaches the central citadel of language. That aspect of the innateness issue will be addressed in due course. For the present, it may be noted that, on the conceptual level at least, internal representations constitute a mosaic of innate and learned forms. If language is indeed, primarily, an additional system of representation found in a particular mammalian species, there seems no principled reason why it too should not consist of a similar mosaic.

But is language really a system of representation? If it is, then we should be able to resolve the Continuity Paradox. We could search for the ancestry of language not in prior systems of animal communication, but in prior representational systems.

But before this can be done, two things are necessary. The first is to show that language may indeed be properly termed a representational system, and to describe the properties peculiar to it. The second is to survey the development of representational systems in evolutionary terms, in order to show that at least a good proportion of the infrastructure necessary for language antedated the emergence of the hominid line. If these things can be done, we can then turn to the development of hominids and determine, first, what other properties were required to create language as we know it, and second, whether it is plausible that just those properties could have been developed by the few speciations that separate us from speechless primates.

Before we begin this quest, one point in favor of the chosen course may be noted. No attempt to derive language from animal communication could hope to tell us anything significant about the origins of consciousness. If language were no more than communication, it would be a process; consciousness is a state. But if language is a representational system, it too is a state. Moreover, if consciousness too is a way of representing to ourselves ourselves and the world around us, then it may be that the origins of the two are closely linked, and that by uncovering the one we may also uncover the other.

===

FOR DISCUSSION AND REVIEW

1. How does Bickerton explain his "continuity paradox" with respect to the evolution of language? What is the paradox?

2. Discuss the terms *formalist* and *antiformalist*. What imbalances exist between these two groups?

3. What is the formalist viewpoint on the evolution of language and its study? Why does Bickerton believe that one cannot ignore this viewpoint in studying his paradox?

4. Outline the differences Bickerton explores between animal communication and language. Include in your discussion the term *productivity* as well as the units of communication each group uses. To what do the terms *holistic* and *entities* refer in this comparative process?

5. Bickerton asserts that the things words refer to are not external entities but, rather, our perceptions of them. How has the study of vervets led to this conclusion? In what ways do we conform to this hypothesis in our language?

6. What is Bickerton's purpose for contrasting animal communication and human language, two obviously distinct and separate systems?

7. What is the importance of the "two-way street" that exists in the relationship between concepts and language?

8. What can be said about the ancestry of language? How does innateness play a part in this ancestry?

9. What solutions, if any, does Bickerton offer for this "continuity paradox"?

Projects for "Language, Thought, and the Brain"

1. Some recent findings on neural asymmetry suggest that the kind of notation or code used in a given task influences how the task may be done. (Recall the comments in "Brain and Language" by Jeannine Heny on the two types of Japanese script, for example.) Using examples from your own experience, think of how using different codes might influence how you do a task. One example might be the use of Roman numerals versus Arabic numerals in multiplication: which can you process faster: "XIX times III" or "19 times 3"? Another example, if you know German, might be the use of familiar modern printing as opposed to the more elaborate script used in early German texts. Write a short essay in which you discuss how codes might affect your efficiency or the way you approach one specific task.

2. Lateral eye movement (LEM) is perhaps the most controversial and difficult to control of all behavioral tests for brain asymmetry. But it is also the most accessible to the lay person. Construct a list of six questions, each of which is either clearly emotional or clearly intellectual. Such questions might be expected to elicit left- or right-eye movements, respectively. An emotional (right-hemisphere) question might be, "What would you do if you saw a poisonous snake?" An intellectual (left-hemisphere) question might involve defining an abstract word or explaining how to compute taxes. Ask four people your questions, and watch their eyes as they answer. Do their LEMs seem to vary with question type? Or do you find (as some suspect) that each person looks relatively consistently in one direction? (Don't forget that a left-eye movement means right-hemisphere activity; you may find this confusing when facing a person in normal conversation.)

3. The nature and extent of therapy available to aphasics—those who have lost language skills as a result of damage to the brain, usually the result of a stroke or traumatic head injury—often make the difference between at least partial recovery and continued, severe language disability. Prepare a report on one of the rehabilitation techniques now in use and explain why it is helpful. If you know someone who has been helped by this technique, see whether he or she would be willing to discuss it with you. You may wish to supplement library research by interviews with speech therapists and others who work with aphasic patients.

You may find particularly interesting a program called Melodic Intonation Therapy, in which aphasics are first taught to sing phrases. Information about this technique can be found in the following two articles: (1) Albert, M. L., R. W. Sparks, and N. A. Helm. "Melodic intonation therapy for aphasia." *Archives of Neurology* 29 (1973), 130–131. (2) Sparks, R., N. Helm, and M. Albert. "Aphasia rehabilitation resulting from melodic intonation therapy." *Cortex* 10 (1974), 303–316.

A different therapy, designed for patients with another kind of aphasia, has been suggested by A. R. Luria. It is discussed in his book *Higher Cortical Functions* (New York: Basic Books, 1966).

4. In a journal article (*Neuropsychologia* 21 [1983], 669–678), a Japanese researcher, Takeshi Hatta, described an experiment in which he asked people to look at pairs of digits, comparing their relative physical sizes and their relative numerical values to see if they matched. If the subject saw a large 7 and a small 2, he was to say "yes." On the other hand, a large 4 and a small 8 required a negative answer. As expected, because the task involved analytical thinking (comparison and mathematics), the left hemisphere showed superior performance. But interestingly, even when he translated the task into some rare Ming-era kanji characters, the left dominance remained. This occurred despite the high visual complexity of the figures and the fact that people seldom use them (they did not even appear in an official kanji list published in 1850). His two types of pairs are illustrated here:

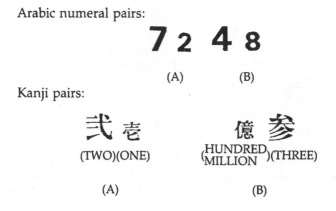

Arabic numeral pairs:

7 2   **4** 8

(A)   (B)

Kanji pairs:

弐 壱   億 参

(TWO)(ONE)   (HUNDRED MILLION)(THREE)

(A)   (B)

In an earlier study, Hatta had found that subjects read a watch (presumably a familiar "holistic" object) with the right hemisphere. Yet, when warned that the watch would be one hour slow or fast, the results reversed, and he found left-hemisphere superiority.

In both cases, the type of task seems more important than the visual stimulus: in the first case, the stimulus changes and hemispherical preference remain the same; in the second, the stimulus stays the same but hemispheric choice changes. What do the two tasks in the first experiment and the second time-telling task have in common that make them demand left-hemisphere processing space?

Design a hypothetical experiment similar in spirit and goal to one of those just cited. For example, think of a situation in which you see or hear the same material, but do two different things with it.

5. Read Geoffrey Pullum's essay, "The Great Eskimo Vocabulary Hoax," in a book with the same title (Chicago: University of Chicago Press, 1991). Write a summary of the "hoax" and its impact on discrediting the Sapir-Whorf hypothesis.

6. Although the Sapir-Whorf hypothesis has been generally discredited today, David Crystal, in the final paragraph of his essay, states that "a weaker version of the Sapir-Whorf hypothesis is generally accepted." Locate several of the recent studies by psycholinguists and report on the light they shed on the relationship between language and thought.

7. The story of "Clever Hans" (see Roger Brown, *Words and Things*, Glencoe, IL: The Free Press, 1958), the extent of the belief in his near-human abilities, the variety of those abilities, and the long struggle to reveal the truth, is a fascinating one. Prepare a report in which you review the events chronologically.

8. A number of films of the various chimpanzee experiments are available. Your media librarian should be able to help you compile a reasonably complete list. Watch at least one of these films in class. Can you detect any of the flaws in the experiments that are mentioned by Kemp and Smith? If so, describe them.

Selected Bibliography

Note: The article by Jeannine Heny in this part contains an extensive bibliography, as do two of the books listed here: Segalowitz's Two Sides of the Brain *and* Springer and Deutsch's Left Brain, Right Brain. *The reader should consult these for a more exhaustive listing of sources.*

Bickerton, Derek. *Language & Species.* Chicago: The University of Chicago Press, 1990. [An interesting exploration of how language systems came to be, how they function, and what they accomplish.]

Blakeslee, Thomas R. *The Right Brain: A New Understanding of the Unconscious Mind and Its Creative Powers.* Garden City, NY: Anchor Press/Doubleday, 1980. [The title is accurate. Thorough exploration of the functions of the right hemisphere; excellent bibliography.]

Buck, Craig. "Knowing the Left from the Right." *Human Behavior* 5 (June 1976), 329–335. [Interesting collection of specific examples of what each side of the brain can do.]

Campbell, Jeremy. *Grammatical Man: Information, Entropy, Language, and Life.* New York: Simon and Schuster, 1982. [An extraordinary and fascinating book; see especially parts three and four.]

Damasio, Antonio R. "Brain and Language." *Scientific American* (September 1992), 88–96. [An intriguing neurophysiological look at the brain and how it is used in language. Helpful diagrams are included.]

Farb, Peter. *Humankind.* Boston: Houghton Mifflin, 1978. [Readable and informative; see Chapter 15 for a broad discussion of a variety of aspects of the brain and its functioning.]

Fromkin, Victoria. "Slips of the Tongue." *Scientific American* 229 (1973), 110–117. [Interesting in themselves, slips of the tongue offer clues to language processing in the brain.]

Gardner, Howard. *The Shattered Mind: The Person after Brain Damage.* New York: Alfred Knopf, 1975. [Chapters 2, on aphasia, and 9, on the brain's two hemispheres, are especially interesting.]

———. *Art, Mind, and Brain: A Cognitive Approach to Creativity.* New York: Basic Books, 1982. [A consistently interesting collection of thirty-one essays, almost all of which were originally published elsewhere.]

———. *Frames of Mind: The Theory of Multiple Intelligences.* New York: Basic Books, 1983. [An interesting synthesizing work, see especially II, 5, "Linguistic Intelligence," and II, 8, "Spatial Intelligence."]

Gardner, R. Allen, B. T. Gardner, and T. E. Vancantfort. *Teaching Sign Language to Chimpanzees.* Albany: State University of New York Press, 1989. [An illustrative study of the processes of teaching sign language to chimps and the trends that parallel language development in children.]

Gazzaniga, Michael S. "The Split Brain in Man." *Scientific American* 217 (1967), 24–29. [A readable early report on the effects of split-brain surgery (commissurotomy).]

Geschwind, Norman. "Language and the Brain." *Scientific American* 226 (1972), 76–83. [Discusses how aphasia and other kinds of brain damage help us understand how language is organized in the brain.]

———. "Specializations of the Human Brain." *Scientific American* 241 (1979), 180–182, 186–187, 189–192, 196, 198–199. [Discussion of hemisphere specialization and of the specialization of particular areas of the brain.]

Jones, Gerald. "Clues to Behavior from a Divided Brain." In *1978 Nature/Science Annual*, ed. Jane D. Alexander. Alexandria, VA: Time/Life Books, 1977. [A nontechnical summary.]

Macneilage, Peter F., M. G. Studdert-Kennedy, and B. Lindblom. "Hand Signals— Right Side, Left Brain and the Origin of Language." *The Sciences* (January/February 1993), 32–37. [A fascinating article that explores the relationships between left-hemisphere brain dominance and language origins.]

Ornstein, Robert E., ed. *The Nature of Human Consciousness: A Book of Readings*. San Francisco: W. H. Freeman and Company, 1973.]An interesting collection of forty-one articles; see especially part 2.]

Penfield, Wilder. *The Mystery of the Mind*. Princeton, NJ: Princeton University Press, 1975. [A personal account of the work of this renowned neurosurgeon.]

Perkins, William H. *Speech Pathology: An Applied Behavioral Science*. 2nd ed. St. Louis: Mosby, 1977. [Somewhat technical but very informative analysis of aphasia on pp. 131–133, 241–247, and 384–387.]

Pines, Maya. *The Brain Changers: Scientists and the New Mind Control*. New York: Harcourt Brace Jovanovich, 1973. [Fascinating chapters on many aspects of the brain; see especially Chapter 7, "What Half of Your Brain Is Dominant—and Can You Change It?"]

Pinker, Steven. *The Language Instinct: How the Mind Creates Language*. New York: Morrow, 1994. [See Chapter 3, "Mentalese," and especially pp. 59–64 on the linguistic determinism hypothesis.]

Potter, Robert. "Language" (videorecording 30 min.). New York: Insight Media, 1989. [An examination of the uniqueness of human language, its development, language and the brain, and a look at the topic cross-culturally.]

Premack, David. *Gavagai! or the Future History of the Animal Language Controversy*. Cambridge: MIT Press, 1986. [As controversial as its title, Premack offers insights as to whether human language is species- and/or task-specific.

Pullum, Geoffrey. *The Great Eskimo Vocabulary Hoax and Other Irreverent Essays on the Study of Language*. Chicago: University of Chicago Press, 1991. [See especially Chapter 19 "The Great Eskimo Vocabulary Hoax."]

Restak, Richard M., M.D. *The Brain: The Last Frontier*. Garden City, NY: Doubleday & Company, 1979. [Readable, intriguing, and authoritative, hemispheric specialization, language acquisition, and much more. Good bibliography.]

Rieber, R. W., ed. *The Neuropsychology of Language: Essays in Honor of Eric Lenneberg*. New York: Plenum Press, 1976. [Although technical, the nine chapters are packed with information.]

Sagan, Carl. *The Dragons of Eden: Speculations on the Evolution of Human Intelligence*. New York: Random House, 1977. [Controversial but fascinating; worth reading.]

Sage, Wayne. "The Split Brain Lab." *Human Behavior* 5 (June 1976), 24–28, 1976. [An interesting and very readable summary of split-brain research.]

Samples, Robert E. "Learning with the Whole Brain." *Human Behavior* 4 [February 1975), 17–23. [Possible implications for education of our emphasis on the left half of the human brain.]

Scientific American. *The Brain*. San Francisco: W. H. Freeman and Company, 1979. [The eleven articles originally appeared in the September 1979 issue of *Scientific American* and deal with a variety of topics related to the brain.]

Scientific American. *Mind and Behavior*. San Francisco: W. H. Freeman and Company, 1980. [Twenty-eight articles, mostly by psychologists, covering a diversity of interesting topics.]

Segalowitz, Sid J. *Two Sides of the Brain: Brain Lateralization Explored*. Englewood Cliffs, NJ: Prentice-Hall, 1983. [A very readable text by a distinguished researcher who discusses "the uses of the left-right distinction between the brain hemispheres" and gives "some perspectives on the limitations of [this] construct." Excellent bibliography.]

Shepard, R. N., and L. A. Cooper. *Mental Images and Their Transformation*. Cambridge: MIT Press, 1982. [Useful for discussion of language and thought.]

Smith, Adam. *Powers of Mind*. New York: Random House, 1975. [Popular and interesting account of the workings of the brain, TM, EST, Rolfing and much more. See especially "II. Hemispheres," pp. 59–182.]

Springer, Sally, P., and Georg Deutsch, *Left Brain, Right Brain*. San Francisco: W. H. Freeman and Company, 1981. [An outstanding book that discusses most of the important research into the nature of hemispheric asymmetries. Excellent bibliography.]

Walker, Edward, ed. *Explorations in the Biology of Language*. Montgomery, VT: Bradford Books, 1978. [Six difficult but important essays focusing on language as a biological manifestation of universal cognitive structure. The second essay deals with aphasia.]

PART ELEVEN

LANGUAGE, READING, AND WRITING

$\mathbf{A}$s we approach the twenty-first century, what is happening to the languages of the world? From the evidence that we have seen and read so far, it is clear that a high percentage of them, and of the cultures that sustain them, are in a state of upheaval. Many languages, mostly indigenous and oral, are dying or recently extinct; many, particularly those of the most literate and technically advanced cultures, are undergoing unprecedented growth and change. It would seem that literacy has become a linguistic criterion for survival. No language in today's world is immune to the influences of international politics, commerce, and the Internet. Even if the burgeoning jargon of the computer world were banished to "Outer Cyberia," as one disgruntled grammarian would have it, the explosion of knowledge in many other fields—combined with the means to communicate it—would still be stretching the world's languages, especially English, with a vast array of new concepts and terms.

The English language is a hub of contention today partly because it is the primary medium of communication in many fields worldwide, and partly because it represents a dominant American culture that threatens the prestige and the very existence of a host of ethnic and minority cultures. Thus it is a language under constant scrutiny. Feminists, Hispanics, blacks, Native Americans, and other groups all challenge the notion of "standard" English. These groups raise a number of vital questions about the nature of languages and the criteria by which to judge their quality and effectiveness. Is one language "better" than another? How does literacy—that is, the ability to read and write—both derive from and contribute to the continuity of a culture? What are the best ways to balance the constant rules of grammar and the inevitable changes of usage undergone by living language?

The six essays in Part Eleven explore these issues in detail. In "Languages and Writing," John P. Hughes lays the groundwork for a consideration of literacy and its importance by explaining the derivation of alphabets. He contends that the original phonemic alphabet came into existence by a great stroke of luck and that its dissemination through succeeding cultures has altered the course of history. A phonemic alphabet placed the capability for written communication, which had been the exclusive privilege of the rich and highly educated, into the hands of the populace.

The next three essays undertake to define a standard of quality in contemporary English language usage. John Algeo ("What Makes Good English Good?") takes aim at some of the most cherished notions of scholars and grammarians, and finds that there are no absolutes. "Because good English is so diverse," he concludes, "to use it in more than a few circumstances requires an equally diverse knowledge and a fine sense of what is appropriate under varying conditions." Charles R. Larson ("Its Academic, or Is It?") and Patricia T. O'Conner ("Like I Said, Don't Worry") take different viewpoints as they consider the effects on American society of the rapidly increasing erosion of traditional grammar in instruction and usage. With humor and without apology, they both affirm the strengths of a successful, long-standing linguistic system.

Barbara Hill Hudson applies her knowledge of English dialects to the interpretation of English and American literature. In "Sociolinguistic Analysis of Dialogues and First-Person Narratives in Fiction," Hudson alerts her students to the regional, ethnic, racial, and historical dialects of fictional characters. She shows how authors use the richness of the English language to portray the status, motivation, and actions of their characters.

In the final article, "Into the Electronic Millennium," Sven Birkerts expresses strong reservations about the effects of computer technology on literacy. He contends that the Internet is replacing the library as a source of information, that the public venue of e-mail chat rooms will supplant personal correspondence by letters, and that the linear, historical, contemplative reasoning gained by the reader of a good book is doomed to disappear into a fragmented, multitrack future. While acknowledging that "no one can really predict how we will adapt to the transformations taking place all around us," he warns us to be alert to the rapid technological changes that might endanger our culture and our language.

51

Languages and Writing

John P. Hughes

Most Americans take mass literacy for granted; they find it difficult to imagine not being able to read and write, and they are surprised to learn that even today a significant proportion of the world's currently spoken three thousand to five thousand languages lack writing systems. In the following selection from his book The Science of Language, *Professor John P. Hughes suggests the limitations that the lack of a writing system can impose. He traces in detail the evolution of writing systems, sometimes logical and sometimes not, from the earliest Cro-Magnon cave drawings to present-day systems. Note his explanation of the advantages of alphabetic systems and the unique nature of their origin.*

It has been said that the two oldest and greatest inventions of man were the wheel and the art of controlling fire. This is probable enough: and if one wished to make a group of three, surely the development of writing must claim the third place. Without a system of writing, no matter how wise or sublime the thought, once uttered it is gone forever (in its original form, at least) as soon as its echoes have died away.

Indeed, it would seem that without a means of preserving wisdom and culture, civilization, which depends on the passing on of a heritage from generation to generation, could not develop. The facts, however, are otherwise: noteworthy civilizations *have* arisen and flourished without possession of any form of writing, usually by forming a class of society whose duty and profession it was to keep in memory what we write down in books (and, too often, subsequently forget). Even the average citizen in such a society took as a matter of course demands upon his memory which we today would consider beyond human capacity.

All the same, one may question whether a really complex civilization—one capable of governing large areas, for instance—could be supported by such a system. If there ever was one, we may be sure it has been grossly slighted by history—which, after all, depends almost entirely on written records. Who, for example, has ever heard the Gaulish version of Caesar's campaigns?

There seems to be no reason to doubt that the many systems of writing which have been developed at different times by various peoples during mankind's long history all grew, by steps which we can and shall trace, out of man's ability to draw pictures.

Suppose you wish to preserve a record of your catching a twenty-pound trout, but happen to be illiterate. The obvious thing to do would be to draw and hang a picture of yourself catching the big fish. It was, apparently, an equally obvious thing to do some fifty thousand years ago, for the caves which yielded us the remains of the Cro-Magnon man first attracted attention because of their beautifully drawn pictures of a procession, perhaps a hunt, of animals. We shall never know whether this was a mere decoration or a record.

Given the ability to draw well enough so that your representations of persons and objects can be readily recognized, it is, of course, not difficult to tell a complete story in one panoramic picture, or in a series of uncaptioned sketches. The range of information that can be conveyed in this way can be greatly extended if a few simple conventions are agreed upon between the artist and his prospective audience: the use of a totem-sign for a certain tribe; considering a prone man to be sick or wounded if his eyes were open, dead if they are closed, and so on. Several tribes of North American Indians made use of this kind of communication (figure 51.1).

In these circumstances, it will be noted, pictures act as a means for the communication of thought, and thus are somewhat like a language in themselves. Indeed, some authorities include this kind of communication among various forms of "language," but we have deliberately excluded it from our definition. It is common and conventional to call this kind of writing *ideographic writing*, and while the term is convenient, this is properly in no sense either language or writing, as we shall proceed to show.

Note, first, that the kind of communication achieved in figure 51.1

FIGURE 51.1   An indian pictographic message. This message of friendship was sent from an American Indian chief to the president of the United States—the figure in the White House. The chief, identified by the lines rising from his head, who is sending the message, and the four warriors behind him, belong to the eagle totem; the fifth warrior is of the catfish totem. The figure at lower left is evidently also a powerful chief. The lines joining the eyes indicate harmony, and the three houses indicate the willingness of the Indians to adopt white men's customs. (From Henry R. Schoolcraft, *Historical and Statistical Information Respecting the Indian Tribes of America*, I, 418.)

is totally independent of the language or languages of the persons who make the drawing and of those who read it. The "text" may be correctly "read" in any language. It is not an effort to record the *language* in which the event is described, but, like language itself, to record the *original events:* we might even say it is a system alternative to language for symbolizing events. And therefore it is not strictly writing; for writing is always a *record or representation of language.*

Ideographic "writing" cannot be strictly language either, for it has two limitations which would make it unworkable as a system for expressing human thought. First, it is not within everyone's competence: some of us have no talent for drawing. This, however, could be offset by conventionalizing the characters to a few simple strokes, not immediately recognizable as the original picture except by previous knowledge of the convention (see figure 51.2).

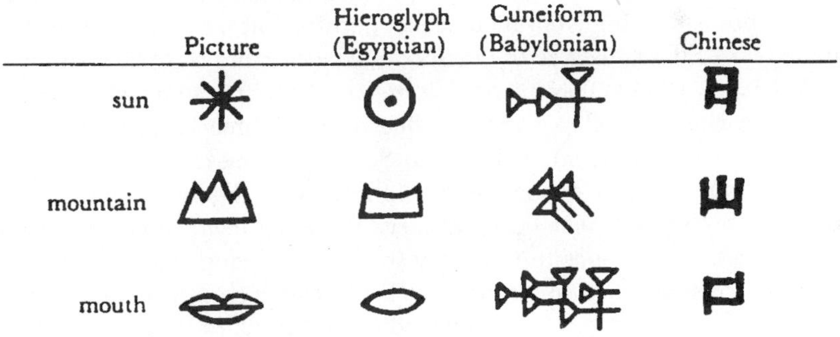

	Picture	Hieroglyph (Egyptian)	Cuneiform (Babylonian)	Chinese
sun				
mountain				
mouth				

FIGURE 51.2   Conventionalized symbols.

But then the second, more serious objection still remains: even with such conventionalization, the system cannot adequately express the whole range of human thought; and to do so even partially will require thousands of characters and a system of such complexity that exceedingly few in the society could master it.

The Chinese people have an ancient and beautiful script which was originally, and still is largely, ideographic. The characters have been conventionalized, but it is still quite easy to recognize their origin, as is shown in figure 51.2. Although there are many mutually unintelligible dialects of Chinese, the same written text can be read by any native (each in his own dialect), and the gist can even be made out by one who knows the principles of the system, but little of the language. Chinese writing is thus one of the strongest forces toward Chinese cultural unity. . . . But it is estimated that 70,000 to 125,000 characters exist (not all, of course, used with equal frequency), and it is said that a scholar takes seven years to learn to read and write Chinese if he already speaks it, while over 80 percent of the native speakers of Chinese are illiterate in their own language.

Where there is considerable divergence between a language and its written representation, as in the case of Chinese or Italian, where many different dialects are written with the same spelling, or in French or English, where the language has changed considerably since the stage for which the writing was devised, a tendency may arise to consider the written language the "correct" language, of which the spoken language is a deformation which should be "corrected" to agree with the writing. This is particularly true when the writing either records, or once recorded, or is believed to record, the speech of a class of society which enjoys prestige, to which many native speakers would like to assimilate themselves.

This, however, always obscures things and puts the cart before the horse. Actually, the prestige class of any society probably least conforms its speech consciously to writing: sure of their status, its members do not worry about betraying an inferior origin in speech or behavior. It is said that if a man's table manners are absolutely disgusting, he is either a peasant or a duke. Writing is, in its essence, nothing but a means of recording language with some degree of efficiency. Whether one form or another of the language is "good" or "correct" is an entirely different question; a system of writing is good or bad according to how it records, accurately or otherwise, whatever form of the language it is aiming to record.

However, because of the prestige of letters in largely illiterate populations (which is so great that *gramarye* has even been thought to have magic power), the opposite tendency to "correct" language according to written forms has been so strong as to lead to such things as the creation of a word like "misle" from a misreading of the word "misled."[1] Many similar examples could be given.

PICTOGRAPHIC WRITING

Any nation which finds occasion to use a form of ideographic writing with any regularity, even if all the writing is the job of one relatively small social group, will probably sooner or later take the simple and logical step to *pictographic writing*. In this case, the written sign, which in ideographic writing is the symbol for an *idea*, becomes the symbol of a *word*. For example, a device like

which represents the floor-plan of a house, now becomes a sign for *per*, the Egyptian word for "house," or of *beyt'*, the Hebrew word for "house."

---

[1] This is an extreme case of what is called "spelling pronunciation." More typical examples are the pronunciation, by Americans in England, of words like *twopence* and *halfpenny* as written.

Another example: the picture

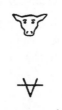

conventionalized to

which of course represented the snout of an ox, now becomes a sign for *alep*, the ancient Hebrew word for "ox."

The advantages of this step for the improvement of communication are evident. The written sign now symbolizes, not an idea, but a word, and a word is a far more precise symbol of a mental concept than any other which can be devised. With a sufficient stock of symbols of this new type, the writer can distinguish among a house, a stable, a barn, a shed, and a palace; whereas with ideographic writing he is pretty well limited to "house" vs. "big house" or "small house" (as there is no separate symbol for the adjective, the bigness or smallness cannot be specified and can range from "largish" to "enormous"). Much ambiguity is avoided: if you have tried to convey messages ideographically . . . you know how easy it is for an intended message "the king is angry" to be interpreted "the old man is sick."

Pictographic writing is, moreover, true writing, since it is a means of recording language, not just an alternative way of expressing the concepts which language expresses.

All pictographic writing systems that we know have developed from ideographic systems, and show clear traces of this, notably in their tendency to preserve ideographic symbols among the pictographic. Thus, the ancient Egyptians had an ideograph for water, a representation of waves or ripples:

〰〰

Eventually they derived from this a sign

〰〰
〰〰
〰〰

standing for the word *mu*, which meant "water." But they often wrote the word *mu* as follows:

And in writing of a river, the word for which was *atur*,

they also added the water sign: *atur* was written

The purpose of these ideographic "determinants" was probably to help the reader who did not know the particular word or sign by giving an indication of its general connotation. Nouns denoting persons were usually given the "determinant" of a little man—

or a little woman—

For, despite the noteworthy increases in efficiency which pictographic writing represents, thousands of characters are still necessary; and one advantage of the ideographic system has been lost—the characters are no longer self-explanatory. (This is only a theoretical advantage on behalf of ideographic script, since, while the ideographic character for a bird should presumably be readily recognized as a bird, in practice the characters have to be conventionalized for the sake of those who do not draw well.)

A considerable number of pictographic writing systems have been developed at different times in different parts of the world, but, Sunday-supplement science to the contrary notwithstanding, quite independently of one another, so that we have no ground for talking about the "evolution" by man of the art of writing. There is no evidence whatever for a First Cave Man who sat with hammer and chisel and stone and figured out how to chisel the first message, after which man made improvement after improvement, until the peak (represented, of course, by English orthography of the present day) was reached. Actually, nations once literate have been known to lapse into illiteracy as a result of ruinous wars and social disorganization.

SYLLABIC WRITING, UNLIMITED AND LIMITED

The step from pictographic to syllabic writing is an easy, logical, and, it might very well seem, self-evident one; yet there have been several nations which developed the first without ever proceeding to the second. It would probably be safe to say, however, that a majority of those who came as far as pictographic writing took the step to syllabic script.

In pictographic writing it is, of course, as easy to develop a stock of thousands of characters as in ideographic; yet, strange as it might seem, there is still always a shortage. This shortage arises because it is extremely difficult or impossible to represent some words in pictures. Take "velocity," for example. Is there any picture you could draw to express this that might not be read as, say, "the man is running"? Or, if you think you could picture "velocity," how would you handle "acceleration"? If you still think you could manage this one, what sort of picture, pray, would you draw for the word "the"?

The first step toward syllabic writing is taken when you permit yourself to cheat a little and take advantage of homophones. There is, let us say, a good pictograph for "the sea"; you use it to express the Holy "See," or "I see" (writing, perhaps, the characters for *eye* and *sea*).

When you have expressed the word "icy" by the characters for *eye* and *sea*, or *belief* by the characters for *bee* and *leaf*, you have turned the corner to syllabic writing. Any relationship whatever between the character and the *meaning* of the syllable it stands for is henceforth entirely irrelevant. The character expresses nothing but a sequence of sounds— the sounds making up one of the syllables of the language.

The first result of this is a gain of efficiency: a decrease in the number of possible characters (since more than one word or syllable can be written with the same syllabic character—in fact a great number can be written with varying sequences and combinations of a rather small number of characters). This gain is largely theoretical, however, for there will still be several thousand characters. The superiority of syllabic writing over pictographic from the point of view of efficiency will largely depend on the structure of syllables in the language using it. If syllables are generally or always simple in structure, a syllabic system of writing may work extremely well.

In every type of language, however, ambiguity and duplication are likely to be discovered in this kind of *unlimited syllabic* writing. It is often uncertain which of various homonymous readings is intended (e.g., does a character for "deep" joined to one for "end" mean "deep end" or "depend"?). And conversely, there are almost always two or more ways to say the same thing.

If the users of a syllabic system have a sense of logic, they will soon tend to adopt the practice of always writing the same syllable with the same character. The immediate result of this is for the first time to reduce the number of signs to manageable proportions: the sequence *baba* will always be expressed by signs expressing BA BA—never by signs for syllables such as BAB HA, BA ABA, 'B AB HA. Hence the number of signs is not so great as not to be within the capacity of the more or less average memory.

Since many languages have only one syllable-type—CV (i.e., consonant followed by vowel)—application of the principle above to the syllabic writing of such a language results in a very simple, logical and efficient system, next to alphabetic writing the most efficient writing possible.

The simplicity and efficiency are likely to prove elusive, however, when applied to languages of more complex syllabic structure. Even so, one almost inevitably arrives at the idea of having a series of signs representing syllables in which each consonant of the language is paired with each vowel: BA, BE, BI, BO BU; DA, DE, DI, DO, DU; FA, FE, FI, FO, FU; and so on. A list of such signs is called a *syllabary*.

Some time after this stage of limited *syllabic writing* has been reached, the thought may occur that the inventory of signs can be further reduced by taking one form, without any specification, as the form for, say, BA; and then simply using diacritic marks to indicate the other possible syllable structures: something like the following:

△ BA   ⬘ BI   △- BU
⬗ BE   -△ BO

This brings us very close to alphabetic writing. The last step in syllabic writing and the first in alphabetic writing might come about by accident; suppose a class of words ends in a syllable -*ba*, and in the course of time the vowel ceases to be pronounced. Now the syllabic sign △ stands for B alone, not BA; and some sign (in Sanskrit *virāma*, in Arabic *sukūn*) is invented to express this situation: e.g., △ will express BA, and △ will express B. By use of this sign the vowel of any syllabic sign can be suppressed, and any sign in the syllabary can be made alphabetic.

A situation like that just described is seen in the Semitic writing systems (Arabic, Hebrew), of which it is often said that they "write only the consonants." Actually, all the Arabic and Hebrew letters were originally syllabic signs, representing the consonant *and* a vowel (see figure 51.3).

ALPHABETIC WRITING

As will be clear by now, true alphabetic writing consists in having a sign for each sound (technically each phoneme) of the language, rather than one for each word or one for each syllable. This is the most efficient writing system possible, since a language will be found to have some thousands of words and at least a couple of hundred different syllables, but the words and syllables are made up of individual speech sounds which seldom exceed sixty to seventy in number, and sometimes number as few as a dozen. Hence an alphabetic writing system can, with the fewest possible units (a number easily within anyone's ability to master), record every possible utterance in the language.

It would seem that the different stages we have traced, from drawing pictures to ideographs, to pictographic and syllabic writing, so logically follow each other as inevitably to lead a nation or tribe from one to the next until ultimately an alphabetic writing would be achieved. But such is simply not the case. Many great nations, for example the Japanese, have come as far as syllabic writing, and never seemed to feel a need to go beyond it. Indeed, in all the history of mankind, alphabetic writing has been invented only once, and all the alphabets in the world that are truly so called are derived from that single original alphabet. It seems likely that but for a certain lucky linguistic accident, man would never have discovered the alphabetic principle of writing. Had that been the case, the history of mankind would certainly have been very, very different.

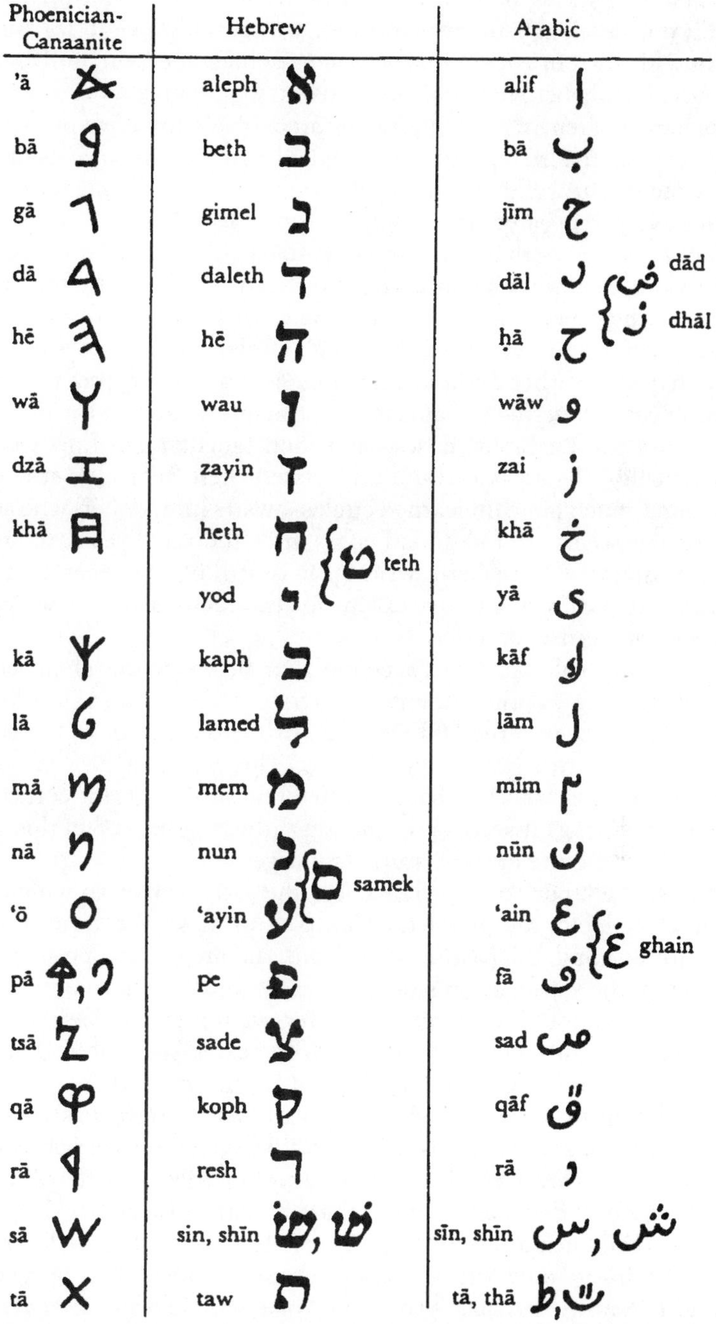

Phoenician-Canaanite		Hebrew		Arabic	
'ā	𐤀	aleph	א	alif	ا
bā	𐤁	beth	ב	bā	ب
gā	𐤂	gimel	ג	jīm	ج
dā	𐤃	daleth	ד	dāl	د dād ض / dhāl ذ
hē	𐤄	hē	ה	hā	ح
wā	𐤅	wau	ו	wāw	و
dzā	𐤆	zayin	ז	zai	ز
khā	𐤇	heth	ח teth ט	khā	خ
		yod	י	yā	ى
kā	𐤊	kaph	כ ך	kāf	ك
lā	𐤋	lamed	ל	lām	ل
mā	𐤌	mem	מ ם	mīm	م
nā	𐤍	nun	נ ן samek	nūn	ن
'ō	𐤏	'ayin	ע	'ain	ع ghain غ
pā	𐤐	pe	פ	fā	ف
tsā	𐤑	sade	צ ץ	sad	ص
qā	𐤒	koph	ק	qāf	ق
rā	𐤓	resh	ר	rā	ر
sā	𐤔	sin, shīn	שׁ שׂ	sīn, shīn	ش , س
tā	𐤕	taw	ת	tā, thā	ط , ث

FIGURE 51.3   Semitic alphabets. The names of the letters of the Phoenician-Canaanite (Old Semitic) alphabet are surmises. Letters in one alphabet which do not have correlatives in the others are set off to the side. The traditional order of the Arabic letters has been modified slightly to stress parallels.

There is a strong probability that it was the ancient Egyptians who first hit on the alphabetic principle; but we cannot prove it, for we cannot show that all or even a majority of the characters which ultimately became the alphabet we know were used in Egyptian texts of any period (though an apparently sound pedigree can be made for a few of them).

Of course, the hieroglyphic writing had a stock of thousands of characters, and might well have included the ones we are looking for in texts which have disappeared or not yet been discovered. What is harder to explain, however, is that when the Egyptians wrote alphabetically, they gave alphabetic values to an entirely different set of characters (figure 51.4). Yet the Egyptians had been using a writing system for literally thousands of years, and had gone through all the stages. It does not seem likely that some other nation came along just as the Egyptians were on the point of discovering the alphabetic principle, snatched the discovery from under the Pharaohs' noses—and then taught *them* how to write alphabetically! There is certainly a mystery here which is still to be solved, and much fame (in learned circles) awaits him [or her] who solves it. If the Egyptians did indeed fail, after three thousand years, to discover the principle of alphabetic writing, it is striking evidence that man might never have had this art except for the lucky accident which we shall now proceed to describe.

Not being able to prove a connection between the alphabet and Egyptian writing, for the present we have to say that the oldest known genuine alphabet was the Old Semitic, ultimate ancestor of the scripts used today to write Arabic and Hebrew. This alphabet had, of course, been a syllabic script. How had it turned that all-important corner into alphabetic writing? It seems probable that it was prompted in this direction by the structure of the Semitic languages.

To us, the "root" of our verb *ask* is the syllable *ask*, to which various other syllables are prefixed or suffixed to make the various verbal forms, for example the past tense (*ask-ed*), the progressive present tense (*is ask-ing*), the third-person singular present (*ask-s*), and so on.

With verbs like *drive* or *sing*, however, we might say that the root is a syllable *dr-ve* or *s-ng*, where the dash indicates some vowel, but not always the same vowel, since we have *drive, drove, driven, sing, sang, sung*. Something is expressed by the alternation of these vowels, to be sure . . . , but the root of the verb is still a *syllable*, even with a variable vowel.

It was probably some kind of (alternating vowel) system like this which led to the situation now characteristic of Semitic languages (which is really just a further step in this direction), whereby the meaning of "driving" would inhere in the consonants D-R-V, that of "asking" in '-S-K. In Semitic languages the "root" of a word is really a *sequence of consonants* (usually three), modifications of the root being effected by kaleidoscopic rearrangements of the vowels intervening.

Thus, anything to do with writing shows the consonants *K-T-B*, but "he wrote" = *KaTaBa*, "it is written" = *meKTūB*, "he got it written" = *KaTtaBa*, "scribes" = *KuTtaBūn*, and so on. Words which seem to us quite unrelated turn out to be, in this system, derived from each other, like *SaLāM*, "peace," *iSLām*, "the Mohammedan religion," *muSLiM*, "a Mohammedan." (From *salām* we get *'aslāma*, "he pacified, subjugated"; *islām* is "subjugation, submission" to God, and *muslim* is "one who has submitted.")

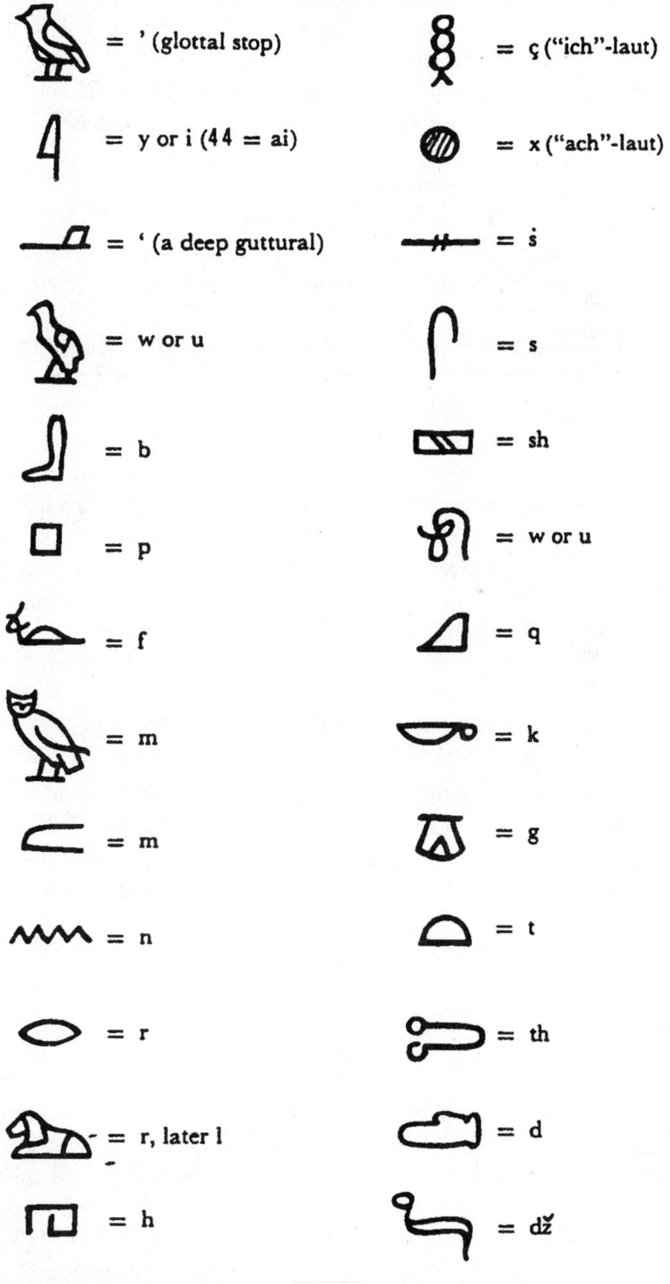

🦅	= ' (glottal stop)	𐎠	= ç ("ich"-laut)
	= y or i (44 = ai)		= x ("ach"-laut)
	= ' (a deep guttural)		= ṡ
	= w or u		= s
	= b		= sh
	= p		= w or u
	= f		= q
	= m		= k
	= m		= g
	= n		= t
	= r		= th
	= r, later l		= d
	= h		= dž

FIGURE 51.4   Egyptian alphabetic characters.

Obviously, no other type of language is better adapted to suggest to its speakers that there is a unit of word structure below the syllable; that BA is in turn composed of B- and -A. This is precisely what other nations might never have guessed. In Semitic, where BA alternates constantly with BI and BU, and sometimes with B- (the vowel being silenced), it is almost inevitable that every user of the language should develop a concept of the phoneme—a notion which is fundamental to the development of true alphabetic writing.

The structural nature of the Semitic languages is, therefore, in all probability the happy accident which became the key that unlocked for mankind, for the first and only time, the mystery of how to record speech by the method of maximum efficiency—one which does not have so many characters as to make learning it a complex art demanding years of training nor require a skill in drawing which few possess, nor consume large volumes of material for a relatively small amount of recorded message.

The consequences of this lucky accident are truly tremendous. If we did not have the alphabet, it would be impossible to hope for universal literacy, and therefore (if Thomas Jefferson's view was correct) for truly representative government. Writing could have been kept a secret art known only to a privileged few or to a particular social class which would thus have an undue advantage over the others. Information could not nearly so easily be conveyed from nation to nation, and the levels of civilization achieved by the Romans and ourselves might still be only goals to strive for. Truly, Prometheus did not do more for human progress than the unnamed scribe who first drew an alphabetic sign.

THE WANDERINGS OF THE ALPHABET

Let us here stress again that as far as can be ascertained from the available records, the principle of alphabetic writing has only been discovered once—hence, in the whole world *there is only one alphabet*. It follows that any people which writes in alphabetic signs has learned and adapted the use of the alphabet from another people who, in turn, had done the same. When the wanderings of this most potent cultural innovation are plotted, it makes an impressive odyssey. But the same would no doubt be true of every other discovery which has figured in an advance of civilization, if the same means existed for following its trail.

The earliest preserved inscriptions in alphabetic script date to about 1725 B.C. and were found in and around Byblos, in the country then known as Phoenicia (now Lebanon). It would seem that an alphabetic script which we might call Old Semitic was fairly familiar in that region at that time, though, as we have said, we cannot establish precisely where this script was invented, or by which Semitic tribe. It has been suggested that several Semitic peoples might have hit on the alphabetic principle at around the same time; but, if so, they seem to have soon adopted a common set of symbols.

This Old Semitic alphabet is of course the ancestor of the Hebrew, Phoenician, and Aramaic systems of writing. From these northern Semites, the knowledge of the alphabet appears to have passed, on the one hand, to the Greeks of Asia Minor, and on the other, to the Brahmans of ancient India, who developed from it their *devanagari*, the sacred script in which the religious rituals and hymns of the ancient Hindus were recorded.

With this exception, it seems that the genealogy of every other alphabetic system of writing goes through the Greeks. And it was because of the structure of *their* language that the Greeks were responsible for the greatest single improvement in the system: the origination of signs for the vowels.

The Semitic dialects had certain sounds which did not exist in Greek. The symbols for some of these, such as *qoph* (Q), the sign for the velar guttural which had existed in Indo-European but had everywhere been replaced by *p* in Attic Greek, were simply discarded by the Greeks (except in their use as numbers, but that is a different story). In other cases, however, the Greeks kept and used the symbol for a syllable beginning with a non-Greek sound, but pronounced it *without the foreign consonant*—so that the symbol became a sign for the syllable's vowel.

Thus, the first sign in the alphabet originally stood for the syllable 'A, where the sign ' represents the "glottal stop," a contraction and release of the vocal cords—not a phoneme in English, but used often enough as a separator between vowels (e.g., oh-'oh), and you have heard it in Scottish dialect as a substitute for T: *bo'le* for *bottle*, *li'le* for *little*. Some dialects of Greek had this sound, and others did not. Those which did ultimately lost it, so that the sign Ɐ (by now written in a different direction, A) everywhere became the sign, not for 'A, but for the vowel *A*.

Other Semitic gutturals had had the tendency to influence adjacent vowels in the direction of O or U, and they accordingly, by the process just described, became the signs for those vowels.

A rather good illustration of what was going on is found in the sign H, standing for the syllable HE. In Ionic Greek, where the sound *h* was eventually eliminated, H became the sign for the vowel *e*. In Sicilian Greek, however, where syllables beginning with *h* still remained, the same H became the sign for *h*—which is our usage also, because we got the alphabet from the Romans, who got it from the Greeks, who followed the Sicilian tradition.

This fact explains deviations in *our* values for the alphabetic signs as compared with those of the standard (Attic) Greek alphabet (see figure 51.5). Since the alphabet had not been invented as a tool for writing Greek, each Greek dialect which adopted it had to modify it a little—to assign different values to some of the signs, and discard the excess signs or use them in new ways, according to the phonology of their own speech.

Early Greek	Attic (East)	Sicilian (West)	Roman and Modern Equivalent
A	A	A	A
ꓭ	B	B	B
ꓶ	⋀	⌐	G and C
◁	△	△	D
ꓱ	E	E	E
ꓶ	[F] (=w)	F (=w)	F
X	Ⲓ	Ⲓ	Z
⊟	⊟ (=e)	H (=h)	H
⊗	⊗	⊙	TH
ꙅ	I	I	I
ꓘ	K	K	K
ꓥ	⋀	⋀L	L
ꟽ	M	M	M
ꓠ	N	N	N
⊞	Ⲭ (=ks)	ⵣ	X
O	O	O	O
ꓶ	⌐	⌐ or ⋂	P
M	‾	‾	‾
Φ	ϙ	ϙ	Q
�535	P	R	R
ꓳ	ϟ	ϟ	S
†	T	T	T
↓	V·	V	V (=u) , W, Y
	Φ	φφ	PH
	X (=kh)	X or + (=ks)	CH (=kh)
	↓	−	PS

FIGURE 51.5   Greek alphabets. Note changes in direction of writing and variation of values between Attica and Sicily (after E. M. Thompson).

While practically all modern nations which have alphabetic writing got it directly or indirectly from the Romans, there are a few to whom the tradition passes directly from the Greeks, in some cases concomitantly with direct northern Semitic influence. Between the third and fifth centuries A.D., the spread of Christianity occasioned the devising of the ornamental and highly efficient Armenian, and the intriguing, delicate Georgian alphabets. And when the feared Goths were marauding throughout Latin Christendom, Ulfilas, child of a Gothic father and a Greek mother, became the St. Patrick of the Goths, Christianizing them and translating the Bible into their language, writing it with an alphabet which, according to repute, he invented, basing it on Greek. Ulfilas' lucky bilingualism not only gave us our oldest extensive records of any Germanic language, but also, it is believed, served as the basis of the Scandinavian "runic" writing, although some think it was the other way around.

Later, in the ninth century, when Christianity reached the Slavic peoples, two principal alphabets, the "glagolitic" and the "Cyrillic" (the latter named in honor of one of its reputed inventors, St. Cyril, who died 869 A.D.; the other inventor was his brother, St. Methodius, d. 855 A.D.), were devised to represent the then most generally used Slavic dialect. From these developed in the course of time the national alphabets of those Slavic peoples who were evangelized from Byzantium—the Russians, the Ukrainians, the Bulgarians, and the Serbs (figure 51.6). (In contemporary Russia the Cyrillic alphabet has in turn been adapted for writing many non–Indo-European languages of the Soviet Union.)

Slavs who got their religion from Rome had to struggle to put their complex Slavic phonology into the Latin alphabet, with what often seem (to English speakers) jaw-breaking results, as seen in names like Przmysl, Szczepiński, and Wojcechowic. The name Vishinsky, as a rough transcription from the Cyrillic, is identical with the Polish name Wyszinski.

From the great Roman empire the art of alphabetic writing passed, by inheritance or adoption, to virtually all the peoples who know it today. They were responsible for many interesting and important innovations in the basic system which there is not space to detail here, but which may be found in any thorough and complete history of the alphabet. We shall just point out a few of the most significant ones.

The Romance-speaking peoples simply inherited their alphabet; in many cases, they did not realize that they were not still speaking, as well as writing, genuine but perhaps rather careless Latin. When they made an effort to write Latin more correctly, only then did they realize that theirs was actually a different language.

It was during the time when Latin was still spoken, however, that the first modifications had to be made in the alphabet—leading to the first diacritic signs. The sound *h* became silent in colloquial Latin in the first century B.C. and in standard Latin by the second century A.D. Thereafter the letter was a zero, expressing nothing, and hence could be used with other letters to express variations: TH for something like T that was not quite a T; GH for something like G that was not a G, and so on.

Cyrillic	Russian	Equivalent	Cyrillic	Russian	Equivalent
ⱔ	а	a	Ȣ	у	u
Б	б	b	Ф	ф	f
В	в	v	Ѳ	ѳ*	f (originally th)
Г	г	g	Х	х	kh
Д	д	d	Ѡ		ō
Є	е	ye	Ш	ш	sh
Ж	ж	zh	Ѱ	щ	shch
Ѕ		dz	Ч	ц	ts
Ꙁ	з	z	Ɣ	ч	ch
Н	и	i	Ъ	ъ*	"hard sign"
І	і*	i	Ꙑ	ы	ÿ
Ћ		d', t'	Ь	ь	"soft sign"
К	к	k	Ѣ	я	ya
Ⰾ	л	l	Ю	ю	yu
М	м	m	Ѥ	ѣ*	ye
N	н	n	Ꙗ, Ꙗ		ē, yē
О	о	o	Ѫ, Ѭ		ō, yō
П	п	p	Ѯ		ks
Р	р	r	Ѱ		ps
С	с	s	Ѵ		ü
Т	т	t			

* These letters were abolished in 1918.

FIGURE 51.6   Slavic alphabets. Some of the Modern Russian letters are given out of standard order for purpose of matching.

Another early diacritic, perhaps the earliest, was the letter G. Words like *signum* had shifted in pronunciation at a very early period from SIG-NUM to SING-NUM to, probably, [seɲo] (where the sign ɲ stands for what is technically a "palatized n," as *gn* in French *mignon* or *ñ* in Spanish *cañón*). This made the G, in this particular position, another zero: and the idea logically arose that any sound could be distinguished from a palatalized correlative by prefixing G to the latter: N/GN; L/GL. Hence Romance languages blossomed with forms like *egli, Bologna, segno, Cagliari*. But Portuguese used the faithful H to express these sounds (*filho, senhor*), and Spanish, which had divested itself of doubled consonants, used a doubled letter (*castillo, suenno*), and later used an abbreviation for a doubled *n* (*sueño*)—for the Spanish *tilde* is nothing other than the well-known medieval Latin MS. abbreviation for an M or N (*tā, dōinū, ītĕtiōĕ*). Thus, the American who reads the Italian name *Castiglione* as *Cas-tig-li-o-ni* is murdering the harmonious genuine sound, since the spelling stands for *Ca-sti-lyo-ne*.

When the practice ceased of using as names of the letters the names of the objects they had pictured (or some meaningless derivative thereof, like *alpha, beta*), there arose the custom of naming a letter by giving (in the case of a vowel) its *sound*, or (in the case of a consonant), its sound *preceded or followed by [e]*. (In English this latter sound has uniformly shifted to [i], so we say the letters of the alphabet [e], [bi], [si], but Frenchmen say [a], [be], [se].) In some exceptional cases, however, phonetic shift has eliminated the letter's sound from its name. Our name for R is [ar] (from earlier [er] by the same change which gives us *heart, hearth, sergeant*). In English pronunciation, however, R is silent after a vowel, so the name of the letter R is *ah*—with no R in it.

Again, our name for *h* is *aitch*, a meaningless word in English but a preservation of French *la hache* "the hatchet"—suggested by the letter's appearance, to be sure.

$$\mathfrak{H} = h$$

—but originally containing its sound; no [h] has been pronounced in French, however, for over a century, so the name of this letter, too, fails to contain its sound . . .

Our present letters J and W are known to have been invented in the sixteenth century. In Latin, since all W's had become V's by the second century A.D., the letter U, however written (V, U), expressed that sound—the choice between the rounded and the angular form being purely a matter of calligraphy. The English language, however, had both the V sounds and the W sounds; so, to express the latter, English printers of the sixteenth century "doubled" the former, writing vv (or uu).

Latin also lacked any sound like English J; but this sound appeared in Old French in words where Latin had had *i*, either as *ee* or as *y* (*Fanuarius* > *janvier; iuvenis* > *jeune*), and printers traditionally used *i* for it. Medieval scribes often extended this letter downwards in an ornamental flourish at the end of a number (thus: xiiij), and no doubt it was this which suggested the adoption in English printing of this alternative form of *i* for the *j*-sound. For quite a while, however, many printers continued to regard i/j and u/w/v as interchangeable and to print *Iohn, starres aboue, A Vvinter's Tale, Fnterlude,* and so on.

We have been able to mention here only a few of the vicissitudes undergone by the alphabet—*the* alphabet, only one, always the same—in its long journey through space and time from the eastern shores of the Mediterranean to the far islands of the Pacific.

FOR DISCUSSION AND REVIEW

1. According to Hughes, "ideographic writing" is "properly in no sense either language or writing." How does he support this statement? Do you agree or disagree? Defend your answer.

2. In general, each character of written Chinese represents one morpheme or one word. Explain the advantages of such a system, which does not involve linking sound to written characters, to the Chinese as a nation. What are the disadvantages?

3. Justify Hughes's statement that "Pictographic writing . . . is true writing."

4. Describe the development of syllabic writing systems from pictographic systems. What are the advantages of the former? How might a limited syllabic system develop into an alphabetic system? Is such a logical progression more or less inevitable? Why or why not?

5. Why is alphabetic writing "the most efficient writing system possible"?

6. Explain how the structure of the Semitic languages and the development of the concept of the phoneme led to the development of the alphabet.

7. Summarize chronologically what Hughes calls "the wanderings of the alphabet." Be sure to explain the important contribution made by the Greeks and how the structure of their language made improvement of this alphabet possible.

8. What is a diacritic sign? Give three examples (draw them from at least two languages). Describe the development of diacritic signs as part of alphabetic writing.

9. Hughes describes the development of an alphabetic writing system as a "lucky accident" and as "truly tremendous." Describe the kind(s) of cultures that might have developed had an alphabetic writing system not evolved. (Consider, for example, Ray Bradbury's *Fahrenheit 451* or George Orwell's *1984*.)

52

What Makes Good English Good?

John Algeo

For more than three hundred years, a battle has been waging over what constitutes good English. Schools have traditionally taught the difference between imply *and* infer, *never to split an infinitive, and that it's between you and* me *and not between you and* I. *In this delightful tongue-in-cheek essay, which first appeared in* The Legacy of Language: A Tribute to Charlton Laird, *Professor John Algeo of the University of Georgia reviews ten key criteria that usage experts and grammarians have used for determining what constitutes good English. As you read, think about which of these criteria you use in judging language usage, including your own.*

Human beings are a peculiar species. We have a rage for order: out of the great booming chaos of the world around us, we obsessively make pattern and regularity. Out of the wilderness, we make cities. Out of experience, we make histories. Out of speech, we make grammars. And in the process of turning chaos into order, we create values.

The human species has been called *homo sapiens*, the earthy one who knows or experiences. But we might as well be called *homo judex*, the judge, because an inescapable human impulse is to distinguish between good and bad. For us, the good is its own warrant. As Mammy Yokum was wont to instruct her physically sound and morally pure, if intellectually disadvantaged, offspring, Li'l Abner: "Good is better than evil because it's so much nicer." Or, as *Webster's New World Dictionary of the American Language*, with which Charlton Laird was associated, defines the word, *good* is "a general term of approval or commendation, meaning 'as it should be.'"

Should is a powerful and distinctly human concept. Wars have been fought over it. Among English speakers, the Grammar Wars began in the seventeenth century, when pedagogues fell out over why and how to teach Latin. One camp wanted to teach grammar as an end in itself, because knowing grammar is good. Another camp wanted to teach grammar only so that young English scholars could read the great works of Latin literature. The two camps were roughly the equivalents three hundred years ago of scientific linguists and literary humanists (if I may use the word *humanist* without calling down the wrath of the Reverend Jerry Falwell). The equivalence is only approximate, however, because the grammar-as-an-end-in-itself advocates of the 1600s had a strong bent toward logic and neatening up the language, whereas the grammar-as-a-tool-for-literature advocates argued that the ancients could hardly have been wrong in the way they used their own language and thus needed no help from grammarians intent on regularizing and improving Latin.

Joseph Webbe, a doughty combatant in the lists of the Grammar Wars, scored against the grammarians in his 1622 book, *An Appeale to Truth*, by writing that

> they haue not onely weakened and broken speech, by reducing it vnto the poore and penurious prescript of Grammar-rules; but haue also corrupted it with many errors, in that they haue spoken otherwise than they ought to doo: well, in respect of rules; but ill in respect of custome, which is the *Lady and Mistress* of speaking.[1]

Our modern Grammar Wars (chronicled by Edward Finegan in his *Attitudes toward English Usage: The History of a War of Words*) have seen a curious realignment of forces. Today it is those whose principal concern is with studying language as an end in itself who are most in sympathy with Webbe's position "that we can neither in the Latine, nor in any other Tongue, be obedient vnto other rules or reasons, than Custome and our sense of hearing,"[2] whereas it is some contemporary men and women of letters who ignore custom and their sense of hearing in favor of "the poore and penurious prescript of Grammar-rules." And so we have spawned a new subspecies, variously called *pop-grammarians* or *usageasters* (the latter by Thomas L. Clark).[3]

The Grammar Wars go on. And, as they were more than three hundred years ago, they are still concerned with the question of what good English is. What makes good English good? A variety of answers have been given to that question, and since the question has been so long with us, it is useful occasionally to summarize the answers that have been given.

What I propose to do briefly in this essay is to look at ten of the grounds that have been proposed for deciding what good English is. I focus on grounds proposed by Theodore M. Bernstein, mentioning a few other writers on usage to show that Bernstein is not a linguistic sport. I single out Bernstein, not because he is particularly better or worse than others of the tribe, but because he wrote a good bit on the subject of usage, because he is typical of the modern man of letters, and because he was kind enough to provide a handy list of criteria for determining good usage.

---

[1] Joseph Webbe, *An Appeale to Truth, in the Controuersie betweene Art, & Vse; about the Best and Most Expedient Course in Languages* (1622). Reprinted in *English Linguistics, 1500–1800*, ed. R. C. Alston, no. 42 (Menston, England: Scolar Press, 1967), 22.

[2] Ibid., 46.

[3] Thomas L. Clark, "The Usageasters," *American Speech* 55 (1980): 131–136.

COMMUNICATIVE CRITERION

In *The Careful Writer* (1965), Bernstein equates good English with successful communication: "What good writing can do . . . is to assure that the writer is really in communication with the reader, that he is delivering his message unmistakably."[4] Porter Perrin has a similar criterion for good English: "So far as the writer's language furthers his intended effect, it is good; so far as it fails to further that effect, it is bad, no matter how 'correct' it may be."[5]

These are pious statements, which, like promises never to curtail Social Security benefits, are made to be broken. Bernstein does not even get out of the introduction to his book before he fractures the ideal of communication: "Let us insist that *disinterested* be differentiated from *uninterested*."[6] He urges this difference as essential to the existence of good English, with no concern for communicating with those readers for whom the two words are synonyms. If Bernstein had been really concerned about successful communication, he would not have advised his readers to avoid *disinterested* in the sense "uninterested" but rather told them not to use it at all, because the word is ambiguous. Bernstein's point about the need for communication is obviously well made, but it is seldom taken seriously by those who make it.

Bernstein goes on to enumerate six other sources for determining good English. It is worth looking at them seriatim.

LITERARY CRITERION

Bernstein adduces "the practices of reputable writers, past and present."[7] This criterion, like that of successful communication, is practically de rigueur in any discussion of usage. It is also a criterion of respectable antiquity. Webbe in 1622 had cited authors like Cicero as models of good Latin, in distinction to the grammarians among his contemporaries who invented rules that imposed more order on Latin than was to be found in classical authors. The authority of the literati was also invoked by Thomas Lounsbury, who used an elegant chiasmus in his *Standard of Usage in English*: "The best, and indeed the only proper, usage is the usage of the best."[8]

As appealing as it may be to English teachers, the literary criterion suffers from several weaknesses. One is the difficulty of deciding which authors are reputable or best and which are not; there is a danger of cir-

---

[4] Theodore M. Bernstein, *The Careful Writer: A Modern Guide to English Usage* (New York: Atheneum, 1965), vii.

[5] Porter G. Perrin, *Writer's Guide and Index to English*, 4th ed. rev. Karl W. Dykema and Wilma R. Ebbitt (Chicago: Scott Foresman, 1965), 27.

[6] Bernstein, xv.

[7] Ibid., viii.

[8] Thomas R. Lounsbury, *The Standard of Usage in English* (New York: Harper, 1908), vi.

cularity—writers who do not use good English (as the decider conceives it) are clearly not reputable or best, however widely read they may be. Another difficulty is that of deciding how far past or present one will look for models of good English: Joyce Carol Oates? Virginia Woolf? Ralph Waldo Emerson? Fanny Burney? Shakespeare? Chaucer? the Beowulf poet? In fact, popular writers on usage cite reputable writers as exemplifiers of good English rather infrequently. They are rather more apt to quote the words of famous authors as examples of blunders by the mighty, Homer nodding, and all that. Since the days of Bishop Lowth, citing errors from the works of great writers (or of one's opponents) has been a game rivaled only by the current popularity of Trivial Pursuit.

SCHOLARLY CRITERION

Bernstein's next criterion for good English is from "the observations and discoveries of linguistic scholars."[9] He carefully qualifies this criterion in two ways, however. First, "the work of past scholars has, when necessary, been updated," and second, "the work of contemporary scholars has been weighed judiciously." That is, *homo judex* is free to change (update) or to ignore (weigh judiciously) whatever he does not like. Although clearly subordinate to reputable writers, linguistic scholars seem like an authoritative group to invoke, especially if you don't have to pay any attention to them. We like being told that the message we are getting is backed by authorities: 9 out of 10 doctors, 64 percent of economists, any and all linguistic scholars. However, the fact that something is said to be recommended by doctors or economists or linguistic scholars is of no importance. What is important is the evidence on which doctors, economists, and linguistic scholars speak. And therefore this criterion is no criterion at all. It is not evidence, but publicity hype.

PEDAGOGICAL CRITERION

The following criterion is even phonier. It is "the predilections of teachers of English, wherever—right or wrong, like it or not—these predilections have become deeply ingrained in the language itself."[10] It is not at all clear that any predilections of any teachers of English have ever become deeply ingrained in our language. There may be one or two trivial matters for which the sweat of English teachers has dripped so incessantly on the stone of real language that it has finally worn a small indentation—the pronunciation of the *t* in *often* is probably one—but on the whole, not only are English teachers overworked, underpaid, and poorly educated, they are also ineffective.

---

[9] Bernstein, viii.
[10] Ibid., viii.

The archetype of the starched schoolmarm who has devoted her life, at the sacrifice of all personal comfort and happiness, to upholding standards and educating into self-awareness the pliable young minds entrusted to her charge is as mythological as Parson Weems's George Washington. Bernstein seems to be remembering with ambivalent nostalgia some Miss Thistlebottom from the eighth grade, who, in the haze of fifty intervening years, has taken on the epic proportions of Candida, Martin Joos's Muse of Grammar.[11] The reality is likely to have been thinner and more wizened. The predilections of teachers of English that have become deeply ingrained in our language are probably a null set.

LOGICAL CRITERION

Bernstein's next criterion is "what makes for clarity, precision, and logical presentation."[12] This is another mom-and-apple-pie criterion. However important clarity, precision, and logic are, our impression of them in language is likely to be a function of our familiarity with particular words or grammatical structures. Those for whom *disinterested* means "uninterested" find that use perfectly clear and precise. The difference between *She be here* and *She here* is clear and logical to anyone who understands it. Those who find such expressions muddled, vague, and illogical have got a problem. But the problem is theirs; it is not one for those who use the expressions. Talk about clarity and logic in language is often an unconscious confession of ignorance and ethnocentrism. What we know, we think logical; what we don't, illogical.

This criterion is often expressed by saying that good writing is the expression of good thinking. Ambrose Bierce, for example, held such a position in his delightfully quirky little book *Write It Right*, subtitled *A Little Blacklist of Literary Faults*, in which he says that good writing "is clear thinking made visible."[13] Bierce is probably best known for his advice to "prefer *ruined* to *dilapidated* since the latter—coming from Latin *lapis* "a stone"—cannot properly be used of any but a stone structure."[14] That is an example of diaphanous, rather than clear, thinking.

A similar standard was adopted by Richard Mitchell, whose *Underground Grammarian* announced in its first issue: "Clear language engenders clear thought and clear thought is the most important benefit of education."[15] One may subscribe to the idea that clear thought is the best possible result of education, while finding the proposition that clear language produces clear thought to be muddled. However, one can for-

---

[11] Martin Joos, *The Five Clocks* (New York: Harcourt, 1967).

[12] Bernstein, viii–ix.

[13] Ambrose Bierce, *Write It Right: A Little Blacklist of Literary Faults* (New York: Neale, 1909; New York: Union Library Association, 1934), 5.

[14] Ibid., 23.

[15] Richard Mitchell, *The Graves of Academe* (Boston: Little, Brown, 1981), 27.

give almost any amount of Mitchell's muddling for the sake of his épée, for example, his palpable hit in saying that "so many [college administrators] seem to be born aluminum-siding salesmen who took a wrong turn somewhere along the line."[16]

The link between good language and clear or exact thinking has been made by many writers on usage. One more example, an older one, will have to suffice. John O'London, who dedicated his book *Is It Good English?* To "Men, Women, and Grammarians," thereby expressing his opinion of our tribe, wrote: "Good English follows clear thinking rather than that system of rules called Grammar which youth loathes and maturity forgets."[17]

A problem with the equivalence of good language and clear thinking is that the latter might be defined as thinking that arrives logically at correct conclusions. T. S. Eliot and John Steinbeck, whom one might suppose to use rather good language, have thought themselves into rather different conclusions. It is hard to see how Eliot and Steinbeck can each be said to be clear thinking on social questions. Or, as Jim Quinn points out, "If good thought made good writing, and good writing made good thought, then Immanuel Kant, Hegel, and Ludwig Wittgenstein are not worth reading."[18]

PERSONAL CRITERION

Bernstein's penultimate criterion is the personal preference of the author, of which he asks rhetorically: "And why not? . . . After all, it's my book."[19] Why not, indeed. This is the most honest criterion Bernstein has set forward. By asserting it, he agrees with a cartoon that appeared shortly after the publication of Nancy Mitford's *Noblesse Oblige*, a popular treatment of the difference between U (upper class) and non-U language.[20] In the cartoon, a tweedy, horsy-looking woman says to her companion at the tea table, "I always say, if it's me it's U."

Everyone is certainly entitled to a choice among linguistic options. And if you can get people to buy a book in which you state your choices, why not? First amendment, free enterprise, and all that. Right on, Ted! Let's throw out all that malarkey about communicating unmistakably, reputable writers, linguistic scholars, English teachers, and logic, and just hunker down with good old ipse dixit. If it's me, it's U. As H. L. Mencken said, "No one ever went broke underestimating the intelligence of the American public."

---

[16] Ibid., 28.

[17] John O'London, *Is It Good English?* (New York: Putnam's, 1925), xi.

[18] Jim Quinn, *American Tongue and Cheek: A Populist Guide to Our Language* (New York: Pantheon, 1980), 76.

[19] Bernstein, ix.

[20] Nancy Mitford, ed. *Noblesse Oblige* (New York: Harper & Row, 1956).

PROFESSIONAL CRITERION

Bernstein's last criterion is a letdown from the preceding high point. He cites his experience in working with language as an editor of the *New York Times* and congratulates himself on the newspaper's "precision, accuracy, clarity, and—especially in recent years [under Bernstein's editorship, presumably]—good writing."[21] All this criterion does is to establish Bernstein's credentials for ipse-dixiting. It is a sad anticlimax. How much better to finish off with a glorious burst of egotistic self-assertion. Well, we can't all be perfect.

People who earn their living by the word, particularly the written word, know how to use words effectively. If they did not, they would not earn much of a living. But effective journalism and even great literature are obviously not the same thing as good English. If they were, only effective journalists and great writers would be using good English. That Bernstein spent many years as an editor, worrying about the language of others, explains how he came to write five books on usage; it does not warrant his claiming special authority to determine what is good language.

STYLISTIC CRITERION

Other writers have offered still further criteria for good English. Some have identified the stylistic characteristics of bad writing and thus by inference defined what is good. Richard Mitchell, the Underground Grammarian, for example, focuses on the sins of wordiness, weasel words (*attempt to, may*), passive verbs with no agent, and "needless neologism."[22] Similarly, Edwin Newman castigates cliches, jargon, voguish words, redundancy, and innovations—or what he imagines to be innovations (they frequently are nothing of the kind).

A digression: the subtitle of Newman's first book (*Strictly Speaking: Will America Be the Death of English?*)[23] identifies him as a disciple of the Armageddon school of usageasters. He, like John Simon, whose *Paradigms Lost*[24] is subtitled *Reflections on Literacy and Its Decline*, sees us as living in the time of the end. It is ironic that the demise of English should be predicted at a time when the language is being used by more people for more purposes in more places around the globe than ever before. Thomas Lounsbury expressed an ironic insight that is as applicable today as it was in 1908, when he wrote it:

---

[21] Bernstein, ix.

[22] Mitchell, 27, 49.

[23] Edwin Newman, *Strictly Speaking: Will America Be the Death of English?* (New York: Warner Books, 1974, 1975).

[24] John Simon, *Paradigms Lost: Reflections on Literacy and Its Decline* (New York: Potter, 1980).

There seems to have been in every period of the past, as there is now, a distinct apprehension in the minds of very many worthy persons that the English tongue is always approaching collapse, and that arduous efforts must be put forth, and put forth persistently, in order to save it from destruction.[25]

In a generation between Lounsbury and Newman-Simon, the anonymous "Vigilans" was another of the Dying-Declining-Doomsters. In his book *Chamber of Horrors* he castigated jargon, which he characterized as involving circumlocutions; long, abstract, unfamiliar words using classical roots; phrases where single words will do; padding; cautious wording and euphemism; vagueness and woolliness; and esoteric expressions.[26]

Our thoughts and our language are certainly intimately related, if they are not in fact the same thing. And pompous language is fair game. It is great sport to expose and snicker at egregious examples of linguistic bombast and thick-headedness, as the Armageddon usageasters are wont to do. But such sport is easy to overdo. The cannons of Mitchell-Newman-Simon-"Vigilans" tend to produce, not a bang, but a whimper—kvetching against petty violations of an idiosyncratic standard of style. It is remarkable that so much has been written, so seriously, about such trivia.

DEMOCRATIC CRITERION

A refreshingly different approach to the subject is that of Jim Quinn, whose *American Tongue and Cheek* is a lusty defense of many of the bugbears of contemporary usageasters. Quinn delights in showing that usageasters frequently do not know what they are talking about and that their criteria for defining good language are nonsense. Quinn is straightforward in stating his own criterion: "For me, the only sensible standard of correctness is usage by ordinary people."[27]

And yet Quinn's own usage populism is also nonsense if taken at face value. Ordinary people and extraordinary people alike make mistakes in using language; mistakes are a part of usage. When people notice mistakes—their own or others'—they correct them. Editing language is just as natural as producing it, and so is passing judgment on some forms of language as better than others. The values we attach to our linguistic options are just as much a part of the language as the options themselves. We are value-ridden, judgmental beings. As a piece of rhetoric, a sortie in the Grammar Wars, Quinn's position is great tactics, but it is weak strategy.

---

[25] Lounsbury, 2.
[26] "Vigilans," *Chamber of Horrors: A Glossary of Official Jargon Both English and American*, intro. Eric Partridge (New York: British Book Centre, 1952).
[27] Quinn, 11.

ELITIST CRITERION

In America we have no official aristocracy, whose speechways might provide a standard for the commoners of the realm. So we make do with a less well-defined group: educated, respected, important people in the community. Their usage is sometimes held up as a model for the hoi polloi of the citizenry. Bergen and Cornelia Evans in their *Dictionary of Contemporary American Usage* write: "Respectable English . . . means the kind of English that is used by the most respected people, the sort of English that will make readers or listeners regard you as an educated person."[28] William and Mary Morris echo the theoretical sentiment, if not the practical sensibleness, of the Evanses. The Morrises define *standard* (which is not the same as *good*, but is related) as "word usage occurring in the speech and writing of literate, educated users of the language."[29]

Another digression: the *Harper Dictionary of Contemporary Usage*, which the Morrises edited, deserves special acknowledgment as among the most ignorant usage guides to have made the big time. My favorite lapse is their explanation of the use of the objective case for the subject of an infinitive. Under the heading "infinitive, subject of the," they write:

> The confusion about the use of "I" and "me" is reflected in such statements as "The first thing for somebody like you or I to do. . . ." *The subject of the infinitive* "to do" must be in the accusative or objective case. Since the objective case of the first personal pronoun is "me," the statement should be "The first thing for somebody like you or me to do. . . ."[30]

The Morrises tripped over their own grammatical razzle-dazzle. In the example they cite, the subject of the infinitive is *somebody*; *you or me* is the object of the preposition *like*. So the example is irrelevant to the point for which it is cited. The Morrises are educated users of the language, but grammatically they are booboisie.

CONCLUSION

There are other criteria we might identify. But these ten are enough to show what the tendency has been. In deciding what makes good English good, commentators have tried to correlate variation with some outside factor—success in communication, literary excellence, scholarly authority (at least nominally), pedagogical effort, logic, personal authority, professional expertise, esthetic style, a democratic majority, or an elite model. The unspoken assumption is that good English ought to be good for something.

---

[28] Bergen and Cornelia Evans, *A Dictionary of Contemporary American Usage* (New York: Random House, 1957), v.

[29] William and Mary Morris, with the assistance of a panel of 136 distinguished consultants on usage, *Harper Dictionary of Contemporary Usage* (New York: Harper & Row, 1975), xxii.

[30] Ibid., 338.

Efforts to correlate goodness in language with something else are all flawed. Good English is simply what English speakers, in a particular situation, agree to regard as good. There are as many kinds of good English as there are situations in which English is used and sorts of participants who use it. Standard English is one sort of good English—good, that is, in the circumstances that call for it—but it is not the only sort.

Robert Pooley says something similar in *The Teaching of English Usage*:

> The English language is full of possible variations. The term "good usage" implies success in making choices in these variations such that the smallest number of persons (and particularly persons held in esteem) are distracted by the choices.[31]

Good English is the cellophane man—you can see right through it. It does not distract because in any given circumstance it is what the participants expect.

To paraphrase Mammy Yokum, "Good English is so much nicer than bad English because it's better." There is no external criterion by which we can judge what is good in language, either standard English or any other kind. Good language is just what the users of the language have decided is good. Their judgments are exasperatingly inconsistent and unpredictable. Moreover, the bounds they assign to the good are disconcertingly fuzzy; those bounds keep changing, as users of the language push this way and that way against them, continually altering the limits of acceptability. Finally, what is good is wholly relative to the circumstances and the speakers. Despite Wilson Follett's asseveration in *Modern American Usage* that "there is a [i.e., one] right way to use words and construct sentences, and many wrong ways,"[32] good in language is multivalent (that's *mul'ti-va'lent* or *mul-tiv'a-lent*, depending on the circumstances).

Because good English is so diverse, to use it in more than a few circumstances requires an equally diverse knowledge and a fine sense of what is appropriate under varying conditions. Charlton Laird made one of the most sensible comments ever written about usage when he observed, in his introductory essay to *Webster's New World Dictionary*, that "good usage requires wide knowledge and tasteful discrimination; it cannot be learned easily."[33] It is appropriate, especially here, for Laird to have the last word.

---

[31] Robert C. Pooley, *The Teaching of English Usage* (Urbana, IL: National Council of Teachers of English, 1974), 5.

[32] Wilson Follett, *Modern American Usage: A Guide* (New York: Hill and Wang, 1966), 3.

[33] Charlton Laird, "Language and the Dictionary." In *Webster's New World Dictionary of the American Language*, Second College Edition. Ed. David B. Guralnik (New York and Cleveland: World, 1970), xxv.

=

FOR DISCUSSION AND REVIEW

1. Which of the criteria that Algeo discusses sound very familiar? Has your speech and/or writing been influenced by any of them?

2. Algeo says that *"should* is a powerful and distinctly human concept." What does he mean? In what ways does each of the criteria Algeo discusses pay homage to the notion of "should"?

3. What is Algeo's attitude toward so-called usage experts?

4. What, according to Algeo, is the problem with the relationship between "good language and clear exact thinking"?

5. What does Algeo mean when he states that "Good English is the cellophane man"?

6. Discuss examples from your experience or observation that support Algeo's conclusion that "Because good English is so diverse, to use it in more than a few circumstances requires an equally diverse knowledge and a fine sense of what is appropriate under varying conditions."

53

≡

Its Academic, or Is It?

Charles R. Larson

Charles R. Larson is professor of literature at American University and has written two books, Academia Nuts *and* Arthur Dimmesdale. *In the following essay, which appeared as a "My Turn" column in* Newsweek *in November 1995, Larson takes a stand for correct usage. He courageously and comically explores the ways in which Americans are misusing apostrophes. He believes that a decline in reading has led to a lack of knowledge about how to use this important punctuation mark. Further, he laments that few people are even concerned about it. For an opposing view on the usage issue, see the next selection, "Like I Said, Don't Worry" by Patricia T. O'Conner.*

If you're 35 years or older, you probably identify a common grammatical error in the heading on this page. Younger than that and, well, you likely have another opinion: "Its all relative"—except, of course, for the apostrophe. Unfortunately, age appears to be the demarcation here. For those in the older group, youth has already won the battle.

I've been keeping a list of places where *its* is misused: newspapers, magazines, op-eds in major publications and, more recently, wall texts in museums. A few weeks ago I encountered the error in a book title: "St. Simons: A Summary of It's History," by R. Edwin and Mary A. Green. My list is getting longer and longer.

Does it even matter that the apostrophe is going the way of the stop sign and the directional signal in our society? Does punctuation count any longer? Are my complaints the ramblings of an old goat who's taught English for too many years?

What's the big deal, anyway? Who cares whether it's *its* or *it's?* Editors don't seem to know when the apostrophe's necessary. (One of them confessed to me that people have always been confused about the apostrophe—better just get rid of it.) My university undergraduates are clearly befuddled by the correct usage. Too many graduate applications—especially those of students aspiring to be creative writers—provide no clue that the writer understands when an apostrophe is required. Even some of my colleagues are confused by this ugglesome contraction.

How can a three-letter word be so disarming, so capable of separating the men from the boys? Or the women from the girls? When in doubt use it both ways, as in a recent advertisement hyping improved SAT,

GRE, and LSAT scores: "Kaplan locations all over the U.S. are offering full-length exams just like the actual tests. It's a great way to test your skills and get a practice score without the risk of your score being reported to schools. And now, for a limited time only, its absolutely free!"

And now, students, which one of the above spellings of the I word is correct: (a) the first, (b) the second, (c) both, or (d) neither? Any wonder why Educational Testing Services had to add 100 points to the revised SAT exams?

It's been my recent experience that the apostrophe hasn't actually exited common usage; it's simply migrated somewhere later in the sentence. Hence, "Shes lost her marble's" has become the preferred use of this irritating snippet of punctuation in current American writing. "Hes not lost his hat; hes lost his brains'." "Theres gold in them there hill's." Or "It was the best of times' and the worst of time's." The latter, of course, is from Charles Dicken's "A Tale of Two Cities'." Or is it Charle's Dickens?

Where will this end? Virtual apostrophe's? At times I wonder if all those missing apostrophes are floating somewhere in outer space. Don't they have to be somewhere, if—as some philosophers tell us—nothing is ever lost? Lately, I've seen the dirty three-letter word even punctuated as its'. What's next?

I'ts? 'Its?

How complicated can this be? How difficult is it to teach a sixth grader how to punctuate correctly?

Heaven knows I've tried to figure it out, agonized about it for years. I remember being dismayed nearly twenty years ago when I was walking around the neighborhood and discovered an enormous stack of books that someone had put out on the curb, free for the taking. Most of the titles were forgettable; hence the reason they'd been left for scavengers or the next trash pickup. However, mixed among the flotsam and jetsam was a brand-new hardback collegiate dictionary. How could this be, I asked myself? Could someone have too many dictionaries? I think the ideal would be one in every room.

Someone was sending me a signal. If words are unimportant, punctuation is something even more lowly. Why worry about such quodlibets? When was the last time anyone even noticed? Certainly, no one at Touchstone Books caught the errors in a recent ad for "Failing at Fairness: How Our Schools Cheat Girls," by Myra and David Sadker. A testimonial for the book reads as follows: "Reader's will be stunned at the overwhelming evidence of sexism the author's provide." You bet, and the blurb writers' lack of grammatical correctness.

If editors at publishing houses can't catch these errors, who can? Errors common to advertising copy have already spread into the books themselves. I dread walking into a bookstore a decade from now and encountering the covers of classics edited by a new generation of apostrophe-challenged editors: "Father's and Sons'," "The Brothers' Karamazov," "The Adventure's of Huckleberry Finn," "The Postman

Alway's Ring's Twice," "A Midsummers' Night Dream." (Who's wood's these are I think I know . . .)

The apostrophe is dead because reading is dead. Notice that I didn't say "The apostrophe's dead because reading's dead." That's far too complex an alteration. When in doubt simply write out the full sentence, carefully avoiding all possessives and contractions. Soon, no one will be certain about grammatical usage anyway. Computers will come without an apostrophe key. Why bother about errors on the Internet? E-mail messages are often so badly written they make no sense. Fortunately, they get erased almost immediately. Everything passes too quickly.

Last week I went to a lamp store to purchase two new floor lamps for our living room: five rooms of lamps and hundreds of styles—except for one minor problem. Not one lamp was designed for reading. Virtually all the lamps illuminated the ceiling; all were designed for television addicts, not readers. So how is one supposed to read *TV Guide*? The place was so dark (was I expected to hold my book up to the ceiling?) I could hardly find my way out. And speaking of TV, what's the plural: TVs or TV's?

Time to stop this grumbling. Thing's fall apart. If I start making a list only of the times the apostrophe is used *properly*, I won't even have to worry about it. I can already hear you say, "Your kidding."

═══

FOR DISCUSSION AND REVIEW

1. Does Larson make a legitimate point about the way we use language, or is he "an old goat who's taught English for too many years"?

2. What are the three uses of the apostrophe in English? Does Larson discuss all three?

3. After reviewing the example of the Kaplan advertisement, how would you answer Larson's multiple-choice quiz in paragraph 6?

4. How realistic do you find Larson's examples? Do any of them strike you as exaggerated for humor or overstatement? Explain.

5. Larson claims that "the apostrophe is dead because reading is dead." What is the connection between reading and apostrophes?

6. What does Larson mean by his last statement: "I can already hear you say, 'Your kidding?'".

7. Can we control the use of written language, or is the misuse of the apostrophe yet another sign of inevitable language change?

54

≡

Like I Said, Don't Worry

Patricia T. O'Conner

*Patricia T. O'Conner discusses our national attitude toward grammar
and usage from a different perspective than Charles R. Larson in the previous article. Both are constructive—just by different means. Larson is
frustrated, yet retains humor and perspective; O'Conner is gentle and
sympathetic, yet doesn't devalue grammar. Rather, she recognizes that
it does serve a purpose—but that purpose is not to denigrate the speakers of the language. O'Conner, a former editor of* The New York Times
Book Review, *wrote* Woe Is I: The Grammarphobe's Guide to Better
English in Plain English. *In the following article, which appeared as a
"My Turn" column in* Newsweek *in December 1996, O'Conner advises
that we lighten up about grammar and usage because we are all prone
to occasional lapses. Rather than become obsessed by error, she thinks
we should nurture our "love [of] talking about words, about language."*

Now that I'm a grammar maven, everyone's afraid to talk to me. Well,
not everyone. Since my grammar book was published this fall, my
friends have discovered a new sport: gotcha! The object is to correct my
speech, to catch me in the occasional "between you and I" (OK, I admit
it). The winner gets to interrupt with a satisfied "aha!"

But people I meet for the first time often confess that speaking with
an "authority" on language gives them the willies. Grammar, they say
apologetically, was not their best subject. And they still don't get it: the
subjunctives, the dependent clauses, the coordinating conjunctions. So
their English is bound to be flawed, they warn, and I should make
allowances. They relax when I tell them that I'm not perfect either, and
that I don't use technical jargon when I write about grammar. You don't
have to scare readers off with terms like *gerund* and *participle* to explain
why an *-ing* word like *bowling* can play so many different roles in a sentence. With the intimidating terminology out of the way, most people
express a lively, even passionate, interest in English and how it works.
As a reader recently told me, "I don't need to know all the parts of a car
to be a good driver."

Grammarians and hairsplitting wannabes have always loved to argue
over the fine points of language. What surprises me these days is the
number of grammatically insecure people who are discussing English
with just as much fervor, though without the pedantry. As a guest author

737

on radio call-in shows and online chats, I've found that the chance to air a linguistic grievance or pose a question in a nonjudgmental atmosphere often proves irresistible. "Is *irregardless* OK?" a caller hesitantly asks. "I hear it so much these days." (No.) Or, "Is *sprang* a word?" (Yes.) "*Media is* or media *are*?" (*Are*, for the time being.) I saw an ad with the word *alright*, spelled A-L-R-I-G-H-T. It is correct? (No, it's not all right.) "If I *was*? Or if I *were*?" (It depends.) I love it when people who say they hated grammar in school get all worked up over *like* versus *as*, or *convince* versus *persuade*, or *who* versus *whom*. Obviously it wasn't grammar per se that once turned them off. It was the needless pedagoguery—the tyranny of the pluperfects, the intransitives, and all the rest. The truth is that people love talking about words, about language. After years as an editor at *The New York Times Book Review*, I can vouch that almost everybody gets something wrong now and then—a dangler here, a spelling problem there, a runaway sentence, beastly punctuation. Those who regularly screw up would like to do better, and even the whizzes admit they'd like to get rid of a weakness or two.

So, is grammar back? Has good English become . . . cool?

Before you laugh, download this. Thanks to the computer, Americans are communicating with one another at a rate undreamed of a generation ago—and *in writing*. People who seldom wrote more than a memo or a shopping list are producing blizzards of words. Teenagers who once might have spent the evening on the phone are hunched over their computers, gossiping by e-mail and meeting in chat rooms. Wired college students are conferring with professors, carrying on romances, and writing home for money, all from computer terminals in their dorm rooms. Many executives who once depended on secretaries to "put it in English" are now clicking on REPLY and winging it.

The downside of all this techno-wizardry is that our grammar isn't quite up to the mark. We're writing more, and worse, than ever before. (If you don't believe this, check out a chat room or an electronic bulletin board. It's not a pretty sight.) The ease and immediacy of electronic communication are forcing the computer-literate to think about their grammar for the first time in years, if ever. It's ironic that this back-to-basics message should come from cyberspace. Or is it? Amid the din of the information revolution, bombarded on all sides by technological wonders, we can hardly be blamed for finding in grammar one small sign of order amid the chaos.

There is evidence of this return to order elsewhere in our society, too. Perhaps the "family values" mantra, for better or worse, is nothing more than a call for order in a culture that seems to have lost its moral bearings. At any rate, laissez-faire grammar bashers who used to regard good English as an impediment to spontaneity and creativity are seeing the light—and it's not spelled L-I-T-E.

But what about those of us whose "lex" education is a dim memory? The very word *grammar* evokes a visceral response—usually fear. If it makes your hair stand on end, you're part of a proud tradition. The earliest grammarians, bless their shriveled hearts, did English a disservice by appealing more to our feelings of inferiority than to our natural love of words. They could never quite forgive our mongrel tongue for not being Latin, but felt that English could redeem itself somewhat by conforming to the rules of Latin grammar. The word *grammar*, in fact, originally meant "the study of Latin." All this may help explain a couple of silly no-nos from the past, discredited by the most respected twentieth-century grammarians: those inflexible rules against splitting an infinitive and ending a sentence with a preposition.

Surely no school subject has been more detested and reviled by its victims than grammar. Some people would rather have a root canal than define the uninflected root of a word. At the same time, the ability to use language well appeals to our need to be understood, to participate, to be one of the tribe. It's no wonder so many of the people I meet confess to being grammatically inadequate, yet fascinated by words.

My message to these people, delivered from the lofty heights of my newly acquired mavenhood, is this: stop beating up on yourselves. It's only a grammatical error, not a drive-by shooting. Words are wonderful, but they're not sacred. And between you and I (aha!), nobody's perfect.

FOR DISCUSSION AND REVIEW

1. According to O'Conner, why are people afraid of grammar? Why do they want to be better at grammar?

2. What effect does O'Conner believe e-mail is having on usage? Does Larson, in the previous selection, agree or disagree with O'Conner? How has e-mail affected your use of language and concern for grammar?

3. O'Conner writes that there is no need for technical jargon when it comes to discussing grammar. She believes that "with the intimidating terminology out of the way, most people express a lively, even passionate, interest in English and how it works." From your experience, is she correct? Explain.

4. What, according to O'Conner, is the relationship between Latin and English?

5. What advice does O'Conner give to people who feel "grammatically inadequate"? Is it good advice, or not? Explain.

6. How would you describe O'Conner's attitude toward language usage? As a student of language, where on the spectrum from prescription to description would you place her?

55

≡

Sociolinguistic Analysis of Dialogues and First-Person Narratives in Fiction

Barbara Hill Hudson

In the following selection Barbara Hill Hudson uses literature to introduce students to the rich diversity of social dialects. But the article also shows how dialect analysis can inform literary analysis. Hudson's table of socially diagnostic features shows how pronunciation, grammar, and vocabulary in dialogue reveal much about a character's social standing. To illustrate her point, she uses these features to analyze passages by Charles Dickens and Dorothy Parker.

Language arts teachers should consider using first-person narratives and sections of dialogue from selected novels and short stories to help students appreciate the diversity in English dialects past and present. In this essay, I suggest ways in which teachers may use findings from linguistic research to help their students examine how dialogue and first-person narratives serve as social mirrors that in many ways reflect language use in various regions among different social-class, ethnic, and racial groups.

SOCIAL-CLASS DIALECTS

Peter Trudgill (*Sociolinguistics*) and others have pointed out that different social groups use different linguistic varieties and that people have learned to classify speakers according to the language varieties they use. Since dialects differ in syntax, phonology, lexicon, and other features, teachers may wish to use a chart similar to Table 55.1 to help students become familiar with some of the most common socially diagnostic features. Even though some students may know about many of these elements, it is still a good idea to go over the chart thoroughly before asking them to attempt an analysis of dialogues or first-person narratives. Of course, as they proceed, the students should be encouraged to add to the chart.

CATEGORY	STANDARD	NONSTANDARD
Phonology		
Pronunciation of *-ing*	"-ing"	"-in'"
Vowel sounds	No dialectal pronunciation indicated in spelling	Great deal of dialect marking in spelling
Contracted pronunciation of verb form followed by infinitive	Clear distinction between the two verbs, or slight reduction of juncture—e.g., *going to* + verb	Moderate to extreme reduction of juncture—e.g., *gonna; I'ngna; I'mana; I'ma*
Loss of initial unstressed syllable	Retention of first syllable—e.g., *arithmetic, remember, about*	Suppression of first syllable—e.g., *'rithmetic, 'member, 'bout*
Verb Forms		
Past tense of irregular verbs	*swim–swam, know–knew, see–saw, take–took*	*swim–swimmed, know–knowed, see–seen, take–taken* or *taked*
Variation in irregular form of present perfect or past perfect tenses	I've *seen* it; I had *seen* it.	I've *saw* it; I had *saw* it.
A- prefixing of verb	He was *running* and *jumping.*	He was *a-running* (or *a-runnin'*) and *a-jumping* (or *a-jumpin'*).
Ain't	Infrequent occurrence	Frequent use of form
Nouns and Pronouns		
Plural forms of nouns	*desks, children*	*desses, chirren* or *chirrens*
Relative pronouns	I bought one of Fred's houses, *which everyone knows are built right.*	I bought one of Fred's houses, *which everyone knows he builds them right.*
	This is a word *whose meaning I don't know.*	This is a word *that I don't know what it means.*
	A man *who doesn't* run around is a good catch.	A man *what don't* run around is a good catch.
Demonstrative pronouns	*this thing, those things*	*this here* (or *'ere*) *thing, them things*
Reflexive pronouns	He washed *himself;* they washed *themselves.*	He washed *hisself;* they washed *theirself* (or *theirselves*).
	He gave the tickets to my friend and *me.*	He gave the tickets to my friend and *myself.*
	The girl next door and *I* went to the show.	*Myself* and the girl next door went to the show.
Possessive pronouns	It's *yours, mine, his.*	It's *yourn, mines, hisn.*
Plural of *you*	*you* as plural form	*yiz, y'uns, youens, youse, you-all, y'all*
Syntax		
Multiple negatives	He *never* cries; he doesn't *ever* cry.	He don't *never* cry.
Fronting of negative auxiliaries	Nobody has said anything; nobody knows anything.	*Ain't* nobody said nothing; *don't* nobody know nothing.
Auxiliary inversion in indirect question	I wonder if he finished the job.	I wonder *did* he finish the job.
Other Features		
Forms of address	*Yes, madam; No, madam; Yes, sir; No, sir*	*Yes'm; No'me* or *No'm; Yes, sorr; No, sorr*
Rough talk	Infrequent use	Profanity, obscenity, name calling, use of derogatory terms
Polite terms	*thank you, excuse me*	*thankye', 'scuseme*
	Softened expressions, euphemisms, modal constructions—e.g., *darn, passed away, Would you shut the door?*	Direct terms—e.g., *damn, upped an' died, Shet the door!*

[Many of these features and others have been discussed in Walt Wolfram (*Study*), Peter Trudgill (*Sociolinguistics*), William Labov (*Sociolinguistic Patterns*), Fernando Peñalosa (*Introduction*), and Elaine Chaika (*Language*).]

TABLE 55.1 **Socially diagnostic features**

As part of this exercise, students should be made aware that the differences, listed as *Standard* and *Nonstandard*, do not represent two discrete social dialects; rather, they should be told, the dialects merge to form a continuum in which there is a higher frequency of use of nonstandard features on the end represented by the speech of members of lower socioeconomic groups and a much lower frequency of use of nonstandard features in middle- to upper-class speech. Social class is reflected in regional, ethnic, racial, and historical dialects.

Students should be challenged to find evidence of social variation not only in the speaker's language but also in nonlinguistic internal evidence in the text, such as indications of employment or wealth. Students may discover that they can locate only a few phonological features that represent differences in the way social classes in general use language, but they may find a large number of syntactic or grammatical features. A particular author may mark regional and ethnic differences more frequently in the language of certain characters than in the language of others.

Below are examples of how a teacher may lead students in an analysis of two passages, both of which contain speakers representing different social groups. If we were to ask students to find the socially diagnostic linguistic features, most of them would be able to do the initial analysis simply by drawing on their own ideas about the way language was used in earlier times. In itself this is a useful learning experience, for it points up the little-understood fact that all members of the speech community are linguists to some extent. It will also serve to highlight some of the subtle ways in which language is used in marking social context. The teacher may begin by having students read the passages by Dickens and Parker and asking them to respond to the following questions on the basis of table 55.1, as well as of their knowledge of language use:

1. How many characters are involved?
2. What are the ages, genders, and social classes of the participants?
3. Describe the status relationships. Who has the higher status? Who has the lower status? Which characters are social peers?
4. In what social setting does the activity take place?
5. In what country or part of the country does it take place?
6. What is the racial or ethnic group membership of each character?
7. What time period does the passage represent? (Broad answers are acceptable—e.g., late twentieth century, the 1940s, during the Civil War.)
8. List any prominent phonological features. What do they tell you about each speaker?
9. List any prominent syntactic features. What do they tell you about each speaker?
10. List any unusual or unfamiliar lexical items. What dialectal or socioeconomic information do you get from these words or phrases?

SAMPLE EXERCISES

Exercise A: Dickens

Dickens, Charles. *Great Expectations*. New York: Signet Classics, 1963, Ch. 13, 113–114.

"You are the husband," repeated Miss Havisham, "of the sister	1
of this boy?"	2
It was very aggravating; but, throughout the interview, Joe per-	3
sisted in addressing me instead of Miss Havisham.	4
"Which I meantersay, Pip," Joe now observed, in a manner that	5
was at once expressive of forcible argumentation, strict confidence,	6
and great politeness, "as I hup and married your sister, and I were	7
at the time what you might call (if you was any ways inclined) a	8
single man."	9
"Well!" said Miss Havisham. "And you have reared the boy,	10
with the intention of taking him for your apprentice; is that so, Mr.	11
Gargery?"	12
"You know, Pip," replied Joe, "as you and me were ever friends,	13
and it were looked for'ard to betwixt us, as being calc'lated to lead	14
to larks. Not but what, Pip, if you had ever made objections to the	15
business—such as its being open to black and sut, or suchlike—not	16
but what they would have been attended to, don't you see?"	17
"Has the boy," said Miss Havisham, "ever made any objection?	18
Does he like the trade?"	19
"Which it is well beknown to yourself, Pip," returned Joe,	20
strengthening his former mixture of argumentation, confidence,	21
and politeness, "that it were the wish of your own hart." (I saw the	22
idea suddenly break upon him that he would adapt his epitaph to	23
the occasion before he went on to say.) "And there weren't no	24
objection on your part, and Pip it were the great wish of your hart!"	25

Analysis

It would be surprising if most of the students didn't recognize the social status of the narrator (Pip), of Miss Havisham, and of Joe. It might be surprising to some of them to learn, however, that even Miss Havisham is speaking in dialect, since readers are not generally aware that Standard English is represented slightly differently in diverse dialects (e.g., American English, British English, Australian English).

Once it is clearly understood that the narrator (Pip), Miss Havisham, and Joe are all speaking in a dialect, it is useful to go over the passage again and have the students pick out socially diagnostic features of all three speakers. One of the things they might discover is that Pip and

Miss Havisham, though both are speaking Standard English, differ slightly in their style of speech. Once Joe has been identified as being a speaker of nonstandard English, it is interesting to analyze how his speech stereotypes him. His speech contains a number of stigmatized forms.

Phonology

Line 5: "meantersay" for "mean to say" (eye dialect "er": the British spelling of the reduced vowel of informal speech in the preposition *to*)

Line 7: "hup" for "up" (hypercorrection: adding initial *h*- inappropriately)

Line 14: "for'ard" for "forward" (consonant elision)

Line 14: "calc'lated" for "calculated" (syllable elision)

Line 16: "sut" for "soot" (regional dialect)

Line 22, 25: "hart" for "heart" (either eye dialect or information about difference in pronunciation of these two words)

With the possible exceptions of "hup" and "calc'lated," these items would not firmly place a speaker in the lower class unless they were combined with other lower-class markers. The "er" in "meantersay" is the common eye dialect way of spelling the British unstressed vowel; British "er" is pronounced something like the American "uh" but is higher in the mouth, as in the tongue placement of the vowel in *bird* in dialects in which postvocalic *r* is not pronounced. This particular spelling could be used simply to indicate informal, relaxed style; however, in combination with the other features of Joe's speech, it very likely is intended to mark him as being less well educated than Miss Havisham or Pip. The pronunciation "for'ard" could be produced naturally in rapid speech, but the apostrophe in this word, along with "calc'lated," suggest that Joe leaves out portions of his words and thus is not well schooled. "Sut" is a regional pronunciation in both England and the United States, but Dickens uses it to indicate that Joe speaks a folk dialect that differs from preferred London speech. The spelling of "hart" probably indicates a dialectal pronunciation that differs from London Standard, though some research on British English would be necessary for the class to make a firm decision on why Dickens used this particular spelling. Any of the items below, under "Syntax," could serve as springboards for further research by students on regional and social variation in British English.

Syntax

Line 7: "I were" for "I was"

Line 8: "If you was" for "If you were"

Line 14: "and it were" for "and it was"
Line 20: "well beknown to yourself" for "well known to you"
Line 22: "it were the wish" for "it was the wish"
Line 24–25: "there weren't no objection" for "there was no objection"

It should be obvious from this list that most nonstandard features contain some form of the verb *be*.

After the students have gone thoroughly over this passage, identifying the smaller features, they can go back one more time to make an assessment of the general social context by looking at the discourse styles of the two speakers (Joe and Miss Havisham) to discover whatever else they can about the social situation. For example, we might ask:

1. Who has the higher social status? Who has the lower?
2. What kinds of linguistic evidence can you point to? (For instance, Miss Havisham is the questioner, and Joe's replies are overly polite.)
3. How does stereotyping of speech contribute to the reader's characterization of an individual as a protagonist (hero), antagonist (villain), or neutral participant?
4. How do developments in the plot match the way in which each character is marked by his or her speech?

Exercise B: Parker

Parker, Dorothy. "The Standard of Living." *Fifty Great Short Stories*. Ed. Milton Crane. New York: Bantam, 1952, 25–26.

Together they went over to the shop window and stood pressed against it. It contained but one object—a double row of great, even pearls clasped by a deep emerald around a little pink velvet throat.
"What do you suppose they cost?" Annabel said.
"Gee, I don't know," Midge said. "Plenty, I guess."
"Like a thousand dollars?" Annabel said.
"Oh, I guess like more," Midge said. "On account of the emerald."
"Well, like ten thousand dollars?" Annabel said.
"Gee, I wouldn't even know," Midge said.
The devil nudged Annabel in the ribs. "Dare you to go in and price them," she said.
"Like fun!" Midge said.
"Dare you," Annabel said . . .
. . . .
"Is there something—?" the clerk said.
"Oh, we're just looking," Annabel said. It was as if she flung the words down from a dais.
The clerk bowed.
"My friend and myself merely happened to be passing," Midge said, and stopped, seeming to listen to the phrase. "My friend here and

myself," she went on, "merely happened to be wondering how much are those pearls you've got in your window."

"Ah, yes," the clerk said. "The double rope. That is two hundred and fifty thousand dollars, Madam."

"I see," Midge said.

The clerk bowed. "An exceptionally beautiful necklace," he said. "Would you care to look at it?"

"No, thank you," Annabel said.

"My friend and myself merely happened to be passing," Midge said.

Analysis

This passage also points out clearly that language use reflects social context. As with the passage from Dickens, we see representatives from two social classes. In this case, the clerk is representative of an upper class, and the young women represent a lower class.

By having the students examine the change in style of speech Midge and Annabel use when they are outside the shop and when they are inside the shop, the teacher can show that language use is one of the behaviors that mark differences in social situations. As part of the overall analysis, students might notice that when the young women speak to each other, they use slang ("Gee"; "Like fun!") and truncated sentences ("Dare you"). They might then observe that when the young women speak to the clerk, they use a very stilted form of language, including the inappropriate use of reflexives ("My friend and myself") and a nonstandard form of indirect question ("wondering how much are those pearls") in attempts to be "correct" in the awesome surroundings of the shop and the presence of the clerk. This phenomenon, called *hypercorrection*, also occurs in the Dickens passage when Joe uses stilted, overly polite, and circuitous language to address Miss Havisham.

The language of the clerk should give the students an opportunity to examine an example of upper-middle-class dialect. Labov (*Sociolinguistic*) has argued that the language of store clerks often reflects that of the clientele. Students should notice the clerk's precise wording ("That is two hundred and fifty thousand dollars"), his polite question ("Would you care to look at it?"), and his use of formal terms of address ("Madam"). As a final exercise, students may be asked to identify paralinguistic features (stance, body movement) that also point out social class or age differences.

This type of analysis can be incorporated in a number of different classes at various levels. Instructors wishing to make use of this model can easily develop lessons planned around both familiar and unfamiliar passages from the standard anthologies available. Listed below are five additional passages that may be used for similar classroom exercises. A resourceful literature teacher should be able to find many other appropriate passages. Students should be encouraged to look for such passages in assigned readings, in the public press, and in their recreational reading.

OTHER SUGGESTED PASSAGES FOR ANALYSIS

Kipling, Rudyard. "The Courting of Dinah Shadd." *Fifty Great Short Stories*. Ed. Milton Crane. New York: Bantam, 1952, 69–70 (near the beginning of section 2: conversation between narrator and Mulvaney).

Main features. The language features here represent a regional dialect that differs considerably from the standard literary language of Kipling's time. The students may not be able to place the dialect within England, but they can analyze the spelling as indicative of pronunciation and can find nonstandard word forms and syntactic constructions.

Wolfe, Thomas. "Only the Dead Know Brooklyn." *Fifty Great Short Stories*. Ed. Milton Crane. New York: Bantam, 1952, 109–113 (whole passage is first-person narrative).

Main features. Phonological features represent a regional dialect, specifically New York City. The passage also contains some nonstandard verb forms and local slang.

Gaines, Ernest J. "The Sky Is Grey." *Discoveries: Fifty Stories of the Quest*. Ed. Harold Schechter and Jonna Gormely Semeiks. Indianapolis: Bobbs, 1983, 320 (whole passage is first-person narrative; section 5 contains dialogue between two young people).

Main features. Phonological features, word forms, syntactic features, and lexical items represent ethnic (black) dialect, with some features also found in the speech of Southern whites. In addition, students can be asked to identify those features that indicate that the two people in section 5 are quite young.

Bambara, Toni Cade. "The Lesson." *Discoveries: Fifty Stories of the Quest*. Ed. Harold Schechter and Jonna Gormely Semeiks. Indianapolis: Bobbs, 1983, 296–298 (whole passage is first-person narrative; dialogue between young people begins on second page of story).

Main features. See Gaines entry.

Malamud, Bernard. "The Idiots First." *Discoveries: Fifty Stories of the Quest*. Ed. Harold Schechter and Jonna Gormely Semeiks. Indianapolis: Bobbs, 1983, 232–233 (dialogue between Mendel and Fishbein begins about one third of the way into the story).

Main features. Syntactic features, phonological features, and lexical items represent ethnic (Jewish) dialect and educational level (consequently, social class). Syntactic features reflect Yiddish influence in the speech of less educated speakers.

WORKS CITED

Chaika, Elaine. *Language: The Social Mirror*. Rowley, Newbury: 1982.

Labov, William. *Sociolinguistic Patterns*. Philadelphia: University of Pennsylvania Press, 1992.

Peñalosa, Fernando. *Introduction to the Sociology of Language*. Rowley, Newbury: 1981.

Trudgill, Peter. *Sociolinguistics: An Introduction to Language and Society*. New York: Penguin, 1974.

Wolfram, Walt. *The Study of Social Dialects in American English*. Englewood Cliffs: Prentice-Hall, 1974.

FOR DISCUSSION AND REVIEW

1. Using Hudson's discussion of the Dickens and Parker passages as model, analyze one of the texts that she suggests on p. 747. As you analyze your passage, be sure to consider the questions that Hudson suggests on p. 742 and to consult the chart of "socially diagnostic features" she presents.

2. From your own reading of fiction, select a passage that is rich in both social and regional dialects. If you are planning to become a classroom teacher, consider selecting a passage that would be age-appropriate for the students you anticipate teaching. Bring your passage to class and be prepared to discuss your reasons for selecting it. Finally, do a formal analysis of the passage, and if you are a prospective teacher explain how you would go about using the passage with your students.

56

Into the Electronic Millennium

Sven Birkerts

Sven Birkerts became interested in literature, particularly contemporary European texts, while working as a bookstore clerk, and sustained that interest after he began teaching expository writing at Harvard in 1984. Author, educator, and literary critic, Birkerts earned the National Book Critics Circle Award in 1986 for his first book, Artificial Wilderness: Essays in Twentieth Century Literature. *His second book,* The Electric Life: Essays on Modern Poetry, *addresses the harmful effects of mass media on common language. This theme continues in* The Gutenberg Elegies: The Fate of Reading in an Electronic Age, *where he cautions against the superficial nature of electronic media. In the following essay from* The Gutenberg Elegies, *Birkerts ponders a future in which technology determines how we communicate, and libraries serve the same function as museums do today.*

Some years ago, a friend and I comanaged a used and rare book shop in Ann Arbor, Michigan. We were often asked to appraise and purchase libraries—by retiring academics, widows, and disgruntled graduate students. One day we took a call from a professor of English at one of the community colleges outside Detroit. When he answered the buzzer I did a double take—he looked to be only a year or two older than we were. "I'm selling everything," he said, leading the way through a large apartment. As he opened the door of his study I felt a nudge from my partner. The room was wall-to-wall books and as neat as a chapel.

The professor had a remarkable collection. It reflected not only the needs of his vocation—he taught nineteenth- and twentieth-century literature—but a book lover's sensibility as well. The shelves were strictly arranged, and the books themselves were in superb condition. When he left the room we set to work inspecting, counting, and estimating. This is always a delicate procedure, for the buyer is at once anxious to avoid insult to the seller and eager to get the goods for the best price. We adopted our usual strategy, working out a lower offer and a more generous fallback price. But there was no need to worry. The professor took our first offer without batting an eye.

As we boxed up the books, we chatted. My partner asked the man if he was moving. "No," he said, "but I am getting out." We both looked up. "Out of the teaching business, I mean. Out of books." He then said that he wanted to show us something. And indeed, as soon as the books were packed and loaded, he led us back through the apartment and down a set of stairs. When we reached the basement, he flicked on the light. There, on a long table, displayed like an exhibit in the Space Museum, was a computer I didn't know what kind it was then, nor could I tell you now, fifteen years later. But the professor was keen to explain and demonstrate.

While he and my partner hunched over the terminal, I roamed to and fro, inspecting the shelves. It was purely a reflex gesture, for they held nothing but thick binders and paperbound manuals. "I'm changing my life," the ex-professor was saying. "This is definitely where it's all going to happen." He told us that he already had several good job offers. And the books? I asked. Why was he selling them all? He paused for a few beats. "The whole profession represents a lot of pain to me," he said. "I don't want to see any of these books again."

The scene has stuck with me. It is now a kind of marker in my mental life. That afternoon I got my first serious inkling that all was not well in the world of print and letters. All sorts of corroborations followed. Our professor was by no means an isolated case. Over a period of two years we met with several others like him. New men and new women who had glimpsed the future and had decided to get out while the getting was good. The selling off of books was sometimes done for financial reasons, but the need to burn bridges was usually there as well. It was as if heading to the future also required the destruction of tokens from the past.

A change is upon us—nothing could be clearer. The printed word is part of a vestigial order that we are moving away from—by choice and by societal compulsion. I'm not just talking about disaffected academics, either. This shift is happening throughout our culture, away from the patterns and habits of the printed page and toward a new world distinguished by its reliance on electronic communications.

This is not, of course, the first such shift in our long history. In Greece, in the time of Socrates, several centuries after Homer, the dominant oral culture was overtaken by the writing technology. And in Europe another epochal transition was effected in the late fifteenth century after Gutenberg invented movable type. In both cases the long-term societal effects were overwhelming, as they will be for us in the years to come.

The evidence of the change is all around us, though possibly in the manner of the forest that we cannot see for the trees. The electronic media, while conspicuous in gadgetry, are very nearly invisible in their functioning. They have slipped deeply and irrevocably into our midst, creating sluices and circulating through them. I'm not referring to any one product or function in isolation, such as television or fax machines or the networks that make them possible. I mean the interdependent totality that has arisen from the conjoining of parts—the disk drives hooked to modems, transmissions linked to technologies of reception, recording, duplication, and storage. Numbers and codes and frequencies.

Buttons and signals. And this is no longer "the future," except for the poor or the self-consciously atavistic—it is now. . . .

To get a sense of the enormity of the change, you must force yourself to imagine—deeply and in nontelevisual terms—what the world was like a hundred, even fifty, years ago. If the feat is too difficult, spend some time with a novel from the period. Read between the lines and reconstruct. Move through the sequence of a character's day and then juxtapose the images and sensations you find with those in the life of the average urban or suburban dweller today.

Inevitably, one of the first realizations is that a communications net, a soft and pliable mesh woven from invisible threads, has fallen over everything. The so-called natural world, the place we used to live, which served us so long as the yardstick for all measurements, can now only be perceived through a scrim. Nature was then; this is now. Trees and rocks have receded. And the great geographical Other, the faraway rest of the world, has been transformed by the pure possibility of access. The numbers of distance and time no longer mean what they used to. Every place, once unique, itself, is strangely shot through with radiations from every other place. "There" was then; "here" is now. . . .

To underscore my point, I have been making it sound as if we were all abruptly walking out of one room and into another, leaving our books to the moths while we settle ourselves in front of our state-of-the-art terminals. The truth is that we are living through a period of overlap; one way of being is pushed athwart another. Antonio Gramsci's often-cited sentence comes inevitably to mind: "The crisis consists precisely in the fact that the old is dying and the new cannot be born; in this interregnum a great variety of morbid symptoms appears." The old surely is dying, but I'm not so sure that the new is having any great difficulty being born. As for the morbid symptoms, these we have in abundance.

The overlap in communications modes, and the ways of living that they are associated with, invites comparison with the transitional epoch in ancient Greek society, certainly in terms of the relative degree of disturbance. Historian Eric Havelock designated that period as one of "proto-literacy," of which his fellow scholar Oswyn Murray has written:

> To him [Havelock] the basic shift from oral to literate culture was a slow process; for centuries, despite the existence of writing, Greece remained essentially an oral culture. This culture was one which depended heavily on the encoding of information in poetic texts, to be learned by rote and to provide a cultural encyclopedia of conduct. It was not until the age of Plato in the fourth century that the dominance of poetry in an oral culture was challenged in the final triumph of literacy.

That challenge came in the form of philosophy, among other things, and poetry has never recovered its cultural primacy. What oral poetry was for the Greeks, printed books in general are for us. But our historical moment, which we might call "proto-electronic," will not require a transition period of two centuries. The very essence of electronic transmissions is to surmount impedances and to hasten transitions. Fifty years, I'm sure, will suffice. As for what the conversion will bring—and *mean*—to us, we might glean a few clues by looking to some of the "morbid symptoms" of the change. But to understand what these portend, we need to remark a few of the more obvious ways in which our various technologies condition our senses and sensibilities.

I won't tire my reader with an extended rehash of the differences between the print orientation and that of electronic systems. Media theorists from Marshall McLuhan to Walter Ong to Neil Postman have discoursed upon these at length. What's more, they are reasonably commonsensical. I therefore will abbreviate.

The order of print is linear, and is bound to logic by the imperatives of syntax. Syntax is the substructure of discourse, a mapping of the ways that the mind makes sense through language. Print communication requires the active engagement of the reader's attention, for reading is fundamentally an act of translation. Symbols are turned into their verbal referents and these are in turn interpreted. The print engagement is essentially private. While it does represent an act of communication, the contents pass from the privacy of the sender to the privacy of the receiver. Print also posits a time axis; the turning of pages, not to mention the vertical descent down the page, is a forward-moving succession, with earlier contents at every point serving as a ground for what follows. Moreover, the printed material is static—it is the reader, not the book, that moves forward. The physical arrangements of print are in accord with our traditional sense of history. Materials are layered; they lend themselves to rereading and to sustained attention. The pace of reading is variable, with progress determined by the reader's focus and comprehension.

The electronic order is in most ways opposite. Information and contents do not simply move from one private space to another, but they travel along a network. Engagement is intrinsically public, taking place within a circuit of larger connectedness. The vast resources of the network are always there, potential, even if they do not impinge on the immediate communication. Electronic communication can be passive, as with television watching, or interactive, as with computers. Contents, unless they are printed out (at which point they become part of the static order of print) are felt to be evanescent. They can be changed or deleted with the stroke of a key. With visual media (television, projected graphs, highlighted "bullets") impression and image take precedence over logic and concept, and detail and linear sequentiality are sacrificed. The pace is rapid, driven by jump-cut increments, and the basic movement is laterally associative rather than vertically cumulative. The presentation structures the reception and, in time, the expectation about how information is organized.

Further, the visual and nonvisual technology in every way encourages in the user a heightened and ever-changing awareness of the present.

It works against historical perception, which must depend on the inimical notions of logic and sequential succession. If the print medium exalts the word, fixing it into permanence, the electronic counterpart reduces it to a signal, a means to an end.

Transitions like the one from print to electronic media do not take place without rippling or, more likely, *reweaving* the entire social and cultural web. The tendencies outlined above are already at work. We don't need to look far to find their effects. We can begin with the newspaper headlines and the millennial lamentations sounded in the op-ed pages: that our educational systems are in decline; that our students are less and less able to read and comprehend their required texts, and that their aptitude scores have leveled off well below those of previous generations.   Tag-line communication, called "bite-speak" by some, is destroying the last remnants of political discourse; spin doctors and media consultants are our new shamans. As communications empires fight for control of all information outlets, including publishers, the latter have succumbed to the tyranny of the bottom line; they are less and less willing to publish work, however worthy, that will not make a tidy profit. And, on every front, funding for the arts is being cut while the arts themselves appear to be suffering a deep crisis of relevance. And so on.

Every one of these developments is, of course, overdetermined, but there can be no doubt that they are connected, perhaps profoundly, to the transition that is under way.

Certain other trends bear watching. One could argue, for instance, that the entire movement of postmodernism in the arts is a consequence of this same macroscopic shift. For what is postmodernism at root but an aesthetic that rebukes the idea of an historical time line, as well as previously uncontested assumptions of cultural hierarchy. The postmodern artifact manipulates its stylistic signatures like Lego blocks and makes free with combinations from the formerly sequestered spheres of high and popular art. Its combinatory momentum and relentless referencing of the surrounding culture mirror perfectly the associative dynamics of electronic media.

One might argue likewise, that the virulent debate within academia over the canon and multiculturalism may not be a simple struggle between the entrenched ideologies of white male elites and the forces of formerly disenfranchised gender, racial, and cultural groups. Many of those who would revise the canon (or end it altogether) are trying to outflank the assumption of historical tradition itself. The underlying question, avoided by many, may be not only whether the tradition is relevant, but whether it might not be too taxing a system for students to comprehend. Both the traditionalists and the progressives have valid arguments, and we must certainly have sympathy for those who would try to expose and eradicate the hidden assumptions of bias in the Western tradition. But it also seems clear that this debate could only have taken the form it has in a society that has begun to come loose from its textual moorings. To challenge repression is salutary. To challenge history itself, proclaiming it to be simply an archive of repressions and justifications, is idiotic.[1] . . .

A collective change of sensibility may already be upon us. We need to take seriously the possibility that the young truly "know no other way," that they are not made of the same stuff that their elders are. In her *Harper's* magazine debate with Neil Postman, Camille Paglia observed:

> Some people have more developed sensoriums than others. I've found that most people born before World War II are turned off by the modern media. They can't understand how we who were born after the war can read and watch TV at the same time. But we *can*. When I wrote my book, I had earphones on, blasting rock music or Puccini and Brahms. The soap operas—with the sound turned down—flickered on my TV. I'd be talking on the phone at the same time. Baby boomers have a multi-layered, multitrack ability to deal with the world.

I don't know whether to be impressed or depressed by Paglia's ability to disperse her focus in so many directions. Nor can I say, not having read her book, in what ways her multitrack sensibility has informed her prose. But I'm baffled by what she means when she talks about an ability to "deal with the world." From the context, "dealing" sounds more like a matter of incessantly repositioning the self within a barrage of onrushing stimuli. . . .

My final exhibit—I don't know if it qualifies as a morbid symptom as such—is drawn from a *Washington Post Magazine* essay on the future of the Library of Congress, our national shrine to the printed word. One of the individuals interviewed in the piece is Robert Zich, so-called "special projects czar" of the institution. Zich, too, has seen the future, and he is surprisingly candid with his interlocutor. Before long, Zich maintains, people will be able to get what information they want directly off their terminals. The function of the Library of Congress (and perhaps libraries in general) will change. He envisions his library becoming more like a museum: "Just as you go to the National Gallery to see its Leonardo or go to the Smithsonian to see the Spirit of St. Louis and so

---

[1] The outcry against the modification of the canon can be seen as a plea for old reflexes and routines. And the cry for multicultural representation may be a last-ditch bid for connection to the fading legacy of print. The logic is simple. When a resource is threatened—made scarce—people fight over it. In this case the struggle is over textual power in an increasingly nontextual age. The future of books and reading is what is at stake, and a dim intuition of this drives the contending factions.

As Katha Pollitt argued so shrewdly in her much-cited article in *The Nation*: If we were a nation of readers, there would be no issue. No one would be arguing about whether to put Toni Morrison on the syllabus because her work would be a staple of the reader's regular diet. These lists are suddenly so important because they represent, very often, the only serious works that the student is ever likely to be exposed to. Whoever controls the lists comes out ahead in the struggle for the hearts and minds of the young.

on, you will want to go to libraries to see the Gutenberg or the original printing of Shakespeare's plays or to see Lincoln's hand-written version of the Gettysburg Address."

Zich is outspoken, voicing what other administrators must be thinking privately. The big research libraries, he says, "and the great national libraries and their buildings will go the way of the railroad stations and the movie palaces of an earlier era which were really vital institutions in their time . . . Somehow folks moved away from that when the technology changed."

And books? Zich expresses excitement about Sony's hand-held electronic book, and a miniature encyclopedia coming from Franklin Electronic Publishers. "Slip it in your pocket," he says. "Little keyboard, punch in your words and it will do the full text searching and all the rest of it. Its limitation, of course, is that it's devoted just to that one book." Zich is likewise interested in the possibility of memory cards. What he likes about the Sony product is the portability: one machine, a screen that will display the contents of whatever electronic card you feed it.

I cite Zich's views at some length here because he is not some Silicon Valley research and development visionary, but a highly placed executive at what might be called, in a very literal sense, our most conservative public institution. When men like Zich embrace the electronic future, we can be sure it's well on its way.

Others might argue that the technologies cited by Zich merely represent a modification in the "form" of reading, and that reading itself will be unaffected, as there is little difference between following words on a pocket screen or a printed page. Here I have to hold my line. The context cannot but condition the process. Screen and book may exhibit the same string of words, but the assumptions that underlie their significance are entirely different depending on whether we are staring at a book or a circuit-generated text. As the nature of looking—at the natural world, at paintings—changed with the arrival of photography and mechanical reproduction, so will the collective relation to language alter as new modes of dissemination prevail.

Whether all of this sounds dire or merely "different" will depend upon the reader's own values and priorities. I find these portents of change depressing, but also exhilarating—at least to speculate about. On the one hand, I have a great feeling of loss and a fear about what habitations will exist for self and soul in the future. But there is also a quickening, a sense that important things are on the line. As Heraclitus once observed, "The mixture that is not shaken soon stagnates." Well, the mixture is being shaken, no doubt about it. And here are some of the kinds of developments we might watch for as our "proto-electronic" era yields to an all-electronic future:

1. *Language erosion.* There is no question but that the transition from the culture of the book to the culture of electronic communication will radically alter the ways in which we use language on every soci-

etal level. The complexity and distinctiveness of spoken and written expression, which are deeply bound to traditions of print literacy, will gradually be replaced by a more telegraphic sort of "plainspeak." Syntactic masonry is already a dying art. Neil Postman and others have already suggested what losses have been incurred by the advent of telegraphy and television—how the complex discourse patterns of the nineteenth century were flattened by the requirements of communication over distances. That tendency runs riot as the layers of mediation thicken. Simple linguistic pre-fab is now the norm, while ambiguity, paradox, irony, subtlety, and wit are fast disappearing. In their place, the simple "vision thing" and myriad other "things." Verbal intelligence, which has long been viewed as suspect as the act of reading, will come to seem positively conspiratorial. The greater part of any articulate person's energy will be deployed in dumbing-down her discourse.

Language will grow increasingly impoverished through a series of vicious cycles. For, of course, the usages of literature and scholarship are connected in fundamental ways to the general speech of the tribe. We can expect that curricula will be further streamlined, and difficult texts in the humanities will be pruned and glossed. One need only compare a college textbook from twenty years ago, to its contemporary version. A poem by Milton, a play by Shakespeare— one can hardly find the text among the explanatory notes nowadays. Fewer and fewer people will be able to contend with the so-called masterworks of literature or ideas. Joyce, Woolf, Soyinka, not to mention the masters who preceded them, will go unread, and the civilizing energies of their prose will circulate aimlessly between closed covers.

2. *Flattening of historical perspectives.* As the circuit supplants the printed page, and as more and more of our communications involve us in network processes—which of their nature plant us in a perpetual present—our perception of history will inevitably alter. Changes in information storage and access are bound to impinge on our historical memory. The depth of field that is our sense of the past is not only a linguistic construct, but is in some essential way represented by the book and the physical accumulation of books in library spaces. In the contemplation of the single volume, or mass of volumes, we form a picture of time past as a growing deposit of sediment; we capture a sense of its depth and dimensionality. Moreover, we meet the past as much in the presentation of words in books of specific vintage as we do in any isolated fact or statistic. The database, useful as it is, expunges this context, this sense of chronology, and admits us to a weightless order in which all information is equally accessible. . . .

3. *The waning of the private self.* We may even now be in the first stages of a process of social collectivization that will over time all but vanquish the ideal of the isolated individual. For some decades

now we have been edging away from the perception of private life as something opaque, closed off to the world; we increasingly accept the transparency of a life lived within a set of systems, electronic or otherwise. Our technologies are not bound by season or light—it's always the same time in the circuit. And so long as time is money and money matters, those circuits will keep humming. The doors and walls of our habitations matter less and less—the world sweeps through the wires as it needs to, or as we need it to. The monitor light is always blinking; we are always potentially on-line.

I am not suggesting that we are all about to become mindless, soulless robots, or that personality will disappear altogether into an oceanic homogeneity. But certainly the idea of what it means to be a person living a life will be much changed. The figure-ground model, which has always featured a solitary self before a background that is the society of other selves, is romantic in the extreme. It is ever less tenable in the world as it is becoming. There are no more wildernesses, no more lonely homesteads, and, outside of cinema, no more emblems of the exalted individual.

The self must change as the nature of subjective space changes. And one of the many incremental transformations of our age has been the slow but steady destruction of subjective space. The physical and psychological distance between individuals has been shrinking for at least a century. In the process, the figure-ground image has begun to blur its boundary distinctions. One day we will conduct our public and private lives within networks so dense, among so many channels of instantaneous information, that it will make almost no sense to speak of the differentiations of subjective individualism.

We are already captive in our webs. Our slight solitudes are transected by codes, wires, and pulsations. We punch a number to check in with the answering machine, another to tape a show that we are too busy to watch. The strands of the web grow finer and finer—this is obvious. What is no less obvious is the fact that they will continue to proliferate, gaining in sophistication, merging functions so that one can bank by phone, shop via television, and so on. The natural tendency is toward streamlining: The smart dollar keeps finding ways to shorten the path, double-up the function. We might think in terms of a circuitboard model, picturing ourselves as the contact points. The expansion of electronic options is always at the cost of contractions in the private sphere. We will soon be navigating with ease among cataracts of organized pulsations, putting out and taking in signals. We will bring our terminals, our modems, and menus further and further into our former privacies; we will implicate ourselves by degrees in the unitary life, and there may come a day when we no longer remember that there was any other life. . . .

Trafficking with tendencies—extrapolating and projecting as I have been doing—must finally remain a kind of gambling. One bets high on the validity of a notion and low on the human capacity for resistance and for unpredictable initiatives. No one can really predict how we will adapt to the transformations taking place all around us. We may discover, too, that language is a hardier thing than I have allowed. It may flourish among the beep and the click and the monitor as readily as it ever did on the printed page. I hope so, for language is the soul's ozone layer and we thin it at our peril.

===

FOR DISCUSSION AND REVIEW

1. Based on your experience, define what Birkerts means by "plainspeak." What role does the increase of electronic communication play in the rise of "plainspeak"? In what ways does it erode what he calls "syntactic masonry"?

2. Reread Birkerts's third prediction about "the waning of the private self." What does he mean when he says that the figure-ground model of the self is ever less reliable? How is the communications "web" weakening the independent self? Do you agree that "doors and walls . . . matter less and less"? Explain.

3. Why does Birkerts call the Library of Congress "our most conservative public institution"? Why is Zich's point of view so important to his argument?

4. Do you agree with Birkerts that we are truly "living through a period of overlap"? Are we really witnessing the death of the written word? After all, a decade ago it was fashionable to talk about "a paperless society," yet the fact that you are reading this book quells that prediction. What will it take to make printed books—and the printed page itself—historical artifacts? How can the electronic communications revolution replace books, magazines, newspapers, and countless other printed documents that are still popular?

5. Comment on Birkerts's concluding thought: "We may discover . . . that language is a hardier thing than I have allowed. It may flourish among the beep and the click and the monitor as readily as it ever did on the printed page. I hope so, for language is the soul's ozone layer and we thin it at our peril."

Projects for "Language, Reading, and Writing"

1. The Japanese language is unique in possessing multiple functioning alphabets. Kanji (the traditional pictographic alphabet), Hiragana (a syllabic alphabet), and Katakana (also a syllabic alphabet, with many of the same symbols as Hiragana, but restricted to foreign or imported words) are often used concurrently. Interview a Japanese scholar or native Japanese speaker to learn how the three alphabets developed, how they are used, and how they overlap and differ. What advantages and disadvantages might result from this multiplicity of alphabets?

2. If you know Russian, or have access to someone who does, prepare a comparison of the Cyrillic and Roman alphabets. Which alphabet is a better fit for Russian? For English? Why?

3. Were you formally taught grammar in school? If not, do you feel that you missed out on something important? Was the instruction you received boring and confusing, or helpful and enlightening to you in your attempts to become a good writer and articulate speaker? Do you feel confident now in matters of grammar, punctuation, and usage? How important are the more apparently nitpicky rules, such as when to use an apostrophe? Ask the same questions of someone from your generation and of other people, both younger and older, and compare the responses.

4. A number of great American writers other than those cited by Barbara Hill Hudson have used regional, class, and ethnic dialects in their fiction. Mark Twain, for example, is reputed to have been one of the greatest transcribers of regional and ethnic dialects. Read several stories by Twain or another author of your choice. Here are some suggested authors, but there are many other possibilities: Flannery O'Connor or William Faulkner (the American South), Kate Chopin (Acadian Louisiana), Howard Frank Mosher (New England), Sherwood Anderson (the Midwest), Sandra Cisneros (the Southwest). Add what you learn about dialect to Hudson's chart.

5. Computers are doing a great service by bringing literacy to minority students in their own language (see "How Do You Say Computer in Hawaiian?" by Constance Hale in Part Eight. Nonetheless, many experts, as Sven Birkerts, fear that in the wider picture they pose a worldwide threat to the written word and thus to the very nature of "literacy." Do you believe that e-mail and Web pages will replace letters and books? If so, will the technological shift degrade literacy worldwide? This question is the subject of active debate in linguistic, journalistic, academic, and computer circles. As a matter of urgent controversy, this issue suggests a number of possible projects:

    a. Read articles in current magazines and journals supporting opposite viewpoints and write a report presenting the arguments on both sides.

b. Invite several classmates to join you in your research, and prepare a debate on the issue.

c. Consider the effect computer technology has had on your own use of the written word. What other effects do you think computers will have on your writing as they continue to improve and you rely on them more and more?

d. Conduct a survey of people's use of books and computers. What effect does their use of computers have on their reading habits? Do people believe that electronic communications will replace books, magazines, and newspapers in their lifetimes?

6. The power of computers has been applied to many aspects of language study. Besides the familiar spelling and grammar checkers, there are programs to translate from one language to another, analyze literary texts, and interpret and reproduce speech for the language-impaired. Research this general area of technology, choose a topic, and write an essay in which you explain how computers are contributing to advances in that area.

Selected Bibliography

The American Heritage Book of English Usage. Boston: Houghton Mifflin, 1996. [A lively and accessible introduction to English usage.]

Barfield, Owen. *History in English Words*. 1953; Great Barrington: Lindisfarne Press, 1988. [An exploration of how knowledge has been shaped by words and language and how language has evolved through writing.]

Bryson, Bill. *The Mother Tongue: English and How It Got That Way*. New York: Morrow, 1990. [An entertaining overview of dictionary and usage traditions.]

Burchfield, R. W. (Editor) and H. W. Fowler. *The New Fowler's Modern English Usage*. London: Clarendon Press, 1996. [Fowler's name stands for "usage" as much as Webster's stands for "dictionary" and Roget's for "thesaurus."]

Cleary, Linda Miller. *From the Other Side of the Desk: Students Speak Out about Writing*. Portsmouth, NH: Boynton/Cook Publishers, 1991. [An invaluable glimpse into the frustrating process of learning writing from the viewpoint of high school students.]

Crystal, David. "The Prescriptive Tradition." In *The Cambridge Encyclopedia of Language*. Cambridge: Cambridge University Press, 1997. [A brief overview of a longstanding linguistic debate.]

Diringer, D. *The Alphabet*. New York: Philosophical Library, 1948. [A detailed history.]

Frank, Francine Wattman, and Paula Treichler, eds. *Language, Gender, and Professional Writing: Theoretical Approaches and Guidelines for Nonsexist Usage*. New York: Modern Language Association, 1989. [Comes with all the authority of the MLA.]

Gelb, I. J. *A Study of Writing*. Rev. ed. Chicago: University of Chicago Press, 1963. [A highly recommended study of the origin and evolution of writing systems.]

Lederer, Richard R. *Anguished English: An Anthology of Accidental Assaults upon Our Language*. New York: Wyrick and Company, 1988. [A fabulous collection of linguistic goofs and mixed-up metaphors.]

Maggio, Rosalie. *The Bias-Free Word Finder: A Dictionary of Nondiscriminatory Language*. Boston: Beacon Press, 1992. [Has an excellent introduction covering how to avoid sexist and other forms of biased language.]

Partridge, Eric. *Usage and Abusage: A Guide to Good English*. New York: Norton, 1995. [A classic usage guide.]

Pyles, Thomas, and John Algeo. *The Origins and Development of the English Language*, 3rd ed. New York: Harcourt Brace Jovanovich, 1982. [See Chapter 3, "Letters and Sounds: A Brief History of Writing," which traces the origin and development of English writing.]

Waite, Maurice, ed. *The Oxford Dictionary and Usage Guide to the English Language*. New York: Oxford University Press, 1996. [A shorter version of the *Oxford English Dictionary* along with an extensive usage guide.]

Glossary

acoustic phonetics. The study of the properties of human speech sounds as they are transmitted through the air as sound waves.

affix. In English, a prefix or suffix (both are bound morphemes) attached to a base (either bound or free) and modifying its meaning.

affricate. A complex sound made by rapidly articulating first a stop and then a fricative. Affricates appear initially in the English words *chin* and *gin*.

allophone. A nonsignificant variant of a phoneme.

alveolar. A sound made by placing the tip or blade of the tongue on the bony ridge behind the upper teeth (e.g., the initial sounds of the English words *tin, sin, din, zap, nap,* and *lap*); also, a point of articulation.

alveolar ridge. The bony ridge just behind the upper front teeth.

ambiguity. Having more than one meaning; ambiguity may be semantic or syntactic.

American Sign Language (ASL, Ameslan). A system of communication used by and with deaf people in the United States, consisting of hand symbols that vary in the shape of the hands, the direction of their movement, and their position in relation to the body. It is different from finger spelling, in which words are spelled out letter by letter, and from Signed English, in which English words are signed in the order in which they are uttered, thus preserving English morphology and syntax.

aphasia. The impairment of language abilities as a result of brain damage (usually from a stroke or trauma).

applied linguistics. Using linguistic theories, methods, or findings to solve practical problems.

articulatory phonetics. The study of the production of human speech sounds by the speech organs.

aspiration. An aspirated sound is followed by a puff of air; the English voiceless-stop consonants /p, t, k/ are aspirated in word-initial position (e.g., *pot, top, kit*).

assimilation. A change that a sound undergoes to become more like another, often adjacent, sound.

back formation. A process of word formation that uses analogy as a basis for removing part of a word; *edit* was formed by back formation from *editor*.

base. In English, a free or bound morpheme to which affixes are added to form new words; *cat* is a free base, *-ceive* is a bound base.

bilabial. A sound made by constriction between the lips (e.g., the first sound in *pet, bet,* and *met*).

Black English. A vernacular variety of English used by some black people; more precisely divided into Standard Black English and Black English Vernacular.

blending. A process of word formation, combining clipping and compounding, that makes new words by combining parts of existing words that are not morphemes (e.g., *chortle* and *galumphing*).

borrowing. A process through which words, and sometimes other characteristics, are incorporated into one language from another.

bound morpheme. A morpheme that cannot appear alone. In English, prefixes and suffixes are bound morphemes, as are some bases.

Broca's area. One of the language centers in the left hemisphere of the human brain.

caretaker speech. Used by people caring for children, ill people, and the elderly. This speech is characterized by simplified vocabulary, systematic phonological simplification of some words, higher pitch, exaggerated intonation, and short, simple sentences.

central. A sound, usually a vowel, made with the tongue body neither front nor back.

clipping. A process of word formation, common in informal language, in which a word is shortened without regard to derivational analogy (e.g., *dorm* from *dormitory*, *bus* from *omnibus*).

coinage. A rare process of word formation in which words are created from unrelated, meaningless elements.

comparative linguistics. The study of similarities and differences among related languages.

complementary distribution. A situation in which two allophones of a phoneme each occurs in a position or positions in which the other does not. See also *free variation*.

compounding. A process of word formation in which two or more words or bound bases are combined to form a new word.

consonant. A kind of speech sound produced with significant constriction at some point in the vocal tract.

conversational principles. What an auditor should be able to expect from a speaker: that the speaker is sincere, is telling the truth, is being relevant, and will contribute an appropriate amount of information.

copula. A linking verb.

creole. A language developed from a pidgin that has a complex structure and native speakers.

culture. The integrated pattern of human knowledge, belief, and behavior that depends upon people's capacity for learning and transmitting knowledge to succeeding generations.

derivation. A process of word formation in which one or more affixes are added to an existing word or bound base.

descriptivism. A grammatical analysis that seeks to describe linguistic characteristics of a language as they exist in current usage. See *prescriptivism*.

diachronic linguistics. Historical linguistics; the study of changes in languages over long periods.

dialect. A variety of a language, usually regional or social, set off from other varieties of the same language by differences in pronunciation, vocabulary, and grammar.

dichotic listening. A research technique in which two different sounds are presented simultaneously, through earphones, to an individual's left and right ears.

diphthong. Complex vowel sounds having one beginning point and a different ending point. The English words *hoist* and *cow* contain diphthongs.

dissimilation. A change in one or more adjacent sounds that serves to make a string of similar sounds less similar.

downgrading. A historical process through which the value of a word declines. Also known as *pejoration*, *devaluation*, and *depreciation*.

Early Modern English. The English spoken in England from about A.D. 1450 to 1700.

Ebonics. A recently coined name for the dialect spoken by black Americans, also known as Black English Vernacular (BEV).

e-mail. Mail sent electronically that has its own informal style and language conventions.

ethnocentricity. The belief that one's culture (including language) is at the center of things, and that other cultures (and languages) are inferior.

etymology. The study of the origins and history of words, both their forms and meaning.

finger spelling. The use of hand gestures to symbolize letters of the alphabet to spell words when no sign is available.

free variation. A situation in which two or more allophones of a phoneme can occur in a particular position. See also *complementary distribution*.

fricative. A sound produced by bringing one of the articulators close enough to one of the points of articulation to create a narrow opening; a manner of articulation.

front. A sound, usually a vowel, articulated with the body of the tongue set relatively forward.

function words. Words (e.g., articles, prepositions, conjunctions) having little reference to things outside of language that indicate some grammatical relationship; the function-word class is small and closed.

functional shift. A process of word formation in English (made possible by the gradual loss of most inflectional affixes) in which a word is shifted from one part of speech to another without changing its form.

generative grammar. The set of rules used to produce the potentially infinite number of sentences within a language.

glide. Sounds that provide transitions to or from other sounds; they are vowel-like sounds, but sometimes act more like consonants. The English words *yet* and *wet* begin with a glide; the English words *my* and *cow* end with a glide.

glottal. A sound made by constriction of the vocal cords (e.g., English *uh-uh* has a glottal stop in the middle).

glottis. The space, within the larynx, between the two vocal cords.

grammar. The system of a language—its phonology, morphology, syntax, semantics, and lexicon—necessary to form and interpret sentences.

Great Vowel Shift. A set of sound changes that affected the long vowels of English during the fifteenth century A.D., and that resulted in many discrepancies between the spelling and pronunciation of modern English words.

Grimm's law. A statement of the regular sound changes that took place in Proto-Germanic but not in other Indo-European languages.

high. A sound, usually a vowel, that is articulated with the body of the tongue set relatively high (i.e., close to the roof of the mouth).

historical linguistics. The study of change in languages over time.

holophrastic speech. The stage of language acquisition in which children use one-word utterances.

ideograph. A character in a writing system that stands for an idea and is, or was, pictorial. See also *pictograph*.

ideolect. The variety of language spoken by one person. See also *dialect*.

illocutionary force. The intentions of a speaker, as far as those listening can discern from the context. *Implicit* illocutionary force is unstated; *explicit* illocutionary force is stated.

Indo-European. A group of languages descended from a common ancestor and now widely spoken in Europe, North and South America, Australia, New Zealand, and parts of India.

inflection. In grammar, an affix that signals a grammatical relationship, such as case or tense. In phonetics, a change of emphasis or pitch during speech.

interdental. A sound made by placing the tongue tip between the teeth (e.g., the initial sounds of the English words *thin* and *then*).

International Phonetic Alphabet (IPA). A set of symbols and diacritical marks that permits the unambiguous recording of any perceivable differences in speech sounds; an alphabet with a different symbol for every sound in the world's languages.

labial. A manner-of-articulation term under which are included the bilabials and the labiodentals.

labiodental. A sound made by bringing the lower lip into contact with the upper teeth (e.g., the first sound of the English words *fat* and *vat*).

larynx. The structure that contains the vocal cords.

lateralization. The localization of a neurological function in one hemisphere of the brain.

lexicon. The vocabulary of a language, especially in dictionary form.

linguistic relativity/determinism. The hypothesis that the structure of a language determines how the speakers of that language view the world.

linguistic relativity hypothesis. The belief that the structure of a language shapes the way speakers of that language view reality. Also known as the Sapir-Whorf Hypothesis after Edward Sapir and Benjamin Lee Whorf.

linguistics. The study of human speech, how it is organized and used.

liquid. A sound in which the vocal tract is not closed off, nor is there sufficient constriction to produce friction; in English, the liquids are [l] and [r], both consonant sounds.

low. A sound, usually a vowel, articulated with the body of the tongue set relatively low, away from the roof of the mouth.

manner of articulation. The way in which the flow of air from the lungs is modified, usually in the mouth, to produce a speech sound. See also *place of articulation*.

mean length of utterance (MLU). A measure of morphemes in the speech of young children; often used to determine the progress of language acquisition.

metalanguage. A language used for talking about language.

mid. A sound, usually a vowel, articulated with the body of the tongue set midway between the roof of the mouth and the bottom of the mouth.

Middle English. The English spoken in England from approximately A.D. 1100 to 1450.

minimal pair. Two words with different meanings that are distinguished only by having a different phoneme in the same position in both words (e.g., in English, *bat* and *pat* are a minimal pair).

Modern English. English spoken from 1700 to the present.

morpheme. The smallest unit in a language that carries meaning; it may be a word or part of a word.

morphology. The study of the composition or structure of words.

nasal. A sound made with the velum lowered so that air resonates in the nasal as well as in the oral cavity and the airstream flows out of the vocal tract through the nose. A manner of articulation.

native speaker. One who has learned a language as a child and therefore speaks it fluently.

Old English. The ancestor of Modern English, Old English was the language spoken in England from about A.D. 450 to 1100.

orthography. Any writing system that is widely used in society.

palatal. A sound made by bringing the tongue into contact with the front part of the roof of the mouth (e.g., the initial sounds of the English words *church, ship, judge, rim,* and *yet,* and the medial sound of *measure*).

palate. The hard front part of the roof of the mouth.

perceptual phonetics. The study of the perception and identification of speech sounds by a listener.

phoneme. A speech sound that is a single mental unit but that usually has one or more physical representations (i.e., allophones).

phonetics. The study of speech sounds.

phonics. The method of teaching beginners to read and pronounce words by learning the phonetic values of letters, letter groups, and syllables.

phonology. The science of speech sounds, including the history and theory of sound changes in a language.

phrase-structure rule. A rule that expands a single symbol into two or more symbols (e.g., S → NP VP).

pictograph. A character in a writing system that stands for a word. See also *ideograph.*

pidgin. A rudimentary language with a simplified grammar and limited lexicon, typically used for trading by individuals who do not speak the same language. Pidgins are auxiliary languages; people do not learn them as native speakers.

place of articulation. The place in the vocal tract where the airflow is modified, usually by constriction, in the production of speech sounds; also called *point of articulation.* See also *manner of articulation.*

pragmatics. The study of speech acts or of how language is used in various social contexts.

prescriptivism. A grammar that seeks to explain linguistic characteristics of a language as they should be. See *descriptivism.*

presuppositions. Those things that the speaker and the listener in a conversation can suppose each other to know; meanings that are presupposed but not overtly stated.

Proto-Indo-European. The hypothetical language from which it is assumed that many languages now spoken in Europe, North and South America, Australia, New Zealand, and parts of India were descended.

psycholinguistics. The study of the relationship between language and psychological processes.

Sapir-Whorf hypothesis. See *linguistic relativity hypothesis.*

semantics. The analysis of the meaning of individual words and of such larger units as phrases and sentences.

semiotics. The study of signs and symbols as they are found in all human populations.

sibilants. Fricatives characterized by a hissing sound.

sociolinguistics. The study of social dialects; the identification and analysis of dialect features that are significant indicators of social class.

Spanglish. A hybrid language spoken by Hispanic Americans combining elements of English and Spanish.

speech community. A group of people who regularly communicate with one another and who share certain speech characteristics.

Standard English. A form of the English language that is most widely considered "correct" by the speech community; it is used by government and the media and is taught in the schools.

stop. A sound produced by completely blocking the airstream; a manner of articulation.

syntax. The study of the structure of sentences and of the interrelationships of their parts.

telegraphic speech. Speech that follows the two-word stage in language acquisition. It lacks function words and morphemes and is characterized by short, simple sentences made up primarily of context words.

trachea. The tubal area extending from the larynx through the back of the mouth as far as the rear opening of the nasal cavity.

transformational grammar. A grammar that is built upon formal operations (transformational rules) that show correspondences between linguistic structures, e.g., active and passive sentences.

transliterate. To represent or spell a word from one language in the characters of the alphabet of another language.

universal grammar. Properties which belong to all human languages giving rise to the belief that the language instinct is biologically determined.

usage. The way in which words and phrases are actually used in a language community. See *descriptivism* and *prescriptivism*.

velar. A sound made by bringing the tongue into contact with the velum (e.g., the final sounds of the English words *sick, rig,* and *sing*). See also *velum*.

velum. The soft, back part of the roof of the mouth.

vocal cords. Muscular, elastic bands within the larynx that, in speech, are either relaxed and spread apart (for voiceless sounds) or tensed and drawn together so that there is only a narrow opening between them (for voiced sounds).

vocal tract. The vocal tract includes the pharynx, the nasal cavity, and the mouth cavity. It is located above the vocal cords and used for the production of speech sounds.

voice-onset-time (VOT). The time between moving the lips and vibrating the vocal cords. In English, /b/ has a VOT of 0 milliseconds; /p/ has a VOT of +40 milliseconds.

voiced sound. A sound made with the vocal cords tensed and vibrating.

voiceless sound. A sound made with the vocal cords relaxed, spread apart, and relatively still.

vowel. A speech sound produced with a relatively free flow of air; vowel sounds are "open" sounds made by varying the shape of the vocal tract.

Wernicke's area. One of the language centers in the left hemisphere of the human brain.

Acknowledgments

"Talking in the New Land" by Edite Cunha. From *New England Monthly*, August 1990. Copyright © 1990. Reprinted by permission.

"Finding a Voice" by Maxine Hong Kingston. From *The Woman Warrior*. Copyright © 1975, 1976 by Maxine Hong Kingston. Reprinted with the permission of Alfred A. Knopf, Inc.

"Native Tongues" by Nancy Lord. From *Sierra*, November/December 1996. Reprinted with the permission of the author.

"Shakespeare in the Bush" by Laura Bohannan. From *Natural History*, August/September 1966. Copyright © 1966. Reprinted by permission.

"Nine Ideas about Language" by Harvey A. Daniels. From *Famous Last Words: The American Language Crisis Reconsidered*. Copyright © 1983 by the Board of Trustees, Southern Illinois University. Reprinted with the permission of Southern University Press.

"Language: An Introduction" by W. F. Bolton. From *A Living Language*. Copyright © 1981 by W. F. Bolton. Reprinted with the permission of McGraw-Hill, Inc.

"True Language?" by the Department of Linguistics, The Ohio State University. From *Language Files: Material for an Introduction to Language*, sixth edition. Copyright © 1994 by The Ohio State University Press. Reprinted with the permission of the publisher.

"Sign Language" by Karen Emmorey. From *Encyclopedia of Human Behavior*, vol. 4. Copyright © 1994 by Academic Press, Inc. Reprinted with the permission of the author and publishers.

"Nonverbal Communication" by George A. Miller. From *Communication, Language, and Meaning: Psychological Perspectives*. Copyright © 1973 by Basic Books, Inc. Reprinted with the permission of BasicBooks, a division of HarperCollins Publishers, Inc.

"Phonetics" by Edward Callary. Copyright © 1981 by R. E. Callary. Revised 1984 by R. E. Callary.

"The Minimal Units of Meaning: Morphemes" by the Department of Linguistics, The Ohio State University. From *Language Files: Material for an Introduction to Language*, sixth edition. Copyright © 1994 by The Ohio State University Press. Reprinted with the permission of the publisher.

"The Identification of Morphemes" by H. A. Gleason Jr. From *An Introduction to Descriptive Linguistics Workbook*. Copyright © 1955, 1961 by Holt, Rinehart and Winston, Inc. and renewed 1983, 1989 by H. A. Gleason Jr. Reprinted with the permission of the publishers.

"Word-Making: Some Sources of New Words" by W. Nelson Francis. From *The English Language, An Introduction*. Copyright © 1963, 1965 by W. W. Norton & Company, Inc. Reprinted with the permission of the publishers.

"Literary Metaphors and Other Linguistic Innovations in Computer Language" by Kelvin D. Nilsen and Alleen Pace Nilsen. From *English Journal*, October 1995. Copyright © 1995 by the National Council of Teachers of English. Reprinted with the permission of the publishers.

"What Do Native Speakers Know about Their Language?" by Roderick A. Jacobs and Peter S. Rosenbaum. From *English Transformational Grammar*. Xerox College Publishing, 1968. Reprinted with the permission of Peter S. Rosenbaum.

"Syntax: The Structure of Sentences" by Frank Heny. Copyright © 1985 by Frank Heny. Revised 1997 by Frank Heny. Used with permission.

"Bad Birds and Better Birds: Prototype Theories" by Jean Aitchison. From *Words In the Mind: An Introduction to the Mental Lexicon*, second edition, by Jean Aitchison. Copyright © 1994 Jean Aitchison. Published by Blackwell Publishers: Oxford UK and Cambridge, MA USA. Reprinted by permission of Blackwell Publishers UK and the author.

"Clive" carton by Angus McGill. Copyright © *London Evening Standard*. Reproduced by permission of Angus McGill.

"The Tower of Babel" by Steven Pinker. From *The Language Instinct*. Copyright © 1994 by Steven Pinker. Reprinted with the permission of William Morrow & Company, Inc.

"Speech Communities" by Paul Roberts. From *Understanding English*. Copyright © 1958 by Paul Roberts. Reprinted with the permission of Addison Wesley Educational Publishers, Inc.

"Social and Regional Variation" by Albert H. Marckwardt and J. L. Dillard. From

American English, second edition. Copyright © 1980 by Oxford University Press. Reprinted with the permission of the publisher.

"Dialects: How They Differ" by Roger W. Shuy. From *Discovering American Dialects*. Copyright © 1967 by the National Council of Teachers of English. Reprinted with the permission of the publisher.

"The Study of Nonstandard English" by William Labov. From *The Study of Nonstandard English*. Copyright © 1970 by the National Council of Teachers of English. Reprinted with the permission of the publisher.

"Pidgins and Creoles" by David Crystal. From *The Cambridge Encyclopedia of Language*. Copyright © 1987 by Cambridge University Press. Reprinted with the permission of the author and Cambridge University Press.

"'It Bees Dat Way Sometime': Sounds and Structure of Present-Day Black English" by Geneva Smitherman. From *Talkin' and Testifyin': The Language of Black America*. Copyright © 1977 by Geneva Smitherman. Reprinted with the permission of the author and Wayne State University Press.

"Girl Talk—Boy Talk" by John Pfeiffer. From *Science*, February 1985. Copyright © 1985. Reprinted by permission.

"'I'll Explain It to You': Lecturing and Listening" by Deborah Tannen. Excerpted from *You Just Don't Understand*. Copyright © 1990 by Deborah Tannen. Reprinted with the permission of William Morrow & Company, Inc.

"Ethnic Style in Male–Female Conversation" by Deborah Tannen. From John J. Gumperz, ed., *Language and Social Identity*. Copyright © 1982 by Cambridge University Press. Reprinted with the permission of the author and Cambridge University Press.

"The Names of Women" by Louise Erdrich. From *The Blue Jay's Dance*. Copyright © 1995 by Louise Erdrich. Reprinted with the permission of HarperCollins Publishers, Inc.

"Men, Women, Computers" by Barbara Kantrowitz. From *Newsweek*, May 16, 1994. Copyright © 1994 by Newsweek, Inc. Reprinted with the permission of *Newsweek*. All rights reserved.

"Comparative and Historical Linguistics" by Jeanne H. Herndon. From *A Survey of Modern Grammars*, second edition. Copyright © 1976 by Holt, Rinehart and Winston, Inc. Reprinted with the permission of the publisher.

"The Family Tree and Wave Models" by the Department of Linguistics, The Ohio State University. From *Language Files: Material for an Introduction to Language*, sixth edition. Copyright © 1994 by The Ohio State University Press. Reprinted with the permission of the publisher.

"A Brief History of English" by Paul Roberts. From *Understanding English*. Copyright © 1958 by Paul Roberts. Reprinted with the permission of Addison Wesley Educational Publishers, Inc.

"Language Change: Progress or Decay?" by Jean Aitchison. From *Language Change: Progress or Decay?* second edition, by Jean Aitchison. Copyright © 1992 Jean Aitchison. Published by Cambridge University Press. Reprinted by permission of Cambridge University Press and the author.

"To Be Human: A History of the Study of Language" by Julia S. Falk. Copyright © 1993 by Julia S. Falk. Revised 1997 by Julia S. Falk. Used with permission.

"Bilingual Education: Outdated and Unrealistic" by Richard Rodriguez. From *The New York Times*, 1985. Copyright © 1985 by Richard Rodriguez. Reprinted with the permission of Georges Borchardt, Inc. for the author.

"It's the Talk of Nueva York: The Hybrid Called Spanglish" by Lizette Alvarez. From *The New York Times*, March 25, 1997. Copyright © 1997 by The New York Times Company. Reprinted with the permission of *The New York Times*.

"Not White, Just Right" by Rachel L. Jones. From *Newsweek*, February 10, 1997. Copyright © 1997 by Newsweek, Inc. Reprinted with the permission of *Newsweek*. All rights reserved.

"Saving California Languages" by Katharine Whittemore. From *Native Americas*, (Fall 1997), Vol. 14, #3, Akwe:kon Press (Cornell University). Copyright © 1995 by Katharine Whittemore. Reprinted by permission of the author.

"How Do You Say Computer in Hawaiian?" by Constance Hale. From *Wired*, August 1995. Copyright © 1995 by Wired Ventures, Inc. Reprinted with the permission of *Wired*. All rights reserved.

"Rearing Children in a Monolingual Culture: A Louisiana Experience" by Stephen J. Caldas and Suzanne Caron-Caldas. From *American Speech* 67, no. 3, Fall 1992. Copyright © 1992 by The University of Alabama Press. Reprinted with the permission of the publishers.

"The Acquisition of Language" by Breyne Arlene Moskowitz. From *Scientific American*, November 1978. Copyright © 1978 by *Scientific American*. Reprinted with the permission of the publisher. All rights reserved.

"Developmental Milestones in Motor and Language Development" by Eric H. Lenneberg. From *Biological Foundations of Language*. New York: John Wiley and Sons, 1967. Copyright © 1967. Reprinted with the permission of Edith Lenneberg.

"Predestinate Grooves: Is There a Preordained Language 'Program'?" by Jean Aitchison. From *The Articulate Mammal: An Introduction to Psycholinguistics*, third edition, by Jean Aitchison. Copyright © 1989 Jean Aitchison. Published by Routledge: London and New York. Reprinted by permission of Routledge UK and the author.

"How Children Learn Words" by George A. Miller and Patricia M. Gildea. From *Scientific American*, October 1987. Copyright © 1987 by *Scientific American*. Reprinted with the permission of the publisher. All rights reserved.

"The Development of Language in Genie: A Case of Language Acquisition beyond the 'Critical Period'" by Victoria Franklin, Stephen Krashen, Susan Curtiss, David Rigler, and Marilyn Rigler. From *Brain and Language* 1, no. 1, 1974. Copyright © 1974 by Academic Press, Inc. Reprinted with the permission of the author and publishers.

"Genie: A Postscript" by Maya Pines. From *Psychology Today*, September 1981. Reprinted with the permission of the author.

"Teaching How to Talk in Roadville: The First Words" by Shirley Brice Heath. From *Ways with Words*. Copyright © 1994 by Cambridge University Press. Reprinted with the permission of the author and Cambridge University Press.

"Language and Thought" by David Crystal. From *The Cambridge Encyclopedia of Language*. Copyright © 1987 by Cambridge University Press. Reprinted with the permission of the author and Cambridge University Press.

"Brain and Language" by Jeannine Heny. Copyright © 1985 Jeannine Heny. Revised 1997 by Jeannine Heny. Used with permission.

"Signals, Signs, and Words: From Animal Communication to Language" by William Kemp and Roy Smith. From *Speaking Act to Natural Words: Animals, Communication, and Language*. Copyright © 1985 by William Kemp and Roy Smith. Revised 1997 by William Kemp and Roy Smith. Used with permission.

"The Continuity Paradox" by Derek Bickerton. From *Language and Species*. Copyright 1990 by The University of Chicago Press. Reprinted with the permission of the author and The University of Chicago Press.

"Languages and Writing" by John P. Hughes. From *The Science of Language: An Introduction to Linguistics*. New York: Random House, 1962. Copyright © 1962 and renewed 1990 by John P. Hughes. Reprinted with the permission of Megadot, Upper Montclair, NJ.

"What Makes Good English Good" by John Algeo. From P. C. Boardman, ed., *The Legacy of Language: A Tribute to Charlton Laird*. Copyright © 1987 by the University of Nevada Press. Reprinted with the permission of the publishers.

"Its Academic, Or Is It?" by Charles R. Larson. From *Newsweek*, November 6, 1995. Copyright © 1995 by Charles R. Larson. Reprinted with the permission of the author.

"Like I Said, Don't Worry" by Patricia T. O'Connor. From *Newsweek*, December 9, 1996. Copyright © 1996 by Newsweek, Inc. Reprinted with the permission of *Newsweek*. All rights reserved.

"Sociolinguistic Analysis of Dialogues and First-Person Narratives in Fiction" by Barbara Hill Hudson. From *Language Variation in North American English*. Copyright © 1993 by The Modern Language Association of America. Reprinted with the permission of The Modern Language Association of America.

"Into the Electronic Millennium" by Sven Birkerts. From *The Gutenberg Elegies: The Fate of Reading in an Electronic Age*. Copyright © 1994 by Sven Birkerts. Reprinted with the permission of Faber and Faber Publishers, Inc.

Author and Title Index

Subject Index